Books of Merit

First Drafts

J. L. Granatstein
Norman Hillmer

FIRST DRAFTS

Eyewitness
Accounts
from
Canada's
Past

Thomas Allen Publishers
Toronto

National Library of Canada Cataloguing in Publication Data

Main entry under title

First Drafts: eyewitness accounts from Canada's past /
[compiled by] J. L. Granatstein & Norman Hillmer.

Includes index.

ISBN 0-88762-113-9

Canada—History—Sources. I. Granatstein, J.L., 1939–
II. Hillmer, Norman, 1942–

FC176.F47 2002   971   C2002-902551-6
F1026.F57 2002

Editor: Patrick Crean
Cover images: (front, from left) Billy Bishop, CP; Pauline Johnson, McMaster University;
    Pierre Trudeau, Sun Media Corporation; Captain James Cook, portrait RN 1782 by
    John Webber, oil on canvas, National Portrait Gallery, Canberra, collection, purchased
    2000 by the Commonwealth Government with the generous assistance of Robert Oatley
    and John Schaeffer; Louis Riel, www.canadianheritage.org ID #21946, Archives of Ontario
    S637; (back) Battle of Frezenburg, courtesy Princess Patricia's Canadian Light Infantry

Page 467 constitutes a continuation of this copyright page.

Published by Thomas Allen Publishers,
a division of Thomas Allen & Son Limited,
145 Front Street East, Suite 209,
Toronto, Ontario M5A 1E3 Canada
www.thomas-allen.com

ONTARIO ARTS COUNCIL
CONSEIL DES ARTS DE L'ONTARIO

The publisher gratefully acknowledges the support of the
Ontario Arts Council for its publishing program

Printed and bound in Canada

For Bill Kaplan and Susan Krever,
friends in good times and bad

Contents

Introduction

In the fall of 1933, during Adolf Hitler's first year in power, the *Toronto Daily Star*'s Matthew Halton was already predicting a second world war. "I have seen and studied," he told his readers after four weeks of touring Germany, "the most fanatical, thoroughgoing and savage philosophy of war ever imposed on any nation." The country was being prepared for conflict, blood and death. "This is not a sensational dream, but a cold fact, and anyone who can read and hear could learn the same in 24 hours in Germany." As the world lurched towards chaos over the succeeding years, Halton excoriated Hitler for nurturing and feeding off an unreasoning hysteria that made his followers thirsty for aggression. "This cancer," he warned from the 1936 Olympic Games in Berlin, "is subtly masked in a garb of belligerent nationalism called Fascism. Watch out for the first signs of Fascism in your own country, and operate on them quickly, because in spite of their seductive exterior virility, they are signs of decay. They are signs that we are despairing of reason, despairing of our fine dreams, of a sane world."

In the pre-television age of swashbuckling foreign correspondents such as Gordon Sinclair, Halton was widely known and read. There was drama and texture to his journalism, as well as a highly charged advocacy. Travelling frequently to Germany from his perch as the *Star*'s man in England, he used language as a blunt instrument against Nazism—colourful, visceral, full of foreboding. As Hitler moved in his shining black limousine towards the Olympic stadium, the brown-uniformed Führer seemed to the young reporter an evil Caesar, surrounded by security and sycophancy. Sinister armed guards formed an impenetrable cordon around him. By contrast, Britain's King George V passed by his public openly, with policemen at only six-foot intervals, their backs to the crowd. This was Halton's straightforward lesson in the contrast between democracy and dictatorship, delivered at a time when almost no one in Canada—or anywhere else—had the courage or perceptiveness to take on Hitler, even rhetorically.

In Hitler's war from 1939–45, Halton transformed himself with ease into the Canadian Broadcasting Corporation's senior radio correspondent at the front. He used the same methodology: intense involvement and a startling vocabulary. "There's an unholy thrill about it as well as fear," he said of the Italian Campaign late in 1943. "You are with good friends. You can laugh and joke. It's when you are watching others do it that you grow older, especially when a vehicle is hit and goes up in a vomit of flame and smoke." By design, he was right in the middle of the action, spouting Shakespeare and attacking his work with the same passion and partisanship that characterized his reporting from Germany in the previous decade. As colleague Charles Lynch recalled in his memoirs, Halton rejected the theory that reporters were better off waiting for the battle to be done, when the full picture became clearer and some perspective could be gained. Armed with an instinct for show business and a loathing of the Nazis, Halton pioneered a new electronic journalism with the freshness and vitality of his bulletins directly from the field. "It was propaganda," Lynch wrote, "though we might not have admitted it at the time. Halton became the first of the great media celebrities. When summoned home to help with the sale of victory bonds, he was a bigger box-office draw than Billy Bishop."

Propagandist, analyst and reporter: Halton was all three. Canadian war correspondents such as Marcel Ouimet, Ross Munro and Gregory Clark adopted his explicitly personal style from the battlefields of World War II. "Monsters in victory and monsters in flight," raged Clark from "somewhere in Italy" on 30 September 1943, "the Germans have added to the imperishable name of Lidice in Czechoslovakia the little name of Rionero in Italy. And," he declared, "I am one of the witnesses." Occasionally there was a hint of admiration for the skill of the adversary's armed forces in Canadian reporting on the war. Still, the Germans were, in Halton's words, a warrior people, their soldiers "savage, cunning young zealots." Canada's wartime reporting rang loudly with an almost theological certitude. Everyone was sure of himself then. Halton had always been sure of himself, and it gave his journalism a memorable edge.

There is a great deal of Matthew Halton in the pages that follow; we were deeply influenced by his approach to reportage in our selections. He made no pretense to the nothing-but-the-facts school of journalism, with objectivity as the goal, even if an impossible dream. He was not preoccupied, in the final analysis, by a concern for balance. "We are surrogates for Everyman," argued longtime *Ottawa Citizen* writer Christopher Young, "not experts, not historians, not public relations men. We hope to provide accurate reportage and intelligent comment, but our perspective is today's view of yesterday's event." Halton would have accepted that traditional summary of journalistic aims—except for the implied distance, even the distance of a single day. He wanted, as his newsman son David has recalled, to be part of the story, not outside it or away from it.

Halton was a harbinger of modern journalism, with its emphasis on context, perspective and analysis. As Anthony Lewis of the *New York Times* points out, "The old image of the print journalist as recording machine has faded. In its place is the journalist who tries to make sense, for the reader, of whatever world he or she is describing."

Halton had a degree from the University of Alberta and a leftish bent acquired at the University of London in the England of the early 1930s. Literary allusions dropped naturally from his typewriter, and he could, in the heat of battle, compare an Italian landscape to a Cézanne painting. Gordon Sinclair, writing for the same newspaper at the same time, enthralled Depression-scarred readers with exotic tales from China, Africa and India. Readers of this book can compare Sinclair's racy and sloppily written gee-whizzery in *Foot-Loose in India* (or the opinionated sentimentality of his 1973 paean of praise to the United States, "The Americans") to Halton's thoughtful and sophisticated exercises in persuasion.

When we began this volume of reportage by Canadians and about Canada, we were looking for good, even eloquent, writing. We ended with a preoccupation with immediacy. More and more we found ourselves drawn to eyewitness records of events, the first drafts of history. Peter Worthington was standing only feet away from Jack Ruby when he killed Lee Harvey Oswald on the November 1963 Sunday in Dallas, Texas, after Oswald had assassinated President John F. Kennedy. Worthington has written about that dramatic moment in his memoirs, *Looking for Trouble*. We prefer, however, the story he quickly spilled out into the *Toronto Telegram* that appeared the day after the killing on 25 November 1963. Dealing with a shock piled on another shock, the newspaper report was rougher, more real. As the British literary critic John Carey notes, such accounts offer history "but history deprived of generalizations. The writers are strangers to omniscience. The varnish of interpretation has been removed so we can see people clearly, as they originally were—gazing incredulously at what was, for that moment, the newest thing that had ever happened to them."

Many good reporters purposely avoid the use of themselves as characters in their own stories, but we frequently gravitated towards precisely that. The more personal, it seemed, the better. We considered, for example, three of Andrew Cohen's articles: a June 1990 *Saturday Night* piece recounting the negotiations leading to the Meech Lake Accord three years before between the federal government and the provinces; a column for the *Globe and Mail*, filed on 17 January 2000 from George W. Bush's Texas, about the execution of a 54-year-old black man who had been convicted of murder; and a *Globe* portrait of the famous (or infamous) investigative reporter Seymour Hersh, published on 10 January 1998.

The first article, "That Bastard Trudeau," came together as the result of classic reporting, a reconstruction of events based on meticulous interviewing and research. Cohen's history of the origins of Meech Lake won three national magazine awards and a bevy of other prizes, and had an impact on the debate then taking place about whether the accord ought to be finally ratified and come into effect. The second piece was a minute-by-minute study of a process the author called "choreographing the dance of death," Texas style. "At 6 p.m., they came for Sammie Felder Jr. . . . At 6:02, they inserted an intravenous catheter into his right arm ('successfully,' noted the official report) . . . At 6:11, they began to administer the poison . . . At 6:15, the doctor looked at his watch, and then he looked again, as if he didn't believe it. Pausing, pausing, pausing—he pronounced Sammie Felder Jr. dead." In the third article, Cohen told of the savaging of Hersh after the publication of his book on the Kennedys, full of damning chronicles of lies, corruption, assignations and policy failures from Cuba to Vietnam.

Which to choose, if choose we must? The Meech Lake article was a groundbreaking account of a major event. It was also beautifully written. But then everything Cohen writes is stylish, and this magazine piece was long and difficult to trim. The Texas story was the right length and extraordinarily moving. The author's idiosyncratic voice came through loudly and clearly: "He wasn't a nice man, our Mr. Felder. He took a pair of scissors to a paraplegic in an apartment house 25 years ago. Didn't think much about it. Now the state, embracing a biblical morality most democracies have long rejected, would take its scissors to him. Didn't think much about it, either."

We decided on the Hersh report, in part because it aimed at the inevitable subjectivity of reportage and in part because it was, very specifically and dramatically, about Cohen himself. The reporting and the reporter, then, all in the same package. The article was not simply directed at the onslaught of denunciation faced by Hersh as he took on the Kennedy legend. Its subject was the baggage all sides carry. Kennedy's loyalists had canonized him. They now circled the wagons and shot back hard at the enemy. The people believed the myth making, and forgave the fallen president his sins. Academics, with their books and views on public display, protected their investment in the status quo. With methods sometimes shoddy and erratic, Hersh made it much easier for his critics by resorting to sensationalism and innuendo; he so clearly hated the Kennedys, who had stolen the moral American dream.

Cohen, a journalist who seldom writes about himself, admitted frankly to his readers that he could not be any more dispassionate than others. He also had his biases and self-interest. He adored Jack and his brother

Bobby. He went to JFK's boarding school in Connecticut. He visited their rhetoric and their graves still. "The romantic in me," he concluded, "says that Mr. Hersh is largely wrong, that his story doesn't entirely hang together, the picture is incomplete. He has his Jack, and I have mine." Yet the journalist in Cohen (and the romantic, too) was troubled. He realized that The Truth has many versions, and that Hersh had found "a truth, which is undeniable and arresting."

We did not feel a compulsion to mark every important event in Canadian life, or to judge what was or is "important." How would that be possible, or even desirable? There was nothing magical about Meech Lake, even though its failure might have precipitated the end of a country. As it happened, we included an interview with Prime Minister Brian Mulroney by two *Globe and Mail* reporters, Susan Delacourt and Graham Fraser, conducted just as Mulroney was attempting to prevent a last-minute unravelling of the accord. We did so because it was strong reportage, the prime minister raw and exposed. It was here that he admitted, disastrously as it turned out, to "rolling the dice" by putting a gun to the heads of the provincial premiers at an eleventh-hour constitutional conference in 1990.

Twentieth century reporting takes up about two-thirds of the book, and there are large contingents of reportage from the two world wars, which did so much to change Canada and make it modern. World War I in particular shocked and shaped Canada. We print, side by side, two 1918 documents, one from the home front and one from the battlefield. Both are social histories of the impact of war. On 24 August 1918, the Kingston *Daily British Whig* published an apparently straightforward narrative on Canada's first street railway conductorettes. Miss Maude Chart had approached Hugh C. Nickle, the general manager of the Kingston, Portsmouth and Cataraqui Electric Railway Company in October of the previous year with an idea. "Women were doing all kinds of work to win the war, and she was quite willing, therefore, to act as conductor while the boys were away doing their bit. The women of England were running trams, and she considered it high time that the Canadians did the same." Chart was hired, the experiment was an unalloyed success and one conductorette became 12, the entire company cohort. The doubters were everywhere, "staid, old-fashioned gentlemen who said that Mr. Nickle had been foolish to give the girls an opportunity to show their ability." The winter would be too cold, the summer would be too hot, the hours would be too long. The writer clearly identified the pessimists as being on the wrong side of history, and yet the article fairly dripped with condescension: Chart looked down "appealingly"; women were "little girls"; the conductorettes performed their duties "with a grace and cleverness" that was "exceedingly creditable and gratifying."

As the *Daily British Whig* wrote about Chart's revolution, the Canadian Corps was in the first days of its final campaign, the Hundred Days, which was to end with the armistice on 11 November 1918. Captain Bellenden S. Hutcheson described his work as a medical officer feverishly trying to save lives as the shells fell all around him, "the possibility of being in the next few seconds in the same plight as the terribly wounded men [he] was dressing," occurring only "every now and then." He saw a company commander with the back of his head sheared off, identifiable only by the name "Captain MacDonald" written on his equipment; a soldier on fire and incinerated by the phosphorous smoke bombs he had been carrying; German wounded, in need of care and grateful for it; a captain leading his company into withering fire as he swung his walking stick nonchalantly, hit in the stomach and then hit again as he lay waiting for assistance; the grey faces of the very young, dead and dying. Hutcheson matter-of-factly itemized the killing he knew to be systematic and deliberate, his prose unvarnished by any reach for style or eloquence.

We found many other reporters like Captain Hutcheson, who were not professional writers and whose reportage spanned many of Canada's centuries: Jacques Cartier on his original meeting with First Nations in 1534; Samuel de Champlain discovering the terrible effects of scurvy; Marie d'Incarnation, founder of the Ursuline Order in Canada, commenting on life in New France; the Frobisher brothers' description of the 1784 fur trade; Sir John Franklin's exploration of the Arctic in 1820; colonial governor Sir Francis Bond Head on the 1837 Rebellion; Lady Agnes Macdonald, horrified by the assassination of Thomas D'Arcy McGee; engineer and inventor Sanford Fleming's breakfast habits; a pioneer woman in the Klondike; Lady Aberdeen and Sir Wilfrid Laurier on the hated Americans; British disapproval of the manners of Prime Minister R.B. Bennett, "partially educated and wholly uncivilised"; the encounter of a young diplomat, John Holmes, with Josef Stalin after World War II: "twinkling eyes and a Giaconda smile in an otherwise immobile face, but freshly painted for the occasion."

This book is a product of our interests, where we live and what was available to us. We read thousands of pages in newspapers, autobiographies, and books of documents and anthologies, and on the ever-increasing number of web sites devoted to historical subjects. We are particularly indebted to the multi-volume Champlain series, one of the too-little-known treasures of Canadian history; to the National Press Club's *A Century of Reporting/Un Siècle de Reportage* (1967); and to Prentice Hall's Canadian Historical Documents series, three volumes edited in the 1960s by Cameron Nish, Peter Waite and R.C. Brown, and M.E. Prang, respectively. It was frustrating to discover how hard it was to locate issues of old Canadian newspapers and magazines; sometimes sources were impossible to track down. The book is modelled on *The Faber Book of Reportage* (1987): editor John Carey provided spare introductions to his selections (and frequently none at all), and explained only where explanations were absolutely required. Where there were footnotes in the original text, we omitted them, and some of the French language entries were deliberately left as they were written.

Colleagues and friends helped us to better reflect the diversity of the country and its history: John Armstrong, Karen Baldree-O'Neil, Janice Cavell, Jennifer Cederwall, Lucie Courchesne, Grant Dawson, Bruce Elliot, Louisa-Joan Everitt, Graham Fraser, Trista Grant, Charlotte Gray, Stephen Hoogenraad, Maria Khan, Vadim Koukouchkine, Hector M. Mackenzie, Steve Mansell, Dominique Marshall, John Milloy, Richard Newport, Mike Orr, Jennifer Pedersen, Ryan Shackleton, Susan Whitney and Nico Zentil. The friendship and advice of our agent, Linda McKnight, was as dependable as ever. Katja Pantzar, Sarah Williams, and Jim Gifford saw a complicated manuscript to press with humour and professionalism. We particularly thank publisher Patrick Crean for his powerful commitment to the project and a searching critique of the first draft that caused us to reconsider many of our ideas.

J.L. Granatstein
Norman Hillmer
Toronto and Ottawa
1 July 2002

First Drafts

The Vikings Come to Vinland

ANONYMOUS

According to Eirik's Saga—*and to archaeological evidence in New-foundland—well before Columbus, Vikings made their way across the Atlantic.*

When Leif Eirikson had been with King Olaf Tryggvason and had been asked to preach Christianity in Greenland the king had given him a Scottish couple, a man called Haki and a woman called Hekja. The king told Leif to use them if he ever needed speed, for they could run faster than deer. Leif and Eirik had turned them over to Karlsefni for this expedition.

When the ships had passed Furdustrands the two Scots were put ashore and told to run southwards to explore the country's resources, and to return within three days. They each wore a garment called a bjafal, which had a hood at the top and was open at the sides: it had no sleeves and was fastened between the legs with a loop and button. That was all they wore.

The ships cast anchor there and waited, and after three days the Scots came running down to the shore; one of them was carrying some grapes, and the other some wild wheat. They told Karlsefni that they thought they had found good land. . . .

Karlsefni sailed South along the coast, accompanied by Snorri and Bjarni and the rest of the expedition. They sailed for a long time and eventually came to a river that flowed down into a lake and from the lake into the sea. There were extensive sandbars outside the river mouth, and ships could only enter it at high tide.

Karlsefni and his men sailed into the estuary and named the place *Hope* (Tidal Lake). Here they found wild wheat growing in fields on all the low ground and grape vines on all the higher ground. Every stream was teeming with fish. They dug trenches at the high-tide mark, and when the tide went out there were halibut trapped in the trenches. In the woods there was a great number of animals of all kinds.

They stayed there for a fortnight, enjoying themselves and noticing nothing untoward. They had their livestock with them. But early one morning as they looked around they caught sight of nine skin-boats; the men in them were waving sticks which made a noise like flails, and the motion was sunwise.

Karlsefni said, "What can this signify?"

"It could well be a token of peace," said Snorri. "Let us take a white shield and go to meet them with it."

They did so. The newcomers rowed towards them and stared at them in amazement as they came ashore. They were small and evil-looking, and their hair was coarse; they had large eyes and broad cheekbones. They stayed there for a while, marvelling, and then rowed away south round the headland.

Karlsefni and his men had built their settlement on a slope by the lakeside; some of the houses were close to the lake, and others were farther away. They stayed there that winter. There was no snow at all, and all the livestock were able to fend for themselves.

Then, early one morning in spring, they saw a great horde of skin-boats approaching from the south round the headland, so dense that it looked as if the estuary were strewn with charcoal: and sticks were being waved from every boat. Karlsefni's men raised their shields and the two parties began to trade.

What the natives wanted most to buy was red cloth; they also wanted to buy swords and spears, but Karlsefni and Snorri forbade that. In exchange for the cloth they traded grey pelts. The natives took a span of red cloth for each pelt, and tied the cloth around their heads. The trading went on like this for a while until the cloth began to run short; then Karlsefni and his men cut it up into pieces which were no more than a finger's breadth wide; but the Skraelings paid just as much or even more for it.

Then it so happened that a bull belonging to Karlsefni and his men came running out of the woods, bellowing furiously. The Skraelings were terrified and ran to their skin-boats and rowed away south round the headland.

After that there was no sign of the natives for three whole weeks. But then Karlsefni's men saw a huge number of boats coming from the south, pouring in like a torrent. This time all the sticks were being waved anti-clockwise and all the Skraelings were howling loudly. Karlsefni and his men now hoisted red shields and advanced towards them.

When they clashed there was a fierce battle and a hail of missiles came flying over, for the Skraelings were using catapults. Karlsefni and Snorri saw them hoist a large sphere on a pole; it was dark blue in colour. It came flying in over the heads of Karlsefni's men and made an ugly din when it struck the ground. This terrified Karlsefni and his men so much that their only thought was to flee, and they retreated farther up the river.

They did not halt until they reached some cliffs, where they prepared to make a resolute stand.

Freydis came out and saw the retreat. She shouted, "Why do you flee from such pitiful wretches, brave men like you? You should be able to slaughter them like cattle. If I had weapons, I am sure I could fight better than any of you."

The men paid no attention to what she was saying. Freydis tried to join them but she could not keep up with them because she was pregnant. She was following them into the woods when the Skraelings closed in on her. In front of her lay a dead man, Thorbrand Snorrason, with a flint-stone buried in his head, and his sword beside him. She snatched up the sword and prepared to defend herself. When the Skraelings came rushing towards her she pulled one of her breasts out of her bodice and slapped it with the sword. The Skraelings were terrified at the sight of this and fled back to their boats and hastened away.

Karlsefni and his men came over to her and praised her courage. Two of their men had been killed, and four of the Skraelings, even though Karlsefni and his men had been fighting against heavy odds.

They returned to their houses and pondered what force it was that had attacked them from inland; they then realized that the only attackers had been those who had come in the boats, and that the other force had just been a delusion.

The Skraelings found the other dead Norseman, with his axe lying beside him. One of them hacked at a rock with the axe, and the axe broke; and thinking it worthless now because it could not withstand stone, they threw it away.

Karlsefni and his men had realized by now that although the land was excellent they could never live there in safety or freedom from fear, because of the native inhabitants. So they made ready to leave the place and return home. . . .

Cabot Comes to North America, 1497

LORENZO PASQUALIGO

Giovanni Caboto, or John Cabot, discovered North America in the service of King Henry VII of England. This letter from a Venetian living in London is one of the first reports of Cabot's explorations.

That Venetian of ours who went with a small ship from Bristol to find new islands has come back and says he has discovered mainland 700 leagues away, which is the country of the Grand Khan, and that he coasted it for 300 leagues and landed and did not see any person; but he has brought here to the king [Henry VII] certain snares which were spread to take game and a needle for making nets, and he found certain notched [or felled] trees so that by this he judges that there are inhabitants. Being in doubt he returned to his ship; and he has been three months on the voyage; and this is certain. And on the way back he saw two islands, but was unwilling to land, in order not to lose time, as he was in want of provisions. The king here is much pleased at this; and he says that the tides are slack and do not run as they do here. The king has promised him for the spring ten armed ships as he desires, and has given him all the prisoners to be sent away, that they may go with him, as he has requested; and has given him money that he may have a good time until then, and he is with his Venetian wife and his sons at Bristol. His name is Zuam Talbot and he is called the Great Admiral and vast honour is paid to him and he goes dressed in silk, and these English run after him like mad, and indeed he can enlist as many of them as he pleases, and a number of our rogues as well. The discoverer of these things planted on the land which he has found a large cross with a banner of England and one of St. Mark, as he is a Venetian, so that our flag has been hoisted very far afield.

The Sea Is Swarming with Fish

RAIMONDO DI SONCINO

> *Within months of John Cabot's first visit to North America in 1497, reports were widespread of the vast quantities of cod on the Grand Banks. Raimondo di Soncino wrote this letter to the Duke of Milan in December 1497.*

. . . the sea there is swarming with fish, which can be taken not only with a net but in baskets let down with a stone, so that it sinks in the water. I have heard this Messer Zoane . . . say that they could bring so many fish that this kingdom would have no further need of Iceland, from which place there comes a very great quantity of the fish called stockfish.

The 1534 Voyage of Jacques Cartier

JACQUES CARTIER

> *Jacques Cartier undertook the first major exploration of the Gulf of St. Lawrence. His account of the land and its inhabitants must have intrigued France.*

If the soil were as good as the harbours, it would be a blessing; but the land should not be called the New Land, being composed of stones and horrible rugged rocks; for along the whole of the north shore, I did not see one cart-load of earth and yet I landed in many places. Except at Blanc-Sablon there is nothing but moss and short, stunted shrub. In fine I am rather inclined to believe that this is the land that God gave to Cain. There are people on this coast whose bodies are fairly well formed but they are wild and savage folk. They wear their hair tied up on the top of their heads like a handful of twisted hay, with a nail or something of the sort passed through the middle, and into it they weave a few bird's feathers. They clothe themselves with the furs of animals, both men as well as women; but the women are wrapped up more closely and snuggly in their furs. . . .

The next day some of these Indians came in nine canoes to the point at the mouth of the cove where we lay anchored with our ships. And being informed of their arrival we went with our two long-boats to the point where they were, at the mouth of the cove. As soon as they saw us they began to run away, making signs to us that they had come to barter with us; and held up some furs of small value, with which they clothe themselves. We likewise made signs to them that we wished them no harm, and sent two men on shore to offer them some knives and other iron goods, and a red cap to give to their chief. Seeing this, they sent on shore part of their people with some of their furs; and the two parties traded together. The savages showed a marvellously great pleasure in possessing and obtaining these iron wares and other commodities, dancing and going through many ceremonies, and throwing salt water over their heads with all hands. They bartered all they had to such an extent that all went back naked without anything on them; and they made signs to us that they would return on the morrow with more furs.

Champlain on Scurvy, 1605

SAMUEL DE CHAMPLAIN

Samuel de Champlain set out to found settlements in New France, but the task was hard, especially in winter, for these vitamin-deprived men.

During the winter a certain malady attacked many of our people. It is called land-sickness, otherwise scurvy, according to what I have since heard stated by learned men. There was engendered in the mouths of those who had it large pieces of superfluous fungus flesh (which caused a great putrefaction); and this increased to such a degree that they could scarcely take anything, except in very liquid form. Their teeth barely held in their places, and could be drawn out with the fingers without causing pain. This superfluous flesh was often cut away, which caused them to lose much blood from the mouth. Afterwards, they were taken with great pains in the arms and legs, which became swollen and very hard and covered with spots like flea-bites; and they could not walk on account of the contraction of the nerves; consequently they had almost no strength, and suffered intolerable pains. They had also pains in the loins, stomach, and bowels, together with a very bad cough and shortness of breath. In brief, they were in such a state that the majority of the sick could neither get up nor move, nor could they even be held upright without fainting away; so that of seventy-nine of us, thirty-five died, and more than twenty were very near it. The majority of those who kept well complained of some minor pains and shortness of breath. We could find no remedy with which to cure these maladies. We opened several of them to determine the cause of their illness.

In many cases it was found that the interior parts were diseased; for example the lungs were so altered that no natural moisture could be seen; the spleen was watery and swollen; the liver very fibrous and mottled, with none of its natural colour; the *vena cava*, both ascending and descending, full of thick, clotted and black blood; the gall tainted. Nevertheless many arteries, both in the mid and lower bowels, were in pretty good condition. In some cases incisions were made with a razor upon the thighs over the purple spots, whence there flowed a black clotted blood. This is what could be learned from the bodies infected with this disease.

Our surgeons were unable to treat themselves so as not to suffer the same fate as the others. Those who continued to be ill grew well in the spring, which in this country begins in May. This made us believe that the change of season restored them to health rather than the remedies which had been prescribed for them.

Champlain Fights the Iroquois, 1609

SAMUEL DE CHAMPLAIN

> *When Champlain and his men fired their arquebuses at the Iroquois, the enemy fled. The long-lasting enmity between the French and the Iroquois had its origins in this encounter.*

Our Indians all night long also kept their canoes close to one another and tied to poles in order not to get separated, but to fight all together in case of need. We were on the water within bowshot of their barricades. And when they were armed, and everything in order, they sent two canoes which they had separated from the rest, to learn from their enemies whether they wished to fight, and these replied that they had no other desire, but that for the moment nothing could be seen and that it was necessary to wait for daylight in order to distinguish one another. They said that as soon as the sun should rise, they would attack us, and to this our Indians agreed. Meanwhile the whole night was spent in dances and songs on both sides, with many insults and other remarks, such as the lack of courage of our side, how little we could resist or do against them, and that when daylight came our people would learn all this to their ruin. Our side too was not lacking in retort, telling the enemy that they would see such deeds of arms as they had never seen, and a great deal of other talk, such as is usual at the siege of a city. Having sung, danced, and flung words at one another for some time, when daylight came, my companions and I were still hidden, lest the enemy should see us, getting our fire-arms ready as best we could, being however still separated, each in a canoe of the Montagnais Indians. After we were armed with light weapons, we took, each of us, an arquebus and went ashore. I saw the enemy come out of their barricade to the number of two hundred, in appearance strong, robust men They came slowly to meet us with a gravity and calm which I admired; and at their head were three chiefs. Our Indians likewise advanced in similar order, and told me that those who had the three big plumes were the chiefs, and that there were only these three, whom you could recognize by these plumes, which were larger than those of their companions; and I was to do what I could to kill them. I promised them to do all in my power, and told them that I was very sorry they could not understand me, so that I might direct their method of attacking the enemy, all of whom undoubtedly we should thus defeat; but that there was no help for it, and that I was very glad to show them, as soon as the engagement began, the courage and readiness which were in me.

As soon as we landed, our Indians began to run some two hundred yards towards their enemies, who stood firm and had not yet noticed my white companions who went off into the woods with some Indians. Our Indians began to call to me with loud cries; and to make way for me they divided into two groups, and put me ahead some twenty yards, and I marched on until I was within some thirty yards of the enemy, who as soon as they caught sight of me halted and gazed at me and I at them. When I saw them make a move to draw their bows upon us, I took aim with my arquebus and shot straight at one of the three chiefs, and with this shot two fell to the ground and one of their companions was wounded who died thereof a little later. I had put four bullets into my arquebus. As soon as our people saw this shot so favourable for them, they began to shout so loudly that one could not have heard it thunder, and meanwhile the arrows flew thick on both sides. The Iroquois were much astonished that two men should have been killed so quickly, although they were provided with shields made of cotton thread woven together and wood, which were proof against their arrows. This frightened them greatly. As I was reloading my arquebus, one of my companions fired a shot from within the woods, which astonished them again so much that, seeing their chiefs dead, they lost courage and took to flight, abandoning the field and their fort, and fleeing into the depth of the forest, whither I pursued them and laid low still more of them. Our Indians also killed several and took ten or twelve prisoners. The remainder fled with the wounded. Of our Indians fifteen or sixteen were wounded with arrows, but these were quickly healed.

The Martyrdom of the Jesuits at Ste. Marie, 1648

FATHER PAUL RAGUENEAU

Jesuit fathers came to New France to spread Christianity among the Indians, but found themselves caught up in tribal wars. The Iroquois sacked and burned Ste. Marie among the Hurons in 1648.

Hardly had the Father ended Mass, and the Christians—who, according to their custom, had filled the Church after the rising of the sun—were still continuing their devotions there, when the cry arose, "To arms! and repel the enemy!"—who, having come unexpectedly, had made his approaches by night. Some hasten to the combat, others to flight: there is naught but alarm and terror everywhere. The Father, among the first to rush where he sees the danger greatest, encourages his people to a brave defense; and—as if he had seen Paradise open for the Christians, and Hell on the point of swallowing up all the Infidels—he speaks to them in a tone so animated with the spirit which was possessing him, that having made a breach in hearts which till then had been most rebellious, he gave them a Christian heart. The number of these proved to be so great that, unable to cope with it by baptizing them one after the other, he was constrained to dip his handkerchief in the water (which was all that necessity then offered him), in order to shed abroad as quickly as possible this grace on those poor Savages, who cried mercy to him,—using the manner of baptizing which is called "by aspersion."

Meanwhile, the enemy continued his attacks more furiously than ever; and, without doubt, it was a great blessing for the salvation of some that, at the moment of their death, Baptism had given them the life of the soul, and put them in possession of an immortal life.

When the Father saw that the Iroquois were becoming masters of the place, he,—instead of taking flight with those who were inviting him to escape in their company,—forgetting himself, remembered some old men and sick people, whom he had long ago prepared for Baptism. He goes through the cabins, and proceeds to fill them with his zeal,—the Infidels themselves presenting their children in crowds, in order to make Christians of them.

Meanwhile the enemy, already victorious, had set everything on fire, and the blood of even the women and children irritated their fury. The Father, wishing to die in his Church, finds it full of Christians, and of

Catechumens who ask him for Baptism. It was indeed at that time that their faith animated their prayers, and that their hearts could not belie their tongues. He baptizes some, gives absolution to others, and consoles them all with the "sweetest hope of the Saints,—having hardly other words on his lips than these: "My Brothers, to-day we shall be in Heaven."

The enemy was warned that the Christians had betaken themselves, in very great number, into the Church, and that it was the easiest and the richest prey that he could have hoped for; he hastens thither, with barbarous howls and stunning yells. At the noise of these approaches, "Flee, my Brothers," said the Father to his new Christians, "and bear with you your faith even to the last sigh. As for me" (he added), "I must face death here, as long as I shall see here any soul to be gained for Heaven; and, dying here to save you, my life is no longer anything to me; we shall see one another again in Heaven." At the same time, he goes out in the direction whence come the enemy, who stop in astonishment to see one man alone come to meet them, and even recoil backward, as if he bore upon his face the terrible and frightful appearance of a whole company. Finally, —having come to their senses a little, and being astonished at themselves,—they incite one another; they surround him on all sides, and cover him with arrows, until, having inflicted upon him a mortal wound from an arquebus shot,—which pierced him through and through, in the very middle of his breast,—he fell. Pronouncing the name of Jesus, he blessedly yielded up his soul to God,—truly as a good Pastor, who exposes both his soul and his life for the salvation of his flock.

It was then that those Barbarians rushed upon him with as much rage as if he alone had been the object of their hatred. They strip him naked, they exercise upon him a thousand indignities; and there was hardly any one who did not try to assume the glory of having given him the final blow, even on seeing him dead.

The fire meanwhile was consuming the cabins; and when it had spread as far as the Church, the Father was cast into it, at the height of the flames, which soon made of him a whole burnt-offering. Be this as it may, he could not have been more gloriously consumed than in the fires and lights of a *Chapelle ardente*.

Marie de l'Incarnation Reports from New France, 1665

MARIE DE L'INCARNATION

Marie de l'Incarnation founded an Ursuline convent in Québec and regularly sent letters back to France with full reports on life in New France.

The hundred girls that the King sent this year have just arrived and already almost all of them are married. He will send two hundred more next year and still others in proportion in the years to come. He is also sending men to supply the needs of the marriages, and this year fully five hundred have come, not to speak of the men that make up the army. In consequence, it is an astonishing thing to see how the country becomes peopled and multiplies. It is said that His Majesty intends to spare nothing, being urged to this by the seigneurs that are here, who find the country and living here delightful in comparison with the West Indies whence they come, where the heat is so extreme one can scarcely live. Those countries are rich because of the sugar and tobacco taken from them, but it is impossible to grow wheat there, and their bread is made of a certain root that necessity forces them to subsist on. But here wheat, vegetables, and all sort of cereals grow in abundance. The soil is excellent for wheat and, the more the woods are stripped from it, the more fertile and bounteous it becomes. Its fertility was very apparent this year because, the army's flour having spoiled on the ocean, enough wheat was found here to supply their needs without harming the provision of the habitants.

However this bounteousness does not prevent there being a great many poor folk here; the reason is that, when a family commences to make a habitation, it needs two or three years before it has enough to feed itself, not to speak of clothing, furniture, and an infinite number of little things necessary for the maintenance of a house; but when these first difficulties are past, they begin to live comfortably and, if they have guidance, they become rich with time—or as much so as is possible in a new country such as this. In the beginning they live on their cereals and vegetables and on wild game, which is plentiful in winter. To obtain clothing and other household utensils, they make roofing planks and cut timber, which they sell at a high price. When they have thus obtained all their necessities, they begin to trade and in this way advance little by little. . . .

I told you in another letter that part of the army has gone on ahead to get control of the river of the Iroquois and build forts on its banks in the most advantageous places. To this I shall add that our Christian Algonkins have gone to camp with their families under protection of the forts and those that guard them. They are hunting where their enemies were accustomed to do so and obtain the greater part of their pelts. Their hunt is so bounteous that it is said they take more than a hundred beaver each day, not to speak of moose and other wild beasts.

In this the French and the Savages help one another. The French defend the Savages, and the Savages provide food for the French by the flesh of the beasts they kill, after they have removed the skins, which they take to the storehouses of the country. Monsieur de Tracy told me a few days ago that he had informed the King of all this and also the other advantages there are in making war upon the sworn enemy of our Faith.

Voyageurs in the Fur Trade in the 1690s

LAMOTHE CADILLAC

The search for furs sent men of New France on long, difficult trips into the interior. This account by Lamothe Cadillac details the conditions of the trade and the endurance of the voyageurs.

If people could realize the labor which is involved in finding beaver skins they would not think so lightly of this commodity, for it should be known that the French trading-party generally leaves Montreal at the beginning of spring, or about the 15th of September, and in this country both seasons are bad—the first, because it is the time when the ice and snow melt, making the current strong and the water very cold, and the second because it is the beginning of the ice and snow. There are many rapids on the way. The Canadians, who are almost always indomitable fishermen, are generally bare-footed and bare-legged, wearing only their shirts; when their canoes cannot make headway against the rapids, they boldly jump into the water and by main strength, all helping one another, they manage to get them along, but not without frequently skinning their feet and legs for the rocks are so cold that their skin sticks to them and the men do not get free without leaving a piece behind them. If this happened only once a day it would be a small matter; but, on the contrary, it happens constantly throughout their entire voyage.

Nor is this all. They frequently come to rapids or waterfalls where it is impossible to take their boats up or down, and it is necessary to disembark at the foot of the rapids and carry the canoes on the men's shoulders through the woods, along with all the merchandise or beaverskins, around the falls before they can re-embark; this is called making a portage. Some of the portages are [two] leagues long.

Thus the Canadians have to make a journey of 300 leagues by this continual and laborious work before reaching Michilimackinac, which shows their strength and vigor and how inured they are to fatigue; it seems incredible that the human body is able to withstand such extraordinary cold.

When they arrive there, instead of trying to recover a little from their fatigue they hasten to continue their journey, and go on as soon as possible. They generally re-equip themselves here with canoes and provisions, after which some go to the north coast of Lake Superior and others to the south, and they follow the rivers into the back country for a distance of 200 or 300 leagues. Some of them, following Lake Michigan, go south to the most distant tribes. The object of all alike is to get beaver-skins.

When the voyageurs have sold their goods they return to Michilimackinac, generally arriving at the beginning of July; here they re-equip themselves anew and go down to Montreal in a convoy, if the commandant of the country thinks it safe. It is plain, therefore, that those who engage in this trade for beaver skins have to travel at least 1000 leagues before getting back to Montreal; but aside from this it is difficult to conceive the dangers to which they are exposed in shooting whirlpools, falls and rapids, which only to think of makes one's hair stand on end.

Nor is this all. They must also risk losing their lives by the hands of the Iroquois, who prepare ambushes in narrow passes along the route and if a man is captured alive he must be prepared to be burned to death by inches. It is true that all necessary precautions are taken to avoid this misfortune, and that it rarely happens that our convoys are defeated.

Marie-Madeleine de Verchères
Tells How She Drove Off the Iroquois, 1692

MARIE-MADELEINE DE VERCHÈRES

Marie-Madeleine de Verchères, 14 years old at the time of her exploit, gave this account some 24 years after the event of her defence of her family's fort at Verchères.

I was five arpents away from the fort of Verchères, belonging to Sieur De Verchères, my father, who was then at Kebek by order of M. Le Chevalier De Callières, governor of Montreal, my mother being also in Montreal. I heard several shots without knowing at whom they were fired. I soon saw that the Iroquois were firing at our settlers, who lived about a league and a-half from the fort. One of our servants called out to me:

"Fly, mademoiselle, fly! the Iroquois are upon us!"

I turned instantly and saw some forty-five Iroquois running towards me, and already within pistol shot. Determined to die rather than fall into their hands, I sought safety in flight. I ran towards the fort, commending myself to the Blessed Virgin, and saying to her from the bottom of my heart: "Holy Virgin, mother of my God, you know I have ever honoured and loved you as my dear mother; abandon me not in this hour of danger! I would rather a thousand times perish than fall into the hands of a race that know you not."

Meantime my pursuers, seeing that they were too far off to take me alive before I could enter the fort, and knowing they were near enough to shoot me, stood still in order to discharge their guns at me. I was under fire for quite a time, at any rate I found the time long enough! Forty-five bullets whistling past my ears made the time seem long and the distance from the fort interminable, though I was so near. When within hearing of the fort, I cried out: "To arms! To arms!"

I hoped that someone would come to help me, but it was a vain hope. There were but two soldiers in the fort and these were so overcome by fear that they had sought safety by concealing themselves in the redoubt. Having reached the gates at last, I found there two women lamenting for the loss of their husbands, who had just been killed. I made them enter the fort, and closed the gates myself. I then began to consider how I might save myself and the little party with me, from the hands of the savages. I examined the fort, and found that several of the stakes had fallen, leaving gaps through which it would be easy for the enemy to enter. I gave orders to have the stakes replaced, and heedless of my sex and tender age, I hesitated not to seize one end of the heavy stake and urge my companions to give a hand in raising it. I found by experience that, when God gives us strength, nothing is impossible.

The breaches having been repaired, I betook myself to the redoubt, which served as a guard-house and armoury. I there found two soldiers, one of them lying down and the other holding a burning fuse. I said to the latter:

"What are you going to do with that fuse?"

"I want to set fire to the powder," said he, "and blow up the fort."

"You are a miserable wretch," I said, adding: "Begone, I command you!"

I spoke so firmly that he obeyed forthwith. Thereupon putting aside my hood and donning a soldier's casque, I seized a musket and said to my little brothers:

"Let us fight to the death for our country and for our holy religion. Remember what our father has so often told you, that gentlemen are born but to shed their blood for the service of God and the king!"

Stirred up by my words, my brothers and the two soldiers kept up a steady fire on the foe. I caused the cannon to be fired, not only to strike terror into the Iroquois and show them that we were well able to defend ourselves, since we had a cannon, but also to warn our own soldiers, who were away hunting, to take refuge in some other fort. But alas! what sufferings have to be endured in these awful extremities of distress! Despite the thunder of our guns, I heard unceasingly the cries and lamentations of some unfortunates who had just lost a husband, a brother, a child or a parent. I deemed it prudent, while the firing was still kept up, to represent to the grief-stricken women that their shrieks exposed us to danger, for they could not fail to be heard by the enemy, notwithstanding the noise of the guns and the cannon. I ordered them to be silent and thus avoid giving the impression that we were helpless and hopeless.

While I was speaking thus, I caught sight of a canoe on the river, opposite the fort. It was Sieur Pierre Fontaine with his family, who were about to land at the spot where I had just barely escaped from the Iroquois, the latter being still visible on every hand. The family must fall into the hands of the savages if not promptly succoured.

I asked the two soldiers to go to the landing place, only five arpents away, and protect the family. But seeing by their silence, that they had but little heart for the work, I ordered our servant, Laviolette, to stand sentry at the gate of the fort and keep it open, while I would myself go to the bank of the river, carrying a musket in my hand and wearing my soldier's casque. I left orders on setting out, that if I was killed, they were to shut the gates and continue to defend the fort sturdily. I set out with the heaven-sent thought that the enemy, who were looking on, would imagine that it was a ruse on my part to induce them to approach the fort, in order that our people might make a sortie upon them.

This is precisely what happened, and thus was I enabled to save poor Pierre Fontaine, with his wife and children. When all were landed, I made them march before me as far as the fort, within sight of the enemy. By putting a bold face upon it, I made the Iroquois think there was more danger for them than for us.

They did not know that the whole garrison, and only inhabitants of the fort of Verchères, were my two brothers aged 12 years, our servant, two soldiers, an old man of eighty, and some women and children.

Strengthened by the new recruits from Pierre Fontaine's canoe, I gave orders to continue firing at the enemy. Meantime the sun went down and a fierce northeaster accompanied by snow and hail, ushered in a night of awful severity. The enemy kept us closely invested and instead of being deterred by the dreadful weather, led me to judge by their movements that they purposed assaulting the fort under cover of the darkness.

I gathered all my troops—six persons—together, and spoke to them thus: "God has saved us to-day from the hands of our enemies, but we must be careful not to be caught in their snares to-night. For my part, I want to show you that I am not afraid. I undertake the fort for my share, with an old man of eighty, and a soldier who has never fired a gun. And you, Pierre Fontaine, with La Bonté and Galhet (our two soldiers), will go to the redoubt, with the women and children, as it is the strongest place. If I am taken, never surrender, even though I should be burnt and cut to pieces before your eyes. You have nothing to fear in the redoubt, if you only make some show of fighting."

Thereupon, I posted my two young brothers on two of the bastions, the youth of 80 on a third bastion and myself took charge of the fourth. Each one acted his part to the life. Despite the whistling of the northeast wind, which is a fearful wind in Canada, at this season, and in spite of the snow and hail, the cry of "All's well," was heard at close intervals, echoing and re-echoing from the fort to the redoubt and from the redoubt to the fort.

One would have fancied, to hear us, that the fort was crowded with warriors. And in truth the Iroquois, with all their astuteness and skill in warfare were completely deceived, as they afterwards avowed to M. De Callières. They told him they had held a council with a view to assaulting the fort during the night, but that the increased vigilance of the guard had prevented them from accomplishing their design, especially in view of their losses of the previous day (under the fire maintained by myself and my two brothers).

About an hour after midnight, the sentinel at the gate bastion, cried out:

"Mademoiselle! I hear something!"

I walked towards him, in order to see what it was, and through the darkness, aided by the reflection from the snow, I saw a group of horned cattle, the remnant escaped from the hands of our enemies.

"Let me open the gates for them," said the sentry.

"God forbid," I answered, "you do not know all the cunning of the savages, they are probably marching behind the cattle, covered with the hides of animals, so as to get into the fort, if we are simple enough to open the gates."

I saw danger everywhere, in face of an enemy so keen and crafty as the Iroquois. Nevertheless, after adopting every precaution suggested by prudence under the circumstances, I decided that there would be no risk in opening the gate. I sent for my two brothers, and made them stand by with their muskets loaded and primed, in case of a surprise, and then we let the cattle enter the fort.

At last the day dawned, and the sun in scattering the shades of the night seemed to banish our grief and anxiety. Assuming a joyful countenance I gathered my garrison around me and said to them:

"Since, with God's help, we have got through the past night with all its terrors, we can surely get through other nights by keeping good watch and ward and by firing our cannon hour by hour, so as to get help from Montreal, which is only eight leagues off."

I saw that my address made an impression on their minds. But Marguerite Antoine, the wife of Sieur Pierre Fontaine, being extremely timorous, as is natural to all Parisian women, asked her husband to take her to another fort, representing to him that while she had been lucky enough to escape the fury of the savages the first night, she had no reason to expect a like good fortune for the coming night; that the fort of Verchères was utterly worthless, that there were no men to hold it, and that to remain in it would be to expose one's self to evident danger, or to run the risk of perpetual slavery or of death by slow fire. The poor husband, finding that his wife persisted in her request and that she wanted to go to Fort Contrecoeur, three hours distant from Verchères, said to her: "I will fit you out a good canoe, with a proper sail, and you will have your two children, who are accustomed to handle it. I myself will never abandon the fort of Verchères, so long as Mademoiselle Magdelon (this was the name I went by in my childhood) holds it."

I spoke up firmly then, and told him that I would never abandon the fort; that I would sooner perish than deliver it up to our enemies; that it

was of the last importance that the savages should never enter one of our
French forts; that they would judge of the rest by the one they got possession of, and that the knowledge thus acquired could not fail to increase
their pride and courage.

I can truthfully say that I was on two occasions, for twenty-four hours
without rest or food. I did not once enter my father's house. I took up my
station on the bastion, and from time to time looked after things on the
redoubt. I always wore a smiling and joyful face, and cheered up my little
troop with the prospect of speedy assistance.

On the eighth day (for we were eight days in continual alarms, under
the eyes of our enemies and exposed to their fury and savage attacks), on
the eighth day, I say, M. De La Monnerie, a lieutenant detached from the
force under M. De Callières, reached the fort during the night with forty
men. Not knowing but the fort had fallen, he made his approach in perfect silence. One of our sentries hearing a noise, cried out: "Qui vive?"

I was dozing at the moment, with my head resting on a table and my
musket across my arms.

The sentry told me he heard voices on the water. I forthwith mounted
the bastion in order to find out by the tone of the voice whether the party
were savages or French. I called out to them:

"Who are you?"

They answered: "French! It is La Monnerie come to your assistance."

I caused the door of the fort to be opened and put a sentry to guard it,
and went down to the bank of the river to receive the party. So soon as I
saw the officer in command I saluted him, saying:

"Sir, you are welcome, I surrender my arms to you."

"Mademoiselle," he answered, with a courtly air, "they are in good
hands."

"Better than you think," I replied.

He inspected the fort and found it in a most satisfactory condition,
with a sentry on each bastion. I said to him:

"Sir, kindly relieve my sentries, so that they may take a little rest, for
we have not left our posts for the last eight days."

I was forgetting one circumstance which will give an idea of my confidence and tranquility. On the day of the great battle, the Iroquois who
were around the fort, were sacking and burning the houses of our settlers
and killing their cattle before our eyes, when I called to mind, about one
o'clock in the afternoon, that I had three sacks of linen and some quilts
outside the fort. I asked my soldiers to take their guns and accompany me
while I went out for the clothes; but their silence and sullen looks convinced me of their lack of courage, so I turned to my young brothers and
said to them:

"Take your guns and come with me! As to you," I said to the others,
"keep your fire against the enemy while I go for my linen."

I made two trips, in sight of the enemy, in the very place where they had so narrowly missed taking me prisoner, a few hours before. They must have suspected some plot under my proceedings, for they did not venture to try to capture me, or even to take my life with their guns. I felt then that when God overrules matters, there is no danger of failure. . . .

An Encounter with the Esquimaux, 1743

SIEUR LOUIS FORNEL

Fornel traveled into the Labrador country in the summer of 1743 and encountered the Eskimo.

Finally, at about two o'clock in the afternoon, we anchored in twenty fathoms of water near the islands. One hour later, eight canoes of Eskimaux appeared at the point. They landed on an island, uttering their usual cries, which we answered, which is equivalent to inviting them to approach. The Eskimaux having re-embarked in their canoes came on board. As we saw them approaching, we armed ourselves. They boarded us and brought aboard eight whale fins which I bartered with them. One hour after their departure, six other canoes of Eskimaux boarded us, and they traded four whale fins. One of these Eskimaux gave us to understand that he was Captain Amargo, and that Captain Araby had ordered him to fire a gun shot at a seal to teach him the use of arms. Before leaving us, he also gave us to understand that he was going to sleep and, in the morning would bring other Indians of his nation to trade with us. I ordered that this chief and his band be given cooked meat, which they ate. They drank fresh water that we gave them. This disproves the story that these barbarians eat only raw meat and drink salt water, which seemed incredible, but they refused bread, wine and whiskey, the use of which was unknown to them. It would be desirable that it be the same with our other Indians. It is only to be feared that, if the Coste des Eskimaux is settled by too many Frenchmen, the liquor habit will be acquired by these barbarians, as has been the case with other Indians. I noticed that many of them were bleeding naturally from the nose, and were drinking it. Our men pretended that fear was the only cause of it. I doubt it, because these barbarians did not seem frightened. Their intention was perhaps to let us understand that they likewise wished to drink our blood. Therefore, as long as they remained on board, we were on our guard.

17 July, 1743

Contrary winds prevented us from leaving the Baye des Meniques. About seven o'clock in the morning, twenty-four canoes of Eskimaux boarded us, followed by eighteen boats which seemed loaded only with women, children and luggage. The boats kept at a distance, undoubtedly fearing to approach. Having uttered their usual cries, which we answered while keeping on the alert, the Eskimaux of the twenty-four canoes came on board where they traded with us about one quintal of whalebone, three canoes, seal clothing and some of their weapons. That is the only profit I made during my exploration in return for the heavy expenses I incurred.

The Expulsion of the Acadians, 1755

LIEUT.-COL. JOHN WINSLOW

Imperial concerns led the British to drive the French-speaking Acadians out of their homes in Nova Scotia. This account by Lieut.-Col. John Winslow, who did not seem wholly happy in his work, describes his orders and the subsequent expulsion.

September 5th—At Three in the afternoon the French Inhabitants appeared agreeable to their Citation at the Church in Grand Pre amounting to 418 of Their Best Men upon which I ordered a Table to be Sett in the Center of the Church and being attended with those of my officers who were off Guard Delivered them by Interpretors the King's orders in the Following words:

Gentlemen—I have Received from his Excellency Governor Lawrance, The Kings Commission which I have in my hand and by whose orders you are Convened together to Manifest to you his Majesty's Final resolution to the French Inhabitants of this his Province of Nova Scotia, who for almost half a Century have had more Indulgence Granted them, then any of his Subjects in any part of his Dominions, what use you have made of them, you your Self Best know.

The Part of Duty I am now upon is what thot Necessary is Very Disagreeable to my Natural make and Temper as I Know it Must be Grevious to you who are of the Same Specia.

But it is not my Business to annimedvert, but to obey Such orders as I receive and therefore without Hesitation shall Delivery you his Majesty's orders and Instructions vizt.

That your Lands & Tennements, Cattle of all Kinds and Live Stock of all Sortes are Forfitted to the Crown with all other Effects Saving your Money and Household Goods and you yourselves to be removed from this his Province.

This it is Preremtorily his Majesty's orders That the whole French Inhabitants of these Districts, be removed, and I am Throh his Majesty's Goodness Directed to allow you Liberty to Carry of your money and Household Goods as Many as you Can without Discomemoading the

Vessels you Go in. I shall do Everything in my power that all Those Goods be Secured to you and that you are Not Molested in Carrying of them and also that whole Families Shall go in Same Vessel, and make this remove which I am Sensable must give you a great Deal of Trouble as Easy as his Majesty's Service will admit and hope that in what Ever part of the world you may Fall you may be Faithful Subjects, a Peasable and happy People.

I Must also inform you That it is his Majesty's Pleasure that you remain in Security under the Inspection and Direction of the Troops that I have the Honr. to Command.

and then declared them the Kings Prisoner's. . . .

October 8th. Began to Embarke the Inhabitants who went of Very Solentarily and unwillingly, the women in Great Distress Carrying off Their children In their arms. Others Carrying their Decript Parents in their Carts and all their Goods Moving in great Confussion & appeard a Sceen of woe & Distress.

Governor General Vaudreuil Reacts to Montcalm's Defeat, 1759

MARQUIS DE VAUDREUIL

> *The climactic battle that decided the fate of Canada took place at Québec in September 1759. Vaudreuil, New France's governor general, was arguably more sensible than his military commander, Montcalm.*

A very unfortunate event has occurred. At dawn the enemy surprised M. de Vergor who was in command at l'Anse-du-Foulon. They quickly gained the heights . . . Montcalm arrived with the first detachment. I was part of the rear guard, and quickened the pace of the militia troops on my route. I had . . . Bougainville advised, who, in an instant, marched from Cap Rouge with the five companies of grenadiers, two field pieces, the cavalry, and all that he had that was useful. Although the enemy had forestalled us, his position was critical. All we had to do was await . . . Bougainville, for while we could attack with all of our forces, he would also be attacked from the rear. But fate was not with us to the extent that the engagement was undertaken too hastily. . . As a result, this is our present position: 1—We are not prepared to revenge ourselves this evening; our army is too demoralized and we could not rally it. If we wait until tomorrow the enemy will be entrenched in an unassailable position. 2—I cannot, and will not, consent to the capitulation of the whole colony. 3—Our retreat thus becomes imperative.

Wolfe's Men Gain the Heights at Québec, 1759

UNKNOWN

This account by an unnamed junior staff officer to General James Wolfe tells how the British made their way to the battlefield of Québec.

... The 6th M^r. Wolfe went up. The ships moved up to Carrouge, the following day the General went in his Barge, and reconnoitred the Coast at less than 200 yards distance all the way up to Pointe de Trempe and there fixt on a place for the Descent, and gave his orders in consequence; Heavy rain delay'd this operation, and the General fearing for the Health of the soldiers, who were much crowd'd aboard the ships, order'd half of them to be landed on the southern shore and Cantoon'd in the Village of St. Nicolas: During this Interval the General went in Captn. Leaske's schooner and reconnoitered close by the shore from Carrouge down to the Town of Quebec. During his absence M^r. Murray and Townshend came aboard the Admiral, and behaved very seditiously in respect of M^r. Wolfe.

The General having observ'd the Foulon, thought it practicable and fix'd on it for the Descent, and the Day following took M^r. Monckton, Townshend and Col. Howe & Captn. Shads the regulating Captn. of the boats to a Post we had at the mouth of the Echemin which is almost opposite to the Foulon, in order to shew them the Places He thought most accessable. The 11th orders were given to prepare for landing and attacking the Enemy, when M^r. Wolfe recd. a Letter sign'd by each of the Brigadiers, setting forth, that they did not know where they were to land & attack the Enemy. The 12th M^r. Monckton came aboard the Sutherland in the morning: after He was gone M^r. Wolfe said to his own family that the Brigadiers had brought him up the River and now flinch'd: He did not hesitate to say that two of them were Cowards and one a Villain.

Captn. Shads (regulating Captain of the boats) on the Eve of the attack made many frivolous objections such as that the Heat of the Tide wou'd hurry the boats beyond the object &c. &c. which gave reason to suspect some one had tamper'd with him: The General told him he shou'd have made his objections earlyer, that shou'd the disembarkation miscarry, that He wou'd shelter him from any Blame, that all that cou'd be done was to do his utmost, That if Captn. Shads wou'd write any thing to testify that the miscarriage was G. Wolfe's and not Captn. Shads that he wou'd sign it. Shads still persisting in his absurdity, the General told him He cou'd do no more than lay his head to the block to save Shads, then left the Cabin. The 12th. the Troops that landed at S^t. Nicolas reembark'd. The Ships mov'd up the River as well to receive them as to draw the Enemies attention upwards. The General gave orders that the Troops for the first attack shou'd get into the Boats during the latter Part of the Tide of Flood, as the violence of The Ebb would make it more difficult, The Ebb uniting to its own force, the Natural Rapidity of The River: M^r. Wolfe was desirous that the Boats shou'd arrive at the Foulon as the Day dawn'd, to answer which They fell down about half hour after three, and arriv'd at the Foulon half after four without striking with the oars, merely by the Force of the Tide which was 9 mile. The Boats were not Discover'd by any of the Enemy's Centinels untill we came opposite to the Battery of S^t. Augustine, to the Centinel's Challenge there, Captn. Fraser answer'd according to the French manner, told them we were loaded with Provisions for the Town, and desir'd them to be silent as there was an English ship of War not far off (The Enemy expected at this time a Convoy of Provision from their ships, which lay at Batiscan) They did not begin to fire on the Boats untill They drew in towards the Foulon. The ships with the Remainder of the Troops fell down some Distance of time after the Flat Boats, so as not to give the Alarm.

Col. Howe with The Light Infantry gain'd the Heights with little loss, the Enemy had an hundred men to Guard the Foulon which were soon dispers'd: M^r. Wolfe was Highly Pleased with the measures Col: Howe had taken to gain the Heights, wish'd that M^r. Howe might outlive the Day that He might have an opportunity of stamping his merit to the Government.

The General stop'd a further Debarkation of the Troops untill the first were well establish'd above, saying if the Post was to be carry'd there were enough ashore for that Purpose, if They were repuls'd a greater number wou'd breed more confusion: The boats were kept empty to be ready to bring off the 1st debarkation in case of Repulse.—As soon as the Heights were carry'd the whole landed with all possible expedition....

[At] 10 o'clock... The Regular Troops made but one Effort and afterwards dispers'd. The Troupes de Colonie and Militia disputed the Copse for some time afterwards, at length by 12 the whole were driven on all sides.

The Death of Wolfe, 1759

CAPTAIN JOHN KNOX

After our late worthy general, of renowned memory, was carried off wounded, to the rear of the front line, he desired those who were about him to lay him down; being asked if he would have a Surgeon, he replied, "It is needless; it is all over with me." One of them cried out, "They run, see how they run." "Who runs?" demanded our hero, with great earnestness, like a person roused from sleep. The Officer answered, "The enemy, Sir Egad they give way everywhere." Thereupon the General rejoined, "Go one of you, my lads, to Colonel Burton; tell him to march Webb's regiment with all speed down to Charles's river, to cut off the retreat of the fugitives from the bridge." Then, turning on his side, he added, "Now, God be praised, I will die in peace": and thus expired.

The Governor Reports on the Isle of St. John, 1770

WALTER PATTERSON

> *In 1770, Walter Patterson became governor of the Isle of St. John, renamed Prince Edward Island 29 years later.*

I arrived here on the 30th of last August, since which time I have been employed in finishing one of the houses built here, by order of Mr. Franklin, in such a manner as I hope will keep out a little of the approaching cold: And in sending to different parts of the Continent for Provisions to maintain my Family during the Winter; added to this Communications to the different parts of the Island being very bad; I will be able to furnish Your Lordship at present, with but a very imperfect description of it.

So far as I have been able, under the above circumstances, to see of the Island: the soil appears to be very good and easyly cultivated. It is of redish colour, mixed with sand; and in most places free from Stones. From this account of it Your Lordship, whom I know to be a perfect judge of Lands, will not believe it to be so good as it realy is, but I never saw finer grass in my life, than grows every place where it is clear of woods. It will produce every kind of grain and vegitables common in England, with little or no trouble; and such as I have seen of the latter are much better of their kinds than those at home, tho' raised in a very slovenly manner.

Captain Cook's Crew Enjoys Nootka Sound, 1778

DAVID SAMWELL

> *Surgeon David Samwell, sailing under Captain James Cook's command, recorded this account of the meeting of sailors' and natives' customs and practices.*

Monday April 6ᵗʰ. The Indians trading about the Ship as usual. We found the Head of our foremast so much damaged that it became necessary to get it on shore to be repaired, this Business & caulking the ship's Sides employed the Carpenters of both Ships. Hitherto we had seen none of their young Women tho' we had often given the men to understand how agreeable their Company would be to us & how profitable to themselves, in consequence of which they about this time brought two or three Girls to the Ships; tho' some of them had no bad faces yet as they were exceedingly dirty their Persons at first sight were not very inviting, however our young Gentlemen were not to be discouraged by such an obstacle as this which they found was to be removed with Soap & warm water, this they called the Ceremony of Purification and were themselves the Officiators at it, & it must be mentioned to their praise that they performed it with much piety & Devotion, taking as much pleasure in cleansing a naked young Woman from all Impurities in a Tub of Warm Water, as a young Confessor would to absolve a beutiful Virgin who was about to sacrifice that Name to himself. This Ceremony appeared very strange to the Girls, who in order to render themselves agreeable to us had taken particular pains to daub their Hair and faces well with red oaker which to their great astonishment we took as much pains to wash off. Such are the different Ideas formed by different nations of Beauty & cleanliness; they were prevailed upon to sleep on board the Ships, or rather forced to it by their Fathers or other Relations who brought them on board. In their behaviour they were very modest and timid, in which they differed very much from the South Sea Island Girls who in general are impudent & loud.

Their Fathers who generally accompanied them made the Bargain & received the price of the Prostitution of their Daughters, which was commonly a Pewter plate well scoured for one Night. When they found that this was a profitable Trade they brought more young women to the Ships, who in compliance with our prepostorous Humour spared themselves the trouble of laying on their Paint & us of washing it off again by making themselves tolerable clean before they came to us, by which they found they were more welcome Visitors and thus by falling in with our ridiculous Notions (for such no doubt they deemed them) they found means at last to disburthen our young Gentry of their Kitchen furniture, many of us after leaving this Harbour not being able to muster a plate to eat our Salt beef from. But as we found the following Maxim, 'No Bankrupt ever found a fair one kind,' hold true in this part of the Globe, & had been stripped of all our Hatchets & iron trade by the beautiful Nymphs of the South Sea Islands, we were reduced to the Dilemma of parting with these Articles or of renouncing all Claim to the favour of these fair Americans, & it may well be supposed that we chose the better part, that we enjoyed the present Day & left the Morrow to provide for itself—& to provide us Tables & Chests to eat our Salt Beef & pork from instead of Plates.

The Fur Trade, 1784

BENJAMIN AND JOSEPH FROBISHER

> *This account by the Frobisher brothers sounds little different than Lamothe Cadillac's a century before.*

The first adventurer went from Michilimakinak in the year 1765. The Indians of Lake La Pluye having then been long destitute of Goods, stop'd and plundered his canoes, and would not suffer him to proceed further. He attempted it again the year following and met with the same bad fortune. Another attempt was made in the year 1767; they left goods at Lake Pluye to be traded with the Natives, who permitted them to proceed with the remainder and the canoes penetrated beyond Lake Ouinipique.

From this period the Trade of that Country was attempted by other Adventurers with various success, and we were among the number in the year 1769, when we formed a connection with Messrs. Todd & McGill of Montreal, for the purpose of carrying on the business, but the Indians of Lake La Pluye, still ungovernable and rapacious, plundered our canoes and would not suffer any part of our goods to be sent further. Before we could be acquainted with this misfortune, our goods for the year following were at the Grand Portage, and we were then too far engaged to hesitate for a moment. A second attempt was made in which we were more successful. Our canoes reached Lake Bourbon, and thence forward we were determined to persevere. Taught however by experience that separate Interests were the Bane of that Trade we lost no time to form with those Gentlemen, and some others, a Company, and having men of Conduct and Abilities to conduct it in the Interior Country, the Indians were soon abundantly supplied and being at the same time well treated, New Posts were discovered as early as the year 1774 which to the French were totally unknown. . . .

Two setts of men are employed in business, making together upwards of 500; one half of which are occupied in the transport of goods from Montreal to the Grand Portage in canoes of about Four Tons Burthen, Navigated by 8 to 10 men and the other half are employed to take such goods forward to every Post in the interior Country to the extent of 1,000 to 2,000 miles and upwards, from Lake Superior, in Canoes of about one and a-half Ton Burthen made expressly for the inland service, and navigated by 4 to 5 men only, according to the places of their destination.

The large canoes from Montreal always set off early in May, and as the provisions they take with them are consumed by the time they reach Michilimakinac, they are necessitated to call there merely to take in an additional Supply, not only for themselves but also for the use of the canoes intended for the Interior Country and the consumption of their servants at the Grand Portage.

Saint John: "The Most Magnificent and Romantic Scene"

EDWARD WINSLOW

The Loyalists, fleeing the victorious republicans, came to British North America. They left behind homes and civilization for a rough, unbroken land. But there were compensations, as Edward Winslow reported in July 1783.

I will not aim at a description of this business. We cut yesterday with about 120 men more than a mile thro' a forest hitherto deemed impenetrable. When we emerged from it, there opened a prospect superior to anything in the world, I believe. A perfect view of the immense Bay of Fundy on one side, a very extensive view of the river St. John's with the Falls, grand Lake (or Bay) and Islands on the other—in front the Fort, which is a beautiful object on a high hill, and all settlements about the town with the ships, boats, &c, in the harbour—'twas positively the most magnificent and romantic scene I have ever beheld.

The Well-off Loyalist Comes to Québec

WILLIAM SMITH

Smith, an able jurist, left his home in New York to come to Québec, via England. His wife remained in New York, however, and he wrote her with instructions—and affection—on what to bring to their new home.

Quebec 28th Octr. 1786

What a Delight, my dearest Janet, to be able to date a Line to you within 600 Miles from you, after writing so many at the Distance of 3000! Our Departure from England had been tolled on to the worst Season of the Year, but the Arbiter of all Seasons gave us a Voyage as favorable as in the best. Thanks to his Mercy, and Praise to his Name! Your Daughter and we had our Parting in London the 27th Augt. Our Embarkation at Portsmouth was on the 29th. and our arrival here, after visiting Guernsey and one of the Western Islands, on the 22 Inst. Not a single Moment of Apprehension! Every Convenience that could be desired on the Passage, and a very hospitable and joyful Reception at our Landing.

It would compleat my Felicity, to have been able to recollect my little Flock about me, but that, if it was possible, I ought in Kindness to oppose, till I have a House, and that furnished; which can't be till the latter End of May; by which Time if you improve the Opportunities *you* have, & I have not, our Supplies may be had from the other Side of the Water, in the

Ships that leave England in March or April . . . As soon as I receive your Directions (which on account of my gross Ignorance must be very clear and particular) I will set the Artificers to work. It shall be your Fault if I have them not ready at your Chateau, long before you make your Entrance into this Capital of the British Dominions in America. . . .

I have heard of, but not seen the House recommended for our Mansion here—but however lodged, you will want a House Keeper & Cook *in one Character*, and a Female Hairdresser, with under Drudges, & two Men Servants (in Addition to the one I brought with me) with a Boy. Think well of this, & if you cannot find them at N York, let Mrs. Mallet have Directions to send them out to me with your Furniture, & direct her to contract firmly with them under the Eye of Mr Rashleigh or Mr. Watson; for as with you so here, the European Poor find so many of their own Condition, as to forget their Stations and Engagemts. There will be a Saving if you can supply yourself at NY. . . .

Perhaps your Orders to Mrs. M may not rise to the Sum comitted, & this will leave you Scope for a little Finery for the Girls of the newest Fashions of which Madam Mallet is no indifferent Connoiseur. The Ladies dress here much as in England when I left it, except that their Hair is not down yet into flowing Tresses, nearly as low as the Elevation made by what at Bath is known by the Name of the *brown Bristle*. It drop'd at a Ball & not one of a 100 Ladies could give it a Name.

I have ordered no Carriage out. So my Lord D advised, and yet he has his Coach, and this Colony is all Town upon the Banks of the River, 90 Miles below this, & 180 above it to Montreal. They use a Calash in Summer, which is a coarse Sort of Double Chair, and a Cariole in Winter or Chariot-Box upon a Slay. The Roads are so good, that the Calashes run 8 Miles an Hour, and are every where practicable for a Chariot in the Environs of this City, very beautifully disposed by Nature, & not meanly improved. But I can ill spare the Time for this Sort of Conversation. . . .

A List of Articles to be bought in Quebec

Scotch Carpets	Com̄ Urns
Com̄ China & Earthenware	Kitchin Tables and Chairs
Comm̄ Mahogany Tables and Chairs	Smoothing Irons
Com̄ Tea Boards	Grid Irons & Frying Pans
Bed Steads	Brushes & Brooms of all Kinds
Iron Potts	(excepting Fire & Hearth
Tea Kettles	Brushes & Whisk Brooms.)

. . . This Place has a most abundant Market: Fish Flesh and Poultry of all Sorts & of the best Kinds. I will send you the Prices, Fowls 9 Pence a Brace, Turkeys 2/- a Brace. Our Markets I think were never so plentiful.

The English Guinea is here 2 3/4, the Shilling 13 Pence. I don't remember that you bought a fat Turkey for 18 Pence. I was glad to see our large Bass here of 40 50 & 60 Weight, Heath[h]en, Snipes &c &c &c; Vegetables all in the highest Plenty & Perfection.

Love and Marriage in Upper Canada, 1800

AMELIA HARRIS

> *Daughter of a Loyalist family, Harris left this account of the courtship of the family's nursemaid.*

In the summer of 1800, my mother had a very nice help as nurse. Jenny Decow had been apprenticed to a relative and at the age of 18 she received her Bed, her Cow and two or three suits of clothing. Those articles it was customary to give to a bound girl and was considered legally of age with the right to earn her own living as she best could. My mother soon discovered that Jenny had a woer. On Sunday afternoon young Daniel McCall made his appearance with that peculiar happy awkward look that young lads have when they are keeping company, as it is called. At that time when a young man wanted a wife He looked out for some young Girl whom he thought would be a good helpmate and, watching the opportunity, with an awkward Bow and blush, He would ask her to give him her company the ensuing Sunday evening. Her refusal was called "giving the mitten", and great was the laugh against any young man if it was known that He had "got the mitten". All hopes of success in that quarter would be at an end, but young McCall had not "got the mitten", and it was customary on those occasions when the family retired to bed for the young woer to get up and quietly put out the candles and cover the fire if any, then take a seat by the side of his lady love and talk as other lovers do, I suppose, until 12 or 1 o'clock, when He would either take his leave and a walk of miles to his home that He might be early at work, or lie down with some of the Boys for an hour or two and then be away before daylight. Those weekly visits would sometimes continue for Months, until all was ready for mariage. . . .

When Jenny had been with my mother about six months young McCall made his appearance in the middle of the week and my Father and some visitors commenced bantering him why did he not marry at once, why did he spend his time and wear out his shoes in the way He was doing. He said he would go talk to Jenny and hear what she said. He returned in a few minutes and said they would be married; in an hour afterwards they were man and wife. They were married in their working dresses, he in his buckskin trowsers and she in her homespun. She tied up her bundle of clothes, received her wages, and away they walked to their Log house in the woods. Thirty years after they used to show me some little articles that had been purchased with Jenny's wages and they appeared to look back upon that time with pleasure. They became rich.

French–English Tensions in Lower Canada, 1804

LORD SELKIRK

> *Selkirk may have been thinking mostly of the colonies he had already and would soon establish in British North America, but his observations on the attitudes of the French- and English-speaking inhabitants of Lower Canada almost a half-century after the conquest make clear that two solitudes existed.*

There is but one opinion as to the universal disaffection of the French Canadians to the British Government, & it seems scarcely to be more questioned than their repugnance is unconquerable. The postillions as they drive along are continually speaking to their horses—generally scolding—one of them ended a string of Oathes with Sacre Anglais!— They have never been reconciled to the British institutions that have been introduced among them—Even the trial by Jury & Criminal procedure are approved only by a few of the most enlightened men—
    The English at Quebec and Montreal cry out in the true John Bull style against their obstinate aversion to institutions which they have never taken any pains to make them understand—& are surprized at the natural and universally experienced dislike of a conquered people to their conquerors & to every thing which puts them in mind of their subjection—In these ideas some individuals of great good sense & liberality (among others Bishop Mountain & Ch. Justice Elmsley) join to a surprizing degree. The English Govt. certainly seems never to have acted with any system as to Canada—the only chance of reconciling the people would have been either to use every effort to change them entirely in language & institutions & make them forget that they were not English—or keeping them as French to give a Government adapted to them as such, & keep every thing English out of sight—neither of these plans has been followed, & the policy of Govt. has been a kind of vibration between them.—at first after 3 or 4 years hesitation it was decided in 1764 to introduce the English Law—the French Lawyers did not like the trouble of learning their trade anew, & found pretexts for remonstrating and stating pretexts of hardships—they were listened to, & from the subsequent contradictory determinations at different times has resulted a complete jumble of Laws & a total uncertainty in many cases what Law is to be the ruler. . . .
    The most likely channel to influence the common peasants would perhaps be thro' the Clergy—but this hold has been almost thrown away, by devolving the entire patronage of the Curés to the Catholic Bishop.—

In addition to this, the law which allows them no tythes from lands held by protestants, operates to give them a needless jealousy, perhaps the silly parade with which a Protestant Bishoprick & Cathedral have been set up at Quebec, may add to this. . . .

It is remarked even in private society how much the English & Canadians draw asunder.—At Montreal where the English have everything there are scarcely any genteel French to be met in society—the gentry of the place and neighbourhood hold Assemblies of their own at Boucherville a few miles off where no English intrude.—At Quebec the example & influence of the Govr has tended to prevent that total separation, but even there they do not appear to live to-gether or amalgamate.—While I was there the Govr gave a ball on Mardi gras—the room held two country dances—nine tenths of the company in the one dance was French—in the other English. . . .

Lac la Biche

GABRIEL FRANCHÈRE

Between 1811 and 1814, Gabriel Franchère undertook explorations of the west and northwest.

On the 4th of June we journeyed on, now in canoes, now walking along the river. At last on the 5th we crossed Lac la Biche, which must be about 15 leagues long and from 8 to 10 wide. While passing the lake we saw a small canoe and when we came up with it we saw that it was paddled by two women looking for eggs, which at this season are abundant on the islands in the lake. They told us that their father was not far away and we soon saw him appearing around a small island. This man told us that he was A. Desjarlais, a former guide in the service of the North West Company, free since the junction of the two companies in 1805. On informing this man that we were without food, we were offered a large number of eggs and he had one of our men embark in the small canoe with his daughters to go to his cabin on the other side of the lake to procure supplies for us. And he accompanied us to the portage, which is perhaps 25 paces long, formed by a beaver dam. Passed a little pond caused by this dam and camped early to await the return of the young man who had gone in search of provisions.

On the morning of the 6th of June, Desjarlais came back with our man bringing about 50 pounds of dried meat and 10 to 12 pounds of tallow. We invited him to breakfast with us. This man seemed reasonably contented with his fate as no one troubled him in his possession of Lac la Biche, which he had as it were preempted, living with his family on the proceeds of the hunt. He asked me to read two letters that he had had in his possession for two years without finding anyone able to read them.

They were dated from Varennes and were from one of his sisters. I even recognized Mr Labadie's handwriting.

Finally after expressing our gratitude for the supplies that he had been kind enough to give us, we left him. . . .

The Americans Take York, 1813

DR. WILLIAM BEAUMONT

The War of 1812 was fought with extraordinary ferocity by both sides, not least in the capture of York by the American forces in April 1813.

April 26, 1813.

Wind pretty strong in the morning, increasing to a strong blow, so that the swells run high, tossing our vessels smartly about. Several seasick—was myself. At half-past four o'clock passed by the mouth of Niagara River. This circumstance baffled our imagination where we were going. We were first impressed with the idea of Kingston, then to Niagara, but now our destination must be Little York. At sunset came in view of York Town & the Fort, where we lay off all night within 3 or 4 leagues.

27th. Sailed into harbor and came to anchor a little below the British Garrison. We now filled the boats and affected a landing, though not without some difficulty and the loss of some men. The British marched their troops from the Garrison down the [hill] to cut us off in landing, and then they had every advantage. They could not effect their [plan]. A hot engagement ensued, in which the enemy lost nearly a third of their men and were soon compelled to quit the field leaving their dead and wounded strewed in every direction. We lost but very few in the engagement. The enemy returned into garrison, but from the loss sustained in the 1st engagement, the undaunted courage of our men, and the brisk firing from our fleet into the Garrison with 12 and 32-pounders, they were soon obliged to evacuate it and retreat with all possible speed. Driven to this alternative, they devised the inhuman project of blowing up their Magazine (containing 300 Bbls. powder), the explosion of which, shocking to mention, had almost totally destroyed our Army. Above 300 were wounded, and about 60 killed dead on the spot by stones of all dimensions falling like a shower of hail . . . A most distressing scene ensues in the Hospital—nothing but the Groans of the wounded and agonies of the Dying are to be heard. The Surgeons wading in blood, cutting off arms, legs, and trepanning heads to rescue their fellow creatures from untimely deaths. To hear the poor creatures crying, "Oh, Dear! Oh, Dear! Oh, my God, my God! Do, Doctor, Doctor! Do cut off my leg, my arm, my head, to relieve me from misery! I can't live, I can't live!" would have rent the heart of steel, and shocked the insensibility of the most hardened assassin and the cruelest savage. It awoke my liveliest sympathy, and I cut and slashed for 48 hours without food or sleep. My God! Who can think of the shocking scene when his fellow-creatures lie mashed and mangled in every part, with a leg, an arm, a head, or a body ground in pieces, without having . . . his blood chill in his veins.

Laura Secord's Heroism

JAMES FITZGIBBON

> Thought to be a mythical event by some, Laura Secord's efforts to warn the British of an impending American assault was attested to by Lieut. James FitzGibbon.

I do hereby certify that Mrs. Secord, wife of James Secord, of Chippewa, Esq., did, in the month of June, 1813, walk from her house, near the village of St. David's, to De Cou's house in Thorold by a circuitous route of about twenty miles, partly through the woods, to acquaint me that the enemy intended to attempt, by surprise, to capture a detachment of the 49th Regiment, then under my command, she having obtained such knowledge from good authority, as the event proved. Mrs. Secord was a person of slight and delicate frame, and made the effort in weather excessively warm, and I dreaded at the time that she must suffer in health in consequence of fatigue and anxiety, she having been exposed to danger from the enemy, through whose lines of communication she had to pass. The attempt was made on my detachment by the enemy; and his detachment, consisting of upwards of 500 men and a field piece and 50 dragoons, were captured in consequence.

I write this certificate in a moment of much hurry and from memory, and it is therefore thus brief.

(Signed) James FitzGibbon,
Formerly Lieutenant 49th Regiment.

The Indians in the War of 1812

LIEUT. JOHN LE COUTEUR

> The Indians had a well-deserved reputation for scalping prisoners. Their presence on the battlefield could impel American troops to surrender—to the British.

24 June 1813

About half an hour before day break, an Indian brought me a message from their Chief intimating that a strong force of the Enemy with Guns and Cavalry were moving upon us by De Cew's. I instantly ordered the turn out, as silently as possible, and ran to Major De Haren who desired the men to be formed instantly. The Indians had all gone off after their own Mode of warfare acting quite independently—we moved after them in a run towards the Beech woods.

Presently we heard one rapid, yet steady, roll of musquetry then a terrific Yell which sounded high above a roll of Artillery & small arms. The Major [ordered me] to gallop on and see how the affair stood, then return to bring the Light Division up to the best position. In a quarter of an hour, I got to the scene of action—some round shot came plunging along the road but the Indian yells were awful and ringing all around an extensive clearing—they concealed and lying down along the edges of the wood, the American force in the clearing in Line with their Guns on their Right and their Cavalry in reserve. The 49th [Regiment] I perceived to be to the Right of the Americans turning it. To these I rode when, immediately, a flag of truce was sent in with an offer to surrender to a British force.

Fitzgibbon wished them to surrender to Him but the American officer said He would not to so small a force. I observed that "the Light Division, Seven hundred men under Major De Haren, was here." "The moment they are here and can protect us from the Indians, we will surrender." They came up in less than twenty minutes and Major De Haren ratified the treaty which Fitzgibbon had entered on. The Yankee Horsemen made a dash through the Indian fire and got off but we took Two Guns, a number of Volunteer officers, and 550 men.

The Indians were very savage—one tomahawked an American close to me during the parley—they would have destroyed them all but for us. All the dead were scalped. Their heads divested of the scalp looked white and clean, some as if they had been washed. I got a capital black horse for a charger on this occasion, saddle & Bridle & Pistols and all.

Major De Haren gave me charge of the [American] Com[man]d[ing] officer, Colonel Boerstler, and the Field officers. Our Division was drawn up in line and presented arms to Him as He rode by. He admired the men greatly: "what fine, smart, well-disciplined Young Men." Then, as he passed the Indians and saw numbers of his poor men Scalped, He first asked: "Oh! What are those? What is that?" I made no answer but turned away my head for I felt for Him. He was badly wounded and seemed horror struck, the tears rolled down his handsome countenance. He was exceedingly sensible of the poor Courtesy which I had occasion to show Him and, when I left Him in the quarters allotted to Him, He was most friendly—a fine Gentlemanly Young man.

The Indians were ticklish friends to deal with. I had for a few days been acting Commissary and Quartermaster as well as Adjutant to the Light Division, having to ride about the Country with an escort, buy Oxen, flour & Rum where I could get them, then do the distribution myself. One day, I refused to give a half-drunken Indian a Hide which He coveted over and above the Meat which had been issued to his tribe when he snatched his Tomahawk and made a motion as if to cut me down. In an instant, however, self-preservation had instinctively made me place my drawn Sword to his throat and He pretended it was a mere faint and, after a growl, [said] "Sago Nitchie". Of course I shook hands with Him but my men would have bayoneted Him, if I had not prevented it. I complained to his Chief and He met with some Indian rebuff.

There was a poor unfortunate American Soldier, a Prisoner in the Indian camp. An old Mohawk Chief had lost his only Son in one of the late engagements and He kept this Young Man as a Victim—it was said to be immolated when He got Him into the back woods. The poor fellow implored us to ransom or rescue Him from his sad fate and shed many tears at the idea of being taken away from civilized man. We settled on a Subscription and offered the Old Chief a Considerable Sum to give Him up to us. No Sum would tempt Him—if the young Man behaved well, He would adopt Him as his Son! A delightful Compliment! Rescue Him we dared not, it would have lost us an alliance of seven hundred Indians, most invaluable allies they were—no surprises with Nitchie on the lookout.

After a few days Our Yankee friend was stripped of his Uniform and toggery of all sorts and clothed in an Indian dress. His hair was shaven, a tuft left on which was ornamented with Feathers and Horse hair and, though it was very lamentable to Him and excited our Sympathy, He looked irresistibly ludicrous. However we got the Old Chief, by Good humour and presents, to adopt Him as his Son which insured his life. He was, notwithstanding, incessantly watched both by night and day. We advised [him] not to attempt to escape till he had a year or two with them as any trick of the sort would cost his life.

Seven Weeks at Sea to Québec

JAMES WILSON

> *It took courage to emigrate under the conditions of passage in the early nineteenth century. This account gives the story of a voyage on the* Mary and Bell *in 1817.*

1817. I sailed on Thursday 15th of May from Dublin, in the brig Mary and Bell, bound for Quebec, commanded by Captain Cunningham; felt my mind awfully impressed on leaving my native land; yet sensible that it is thy will, O God! Do willingly commend myself and family to thee both now and for ever.

17th—This morning the following circumstance happened. The captain seeing a small cask or barrel floating on the waves, took boat in pursuit of it, and on examining found a human body contained therein.

I and my family are now sick, especially my companion: Lord help us to be resigned! We are in thy hands, O God! Chasten us, but not in thine anger, lest thou bring us to nothing.

18th—This day the wind is fair; the vessel sails rapidly. We passed Tusker rock, situate within nine miles of Wexford town, on which is built a light house to be a guide for shipping by night; a family resides therein, paid by government for lighting the house. This evening I was requested to hold a religious meeting, which I consented to, having obtained leave from the captain of the vessel; a great number attended on the occasion, whilst I said a few words on the 3d chapter of 2d Peter. The people waited on God in a becoming manner; I trust not in vain.

19th—The people are mostly all recovering from their sickness, consequently there is more order and regularity observed.

20th—This day the wind is fair; the ship sails nearly five miles an hour, The rocking of the vessel has brought on sickness again to many of the passengers. My wife is quite unwell, and myself also; but thou art my portion, O Lord, my God!

21st—This morning is quite calm: the sky clear. About twelve o'clock, the waves swelled prodigiously, the ship making five miles an hour and through its excessive motion extreme sickness prevails. O my God! Save me from a murmuring spirit, and help me to cast my care on thee.

22d—It is now eight days since I left Dublin bay, never more, I suppose, to return. I find it a serious thing to go to America; it is attended with much pain of mind, sorrow, sickness and affliction. How few consider this, till they find themselves on the wide extended ocean then 'tis too late to wish themselves back! I think those who enjoy the comforts of life in abundance in Ireland, have no right to leave a certainty for an uncertainty. At least without a satisfactory evidence of their removal being of God, but, alas! how few consult him on any occasion.

This evening several huge fish were seen sporting on the waves; this it seems indicated an approaching storm, which lasted the whole of the night.

23d—This day nothing particular occurred; many of the passengers continue sick: my wife and I are still unwell, and my children also; but my trust is in thee, O Lord, my God!

26th—Being much afflicted with sickness these few days past, I have been unable to write, but thanks be to God, now feel better. I never witnessed such a scene before as the storm which we had on Friday night. About eleven o'clock, the captain being just gone to bed, it began, on which he immediately got on deck and ordered all the sails down, which being done, restrained the motion of the vessel; nothing could equal the awful change that took place—the vessel rolled from side to side, and overturned all the passengers' boxes, pans, kettles, and vessels of water, in such a manner as that no tongue can express, or mind conceive the state we were in—all, I may say, expected every moment to be swallowed in the great deep. My mind was seriously impressed on the occasion, but my whole soul was stayed on God. The captain had, by his own account, three dozen of plates broken, besides several bottles of porter. This storm continued partly till Sunday evening. . . .

June 2d—On Saturday night we had another storm, which continued the whole of Sunday; and although it was not so violent as the one we had . . . yet I may safely say, the consequences were of a more serious nature. Through the violent agitation of the waves, the vessel heaved from side to side so vehemently as to produce the utmost confusion; the people could scarcely remain secure in their beds; their chests and other articles of use were all thrown into one common heap: in short, I never witnessed such disorder before. I felt my mind deeply impressed on the occasion, and firmly stayed on the God of my salvation. The vessel sailed near ten miles an hour part of this day, till the shifting of the wind caused a decline in sailing.

5th—We are now three weeks this day at sea, and by this time, have a tolerable knowledge of what kind of provisions are most needful for a voyage to America:

And 1st Oatmeal, and cutlings are much used, molasses also; potatoes are of the greatest value, nothing more so in my judgment. Salt, or hung beef, pork, bacon or hams, are all excellent in their use; veal when salted, and afterwards watered, then boiled with beef or bacon, will produce a soup very desirable. One family here, brought a quantity of fowl in pickle, which when watered, eat very delicious. Coffee is much preferable to tea, the water being so bad, as to render the tea rather insipid and tasteless: bottled ale is good for drink, but in my opinion, cyder when mixed through water, is a much better and cooler drink for the stomach than any other; a constant thirst being common to all on sea. As to spices, pepper, and ginger is mostly used. Flour is essentially necessary; cake bread or pan cakes being very applicable to weak constitutions. Eggs are much used, and when well grazed, or put in salt pickle for six hours, and well packed, will keep fresh a considerable time, this I found by experience. Good port wine is very reviving on sea, when used moderately; but spirits is not so very necessary here. I conceive pickled cabbage to be very useful, such kind of diet only answering whilst sickness prevails; I therefore recommend it. Biscuit is much used by seamen, and the only way for passengers to take it is, to pour boiling water on it, and when steeped a few minutes toast it before the fire, then butter it, and it will eat as pleasant as loaf bread, but not otherwise: oat bread well baked in an oven, will answer well with either tea or coffee; cheese will be very needful; split peas for soup, and lastly, vinegar, butter, and potted herrings.

To preserve new milk for a voyage, take a large or small jar or jars, and clean them remarkably well, and when done, put the milk therein, and after securing it well by corking it close, put the jar or jars into a large pot of water, and boil them over a good fire, and when done, pack them in a hamper, or some other place, and it will keep sweet the whole of the passage. This has been tried by a man of truth and credit, who went last season to Philadelphia, and used the milk there after his arrival, it retaining its natural sweetness. There is a diet much used here, vulgarly called "beggars dish," composed of peeled potatoes and either beef or bacon cut in thin slices, and mixed through them, affords a pleasant meal, the soup is much esteemed, being seasoned with pepper. Delft ware will not in any wise answer in common use, I would therefore recommend tin poringers, or small wooden noggins and trenchers, these will be found best at sea, as the constant motion of the vessel will have a tendency to break any other: a tin kettle in the form of a D will be found very useful in boiling meat or any other food, as it can hang on the bars of the grate at any time, this will be highly accommodating, especially where so many families are boiling their food at one time. The kind of apparel I would recommend to male passengers would be, short jackets or waistcoats with sleeves, a dark handkerchief for the neck, and coarse trowsers:—for women, a long bed gown, or wrappers with dark shawls or handkerchiefs, as cleanliness cannot be observed with any degree of precision. It is necessary to provide strong chests or boxes for a voyage, well secured with good locks and hinges; or otherwise it is impossible to preserve property: I am sorry to have it say, in this vessel there has been much plunder committed, for want of being duly prepared against it. . . .

9th—This day is fine, and affords much pleasure to the passengers who are chiefly on deck, except a few who are weak and sickly. My dear wife being one of these, is a good deal confined to her bed. She is this day better, thanks be to God. Our vessel is sailing well today, with a fair wind. We hope ere long to be favoured with a sight of Newfoundland banks, if this was once effected, we then, it seems, would be liable to no danger arising from storm.

Yesterday we were cut short of our allowance of water, from three quarts per day to each passenger, to five pints, (government allowance) and from the badness of it, together with the small quantity given, serves to increase the distress of mind which arises daily; and never did the children of God pant, and long more eagerly for the water of life, than the people do here for the clear spring water: but when will they long for the fountain of living waters? I fear some never; I hope others in due time.

11th—Yesterday being quite unwell with a violent pain in my head, I was chiefly confined to my bed, but this day feel much better. Glory be to God. Our vessel is gaining these few days by means of foul winds, and a constant swell in the sea. Both render our passage tedious and disagreeable. Our captain says he never remembers such severe weather this season of the year before: "but the end of all things is at hand." May I be sober, and watch unto prayer. . . .

21st—We have at length arrived at the banks this morning; the captain sounded for bottom, and found it 54 fathoms. A thick fog covers every part of this region, with a heavy mist of rain. The vessel sailed from four o'clock yesterday evening till twelve to day, about 7 miles an hour and now sails slowly this evening, through means of a dead calm, yet we humbly hope very soon to land at Quebec.

22d—This blessed Sabbath is spent by many of the passengers in fishing, fish being very numerous in this part of the sea. . . .

23d—This morning several vessels are in view, all employed in fishing, this part of the deep supplying chiefly every part of the world with fish, and is resorted to at this season by fishermen of almost all nations who trade in this line of life. A thick fog covers the whole sea in this place, and is, I think, unwholesome in the highest degree. I expect a few days will bring us to the gulf of the great river St. Lawrence—this will be truly pleasing to our longing minds. . . .

July 3d—We are this day seven weeks on the great deep, urging our way often against fierce contrary winds and heavy tempests, and as frequently detained by a settled calm; this has been our case since we left America; yet blessed be the Lord, he has brought us to the river Saint Lawrence, at the entrance of which may be seen a large wood, or forest, abounding with stately trees, which afford great pleasure as we sail along. This morning and yesterday we made no way, by reason of a dead calm, but at two o'clock a brisk wind arose, and we now proceed at the rate of eight miles an hour; we therefore expect, being now far up the river, that our danger is over, and hope the rest of our passage will be pleasant and agreeable.

4th—This morning (as is usual in drawing near Quebec), about six o'clock, a pilot came on board to steer us safely up the river; it appears no vessel dare approach the city without one. This had a tendency to appease the minds of the people at large, being now convinced that we are near our landing place. The stately mountains ascending over each other, are truly grand along the sea shore on the left, and it seems to continue all the way to Quebec. The people now seem to forget all the misery, sickness, and sensible trials they have passed through, as all enjoy health, and are looking forward with eager desire to a speedy deliverance, and are thereby comforted, expecting to reap the benefit of an exertion truly great and awful, in leaving one kingdom for another.

Sir John Franklin Explores the Arctic Lands, 1820

SIR JOHN FRANKLIN

> Later to be lost with his crew in the high Arctic, Sir John Franklin also explored the Arctic terrain.

Besides the Indian population in the NW parts of America there is now a numerous race of Half Breeds offspring of the European and Canadian residents, who for the most part intermix with the Indians, and in general

follow their habits and character. They consider themselves to be superior to the Indians on account of their birth, but these are unwilling to
admit their superiority merely on this score, and will only estimate their
qualifications according to the respective merits they evince as good
Hunters. Many of them display great ability in the Art, and frequently
make more ample returns both of skins and provision than the Indians. A
few are employed as Interpreters, and some who have had the benefit of
education as Clerks. They all appear to possess considerable genius and
great aptitude for learning and I think it is much to be regretted that
the blessings of education and instruction have not been more generally
imparted to them. Many of the Vices and Errors which they now possess
would thereby have been removed, and their conduct would in all probability have been governed by correct principles, and not exposed to the
guidance of chance, or the impulse of uninformed reason.

The residents, both Traders and Voyageurs, usually take their female
partners from this class, but it appears to me that exemption from fatigu-
ing work, a better dress and some few luxuries are the only benefits which
these women gain by living at the Establishments. They are not admitted
to the Traders table on account of the prejudice of the Indians, nor to share
the comforts of domestic society. And I fear very few attempts have been
made to instruct or inform their minds. They are permitted to remain
in the state of lamentable ignorance both as to morality and religion in
which they were brought up, and the consequence generally follows, that
they prove faithless; and indeed it could hardly be expected that chastity
should be regarded, by persons who have not been early taught to consider it as a Virtue. The principal occupation of these women exclusive of
attention to their children, of whom they are passionately fond, seems to
be dressing skins, sewing, and garnishing leather with porcupine quills,
for shoes or parts of dress, and in this work they display great taste and
ingenuity, and no small skill in extracting the proper colours from different materials to stain their quills. Both Companies I understand have
wisely prohibited their Servants from taking any Indian woman.

Alcohol and the Indians

GEORGE SIMPSON

*The Governor of the Hudson's Bay Company argues for the continuation
of the trade in liquor, 1822.*

It is not my province to go into this subject in a moral point of view and
shall therefore confine my opinion thereon as to the effect such restric-
tion might have on our Trade. If the quantity of Spirits given to Indians
was calculated I am satisfied it would not amount to a pint per man annu-

ally on an average, which may give some idea of the extent of Crime likely to result therefrom; and I'll venture to say there are not three murders committed annually on the average of the last Ten Years in the whole tract of Country occupied by the Hudson's Bay Coy. from inebrity. As an article of trade it is not generally used and I do not suppose we make Ten packs of Furs p. annum by it: it is, however, the grand Stimulus to call forth the exertions of the Indians and I have often heard them reason thus, "it is not for your Cloth and Blankets that we undergo all this labor and fatigue as in a short time we could reconcile ourselves to the use of Skins for Clothes as our forefathers did, but it is the prospect of Drink in the Spring, to enable us to communicate freely and speak our minds to each other that carries us through the Winter and induces us to Work so hard." This I really believe to be the case, and that if Spirits were withheld it would materially discourage them and produce a lassitude which Weight of other property could not remove.—

In the Provision Countries it is, however, a very principal article of Trade and indispensibly necessary: the Plain Indians are a bold, independent race, Dress entirely in Skins and with them Tobacco and Spirits are the principal commodities, a Quart of Mixed Liquor will at times procure more Pounded Meat and Grease than a Bale of Cloth, indeed our whole profit in that Trade is upon those articles, and if Provisions were paid for in Dry Goods they would eat up all the gains of the Fur Trade. I therefore sincerely hope the Committee will take due time to examine this subject and that they will not prematurely determine thereon as it might be very injurious to the interests of the Concern. . . .

Eskimos Speak of the White Man

KNUD RASMUSSEN

Rasmussen spoke the native tongue and reported on Eskimo attitudes as passed down by oral tradition.

The Arviligjuarmiut still had many recollections of their first meeting with white men, and the sober manner in which they told of these experiences, now almost a hundred years old, is good evidence of how reliable the Eskimos can be as narrators if only they have to do with people that understand them. I emphasize this here because it is not uncommon that travelers assert that an Eskimo can be made to say almost anything. This quite unwarranted accusation is effectively discounted through the following accounts.

It was not always an easy matter to obtain people's true meaning as to how they appraised the white man . . . Often one had the feeling that they regarded him in quite the same manner as many white men look upon the

Eskimo—as being inferior to themselves, as a sort of powerful barbarian to whom particular deference was due, because he was bigger and stronger than themselves and had an outfit and instruments of power far in excess of their own. A strong nation, that lived in a great, distant land. Nor could the old orthodox Eskimos disregard the fact that the white men, like the Indians, were the bastards of an arrogant and disobedient woman and a dog. Still, all who had met white men could not help admiring them and subjecting themselves entirely to the superiority of their will. A further fact that increased their respect was that they always believed the white man's resources were inexhaustible. When they came sailing in their ships or journeying with their dog sledges they always brought along a wealth of implements and food that must always impress people in a poor country. And they had many accomplishments that made them superior to the Eskimos. They knew how to find their way and exactly determine their position by the sun. They could draw marvelous maps of land that they now saw for the first time, and they could reproduce the people they met themselves and their appearance by means of lifelike pictures that were made in some incomprehensible manner. But above all was their invention of the firearms, which made them both terrible enemies and impossible to compete with in the struggle for food. On the other hand, the Eskimos were always their superiors in their ability to live in their cold land, in building snow huts, in driving dogs and in paddling a kayak. In these very elementary accomplishments the white men were always inferior, and in many ways quite dependent upon the Eskimos themselves while in their country. But whatever opinion one formed of the qablunait, all agreed that they had to be treated with the very greatest caution. All these points of view were explained to me one day by old Kuvdluitsoq, and in conclusion he as it were summarized his views and his appraisal in the following sentence[s]:

"It is generally believed that white men have quite the same minds as small children. Therefore one should always give way to them. They are easily angered, and when they cannot get their will they are moody and, like children, have the strangest ideas and fancies."

Scots and Religion in Cape Breton, 1834

REV. JOHN STEWART

> The Glasgow Colonial Society sent out immigrants and clergy to British North America.

Since my arrival in this Island I have been so throng[ed] with business of one kind or other that little time was left me for epistolary correspondence. I have performed a circuit of the Island with the exception of the northern parts preaching and baptizing from settlement to settlement. It is no easy matter to travel here and you would not require to send any man here either of a weakly habit or accustomed to very delicate living.

In this Island we have a large Population of Scots by far the majority of them Highlanders. According to the best estimate I have been able to make, the number of Presbyterians, almost all attached to the Church of Scotland, amounts to upwards of 11,000. These are scattered over a wide surface as must be the case from the manner in which the land is granted to them. Along the Lakes and rivers of the Island the land is parcelled out in Lots of 200 acres each. On each of these lots you have a house, so that between every house, at an average, is a 1/4 mile, consequently when you hear of a settlement you understand that a great distance lies between its extremes. The settlers behind the front, are called back settlers, who are in general extremely poor.

The prospects of the Kirk in this island are encouraging. Our people are for the most part separated from the Rom. Catholics and no dissenters hardly among them. Although the Rom[s]. are more numerous in the mean time, this will not be the case long, as God in his providence has opened up a way for the instruction of our poor expatriated countrymen who formerly were the butt of the Ro. Catholics and often had to go to the priest for some little instruction. Many of them in this way became Rom. C[s]. but I doubt not that these shall return to us except the allurements of the <u>harlot</u> prove too powerful for them.

There are now in operation in this Island 13 churches in connection with the church of Scotland of which 3 have been commenced since I commenced itinerating and the other two will be commenced in spring. The commencement however is nothing, but the finishing is something. Not one of these is yet finished nor nearly so, and I do not see how they can be finished for many years to come. The people are extremely poor, though, blessed be God for it, plenty of food for man and beast is to be found ... If I could by possibility get about £300, all these churches would be built within three years or a little more. I have given already a good part of my salary to encourage the people, and such is the effect of this little help that they are straining every nerve to follow up my directions. But still they have no money and without some money the work cannot go on. Tradesmen will not work without payment, and though wood can be furnished for their work yet no money can be got for their pay. If we had then, what would pay wages to tradesmen, materials would be furnished by the people. Glass, nails etc. etc. are to purchase from Merchants, and they will take the produce of the country for these articles. Will our Dear Friends not help us a little, and the Lord shall reward them.

You would be delighted to see the willingness of the people to hear the word of God, and the manifestations of a spirit of enquiry among them. I have seen them in numbers around me shedding tears profusely either for their sins' or for joy that they had the opportunity of hearing the words of life . . . If but £50 a year could be sent for helping these erections, they would be finished in a few years and we could meet with comfort. At present it is impossible to meet in these houses unfinished as they are. I met the people of this settlement last sabbath in the church here, but the cold was so intense that my teeth were chattering, and could hardly articulate before concluding. The house is indeed closed in, without ceiling, without seats, and without a stove, an absolute necessary at this time of year in this cold climate. . . .

This day I had a Messenger from the people in this settlement offering me £150 a year half cash, half produce at cash price. I cannot in the mean time give them an answer as I mean [to itinerate] till the month of Sepr. 1835. They are clamoring [for my] settling among them and they are ready enough [to promise] but slow to perform. Not perhaps from want of will [but from want] of means. I have an offer also from McLennan's Mountain Pictou [County, near New Glasgow] of £150 all cash. To this I mean not to return an answer till the month of June. Around the Bay where I now sit are about 170 families almost all Highlanders, many of whom cannot speak a sentence of English. I mean to give you this early notice that I shall not settle here, nor on the Island except on the condition of receiving £50 a year for 3 years to come. The expense at which I must be in building a house and procuring necessaries will plunge me in debt; the first years from which I shall not be able to extricate myself as happens with some of our Ministers in N. America. It is not that I am in love with money that I make this demand but because I do not see that I can get on without it. I cannot calculate on getting payment from the people though in their anxiety to be possessed of a Min^r. they make such an offer. . . .

Building a House in the Backwoods

CATHERINE PARR TRAILL

It was the latter end of October before even the walls of our house were up. To effect this we called "a bee." Sixteen of our neighbours cheerfully obeyed our summons; and though the day was far from favourable, so faithfully did our hive perform their tasks, that by night the outer walls were raised.

The work went merrily on with the help of plenty of Canadian nectar (whiskey), the honey that our *bees* are solaced with. Some huge joints of salt pork, a peck of potatoes, with a rice-pudding, and a loaf as big as an enormous Cheshire cheese, formed the feast that was to regale them during the raising. This was spread out in the shanty, in a *very rural style*.

In short, we laughed, and called it a *picnic in the backwoods*; and rude as was the fare, I can assure you, great was the satisfaction expressed by all the guests of every degree, our "bee" being considered as very well conducted. In spite of the difference of rank among those that assisted at the bee, the greatest possible harmony prevailed, and the party separated well pleased with the day's work and entertainment.

The following day I went to survey the newly raised edifice, but was sorely puzzled, as it presented very little appearance of a house. It was merely an oblong square of logs raised one above the other, with open spaces between every row of logs. The spaces for the doors and windows were not then sawn out, and the rafters were not up. In short, it looked a very queer sort of a place, and I returned home a little disappointed, and wondering that my husband should be so well pleased with the progress that had been made. A day or two after this I again visited it. The *sleepers* were laid to support the floors, and the places for the doors and windows cut out of the solid timbers, so that it had not quite so much the look of a bird-cage as before.

After the roof was shingled, we were again at a stand, as no boards could be procured nearer than Peterborough, a long day's journey through horrible roads. At that time no saw-mill was in progress; now there is a fine one building within a little distance of us. Our flooring-boards were all to be sawn by hand, and it was some time before any one could be found to perform this necessary work, and that at high wages—six-and-sixpence per day. Well, the boards were at length down, but of course of unseasoned timber: this was unavoidable; so as they could not be planed we were obliged to put up with their rough, unsightly appearance, for no better were to be had. I began to recall to mind the observation of the old gentleman with whom we travelled from Cobourg to Rice Lake. We console ourselves with the prospect that by next summer the boards will all be seasoned, and then the house is to be turned topsy-turvy by having the floors all relaid, jointed, and smoothed.

The next misfortune that happened was that the mixture of clay and lime that was to plaster the inside and outside of the house between the chinks of the logs was one night frozen to stone. Just as the work was about half completed, the frost suddenly setting in, put a stop to our proceeding for some time, as the frozen plaster yielded neither to fire nor to hot water, the latter freezing before it had any effect on the mass, and rather making bad worse. Then the workman that was hewing the inside walls to smooth them wounded himself with the broad axe, and was unable to resume his work for some time. . . .

Every man in this country is his own glazier; this you will laugh at: but if he does not wish to see and feel the discomfort of broken panes, he must learn to put them in his windows with his own hands. Workmen are not easily to be had in the backwoods when you want them, and it would be preposterous to hire a man at high wages to make two days' journey to and from the nearest town to mend your windows. Boxes of glass of several different sizes are to be bought at a very cheap rate in the stores. My husband employed himself by glazing the windows of the house preparatory to their being put in. . . .

A Rude, Coarse, Familiar People

SUSANNA MOODIE

The sister of Catherine Parr Traill, like her a British emigrant to Upper Canada, comments on American immigrants.

All was new, strange, and distasteful to us; we shrank from the rude, coarse familiarity of the uneducated people among whom we were thrown; and they in return viewed us as innovators, who wished to curtail their independence, by expecting from them the kindly civilities and gentle courtesies of a more refined community. They considered us proud and shy, when we were only anxious not to give offence. The semi-barbarous Yankee squatters, who had "left their country for their country's good," and by whom we were surrounded in our first settlement, detested us, and with them we could have no feeling in common. We could neither lie nor cheat in our dealings with them; and they despised us for our ignorance in trading and our want of smartness.

The utter want of that common courtesy with which a well brought-up European addresses the poorest of his brethren, is severely felt at first by settlers in Canada. At the period of which I am now speaking, the titles of "sir" or "madam" were very rarely applied by inferiors. They entered your house without knocking; and while boasting of their freedom, violated one of its dearest laws, which considers even the cottage of the poorest labourer his castle, and his privacy sacred.

"Is your man to hum"?—"Is the woman within?" were the general inquiries made to me by such guests, while my barelegged, ragged Irish servants were always spoken to, as "sir" and "*mem*," as if to make the distinction more pointed.

Why they treated our claims to their respect with marked insult and rudeness, I never could satisfactorily determine, in any way that could reflect honour on the species, or even plead an excuse for its brutality, until I found that this insolence was more generally practised by the low, uneducated emigrants from Britain, who better understood your claims to their civility, than by the natives themselves. Then I discovered the secret.

The unnatural restraint which society imposes upon these people at home forces them to treat their more fortunate brethren with a servile deference which is repugnant to their feelings, and is thrust upon them by the dependent circumstances in which they are placed. This homage to rank and education is not sincere. Hatred and envy lie rankling at their heart, although hidden by outward obsequiousness. Necessity compels their obedience; they fawn, and cringe, and flatter the wealth on which they depend for bread. But let them once emigrate, the clog which fettered them is suddenly removed; they are free; and the dearest privilege of this freedom is to wreak upon their superiors the long-locked-up hatred of their hearts. They think they can debase you to their level by disallowing all your claims to distinction; while they hope to exalt themselves and their fellows into ladies and gentlemen by sinking you back to the only title you received from Nature plain "man" and "woman." Oh, how much more honourable than their vulgar pretensions!

I never knew the real dignity of these simple epithets until they were insultingly thrust upon us by the working-classes of Canada.

But from this folly the native-born Canadian is exempt; it is only practised by the low-born Yankee, or the Yankeefied British peasantry and mechanics. It originates in the enormous reaction springing out of a sudden emancipation from a state of utter dependence into one of unrestrained liberty. As such, I not only excuse, but forgive it, for the principle is founded in nature; and, however disgusting and distasteful to those accustomed to different treatment from their inferiors, it is better than a hollow profession of duty and attachment urged upon us by a false and unnatural position. Still it is very irksome until you think more deeply upon it; and then it serves to amuse rather than to irritate.

And here I would observe, before quitting this subject, that of all follies, that of taking out servants from the old country is one of the greatest, and is sure to end in the loss of the money expended in their passage, and to become the cause of deep disappointment and mortification to yourself.

They no sooner set foot upon the Canadian shores than they become possessed with this ultra-republican spirit. All respect for their employers, all subordination, is at all end; the very air of Canada severs the tie of mutual obligation which bound you together. They fancy themselves not only equal to you in rank, but that ignorance and vulgarity give them superior claims to notice. They demand in terms the highest wages, and grumble at doing half the work, in return, which they cheerfully performed at home. They demand to eat at your table, and to sit in your company; and if you refuse to listen to their dishonest and extravagant claims, they tell you that "they are free; that no contract signed in the old country is binding in 'Meriky;' that you may look out for another person to fill their place as soon as you like; and that you may get the money expended in their passage and outfit in the best manner you can."

The Lieutenant-Governor Reports
on the 1837 Upper Canadian Rebellion

SIR FRANCIS BOND HEAD

I have the honour to inform your Lordship that on Monday, 4th inst., this city was, in a moment of profound peace, suddenly invaded by a band of armed rebels, amounting, according to report, to 3000 men (but in actual fact to about 500), and commanded by Mr. M'Kenzie, the editor of a republican newspaper; Mr. Van Egmond, an officer who had served under Napoleon; Mr. Gibson, a land-surveyor; Mr. Lount, a blacksmith, Mr. Loydd, and some other notorious characters.

Having, as I informed your Lordship in my despatch, No. 119, dated 3rd ultimo, purposely effected the withdrawal of her Majesty's troops from this province, and having delivered over to the civil authorities the whole of the arms and accoutrements I possessed, I of course found myself without any defence whatever, excepting that which the loyalty and fidelity of the province might think proper to afford me. The crisis, important as it was, was one I had long earnestly anticipated. . . .

As the foregoing statement is an unqualified admission on my part that I was completely surprised by the rebels, I think it proper to remind, rather than to explain, to your Lordship, the course of policy I have been pursuing.

In my despatch, No. 124, dated 18th ult., I respectfully stated to your Lordship, as my opinion, that a civil war must henceforward everywhere be a moral one, and that, in this hemisphere in particular, victory must eventually declare itself in favour of moral, and not of physical preponderance.

Entertaining these sentiments, I observed with satisfaction that Mr. M'Kenzie was pursuing a lawless course of conduct which I felt it would be impolitic for me to arrest.

For a long time he had endeavoured to force me to buoy him up by a Government prosecution, but he sunk in proportion as I neglected him, until becoming desperate, he was eventually driven to reckless behaviour, which I felt confident would very soon create its own punishment.

The traitorous arrangements he made were of that minute nature that it would have been difficult, even if I had desired it, to have suppressed them; for instance, he began by establishing union lists (in number not exceeding forty) of persons desirous of political reform; and who, by an appointed secretary, were recommended to communicate regularly with himself, for the purpose of establishing a meeting of delegates.

As soon as, by most wicked misrepresentations, he had succeeded in seducing a number of well-meaning people to join these squads, his next step was to prevail upon a few of them to attend their meetings armed, for the alleged purpose of firing at a mark.

While these meetings were in continuance, Mr. M'Kenzie, by means of his newspaper, and by constant personal attendance, succeeded in inducing his adherents to believe that he was everywhere strongly supported, and that his means, as well as his forces, would prove invincible.

Louis-Joseph Papineau, 1838

UNKNOWN

Louis Joseph Papineau is the son of Joseph Papineau, a notary in Montreal, who is still living, although ninety years of age. He has ever been denominated by the Canadians as "Father of the Patriots," but not a patriot either in the spirit or sense in which it is now applied to his son. This aged individual has never been the enemy of Great Britain, neither was he opposed to the Government at a period when it was generally believed by the Canadians to be the intention of England to make innovations on the institutions and privileges guaranteed to them at the conquest of the country. Yet, naturally jealous and fearful of such consequences, he was induced to take the chair at a large public meeting held on the Champ de Mars, against the then projected union of the Upper and Lower Provinces, at which a petition was voted to the Sovereign, and afterwards signed by eighty thousand Canadians, expatiating on the blessings they enjoyed under the Constitution as it then stood, and still stands, and praying that it might remain unaltered.

Such was the spirit of the aged parent of the rebel Papineau. We have been induced cursorily to mention him, merely to show that the revolutionary opinions of the son were not inculcated from early youth, but merely the out-breakings of a discontented mind, embittered by events and disasters of his own seeking. On the contrary, we have reason to believe that the aged Papineau earnestly endeavoured to check the rebellious principles exhibited by the son in all his actions for several years past, being fully convinced that he was guided and governed in all his extravagant and rebellious designs far more from vanity and ambition than from any conviction that his patriotism, so called, could lead to the welfare of his country, or that he had the means or ability of carrying his measures into effect.

Had his cause in any one principle been a just one; had there been one shadow of excuse that might have been urged in extenuation for the blood that he has been principally the cause of spilling by this patriotic rebelry; had, we say, his country taken up arms at his suggestion, and in a right cause, Papineau never could have sustained the character of a leader; he never could have been their chief, for it is well known he never through life possessed one generous feeling of moral or physical courage; and the absurdity of the supposition is great that the Americans would risk a war with Great Britain to assist the Canadians in gaining their independence, for the purpose of installing Papineau chief of the Canadian nation as dictator; or that Great Britain would quietly submit to have the province wrested from her, to the destruction of the lives and properties of those emigrants who had left the home that was dear to them to establish themselves in Canada, to enjoy, as they naturally expected, the protection of the British Government; or that if he, Papineau, could succeed in separating the Canadian nation from Great Britain, that the Americans would allow them to remain so near to them without immediately attaching them to the Great Republican Family, which would be a sad exchange for the tyranny of England—so termed by General Papineau.

The individual we have here alluded to is about forty-nine years of age, and of mild and courteous manners, which have no similarity with his opinions or appearance. In height he is about five feet eight, and inclining to the *embonpoint*. His features, which are prominent, have something of the Jewish cast, which is much added to by his dark hair and eyebrows, which are thick and arched, giving much fire to the eye. He is undoubtedly a man of much information, and in society his conversational powers are most fascinating. It cannot but be deplored that an individual so gifted should be led by motives of ambition to seek his own ruin, instead of employing his talents for the benefit of his fellow men.

Durham on Lower Canada, 1838

LORD DURHAM

> *Sent to the Canadas as governor-in-chief in 1838, Lord Durham quickly formed clear views on the difficult relations between French- and English-speakers.*

Durham to Glenelg, from Castle St. Louis, Quebec, August 9, 1838. Secret and confidential.
The first point to which I would draw your attention, being one with which all others are more or less connected, is the existence of a most bitter animosity between the Canadians and the British, not as two parties holding different opinions and seeking different objects in respect to Government, but as different races engaged in a national contest.

This hatred of races is not publicly avowed on either side. On the contrary, both sides profess to be moved by any other feelings than such as belong to difference of origin; but the fact is, I think proved by an accumulation of circumstantial evidence more conclusive than any direct testimony would be, and far more than sufficient to rebut all mere assertions to the contrary. If the difference between the two classes were one of party or principles only, we should find on each side a mixture of persons of both races; whereas the truth is that, with exceptions which tend to prove the rule, all the British are on one side, and all the Canadians are on the other. What may be the immediate subject of dispute seems to be of no consequence; so surely as there is a dispute on any subject, the great bulk of the Canadians and the great bulk of the British appear ranged against each other. In the next place, the mutual dislike of the two classes extends beyond politics, into social life, where, with some trifling exceptions again, all intercourse is confined to persons of the same origin. Grown-up persons of a different origin seldom or never meet in private society; and even the children, when they quarrel, divide themselves into French and English like their parents. In the schools and the streets of Montreal, the real capital of the province, this is commonly the case. The station in life, moreover, of an individual of either race seems to have no influence on his real disposition—towards the other race; high and low, rich and poor, on both sides—the merchant and the porter, the seigneur and the habitant—though they use different language to express themselves, yet exhibit the very same feeling of national jealousy and hatred. Such a sentiment is naturally evinced rather by trifles than by acts of intrinsic importance. There has been no solemn or formal declaration of national hostility; but not a day, nor scarcely an hour passes without some petty insult, some provoking language, or even some serious mutual affront occuring between persons of British and French descent. Lastly, it appears upon a careful review of the political struggle between those who have termed themselves of the loyal party and the popular party, that the subject of dissension has been, not the connexion with England, nor the form of the constitution, nor any of the practical abuses which have affected all classes of the people, but simply such institutions, laws, and customs as are of French origin, which the British have sought to overthrow, and the Canadians have struggled to preserve, each class assuming false designations and fighting under false colours—the British professing exclusive loyalty to the Crown of England, and the Canadians pretending to the character of Reformers...

I have no hesitation in asserting that of late years they have used the Representative System for the single purpose of maintaining their nationality against the progressive intrusion of the British race. They have found the British progressing upon them at every turn, in the possession of land, in commerce, in the retail trade, in all kinds of industrious enterprise, in religion, in the whole administration of government, and though they are a stagnant people, easily satisfied and disinclined to exertion, they have naturally resisted an invasion which was so offensive to their national pride.

The British, on the other hand, impeded in the pursuit of all their objects, partly by the ancient and barbarous civil law of the country, and partly by the systematic opposition of the Canadians to the progress of British enterprize, have naturally sought to remove those impediments and to conquer without much regard to the means employed, that very mischievous opposition. The actual result should have seemed inevitable. The struggle between the two races, conducted as long as possible according to the forms of the constitution, became too violent to be kept within those bounds. In order to preserve some sort of government, the public revenue was disposed of against the will of the Canadian people represented by their Assembly. The consequent rebellion, although precipitated by the British from an instinctive sense of the danger of allowing the Canadians full time for preparation, could not, perhaps have been avoided.

A Lady at York Factory, 1840

LETITIA HARGRAVE

A very chatty letter home by the wife of a Hudson's Bay Company trader at York Factory.

To Mrs. Dugald Mactavish
York Factory Septem^r 1840

My dear Mama

We arrived here on Monday the 10th of Augst after an unusually short passage. We got on shore meaning stuck on the bar on Sunday evening 15 miles from York, fortunately the bottom was soft mud & except that there was much confusion & the men took the oppor^y to get tipsy, the weather being calm we lay quietly altho' a good deal on one side, & no harm was done. In consequence of our guns, Mr Finlayson & Willie came off in a small boat about 9 at night. They remained all night but W^m returned at day light with the dispatches—We waited for the afternoon tide & left the ship at 4 oclock sticking fast. She got off next morn^g & reached York in 3 hours & I can give you very little idea of my feelings as for some days or weeks I had been so wretched that Hargrave thought if I went on shore at all it w^d have been rolled & carried in a blanket. I could neither eat sleep nor speak & my pulse was often 120. I c^d not take medicine as I told you we had the cuddy for our cabin & the Mess was there & the Cap^n always in it. My 1st exploit on being lowered into the yawl, was to turn my back to the company & cry myself sick. After which I began to look about me & feel less disconsolate. I had no sooner got out of the yawl than I felt better & have ever since got stronger & as for fatness I am getting on well & my neck is as well covered as when I left Stromness.

On reaching the Quay here we found Mr Gladman & a Mr Manson Chief trader from F^t Vancouver who goes home by the ship this season. Hargrave introduced them both & then took Miss Ross & me away up. On looking round we found M^r & Mrs Finlayson behind together,

Mr Gladman & Miss Allan, & Mrs Potter & Mr Manson likewise arm in arm. Poor Mrs Potter had resisted Mr Mansons politeness as long as she civilly could, but after walking a few paces she said she would wait for Marg^t & Mrs Turner & by this means gave him a hint of which he availed himself but he nevertheless escorted them to the Fort—

Dugald certainly asperses Willie when he accuses him of reserve. At least there is nothing of the kind to me, he is quite open & frank & except that he looks older than I had expected he has not in my opinion lost his looks. He looks stout & strong, [his] expression wch I think used to be mild, is now knowing and acute. He seems very active & pads about as if he had the whole charge of the Factory, & is in the store from 1/2 past 4. A.M. till 8 at night, but this will not long be the case & the summer work will soon be over. I w^d not have known him altho' Hargrave sent him down to the Gun room where I was waiting expressly for him, I w^d not have ventured to speak. He says he w^d never know he had seen me before & was greatly shocked by the thin cheeks and hollow eyes I brought on shore. Not to speak of my fingers wch were so reduced that I lost my rings punctually when in bed & had to get them tightened with ribbon. W^m had a letter from John by the ship, he had had an attack of fever in Feb^r but he wrote in good spirits & was quite well again. It was by far the best written letter I had seen from him, & there was no mispelling from 1st to last. I hope that wherever it may be my lot to go I shall never be shut up in a cabin with 3 ladies & servants. The constant clack clack & the impossibility of being one moment alone had worn me out completely. Had I had the power to get a little time to myself I w^d not have been so miserable, but if I were 1/2 dead & lay down on my berth—one or other of them was sure to squat on the ledge of my bed & all out of kindness.

Mrs Finlayson was very kind & gave indeed pressed me to lie down all day in her bed but somehow I never did so but when she compelled me. Her husband & she were both very kind, & altho he was in charge here we had our own house—at least the larger part & he even offered to leave it altogether.

The mosquitoes were nearly over but Mrs F. & Miss Allan suffered a good deal. Indeed the latter had to get Dr Gillespie as her face & eyes swelled as if she had been stung by bees. They did not touch Miss Ross or me. The day after our arrival, a boat from Norway House brought Mr Evans a Wesleyan missionary who is there with his family, consisting of his wife & daughter a Miss of 17. He dined with us next day & Mrs Fin^n as usual began her lamentations about Mrs Turner having turned out such a light frivolous character that she was resolved to send her home again. The minister said nothing but next morn asked Mr F. if he would allow him to take her to Norway House as his servant. Mr F. told him plainly that he was sending her back in consequence of having been drunk on board & having stolen rum from the steward. Mr E. was nothing daunted, said she w^d have no temptations at his house & that she might reform. She is a regular cook & he agreed to give her M^r F's wages viz. 20 guineas. Poor wretch she left this in a boat with him & 19 men on the 18th in dreadful weather, one foot a sore of broken chilblain. I think she has not met with sympathy, I neither liked her nor the other who is a grumbling discontented hypocritical sinner, & told Marg^t that Mrs F. "was no lady" altho' the poor thing seems to take greater care of her than herself. The constant fightings that went on were sickening. Mrs Potter is particular about her fare & says she cares not where she goes if she gets good meat & a comfortable feather bed—Marg^t is very satisfactory & quiet, works very neatly & is a great hand at making drawers flannels &c. & sorting M^r Hs clothes having learned from her father—She will have a very easy time of it as she has nothing to do, but our bedroom & the stove is lighted at 5 A.M. by the butler, an elderly conceited Canadian called *Gibout* an old servant of Uncles. When we landed Hargrave was shocked at the change in Crosbies appearance, & on speaking to the D^r he said he was threatened with consumption & must leave the Coast & go to the Interior. Crosbie resisted but must go as they may kick their servants about as they please. Willie says he is a great blackguard but he was a good servant & looked highly civilized. Nevertheless I like old Gibout best, he is very respectable & the delight he takes in toiling for me is refreshing. Crosbie cooked well particularly in the article of tarts, the very look of wch are enough for me, I was so sickened with rhubarb in Lond^n & on board—The usual dinner for our mess meaning the 3 ladies & me was—a roast of venison at the top 3 geese at the foot, 4 ducks on one side 6 plovers on the other, a large Red river ham (whole leg) & potatoes & mashed turnips or boiled lettuce. For something green when they have broth they put lettuce & the bitterness is surprizing—They have radish & lettuce after dinner.

I am getting a superfine blue cloth gown but do not see how I am to wear it as I cant bear a cap on my head, the room is so close, & the fires quite small. There are 3 windows in it. We have 2 sittingrooms, but the kitchen in our house is not used except in Winter. Marg^t has had fires in it all along. It is very large. I had nearly forgot to say that we had sermon from Mr Evans the Sunday after our arrival. In illustration of the ingratitude of the human heart he reminded us of how unnecessary it was to tell children to ask for what they wanted & what labor it cost to make them express feeling of thankfulness. For instance how constantly parents had to desire them to say "Thank you Sir" & "Thank you Ma'am". I c^d scarcely help laughing at the simplicity. He preaches well but quietly as if he were addressing them.

I only observed one or two 1/2 breeds, one was a woman the only female except ourselves & Mrs Potter & Marg^t She had a baby with her & its unhappy legs wrapt up in a moss bag. It looked like a mummy. I have not been near enough to inspect closely but I shall make Marg^t fetch a child over without the mother that I may examine it. The moment it is born they get the bag stuffed with soft moss wch has been in readiness & stuff the wretch into it up to the neck, bind it tightly round like a mummy, so as to make it as firm & flat as a deal board, then fasten it around their own back & work away about what they have to do. They dont mind the moss being wet & dirty but consider it a great convenience that they have no trouble shifting [it] at least for a long time. The Indians all walk wth their feet turned in from this discipline & their arms are as stiff as if there was not a joint in them. While the whites gentle & simple are running about perspiring with haste the Indian stalk along the platforms with their backs bent as if it were entirely for pleasure that they were wheeling barrows. They march so slowly & look so stately that they remind me of people on the stage. The women always come to the Fort in pairs, the older 1st the younger behind her & they also look very dignified & demure. The men wear long blue capots like childrens surtouts (very long) & hoods either hanging down or on their head, scarlet leggins, not trowsers & gay scarlet military sashes round their waist. Squaws never move without their blanket common coarse often dirty affairs. They fold them like a scarf, not a shawl. The wee'est girls have them. One of the pigs comes to my window with red currants in the corner of hers wch is black with dirt. Hargrave bought 2 lbs of peppermint drops at Stromness & they laugh aloud when I give them some. They dont know a word of English or French. When I want flowers or berries I show them a specimen & give them a shove & off they go. It never happens that they fail.

I was much surprized at the "great swell" the Factory is. It looks beautiful. The houses are painted pale yellow. The windows & some particular parts white. Some have green gauze mosquito curtains outside & altogether the effect is very good. Our house is a good size, 1 bedroom off each sitting room & men servants rooms off the kitchen a very large closet off the diningr^m. I had nearly forgot my piano. It is a very fine one & the handsomest I ever saw. The wood is beautiful & Mr Finlay[son] is croaking for one the same. M^rs F does not play except to accompany herself. I was astonished at its appearance as I did not expect the cast to be any great thing. The hinge of the lid, & the lock have created a sensation among the geniuses here from the uncommon elegance of their contrivance & mechanism. There was not a scratch upon it nor a note out of tune. The form of the pedal is magnificent & the wood beautifully marked. Mr Gladman has a barrel organ in wch are a drum & some other instruments. It is never silent, the family imagine themselves so fond of music. Willie maintains that it was nothing but weakness & want of sense that made Gladman cause the disturbance between Uncle & Dugald. The whole family make it their duty to gather gossip & to detail it to all & sundry—Gladman heard some stories of Dug^d as he did of others & repeated them to Uncle who without inquiry attacked Dug^d who made no attempt to explain or as others w^d have done denied at once when every thing was false. But he quarrelled & scorned them. Willie says Gladman has always been kind & friendly to him & has no idea he did any harm to Dug^d. At any rate Uncle & he are great enough now. I daresay Mr Christie has been at Kilchrist. One of Uncles wives was sister to his wife—

When papa was in London Mrs Webster told him that they thought I was in the family way. I did not myself think so, & from my illness on my way from London to Stromness I suppose I was right. Now however I have no doubt of it. Dr Gillespie is very clever. He had an interview with Dr Elliott who thought him as intelligent a person for his age as he had met with. I dont think he is above 23. He looks curious but is very agreeable & nothing c^d be more attentive than he was on the voyage. His father is Kilberry's Edin D^r & he was a g^t friend of Dr MacIntosh. I am taking more iron powders & he says I am as well as I could possibly be. I feel that I owe my being extant at all to Mrs Webster & Dr Elliott. I had a long letter of instructions from her at Stromness & have not had the slightest return of my London complaint. My throat is also well & on looking at it for the 1st time since I left Lon^n I found it away to nothing not the slightest remains of swelling & the cold I suffered on board was past mentioning. Mrs Fin^n & Miss Ross c^d not stand a fire for fear of gun powder & as I was constantly taking *dwams* even at dinner from perfect cold among the ice, the D^r always ordered a fire as he said the dampth from the bare floor which was constantly washing & never dry was enough to hurt me, yet as M^rs F's feet & hands were covered with chilblains & she w^d not have a fire an her own account, I w^d not allow her to be applied to on mine. I will write papa Polly & Flora. I was very glad to get y^r letter the day we were to leave Stromness.

Hargrave joins me in kindest love to you & the boys & believe me ever dear Mama y^r m^o affec^te daughter

Letitia Hargrave

Sealing off Newfoundland, 1840

J.B. JUKES

March 18, 1840.

Generally, however, the young ones did not attempt to stir as we approached them, and quietly suffered themselves to be knocked on the head with the gaff, and skinned on the spot. I saw one poor wretch skinned, or sculped, while yet alive, and the body writhing in blood after being stripped of its pelt. The man told me he had seen them swim away in that state, and that if the first blow did not kill them, they could not stop to give them a second... As this morning I was left alone to take care of the punt while the men were on the ice, the mass of dying carcasses piled in the boat around me each writhing, gasping, and spouting blood into the air nearly made me sick. Seeking relief in action, I drove the sharp point of the gaff into the brain of every one in which I could see a sign of life. The vision of one poor wretch writhing its snow-white woolly body with its head bathed in blood, through which it was vainly endeavouring to see and breathe, really haunted my dreams.

Death in Quarantine, Grosse Île, June 1847

GERALD KEEGAN

Desperately escaping the famines in Ireland, thousands fled to the New World. For many, the voyage to a new life ended tragically at the quarantine station on Grosse Ile, downstream from Québec City.

Leaving the cemetery with the priest, I thanked him from my heart, and ran to the quay. My heart was in my mouth when I saw on it Aileen, standing beside our boxes, and the ship, having tripped her anchor, bearing up the river. "What makes you look so at me, Gerald? I have come as you asked."

"I never sent for you."

"The steward told me you had sent word by the sailors for me to come ashore, that you were going to stay here. They carried the luggage into a boat and I followed."

I groaned in spirit. I saw it all. By a villainous trick, the captain had got rid of me. Instead of being in Quebec that day, here I was left at the quarantine station. "My poor Aileen, I know not what to do; my trouble is for you." I went to see the head of the establishment, Dr Douglas. He proved to be a fussy gentleman, worried over a number of details. Professing to be ready to oblige, he said there was no help for me until the steamer came. "When will that be?" Next Saturday. A week on an island full of people sick with fever! Aileen, brave heart, made the best of it. She was soaking wet, yet the only shelter, apart from the fever sheds, which were not to be thought of, was an outhouse with a leaky roof, with no possibility of a fire or change of clothing. How I cursed myself for my rashness in making captain and mate my enemies, for the penalty had fallen not on me, but on my Aileen. There was not an armful of straw to be had; not even boards to lie on. I went to the cooking booth, and found a Frenchman in charge. Bribing him with a shilling he gave me a loaf and a tin of hot tea. Aileen could not eat a bite, though she tried to do so to please me, but drank the tea. The rain continued and the east wind penetrated between the boards of the wretched sheiling. What a night it was! I put my coat over Aileen. I pressed her to my bosom to impart some heat to her chilled frame, I endeavoured to cheer her with prospects of the morrow. Alas, when morning came she was unable to move, and fever and chill alternated. I sought the doctor, he was not to be had. Other emigrant ships had arrived, and he was visiting them. Beyond giving her water to assuage her thirst when in the fever it was not in my power to do anything. It was evening when the doctor, yielding to my importunities, came to see her. He did not stay a minute and writing a few lines told me to go to the hospital steward, who would give me some medicine. Why recall the dreadful nights and days that followed? What profit to tell of the pain in the breast, the raging fever, the delirium, the agonizing gasping for breath —the end? The fourth day, with bursting heart and throbbing head, I knelt by the corpse of my Aileen. There was not a soul to help; everybody was too full of their own troubles to be able to heed me. The island was now filled with sick emigrants, and death was on every side. I dug her grave, the priest came, I laid her there, I filled it in, I staggered to the shed that had sheltered us, I fell from sheer exhaustion, and remember no more. When I woke, I heard the patter of rain, and felt so inexpressibly weary I could think of nothing, much less make any exertion. My eye fell on Aileen's shawl, and the past rushed on me. Oh, the agony of that hour; my remorse, my sorrow, my beseechings of the Unseen. Such a paroxysm could not last long, and when exhausted nature compelled me to lie down, I turned my face to the wall with the earnest prayer I might never awaken on this earth.

Lord Elgin on the French Canadians, 1848

LORD ELGIN

> Lower Canada was in a state of high tension in 1848, with English merchants calling for annexation to the U.S. Governor Elgin began looking to the French speakers as a bulwark of the British connection.

Elgin to Grey, May 4, 1848. Private.
I must moreover confess that I for one am deeply convinced of the impolicy of all such attempts to denationalize the French. Generally speaking they produce the opposite effect from that intended, causing the flame of national prejudice and animosity to burn more fiercely—But suppose them to be successful what wd be the result? You may perhaps *americanise*, but, depend upon it, by methods of this description, you will never *anglicise* the French inhabitants of the Province.—Let them feel on the other hand that their religion, their habits, their prepossessions, their prejudices if you will, are more considered and respected here than in other portions of this vast continent which is being overrun by the most reckless, self-sufficient and dictatorial section of the Anglo Saxon race,

and who will venture to say that the last hand which waves the British flag on American ground may not be that of a French Canadian?

A Fugitive Slave in Canada

THOMAS HEDGEBETH

> *Hundreds of escaped slaves made their way to the Canadas before the American Civil War. There was prejudice, but "as much freedom as a man can have."*

I came here a year last spring, to escape the oppression of the laws upon the colored men. After the fugitive slave bill was passed, a man came into Indianapolis, and claimed John Freeman, a free colored man, an industrious, respectable man, as his slave. He brought proofs enough. Freeman was kept in jail several weeks,—but at last it turned out that the slave sought, was not Freeman, but a colored man in Canada, and F. was released. The danger of being taken as Freeman was, and suffering from a different decision, worked on my mind. I came away into Canada in consequence, as did many others. There were colored people who could have testified to Freeman's being free from his birth, but their oath would not be taken in Indiana.

In regard to Canada, I like the country, the soil, as well as any country I ever saw. I like the laws, which leave a man as much freedom as a man can have,—still there is prejudice here. The colored people are trying to remove this by improving and educating themselves, and by industry, to show that they are a people who have minds, and that all they want is cultivating.

I do not know how many colored people are here—but last summer five hundred and twenty-five were counted leaving the four churches.

Hunting the Buffalo

HENRY YOULE HIND

> *Explorer and proponent of western settlement, Hind saw the buffalo before over-hunting killed off the great herds.*

... The ranges of the buffalo in the north-western prairies are still maintained with great exactness, and old hunters, if the plains have not been burnt, can generally tell the direction in which herds will be found at certain seasons of the year. If the plains have been extensively burnt in the autumn, the search for the main herds during the following spring must depend on the course the fires have taken. Red River hunters recognized two grand divisions of buffalo, those of the Grand Coteau and Red River, and those of the Saskatchewan. Other ranges of immense herds exist beyond the Missouri towards the south, as far as Texas and Mexico. The north-western buffalo ranges are as follows. The bands belonging to the Red River Range winter on the Little Souris, and south-easterly towards and beyond Devil's Lake, and thence on to Red River and the Shayenne. Here too, they are found in the spring. Their course then lies west towards the Grand Coteau de Missouri, until the month of June, when they turn north, and revisit the Little Souris from the west winding round the west flank of Turtle Mountain to Devil's Lake, and by the main river (Red River), to the Shayenne again. In the memory of many Red River hunters, the buffalo were accustomed to visit the prairies of the Assinniboine as far north as Lake Manitobah, where in fact their skulls and bones are now to be seen; their skulls are also seen on the east side of the Red River of the north, in Minnesota, but the living animal is very rarely to be met with. A few years ago they were accustomed to pass on the east side of Turtle Mountain through the Blue Hills of the Souris, but of late years their wanderings in this direction have ceased; experience teaching them that their enemies, the half-breeds, have approached too near their haunts in that direction. The country about the west side of Turtle Mountain in June 1858 was scored with their tracks at one of the crossing places on the Little Souris, as if deep parallel ruts had been artificially cut down the hill-sides. These ruts, often one foot deep and sixteen inches broad, would converge from the prairie for many miles to a favourite crossing or drinking place; and they are often seen in regions in which the buffalo is no longer a visitor. The great western herds winter between the south and north branches of the Saskatchewan, south of the Touchwood Hills, and beyond the north Saskatchewan in the valley of the Athabaska; they cross the South Branch in June and July, visit the prairies on the south side of the Touchwood Hill range, and cross the Qu'appelle valley anywhere between the Elbow of the South Branch and a few miles west of Fort Ellice on the Assinniboine. They then strike for the Grand Coteau de Missouri, and their eastern flank often approaches the Red River herds coming north from the Grand Coteau. They then proceed across the Missouri up the Yellow Stone, and return to the Saskatchewan and Athabaska as winter approaches, by the flanks of the Rocky Mountains. We saw many small herds, belonging to the western bands, cross the Qu'appelle valley, and proceed in single file towards the Grand Coteau in July 1858. The eastern bands, which we had expected to find on the Little Souris, were on the main river (Red River is so termed by the half-breeds hunting in this quarter). They had proceeded early thither, far to the south of their usual track, in consequence of the devastating fires which swept the plains from the Rocky Mountains to Red River in the autumn of 1857. We met bulls all moving south, when approaching Fort Ellice; they had come from their winter quarters near the Touchwood Hill range. As a general rule the Saskatchewan bands of buffalo go north during the autumn, and south during the summer. The Little Souris and main river bands, go north-west in summer and south-east in autumn. It is almost needless to remark again that fires interfere with this systematic migration, but there are no impediments which will divert the buffalo from their course. The half-breeds state that no slaughter by large parties of hunters or Indians can turn large herds from the general direction they have taken when on the march; want of food is alone able to make them deviate from the course they have taken. The approach of numerous herds can be recognised by a low rumbling sound they occasion, if the weather be calm, fully twenty miles before they arrive, this warning is best perceived by applying the ear to a badger hole. During the rutting season they can be heard bellowing for a great distance on a still night. When we arrived at the Sandy Hills on the South Branch, the Crees, on being asked if the buffalo were numerous near at hand, answered, "listen to-night and you will hear them." The summer and fall buffalo hunts are the grand events of the year to the Red River settlers, in fact the chief dependence for a livelihood of the greater part of the population. The start is usually made from the settlements about the 15th of June for the summer hunt, the hunters remaining in the prairie until the 20th August or 1st of September. One division (the White Horse Plain) goes by the Assinniboine River to the "rapids crossing place," and then proceed in a south-westerly direction. The other, or Red River division, pass on to Pembina, and then take a southerly direction. The two divisions sometimes meet, but not intentionally. Mr. Flett in 1849 took a census of the White Horse Plain division near the Chiefs' Mountain, not far from the Shayenne River, Dacotah Territory, and enumerated 603 carts, 700 half-breeds, 200 Indians, 600 horses, 200 oxen, 400 dogs and one cat. . . .

After the start from the settlement has been well made, and all stragglers or tardy hunters have arrived, a great council is held, and a president elected. A number of captains are nominated by the president and people jointly. The captains then proceed to appoint their own policemen, the number assigned to each not exceeding ten. Their duty is to see that the laws of the hunt are strictly carried out. In 1849, if a man ran a buffalo without permission before the general hunt began, his saddle and bridle were cut to pieces, for the first offence; for the second offence of the same description his clothes were cut off his back. At the present day these punishments are changed to a fine of twenty shillings for the first offence. No gun is permitted to be fired when in the buffalo country before the "race" begins. A priest sometimes goes with the hunt, and mass is then celebrated in the open prairies. At night the carts are placed in the form of a circle with the horses and cattle inside the ring, and it is the duty of the captains and their policemen to see that this is rightly done. All camping orders are given by signal, a flag being carried by the guides, who are appointed by election. Each guide has his turn of one day, and no man can pass a guide on duty without subjecting himself to a fine of five shillings. No hunter can leave the camp to return home without permission, and no one is permitted to stir until any animal or property of value, supposed to be lost, is recovered. The policemen, at the order of the captains, can seize any cart at night-fall and place it where they choose for the public safety, but on the following morning they are compelled to bring it back to the spot from which they moved it the evening previous. This power is very necessary in order that the horses may not be stampeded by night attacks of the Sioux or other Indian tribes at war with the half-breeds. A heavy fine is imposed in case of neglect in extinguishing fires when the camp is broken up in the morning. In sight of buffalo, all the hunters are drawn up in line, the president, captains, and police being a few yards in advance, restraining the impatient hunters. Not yet, not yet, is the sub-dued whisper of the president; the approach to the herd is cautiously made. Now! the president exclaims, and as the word leaves his lips the charge is made, and in a few minutes the excited half-breeds are among the bewildered buffalo. Blind buffalo are frequently found accompanying herds, and sometimes they are met with alone. Their eyes have been destroyed by prairie fires; but their quickening sense of hearing and smell, and their increased alertness enable them to guard against danger, and makes it more difficult to approach them in quiet weather than those possessing sight. The hunters think that blind buffalo frequently give the alarm when they are stealthily approaching a herd in an undulating coun-try. When galloping over stony ground blind buffalo frequently fall, but when quietly feeding they avoid the stones and boulders with wonderful skill. . . .

George Brown on the Charlottetown Conference, 1864

GEORGE BROWN

> *Leader of the Upper Canadian Grits and owner of the* Toronto Globe, *Brown had a shrewd eye and an engaging way with words.*

George Brown to Anne Brown, September 13, 1864, from Halifax.
Our party from Quebec consisted of Cartier, John A. [Macdonald], Galt, McDougall, Campbell, Langevin, McGee and myself—beside the clerk of the Executive Council Mr. Lee, the clerk of the Attorney-General, Mr. Bernard, and a shorthand writer. We had great fun coming down the St. Lawrence—having fine weather, a broad awning to recline under, excellent stores of all kinds, an unexceptionable cook, lots of books, chessboards, backgammon. . . .

From Gaspe our course was direct to Charlottetown, the little capital of little Prince Edward Island. I was up at four in the morning!—Thursday morning—to see the sun rise and have a salt water bath. We had just reached the westerly point of Prince Edward and were running along the coast of as pretty a country as you ever put your eye upon. The land all along the shore rises gradually up from the sea for a space of two or three miles, and this slope all round the island is well cultivated and when we passed was clothed in bright green verdure.

About noon we came to an inlet which we entered, and running up for some miles what appeared to be a river but was in fact but an inlet of the sea, amid most beautiful scenery, we came suddenly on the Capital City of the Island. Our steamer dropped anchor magnificently in the stream and its man-of-war cut evidently inspired the natives with huge respect for their big brothers from Canada. I flatter myself we did that well. Having dressed ourselves in correct style, our two boats were lowered man-of-war fashion—and being each duly manned with four oarsmen and a boatswain, dressed in blue uniform, hats, belts, etc., in regular style, we pulled away for shore and landed like Mr. Christopher Columbus who had the precedence of us in taking possession of portions of the American continent. . . .

On Friday [Sept. 2] we met in Conference and Canada opened her batteries—John A. and Cartier exposing the general arguments in favour of confederation—and this occupied the time until the hour of adjournment at three. At four o'clock, Mr. Pope gave us a grand *Déjeuner à la fourchette*—oysters, lobsters and champagne and other island luxuries. This killed the day and we spent the beautiful moonlight evening in walking, driving or boating, as the mood was on us. I sat on Mr. Pope's balcony looking out on the sea in all its glory.

On Saturday, the Conference resumed its deliberations, and Mr. Galt occupied the sitting in opening up the financial aspects of the Federation and the manner in which the financial disparities and requirements of the several Provinces might be arranged.

When the Conference adjourned, we all proceeded on board our steamer and the members were entertained at luncheon in princely style.

Cartier and I made eloquent speeches, of course, and whether as the result of our eloquence or of the goodness of our champagne the ice became completely broken, the tongues of the delegates wagged merrily, and the banns of matrimony between all the provinces of B.N.A. having been formally proclaimed and all manner of persons duly warned there and then to speak or forever after to hold their tongues—no man appeared to forbid the banns and the union was thereupon formally completed and proclaimed! . . .

On Monday the conference resumed its sittings, when I addressed the members on the Constitutional aspects of the question—the manner in which the several Governments general and local should be constructed —and the Judiciary should be constituted, what duties should be ascribed to the general and local legislatures respectively and so forth. My speech occupied the whole sitting. At four, we lunched at the residence of Mr. Coles, leader of the Parliamentary Opposition. He is a brewer, farmer and distiller and gave us a handsome set out. He has a number of handsome daughters, well educated, well informed and as sharp as needles. The evening I passed on board the steamer, playing chess and catching lobsters over the side of the steamer.

Hot Times in Old Québec

ALFRED TOWNSEND

Sillery, Canada East
20 January 1865

Dear Carrie:

If I were a younger man, I think I should never come back to Bideford to live my life out. These Canadian folk know how to enjoy themselves. My word. Never a dull moment, as they say. Not here, there isn't. I've just about made my deal with the shipper, and I'm leaving for New York in a fortnight or so, and I don't mind saying I'm a bit loathe to go. We've had a gay time here, and no mistake. And only a little bit of a place, this is, when you come to compare. Eight miles out of Quebec, we are, and only tracks, you might say, more or less tunnels, in the snow—sometimes eight feet deep, they are, between the house and the road, and then the eight miles. But do people sit at home warming theirselves? They do not. Up and at it, night and day. I know what you'll say, "It's those Frenchies, there. We always knew they were a gay lot." Well, my girl, you're wrong this time. Not that they aren't gay, of course, but it's the English soldiers that mostly are to blame, in my opinion. And then there's the Governor General, living right here. Fine big house like Buckingham Palace, pretty well, it is. Called Spencer Wood, or some such name. Twice as long as a church, and with a verandah all along the whole front of the house. Posts all along, and arches in between. The house is white, and has a lot of cedar trees growing in front. Might be all right come summer time, but just now, it being all white, and the snow behind it being all white too, it's not so much, only for the size. And there's lots going on there, all the time. Soldiers tracking up there on snowshoes, to show themselves off, in their fur coats and hats, to the Governor, and strings of sleighs, all jingling with bells, and the ladies in them so covered up with furs and veils and cloaks till there might as well be a nest of ferrets in the cariole (that's what they call these little low sleighs) for all a man can see of a face.

The officers of the regiments play pretty high, with the customs of this country, if you ask me. They swank around with sleighs built to order just for themselves, and trimmed here and there with the colours of their regiment. And then, not content with that, they buy great big buffalo robes, or bearskins they might be, and have them trimmed around the edge with their colours. What are they going to do with the likes of that kind of thing when they go home? Ten to one his regiment won't be here more than maybe a few months, the way it seems to be.

Col. Monck, he's the Gov. Gen's brother, he got one of these fancy sleighs, and he's off down to the rink, or off to the Cone, or calling on some nob every day, with a tandem pair. Don't they just lick through the roads, though!

There's no waiting here, for summertime, like Ascot, or the Derby, to start the racing. Canadians race their horses all the time, winter and summer, just as long as the roads are dry enough to set a pair of wheels on. In wintertime, it's sleighs. They tell me it's already eight years since the Queen gave a prize for the fastest horse in her remaining part of North America. The part that doesn't belong to us any more hasn't got any race started that long ago. You might be wondering how they race in the winter, when, as I've told you, they've got six to eight feet of snow in front of every house in Sillery, and in Quebec too, the city, I mean, and nobody does anything about it but shovel a little tunnel through. The city seems sunk down into the snow, I don't know what they COULD do about it, come to think of it. Well, the race is on the river—on the ice, that is. Put up rows of fir trees (mostly what they call spruce, here), to make the race track, and away they go.

There's the English officer, with his blood horse, and there's the French Canadian with his shaggy black horse, hardly bigger than a pony, really. And the officer yells "Hi!," and the Frenchy yells "Avant!" And away they go, running like the very devil. And it isn't always the blood horse that wins either. The little black chap, you see, is maybe more used to racing on the ice. The Canadians do it all the time. The rivers are like roads to them, in the winter. "Ice bridge," they call it, when the river freezes over. I heard about this ice-bridge, and like a fool, thought it would be a bridge built up in the air. I didn't admit that, to anybody though. And even with the "ice-bridge," things can be pretty exciting sometimes. I cut this piece out of the paper, a magazine, that I saw. I didn't suppose you would believe me, if I told you myself. And the man says it a lot better than I could.

Occasionally serious accidents occur while driving upon the snow over frozen rivers or lakes in sleighs or carioles. Pleasure parties suddenly become engulphed without the slightest premonitory warning of their danger, when every strenuous exertion become necessary in order to save their lives. Their first object is to make sure their footing upon strong ice, when they immediately seize hold of a noose attached to the sinking horse's neck, when they pull-pull-pull remorselessly with all their might until the poor animal is almost strangled. When his breathing becomes thus checked, he rises at once gently to the surface and is hauled on to the ice. So soon as the noose is relaxed respiration becomes restored, and in a few minutes the horse canters on the snow as nimbly as before. These processes of emersion and semi-strangulation not infrequently take place several times during one day.

I haven't seen that, myself, yet, but there's no doubt but with all the cavorting that goes on on the little river here (St. Charles)—and not so little either, but only to compare with the St. Lawrence, which is like a sea all by itself—a power of occurrences do take place.

'Tisn't only the racing or the driving just for the fun on the river. There's many a sleigh down there this minute cutting out huge blocks of ice, quarrying it, you might say. This is for keeping the food from spoiling. Every nob has an "ice house," not a house made of ice, though the young folk do that, too, but to keep ice in. What do you think of that, old lady? Mostly they drive their "berlots," down for that job. You say that word "bare low." They dig an excavation in the ground and build half the house more or less under ground. Then there's sawdust put in, and when the ice is some feet thick in the St. Lawrence, out they come with their "berlots." And pretty uncomfortable contraptions they are, to my eye. The driver sits on just a strip of leather, strung up between two uprights.

They make a great hole with a cross cut saw about six feet long, with teeth like a crocodile. Two or three men to a berlot. They quarry the blocks out, and heave it up onto the sleigh. When they've got the load as high as the horse can pull, they track home again. It takes the best part of a week, going on like this, to fill some ice houses. They tell me that properly built, with sawdust underneath and on top, this ice will last until next September. Maybe longer. Taking into account the summer, which is uncommonly warm, in these parts, that seems a remarkable thing, to me. The whole enterprise looks pretty uncomfortable, but the men don't seem to mind. The old sleigh bells are ringing, and the harness creaking away and jingling in the cold, and the men wrapped up with furs pretty well incognito.

Funny thing I saw the other day. Up at Spencer Wood, maybe I told you, the Governor General's sister-in-law is staying just now. Her husband being the G.G.'s brother, Colonel Monck. Well, Mrs. Monck, of course, has a little cariole made up just to suit her. Red as a hunting jacket. Slung low to the ground these things are. A real big dog could just about step over a cariole, would hardly need to leap. I was driving along behind her, the other day. Couldn't see her, of course, her being so smothered up in furs, as I said, but I recognized the fit out. And driving along ahead of her was a very smart turn-out, Colonel somebody or other, to judge from his looks, and a lady with him. (This was a real lady, not one of your muffins.) He was driving "tandem," one horse ahead of the other and very smart they looked. Well, here we were, jingling along like a bell ringers concert, and suddenly the front sleigh, with the colonel in it, tipped over sideways and tossed the col. and his lady into eight feet of soft snow. The horses and the shafts broke from the sleigh, and ran demented along the road. Well, this happens, nobody hurt, and Mrs. Monck right behind sat up straight and sudden in her cariole like a hare out of hole. She laughed and laughed. Surprised me. She doesn't laugh very easily, I hear. Built something in the fashion of the Queen, a bit on the dumpy side. Mind of her own, too. Caught a glimpse of her at the Sergeant's Ball, the other night. No, I wasn't dancing, just looking on to see what I could see. She didn't dance much, fearful of tearing her lace flounces, somebody said. And where every other woman there had about seven pound of hair, false, that is, mounted up on their heads, the higher the better, the Honourable Mrs. Monck had hers parted straight down the middle and brushed back like two blackbirds wings, with only a little knot of her own hair, about the size of a biggish snail, coiled about at the back of her neck. Independent.

Hard to say what these folk do in the summer. A man would almost think they had to have snow and ice and frozen ears before they were enjoying themselves. There's these outside "rinks" for skating, with carpets spread out for the ladies who don't want to skate, and tea and coffee and cakes on little tables, and a band playing away like mad.

I'm too old to learn to skate, now, and I'm telling you what you'd know anyway, I wouldn't fancy myself on one of these flat little sleds that are all about. Tarboggins. But I've broomed a few iron stones along the ice. Too cold here for the granite. Cracks them. And I'd like to take a turn at what they call "ice-boating." What would you think of racing in a boat on a river in the winter time, ice right down to the bottom, I should think. Not done with a proper boat, of course, but what else would you call a vessel with mast and sails, that can go like hell for leather, all down the river? The boat is a kind of floor, shaped in a triangle, set up on great iron skates. One of these skates at the stern is worked with a tiller; this makes a helm. "Wear" and "Tack" is precisely the same, they tell me, as with an ordinary sailing yacht. Maybe it's just tales, having me on, but they say that some have done five miles in five minutes, on one of these boats. Maybe I'll have a try, before I come home.

Yrs aye

ALF.

Five or six people lie down flat on the floor, on these boats.

Nova Scotia, Confederation and the Fenians, 1866

CHARLES TUPPER

> *Premier Tupper used the Fenian menace as an argument for Confederation in the Nova Scotia legislature.*

The information coming to us from hour to hour shows the existence and widespread ramification of the Fenian organization. What ought to be the conduct of a patriot and a statesman in the face of a danger like that? The men who will be held responsible for all [the] horrors [of an invasion of British North America] will be the men who are resisting intercolonial union and indoctrinating our people with sentiments that may shake their allegiance to the crown.

In the presence of a common danger like that the duty of a patriot and statesman would be to sink all differences and combine for the purpose of protection the rights and liberties of British North America. Let the aegis of British protection be withdrawn and what can Nova Scotia do in the face of such danger? Simply nothing.

I will now ask the house if I were corrupted by American gold, enamoured of American institutions, believing that the best thing that I could do would be to transfer this country to the United States of America, what are the most effective measures that I could take? Would it not be to keep the provinces disunited and repel the protection of the mother country, and then button-hole every man whom I could influence, and undermine his confidence in our institutions by whispering into his ear the insidious statement that Great Britain could not protect us—that the power of the United States was too gigantic—that Great Britain herself would fail to protect even the city of Halifax against such ships as were now possessed by the American government? And when I had indoctrinated the minds of my countrymen with that idea, I would tell them that the best plan is to reject the policy of the imperial government.

We all know that the feeling of loyalty to one's country, the pride in its institutions, lies to the fact that [its] institutions are able to afford protection to life and property. Therefore, the moment you have carried conviction to the minds of the people that Great Britain is unable to protect us, and that they stand in the presence of so gigantic a power that it has only to will to take them, then you undermine their loyalty. Now we have Mr. [Joseph] Howe in that attitude; since his return, in the streets, and in the clubs, and in the presence of the highest authorities in the land, you find him constantly holding forth the doctrine that Great Britain is impotent to defend this province—that though British America might unite, yet with even Great Britain at her back, all she could do would not prevent [our] being swept away when the American government wished it. If I stood in a position like that, the honourable member for Halifax [Annand] might be justified in making us an object of suspicion and throwing out his taunts and innuendoes about base bribes having influenced public men.

Holding the sentiments I do—believing that the crisis has come when we must decide whether we shall be annexed to the United States or remain connected with the parent state, I would be the blackest traitor that ever disgraced a country if I did not by every means in my power urge upon this legislature to prove equal to the emergency and take that course which, in a few months, will secure that consolidation of British North America and the connection with the crown of Great Britain which I believe, which I know, it is the sincere wish of the people to secure, and which can alone place these provinces in a position that will at once give them dignity of position and ensure their safety.

The Governor General on the Fenians

LORD MONCK

Ottawa, June 6, 1866

My dearest Henry,

As you will probably see accounts in the papers of the invasion of Canada by the Fenians, I send you one line to say that about nine hundred of them crossed from Buffalo to Fort Erie on Friday last and had a skirmish with some Volunteers which satisfied their appetite for fighting—as they recrossed the river on Saturday night leaving about sixty of their number prisoners in our hands. The main body were immediately arrested by the authorities of the United States and are now prisoners at Buffalo to the number of about 750.

In great haste to catch the mail.

Ever your most affectionate father,

MONCK

Ottawa, June 7, 1866

My dearest Henry,

I have only time to write you a short line to tell you that we are all alive and well, thank God! notwithstanding the Fenian invasion! There has been no second attack on Canada, though there are reports of lots of Fenians on the frontiers; however, we are thoroughly prepared for them, and, as the Government of the United States has directed the arrest of all their leaders, I think they are in rather a bad way. I have heard today that Mr. Sweeney has been actually arrested and that a warrant has been issued for the apprehension of Mr. Roberts.

All seems to be going well in New Brunswick for the cause of union. . .
God bless you, my dearest boy.
Believe me every your fond father,
MONCK

Fighting the Fenians at Ridgeway, 1866

T. WATKIN JONES

> *The Fenians advanced into Upper Canada at the beginning of June 1866 and faced a force of militia. The invaders won the battle but lost the war when they retreated back to the U.S.*

Hamilton, 10th July, 1866

My dear Ellen

I'll try now that I have time to give you a short account of this Fenian invasion. As there was some apprehensions of a Fenian attack we were ordered to hold ourselves in readiness to march at a moments notice—so on the 1st of June about 6.30 am the city was aroused by the noise of three big battery guns which are at the drill shed being discharged, this being the preconcerted signal every one of course knew what it meant. I had got up early that morning to ride a young horse that needed exercise so upon hearing the guns I postponed my ride for an indefinite period and getting some breakfast put on my uniform and accoutrements and started for the drill shed. When I got there I found about 100 of our fellows, and the rest came running in in dozens. When we were all assembled the roles of the different companies were called and our arms and accourtrements inspected. When we were marched to the railway station where a special train was waiting for us, so away we went not knowing and not caring where, so long as we had a chance to have a brush with the "Finnegans". How little did we then think that our hopes were so near being realized— about 4.30 pm we arrived at a place called Dunville, on the coast of Lake Erie and as there was no barrack accomodation for troops, we were billetted on the inhabitants. Our adjutant (Captain Henry) showed very good discrimination in this for he arranged it so that the men were all sent to the same social class as that to which they belonged in Hamilton—for instance fellows in No 3 and 5, who work in the shops of the Great Western railway works, Blacksmiths, Machinists, Strikers etc were all sent to the taverns, whilst other companies not composed of such rough material were sent to the shop keepers and the fellows in No "one" and a few of No "Six" were billetted upon the nicest people in the place. This of course was done to give the people as good an impression of the regiment as possible. I and three others were sent to the house of a Doctor Hart. He is very well off and doesn't practice but is an extensive ship owner on the lakes. They were all very kind to us, gave us nice rooms and said they were expecting us after we cleaned our traps and selves. We had a very nice dinner and began anticipating some fun as there were two young ladies and a pretty governess, all very musical. The news the people had in Dunville was—that the Fenians had crossed from Buffalo—to Fort Erie in the night and were advancing to destroy the Welland Canal—that they had cut down the telegraph posts and burnt the railway bridges to prevent the trains from bringing troops. When we heard this we knew that our stay in Dunville would be but a short one, so we determined to make it as agreeable as we could, so we asked the young ladies for some music, one of them sat down and opened the piano and Georgey MacKenzie (He was shot afterwards) hunted up a music book for her and she had just commenced that song from Sir Walter Scott's "Lady of the Lake" which begins "Soldier rest, thy warefare's o'er" when as if to give a direct lie to the statement twang twang goes a bugle in the street and on throwing up the window we saw "Stair" our orderly-bugler and the six company buglers standing in the street making the quiet little town echo, again with "The Assembly" so our flirting in the evening, like my ride in the morning, had to be "indefinitely deferred". So hastily getting into our accoutrements we said good bye and rejoined our comrades when we fell in by companies. The rolls were called and not a man was absent, so we took the train again and came down to Port Colborne, where we found the Queen's Own Rifles, from Toronto. It was about 10 pm when we got there and the "Queens Own" fellows came alongside the train and enquired through the windows for any 13th men they knew. The "Queens Own" were billetted and as there was no more room we were ordered to remain in the train all night. About 3 am on Saturday morning the Queens Own were assembled and remained in the street for a while after which they were placed on the train with us, until 5 am when we steamed slowly down towards Ridgeway, for fear the rails might have been tampered with. I must tell you before I go any farther that the whole force was under the command of our Colonel "Booker" and that he has showed himself (altho' a good drill) to be quite incompetent to command men in danger, and that he does not see far enough ahead to provide for the comfort of the men or for any exegency that may arise—in addition to which he is a conceited, arrogant, cowardly, nervous poltroon. He had orders from Colonel Peacock of the 16th who commanded a large force of Regulars and Volunteers, two batteries of horse artillery and a troop of Volunteer cavalry to form a junction with him and on no account to risk an engagement, but some one told him that the Fenians were only 200 strong, and all drunk so his vanity suggested what a fine thing it would be to go himself and destroy them all without any assistance from the regulars, and instead of 200 drunken men, he found 1500 well armed in a strong position, and under an officer of bravery and experience.

However we steamed slowly and cautiously from Port Colborne to Ridgeway where we left the train and fell in upon a road that ran at right angles to the railway, here we loaded with ball cartridge and advanced towards the Fenian position in the following order, The "Queen's Own" being Rifles of course were the advanced guard, then we came and then the York Rifles (a single company) as a rear guard. We marched down in quarter distance column—that is each company extending right across the road, from fence to fence, and one company 4 paces in front of another—so on from rear to front. After advancing a while in this order two companies of the "Queens Own" were sent, one on each side of the roads, to skirmish the woods we advanced that way for a long time, without seeing anything and began to think the Fenians must have retired when just at half past seven bang goes a rifle upon one side of the road—then a couple of dozen shots in quick succession. Then four more companies were sent forward to reinforce those already at the front. They kept advancing and the Fenians retiring for about half a mile—even the main body, following along the road in their rear acting as a reserve and both keeping up a heavy fire all the time. By this time the Fenian outposts had fallen back upon their reserves—where they made a stubborn resistance and took shelter behind some breast works they had thrown up and poured a tremendous fire upon our skirmish line. However nearly all their bullets were too high. After a while Major Gilmore of the "Queen's Own" said that his mens ammunition was getting exhausted and asked Colonel Booker to relieve them, so our right wing—Nos 1, 2 and 3 companies deployed upon No 3 and then extended in skirmishing order up a road that ran parallel to the Fenian front. They had built barricades of rails, wood, earth, stones and every thing they could get their hands on. They had the fences of every field barricaded in this way and in every bit of high ground they had dry rifle pits and regular trenches and had taken possession of a brick farm house on their right which they had filled with their best shots, their commander Colonel Sheil must be a long headed fellow as he has seen a great deal of this sort of thing in the American war.

When we extended in skirmishing order along those woods up the road I spoke of before the bugle sounded "advance" and never was order more promptly obeyed. It would have done your heart good to see the way our fellows dashed at the fence of the road, climbed over and took up their dressing on the other side. I had felt rather queer before but, now I began to feel pretty jolly. Up to this none of the balls came very near us, but now they came screaming about our ears and cutting up the young wheat about our feet, but still most of them were too high.

At this time the Fenians held a large orchard with both their wings behind breast works on their right and left and the Queens Own were about 250 yards from them, with their supports about 100 yards in their rear. We advanced at the double until we came to where the rifles (Queens

Own) were when they retired through our spaces and left nothing but the enemy in our front. We found that it was impossible to dislodge them by firing, so we advanced upon them. When they retired leaving a lot of stuff behind them, rifles revolvers canteens etc we took possession of the orchard and breast works and they got behind more breast works. We hammered away at them for a while when they again retired. Here the bugle again sounded "Advance" and we came on at the double and as soon as we got within 100 yards of them they turned and bolted into another breastwork. In this advance we lost a good many of our fellows—none killed but a good deal hit. The Fenians were nearly all armed with 7 shoot-ing—Spencer rifles—but though they fired faster they were inferior in accuracy and range to our Enfields. Things went on in this way until we drove them over six big 30 acre fields and an orchard. Then Colonel Booker got a message from Colonel Peacock to say that he could not march for two hours later than he expected this put Booker into a stew for although we were beating them so far, yet he thought he was mistaken in finding more than 200 drunken men. Then they took shelter in a wood in their rear and hiding behind the enormous maple trees opened a furious fire upon us. We could very seldom see them but we fired wherever we saw the flashes of their rifles. They were very careful to not expose themselves but nevertheless we managed to pin a good many of them, two of their of-ficers were on horseback and a great many fellows had a shy at them. I dont know whether the officers were killed as they carried all their dead away nearly—but I saw the horses two days after and they were completely rid-dled, one was shot through the saddle besides several other bullet holes. We were in pretty good shelter at this time and were driving them out of this woods when we heard the bugle away in our rear and Rossconnel, our old "Sergeant Major" roared out "Hurrah my lads we have em this time" for they were vexed at not getting a chance to cross bayonets with them. When to our surprise instead of "Advance" it was "Retire".

We looked rather blank at each other and each said to his comrade "There must be some mistake". When the bugle again sounded "Retire" and "Double" so then the captains of companies said "Go on with your firing—men" "That bugle can't apply to us" but still it sounded "Retire" "Double" "Retire" "Double" until Major Skinner who commanded our right wing said "We had better obey orders" "perhaps they are outflank-ing us" or leading us into a trap.

If the bugle had only sounded "Retire" we could have kept up a fire all the time we retired, but as "double" was sounded this was impossible, so as soon as our fire ceased the Fenians came to the edges of the woods yelling and screaming and pouring volley after volley into us. It was then we lost most of our men—all this time the "Queens Own" that we had relieved were drawn up on a road in our rear acting as a reserve. When we were about half way across the fields to form in rear of our reserve some of the "Queens Own" officer raised a cry of cavalry and Booker without a moments reflection immediately formed square—and sounded "form square" to us skirmishers, each of our companies formed "close column of sections" (that is the way a single company forms square) and waited to see from what quarter the cavalry would make their appearance. The Queens Own formed a battalion square on the road. The very worst thing they could have done for they were in a very exposed position and incapable of returning the Fenian fire, while every shot that they sent into the square must hit somebody. They began to drop so fast that Booker ordered them to retire in a square. This is a most difficult thing even on good ground, but situated as they were, was an impossibility so they got mixed up and finally broke running through to one of our companies that had just returned from supporting the skirmishers and were endeavouring to fall in on the rear of the reserve—they trampled on a lot of our fellows and ran along the road in the direction of Ridgeway—with our Gallant Colonel at their head.

I know when my company got back to the rear we had neither reserves, Colonel or ammunition to depend upon. Skinner our major stood upon a bank beside the road and shouted "Thirteenth"! I know you'll stand" and about 200 of us fell in alongside him and we're going to extend up across the fields in skirmishing order—but when he saw we were alone he said, "Its no use lads. It would be only madness and God knows we've lost enough already" At this moment Lieut Percy Routh of No 4 company fell hit in the left side and 3 of the men were knocked down the same moment and several hit slightly, so we retired—making a halt at every defensible turn of the road and holding the enemy in check, carrying the fellows who were hit and swearing loud and deep against the comrades who had left us to our fate and our Colonel who went with them. Major Gilmore of the "Queens Own" and a couple of companies who were skirmishing on our left stood like men and Gilmore and two of his officers gave our major great assistance in keeping the enemy at bay until we reached Ridgeway —where we remained above half an hour. The Fenians never attempting to come in so long as we remained there. So we drank all the whiskey in the place (There's only one small tavern) and forgot to pay for it and I tore up my handkerchief and the tails off my shirt to bandage fellows wounds.

Our men and the Queen's Own now wanted to go back to fight again or to go join Colonel Peacock or to take possession of Fort Erie. Anything but go back to where we came from, but our Colonel with his usual foresight had forgotten all about having ammunition carried after us, and, as ours was almost gone there was nothing for it but to tramp it back to Port Colborne. Next morning at 1.30 am we were aroused by our bugles and heard intelligence that the Fenians had been strongly reinforced in the night, and were marching to attack us, and destroy the works of the Canal. We all fell in expecting to be under fire in five minutes, so did our Colonel for when he found that the train with the sick and wounded would not leave for an hour he hired a horse and trap and drove away by himself towards Hamilton, without saying a word to anyone and then reported that the men were so demoralized that he could do nothing with them.

There was no truth in the report for the Fenians hooked it to Fort Erie, the moment they got a chance and in the night crossed over to Buffalo just a few hours before the Regulars came there, 3 loads of them had gone across and taken all the dead and wounded, but the fourth load was captured by the US gunboat Michigan—with O'Neil and all his officers but the American Government afterwards let them all go on their own recognizances. We remained in Port Colborne for a long time, doing garrison duty and were worked awfully hard and as a lot of Fenians who couldnt manage to get across the river were lurking about the woods we were scouring the country after them, day and night, and picked up 115 of them in small lots and the Welland Volunteer Artillery captured 65 so we have now pretty nearly 200 of them. What I suffered most from was loss of sleep as we were very seldom a night in bed, and even then up at 3.30 am every morning. Colonel Villiers of the 47th was intrusted with the defence of the Canal and he was determined he would not be caught napping. . . .

Your affectionate brother
T Watkin Jones

Nova Scotia "Celebrates" Confederation, 1867

UNKNOWN

> Not all provinces in the new Dominion of Canada were enthusiastic about Canada. Nova Scotia, for example, looked on July 1 as a day of mourning.

"Dominion Day," July 1, was enthusiastically observed as a public holiday all over the Canadas, east and west. Picnics, bonfires, torchlight processions, and reviews of volunteers took place at various points, business was for a while suspended, and the people gave themselves up to relaxation and sport.

The local Government of Nova Scotia refused to allow the Queen's printer of the province, who is a member of the Dominion Parliament, to publish the proclamation of his Excellency the Governor General enjoining the due observance of July 1 as the anniversary of the formation of the dominion of Canada. Thereupon the Administrator of the Government of the province published it upon his own authority, and caused it to be placarded throughout Halifax.

A private letter, from Yarmouth, Nova Scotia, dated July 4, published in the New York papers, says that on "Dominion Day" there was no celebration, and that but two flags were displayed in the town. On Saturday, however, they celebrated July 4 by firing an American national salute of thirty-six guns at sunrise, noon, and sunset, and American flags were displayed all over the town.

D'Arcy McGee Assassinated, 1868: I

AGNES MACDONALD

> *The wife of the Prime Minister left this diary account of McGee's assassination.*

This is how it was, that dreadful night at half-past two o'clock on the Tuesday morning. Tuesday the 7th my husband came home from a late sitting. It had made me a little uneasy his being away so long, to begin with I knew he would feel tired and then a sort of dread came upon me . . . something might happen to him, at that hour coming home alone. About a 1/4 past 2 I felt so restless . . . when I heard the carriage wheels and flew down to open the door for my husband. We were so cosy after that—he coming in so cheery—with news of the debate—and sitting by my dressing room . . . I was almost half asleep when I was roused by a low, rapid knocking on the front door—in an instant a great fear came upon me—springing up I threw on a wrapper just in time to see John throw up the window, and to hear him call out "Is anything the matter?". The answer came up fearfully clear and hard . . . "McGee is murdered—lying in the street—shot thro' the head". The words fell like the blow of an iron bar across my heart. . . . My husband and brother went down to the spot immediately and did not return until 5. I sat trembling with fear and horror . . . for one could not tell how many more assassins might be lurking in the grey lit streets. . . We felt at once that the shot was fired by a Fenian. When John came home he was much agitated—for him whose self command is so wonderful. . . All Tuesday was so wretched—news coming and going—all were on the alert for the finding of the base coward who had done the foul deed. . . John's face was white with fatigue, sleeplessness and regret and yet he never gave in or complained or was other than cheerful to me and kind. I lay on the sofa till the afternoon half paralysed! My reading party came and went, I had forgotten them.

D'Arcy McGee Assassinated, 1868: II

UNKNOWN

This morning shortly after two o'clock the city was thrown into a state of horror and alarm by a report that the Hon. Thomas D'Arcy McGee had been assassinated at the door of his boarding-house in Sparks street. At first the dire intelligence was scarcely credited. But few who heard it could resist the desire to enquire into the correctness of the statement, which upon investigation turned out to be only too true. During the evening the appointment of Dr. Tupper as Commissioner to England had been under discussion in the House, and the honorable gentleman had addressed the Commons at some length on the subject. After the adjournment he must have left the Parliament Buildings almost immediately, as the House had not risen more than twenty minutes before he was found lying murdered on the sidewalk in a pool of blood in front of the Toronto House, where he resided. It appears that a servant in the boarding-house heard some one at the door and a shot fired. Going to the door at once she discovered the body of the murdered man lying on the planks, and at once gave the alarm. From the nature of the wound and the position in which the body lay there can be no doubt but that the murder was coolly done, and that instantaneous death ensued. The deceased was found lying on his back, his hat not even displaced from his head and his walking cane under his arm. The bullet entered at the back of the neck and came out of his mouth, destroying his front teeth and lodging in the door about two inches above the latch-key hole. It is evident, from these facts, that the honorable gentleman must have been in the act of opening the door, stooping to find the keyhold with his head close to it, and his cane under his arm, and that the assassin must have approached him cautiously, and putting the pistol to his head behind his ear, discharged it and fled.

The fearful news soon spread among the members of the Legislature, few of whom had retired to rest, and ere long the place was filled with his sorrowing friends and admirers, whose deeply expressed detestation of the cowardly crime will find an echo in every honest breast. The Premier and the Premier of Ontario, with many others, hastened to the spot, and every effort was at once set afoot to discover the perpetrator of the crime, which for audacity and cold-bloodedness stands unequalled in our history.

The Riel Rebellion, 1870: I — Meeting Louis Riel

ROBERT CUNNINGHAM

> *Louis Riel and his Metis followers seized control of Fort Garry in late 1869 and tried to bargain with Ottawa. This extraordinary account, appearing in a newspaper unfriendly to the rebels, captured something of the man and the time.*

Knowing it to be useless to expect to obtain entrance to any hotel in Winnipeg, without the express sanction of President Riel, I drove up to the Fort for the purpose of obtaining that sanction, and intimated to the sentinel that I wanted to see President Riel.

"M. le President is out," said the sentinel, "Would Monsieur go in till his return?"

Monsieur was very tired and would prefer going to a hotel and call on M. le President in the morning.

"Monsieur had better go in: in fact Monsieur must go in; these are the orders."

"Whose orders?" I asked.

"The orders of Monsieur le President," said the sentinel, giving the Indian pony a blow with the butt end of his musket, urging him through the gate. Once in I saw there was nothing for it but to remain in, so I got out of my crate, and guided by a half-breed who had come out of a small one story house I was conducted to the guard room. The room was a low roofed apartment about twelve feet square with a red hot stove in the centre, and with about twenty men seated on tables, chairs, and the floor, smoking assiduously their Indian pipes. On my entrance each man rose, looked curiously at me, smoked more assiduously than ever, and then sat down again. I had my valises in hand, and after I had got to the centre of the room, I felt somewhat in a quandary as to what I should do or where I should go, when one of the gentlemen came to my assistance and said [in] patois English "Will Monsieur give me his baggage? and I will put it to the right place."

Monsieur was only too glad to get rid of his incumbrances, so he gladly gave them up to his obliging friend, and remained staring around him.

"Will Monsieur take a seat by the stove?" said another friend. Monsieur thanked him and took the proffered chair and sat down by the stove.

"Does Monsieur require any food?" said another friend. Monsieur had supped, and thanked his friend for the hospitable inquiry.

Monsieur sat a long time by the stove. Eleven, twelve, one, two o'clock came, but none of them brought M. le President. Monsieur began to doze by the stove, and the half-breeds began to doze too, and matters were beginning to get very sad and lugubrious and melancholy, when one of the half-breeds rose and said, "Monsieur had better go to bed," Monsieur was exactly of the same opinion, so he got up from his seat by the stove, put on his overcoat and was just beginning to put on his buffalo-coat, when my friend said, "Monsieur must sleep here."

"Where?" I inquired.

"Here," said he, taking me into [an] adjoining room, and pointing out a buffalo-robe spread on the floor; "that is Monsieur's bed."

I urged that I had travelled some eighteen hundred miles, was very tired, and would like a more inviting bed than that. Could I not go to a hotel? My friend was truly sorry; but M. le President's commands must be complied with—that was Monsieur's bed for the night.

"Then I am a prisoner," I said.

"That is so—by the orders of M. le President," said my friend, turning on his heel and walking off; so I lay down on the buffalo robe tired and jaded, and I fell asleep, and did not dream at all that night; I was even too tired to dream.

About six in the morning I was awakened up by the stir in the adjoining room; so I arose, went into the room, and found it very much as I had left it in the evening previous. The stove was still red hot, about a score of half-breeds, in their shirt sleeves, sat on chairs, tables, and the floor, smoking, and as I entered each rose and gave me "Bon jour" in the most kindly and hospitable manner. In self-defence I got out my own pipe, and began to smoke as vociferously as the rest; but whether, struck with my smoked and tanned appearance, or whether instigated by an innate sense of what was due to a dirty stranger, one of the half-breeds laid down his pipe, filled a tin basin with water, and coming over to me, said, "would Monsieur wash?" Monsieur was only too glad of the invitation, so he thanked his friend, and washed abundantly. He then sat himself down and began to smoke again. Whilst sitting smoking, one of the half-breeds took a seat beside him, and entered into conversation with him.

"Monsieur is from Canada, is he not?"

"That is so."

"Is Monsieur the *Gazette* man expected?"

"He was." My friend was delighted to meet the *Gazette* man, and shook hands with him heartily, and the other half-breeds who had gathered around shook hands too.

"Monsieur had come to get news had he not? Monsieur wished to know what we wanted? Monsieur wished to tell the people of Canada why we had taken the front, and taken up arms? Was that what Monsieur had come for?"

"That was what Monsieur had come for."

"Shall I tell Monsieur what we want?" said he, turning to his confreres.

"Oui," resounded all around, so my friend resumed "we want to be treated as free men. Your Canada Government offered to pay three hundred thousand pounds to the Hudson Bay Company for the Rivière Rouge Territory. Now, what we want to know, and we will not lay down our arms till we know what they mean to buy. Was it the land? If so, who gave the Hudson Bay Company the right to sell the land? When the Canada Government bought the land did they buy what was on it? Did they buy us? Are we the slaves of the Hudson Bay Company?"

"Non!" resounded on all sides.

"No, we are not slaves. But remember, and you may tell Canada people this when you go home, that we are not the cruel murderous men we have been described. We do not want to kill any one in this quarrel. We have hurt no one yet, nor do we mean to do so. Let the Canadian Government come and treat with us as free men, and we will lay down our arms, and go to our homes." And here it may be convenient to say a word or two about these

French Half-Breeds.

It is allowed on all hands by every one who knows anything about the French half-breeds, that since this difficulty began, they have been grossly maligned. They have been pictured as an ignorant, savage race—worse in many respects than the Indians themselves—and capable of engaging in any atrocity. But nothing can be further from the truth. From what I saw of them, and heard of them, they are quite the opposite of all this. To me, they seemed a kindly race of people, courteous in the highest degree, and hospitable to a proverbial extent. True, they are, evidently, a rather credulous people, and from their strong religious prejudices, can be made, to a considerable extent, the tools of the priests. Nor are they by any means ignorant of political questions. It is probable that there is not one half-breed in the Red River Territory, who has not several relations in Dakotah or Minnesota, from communication with whom they have gathered a pretty comprehensive idea of the political system at work in the States and Territories of the United States; and though this information by no means leads them to desire Annexation in preference to British connection, at the same time it has educated them up so far as to have some true appreciation of what rights naturally belong to them in any connection whatever. The half-breeds are not savages by any means; on the opposite, if properly treated, they might be a peaceable, industrious, harmless people.

As ten o'clock approached—the hour at which I was positively assured the President would appear—I felt somewhat anxious. I had seen some pen and ink sketches of the President, in which he was portrayed by one as an Alexander, and by another as a Napoleon; and the prospect of meeting with either an Alexander or a Napoleon was surely enough to fluster most men. I was sitting eagerly waiting his arrival, when I heard a commotion in the next room, and on inquiring as to what was the occasion of it, I was told that M. Le President had at length arrived. On hearing this I got up and made my way into the room, where, amongst the assembled half-breeds, I saw two new arrivals. One of them was of a semi-priestly appearance, fair-haired, closely shaven, with a cringing, cunning way with him, which at once suggested to my mind my old acquaintance with Uriah Heep. He introduced himself as Mr. O'Donohoe, and began to converse in a way that more and more confirmed the Uriah idea. But there was another newcomer in the room. He was a man about thirty years of age, about five feet seven inches in height—rather stoutly built. His head was covered with dark, curly hair; his face had a Jewish kind of appearance, with a very small and very fast receding forehead. This, I was sure, was M. Le President Riel, and he stood gazing at me in the most piercing manner, at least, there is no doubt, he thought so. I did my utmost to realize in him a Napoleon or an Alexander, but it was a failure—a dead signal failure,—I could not get beyond the fact that there stood before me a Linen Draper's assistant. There could be no mistake about that, and though he stood looking at me full ten minutes, he could not put the Linen Draper out of my mind, and if he had continued to gaze till now, the result would have been all the same. He was clad in a light tweed coat and black trousers, and he seemed exceedingly proud of them and well he might be, for it is as certain as the fact that he wore them, that these clothes were purchased with the price of his poor widowed mother's only cow.

"I don't know who you are," the modern Alexander at last condescended to remark, after having tried hard to impress upon me the Napoleonic theory.

In reply to this curt remark, I observed that no doubt could possibly attach to his Excellency's statement, but in order to enlighten him I begged to present him my credentials. He took them, read them, and coolly put the documents in his pocket. A brief parley then ensued. I observed that the people of Canada were anxious to know all about this Red River affair.

M. Le President observed that he thought the people of Canada knew all about it already "Look here, and here, and here," said he, pointing to great blotches of ink on the desk, "Some ink has been used, has it not, in writing facts—what more do you want?" and the Modern Alexander seemed to think he had said a very good thing, for he laughed complacently and Uriah Heep wriggled and grinned too. I endeavoured to show that what the people of Canada desired were to have the facts of the case laid before them in a plain, honest way. True, they had read a great deal about the affair, but most of what they had read had come through American channels. All they had read might be good, genuine facts—if so it would do no harm, to allow these facts to be restated.

Mr. Le President made no direct reply to this; but smote his hand violently on the desk, and said "we are in the right, we are in the right!" and walked off in company with Uriah Heep. They had a long conversation together; in the course of which, as I learned afterwards, Uriah cringingly insinuated that I was a spy. A Council was then called, and the matter was debated as to whether I should be allowed to remain or no. O'Donohoe made a speech, as I learned and argued strongly for my expulsion; all the Americans, and most of the Half-breeds took a different stand, and maintained strongly that I should be allowed to stay. M. Le President said nothing. The Council adjourned without coming to any definite conclusion on the point, and Riel once more appeared, and walked up and down the floor like a man enduring the utmost mental agony. He ran his hand through his hair—he scratched at his nose till he peeled the skin off the point of it—now he would pause and gaze at me with the most piercing air, and then he would start off again, tearing at his hair and scratching at his nose more assiduously than ever. After promenading about half an hour—he paused, gazed at me—and coming over, said "will you want anything if you have to go back." As he spoke in the most broken of English I did not exactly comprehend the purport of the enquiry, and asked for an explanation, when he got into a tremendous passion—"G—d d—n," said he, "don't I speak plain, I ask you will you want anything if you have to go back." I deprecated the wrath of the modern Alexander, and endeavoured to show him that such an outburst of feeling was at once superfluous and entirely unwarranted. As regarded going back, if I had to go I would want nothing from him; but I hoped he would think better of it and allow me to remain. He had said he was in the right. If so my remaining could do no harm to his cause but the opposite. He gathered down his brows and looked thunder at me, no doubt imagining I was terribly afraid, and walked off; but I was not afraid at all. I had measured the man at the first glance, and saw where the pen and ink sketches had made the mistake. They credited him with military genius and ambition—and had failed to appreciate the fact that he was a vain-glorious creature, so elated by the position he had attained to, that any particle of common sense he ever had owned had been eliminated from his being, and that though he read no book but the Life of Napoleon, he was the mere tool of a certain party, who used him for their purposes as they listened and laughed at him.

The Riel Rebellion, 1870: II — Executing Thomas Scott

ALEXANDER BEGG

> *Recorded in his diary by Begg, this account is as close as we have to an account of the execution of Thomas Scott on Riel's order. Scott was a troublemaker, very anti-Metis, but still his killing made Riel a fugitive.*

Friday, 4th March, 1870

The weather to-day was clear warm and pleasant.

This morning the news spread that Thos. Scott one of the prisoners was condemned to be shot to-day at twelve O'Clock—this was not believed at first by anyone but some time after when it became known that the lumber and nails had been procured for his coffin people began to realize it. Rev. Geo. Young at the request of Scott went and stayed with him to prepare him for his end. Paper pens and ink were furnished the doomed man to write to his friends. At about twelve O'Clock a.m. a large crowd gathered around the side door leading into Fort Garry. Scott was then brought out—it is said he prayed as he walked—a bandage was then put over his eyes and he knelt.

The following men were detailed to fire the fatal shots.

P. Champagne.	François Thibault.
Marcell Roi.	Augustin Parisien.
Cap Dechamp.	A canadian that used to work with Dr. Schultz.

On a given signal four of the guns were fired (two missing fire) and Scott fell forward pierced in four places—he was not yet dead but struggled on the ground. The Canadian then went up and shot Scott—the ball from the revolver passed in at the ear of the unfortunate man and passed out at his mouth. The corpse was then put into a rough coffin and placed in one of the bastions. A deep gloom has settled over the settlement on account of this deed.

Marking the International Boundary

SAMUEL ANDERSON

Marking the 49th Parallel, the border between Canada and the U.S. through the west, was no easy task, as this letter of December 1872 makes plain.

All this time I had a party at work cutting out the Boundary Line which commenced in a swamp a mile and a half [2.4 km] north of my camp, and in accordance with the terms of the treaty was to be taken due south till it intersected the 49th Parallel of Latitude. This due South line entered the woods close to my camp, and the working party consisted of 12 Indians under the direction of 4 of my own men. They made poor progress at first, as the timber was heavy and the ground under foot, swampy, in which the men sank up to their knees. This obliged us to transport all the camp equipage and provisions for the use of the party, on their own backs. It was as much as our men could do to struggle along with no loads at all, but our Indians thought nothing of carrying 100 lbs. [45 kg] of flour, or 100 lbs. of pork on their backs, with a leather strap across their forehead, and occasionally across their breast. It was a most curious sight to see a party of 12 of these men marching along in "Indian" file with the loads on their backs and hopping over fallen trees and struggling thro' the swamp. Every now and then they halted and smoked their pipes.

The first clear night we had, the surface of the stream at the camp froze, and the swamps were partly frozen, but for some days during which time the ground was partly wet and partly frozen, the men suffered considerable discomfort and even hardship and several of the Indians left, so that at one time I had only 5 of them remaining. They were unaccustomed to continued hard work, and being miserably clad they suffered considerably. I supplied them with mocassins and tents, and they had as much food as they could eat, but the work was too much for them. Fortunately at this time I heard that there was a gang of Indians lately employed on the Government road between the Lake of the Woods and Fort Garry and now paid off, so I sent for them and in about 5 days they arrived, 7 of them, but imagine my consternation when they appeared bringing all their camp, their wives and children and old people. There were 6 women and about 12 children, and several old men. My original party was then 6 miles distant, down the cutting and about 5 or 6 hours journey. I set these men to work at once carrying pork and flour down the cutting, and in two successive days they made two trips, and transported sufficient food to last for 15 days. I only succeeded in getting the men themselves to go and join the working party, on the condition that the families were to remain with me and be fed from my supplies! I agreed to this and I told them I should deduct from their wages, the value of the food consumed by their families. . . .

The cutting 15 ft wide was now completed for 11 miles from the commencement in appearance it showed out as a great lane thro' the woods and being a perfectly straight line could be seen for many miles till in the distance only a fine cut could be distinguished. It was necessary to take fresh observations to see that the line was quite correct, and this was accomplished the following night, when the cold was very intense 30 below zero. The Indians worked bravely, and at last the line which was cut for 16 miles [26 km] ran into the open Lake. The approach to the Lake was most uninteresting, in fact it would be difficult to say within two or three miles where the Lake began. The trees a small species of larch, called Tamarack in this country, became gradually smaller and more open, and at last there was only thick bush and when this came to an end there was an open marsh with grass showing above the snow. Beyond this there were more bushes, so that it seemed as if we never should come to the open Lake. After crossing half a mile of the frozen marsh covered with snow, then there was ice, as clear as crystal and 12 inches thick. One could see thro' the ice, as if it was plate glass. It was the most beautiful ice I had ever seen, frozen at a time when the air was motionless, and there was only an occasional crack to be seen to enable one to judge how thick it was.

At last after cutting thro' a belt of bushes, there was the open Lake beyond. Half ice and half snow the southerly winds had caused such a surf, that at last it froze in heaps. After crossing 100 yards of this, the ice was in places flat and in other places crushed up into heaps, but quite opaque. The Lake is notorious for storms, and in the lulls between the storms the water freezes, and then the ice becomes broken up and frozen again, till at last the whole surface of the Lake presents a very wild scene, for 30 miles nothing but ice. It was blowing a gale of wind, the day we reached this spot, and the appearance of the whole party journeying over this frozen district muffled up in blankets and furs reminded me of Arctic explorations. We cut a hole with axes in the ice and set up a long pole which we had brought along for the purpose, put a flag on it and left it, for the information of our surveying parties, who will be visiting this spot at Christmas time.

I should like the old Plenipotentiaries who decided this Boundary Line by Treaty in 1818 to be resuscitated for a short time in order to come and live at this spot. They would probably have then decided to fix it in some other locality, instead of a swamp, where it will be difficult to find a spot for setting up a permanent mark. Finding that our line ran into the Lake, and ended in the Lake I was saved all further trouble, so after been nearly blown off our feet in the wind in this exposed locality, the whole party beat a retreat and reached the camp at nightfall.

Bread and Beans in a Lumber Camp, 1883

JOSHUA FRASER

> In 1883, Joshua Fraser, the son of an Ottawa Valley clergyman, wrote with enthusiasm about the two staples of shantymen's meals in the Ottawa and Madawaska lumber camps: home-baked bread and beans.

And you would be amazed at the general excellence of the cooking that is done by these fellows. Where will you find such bread as is made in their immense pots, buried in and covered over by the hot ashes at the end of the *camboose*? Not a particle of the strength and fine flavour of the flour is lost by evaporation, as in the case of a stove or open oven: It is all condensed in the bread. Then it is strong and firm, and yet—and this is the mystery to me—it is light and porous as that of any first-class housewife's.

And what shall we say about the beans? They are simply *par excellence*. They are baked in the same kind of pot as the bread, the lid being hermetically sealed to the rim by dough, and then buried in the hot ashes. The beans are first thoroughly sifted, washed and boiled, and then large slices of fat pork mixed with them. The pot is then placed in its deep bed of hot ashes, and as in the case of the bread, not a breath of steam or of the essence of the bean is allowed to escape. The fat pork, becoming dissolved by the heat, and of course, neither fried nor boiled as in other processes, becomes amalgamated with the beans, and when the whole is considered sufficiently cooked, a mess is ready, which, for succulency of flavour, and savoury richness of nutrition, will completely throw the shade the famous pottage for which Esau bartered his birthright.

Sandford Fleming Breakfasts on a Lake Steamer, 1884

SANDFORD FLEMING

> *The creator of Standard Time, railway engineer and traveler Sandford*
> *Fleming also wrote of his journeys.*

The breakfast hour is seven, but I had had some experience of the preceding evening's supper. Appetite must possess to many a somewhat
tyrannical mastery, if we are to judge by the demonstrative determination
to obtain seats at a steamboat table. With us there were four relays of supper, and it was an effort to find a seat at any one of them. Who has not
noticed, under such circumstances, the rows of men and women who
place themselves, with suppressed impatience, behind the seats, standing
in the most prosaic of attitudes, in expectation for the word that the meal
is ready. I was myself content to take my place at the fourth table, so that I
could eat what I required with deliberation. With this experience, I was
in no hurry to rise, so it was about nine o'clock when I entered the long
saloon. There were a few stragglers like myself present, probably influenced by the same philosophy, who were seated here and there at a table
on which lay the scattered remains of the fourth breakfast. On these
lake boats the attendants are called "waiters", not "stewards" as on ocean
steamers, and if there be a difference of nomenclature, there is certainly
no identity of manner. The steward of the ocean steamer is the most
benignant, courtly, kindly, considerate person in the world, and, as a rule,
his virtues in this respect are sufficiently appreciated. On this boat I
addressed one of the waiters, I thought politely enough, and gave my
orders. I was met by the rugged reply, in the hardest of tones, "Ye cannot
have hot breakfasts if ye lie in bed." The man's axiom was certainly borne
out by fact. There was no breakfast, in the sense of the word, and what
there remained was not hot. But the coffee was exceptionally good, and
with a crust of bread I thought that I might have fared worse. Possibly the
owners of the new steamers to be placed on the lakes next summer will
introduce some improvement in the stewards' department, which the
ordinary traveller, they may be assured, will duly appreciate.

Opium Smoking in British Columbia, 1884

EMILY WHARTON

> *B.C. opinion was sharply anti-Chinese. One charge made by exclusionists*
> *was that Chinese encouraged opium smoking and used the drug to entrap*
> *women. This Commission testimony gave scant support to this idea.*

Victoria, B.C., August 9th, 1884

Emily Wharton, examined:

Q: What is your name?
A: Emily Wharton.
Q: What age are you?
A: I am twenty years of age.
Q: How long have you been an opium-smoker?
A: About four years.
Q: Did you learn to smoke opium in Victoria?
A: No; I learned in San Francisco.
Q: Why did you commence to smoke opium?
A: Why do people commence to drink? Trouble, I suppose, led me to smoke. I think it is better than drink. People who smoke opium do not kick up rows; they injure no one but themselves, and I do not think they injure themselves very much. I know opium-smokers who are sixty-five and seventy years of age. There is a man over there who has smoked opium for thirty years.
Q: Have you read De Quincy's Opium Eater?
A: I have.
Q: Had that book anything to do with leading you to become an opium-smoker?
A: No; I was an opium-smoker before I read his book. I believe he has drawn more on his imagination than on experience.
Q: Do you realize the pleasures and visions he dilates on?
A: No; nor I believe does any opium-smoker. I believe De Quincy's book is a pack of lies.
Q: If it does not afford you any such pleasure as that author describes, why do you smoke?
A: Because I must; I could not live without it. I smoke partly because of the quiet enjoyment it gives, but mainly to escape from the horrors which would ensue did I not smoke. To be twenty-four hours without smoking is to suffer worse tortures than the lost.
Q: But does not the smoking make you wretched, just as drinking would?
A: No; I require about twelve pipes, then I fall into a state of somnolence and complete rest. When I awake I feel all right, and can attend to fixing-up the house. I am brisk, and can work as well as anybody else. I do not feel sick or nervous, neither have I the inclination to smoke more opium.
Q: Then why do you return to the use of the drug?
A: Ah! that's it; there is a time when my hands fail me; tears fall from my eyes; I am ready to sink; then I come here and for a few bits have a smoke which sets me right. There is too much nonsense talked about

opium-smoking. Life without it would be unendurable for me. I am in excellent health; but, I suppose, every one has their own troubles, and I have mine.

Q: I do not want to be offensive, but are you what is called a fast woman?

A: I am. But you would be greatly mistaken if you imagined that all the women who come here to smoke are of that character. In San Francisco I have known some of the first people visit opium houses, and many respectable people do the same here.

Q: Are women of your class generally addicted to opium-smoking?

A: No; they are more addicted to drink, and drink does them far more harm. Drink excites passion, whereas this allays it; and when a fast woman drinks she goes to ruin pretty quick.

Q: You have for four years been accustomed to go to opium dens such as this, how have you been treated by the Chinamen whom you have met in such places?

A: They never interfered with me in the least. Waking or sleeping, one act of rudeness from a Chinaman I have never experienced. In that respect they are far superior to white men. Unless you speak to them they will not even speak to you; and, indeed, after the first whiff of the opium you have no desire to speak. You rather resent having to speak or being spoken to; and when you want the smoke the desire to get your pipe ready is far too earnest a business to allow of any desire for idle talk. But I have known Chinamen who were not opium-smokers, and I believe they are far more certain not to offend or molest a woman then white men, especially white men with a glass in.

Q: You express yourself well, you have been educated?

A: Yes; I was well educated, but that is neither here nor there now. We will not go into that. Of course I have not given you my real name.

Q: Have you anything else to add bearing on opium-smoking in connection with the Chinese here in Victoria?

A: No; I will say this, though: that if opium houses were licensed as drinking saloons are one need not have to come into such holes as this to smoke. There would be nice rooms with nice couches, and the degradation would be mitigated. At all events I think the government that will not license an opium saloon should shut up public houses and hotels where they sell vitriol for whiskey and brandy, and where men kill themselves with a certainty and rapidity beyond the power of opium.

Q: Is there anything else?

A: No.

Anti-Chinese Sentiment in British Columbia, 1884

R.F. JOHN

South Saanich, B.C., August 30th, 1884.

Sir,—In reply to your circular of the 22nd August, asking for information respecting the Chinese in the constituency I represent, I have to state for the information of the Commission that, from enquiries made by me, the total number of Chinese resident in this (Victoria) district is about 200. So far as I can learn there is but one Chinese female in the district. A majority of them are employed in market-gardening, others are engaged in chopping cord-wood and in making charcoal; a good many own teams and do their own wood-hauling.

Of the above number about twenty are now in possession of leased property. As very important facts relative to the Chinese evil, in British Columbia, have been repeatedly laid before the Dominion Government, and Parliament, and also before the Commission, it is quite unnecessary for me to comment at length upon the Chinese question.

I would, therefore, briefly state that I am a vigorous opponent to any further influx of Chinese into this province or any other portion of the Dominion, for the reason that they are a most undesirable class of people, and as we have nothing whatever to gain from their presence. The most important industries are being absorbed by them, and a large number are gold and coal mining, to the great detriment of people of our own nationality.

The manufacture of boots and shoes in this province is almost entirely in the hands of Chinamen. They also manufacture large quantities of cigars and market-gardening is monopolized entirely by them. It is useless for farmers and others to compete against them in either of the above-named industries, in consequence of their economic mode of living and habits generally.

During the past three years the influx of Chinese has been very large. The employment of Chinese on the Canadian Pacific Railway in this province is a very serious injury to the country. There is no use whatever to encourage large numbers of laborers to British Columbia at the present time, as their places are already occupied by Chinamen. I am pleased to say, as a rule, farmers do not employ Chinamen.

When the Canadian Pacific Railway is completed, and the thousands of Chinese who are now employed on that work are turned adrift, I shudder to think what will be the consequence to the interests of this province. British Columbia has many valuable resources, and should in the course of time become one of the leading provinces in the Dominion; but if her progressive development is to be left to the Chinese, and her wealth carried to China, then Canada's Pacific province will, in my humble opinion, be ages behind.

In order to alleviate and prevent a further influx of Chinese, the Dominion Parliament should pass an Act at its next session, prohibiting the further immigration of Chinese into any of the Canadian provinces, and British Columbia in particular.

And unless an effort is made, and not a feeble effort either, the present distinguished leaders in Canadian politics will live to regret that they did not pay heed to this great question in time.

R.F. John, M.P.P.
To N.F. Davin, ESQ.,
Secretry Chinese Commission, Ottawa.

Canada's National Game: Lacrosse

THE MARQUIS OF LORNE

A former Governor General offers his comments on sport in the Dominion.

The game of lacrosse is frequently played at Quebec and Montreal, and should be witnessed if possible by any traveller desiring to see a peculiar national pastime. It is a game requiring great speed of foot and quickness of eye and hand. The Cauchnawaga Indians, living above the Lachine Rapids, are adepts at the sport, but are usually beaten by a well-selected team from the Montreal clubs. The game, like all those which are the prettiest to see, is played with a ball. This is made of porous india-rubber, and is rather smaller than a cricket ball. The players are ranged against each other in couples throughout the length of the field, so that wherever the ball alights there may be two contestants for its possession. It must be sent through two goal posts. No player is allowed to touch it except with the lacrosse stick. This is a strong curved piece of ash or other tough wood, in shape like a hockey stick. From the end of the curve at the top a netting is stretched down towards the handle, so that the ball may be caught in it. By giving the stick a peculiar swing the ball may be sent sling-fashion from this netting in the curve, and can be thrown for 150 yards. The attitude of the players would be fit subjects for sculpture, for both in slinging, and in running with the ball on the lacrosse, and in avoiding the pursuit of the opponent, there is no posture of agility, strength, and fleetness unrepresented. No game is more exciting to the spectators, for there is no pause or stay in the contest. At one moment the struggle is in front of one goal, and the next instant the ball has been caught and hurled away to the other extremity of the field, and a fresh set of combatants are called into action. The teams now consist of twelve men on each side, but in old days the Indians played it in numbers, and "good at game, good at war," was a saying with them, much as it is with our fox-hunters, who call their sport a mimic war. Football is our nearest approach to lacrosse, and knocks as hard are given in the one as in the other game, but the injuries at lacrosse are more likely to be in the head, as in following a man who has the ball, strokes are delivered at his stick which often fall on hands, arms, shoulders, and head. Catlin says that in his day these games afforded the squaws the only opportunity they had of paying off their husbands for any injury they had received from them, for it was the women's privilege on these occasions to be allowed to flog their husbands into the ball-fight, and that lazy or timid men could be seen flogged into the contest by their downtrodden women, who laid on the "birch" with a will. No such incentive is necessary with our Canadian brothers, who are as fond of manly sports as are the English at home. There is no finer game than lacrosse, now the national game of Canada, and there are, the world over, no finer young fellows to engage in such contests than our Canadian players.

A Diary of the 1885 Northwest Rebellion

WALTER F. STEWART

> *Stewart was a staff sergeant in the Midland Battalion, one of the militia units mobilized to put down the second Riel Rebellion.*

May 6—Spent a good deal of the morning with Ted in Major Boulton's tent. Going to start tomorrow on our march to storm Batoche, where the enemy is strongly entrenched and commanded by Louis Riel. All anxious to be on the march. Visited the Fish Creek battle field with the rest of the staff sergeants, Sgt. Major Sproule, Lou McDougall and Hooper. Expected to go with Ted and Sandy Stewart but they did not want to go with me. Picked up a few relics and were shown the field by Sgt. Hughes of the 90th. Saw dead horses, broken wagons and dead Indians, and graves being dug. The smells were none too good. Got separated from the rest of my companions in the woods covering rough ground. Wandered back to camp alone to view the scenery. Well, it was nice to be alone once more with my thoughts and situation. Saw neat log houses and farms, belonging to the rebels, some in ruins. Land very rich. Had Will Shepherd of Winnipeg and some of the Shell River boys, Ted among them, spending the evening with us. In brigade orders, "The whole brigade will move on Batoche tomorrow, in full marching order. The Regulars, 60 men, to go up-river on the steamer "Northcote." An alarm was sounded at midnight but turned out to be a hoax.

May 7—Made an early start and began the never-to-be-forgotten march of 16 miles to Batoche, the Grenadiers supplying the advance guard, next to Boulton's Scouts. Next came the 90th, followed by artillery "A" battery of Kingston, 2 guns, and Winnipeg Field Battery, 2 guns. Then the Midlanders in support, followed by the mounted men. Behind the regiments came the 150 teams with supplies, tents, ammunition, all well guarded. Only marched till noon, about halfway. Then stopped to reconnoitre, by sending out mounted scouts, 100 of them, in all directions to make a general survey of all the surroundings. Our paymaster, Capt. Reid, acted as guide, being a land surveyor who had surveyed this part of the country a few years previous; knew it well. Some of Boulton's men came back bringing a prisoner they had captured; had sighted some of Riel's scouts in the distance, gave chase and lassoed one. This captive was soon being most thoroughly pumped by the General and staff, who found out as much as they could about Riel and his gang. Find that they are well prepared for us. All quiet in camp at bedtime.

May 8—The whole camp astir early, the opening scene being putting down tents, packing up and storing away on the wagons. Then all on the march for Batoche, 8 miles north. But wondered why we were being led off in an easterly direction. What did this mean? Following no trail we were marching east across country and led by one horseman, our Capt. Reid. Going east a distance we turned north again. We later found out the reason for us taking this circuitous route and that was: the trail would lead through a thickly wooded country where a concealed enemy could have crept up on us and created some havoc among our ranks. The one we were taking was all over open prairie land. Besides, we avoided the enemy rifle pits and hidden trenches they had along the valley of the Saskatchewan.

Made very slow progress as the General kept up a continual reconoisance during which times halts were called lasting from 10 to 20 minutes. Stopped an hour for dinner. Moved on again at 1 p.m. Once more we were on the march. The usual halts were made and became weird. During these halts everything became quiet; stillness and peace seemed to reign on all sides. Each individual seemed to be completely wrapt up in his own thoughts and when the order came "to advance", we felt as if we were suddenly awakened out of a sleepy dream. Everything bore a very strange aspect to me: the sun, the different shadows it threw; the water in the ponds, the trees with their newly budded foliage; in the distance, seemed altogether different. Nothing seemed to be quite our usual environment. Then the questions were very often asked among ourselves as to what we were going to do tonight. We must be close to the enemy.

At about 5 o'clock we halted at or on a beautiful plain. Orders came that here we would bivouac for the night in our blankets with sweet heaven for a roof. The wagons were formed into a karaal or circle, tongues turned inwards. Each unit was given its limited space inside the wagon fort. A night piquet was paraded and deployed outside the wagons forming a circle guard. Then we all went for a wash in the slough (pronounced slew). The tension was broken as jokes were cracked, ribs punched. But the fun came when an English officer said the horse didn't exist that he couldn't ride. One of our scouts brought him one, a bucking young stallion that no one could ride but its owner. The officer spread-eagled over the prairie in ten seconds. To blankets. Next stop Batoche, five miles away.

May 9—Up at 5:30, breakfast at 6. On the march by 6:45. All in fine spirits, though the night was a bit chilly with frost. Not a snore had been heard at night. All our baggage, tents, teams and wagons we left in charge of the teamsters, who were armed and trained for trouble; nearly all were deadly shots anyway. I left the battalion cash box with Quarter Master Captain Clemes, who commanded the brigade of Teamsters. The cash box contained $4,700 and was in my charge as Paymaster Sergeant. But I wanted to join the firing line. So with Col. Williams' permission I gave it to Clemes to look after, as he was staying, leaving me to march with my Regiment. The mounted scouts leading.

At 8:30 a.m. we heard heavy rifle firing going on away in advance which we knew must be the steamer "Northcote" opening fire on the enemy and were having it hot and furious. "A" battery fired a blank to let them know we were coming and we then quickened our march. We were supposed to engage the enemy on shore at the same time those on the boat engaged them from the river and in that way pepper them from two sides. But the boat got there too soon. Suddenly our advance guard was fired upon and the real Riel battle was on. Our scouts charged and drove the enemy scouts back to their lines. The regiments were at once deployed to right and left in skirmishing order and advanced. The Midlands on the left flank, the Grenadiers on our right, the 90th on their right, with the mounted dismounted working on the extreme right flank of all. The Gatling gun about centre, artillery following on the rear.

As we advanced the firing became more intense, but we got no sight of the enemy; they were well hidden in their rifle pits. Two companies of the Midlands were ordered to support the guns. Gunner Phillips fell wounded and rolled down into the ravine. One of our companies ("C") was sent to charge down and rescue him which was done in a few minutes without losing a man. It seemed to us all that this was a rather different way of fighting from what we had expected. We calculated on seeing the enemy anyway. We were all fully under the impression that in aiming our rifles we would have something to aim at in the shape of human forms; in this we were disappointed, for instead we had hideously painted grinning idiots and puffs of smoke from among the trees to fire at. And they were in prepared positions, well protected, while we were in the open working forward to take theirs away from them. And that is going to be some job.

Suddenly a burst of flame and smoke was seen directly in front of us coming down with the wind at a terrific rate towards us: a bush and prairie fire. I knew what it was, and started by the rebels probably to blind us for a time and to enable them to creep up and break up our formation, but we back-fired and checked it.

Orders were at once given to strengthen the skirmish line on our right and in that way keep a strong body to repel any sudden attack made by the enemy on our right flank. Many rifle pits were being dug here by half breeds, as well as on our left. Thus we were under a constant cross fire. Our Midlanders drove a good number of the enemy from among bushes and small ravines who were creeping up under the cover of the fire and smoke. The blood-curdling war whoops of the Indians cut the air; the sounds were very horrible. The fire was eventually put out by our beating the flames with branches.

Late in the afternoon the General began to appear a little uneasy as to how he was going to hold the position already taken, if he had to retire back the six miles to our camp. The teams must bring up the camp to us, was the only alternative, and must be done before dark or the enemy might maneuvre around and cut our supplies off. The General merely gave the order that things were done the Canadian way he always so much admired.

Mounted men were sent back on the gallop; in two hours all the camp arrived; picks and shovels were out and handled by eager men, soldiers and teamsters, and a rough fort or zareba was built of dirt. In the meantime we kept up a dropping fire on the enemy, still hidden, and watching for any opportunity to harass us in any movement we made.

Then shortly before dark our move was to retire for the night in our zareba or fort. About half a mile to our rear was open ground well exposed to enemy sharpshooters who were well hidden in bush and rifle pits. This kind of retirement required skill and knowledge. Our dead and wounded had been carefully carried in; now our tactics were to fall back facing the enemy and keep up incessant firing and watch our flanks. This was done with the loss of only two men killed and three wounded. Gat-Gunner Howard was in his element as he pumped 300 shots a minute into the still well hidden ranks of the enemy.

The evening and a good part of the night was spent in throwing up earth works and ditching, enlarging our enclosure to about 500 feet long by 300 feet wide, the long side, of course, to the enemy. The enemy kept up a dropping fire on us. If we showed a light of any kind, even a match, it at once drew their fire. Moore of the Grenadiers was shot dead in the act of lighting a match to search for his baggage on a wagon. The casualties for the day were 6 killed and 12 wounded for the first day.

May 10—Had very little sleep all night, Lou Macdougald and I bunked together on the ground among the horses and men, all much crowded in our small space inside the enclosure; with about 250 wagons, 900 horses and about 1250 men. It was just a little close. All day we skirmished and advanced a little; our front extended about two miles, our left flank resting on the river bank, the position of ours, the Midlanders, and the right flank on the hills away to the east of us.

Our Colonel (Williams) was always eager for a charge on the rifle position with the bayonet, but I think he was discouraged in the project by the staff or by the General himself. It was a very peculiar feeling when first coming under fire. You feel inclined to, and in fact do, constantly keep ducking your head as you hear the ping and zip of the bullets as they come whistling about you. This is only nervousness and soon passes off. One thing we all soon learned to do admirably, and that was to take cover. We did not require any teaching.

Towards the end of the day we all began to feel somewhat discouraged. We saw nothing of the enemy although they were not more than 300 or 400 yards from us, and some were even closer but all hidden in the bush and deep ravines. We were more in the open but we made the most of every bit of rising ground, stumps and trees. One of our men had his rifle struck fair on the muzzle. The bullet passed down the barrel, destroying the rifle, blew open the breech block and there it lodged in the breech. This saved the man's life, for otherwise he would have been hit on the head or face.

The day closed with very few casualties: one killed and three wounded. The evening was spent in sniping at the enemy on the roofs of houses and the church near the village at a distance of about 300 to 500 yards. Fires and lights all out at dusk, no tents put up; all slept in the open.

The air was pretty cold at night; severe frosts and still some patches of snow on the ground. Shortly after turning in, had a night alarm; the picquet exchanging some shots with the enemy's picquet. Part of our picquet was driven in at one point.

May 11—All the camp raised at the first peep of dawn, fearing an attack which generally takes place at this particular time. When I threw off my blankets, which I had completely over my head, a lot of snow fell on me, covering my face. On getting up I found that we had quite a fall of snow during the night and a hard frost. The surroundings were anything but comfortable. The enemy did not disturb us, they allowed us to eat our breakfast in peace.

After breakfast our men marched out and took up their usual positions: the Midlands on the left flank, resting our left on the deep ravine in which the Saskatchewan runs; to the right of our regiment were the Grenadiers, extended some distance away to the right in bush, and behind a low ridge to the right of them came the 90th, and the Mounted Infantry, dismounted, which consisted of Boulton's men, French Scouts, and the Intelligence Corps commanded by Dennis. The artillery remained in camp throughout the morning.

I stayed in the zareba for an hour or so waiting for the ball to open on the firing line. With the exception of an occasional shot now and again nothing of an exciting nature occurred for an hour or two. About 9:30 a.m. I took my rifle, revolver and ammunition, some hardtack in my haversack and struck out for our position. On arriving there, I found our men holding a good position under pretty fair cover in the woods, Capt. Grace in charge. Made my way among the men until I reached those far-therest in advance, near the edge of ravine.

Thought I would do some scouting on my own account, so advanced on all fours down into the ravine where the enemy was hidden, and reached a position within 200 yards of their advanced position, taking cover among low bushes but which afforded no protection as far as being bullet proof. Had a good survey of the surroundings, including the ene-mies' rifle pits, and was so close that I could hear them talking.

Several of the Indians and Breeds, I observed, crept up towards our position on the right of where I was lying, evidently to get a shot at some of our fellows. They came so close to me that I could hear them whisper-ing, and if I had moved a twig they could have observed it and riddled me with bullets, but I lay perfectly still, hardly breathing. Our men on the high ground either heard them or saw them, however; they opened fire and soon drove them back to their original position about two or three hundred yards in front of me. As they got farther off and about disap-pearing I opened fire with my rifle and quickly rolled over, changing my position. Lucky thing for me I did, for they returned the fire, their bul-lets tearing the grass and shrubs about where I had been lying.

Soon our men began moving down to me, creeping through the bushes down the slope until we had a line formed from our left front, nearly to the river's edge. This protected our flank completely. In about an hour our commander, Col. Williams, came to us and complimented me on the position I had taken. Orders were given to have axes brought down and the bushes were cleared. Later two guns of the Winnipeg Field Battery were placed in position and shells were thrown into the ravine ahead of us and across the river at the houses and the Indians lurk-ing in the woods. We were kept, about 20 of us, to support the guns.

We could hear the Indian yells and the war-whoops and some cries of distress, so we knew our shots were telling. Some of the houses across the river received shells right through the roofs, blowing them to pieces. A panic seemed to take place among the inhabitants, who seemed to run in all directions. Some took to their horses and scampered off, but the enemy lying in wait nearer to us were not idle. Quite a number of them began to creep up on us and when in a good position in their nearest rifle pits, began a sharp rifle fire on us at pretty close range. We took up the same idea and returned their fire with interest, but there was nothing to be seen but puffs of smoke, into which we directed our fire.

We could not dislodge them, and as we had little or no cover, Col. Williams extended us and ordered a charge right into them. This we did in gallant style, driving the rebels before us from one rifle pit to another, but they made no stand, only running and firing as they went. We advanced about 500 or 600 yards, keeping up a running fight, until we came in sight of the cemetery, from which we received a hot fire.

Having so few men, the Colonel decided that we should retire. Besides, it was late in the evening, and time to fall back on our entrenchments for the night. As we fell back the fire of the enemy slackened. They did not follow us, thinking, probably, that we would lead them into a trap. When going back to our camp, Col. Williams exclaimed, "Men, we can rush the enemy and take Batoche tomorrow."

If the day's work did not accomplish much in the way of advancing our position, it had the desired effect of giving us confidence in ourselves and our Colonel, for we knew where he would lead, we would follow. We also saw he was bent on new tactics. But there was the General's staff clique to reason with. This clique seemed to hold together, and do nothing decisive, and would allow no one else to do anything. We were all getting desperate from being held in check so long, doing nothing, but advance a little through the day, taking certain positions and then in the evening retire to our trenches having to do all the work over the next day.

We felt it was nothing but a lazy siege. We were losing men every day and did not know what kind of work we were doing on the enemy. We had so far seen nothing but puffs of smoke, and heard the defiant yells of the Indians. As we went to camp that night we felt disgusted with the whole business, and looked forward to the next day when surely something would be done.

I went over to the part of the entrenchments where Boulton's men were and had tea with Ted Brown, Billy Duncan, Sandy Stewart, and Joe Burton. Later I turned in with them, sharing Ted's blankets (poor Ted's last sleep on earth). We were all tired so went to sleep in spite of the firing that was kept up through the night. Casualties were about six killed and 12 wounded.

May 12—The memorable day, the one ever to be remembered by those who lived through it.

Early breakfast and all were ready for orders. Every man in the whole brigade felt that the crisis had come. There would be something decisive done on this day, the 12th of May. What would be the first move? General Middleton with a mounted force could be seen away to our right front moving cautiously among the low lying hills. Col. Williams, our commanding officer (Midland Btn.), stood for some moments with his adjutant, Capt. Poston, watching the movements of the General and staff as if waiting to see them out of sight. Then suddenly he gave the following orders: "Men, I want you to fall in quietly at once. You will receive no orders farther than that "A" & "C" Companies will move off in fours and take the positions we had yesterday and there will be no talking. No orders given by company commanders."

We then moved to the woods overlooking the ravine at about 10 a.m. On arriving there Col. Williams formed the companies into a square and addressed us in words scarcely above a whisper as follows:

"I have not received any orders to do what I am going to do. Batoche can be taken and will be taken today. We will advance through and along this ravine. I only ask you to follow me, and we will go as far as we can. We will then be supported by the Royal Grenadiers and the 90th Rifles."

There was no order to fix bayonets. Each man had previously been served with 100 rounds of ammunition. The forward movement through the bush and ravines then began cautiously and without firing, merely feeling out the hidden enemy.

Ten minutes passed. Then suddenly a scattered firing came from across the river on our left. We pushed on then more rapidly and were presently met by a volley of shots on our front. Every man dropped to cover and returned the fire. We had at last located the enemy.

Col. Williams cautioned us to take cover and lie low. "We will hold this ground until the Grens and 90th come up on our right."

We could see nothing but banks and bush on our right. All the rifle pits of the enemy were still ahead of us and we knew a hot reception awaited us. A few of our men fell and there were many had very narrow escapes.

The firing now became heavier from both sides. Then the reinforcements arrived and our whole line was extended a full mile east. The advance all along the line then began in earnest. Firing as we went in rushes, then taking what cover we could. There was no volley firing. Every man regulated his own shooting. Then a small fenced-in cemetery was reached. Here our men passed round either side, then doubled up to re-form the line beyond. At this point the Indians and halfbreeds put up their real fighting. Running from rifle pit to rifle pit firing as they went, they fell back, stubbornly contesting every foot of ground.

Snipers from across the river, 200 yards away on our left, kept up a steady firing that worried our flankmen. Very heavy firing could be heard on our extreme right, where we knew the 90th were having a hot time. All the mounted men, including Boulton and French's Scouts and the Surveyors Corps, leaving their horses behind, joined the infantry and further extended the line from the right flank of the 90th.

Everything was done to prevent the Indians from getting around to attack us in the rear. Suddenly when rounding a bend at the foot of a rise, the village of Batoche came into view. It stood well out in a large clearing. Several neat-looking houses and stores could be seen. But to take that village, we all quite understood that the hottest fighting of all could take place.

There were at least 200 yards of open ground for us to cross, that afforded no protection, while the enemy had the protection of their houses and stores on our immediate front with dense bush on our two flanks. There was a short pause made at the edge of the bush. Every man held to his last bit of cover before emerging into the open on the final charge to take the village.

We, on the extreme left of the line, stormed the first houses, drove the enemy out and took possession. By this move we protected the left flank of the whole line. We poured a heavy fire into the enemy across the street and in the bush to our left. Every window inside and every corner of that house outside was filled by our men.

Captain French led us here, but was shot dead as he and I stood firing out of the same window. His body was carried down the narrow stairs and reverently laid out on the floor in a small back room for the time being. Other men were shot down in this hell-hole: Laidlaw, Wrighton, Christie, Barton of the Midland and one of the Grenadiers.

The house was heavily bombarded from the houses across the street until the whole line with a rush advanced across the open and a plowed field right through and around the stores and houses and for a half mile and in some cases fully a mile beyond. The village was ours. The day was won after four days and three nights of constant engagements with the enemy. The enemy from the first held a well prepared and almost impregnable position, stretching for miles in all directions and all in bush and ravines. Dugouts were everywhere.

As our men reached the village they went through every house and store. In one building a trapdoor leading into the cellar was discovered. On the closed trapdoor a heavy pole five or six inches in thickness stood wedged between it and the rafters above. It was surrounded at the base with a pile of rocks. This was the prison. Inside were prisoners previously collected on the prairies by Riel's soldiers, consisting of surveyors, storekeepers and settlers, some 17 altogether, and for more than 18 days had been confined in this 10 x 12 hole without light or ventilation and very little food.

They were a sickly looking lot when we released them, but they were glad to be alive. They were quickly assisted back to our fort for a square meal. They just hugged us, some broke into tears.

In about an hour after taking Batoche between 200 and 300 prisoners were taken by our men. They were all halfbreeds, the Indians having taken to the woods. There were many incidents of note during this final charge of the 12th day of May 1885.

One was where little Marcile Gratton, a French halfbreed girl aged 10, ran across our line of fire and was shot dead on the doorstep of one of the stores. She wanted to be with her mother. Our boys gathered round the little dead thing as she lay in her frantic mother's arms, who kneeling on the step rocked her as she had when a baby, trying to get her to speak. She couldn't believe that her child was dead.

Suddenly a figure was seen to break away from among the group of prisoners, then under guard, farther up the street. Bareheaded and in shirtsleeves he bounded like a panther through the crowd, pushing our men right and left until he came to the mother and the little dead girl. He stood for a moment looking down at them, his long black hair half covering his face. Then dropping to his knees he stroked his little daughter's hair gently, reverently. "Our poor little Marcile—est mort."

He passed his other arm about his wife's shoulder and the tears welling in his eyes dropped on the little girl's dead hand. The group of soldiers looking on were deeply touched by the scene that was being enacted at their feet. "I'd sooner let them keep Batoche than to have hurt one hair of that poor little girl," one soldier was heard to say.

Then one officer was heard to exclaim, "General Middleton, only yesterday, sent orders to Riel, to have all their women and children put in one place under a white flag and every man would respect it." The reply that Riel returned was the "if one woman or child was even hurt by our fire, he would have all the white prisoners in his possession shot." (By now we had all these prisoners safe in our camp.) No one knew what to do or say.

The father slowly rose to his feet, assisting his Indian wife to hers. He took his little Marcile in his arms and they slowly made their way, towards the setting sun and the ravine, where a few hours ago we were fighting our way toward the finish of the campaign. Such is life. Such is death.

We camped that night behind the building at Batoche, slept in the open under the canopy of heaven and slept well; we were good and tired, every one of us. Then in counting up our dead and wounded for the day earlier in the evening, there were 10 killed and about 35 wounded, some badly. But worst of all, my cousin and partner at Shell River, had been shot and instantly killed. Captain Ted Brown, while leading his men, had been picked off by a sniper.

Victory over Riel, 1885

MAJOR-GENERAL FREDERICK MIDDLETON

Middleton, a British officer, commanded the Canadian forces against Riel. No Napoleon, he had trouble with his Canadian subordinates, but he won nonetheless, as his letter to the Minister of Militia describes.

To Hon. A.P. Caron.
From Batoche N.W.T. 12th.

Since my last evening despatch to you, have ascertained some particulars of our victory, which was most complete. I have myself counted Twelve half-breeds on the field, and we have four wounded breeds in hospital and two Sioux. Among the wounded breeds is one Amboise Joubin, a councillor and Joseph Delorme. As far as I can ascertain Riel and Gabriel Dumont, left as soon as they saw us getting well in but cannot ascertain for certain, which side of the river he is, but think he must be this side, as the scow was the other side. The extraordinary skill displayed, make rifle pits at the exact proper points and the number of them is very remarkable and had we advanced rashly or heedlessly; I believe, we might have been destroyed. As I told you [I] reconnoitred to my right front with all my mounted men yesterday morning, with a view to withdrawing as many of their men from my left attack, which was the key of position and on my return to Camp forced on my left, and then advanced the whole line with a cheer and dash worthy of the soldiers of any army. The effect was remarkable. The enemy in front of our left was forced back from pit to pit and those in the strongest pit facing east found them turned and our men behind them. Then commenced a sauve qui peut and they fled, leaving blankets, coats, hats, boots trousers and even guns in their pits. The conduct of troops was beyond praise. The Midland and Tenth vieing with each other, well supported by the Ninetieth and flanked by the Mounted portion of troops. The artillery and Gatling also assisted in the attack with good effect. When all behaved so well it might appear invidious to mention particular names, still there are always some who, by good luck are brought prominently before the eye of the commanding Officer and these names I shall submit to you later on. My staff give me every assistance and were most energetic and zealous. The medical arrangement under Brigade-Surgeon Orton was as usual most excellent and efficiently carried out. I have to regret the death of three officers as well as two soldiers, but they died nobly, and well. I found no want of ammunition among the enemy or food in spite of what has been said to the contrary, and we found large quantities of powder and shot. Nearly the whole of rebel's families were left and are encamped close to the river bank; they were terribly frightened, but I have reassured them and protected them. There is a report that Gabriel Dumont is killed but I do not believe, though I think it likely he is wounded. One of the killed has been recognized as Donald Ross one of the Council. Yesterday evening just as the action was finished, the "Northcote" and "Marquis" steamers arrived up. The latter having twenty-five police on board. It appears that the "Northcote" had a hot time of it, as the rebels fired at it very heavily and though it was well fortified the rebels managed to wound two men slightly. The "Northcote" got on a shoal for a short time, but managed to keep the enemy off, and to get off themselves. Finding that owing to the barges alongside they could not go up stream again they decided to run down to the Hudson Bay Crossing get rid of them and return. At the Crossing, they found the other steamer and came up together. This morning I sent out one of the Catholic priests with a letter addressed to Riel as follows:—

Batoche May 11th.

Mr. Riel:—I am ready to receive you and your council and to protect you until your case has been decided upon by the Dominion
Government.

Fred Middleton
Major-General
Commanding North-West Field Forces.

I propose marching tomorrow for Prince Albert by the Lepine trail
and expect to arrive there the day after. Sending my wounded up by
Steamer "Northcote" to-day to Saskatoon; the other steamer dropping
down to Lepine Crossing to take my force across the river. I cannot of
course be certain but I am inclined to think the complete smash of the
rebels will have pretty well broken the back of the rebellion. At any rate
it will, I trust, have dispelled the idea that half-breeds and Indians can
withstand attack of resolute whites properly led and will tend to remove
the unaccountable scare that seems to have entered into the minds of so
many in the North-West as regards the prowess and powers of fighting
of the Indians and breeds. There is not a sign of the enemy on either side
of the river for miles. After entering Prince Albert I propose proceeding
south to Carlton and Duck Lake cleaning out & punishing the Indians in
the pines and so on to Battleford.

(Signed) Fred Middleton

Riel's Last Interview

NICHOLAS FLOOD DAVIN

*Journalist Davin secured an interview with Louis Riel shortly before his
execution.*

Entered his cell, I looked round and saw that the policeman had moved
away from the grill. I bent down, told Riel I was a Leader reporter in the
guise of a *prêtre*, and had come to give his last message to the world. He
held out his left hand and touching it with his right said: "Tick! Tick!
Tick! I hear the telegraph, *ah, ça finira*." "Quick," I said, "have you anything to say? I have brought pencil and paper—Speak."
    Riel: "When I first saw you on the trial I loved you."
    "I wish to send messages to all. To Lemieux, Fitzpatrick, Greenshields.
I do not forget them. They are entitled to my *reconnaissance*. Ah!" he cried,
apostrophizing them, "You were right to plead insanity, for assuredly all
those days in which I have badly observed the Commandments of God
were passed in insanity (*passé dans la folie*). Every day in which I have
neglected to prepare myself to die, was a day of mental alienation. I who
believe in the power of the Catholic priests to forgive sins, I have much

need to confess myself according as Jesus Christ has said, 'Whose sins you remit they are remitted.'"

Here he stopped and looked in his peculiar way and said:

"Death comes right to meet one. He does not conceal himself. I have only to look straight before me in order to see him clearly. I march to the end of my days. Formerly I saw him afar. (Or rather "her" for he spoke in French). It seems to me, however, that he walks no more slowly. He runs. He regards me. Alas! he precipitates himself upon me. My God!" he cried, "will he arrive before I am ready to present myself before you. O my God! Arrest it! By the grace, the influence, the power, the mercy divine of Jesus Christ. Conduct him in another direction in virtue of the prayers ineffable of Marie Immaculate. Separate me from death by the force the intercession of St. Joseph has the privilege to exercise upon your heart, O my God! Exempt me lovingly by Jesus, Marie and Joseph, from the violent and ignominious death of the gallows, to which I am condemned.

"Honorables Langevins, Caron, Chapleau, I want to send them a message, let them not be offended if a man condemned to death dares to address them. Whatever affairs hang on you don't forget, 'What shall it profit a man to gain the whole world and to lose his soul?'

"Honorable Messrs. Blake and Mackenzie, I want to send them a message. For fifteen years you have often named me, and you have made resound the echoes of your glorious province, in striking on my name as one strikes on a tocsin. I thank you for having contributed to give me some celebrity. Nobly take from me an advice nobody else will dare to give you. Prepare yourself each day to appear before your God.

"The Vice-Regal throne is surrounded with magnificence. He who occupies it is brilliant, and my eyes cannot fix on him without being blinded. Illustrious personages the qualities with which you are endowed are excellent. For that reason men say 'Your Excellency.' If the voice of a man condemned to death will not appear impertinent to you; it vibrates at the bottom of the cells of Regina to say to you: Excellencies! you also, do not fail to hold yourself in readiness for death, to make a good death, prepare yourself for death!

"Sir John Macdonald! I send you a message. I have not the honour to know you personally. Permit me nevertheless to address you a useful word. Having to prepare myself for death I give myself to meditation and prayer. Excuse me Sir John. Do not leave yourself be completely carried away by the glories of power. In the midst of your great and noble occupations take every day a few moments at least, for devotion and prayer and prepare yourself for death.

"Honorable and noble friends! Laurier, Laflamme, Lachapelle, Desjardins, Taillon, Beaubien, Trudel, Prud'homme, I bid you adieu. I demand of God to send you the visit of Death only when you shall have long time desired it, and that you may join those who have transformed death into joy, into deliverance and triumph.

"Honorable Joseph Dubuc, Alphonse, C. Lariviere, Marc. A. Girard, Joseph Royal, Hon. John Norquay, Gov. Edgar Dewdney, Col. Irvine, Captain Deane, I would invite them to think how they would feel if they had only a week to live. Life here below is only the preparation for another. You are good Christians, think of eternity. Do not omit to prepare yourself for death.

"O my God! how is it death has become my sweetheart with the horror I feel towards her? And how can she seek me with an attention proportioned to the repugnance she inspires. O Death! the Son of God has triumphed over your terrors! O Death I would make of thee a good death!

"Elezear de la Grinodière! Roger Goulet, and you whom I regard as a relative, Irené Kérouak, prepare yourself for death. I pray God to prolong your days. Louis Schmidt, I ask of the good God to enable you to come to a happy old age. Meanwhile prepare yourself for death. Listen to the disinterested advice of one condemned. We have been placed in this world of pain only for the purpose of probation.

"And you whom I admire and respect, glorious Major General Middleton, you were kind to me, you treated me nobly. Pray see in my words the desire to be as little disagreeable as possible. Life has been smiling and fortunate for you, but alas! it will also finish for you. General, if there is one thing I have appreciated more than being your prisoner of war it is that you chose as my guard Captain Young, one of the most brave and polite officers of your army. Captain Young! Be not surprised that I send you a message through the Leader newspaper which I understand with *reconnaissance* has not called out against me, prepare yourself all your days. Death also disquiets himself about you. Do not sleep on watch. Be ever well on your guard.

"And you whom death spares and does not dare to approach and you whom I cannot forget, Ancien Preacher of Temperance, Chinuiquy, your hairs are white. God who has made them white slowly, wishes to make your heart white right away (*tout d'un coup*). O be not angry at the disinterested voice of a man who has never spoken to you, to whom you have never given pain, unless it be in having abandoned regrettably the amiable religion of your fathers. The grace of Marie waits for you. Please come."

The prisoner paused, and in the pause one heard the skirr of the spurred heel of the Mounted Policeman and the neighing of one of the horses in the stables hard by, and I said:—"Is this all? Have you no more to say?"

"No more," replied Riel, "Father André has been here. He has told me there is no hope, that he has a letter from my good friend Bishop Grandin. I have made my confession. I have taken the Sacraments. I am prepared. But yet the Spirit tells me, told me last night I should yet rule a vast country, the North-West, with power derived direct from heaven, look!" and he pointed to the vein in his left arm, "there the spirit speaks, 'Riel will not die until he has accomplished his mission' and—"

He was about to make a speech and I left him with some sympathy and no little sadness. I felt that I had been in the presence of a man of genius *manqué*, of a man who, had he been gifted with judgment might have accomplished much; of one who, had he been destitute of cruelty might even command esteem, and as I rode over the bridge and looked down on the frosty creek, and cast my eye towards the Government House where happy people were perhaps at dinner at that hour, I said to myself, "Why did he murder Scott? Why did he seek to wake the bloody and nameless horrors of an Indian massacre? Why did he seek the blood of McKay and his fellow peacemakers? Unhappy man, there is nothing for it. You must die on Monday."

Here as I passed near the trail going north-west the well-known voice of a home-returning farmer saying "Good night" woke me from my reverie. In twenty minutes I was seated at dinner. I joined in the laugh and the joke, so passing are our most solemn impressions, so light the effect of actual tragedy. Our emotions are the penumbras of rapid transitions of circumstances and vanishing associations and like clouds we take the hue of the moment, and are shaped by the breeze that bloweth where it listeth.

Exploring for the Beothuck, 1886

JAMES P. HOWLEY

Newfoundland's indigenous Beothuck had long been extinct when Howley set out to discover artifacts and remains.

August 7th. Beautiful, calm warm day. Went over to Little Muddy Hole to lay off a plot of land for a man named Hooper. I engaged his son-in-law to come with us as pilot to gratify an old-time longing to explore a Red Indian Burying place on Swan Island which I had been unable to locate. We had a nice time across to the island and reached the place early. It is situated on the eastern end of the island just inside two white island rocks. One would never find the place without being shown . . . It was a sort of a semi-cavern. The floor of this cavern was a mass of large loose angular fragments of rock intermixed with gravel and sand. Amongst all this loose debris we found fragments of birch bark and of human bones. There was quite a lot of bark and most of it was as sound as the day it was placed there. Some pieces exhibited rows of small holes showing where the pieces were stitched together. The place had been ransacked so often that almost everything worth having had been carried away. I was informed that some of the people of the nearby settlements had carried away large quantities of carved bones such as usually accompany the dead bodies of

the Beothucks. Everything within reach had been removed except the
few broken fragments of human bones. The rocks covering the remains
were supported upon horizontal pieces of sticks laid across the cavity.
Most of this wood was very much decayed and had given away under the
heavy top weight so that now all was a jumbled mass of debris. Some of
these sticks exhibited clear evidence of having been hewed off with stone
axes, but the majority were evidently cut with steel implements. After
removing several of the larger masses of rock and getting down to the
more gravelly soil we commenced to dig with pick and shovel. We rooted
and delved for sometime, but were only rewarded with an occasional frag-
ment of much decomposed bones. At length we unearthed a few carved
ornaments of bone or ivory. The men became very eager in the pursuit
and tried to outdo each other in procuring relics. Mike Cole, the most
eager of the lot, who managed to crawl in on hands and knees as far as
possible under the cliff and rooted away with both hands, soon began to
find a number of these ornaments. They consisted of narrow flat strips of
bone, wide at one end but tapering away towards the other in which a
small hole was drilled through. Some of these at the wider end were cut
square across, others obliquely, while one or two were forked or swallow-
tailed. All had some sort of rude design carved on both sides, but the
designs all varied, there were no two exactly alike. All had the small holes
drilled at one end and it was pretty evident they were intended to be tied
onto something by strings. There were also a number of square or oblong
blocks of ivory about an inch and a half wide and 1/2 inch in thickness.
These were carved on one side only, very elaborately. What the designs
indicated or for what purpose the blocks were used can only be conjec-
tured. I have an idea they were used for gaming, somewhat in the manner
of our dice throwing. Some of the designs looked as if intended to represent wigwams, conical-shaped figures wide at base and running to a point.
One differed from all the rest. It had a figure exactly like the letter H
in the middle with a fine fringe around the edges. The other ornaments
found were small circular disks of bone and shell with holes in the middle.
A few fragments of iron and some fragments of clay pipes, evidently of
French manufacture. The latter would seem to indicate that the Beothucks smoked, though all authorities say not. Numerous fragments of
broken shells of mussels and clams, some pieces of lobster claws. Very few
flint chips were seen. There were several fragments of iron pyrites, or
firestones. A few fragments of bows and arrows, all much decayed but still
retaining traces of the red ochre with which they had been smeared. We
did not find any arrow or spear points. There were no perfect skulls,
merely fragments of such, but some loose human teeth. There were several small bones of animals and birds. A dog's and pig's tooth.

   We set to work again after dinner and gave the place a great overhaul-
ing. One of the men, Connors, a St. John's man, did not hold with such

ghoulish work and would not leave the boat or take any part in the search. He said neither luck nor grace would follow our robbing the dead in that manner. I must confess it looked like a great act of desecration. But then to add to the weird scene in the cave amongst the crumbling dust of the poor Red men, all at once an awful storm of thunder and lightning came on. The thunder reverberated amongst the rocks and seemed almost to loosen them from their foundations. They seemed to groan and give out hollow sounds as if disapproving of our operations. We actually feared the loose fragments of rock above would tumble down upon us. This altered the whole aspect of things. It soon became apparent that the lads were thoroughly frightened though they would not admit it. All their excitement; their merriment; their talk and joking ceased at once.

The Great Hull Fire of 1886

ANONYMOUS

In urban Canada, fires could spread very quickly and sometimes whole towns were consumed. The fire at Hull, Québec, was thought to have begun in a bakery.

Shortly after one o'clock on Sunday morning citizens of Ottawa were startled by the vigorous pealing of the Hull church bells, and considerably more so when on rushing to doors and windows AN ALARMING ILLUMINATION met their view. "The unfortunate place will be swept this time," was the remark of many, and in a comparatively short period, despite the very late—or rather early—hour, numbers of citizens were wending their way to Parliament hill and other points of vantage for the purpose of ascertaining something about the extent and locality of the fire. In a short time the bells of 'the' Basilica also pealed forth their alarming notes, and hundreds of residents of the lower portion of the city who had not been awakened by the first alarm were soon hurrying over to the assistance of their friends and relations in the transpontine city, who seemed in imminent danger of being irreparably ruined. Among others a representative of *The Citizen* was quickly at the SCENE OF THE DISASTER and discovered that the fire had originated in the bakery of Ald. Landry, who had been awoke by a neighbour about one o'clock, having only retired half an hour previously and had merely managed to escape with his family, so quickly did the flames engulph his dwelling, bakery and stables, which are adjoined. Public alarm was given almost immediately, the city and church bells being vigorously rung, and all Hull in a few minutes seemed to be abroad, trembling and terrified at the alarming aspect of the situation. A slight breeze prevailed at the time, and the dense rows of old and wooden buildings contiguous on every side to the burning bakery promised the most appalling results. As usual the Jacques Cartier Fire Company turned out with promptitude, and soon had their hand-engine in an advantageous position for attacking the flames. Chief Genest and his gallant company were, however, hampered from the very first by THE WANT OF WATER. They had to get their supply from barrels, and just when they had succeeded in checking the fire a bit with the contents of the puncheons on hand, the supply would run out, and before others arrived the flames would have regained their lost vigour. The Eddy engine, too, lost no time in getting out, but the buildings all around were of such inflammable nature that before the engine could get steam up and a line of hose laid the fire had assumed ALARMING PROPORTIONS. In every direction, north, south, east and west the flames leaped from roof to roof, pursuing ruthlessly the panic stricken men, women and children, who hastily gathered up articles from their little stock of household goods, fled with them to places of supposed safety and depositing their burdens rushed back again and again until the fierce heat forbade any further trips. The man who secured a horse and cart thought himself possessed of a priceless blessing. While some were thus employed in removing their stuff, others organized a strong bucket brigade to endeavour to check the advance of the fire northward and westward, into the heart of the city, and also possessed themselves of axes and ropes with the idea of PULLING DOWN THE BUILDINGS and thus creating a gap. The fire was too close for the last mentioned scheme to be worked to advantage, but the bucket brigade were most successful, and after a couple of hours' toil, heaving water upon the steaming roofs and scorched fronts of the buildings on the north of Philemon and on the west of Duke street, they managed to check the progress of the flames in these two directions, though on the south side of Philemon street several houses were burned to the ground, and those on the east of Duke street were likewise demolished. In the meantime strong efforts were being made to check the flames in their progress towards the post office on Main street, the Wright wood yard, and the lumber piling ground beyond. The Union steam fire engine had been sent over by the Chandiere lumbermen soon after two o'clock, and shortly threw a powerful stream continuing to do excellent service throughout the night. A line of hose had also been laid from the force pump at Eddy's, established so that there were all told four streams at the disposal of the fire fighters, and THE "CONQUEROR" loaned by the Ottawa authorities was expected to make an effectual fifth, but unfortunately it was after three o'clock before it arrived, and from difficulty experienced in getting a water supply, lack of sufficient hose laid out, and other causes, the assistance it rendered was not great until very late when the fire was well under control. On and on the flames leaped towards the

Main street, the buildings in their track melting like wax at their approach. Soon the rear portion of the new Dorion block of fine stores was all in a blaze. The mass of flames at this point was greater probably than at any other time during the night, and with astonishing rapidity they licked up everything within their reach. Across the way the new post office stood, a massive stone building which it was expected would by its resistance do much to check the progress of the fire. But it had a weak spot, as was ere long made apparent. Of a sudden the wooden tower, yet unfinished, from sheer heat from across the street burst into a mass of flame, and not a drop of water being thrown upon it, burned brightly and merrily, the pyramid of fire away aloft forming a GRAND BUT APPALLING SIGHT for it became evident that the noble building was doomed unless help speedily arrove. No help was forthcoming, and the fire made its way down through the building, until nothing remained standing but the four bare walls of what a few hours ago had been one of the sights of Hull—a building of which any city might have been proud. Fortunately the mail matter and important books had been placed in the vault and were secure from danger. The flames also spread along the south side of Main street to the east and west of the post office. To the east Wright's woodyard was attacked, and a considerable quantity of light four foot cord was consumed before the fire was stayed, leaving several hundred cords untouched, and averting a serious threatened danger to the lumber piles along the river below from the huge sparks which must have flown had this wood caught. West of the post office the flames spread to two fine two storey frame buildings, which afforded an easy prey, and across Langevin street the fire also leaped, but with the aid of the fine stream thrown from the Union engine these were soon extinguished and the fire in this direction was at an end. In one other spot only had it to be fought. This was at the juncture of Main and Albert streets, and here right gallantly was it ATTACKED AND CONQUERED the block at the extreme point miraculously escaping and the flames being prevented from getting the threatened hold in the Inkerman street direction, where, if it had once caught, whole blocks were likely to have perished. It was about six o'clock when the complete mastery was obtained over the fire, and persons who had so far escaped could breathe freely and set about gathering in their effects. All day long the ruins smouldered and over and anon broke out here and there into a brisk blaze but the Eddy engine, which had kept up steam, subdued the flames as soon as they reared their heads, and no fear of further loss was expected.

A Fiendish Incendiary.

There is very little doubt that this disastrous fire, which, has devastated several blocks in the principal portion of the city, covering an area of about twenty acres of the most valuable property in Hull, and putting about two hundred families destitute on the streets, was the origin of a fiendish incendiary. Mr. Landry's steam bakery, where it took, adjoins his dwelling house, and is in operation only from midnight to 8 a.m. daily, Sunday morning excepted. There was therefore no steam on after 8 o'clock on Saturday morning. Mr. Landry had been all over the premises, which adjoin his dwelling and have a communicating door, between MIDNIGHT AND TWELVE THIRTY. He had found nothing wrong and no sign of fire, and had retired at the latter hour. On being awakened at one o'clock he still saw nothing wrong on re-entering the bakery. On opening the outside door, however, the draft admitted a sheet of flames from the outside, indicating very strongly, if not clearly, that the premises had been deliberately fired from the exterior, as there is no other way of accounting for a fire originating there at that time of night. If the incendiary for any purpose desired PERSONAL VENGEANCE on Ald. Landry he certainly had it most completely, as he lost his dwelling house, bakery and stables, with all their respective contents, including two car loads of flour and a car load of hay, which had just been laid in his valuable machinery, a good cow, and a horse which he had lately purchased and for which he is said to have refused $400; on none of which did he have a single cent of insurance. Mr. Landry's loss is estimated at $10,000. His safe and contents were saved, as also two horses.

Women's Advice to Prairie Settlers, 1886

MRS. J. ALEXANDER ET AL.

> Governments and railways ran active propaganda campaigns to persuade reluctant settlers to come to the West.

Advice to New Comers.

The following answers are given to the request "Kindly give any advice that may be of service to incoming mothers, wives, daughters, sisters, and any practical information or any household receipt that may be of service to them." In these answers much will be found of service and value to the intending settler.

Mrs. J. Alexander, of Sourisford, Southern Manitoba.—"Bring plenty of blankets and bedding, also body-clothes. A good supply of yarns is useful. Bring no furniture or kitchen furnishings."

Mrs. S. Ballantyne, of Emerson, Southern Manitoba.—"Men with means or men without means who are paying rents in the old country will certainly better their condition by coming here. If poor, those of the family old enough to work will find employment, and thus aid the family in getting a start, and our Canadians are very charitable in the way of helping decent poor men to erect buildings without charge, and they also aid such in many other ways. I was born in Scotland, lived there till I was 21 years of age, and emigrated to the Province of Quebec, lived there over two years, came to Ontario, lived on a farm 18 years, in the city 14 years, and in Manitoba over 8 years, and should know of what I speak, and I must say without fear of contradiction, or an attempt at such, by any person who has lived in Manitoba, that for soil, climate, weather and delightful seasons, it stands unrivalled by any country yet known. Our present fall weather cannot be equalled in any country on the globe."

Mrs. N. Bartley, of Wattsview.—"Plenty of warm clothing, also bedding, dishes, knives and forks, and any useful article (such as a sewing machine, if a good one) that can be packed easily, instead of disposing of it for a trifle, as is generally the way when setting out and leaving their homes."

Mrs. E. Beesley, of Marlborough, near Moose Jaw.—"Would wish all to come who are willing to work. They soon make for themselves and families comfortable homes, and will be independent, as there is plenty of good land to be easily obtained. It is a healthy climate. I can write from experience, as I came myself in poor health, and since settling here have enjoyed the best of health, and have not paid one cent for medicine."

Mrs. A. Bethune, of Archibald, Southern Manitoba.—"Families should first husband their finances to the greatest extent possible, only buying for the first year or two those articles they cannot possibly do without, and don't pay anybody for anything you can do yourself. Be sure your farm is high and dry before you spend a dollar on it. On arrival, get your garden planted with the necessary vegetable seeds, look after your garden well, have your cellar frost-proof, get a few little pigs from your neighbours, and buy nothing you can raise; buy a cow and feed her well, and if you don't get along well in Manitoba you won't do so anywhere else, I'll assure you."

Mrs. N. Brown (Rev.) of High Bluff, Man.—"This is a splendid country for industrious people, but every one coming here should know how to work. There is nothing here that I consider any drawback to people who wish to make a good home for themselves. Of course they must not expect the same luxuries and social advantages of older countries. Although the winter here is very cold, yet the air is dry and healthy, and (although 25 years of age when I left England, and consequently knowing all about it) I prefer the winters here to those in England."

Mrs. E. Butcher, of Glendinning, Man.—"All the advice I can give to those coming out is not to expect too much for the first or second year, but with industry and perseverance, a contented disposition, and a willingness to be cheerful under any difficulties that may arise, and in the course of a few years any family can make themselves a comfortable home. I suppose the cold winter is the greatest objection intending emigrants have to Manitoba. I have now been here four winters, but neither myself nor children have suffered from the cold. We have a comfortable log house, and our stove keeps up and downstairs warm. It is now the 9th of November (1885), and we ploughed up to the 3rd; last year we ploughed until the 16th. I have not felt the cold more than in Ontario, in which country I was born and raised, although we have more degrees of frost; the air being drier, the cold does not seem to penetrate as much. I have been out riding with the thermometer 25 degrees below zero and in a blinding snowstorm, yet did not suffer from cold. Of course I was well and warmly clothed."

Mrs. G. Butcher, of Russell P.O., Shell River, Man.—"Don't be prejudice in your minds in favour of English methods of cooking, baking, washing, etc., or be too proud to ask advice when you come. You will find new methods here more suited to the country and your altered circumstances. Every housekeeper here learns to be baker, laundress, tailoress, soap and candle maker, and dairywoman. New settlers can be taken by the hand by earlier arrivals, and information, receipts, etc., are freely tendered to those desirous of learning. There is great social freedom amongst settlers, so that it would be superfluous to give any recipes. Learn to knit, bring plenty of good woollen underclothing, fishermen's knitted jerseys, and boys' good tweed suits. Boys' clothing here is difficult to obtain."

Mrs. S. Chamber, of Birtle, Man.—"Provide yourselves with warm substantial clothing for the winter, strong boots, etc. Do not burden yourselves with heavy articles of furniture. Our houses are small, and all that is necessary can be procured here. I have kept tender house-plants blooming in the winter here. The summers are delightful."

Mrs. A.C. Clarke, of West half of Sec. 34, TP. 1, Range 15 West, Cartwright.—"I would advise mothers and wives to bring lots of girls with them. Daughters and sisters, come prepared to go housekeeping for some poor bachelor."

Mrs. C.C. Clitten, of Bird's Hill.—"To women settling in the country I would suggest that they pay some attention to gardening, and bring seeds with them; all the small fruits will grow in great perfection here. Make a point of setting out raspberries, currants, and strawberries, as soon as possible; these all grow wild here, and of very fine flavour, and they also add so much to the comfort of the home. Native hops and grapes are here, and I am told that the cultivated cherry and fine plum do well here planted in bluffs, only enough cleared for their growth, the native trees protecting them till they get their growth, then clear away from them."

Mrs. W. Cooper, of Treherne.—"If you intend to help to farm— 1. Bring good, warm, strong, serviceable clothing; study comfort in choosing, more than fashion. 2. If your husband's means are small, be sure to do your utmost to have a cow, some chickens and pigs. 3. Lend a helping hand to the men not supposing it is out of a woman's sphere, as the first year brings lots of extra work on the men. 4. Pay as you go, if possible.

5. Bring a few simple medicines with you, or procure them in town, before going in the country on your farm."

Mrs. P.W. Davies, (Rev.), of Chater.—"Do not come thinking to have a fortune in a year or so. Many have come expecting this; some have succeeded in it, others have been disappointed. Too many come expecting to commence here just where they left off in some other country, where perhaps their parents or friends have been years working away to get the home they are leaving. Of course they will be disappointed, for they cannot have everything at their hands just as they have in old settled places. But come determined that, with the blessing of God, you will have a home for yourself and children, and do not be above work, but rather willing to turn your hand to any respectable work that may present itself, and there is sure success."

Mrs. D.G. Dick, of Dominion City.—"Do not come expecting to find a Paradise. Eve was the only woman that found one, and she was not contented in it."

A Frenchman on Québec, 1891

PAUL BLOUET

A shrewd French observer, Blouet visited Canada and wrote about his linguistic compatriots.

I have been told that the works of Voltaire are prohibited in Quebec, not so much because they are irreligious as because they were written by a man who, after the loss of Quebec to the French Crown, exclaimed: "Let us not be concerned about the loss of a few acres of snow." The memory of Voltaire is execrated; and for having made a flattering reference to him on the platform in Montreal two years ago, I was near being "boycotted" by the French population.

The French Canadians take very little interest in politics—I mean, in outside politics. They are steady, industrious, saving, peaceful; and so long as the English leave them alone, in the safe enjoyment of their belongings, they will not give them cause for any anxiety. Among the French Canadians, there is no desire for annexation to the United States. Indeed, during the War of Independence, Canada was saved to the English Crown by the French Canadians, not because the latter loved the English but because they hated the Yankees. When La Fayette took it for granted that the French Canadian would rally round his flag, he made a great mistake; they would have, if compelled to fight, used their bullets against the Americans. If they had their own way, the French in Canada would set up a little country of their own, under the rule of the Catholic Church, a little corner of France two hundred years old.

The education of the lower classes is at a very low stage: thirty per cent of the children of school age in Quebec do not attend school. The English dare not introduce gratuitous and compulsory education. They have an understanding with the Catholic Church, who insists upon exercising entire control over public education. The Quebec schools are little more than branches of the Confessional box. The English shut their eyes, for part of the understanding with the Church is that the latter will keep loyalty to the English Crown alive among her submissive flock. . . .

The French Canadians are multiplying so rapidly that in very few years the Province of Quebec will be as French as the town of Quebec itself. Every day they push their advance from East to West. They generally marry very young. When a lad is in the company of a girl, he is asked by the priest if he is courting that girl. In which case he is bidden go straightway to the altar; and these young couples rear families of twelve and fifteen children, none of whom leave the country. . . .

What is the future reserved to French Canada and indeed, to the whole Dominion?

There are only two political parties, Liberals and Conservatives, but I find the population divided into four camps: Those in favour of Canada, an independent nation; those in favour of the political union of Canada and the United States; those in favour of Canada going into Imperial Federation; and those in favour of Canada remaining an English Colony or, in other words, in favour of the actual state of things.

Of course the French Canadians are dead against going into Imperial Federation, which would simply crush them, and Canadian "Society" is in favour of remaining English. The other Canadians seem pretty equally divided.

It must be said that the annexation idea has been making rapid progress of late years among prominent men as well as among the people. The Americans will never fire one shot to have the idea realised. If the union becomes an accomplished fact, it will become so with the assent of all parties. The task will be made easy through Canada and the United States having the same legislation. The local and provincial governments are the same in the Canadian towns and provinces as they are in the American towns and States: a house of representatives, a senate, and a governor. With this difference, this great difference, to the present advantage of Canada: whereas every four years the Americans elect a new master, who appoints a ministry responsible to him alone, the Canadians have a ministry responsible to their Parliament—that is, to themselves. The representation of the American people at Washington is democratic, but the Government is autocratic. In Canada, both legislature and executive are democratic, as in England, that greatest and truest of all democracies.

The Bounty of the Okanagan, 1892

CHARLES MAIR

Canada-firster Mair went to British Columbia's Okanagan in 1892 and was dazzled. But the separateness of B.C. worried him.

There are glorious mountains here, swarming with grizzly bears, jumping deer and wapiti, with here and there big-horns & goats; the lake beside me rivals Loch Lomond, only that it is 75 miles long; there is a climate which might fetch the angels down to build their tepees here; there are Siwashes, half-breeds, English & French, mincos, Chinamen, English bloods spending their money & dressing like cowboys . . . This is the gold range & lies west of the Selkirks. Placer digging is going on a few miles from this point & large purchases have been made by an English syndicate below here of a group of claims whither stamp mills and other appliances are being sent by every trip of the Lake boat. Next year will see wonderful excitement in this region, for it is a gold-bearing, not a silver, country. The valleys spread everywhere among the mountains, this Okanagan valley being the most extensive in the Province. They are not large, but are very productive. Every kind of fruit matures here except oranges & lemons & I fancy they will ripen too. The almond tree is in full bearing & melons, musk & water, cantelopes &c are fed to pigs. I never saw such hops as are grown on the Aberdeen estate—only planted this spring. What with fruit, fine vegetables such as tomatoes, hops, vines & wine-growing this region will be an exceedingly rich one. The one draw back is that a lot of political shysters at Victoria and old chaps who packed in over the mountains from Oregon and Washington many years ago have got hold of all the best land, both bottom and mountain. These people know nothing of Canada. In fact they deride everything Canadian, and the sooner the country is municipalized the better so that they may be forced to sell to better men.

One thing I am satisfied about, that this country will support a very large population yet, for the area is great, and it is important that Canadians should come in. But they must have plenty of money. This is no country for a man without means. Bottom lands sell at $60.00 an acre, and mountain (range) land in proportion. But on the other hand a family can not only live but make money easily on 20 acres of good bottom or bench land here. The mining enterprises springing up make an easy & good market supply right at the door & there is the whole North West to supply with fine fruits &c. It will be a very rich Province, but it must be *Canadianized*. It is not that yet. The feeling is "British Columbia", first last & always, & the people know nothing of the mixed farming industries of the East. There are thousands of cows & no butter or milk. Butter is all imported. Milk is tinned. But I have not time to go into matters. I may say there is no politics here, which is a blessing in one way. You never hear the word Canada, and you never hear the word annexation. It is a Province *sui generis*, each valley with its little secluded community, shut off until yesterday from the outer world, and resembling in some ways, the Swiss Cantons.

On the Klondike Trail, *1898*

W.H.T. OLIVE

Olive led a party of men up the Klondike Trail in 1898. The lure was gold, but the way to the ore was hard.

When we decided to break the trail, I rounded up my men and got everything ready, allotting to each man a particular part in the journey. Although the White Pass Trail had been blazed by Bill Moore in 1896, thousands still used the Chilcoot Trail. We were headed for the White Pass. Those who had snowshoes were to go ahead and break trail. The hand-drawn sleds followed. These sleds were only lightly loaded with provisions to take them to Bennett. It was slow work, plodding along, and the day closed in. The men were tired and ready to rebel when they saw a tent with smoke curling out of its stovepipe, bearing the sign, REFRESHMENTS, LIQUORS AND TOBACCO. A whoop went out from a few of the gang. "Happy day!" they shouted, and entered. Inside were two men playing cards. They came forward, smiling at the fact that at last the rush had commenced on the trail.

"What's the chance of stopping for the night?" I asked.

"Every chance in the world. How many?"

"Ten. What's the charge?"

"Fifty cents the night. Your own blankets and the ground."

"How about meals?"

"Righto! The larder is low, but we can give you a meal. Nothing fancy, for fifty cents. You'll pay double when you get a little farther on the trail."

One of my men spoke up, "Say, boss! Where's the drink you promised for breaking trail."

"Alright, line up, boys," I said. "What's the price?"

"Twenty-five cents."

"Mine's a beer," ordered one of the men.

"Sorry, gentlemen, beer freezes."

"Give me a whiskey, then."

"House of Lords, eh?"

"Good label," said another, "but it looks old."

"Ten whiskeys and hurry up, we're freezing," I said. "All ready? Then here's to the *Ora, Nora,* and *Flora.*" We raised our glasses, swallowed the contents, then spluttered and coughed.

Someone said, "What in hell brand is that?"

"Our special blend—'White Pass special.'"

"Get us the meals!" One man ordered the other, "Jake! Set up meals for ten."

We hugged the pot-bellied heater to get a thorough warming. Jake was gone a long time, but we were warm and our pipes tasted good. After an hour or so our meals were ready and at last we heard the welcome words, "Come and get it, boys! Moose meat for ten."

The boys decided to have an appetizer. "Fill 'em up again, Mister!" The glasses were placed on the bar, which was a rude structure. The glasses were clearly made for profit, their bottom halves being solid glass. After the second drink we all lined up to the rough table, which was a couple of planks set on two barrels, and began our meal. From time to time during the meal the boys glanced at each other; their looks seemed to say, "I don't know what you think, but my moose meat is damned tough." After the meal the proprietor suggested a little game before turning in. Several responded and after the game found they were "minus dollars." We laid our beds around the heater for warmth.

The proprietor said, "Now, boys, if you feel cold in the night, here's plenty of wood." It was a cold, long, bitter night. One man after another, not being able to endure any longer trying to sleep on the ground, got up, stoked up the fire and sat around it, waiting patiently for daybreak.

"Say, Boss," one of the men said, "they tell me we are only six miles from Skagway. At this rate we'll be ten days getting to Bennett." Many wanted to turn back, but after much shaming and persuasion on my part, they decided to stay on.

We started at daybreak on our journey, but had not gone far before we came across the carcass from which our supper was supplied. "The sons of guns," we exclaimed, "dead horse!" The steaks had been chopped out with an axe. We called that place Dead Horse Camp, and it was always alluded to as such.

The Dangers of Americanization

ISHBEL, LADY ABERDEEN

The wife of the Governor General kept a full diary with long reports on politics, people and affairs. Her fears of the values brought by American immigrants were written in August 1895.

A large number of immigrants from the U.S.A. are arriving, many of them originally Eastern Canadians, who have by no means realized their golden dreams of the Western States. It is to be hoped that they will leave all U.S.A. ideas behind them & realize that they have returned to a country where freedom & liberty exists for all & not for some, where law & order are respected, & where treaties with Indians are respected. A great number of these new immigrants are doing well & are heartily glad to be British citizens, but there is a remnant who would like to introduce American ideas as to what conduct "in the West" should be. These must be dealt with ruthlessly, & the magistrates & N.W. Mounted Police are determined that this shall be the case, if they can manage it. Our desire for the country to be filled up must not lead to any undue leniency towards these newcomers.

The 1896 Election:
Sir Charles Tupper Leaves Office Grudgingly

ISHBEL, LADY ABERDEEN

When Wilfrid Laurier won the 1896 election, the Tories were out. But as Lady Aberdeen makes clear, Prime Minister Sir Charles Tupper went complaining all the way.

Young Sir Charles came with a message from his father to say that according to Press reports the Government had been defeated, but many of the majorities were v. small, & no statement could be made until there had been recounts. On Thursday evening came a telegram from Sir Charles saying that it would facilitate the course of public business if His Excellency were to come to Ottawa for a few days. Now we had expected him to come to Quebec if he wanted to resign right away, & it was manifestly impossible for us to leave at the moment, as H.E. had made a special request to Admiral Erskine to bring his ships up from Halifax for Dominion Day, when a great meet of bicyclists was to take place from all parts of Canada. It was considered that it would do these young men good to have an opportunity of seeing the British warships. Admiral Erskine very kindly consented at once & brought up the *Crescent*, the *Intrepid* & the *Tartar*. He & Mrs Erskine came to stay with us, & we gave them a grand State dinner on Monday the 29th, & a Ball on the 30th, both of which events went off very well. The weather turned rather cold for the dinner & made sitting out on the Terrace chilly work, but the Ball night was much better & the Terrace & the lower Tennis Court were covered with people sitting out all the night. The searchlight played about the Terrace—the arrangement of fir trees with light all amongst them looked very pretty & the broad temporary staircase from the Ball room to the supper room below was a distinct improvement.

On the Wednesday the much talked of Bicycle Meet was held as part of the celebrations of Dominion Day. H.E. & the children & the Erskines went down to see the procession at 10:30, but there were by no means the promised 5000 wheelmen. Some of the staff took part in the procession. In the afternoon we went to the Bicycle Races, at which there were great crowds of people, but which appeared to me a somewhat dreary affair. There is so much sameness & so much mechanism about bicycle races & whatever bicycle riders may look as they are going along the road in an ordinary attitude, their racing posture is too hideous for words.

On the same evening A. & Capt. Sinclair & Capt. Wilberforce went to an official dinner at the Lieutenant Governor's & I with Marjorie, Miss Wetterman & Mr Ferguson went to a concert arranged in connection with the bicycle meet. It was not up to much. At 11 p.m. H.E., Capt. Sinclair & I started off on our journey here, according to arrangements made with Sir Charles Tupper. He wrote saying that he quite understood that we could not come sooner, & declining our invitation to come & stay at the Citadel.

In the interval he had addressed a letter to H.E., in which he more than hinted that he [i.e. A.] had gravely departed from the precedents followed by his predecessors & had infringed the principle of self-government.

We arrived here at 1:40 p.m. on Thursday & Capt. S. went at once to the Office & to see Sir Charles & to appoint an hour for his coming to see A. Three thirty was suggested, but the old gentleman preferred to come at three. It was his birthday, & seemingly neither all his recent arduous fight nor its results, nor the extreme heat affected him. The plucky old thing came down blooming in a white waistcoat & seemingly as pleased with himself as ever. He did not at all appear as the defeated Premier come to render an account of his defeat & of its causes to the representative of the Sovereign. Not he! Down he sat & for an hour & a half harangued H.E. on the enormity of sending Minutes to Council [under cover] to the Clerk of the Council, asking for information on various points before certain Orders in Council could be signed as for instance in the Chignecto Ry case. He quite ignored the fact that this was the usual custom [& form of procedure (as shown by the office records)] & that the Governor General may go on asking for information as long & as often as he likes. He held that it was most unfortunate that these Memoranda should be recorded as part of the Minutes of Council. Doubtless this is so [from the retiring Government's point of view] when bearing in mind the nature of some of the Orders-in-Council, but the fact that they are recorded is one of their values, & they can never be made public outside Privy Councillors save by the consent of the Governor-General.

Then he went on to the elections, showed conclusively to himself that Laurier had no majority on any one point of policy, instancing especially the trade & the school questions. Then he announced his intention of waiting until after the 7th to decide what to do when the recounts were all over, & hinted the procedure he might take if he met Parliament. Then came some discussion as to whether he should recommend Senators & judges or rather how he should provide especially for Monsieur Angers— a talk about the proposed appt of Mr Payne his own Secretary, to be Asst Clerk of the Privy Council, although he had not passed the prescribed examination, & a few words about the Allan Line. H.E. said but little at the time & gave his visitor tea at the end; but after a great talk he & B. went to work. H.E. drew up a Mem. about the Minutes of Council & the custom observed by his predecessors, & Capt. S. worked at a draft for a letter on the whole position. The two were finally combined & if I can, I shall get a copy to bind up with these journals. [It will be printed presently, as it is to be moved for in Parlt.] It is a Mem. likely to have real results, inasmuch as it lays down the principle that a defeated Govt & more particularly one formed as this one was, after Parlt had ceased to exist & afterwards routed at the polls, had no right to make death-bed appointments of the following character:

   I. *Life appointments*—such as Senators, Judges, Revising Barristers, etc.
  II. *New appointments*—where new posts are actually created or where the office has been vacant for more than a year.
 III. *Appointments not authorised* by statute, such as that of Mr Payne—or that of M. Joncas to Mr Gregory's post when the latter [was not suitable] for superannuation [under the rules] & was perfectly well.

This letter was delivered yesterday evening & this morning at 11 Sir Charles came for another two hours interview.

   He was very much annoyed, & although he had to confess [that] his contention concerning the Minutes of Council [was wrong], & something he said about the Chignecto Ry wrong, yet on he went, maintaining that he was right & concluding with the ultimatum that he would have to resign not on account of the defeat at the polls, but on account of H.E.'s unconstitutional action [and "withdrawal of confidence"]. He asked that the letter might be altered in some details where he thought that statements of his own at the previous interview had been misrepresented & in order that it might be formally submitted to his colleagues. So B. has been hard at work re-arranging, & then after submitting the whole thing to H.E. & going over it with him, turning it from a letter to an official Memorandum & greatly improving it. The value of his help & of his calm wise judgement & clear-headedness & firmness is beyond words. It is difficult to see how we could have got through this time without him. It is hard upon him to have to work on day & night, for that is what it comes to.

Ukrainian Immigrants Come to Canada, 1897

DMYTRO ROMANCHYCH

For almost all immigrants, coming to Canada was traumatic, not least because of the foul conditions on immigrant ships and the difficult weather on the North Atlantic.

After a short wait in Hamburg, one and a half thousand Ukrainian emigrants were loaded into a very old but not very large ship, the Arcadia. It was a boat that had steam engines as well as sails which were hoisted when a favourable wind was blowing. Under the top deck there were about a dozen passenger cabins where the "city-coated gentlemen" travelled. Under the second deck were the galleys and the dining room. Below water level, under the third and fourth decks, there were no cabins, only one big space with rows of iron bedsteads, three or four storeys high. In the lower beds the women and children slept, and in the upper beds, the men and boys. If one wished to reach the upper storey, an iron ladder had to be used.

We stopped over at Antwerp, in Belgium, where the boat took on ballast, hundreds of barrels with cement. We stayed at Antwerp for five days. Nobody was permitted to leave the boat, and only Bodrug and Negrych [Iwan Bodrug and Iwan Negrych, both teachers] managed somehow to get off the boat and view the city. On the boat it was unbearably hot, and below deck an unbearable stench made breathing difficult.

Probably no Ukrainian emigrant ever experienced such a dreadful ocean crossing as we did on our Arcadia. When we left the English Channel and entered the open sea, the weather was beautiful for the first few days. The sun was shining all day, the sea was calm, and it was a pleasure to travel. Above our heads flew loudly-shrieking flocks of seagulls, and in the water whole herds of dolphins accompanied our ship as if they had never seen a boat before. When about half-way across the Atlantic, the weather suddenly changed one evening and a storm broke out, a real hurricane accompanied by a deluge of rain. In no time the sea was transformed into high mountains with white tops. One moment we were on top of these foaming mountains and the next we were thrown into what seemed a bottomless abyss . . . The ballast shifted, and our boat began to list to one side . . . People were holding on tightly to their iron bedsteads, and many started to pray, until all became seasick. The seamen apparently anticipated the storm, because they herded us all below deck and closed the hatches. Passengers who had been warned about seasickness before they started the voyage were also told that garlic, onions, whiskey, and Hoffmann's drops were good remedies against seasickness. People were not overly stingy with these remedies, and they partook of them as much as they could stand. As a result of them, such terrible smells developed below deck during the storm that even the stewards who ventured in became sick. They swore and cursed, but as they did it in German, which few people understood, it had little effect.

The storm lasted three days without a break, and somehow we survived it without great losses. Only two persons died, an old man and a child. On the fourth day the storm stopped as suddenly as it had started. People breathed in relief and all went to sleep exhausted. Suddenly, during the night, a loud blast and a shock which rattled our iron bedsteads woke us up. People were asking, frightened, "What happened?" Those who could, hurried to the top deck, and were amazed to learn that the boat was surrounded by ice. The crew was patching up a hole below, pumps were throbbing, and our boat was trying to free itself from the icy embrace by moving backwards and forwards. The siren was blowing all the time to prevent eventual collision with some other boat, because it was foggy and one could hardly see a few yards ahead.

We remained ice-bound until morning. The boat was imprisoned by the ice and could not move. The captain ordered all passengers on deck, and we obeyed the order. Bodrug interpreted the captain's commands. We were ordered, when the whistle blew, to run from one side of the boat to the other as fast as we could, and back again. We repeated this manoeuvre many times. The boat began to sway, broke the ice which was surrounding it, and began to move forward slowly. Our baggage, which was stored below, became soaking wet during that storm, and we suffered great losses.

We wrestled with the ice floes for three days, and only on the fourth day we reached the open sea, which was as calm and smooth as a mirror. After another two and half days of sailing against the wind on the St. Lawrence, we finally reached Quebec and Canada. We had been at sea twenty-one days.

Canada Goes to War, South Africa, 1899

LORD MINTO

> Governor General Minto was determined to bring Canada into the South African War and, despite Sir Wilfrid Laurier's concerns, he got his way. This letter to the Colonial Secretary Joseph Chamberlain explained the problems and detailed the contingent.

CO 42/869, Minto to Chamberlain, Secret
Oct. 20, 1899

I have the honour in reply to your cable despatch of October 3rd to forward a Privy Council Order, authorizing the despatch of 1,000 volunteers, to serve with Imperial troops in South Africa.

It is intended that this force should be organized as a Regiment of two Battalions, and that it should be commanded by Lieutenant Colonel Otter, an excellent officer, who served with distinction in the North West Campaign, in 1885, and is at present commanding the Toronto District. . . .

My Government is in treaty with the Allan Line Company for the use of the s.s. "Sardinian", which it is calculated will be capable of conveying the whole contingent, and she is expected to sail from Quebec on the 31st instant.

Though the possibility of an offer being made to Her Majesty's Government of Canadian Troops for service in South Africa has been for some months enthusiastically discussed throughout the Dominion, the proposal has been surrounded by difficulties, the leading features of which I will endeavour to place briefly before you.

The first intimation I received that an offer of troops from Canada would be favourably considered by Her Majesty's Government, was conveyed to me in a private letter I had the honour to receive from you, dated July 3rd, in which you informed me, "that if a really spontaneous request were made from any Canadian force, to serve with Her Majesty's troops on such an expedition it would be welcomed by the Authorities", and I then informed Sir Wilfrid Laurier of this portion of your letter, and allowed him to take a note of the above quoted sentence.

Since then I have had frequent interviews with him on the subject and he has repeatedly promised me a decision from his Cabinet, but till a few days ago, no decision had been come to, and moreover the Canadian public, as far as I know, had never been officially informed, as it might, and I think, ought to have been, that Her Majesty's Government was ready heartily to accept a spontaneous request from a Canadian force to serve with Her Majesty's troops.

In all my conversations and correspondence with Sir Wilfrid, whilst drawing his attention to the important bearing the offer of a Canadian Contingent might have on Imperial questions, I have carefully impressed upon him the necessity of discouraging any idea that Her Majesty's Government have in any way asked for troops.

My communications however, in default of any action being taken by the Government, remained confidential; while at the same time a considerable amount of irresponsible rumour was allowed to circulate, opinions as to the offer of a contingent were given in the Dominion Parliament and elsewhere, and preparations were made for the possible despatch of a force which of course could not be kept secret.

In the meantime the more critical the position in South Africa became the more military enthusiasm increased here, and the more apparent became the indecision of the Government, till the more or less garbled versions published in the Press of your cable to me of October 3rd, brought things to a head.

The mischievous idea that the Mother Country had asked for troops was encouraged by the Press and my Ministers were intensely annoyed by the general sense of your cable as it appeared in the newspapers, indicating to the public what had never been officially confided to it, namely, the willingness of Her Majesty's Government to accept Canadian troops, and alluding also to irresponsible offers to raise troops, of which my Ministers were officially ignorant.

The effect of this semi-publicity of the telegram was undoubtedly to force the hands of the Government and oblige it to come to a decision of some sort, whilst the Military enthusiasm throughout Canada, with the exception of Quebec, finally decided what that decision should be.

The above is I think a general outline of what has occurred, but what is of far greater interest are the reasons for the irresolution of the Canadian Government in the face of the intensely Imperial sentiments expressed throughout the country. Undoubtedly the chief opposition has emanated from Quebec, but it would be unfair to say that the population of the Province has been generally adverse to the movement, when French Canadian Officers and men are volunteering freely, and when there have been notable instances, such as that of Mr. Prefontaine, the Mayor of Montreal, of hearty approval of the offer of a contingent.

Nevertheless the difficulty and delay which has arisen has undoubtedly been due to Quebec influence vehemently expressed in the Cabinet by Mr. Tarte, Minister of Public Works. Mr. Tarte bases the opposition of Quebec entirely on what he considers constitutional grounds, namely that a Colony should not accept pecuniary or military responsibility on behalf of the Mother Country, unless that Colony has some representation in the Councils of the Mother Country. He considers that at any rate in the present instance, the Dominion Parliament should have been summoned, when he would heartily have supported the despatch of a contingent, or any vote for necessary funds, always recognizing the fact that Imperial Colonial representation would have eventually to be dealt with. He considers that the present offer of troops on the part of Canada establishes a precedent for her responsibility to furnish troops on the occasion of any war, however small, in which the Empire may be engaged. I have endeavoured to explain to him that there would not appear to me to be any dangerous precedent as regards colonial responsibility in the acceptance by the Old Country of a spontaneous offer from the Dominion on the present occasion, and that there could be absolutely no recognized responsibility on the part of the Colony in this direction; and I have told him that though his arguments might be theoretically sound, the case had not arisen in which any responsibility for assistance from the Colony was claimed, and that I thought he would have done well under the circumstances to recognize the strong demonstration of feeling which had been manifested throughout Canada, rather than raise the question of responsibilities which had certainly as yet never been seriously considered. As to the latter point he appeared inclined to agree with me, and assures me that he will now do all in his power to assist the despatch of the troops.

I am not at all prepared to say to what extent Mr. Tarte's views may have been influenced by want of sympathy for British enterprise, by ultramontane pressure, or by anxiety for the security of the Quebec vote, but the views he has expressed to me no doubt represent the platform upon which he intends that the Government should defend its action. The immediate consequence of the line he has adopted has been that the Government under his influence has been compelled to minimize the official appearance of Canada's offer, and to give it as far as possible the character of a volunteer expedition with a small amount of Government assistance.

The General wish throughout Canada has been to offer a thoroughly representative force, and to pay for it out of her own pocket, and it has naturally accentuated any racial feeling that exists between French and English, and has been all the more galling to the latter to realize that French influence in the Cabinet has overruled British inclination.

On the other hand Mr. Tarte being a strong man, I should not be surprised after the present Military enthusiasm has passed over, to see the question of Colonial responsibilities in connection with Imperial representation seriously brought before the country and with a considerable amount of solid support. The question is of course far too large a one to do more than allude to here, but the present disappointing difficulties may perhaps assist to work out an Imperial problem as yet only in its infancy.

Getting the Royal Canadian Regiment to South Africa

C.F. HAMILTON

> *Hamilton was a reporter for the* Globe *and he sent this letter, dated November 11, 1899, to his editor, J.S. Willison.*

This is in many respects an ill-found transport, and when letters filter back a big chorus of grumbling may be expected. She is a good strong ship, but is over-crowded. She should not carry more than 500 men. The fellows (& everyone) are terribly close packed & in some respects very uncomfortable, but in wonderfully good spirits. I shall write something dealing directly with the vessel, so as to head off the anonymous correspondents in the ranks, with which the ship swarms.

The regiment is getting into shape. There are a good many good officers and some who are useless. That, of course, was to be expected; the gov't really seems to have done the best it could, & could not of course in every instance tell what sort the men are. The officers from Toronto are very well selected. A mistake has been made in sending some of the very young subs—our men are not English Tommies to follow an "officer boy." A good deal of the dead wood is among these. The pick of the young chaps is young Caldwell, W.C. Caldwell's son. He is a choice man & should make his mark.

We have a passenger who is worth his weight in gold. Captain C.C. Todd of the 2nd Royal Dublin Fusiliers. My diary which I am sending indicates what he has done. Privately, he is the only man on board ship who knows how to run a troopship. The vessel was filthy, & was approaching the tropics when he took hold. But for him we would have had pestilence on board & a horrible time. Now she is clean as a new pin. The Canadian gov't owes him some very handsome recognition. He is, I should say, a poor man, as officers go, with his own way to make in the world. He volunteered his services and is brimful of energy & organizing power. Very tactful, too, & well liked by the men whose arrangements he has to supervise.

The Victory of Paardeberg

ALBERT PERKINS

> *Canada's first victory on a foreign field was won at Paardeberg in late February 1900. Perkins, a New Brunswicker with the Royal Canadian Regiment, sent this diary extract to his hometown newspaper.*

Feb. 25—Yesterday did not write. We shifted our position to another kopje. The day was cold and dark like November. Was sick like lots of others. Last night I was on duty; it was awful. The rain fell in torrents, we were wet, cold and hungry and ate half raw meat. Were issued two biscuits. Miles of transports came in yesterday so we may get more. Fighting is the easiest part of the campaign. No soles on shoes, buttons all gone, no knees in trousers, nor seat; Hudlin would not wear them. It is enough to make one yearn for civilization. Guess the rainy season is on for it rains every night and day. Last night the searchlight at Kimberley gave us quite a light at times and was company for the sentry. The wind blew so that our enemy could have advanced very close without our hearing them.

Feb. 26—Weaker still, and we have nothing to eat. The rest of the batt. have been down near the river. Some of us had to make the trip down and back. When we got back we just fell down, our legs almost refused to move. Have been on less than half rations for nearly two weeks. It didn't rain last night so we slept a little. Wish I had a burnt crust or any old thing. Have heard that French or some one has inflicted a severe defeat on the Boers a few miles from here. The gunners say they can shell the Boers out of their position in a few hours, but that is not the game it seems. The idea is to keep these here as a bait. Some trying to relieve them have been captured. Then by keeping these here other generals can operate the easier. We are moving our trenches near those of the enemy. We don't know what is going on outside ourselves, but hope it is encouraging for you all.

Feb. 27 (Majuba Day)—Very lucky to be able to write. We are almost in the Boer lines and quite a few have given up and are passing to the rear. We laugh and talk with them. G Co. lost heavily. Herb Leavitt was shot right through with an explosive bullet. Yesterday right after writing we marched down the hill and took position on the river bank near the trenches. We had something to eat, then after dark took our position in the trenches. They are dug at night running at right angles to the river. At 2 a. m. we arose and advanced. We had gone about three hundred yards when orders came to entrench. We had only been at it a few minutes when we again got orders to advance. It was pitch dark and we had only gone about 100 yards when such a fire opened on us. I saved myself by a miracle almost. There was a perfect hail of bullets. We dropped like a flash, crawled and after a while got up and ran back to the trench, where we lay till some time ago. Then we advanced up this trench a hundred yards from the Boers. We have quite a lot killed. Our company suffered far the most. The Canadians did it all. Now it seems this crowd will surrender. Riggs, Scott, Withers, Johnston, and perhaps more of our company have been killed. Canadians did not receive support. Horrible work; Leavitt hardly expected to live. Boers surrendered to Canadians. Roberts said we did excellent work.

Am now in the Boer laager. Have tea, flour, meal, and have been cooking. Hundreds of rifles and tons of ammunition left here. Thousands of prisoners. Cronje took breakfast with Roberts.

G. Company took all the fire. Boers had families with them. Could get hundreds of souvenirs. Never felt worse than for Herb. Donahoe lost his leg. Men horribly shot; were within fifteen yards of trenches when Boers opened fire, and built trench less than 100 yards from theirs. Herb Leavitt walked over four hundred yards after he was shot.

28th.—Last night we lay around a fire and cooked. Walker made cakes, flour and oatmeal, fried in fat. I made tea. Not hungry, had a good sleep and am going on fatigue. Found lots of rifles taken from British troops at Magersfontein. Most every one has a kettle or pan. Boers have little kettles, pots galore (or had).

The Brutal Sameness of Prairie Towns, 1902

BERNARD MCEVOY

Let it be confessed that the architecture of these new Western towns—
and I need make no invidious comparisons, for with very few exceptions
they are all "much of a muchness"—is principally governed, in the main
streets, by commercial considerations and by the exigencies of necessity.
On the way from Calgary to Edmonton you can see, at one or other of the
score of stations that intervene, the whole process of town-building. The
unit, the primal cell—the germ, as it were—is the store, and the store, in
most instances, is simply a magnified packing-box. A man sends a few carloads of lumber to a township site, gets hold of a carpenter, and the big
packing-box for commodities is built. Nowhere is the adventurous spirit
of trade more manifest. A few oblong holes are punched in for windows in
the upstairs department, and of course there are the large store-windows
below. Something in the way of nice architecture might be done with the
gable end of the roof, but the merchant likes to have the front boarding
carried up square and high to hide the roof, in fact, he likes it ugly. A plain
boarded parallelogram, reaching seven or eight feet above the ridge,
strikes him as about the thing. You can't see the roof then; in fact, you
would not know there was a roof. What could be better? The spirit of
competition soon attracts another merchant, and we may be very sure
that he will make an effort to outdo the first man in ugly utility. He will,
perhaps, have no apertures or break of any kind in the vast square of
boarding above his store windows. By and by people build houses to live
in, and an hotel; and naturally the same conditions prevail. The packing-
box style of architecture is established for the buildings of the early years
of every settlement. The people would consider it a waste of money to
employ an architect, and the packing-box style of architecture needs
none. The object is to get a place to store goods, or to live in, that will cost
as little as possible; and it must be owned that there is but little native
appreciation of beauty in the colonizing Anglo-Saxon. The trail of "Early
Commercial" is over all these new towns, and it takes scores of years
before they appreciate Early English or any other more beautiful style of
building. Even the Doukhobors build better than your prosaic and pushing Anglo-Saxon, whose imaginative soul and shrewd intelligence are
set on dollars to the exclusion of everything else, and who thinks nothing
of desecrating a beautiful landscape with the most detestably ugly buildings that can possibly be erected. Thereby much bad taste is nurtured
among children, and necessarily prosaic lives are made still more prosaic
and featureless. When the people in these towns "get up" a little, they
travel, see better buildings, and by degrees a better style of architecture

creeps in. They begin to acquire what are called "residential streets," and the packing-box architecture gives place to something much more tolerable so that you may see both at Edmonton and Calgary, notably in the latter place, buildings of most satisfactory and pleasing design.

The Red Light District in Dawson

LAURA BERTON

The social season ended, too, with the coming of continuous daylight, and Miss Hamtorf and I indulged our mutual enjoyment of long walks. These had become a daily fetish with us, for we considered them necessary to our health. One of our married friends met us labouring up the hill on one of these excursions and laughed out loud.

"You girls make me laugh," she said. "You tire yourselves out with your everlasting walking, thinking to improve your health or your complexions or something. And what good does it do you? Look at the women in Klondike City. They don't bother about exercise. They work hard all night, sleep all day, drink and eat all they can get and they're always the picture of health."

We had to agree with her. We often ran into these women as they strode in pairs along Fifth Avenue on shopping tours, and far from looking evil or jaded they were for the most part fine, healthy specimens invariably with a peaches-and-cream complexion. Their profession was tolerated by the police—as long as it was practised in Klondike City and not in Dawson—but they were not allowed to mingle at any of the community gatherings. I was at one concert in the A.B. Hall when three of these handsome and full-figured sirens, led by Sweet Marie, entered the place and "brazenly" (as all decent women agreed) seated themselves in an open box in the gallery. An undercurrent of excitement ran through the audience, but in a moment a Mountie appeared in the box, spoke a few words, and the women departed. Over these people—indeed over anybody who didn't behave—the Mounties held the threat of a "blue ticket": an order to get out of town on the next boat.

Klondike City, the restricted district where the painted ladies lived, and which was better known as Lousetown, was on the far side of the Klondike River and connected to Dawson by a splendid cantilever bridge. There was, of course, a good deal of gossip concerning those men who crossed the bridge and entered that forbidden but very sunny-looking land beyond the pale. During the bright summer nights, of course, it was impossible for any man bent on this errand to avoid scrutiny.

The little houses, as those virtuous ones who remained on the right side of the river could easily see, stood in neat rows and (as the wires showed us through field glasses) each was installed with electric light and telephone. The occupant's business name was plainly painted on the door.

Miss Hamtorf and I soon became consumed with curiosity to see at close range something of the set-up of the forbidden city, and so she and I, one summer's afternoon, set out on what was ostensibly a berry-picking expedition along the banks of the Klondike. But as soon as we were rid of the prying eyes of the town we faced about and, slinking along by devious paths and rocky hillsides, we reached the plateau directly above Louse-town.

Climbing stealthily, and a little shamefacedly, down the rough, bush-enshrouded bluff which backed the area, we soon found a secluded clump of shrubs from which we could observe unnoticed the goings-on below.

If we anticipated any shameful sights we were disappointed and con-founded, for the scene below us was one of unparalleled gaiety. Indeed, it might have been lifted straight from a Brueghel's canvas. At the back doors of the tiny frame houses, the whores, laughing and singing, calling out to each other and chattering like bright birds, were making their toilets for the evening. Some were washing their long hair—invariably bright gold or jet black—drying it in the sun and leisurely brushing it out. Others were just reclining languorously and gossiping with their neigh-bours. Some were singing lyrically. All were in their chemises. Our eyes started from our heads as we gazed down on them, for these garments were quite short, scarcely down to the knees, and every woman's legs were quite bare. The chemises were also sleeveless, which seemed equally immodest, and cut with a low round neck. As they were made of coloured muslin—pink, blue and yellow—the effect was indescribably gay.

This cheerful picture was further enhanced by the comings and goings of waiters from the neighbouring hotel, carrying trays of bottles and glasses or platters of food covered with linen napkins. I must say that as the scene comes back to me now after forty years, and it is one that comes back continually—the bright colours, the cheerful sounds, the brilliant sunshine, the great river flowing majestically in the foreground and the encircling shoulder of the green hillside carpeted with wild flowers—it is more reminiscent of a gay Technicolor film than of the setting of the largest red-light district north of the fifty-four-forty line.

Signor Marconi and Wireless Telegraphy

UNKNOWN

In December 1901, Guglielmo Marconi sent a message from Signal Hill in St. John's, Newfoundland, to Britain.

Signor Marconi is today the most celebrated man in the world and his name stands out in bold prominence above all others as the greatest genius of the age. He has achieved a success that, in the words of Paul Kruger, has staggered humanity. Wireless telegraphy at long distances is an accomplished fact, for Marconi has spoken to a man one thousand nine hundred miles away, with no other medium than that which existed on the morning that Noah came out of the ark. Nature grudgingly gave out THE GREAT SECRET; but bit by bit Marconi made the bold venture and subdued the hidden secrets of dame nature to obey his own will. The very thought of it sets one aghast. The humble genius who received the Telegram reporter at the Cochrane Hotel makes no vain-glorious boast about what he has achieved. He is as modest as a school boy, and one would not think he was the wizard who wrought this all-inspiring wonder of science, that at once realizes the tales of the Arabian nights and the stories of Jules Verne. It is no wonder that New York stood astounded and refused to believe the news when it was flashed over the wires on Saturday night. Newspapers were skeptical and before sending the report to their printers wired for CONFIRMATION OF THE NEWS. The citizens of St. John's even doubted the truth of it on Saturday night. They had cast an occasional glance up at Signal Hill the past few days while the experiments were going on. They had seen electrically charged kites whirling in the storm-tossed air over Signal Hill now and then. But they did not attach much importance to the matter. They knew that Mr. Marconi was making experiments, but up to Saturday they had failed. This was not the case, for he had succeeded in getting from the Lizard, Cornwall, the letter S (. . .) of the Morse Code distinctly at 11:30 on Wednesday, TWENTY-FIVE DIFFERENT TIMES, and the same success was expected on Thursday. In order that there would be no doubt about the genuineness of those messages, Mr. Marconi cabled to friends in charge of the transmitting apparatus at the Lizard to verify the signals and have them reported at a prearranged moment. This made assurance doubly sure, and there remained no doubt in the mind of Mr. Marconi that what he dared hope to do when he established an elaborate apparatus at Cornwall last August, was accomplished. It was the faith and confidence in himself that prevailed on the company to allow the establishment of a station at Lizard Point, on the coast of Cornwall. This was kept in the background FEARING A POSSIBLE FAILURE. The published object of Marconi's visit to our shores was to install on Signal Hill or some other favourable point the necessary machinery to communicate with the ocean liners passing the coast of Newfoundland. The Chart of the Wreck published by Mr. Murphy, superintendent of Marine and Fisheries Department, had awakened the world to the advantages that would be derived from establishing a wireless station on this coast to warn ocean-going steamers from their threatened doom of being lost on the rocks in the vicinity of Cape Race. From experiments made at NANTUCKET, NEW YORK, AND OTHER PLACES, Mr. Marconi knew that his success would be repeated here and he would be able to pick up ships two hundred and fifty or two hundred miles to the south. This is the summer route of the ocean liners. Perhaps if the atmospheric, topographical and mineralogical conditions at Signal Hill, St. John's, were favourable, Mr. Marconi would be able to reach even the winter track of steamers, four hundred and fifty miles to the south. Marconi had all this outlined in mind, but his greatest hope was centered at the Lizard, in Cornwall, nearly two thousand miles away. Whilst having great confidence in this he dared not give it out to the public through newspaper representatives, fearing a possible failure. He had installed in August last an electrical transmitting apparatus OF THIRTY HORSE POWER at Lizard, in a way so quiet that it attracted very little attention. Now it has accomplished its work and astounded the world. In telling about it to a Telegram reporter last night, Mr. Marconi said that if the distance had been ten miles greater it may be that the power would not be sufficiently strong to transmit the message, and that the thirty horse power apparatus was taxed to its full capacity in making the recorder give an intelligible sound at Signal Hill. The sound was quite distinct, but very faint, and it was only frequent and uniform repetition of the letter S (. . .) of the Morse Code that could leave no doubt. This could be easily remedied, and, as the principle had been exhibited, the triumph was in NO WISE THE LESS. Wednesday the eleventh of December, 1901 will be put down as the memorable day in the history of the world—the day on which one of the greatest achievements in science was accomplished. It will be a proud boast for the people of Newfoundland to say in the words of the poet when looking back upon it, Magna pars quorum fuimus. We heartily congratulate Signor Marconi on his success. There is a fascination in imagining him sitting at his table in the building on Signal Hill, with watch in hand, waiting for the hand to point to the moment agreed upon with his friend on the other side of the Atlantic. The hand moves slowly around, the scientist's mind is STRUNG TO A POWERFUL TENSION. Will the dreams of his life—of his soul's ambition—be realized? A quiver like an angel's breath breathes over the receiving instruments, and the delicate recorder begins to move, low as a whisper of a dying child at first, but in half a minute gaining strength. The secret of the ages was being yielded grudgingly, as it were, to the listening ear of the high priest of electrical science—Signor Marconi. The sounds were now distinct, and what ravishing music they made when the three dots of that letter S (. . .) were repeated, GROWING STRONGER EACH TIME. A new spirit was born to science with a tip of its wing on each side of the ocean. The old Atlantic cable heard the news; quivered and groaned. Telegraph cable stocks slumped on the market Saturday evening, and there was fever heat excitement among business men. As soon as Signor Marconi had made up his mind there was no doubt about the success of his experiment, he called on his excellency Governor Boyle Saturday afternoon and gave him the first information which was immediately cabled to THE BRITISH GOVERNMENT AND THE ADMIRALTY. Among foreign newspaper correspondents, Mr. T.J. Murphy was the first to get a message, one hundred and fifty words off to the New York Journal, and M.A. Devine to the Montreal Star. Both these papers cabled yesterday for five hundred additional words, and photographs of Signal Hill, etc. All the big newspapers sent for special despatches, the news being regarded as the most important that has ever fallen on the world of science. Mr. Marconi said last night "Some of the New York people refuse to believe it", well, that's not to be wondered at. No doubt they will believe by and by.

Pauline Johnson on the Blackfoots, 1902

PAULINE JOHNSON

Mohawk poet Pauline Johnson was hugely popular in Canada. This newspaper piece recounts her trip west on the Canadian Pacific Railway and the passengers' encounter with Blackfoot Indians.

Traffic had congested but 24 hours when the C.P.R. took us over as its guests. For a week it has "boarded" thousands of transients at the very best hotels, the dining cars, the cafes. The company has spared no pains, no money, so long as their patrons could be royally treated. At Gleichen more than six hundred of us were the guests of the C.P.R. for two days. At Calgary 800, at Banff and at Field another five or six hundred—all treated like Princes at the expense of the road that is hourly dropping unestimated thousands. One million dollars will hardly cover the loss, and yet every official smiles through it all, and the public are treated with a consideration open-handed enough to almost border on extravagance, and even the ever-exacting American tourist remarked loudly that after "free meals" had been declared to the traveling colony at Gleichen neither service nor menu in the two dining cars, "St. Cloud" and "Frogmore," fell off one jot.

An Interesting Discovery.

But just here a delightful surprise awaited us all, an indefatigable Detroiter who wandered up prairie trails, ever searching for information, discovered mushrooms, of that large, luscious, shell-pink variety that only comes from wild stretches of field, and that have a flavor far more delicate and appetizing than those found in the city markets. Buckets, baskets, and even hats were requisitioned, and we supplied the dining cars for every meal with these delicacies. The Detroiter gave us impromptu lectures on edible fungi. He was a man of most extensive information, had travelled the world over and kept his eyes open, but he told us he had never seen such quantities of mushrooms together as these. We gathered bushels of them daily. I hardly think the Indians eat these fungi, or else the enormous camp of Blackfoots would have been up betimes and secured our breakfasts while we yet dozed in comfortable berths, for their tepees arose, smoke-tipped and conical, not 500 yards from the siding where we lay. The Indians made a good thing out of the c.p.r. mishaps, for the tourists hired horses from them at "a dollar a ride," and even the tender-foot would vault into the Mexican saddle and ride away across the prairie. The sturdy, shaggy inappi laying back on his ears and loping away with the long, clean, rocking motion never seen except in the prairie-bred animal. Only one lamentable accident occurred, in the evening, when we had base-ball and horse races. In the latter a fine gray pony, the property of a splen-didly handsome blanket and buckskin clad Blackfoot, plunged into a badger hole, fell, and instantly expired with a broken neck. And just here it is time to refute an aspersion too frequently laid upon our wilder Indian tribes of the great west. The prejudiced white man will tell you that the Indians will eat anything, animals that die of disease, unclean portions of meat, etc. The detractors of the redman, and there were plenty of them aboard, assured the crowd that "the Indians will have a great pow-wow, and the feast of the dead horse" over the unlucky animal that lay near the track. But the next morning and the next night, and yet another morning came and waned, and the horse lay where it had fallen, and the Blackfoot braves shook their heads when asked about a "feast." A goodly collection was taken up for the owner, which reward he deserved, as his steed had expired in making "a white man's holiday."

Class Distinctions.

This identical brave exhibited great appreciation of class distinctions. A curious Chinaman came forth from his car and a tourist asked the Black-foot: "Is this your brother?" indicating the Mongolian. Such scorn and hauteur as the reply "No" expressed, such a lifting of the red chin, and indig-nant glance. It amazed some, but I was proud of my color-cousin of the prairie, and of his fine old aristocratic red blood, that has come down through the centuries to pulse in his conservative veins. We visited the camp; a group of some dozen tepees, neat, orderly and picturesque, were bunched against the southern rim of the prairie. Great herds of fat cattle and excellent ponies grazed near by, for the Blackfoot is a thrifty person, and his wife is a marvel of dexterity in needlework. Beside every tepee was a travois, the peculiar vehicle that supplies the place of a cart. It is a fixture like two shafts, fastened at the lower end by a horizontal pole, firmly lashed in place by deer sinew. An immense amount of duffle can be stowed on this contrivance, and when the band "treks" the clothing, utensils, tepees and the smaller children are all packed atop the travois, a horse or dog is harnessed between the shafts, and the cavalcade starts up the trail.

Inside the Tepees.

The interior of the tepees was a delight. A fire burned in the centre, the smoke ascending through the apex of the canvas. Beautiful beadwork, buckskin garments, fringed and ornamented elaborately, hung about in profusion. Well-blanketed women cared for tiny children, whose painted cheeks glowed vermillion and yellow in the fire and sunshine. The gay coloring of the tepees, the silently-moving, graceful figures of the red folk, the sleek, fat herds, the camp fires, and the glorious carpet of coral-colored prairie flowers, the over-hanging blue of the wide territorial skies, the far-off Rockies, with their snowy coronets, made a picture beyond the limitations of the artist's brush or pen, and always and ever the vivid scarlet of the tunics of the Mounted Police. We sighed a keen regret when the engineer sounded a long series of whistles to get us aboard, for word had been flashed from Calgary that the Bow River had been conquered and that our 48-hour blockade was broken.

The Crack Shot of the Empire

UNKNOWN

The crack shot of the British Empire, the man who had competed against the best marksmen gathered together under the British flag, and who had defeated them all, Private S.J. Perry, formerly of F Company, Royal Grenadiers. Toronto gave a warm welcome home last night. The winner of the King's Prize at Bisley, whose keen eye and steady nerve won for him the most coveted trophy that an Imperial marksman can strive for, accepted the honors showered upon him with characteristic modesty, and even made light of the victory which has made the name of Pte. Perry familiar in Great Britain and her colonies, and has proved, too, that in Canada lives the best shot in his Majesty's dominions.

"How long is it since you commenced shooting?" was asked Pte. Perry last night as he stood in the Union Station, surrounded by questioning relatives and admiring friends.

"Oh, I don't know," he replied pleasantly. "I guess it was when I had my first pea-shooter."

Dressed in his khaki uniform, that of the Dominion Rifle Association at Bisley, with the soft slouch hat thrown back on his head, bronzed of countenance, and looking the picture of health, Pte. Perry faced the thousands of Toronto's people, men, women and children—more women than men, by the way—who had gathered to do him honor. He came in by the Canadian Pacific train due at 7:30 last evening, and long before that time Front street from Bay to Simcoe, and all the avenues leading to the station, were black with the crowds that were patiently awaiting the sight of King's Prize winner.

Thousands of Militiamen.

The military arrangements for the street parade, as previously adopted, were carried out perfectly. Lined up on Front street were the Governor-General's Body Guard and band, the Toronto Light Horse (dismounted), the 9th Field Battery, the Queen's Own Rifles and band, the Cadet Band, the Army Service Corps and the veterans. Hamilton had sent to Toronto the 91st Highlanders, under command of Lieut. Col. Logie; the 13th Regiment, under command of Lieut.-Col. Stoneman; the 4th Field Battery, under command of Major Tidswell, and the Army Medical Corps, under command of Major Rennie. The 91st Highlanders, which is the newly-formed regiment in Hamilton, excited considerable comment and admiration here, their handsome costume being quite a novelty to the thousands who saw them marching through the streets, headed by their pipe band. Inspector Hall had a squad of thirty policemen to look after the crowds along the line of march, and the men at the Union Station were all needed, for after the announcement that "the train is in" there was a mighty cheer from the crowd, and a general rush was made towards the station. The police kept the crowd back, however, and only a privileged few were allowed on the lower platform.

Making a Life on the Prairies, 1903

C. SCHACK

I came to Calgary from Germany in October, 1893, with empty pockets, and when the first spring arrived I was sixty dollars in debt. I lived in Calgary for three years, earning enough money to buy a few head of cattle, which I gave out on shares. I cannot say that this was a success, as parties did not look after them properly, so I made up my mind to get a farm of my own, and I must say I did not like Canada very much until then.

I homesteaded a quarter section and bought another quarter section for which I could only make a small payment and gave a mortgage for the balance, which I paid as it became due. I started with five cows and three small horses. My farm was in a bad state of cultivation, the man I bought the farm from advised me not to do any farming at all as it would not pay, but it was no wonder it would not pay: four years in succession grain had been sown on the stubble on the same piece of ground, and as I bought the place in the beginning of May, I could only plow a little, the balance I sowed on the old stubble for the fifth year. The grain came up well, but soon rose bushes and weeds covered all of it; the grain at that time was about five inches high, the weeds ten inches. I set the mower to work and cut the whole clean to the ground. My neighbors were laughing at my proceeding, but when I threshed I got fifty bushels of oats to the Acre. Since then I have farmed every year from one hundred to one hundred and twenty acres and had never any less than seventy bushels of oats to the acre.

I have so far only spoken of oats, but do not mean that this is the only crop grown here; in fact, I have seen splendid fields of spring wheat yielding fifty bushels No. 1 to the acre; also barley has proven a great crop, as it has yielded between forty to fifty bushels to the acre. The best of all this country is good for is fall wheat. I have watched my neighbors for the last four years raising fall wheat, and came to the conclusion that this is the crop for the future. This fall I have sown forty acres and have made preparations to sow three hundred acres next fall. This may sound big, but I will only show my confidence in wheat growing. I may state that my farm today consists of six hundred and forty acres of land, with buildings worth six thousand dollars. I keep now, over one hundred head of cattle, thirty head of mostly Clyde horses. I intended to sell this place, and asked fifteen thousand dollars. I was offered fourteen thousand by Mr. Henderson, of Sarnia, Ont., but would not let it go. Besides this farm, I own another six hundred and forty acres of land and considerable town property, and feel satisfied with my earnings for the last ten years.

Sir Wilfrid Laurier on the United States

SIR WILFRID LAURIER

We live by the side of a nation . . . a nation for which I have the greatest admiration, but whose example I would not take in everything, in whose schools for fear that Christian dogmas in which all do not believe might be taught, Christian morals are not taught. When I compare these two countries, when I compare Canada with the United States, when I compare the states of the two nations, when I think upon their future, when I observe the social condition of civil society in each of them and when I observe in this country of ours, a total absence of lynchings and an almost total absence of divorces and murders, for my part, I thank heaven that we are living in a country where the young children of the land are taught Christian morals and Christian dogmas. Either the American system is wrong or the Canadian system is wrong. For my part I say and I say it without hesitation. Time will show that we are in the right, and in this instance as in many others, I have an abiding faith in the institutions of my own country.

Dining in the West

HOWARD A. KENNEDY

The Westerner "lives well." That is to say, he has plenty of good food; but he does not always make the best use of it, and in feeding, if in little else, I should not advise old-country folk to adopt the new-country ways in a hurry. The American, and the Canadian also, generally take too much meat, made as indigestible as possible in the frying pan; and they scarcely draw that distinction between summer and winter diet which the climate suggests. They also take too much tea. I have travelled over the prairie with an old freighter who fed himself—and me, as I remember with pain—at every halt, making five times a day, on fried salt pork, bread, and boiled tea. The western farmer is not a primitive barbarian like that, but he still boils his tea, and the copper-bottomed tea-pot is left simmering indefinitely on the stove for casual use.

As a rule, however, there is plenty of variety in the farmer's bill of fare. He takes porridge and milk for breakfast as well as his fried pork or beef-steak, salt pork being chiefly used in summer and fresh frozen beef in winter. Many of the Americans come in with a habit of taking coffee, but soon fall in with the ways of the country and give it up for tea. Bread making is not as common an art as it should be, and thick bannocks or scones are commonly used when there is no baker within reach. For dinner, besides the regulation meat and potatoes, and bread and butter and tea, the Canadians, and of course the Americans, will have their round flat pies, containing fruit sandwiched between the upper and under crust—an article known distinctively as American, but exactly similar to the pies I have seen exposed for sale by market women in the old country. There will also be plenty of stewed fruit; either the fresh barrelled apples bought by the well-to-do farmer, or dried apples and apricots, or the small fruits that grow wild almost all over the West, such as strawberries, raspberries, black and red currants, gooseberries, chokecherries, huckleberries, and cranberries. The supper, taken as soon as the day's work is done, is practically a repetition of the breakfast or dinner, with the porridge perhaps left out. Alcoholic drinks are very seldom used or even kept in the house; and, though many a Westerner who abstains at home will not refuse a nip when he goes to town, total abstinence is much more common out there than in the old country.

The Railway Comes to Lloydminster

MRS. W. RENDALL

Access to the railway meant the difference between life and stagnation for Canadian towns. In 1905, the Canadian Northern Railway came to Lloydminster, Alberta.

Lloydminster is now quite a little town, the rail is up and our station is quite a pretty addition to the town. Little did I think that the whistle of an engine would ever sound so sweet. The passenger service is not properly organized yet as the line is still in the hands of the construction party, but, as soon as the line is completed and handed over to the c.n.r. company, then we shall have a regular service. It is hard for you in the old country, surrounded by every comfort and luxury, to realize in the smallest degree what we have all been put through the past two years in comparative isolation, sometimes without the slightest idea of what was going on in the outside world for a fortnight or three weeks together. For the winter we have been comparatively at the mercy of the weather for news and provisions. All have had to come by road from Saskatoon, and, when they did come, the price of the commonest necessaries was enough to make the pluckiest feel downhearted when we saw the capital we had thought was ample to carry us on for a year or so vanishing like dust almost in bare living. "It will be different when the train is in" became the stock phrase. It was weary waiting and many of us had almost lost heart until one day we heard the rails were laid within two miles of Lloydminster, and, in less than a week later, the first train steamed into Lloydminster. Since then there has been quite a revolution in the price of everything. Flour for which we had paid 5 dollars per 100 lb. bag is now $2.80 top price, and everything else in proportion. Lumber, too, is coming down in price. Town lots have been on the market and bought at high prices. Everyone is now building lumber houses instead of the log shack of the "old timers", bricks, too, are being extensively used for building, and this winter will probably be a pretty severe test as to whether they will stand the climate or no. To those like ourselves, who were among the first to arrive up in the Colony in May 1903 when at most one dozen tents were all that could be seen on the bare prairies, but now large Hotels are in course of erection, and there are stores of all kinds, a fine building for the Branch of the Canadian Bank of Commerce, Drugstore, printing office from which is issued weekly our newsy little paper, the "Lloydminster Times", it is just marvellous. This season has been a good season on the whole for the harvest, but everything has to be done with such a rush, the summer season is so short. One needs an infinite amount of patience in this climate, the late and early frosts play awful havoc. This year we have had 50 acres under cultivation. . . .

The Salvation Army Takes Over Joe Beef's Saloon, Montreal

W.H. DAVIES

The lure of the open road after the turn of the 20th century attracted some adventurers. Davies recorded his experiences, including this account of Montreal.

Now, once upon a time, there lived a man known by the name of Joe Beef, who kept a saloon in Montreal, supplying his customers with a good free lunch all day, and a hot beef stew being the mid-day dish. There was not a tramp throughout the length and breadth of the North American

Continent, who had not heard of this and a goodly number had at one time or another patronised his establishment. Often had I heard of this famous hostelry for the poor and needy, and the flavour of its stew discussed by old travellers in the far States of the South. When I thought of this, I knew that a companion for any part of America could most certainly be found on this man's premises, and I would there hear much valuable information as to the road I was about to travel... I was strolling along with these thoughts, when I met the man of my desire, leaning lazily against a post. Not wishing to accost him outright, and yet eager for his conversation, I stood beside him lighting my pipe, striking several matches for this purpose and failing owing to the wind blowing in small gusts. Seeing my dilemma, the man quickly produced matches of his own, and, striking one, held it lighted between the palms of his hands, leaving just enough space for the bowl of my pipe to enter. For this I thanked him, and secondly, invited him to a drink, asking him where we should go, being in hopes he would mention Joe Beef. "Well," he answered, pointing to the opposite corner, "the nearest place is French Marie's." We entered that place and, in the course of conversation, I told him how I had beat my way from state to state, but that this was my first experience in Canada. "The United States," said this man sagely, "are nearly played out, and of late years there are far too many travellers there. You will find the Canadian roads better to beat, and the people's hearts easier to impress, for they are not overrun. When did you get here?" Knowing that this man was under the impression that I had just beat my way into Canada from the States, and not willing to undeceive him, I answered quickly "This morning," and for a time changed the conversation into a praise of the beer. "Where are you going to sleep?" he asked. "Meet me here in half an hour, after I have begged the price of my bed, and a drink or two—and we will both go to Joe Beef's, where I have been for this last week." Not wishing to lose sight of this man, I told him that my pocket could maintain the two of us until the next day. "All right," said he, appearing much relieved, "We will go at once and settle for our beds, and come out for an hour or so this evening." Leaving French Marie's we walked beside the river for some distance, when my companion halted before a building, which I knew must be Joe Beef's, having just seen two seedy looking travellers entering. We followed, and to my surprise, I saw it was a rather clean looking restaurant with several long tables, with seats and a long bar on which the food was served. But what surprised me most was to see a number of Salvation Army men and officers in charge of this place. Without saying a word to my companion, I took a seat at one of the tables, to order a beef stew, asking him what he would have, and, for his sake, the order was doubled. "When Joe Beef kept this place," whispered my companion, "he was a true friend to travellers, but you don't get much out of the people except you pay for it!"

Although I winked at him, as though the same thoughts were mine, I noticed that the meals were well worth what was charged for them, and, in after days, I often compared this place favourably with similar institutions in London, that were under the same management, and where men did not get the worth of their money.

The Collapse of the Québec Bridge, 1907

ANONYMOUS

END OF QUEBEC'S NEW BRIDGE COLLAPSED: OVER EIGHTY WORKMEN MET TERRIBLE FATE.

An Awful Calamity on World's Greatest Bridge, in Course of Construction.

STEEL STRUCTURE FELL WITHOUT ANY WARNING.

Locomotive and Three Cars of Iron on Bridge at Time of the Catastrophe.

Many Crushed to Death, While Others Were Drowned in the St. Lawrence—Number of Workmen Were From United States—Heartrending Scenes Around Place of Disaster—Bodies Being Recovered—Confidence May be Destroyed in the Gigantic Enterprise, Which Was the Hope of Quebec—Navigation Unimpeded.

(Special Despatch to the Globe.)

The Dead	84
Bodies Recovered	16
Money Loss	$1,500,000

Quebec, Aug. 29.—One of the most terrible disasters in the history of bridge building in America took place at 5:45 o'clock this afternoon at the Quebec bridge, five miles up the river from this city, when the south anchor column and the 800 feet of the cantilever span projecting from it over the river collapsed, and carried down with it scores of the workmen who were engaged in the operations. The bridge structure is the greatest of its sort in the world, and the survivors of the disaster speak in terrified tones of the fearful sights and sounds when thousands of tons of steel, with a grinding noise quite indescribable, crashed down into the river. The disaster was utterly unexpected. At one moment the men were swinging beams into position and rivetting them, and at the next the vast mass was hurtling down with the poor fellows clinging to it or crushed beneath the wreckage long before the river received them.

At the moment of writing the total number of dead can only be roughly estimated, and estimates range from eighty to over ninety men, the greater number being citizens of the United States and employees of the Phoenix Bridge Company, the contractors. In the vicinity of the disaster a big rescue corps is at work recovering the dead and aiding the injured. Sixteen bodies have been recovered. Two families have lost three members each, and in two homes three dead bodies lie side by side, while in one of them a fourth member of the family lies injured. The bulk of the injured are being transferred to the hospital at Levis.

The cause of the disaster is as yet unexplained, but survivors agree in saying that it occurred at the moment when a locomotive with three cars of steel went out upon the bridge.

According to latest reports this calamity will not interfere with the navigation of the St. Lawrence channel. Since the bridge fell vessels have already been sent through to ascertain the exact situation. The loss is estimated at $1,500,000.

Eighty-four Men Lost.

It will probably be found that eighty-four men have lost their lives in the disaster. The bridge fell exactly at twenty-three minutes to six this evening. Just as many of the workmen were preparing to leave. It was, however, so horribly effective in wiping out the lives of the men employed on it that very little is known as to how the disaster happened, and those who are left are so completely benumbed by the horror of the situation that they can do little to aid.

The Southern End.

It was the southern extension of the bridge which collapsed, and this was rapidly nearing the zenith of the immense steel arch which was to span the river. For eight hundred feet from the shore the massive steel structure reared an arch with no support but the piers from the shore and one pier erected in the river a hundred or more feet from the shore, while the outward extremity was 180 feet above the water.

Shook the Neighborhood.

Suddenly those on the northern shore saw the end of the half arch bend down a little and a moment later the whole enormous fabric began to break, slowly at first, then with a terrific crash, which was plainly heard in Quebec, and which shook the whole countryside so much so that the inhabitants rushed out of their houses, thinking that an earthquake had happened.

Eight Men Escaped.

At the time of the collapse it is estimated there were ninety-two men working on the bridge. Of these eight have been so far rescued alive, being picked up immediately after the disaster by boats. Of the other eighty-four, so far sixteen have been recovered, all dead, and it is feared that all the rest or most of them have been either drowned or crushed by the falling girders.

Wounded Pinned in the Wreckage.

The horror of the situation is increased by the fact that there are a number of wounded men pinned in the wreckage near the shore. Their groans and shrieks can be plainly heard by the anxious crowds who are waiting at the water's edge, but nothing so far can be done to rescue them or relieve their sufferings in the slightest degree. There are no searchlights available, and by the feeble light of lanterns it is impossible to even locate the sufferers, so that for the present nothing whatever can be done but leave them to their fate.

Many are Bereaved.

The awful completeness of the catastrophe seems to have paralyzed the sensibilities of everybody near the place. There is scarcely a family in the village of St. Romuald and New Liverpool that has not been bereaved, while in some cases five and six men of a single family have been killed. Driving through the villages from almost every house are heard the sounds of lamentations of women. Most of the men are gathered around the approaches to the place where the bridge was, some aiding in the efforts to rescue those who are still alive, and others waiting around for news, or helping to dispose of the bodies of the dead as they are found.

Receiving the Report.

The disaster has produced an extraordinary effect in this city, and is regarded as a national calamity. A few minutes after the crash was heard here a telephone message came from Sillery that the whole southern half of the bridge had fallen into the river. For a long time people refused to believe that such a thing was possible, and crowds gathered around the newspaper offices waiting for further news, which did not come for over an hour. Then the original report was confirmed, with the addition that practically every man working on the bridge at the time had been killed. It was known that there were about a hundred men at work on this part of the bridge, and the tidings caused the most intense anxiety, which gradually grew to a despairing certainty that one of the most terrible disasters that had ever occurred in Canada had taken place.

Cause is Unknown.

The number of the dead is variously estimated at from eighty to ninety, but the few left of the men who were working on the structure state that there were about ninety-two working on the bridge at the time of whom but eight have been taken out alive, so that in all probability the list of the dead will be about 84. Nothing is known of the cause of the disaster. There was nothing of an untoward nature reported that could give the slightest indication during the past few days that the huge structure was in a dangerous condition. It was built on such immense lines that it did not seem possible that it could break down.

All is Conjecture.

Whether it was caused by defect in the materials or by an error in the calculations of the architect is a mere matter of conjecture. The one certain fact is that where this afternoon there was almost the half of a bridge that was to have been one of the engineering wonders of the world, with a small army of mechanics and workmen, there is nothing but a mass of fantastically twisted iron and steel wreckage, and a terrible number of corpses floating down the river or crushed in between the fallen girders.

The bodies rescued so far are in a terrible state, crushed and broken until they can scarcely be recognized. Only one man was taken from the bridge alive, and he was so frightfully injured that he died a few minutes after being taken to his home. Work was going on as usual, the men being employed in placing the immense girders in position. In this work a track had been laid on the bridge and an engine with freight cars and several heavy moving cranes were employed in getting the steel into position.

Skilled Mechanics Have Perished.

Amongst the employees who met their death were a number of skilled mechanics brought by the Phoenix Bridge Co. from Pennsylvania, as well as a number from this district, while most of the labor was furnished by French-Canadians from the neighborhood, and half a hundred Indians from Caughnawaga, near Montreal. Few of these escaped, except six of the Indians, who had a dispute with their foreman this morning and quit at noon. The survivors state that some thirty Indians were killed, while the six who left the work were saved. These were John Spleen, Louis Canadian, Thomas Montour, Dominick McComber, Alex Beauvais and John Morton, all of Caughnawaga. Several Government tugs will leave for the scene of the disaster in the morning, and preparations will be made for finding as many of the bodies as possible, while necessary arrangements will also be made to prepare for an examination which will allot the responsibility for the disaster. . . .

Was It Engineer's Error?

Mr. M.P. Davis of Ottawa, however, who was the contractor for the anchor pier, states that this is still in good condition. There are only two choices. Either the engineer miscalculated the powers of resistance of iron, steel and stone in preparing his plans and specifications or the contractors did not secure perfect materials. This will be decided later when the Government inquiry is held, which must inevitably start in a few days.

Election Campaigning in Newfoundland, 1909

MAJOR PETER CASHIN

In this election (1909), my uncle, Louis Mullowney of Witless Bay was the driver from the Goulds to Ferryland. The messenger was Alphonsus Mullowney. Uncle Louis had a very fast horse. When he hauled out on the main road after leaving the Goulds, he noticed that he was being followed, and he recognized the individual who was following him. He was Patrick Tobin of Witless Bay, accompanied by James Burke of the same place, both strong political opponents of my father. It appears that during the course of a political meeting which my father was addressing in the open air at Witless Bay, Tobin had hidden himself under a fish flake, continually heckling and using insulting language. Father ascertained that the heckler in question was Tobin. When Uncle Louis arrived at Tors Cove on his way to Ferryland, he telegraphed my father that he was being followed by Tobin and asked him if he had any suggestions to make. Father replied immediately to Uncle Louis, telling him that when he arrived at Cape Broyle he should drive right over into our back yard. He figured that Tobin would follow Uncle Louis and he figured right. Prior to the arrival of the two horses and carriages, Cashin sent Jack Harvey, who was then working with us, for the local police officer. At that time the police officer in question was Constable Thomas Lynch, who was highly respected in the community. He told Lynch that he wanted him to look after the ballot boxes when they arrived, as my uncle would be staying at Cape Broyle for a cup of tea. We knew that it would take an hour or a little more for these two horses to come from Tors Cove. Shortly before the expiration of an hour, father ordered me to light the lantern. It was late at night and there was no electric light along the shore at that time. Finally we heard the horses come down over the hill, and eventually both of them arrived in our back yard. I accompanied father out into the yard with the lantern, so that he could see who the people were. The first arrival was my uncle with the official messenger. Then Tobin and his friend Burke arrived. Father asked Uncle Louis what was all this about, and he replied that Pat Tobin and Jimmy Burke had been following him all night. At once Father went to Tobin's carriage. I held the lantern so that he could see both Tobin and Burke. Immediately he asked them what they were doing on his property, whilst at the same time he reached up and grabbed Tobin by the collar, pulled him out of the carriage and gave him an awful beating. He hit Tobin several times, knocking down a new fence which was being erected. Burke, who was just a little man, started crying and bawling, saying, "Oh, Mr. Cashin, do not do this." Then father took hold of Burke, hit him a few times, and finally threw him at Tobin. Following this, he threw both Tobin and Burke back into their carriage and told them in no uncertain language to get out of his yard. They proceeded to Ferryland where the district magistrate, at that time Dr. Freebairn, was located. They wanted to take action against father for assault. I understand that Dr. Freebairn told them that they had no legal case, as they had trespassed on Cashin's property. These two individuals (Tobin and Burke) stayed in Ferryland all night. The following day, they procured the protection of Constable Cleary of Ferryland to take them through Cape Broyle. They were afraid to drive through the settlement on their own in case Cashin would again attack them. Tobin certainly suffered for the personal insults he had thrown at father at that particular public meeting in Witless Bay. On the other hand, it was just another example of the violent temper with which my respected father was unfortunately afflicted. He was at that time a minister of the Crown, and in my personal view, now that I have become, as it were, indoctrinated in the hurly burly of political life, I consider that father would have treated poor Tobin and Burke with greater effect, if he had completely ignored them. It certainly would have been more dignified on his part.

A Home Helper on an Alberta Ranch, 1911

ANONYMOUS

Such is the demand for helps in the West that no sooner had the writer arrived at her destination (a Women's Welcome Hostel in a large Western town) than she was almost literally snapped up by a rancher, handed in to his democrat (a two-seated rig) with her boxes, and forthwith driven fifteen miles to his horse ranch, consisting of a section and a half (960 acres) of land with—not a log hut—but a two-storied house built of the cleaner and more easily manipulated lumber. The building sits, as it were, on the prairie, for ranchers have no time to surround their homes with flower gardens, there are no trees to speak of in Southern Alberta, though a belt of young poplars is planted in the vicinity of the house as a wind-break, and the vegetable patch is situated a short distance away.

As the help enters the house she must live up to her character for adaptability, vouched for in her emigration papers, for the doorstep is represented by two ill-balanced crates and unless she treads warily with due regard to the centre of gravity, she will disarrange the makeshift masonry and herself sustain a nasty fall.

It is already dark, and while her employer unhitches the horses she makes acquaintance with his wife who has a few weeks' old baby—heralded by neither doctor nor nurse—and two elder children who share with their father the sleeping accommodation offered by three chairs and a box ottoman, while the mother occupies the bed.

The planning of the house is ambitious. It is large, even for that part of the country where the ranchers are fairly prosperous, for the owners have advanced ideas on the subject and value the admiration of their neighbours. Unfortunately, however, a series of indifferent harvests (horse ranchers are every year depending more and more on grain for their livelihood) followed the initial stages of house-building so that only the actual necessaries in the way of walls and floors are completed. Few of the rooms have doors, the front stairs are not put in, gaping apertures are protected by laths of wood, and there is as yet no attempt at sanitation.

The help's room is upstairs and is a fairly large one. It is provided with a bed and bedding and a jug and basin on a trestle—nothing else. A "mirror" is brought from town for her later. This aid to toilet reflects her image it is true, but the image appears upwards and sideways at once, as it were, and has been happily described as "the sea-sick kind." The hired men (they are now cow-boys only in name), also sleep upstairs. Their room is provided with one bedstead and one rug but as they never appear to remove their clothes perhaps other furniture would be superfluous. One is an East-Ender, sober and industrious, but aggressively talkative and somewhat coarse in behaviour. The other is a Swede, also a hard worker but unfortunately addicted to bouts of intemperance. It was said that his previous companions (he had worked with a bridge-gang) had corrupted his morals.

With the first stream of sunlight the help must be up to prepare the six o'clock breakfast, to strain the milk brought in by the men who have risen earlier, scald the cans, etc.

The kitchen range is a delightful fresh acquaintance to the new-comer. It is square, bright-looking, standing out into the room and constructed to burn either wood or coal. The latter is seldom used as old wooden posts are nearly always available for fuel in default of fresh logs, and coal is frequently prohibitive in price. Some of the ranchers among the hills have coal on their own "place" which they dig out of the ground but this is by no means usual.

Breakfast consists of porridge (invariably of porridge and a great deal of it) also home-cured bacon, home made bread, and butter churned on the ranch. Dinner is at twelve and supper, or what we should call high tea, about seven. It need scarcely be explained that the cuisine depends solely on the skill of the housewife and when it is realised that her duties also comprise cleaning, laundry work, mending and making clothes, seeing after the children, besides social duties and such other details as curing a pig, pickling meat, and occasionally helping the men outside during the busy times of haying and harvesting, the magnitude of her work may be appreciated.

The help fresh from "the old country" as they say out there, must not be shocked at the sight of the master of the house and his hired men performing their ablutions,—face and hands that is to say, no more extended cleansing process ever appears to take place and combing their hair in the kitchen in close proximity to, and accompanying, her preparations for dinner. Shaving on Sundays or preceding a visit to town also takes place in the kitchen, indeed that apartment witnesses all that occurs in the house, for where labour is scarce and highly paid considerations of time and labour saving have to be borne in mind.

Inside the door of every ranch is placed a pail of water so that, in hot weather thirsty incomers may conveniently take a pull at the "dipper." A supply of water is generally kept handy in pails as the well is outside the house. Only a few of the more well-to-do farmers have a windmill to pump a supply to the house.

The dining-room, if there is one, is only used when company is expected. On these occasions the conduct of the whole house undergoes change. Extra sweeping and dusting takes place, the children are washed and their hair brushed, quantities of cakes and lemon pies are baked—even table napkins are provided for the guests who may have driven some twenty or thirty miles by buggy or on horseback.

The days are busy. Washing up descends to a mere detail, even after ten or twelve people. Cleaning must be done: not scrubbing, for a scrubbing brush appears to be an unknown article in the West. Vegetables must be got in from the garden—the men have probably forgotten to do it and they must not be disturbed in their work. One whisk is used for sweeping the whole house. Multiplication of utensils is expensive and takes time. This light whisk is effective and thoroughly adapted to the rough floors of the country. Hair brushes are practically never seen. Perhaps a consignment of plums or peaches bought in town must be "put away" in sealers, that is, bottled for future use. The day has not yet come when Alberta can grow fruit although, with characteristic optimism, Canadians talk of the time when vineyards will alternate with tracts of corn. Dinner must be cooked, but not dished up till the men appear in sight for they are apt to be unpunctual. Here is opportunity for an exhibition of dexterity on the part of the help who has not been brought up to her job. Getting heated and flushed over refractory baking tins and saucepans she must still appear neat, cool, and smiling at her place at table without undue delay and must, let us hope with no exhibition of greediness, be the first to lay down her knife and fork in order that she may clear away the dishes and produce the second course. Her moral character also undergoes training for she must take in good part any sarcastic remarks as to the lack or superabundance of seasoning in the food and remain imperturbable though the spoilt son of the house willfully throws his plate of gravy on the table-cloth which has been washed and ironed with so much care the day before.

If it be washing day the water must all be fetched in pails and boiled up on the stove to fill the washing machine, the working of which furnishes a rigorous and prolonged course of physical exercises. The help must learn to wriggle under barbed wire fencing without coming in contact with it. All fencing is of barbed wire. What one has to fetch is almost invariably on the other side of a fence; and as there is little time for mending the large triangular tears inflicted by the wire, experience breeds care.

The reader will have already realised how necessary it is for the intending emigrant to be *strong*. She must never complain of headache or fatigue or she will be dubbed a grumbler and her character will suffer for all time when she is discussed by her mistress. She must always be ready, and willing to undertake any oddments in the way of work that may occur and if she carry with apparent ease heavy weights such as pails of milk and cream and baskets of clothes she will win much approbation from her employers, who, having squeezed her fifteen or twenty dollars a month salary from none too large an income, will flatter themselves that their money has not been badly invested.

It must not be supposed for a moment, however that the health of the emigrant will suffer by such a life of manual work. On the contrary it will probably improve. The air is magnificent, buoyant and exhilarating to a degree. The sun shines practically all day and every day and in summer time, however hot the day may be, the nights are cool and bracing. She will find her appetite improving to a surprising extent in spite of plain, frequently unappetising menu. Fresh beef is not always obtainable—or is too extravagant fare for farmers, so veal, fresh or corned takes its place, or pickled pork. Bacon is a great stand-by and frequently for many weeks together constitutes the sole form of meat. Should the bacon by chance have become maggoty through an unperceived hole in the sack in which it has been hung—well, is it to be expected that a large piece should be wasted?

Society? The help will find that the ranchers of Alberta are of many nationalities and of every class from the newly married couple financed from home and playing at ranching, who choose their window curtains from Harrod's latest price list to the genuine pioneer, the poor man who, having collected his experience as a hired man, takes up a homestead (free grant of 160 acres) in the north, and after building the most primitive of shacks, sets to work, through long and laborious days to clear the land of timber, brush and stone with the aid of axe and pick alone.

The home help will doubtless before starting have settled in her own mind that the better the class of people with whom she finds employment, the greater her comfort and happiness. This is so to a certain extent, but she must not imagine that her work will be proportionately lighter. Far from it. Ranchers' wives employ helps, not because they desire a refined and pleasant companion, but either because they are too delicate to do their own work, in which case all the work falls to the lot of the hired lady,

or because they are rich enough to allow themselves more leisure for visiting and seeing after the children, in which case the hired lady has to take
the heavy end of the work, or what would be called over here, the menial
tasks. Widowers with children pay fairly high salaries for housekeepers
—about thirty dollars a month—but the position is harder and more
responsible....

Life in the West, for women at any rate, is very hard and, like most
hard things, very useful. It is also very fascinating and the writer's advice
to intending home helps is "Go, but first divest yourself of all your present ideas of the niceties of life." Keep your ideals, they are good things to
keep by one though it may not always be possible to coin them into such
small change as daily washing up, peeling potatoes and cleaning floors.
And do not for a moment flatter yourself that culture will be of any financial
value to yourself.

There is no particular prospect for a help other than matrimony,
which is a strong, a very strong, probability, and it may also be possible to
"start something" with a few years' savings and make a success of it, but
there is surely very great satisfaction in being where one is most wanted.
Canada needs women very, very badly and the women whom the West
needs must be *strong and energetic*—but not too cultured.

Nellie McClung on Discrimination Against Women

NELLIE MCCLUNG

"I remember one day when I was leaving for a ten-day lecture tour I
bought an Accident Insurance Policy for five thousand dollars at the railway wicket, paying two dollars and a half for ten days' insurance", wrote
the famous western feminist and author. "I had often done this before but
had never really read the blue slip which I had received. But on this day I
went over it carefully. It contained some excellent clauses, all beginning:
'If the insured be male.' It told how much he would be paid in case of total
disability, partial disability, the loss of a hand or a foot or an eye, but always
the sentence began in that ominous way: 'If the insured be male.' I wondered what the company had for me. On the other side of the slip I found
it. In a little enclosure, fenced off in black, as if someone were already
dead, appeared this inscription:

"'Females are insured against death only.'

"When I went back to the office I sought out the man who had sold
me the policy and laid the matter before him.

"'Why is it,' I asked, 'that you take a woman's money and give her
lower protection than you give men?'

"He said he didn't know anything about it, but he would find somebody who might know. The next man assured me that he didn't know that

women ever bought accident policies. He didn't know they could buy them, but he would take me in to see Mr. Brown; Mr. Brown would know. Mr. Brown did know. Mr. Brown knew so well he was rather impatient with me for asking.

"'Don't you know,' said Mr. Brown severely, taking off his glasses, as if to let his brain cool, 'that women are much more highly sensitized than men, and would be more easily hurt in an accident, they would be a victim of pure nerves, would like nothing better than to lie in bed for a week or two, and draw her seven-fifty a week. there would be no end of trouble.'

"'But, Mr. Brown,' I said 'what about the clause relating to the loss of hand or foot? You would not be altogether dependent on the woman's testimony in that, would you? You could check them up if they are pretending, could you not?'

"Mr. Brown's face indicated that he couldn't be bothered answering any more foolish questions. He put on his glasses, and I knew I was being dismissed. I thanked Mr. Brown for his information and told him that I hoped to have an opportunity of bringing the matter before the next convention of insurance men.

"Mr. Brown looked up then quickly.

"'Have the insurance men invited you to speak to them?' he asked sharply.

"'No,' I answered truthfully. 'They haven't. But they will.'"

The Sinking of the Titanic, *1912*

M. GRATTAN O'LEARY

> *Grattan O'Leary of the* Ottawa Journal *became one of the icons of Canadian journalism. In 1912, he was a junior reporter, and rushed to New York to interview survivors after the sinking of the* Titanic.

New York, April 19—With her band playing "Nearer My God to Thee", with gallant Capt. Smith like a true Briton standing on the bridge sublimely heroic, calm and masterful to the last, with hundreds of men and women kneeling in prayer and crying out "My God we're lost" amidst the splintering of steel, the rending of plates and shattering of girders, the proud Titanic, giantess of the sea, went to her ocean fate off the banks of Newfoundland.

This was the story of disaster and death brought to a despairing grief-stricken continent at nine o'clock last night by the woe-freighted Cunarder Carpathia.

The story she brought home was one to crush the human heart with its pathos.

It is the story of a ship of death and yet it is relieved of its gloom, as a rainbow spans a landscape, by the noble action of scores of men who freely laid down their lives that mothers, wives, and sisters might live, brightened too by the fortitude of women in the face of the most awful peril and inevitable death.

Through the courtesy and kindness of the Associated Press office here The Journal representative was enabled to secure a pass through the walls of policemen who beat back a frantic mob of almost twenty-five thousand men and women as the Carpathia, freighted with her argosy of woe, reached the dock, and from the mouths of sunken-eyed wan-faced survivors he heard the true story of how the Titanic went to her doom.

Told in disjointed, almost hysterical fashion it was an awful word picture of the calamity, full of horror, panic and confusion. As brought to this port last night, the toll of death must be placed at 1,601, and the total number of those saved at 745, the ill-fated ship having had on board 2,346 souls.

Chas. M. Hays went down with the mass of wreckage. Almost his last words were spoken to Col. Archibald Gracie, U.S.A. He seemed to have had some strange premonition of impending danger.

"The White Star, the Cunard and the Hamburg-American," said the Grand Trunk President, "are devoting their ingenuity and sole attention in vieing one with the other to attain the supremacy in luxurious ships and in making speed records. The time will soon come when this will be checked by some appalling disaster."

A few hours later the disaster came and Mr. Hays was dead.

According to the evidence of the survivors, the Titanic was steaming at about eighteen knots an hour when she crashed into the iceberg that sent her to the ocean bottom two thousand fathoms deep.

She slid upon a ledge of the icy mountain, her bow crushed and shattered into a mass of crumbled steel, hung there for a few brief moments and fell back into the water.

The awful suddenness and force of the shock exploded three of her boilers and quickly she began to go under.

It was shortly before the mystic hour of twelve.

Lights gleamed from a thousand port holes, as the sea giantess swept through the light swell. A light south-west gale was blowing. The weather was comparatively clear, the air cold and raw. It being Sunday night, most of the cabin passengers were in their staterooms and many had gone to bed, feeling secure in this last supreme effort of man to overcome the elements.

The air was still and only the steady vibration of the great mechanism in the steel pens below and the rhythmic beat of propellers out of the foaming wake behind were heard.

A few miles ahead like a white, ghost-like mountain of death and destruction, a jealous iceberg of the northern sea was silently, but quickly approaching. A minute or two later this massive body of ice which had been shrouded from the view of men in the "Crow's Nest" by a mist, seems to have suddenly risen up in the ship's pathway.

"Stop! Full speed astern!"

These were the signals immediately telegraphed the engineers.

But it was too late.

The blow of fate had fallen.

The Titanic was hurled with the force of forty-five express engines against a glacial mountain afloat.

The terrific impact racked every frame, strained every vaunted barrier of steel, crumpled the bow into a shapeless mass of broken plate and instantly without the warning of a single moment, crushed the life out of nearly two hundred of the crew who were sleeping in the forecastle, well up to the bow.

The momentum of the steamship developed from its 46,000 tons carried her well upon a hidden ledge of ice. A moment or two and she lifted on her port side, slipped from the ice, ripping and tearing her bottom plates and settling back into the sea.

And yet there was no such terrific shock from the impact felt in the cabins, as might be expected, according to the stories of the survivors. But in the engine room and stokeholds havoc was wrought. Valves were wrenched loose, steam joints broken and the huge boilers themselves trembled from the shock. Scalding steam filled every corner and the men were unable to see and were scalded to death in their steel-walled pens.

The bulkhead doors were instantly closed by a hydraulic device, but the whole structure was so weakened that this was of little avail. Rivets had been cut from plates, and water rushed in through a hundred yawning seams.

The longitudinal girders, driven back by the hammer-like blow of the collision, had loosened and started bulkheads, weakening them for the irresistible thrust of the water yet to come. Plates at the bottom were broken and bent while crossbeams were snapped as if of glass.

The great engines were wrecked and wrenched at their fastenings, and live coals were hurled from the huge furnaces burning the firemen and sending them terror-stricken for safety.

So far as the mechanism of the ship was concerned she was doomed from the first blow. Man's great engineering feat was humbled, and the might which had been Titanic was only human. Man was left to fight his battle for life practically unaided by the powers of the fabric which he had called into being.

A minute after the impact the shrieks of passengers echoed through cabins and steerage alike. Decks which had been almost deserted now teemed with human beings. The instinct of natural self preservation drove them from every hidden recess of the hulk of steel. Women with jewels worth millions gleaming on the fingers, men of international fame, immigrants who had scarcely more than the pittance required for their entrance into a new land, all were levelled into one class in scarcely the twinkling of an eye. A reign of terror was let loose.

But the blood of the Anglo-Saxon runs cold and often coldest in the time of peril and discipline soon asserted itself among the crew.

Officers quickly reassured many of the women, themselves not yet realizing the extent of the calamity to the ship. Then an explosion of one of the boilers created a new and wilder panic, and the rush for boats threatened to become a stampede. But the tradition and unwritten law of the sea must assert itself and the cry "Women and children first" was relayed from man to man.

Some of the men steerage passengers, driven to desperation through the realization of inevitable death, tried to force themselves in among the women and children, and the officers shot them down without mercy. Standing on the bridge, Captain Smith shouted directions through a megaphone.

Into the last lifeboat that was launched from the side of the ship the grim old sea dog himself lifted an infant into a seat beside its mother. As the gallant officer performed this final act of humanity, several who were already in the boat tried to force him to join them, but he turned away resolutely towards the bridge, where what he believed to be his duty called.

It was the spirit of Rodney, the spirit of Drake.

Lying over on her port side, the task of lowering boats from the davits on the starboard was a dangerous and difficult task, and yet throughout all these awful moments of anguish deeds of heroism were performed. Women threw their arms about the necks of husbands and begged that they should not be taken aboard the boats. They would prefer to remain and go down with the wreck by their husbands' sides.

But they were urged into the boats, after a last kiss and embrace, lowered down the 90 feet which separated them from the water, and quickly rowed away in the night, never again to look upon the faces of the loved ones whom they had left behind.

Many of them had been placed in the boats while in a state of prostration. Soon all the available boats would be launched and over a thousand souls remained to be saved.

The brave wireless operator had been sending forth into the uncharted regions of the air his call for aid, and this was the one surviving hope. And there were many women yet who had not, or could not be saved, for want of room in the boats available.

As the last two of these craft were being lowered over the side the lights of the saloon and cabins were suddenly extinguished.

No more could the now awe-stricken passengers depend upon electricity as their ally, and the operator was slowly and feebly calling his final "s.o.s." with what power was left in his storage batteries.

A black night of despair fell upon all. Above the din of hissing steam and babel of voices and shouts rose a woman's shriek, "O Christ, save us if Thou will."

An awful report drowned everything and shook the fast sinking ship from stern to stern as another explosion came from the boiler room. Again the remaining women shrieked in despair, and it seemed as if hell had outclimaxed itself at last.

The last, the final, boat was crowded to its utmost capacity and rowed away in the night, and some 1,600 souls were left behind. With powerful strokes the small boats were rowed away from the scene of the disaster. It was feared that they might be carried down with the suction that surely must be caused by the sinking of the wreck.

Suddenly all were thrilled when the strains of "Nearer My God to Thee" were heard and members of the ship's bands were noticed through the twilight gathered together on the after deck. The dim outline of Captain Smith was seen hanging to the bridge. He had done all any mortal could do for the safety of the 2,000 lives entrusted to his care and was prepared for the end.

It was stated by some of the survivors that the veteran captain had blown out his brains just as the ship was sinking. This, however, was very vigorously denied by a score of others. All agreed that Captain Smith showed sublime courage throughout the hours of terror and that almost equal bravery and calm judgment was displayed by the officers and crew.

Only a few of those in the boats saw the Titanic go to her ocean grave. Most of the boats were long since out of seeing distance when the once mighty liner broke in two and was swallowed up by the yawning waters while frantic men clung desperately to wreckage of every kind, now all that was left of the farthest cry in the linking of two continents.

Neptune had taken the empress of the sea captive to his hidden realm, but the night of horror had not ended for those who had escaped in the boats. The women were only half clothed in many instances and suffered terrible hardship. The awful dread that perhaps after all the shadowy call of brave wireless operators had not been heard was borne upon them as hour succeeded hour, and no steamer hove in sight. There was nothing to eat, nothing to drink and half perished, semi-hysterical with grief and fear, two of the women perished after being finally taken on board the Carpathia. Some of the boats were partially filled with water in which women stood up to their knees.

Of the two collapsible canvas boats, only one could be accounted for, although it is believed that both put out to sea. Had it not been for the lack of boats, it is doubtful if the loss of life would have been half so great. Only sixteen boats were picked up.

Some of the men tried to make rafts by tying chairs together and clinging to them but only a few were saved by this means.

Many of the survivors say that the cries for help of those left on the sinking ship were heartrending and never-to-be-forgotten. There are many rumors that in some respects the Titanic was not completed.

It is alleged that workmen were rushed to have the ship ready for the day upon which she was booked to sail and that consequently several little things were left undone. Life boats were not supplied with food and other necessities and several survivors say that had not the Carpathia received the wireless message just when she did they would have been left to drift the seas in hunger and might all have perished by starvation.

If a desperate naval battle had been fought in New York waters and the city awaited the coming of the dead and wounded from the scene of action, this city could hardly have presented a more realistic picture of war heroes than that of which the Red Cross officers were the centre and a frenzied mob of twenty thousand persons was the setting.

The uniforms of two hundred nurses and Red Cross attachés mingled in the picture with the trim garbs of the ambulance surgeons and the chaste costumes of sad-faced sisters of charity. Ten score city policemen guarded the roped cordon lighted up at intervals with green lanterns, whereby the guardians of the city's peace kept back at a distance of seventy-five feet the throng that kept pressing over-eagerly toward the pier where the Carpathia was docked.

Within the shelter of the pier sheds were huddled nearly a thousand of the friends and relatives of the rescued and the lost. To them had been issued special passes. Many of them were weeping and sobbing without restraint. Outside in the murk and drizzle of the forbidding night, stood ominous lines of ambulances to which nearly all the hospitals in the city had contributed their quota. There were black funeral vehicles from the shops of the undertakers, too, conveying their own grim message, and the city coroners were there ready to do their work.

While the long lines of wounded were being tenderly borne ashore at the pier where the Carpathia was berthed, the adjoining pier had been converted into an improvised hospital ward to which the injured were taken for treatment. There were installed all the suggestive paraphernalia of cots, stretchers, operating tables and surgical appliances, while skilled nurses with deft fingers were preparing bandages for ready use.

Through the entire section of which the new Chelsea piers are the focus, ordinary street traffic was wholly suspended and held rigidly in check by lines of police reserves who stood like sentinels guarding the reservation selected for some great field hospital.

Reaching a Prairie Homestead

JAMES M. MINIFIE

Our vehicle was no covered wagon, with canvas top strung over hoops, as depicted in western movies. It was an ordinary farm wagon, painted green. It boasted a sturdy pink running-gear, which could be used for hauling lumber, and a tough wagon-box of hickory-wood, to which two additional tiers could be fitted to hold seventy-five bushels of flax. The basic box survived years of rough trails and exposure to wind, snow, sun, and rain until it was retired to serve another term as a coal-bin. For the trip home from Morse my father brought extra horse-blankets to protect the load in case of thunder-showers. A spring seat was fixed on the wagon-box and on it was perched my mother in her neat brown tweed dress and jacket, with a brown felt hat turned up at the side, secured by a grouse-foot pin with a silver mount. My brother and I arranged ourselves as best we could over the trunks and supplies my father had bought, but it was not a very comfortable ride. We averaged three miles an hour, so it was after three o'clock by the time we pulled into the Halfway House, weary and bruised from the alternations of walking, scrambling back on the wagon, and riding. From time to time we had varied the monotony of the wagon floor by climbing onto the seat, which at least had springs, but they absorbed few of the potholes, stones, and ruts of the prairie trail.

My father stood up to drive. I was fascinated by the shouted commands "Gee" and "Haw", which I had not heard before and which meant swinging to the right or left, and a more general command which I identified as "Uriah!", but which seemed to be a short form of "Where are you?", an incitement to push into the collar and get moving. Old Mike was a willing horse, always up to his side of the whippletree, but Meg was a narrow-chested, disillusioned barren female who let her willing partner do most of the work, since he seemed to like it. Occasionally she bit him to emphasize her point. My father evened this up for Mike by adjusting the whippletree slightly, so that he had the lighter load; but they were not an easy team to drive. That was one reason my father was ready to stop so early in the afternoon....

We were up early in the morning, relieved to find that little damage had been done by the storm either to the groceries or to the trunks. The horse-blankets had deflected most of the water. On this optimistic note we set out. The rain had swollen the creek, but the consensus was that the water would not be above the axle. With that assurance my father put Mike and Meg to a trot and we splashed and bumped through. The bottom appeared to be all boulders, and I feared for the axles, but they held, and momentum carried us through and up the far bank in a terrifying rush. After four hours we stopped for sandwiches and a thermos of tea my mother had brought. Thirty-six miles south of Morse, my father warned that he was going to leave the road, such as it was, and head south-west across the prairie for the next six miles. We soon picked up a faint trail which wandered about, dodging hills and skirting sloughs, but maintaining a generally south-westerly direction. Those were the longest six miles I ever travelled. I walked most of them.

My English boots were not ideal for a long hike and I was limping by the time a peaked roof peeped over the next rise. My father warned me that this was not our house. He pulled up to let me climb aboard. As we skirted the rise we saw a two-storey house, white with green trim, and a big red barn topping a stone stable. In between the two, a dozen cows milled about, followed by a stout woman with a box in one hand and a pail in the other, who was trying to milk whichever cow stood still long enough.

"That's Mrs. Annis," my father explained. "And that black poll-Angus she's milking is our cow. Hey, there, bossie!" he shouted as we drove up. Acknowledging the greeting our cow switched her tail in Mrs. Annis's face and kicked the bucket over.

"She's a mean, miserable cow," Mrs. Annis said to my father, "and she held her milk back. Anyway it's on the ground now, and I guess there goes your cream for supper. Better let me give you some." Then, as she realized who we were, Mrs. Annis roared a welcome and asked my mother how she liked the West.

"Not very much," my mother said truthfully; it had been a poor introduction.

"After you've milked twenty cows twice a day, you'll love it!" Mrs. Annis replied. Then, repenting her flippancy, she handed half a bucket of milk up to my father and urged us all to stay for supper. We declined. We were all desperately anxious to end this interminable journey; I wanted to see our home and get everything unloaded and unpacked. I was tired of wandering about like an Arab. So my father put a halter over the cow, tied her to the wagon, and started up. She was stubborn and unwilling to follow, so I was deputed to follow her on foot and stimulate her with a switch. She responded grudgingly, and the last half-mile was a martyrdom for us both—self-inflicted in her case.

As I inquired for the hundredth time, "When shall we get there, Daddy?" we topped a small rise. "There she is," said my father with a note of pride in his voice. "Built her myself, every nail and board." He said it reverently.

On a knoll a quarter of a mile away stood a small unpainted brown shed. It was exciting, but at the same time disappointing after Annis's splendid establishment. A little to the left on another knoll was a smaller shed, the stable, snuggling against two ricks of hay. We skirted the pasture, fenced in with two strands of barbed wire. . . .

Inside, the room was dark, filled with the aroma of eggs frying in butter. There was a shiny, glittering cooking stove with a couple of saucepans, a kettle, and a frying pan; a very tall table of unpainted pine, two yellow kitchen chairs, and an empty orange-crate. Nailed to a two-by-four was a calendar for the year before from the Northwest Life Insurance Company, featuring a flight of ducks taking off from a slough. The floor was rough boards with wide cracks, innocent of paint or varnish, but showing marks of mud and manure through a dark stain. Pearson and my father hauled the two portmanteaus inside.

There was no bag, basket, or container in the shack for my father's dirty clothes, all of which had simply been thrown in a corner—all, that is, but some woollen underwear, which I found hanging on fence posts. My father explained later that last fall, after a trip to town, he discovered that he was lousy. To ensure that the house-of-his-own-building did not become infested with vermin, he stripped to the buff, hung his underwear on fence posts for the winter, had a quick dip in the slough, and pulled on a clean set. By springtime the frost had taken care of lice and nits; none of our visitors brought any visitors with them. Other homesteaders were not so lucky, but we were spared the misery of lice or bedbugs, for which in those days virtually the only insecticide was to burn the place down. Homesteaders three or four miles west of us nearly went crazy trying to get rid of bedbugs. We avoided visiting them as soon as the word got about, but if they had turned up needing shelter in a blizzard, we could not have turned them away, though we might have emphasized the attractions of barn accommodations. Fortunately our hospitality was never put to this test; the only parasite we had to beware of was an occasional tick, which Tim picked up, I suppose, from the cattle.

As soon as we got into the house, my mother started to move dirty clothing out of corners into four sacks, but the room still looked dim and dreary. . . .

The first night at home was awesome. We had expected to be oppressed by silence. Instead the night air vibrated with an orchestra of thousands of frogs, their notes swelling and falling in a rhythmic diapason that enveloped earth and sky. The pasture by the house had half a dozen little sloughs, each with its quota of frogs. It was like trying to sleep in the middle of grand opera. Above the frogs' chorus was a more sinister aria, the ululating wail of coyotes enjoying the remains of a dead horse. My brother and I shivered and snuggled closer together under the blankets on a mattress thrown on top of the flax bin. We soon learned to sleep quietly, or risk immersion in the sea of flax.

Bunkhouse Men and Booze

J. BURGON BICKERSTETH

I forget whether you have a clear idea what this place, Marlboro, consists of or not. There are a hundred and fifty men employed in installing the cement plant. A few of these are married, and have their own shacks; others are banded together in groups of two or three, and have built themselves little shacks or log houses—this is rather the more permanent element, they feed in the cookhouse, but sleep and spend the evening in their own shacks; and lastly, there are three or four bunkhouses, where the bulk of the men sleep and spend practically all their time when not at work. The bunkhouse men are of all nationalities, and the foreign element generally keeps together. Two of the bunkhouses are predominantly English-speaking.

When I am here I spend almost every evening in the camp. Take last night as an instance. After supper, which I had in my own shack, consisting of fried eggs, bread and marmalade, and tea, two or three of the men came up to help me finish the inside of the church. It is curious that one of my chief helpers has been a strong Roman Catholic. After an hour I went out, with some of the latest Edmonton and Winnipeg papers under my arm, bound for one of the English speaking bunkhouses. It had been sleeting and snowing a horrible wet snow all day, so the whole camp was inches deep in slush, mud, and standing water—it was cold and very damp.

Imagine a long low building of lumber, covered with black tar paper; it looks dingy enough. The door when opened lets out an atmosphere reeking with coal oil, bad tobacco, and wet socks. On the right are two tiers of wooden bunks, each tier consisting of two bunks side by side. The men are pretty closely packed. A bench runs along by the bunks, and this, with several boxes and tree stumps, forms the sitting accommodation. The floor is covered with mud and slush, brought in by many pairs of boots—the said boots, with the socks which belong to them, are hung up in various advantageous positions near the central heater in which a huge wood fire is roaring.

The men themselves, in various forms of *deshabillé*, are sitting and sprawling about on the benches, smoking and talking; while some are so tired with the day's work that they are already rolled up in their blankets and snoring. Round the stove they are all English-speaking, but at the far end there are three or four Italians jabbering away, and, just on my left, as I enter, are some swarthy-looking fellows who look like Spaniards. At any rate they are Dagos, which is a convenient term, and includes any dark-visaged individuals, such as Spaniards, Italians, or Galicians. As I live in the place, I knew a good many of the men, and, after distributing the papers, I stayed and had a long chat. The other night (a Sunday) we had a service in this bunkhouse. The men sang so long, I thought they would never stop, while the accompaniment was a concertina and two mouth organs, the latter played by two Baptists with more noise than discretion.

Generally speaking, the average man in a camp seems to have two great topics of conversation—whisky and women. There are some men who have spent a good part of their lives in bunkhouses, and, when the day's work is over, it is a difficult job to attract them out into any higher or more civilizing atmosphere. They are generally shy, and often ignorant and prejudiced. One can only hope to make a beginning by going into the bunkhouses, taking them good literature, getting to know them and helping them individually. Often the work seems slow, and there is little visible result.

The greatest curse of this country is undoubtedly drink. *By law* no alcoholic drink is allowed in or near a construction camp of any description, but "boose" gets in occasionally, and then fellows will get drunk before mid-day. In many cases it is fearfully pathetic. Men fly to the wilds to escape drink, but even there unscrupulous people pursue them with it.

Often for two or three weeks there is not a sign of whisky in the place. Then, all of a sudden, some "bootlegger," as the man who brings in the drink is called, sneaks into camp with a bagful, or a bunch of men come up from Edmonton with their pockets bulging, and the whole camp seems to go mad. It seems as if this class of man has to drink, and too often the authorities wink at it. All the boss wants to do is to keep his men, and if he thinks he can handle them better by shutting his eyes to the drink—or even by facilitating its arrival—he probably will do so. Morals don't enter into the question at all, and often it is not only drink but worse forms of vice which are tolerated and even provided. In this camp, however, the authorities have done all they possibly can to keep bad influences out.

The havoc which whisky works when you get it into a construction camp is hard to describe. Here in this camp, for instance, is the cook, an Englishman from Liverpool eight years ago—a man who is a real master of his art, and has been earning 100 to 125 dollars (£20 to £25) a month; plus board and lodging, ever since he came to this country. On Saturday night he was in my shack, and over a desultory game of draughts we touched on the drink question. He was sensible enough too, and told me he could have saved thousands of dollars by investing them profitably in real estate, had it not been for alcohol. Yet, yesterday and to-day, he has been half-crazy with whisky—the meals have all been at sixes and sevens, and a bunch of 70 or 80 men kept waiting for their dinner, although they have only half an hour at noon. This is a most unpardonable offence in their eyes, and they were ready to pull down the cook-shack over his ears.

Very often it is the hard drinkers who are the best workers, and for this reason a man who neither drinks, smokes, nor swears is apt to be considered soft and not much good. It almost looks as if the very fact that they are a rowdy bunch who go on the drunk, makes them in their sober intervals first-rate men at their job. To create any public opinion on the drink question seems totally impossible. Excess in drink is looked upon as a necessary evil, or, it would be more true to say, a necessary pleasure. Some drink openly—some secretly—while some try to keep off it out here, but talk perfectly frankly about going "on the drunk" when they reach Edmonton.

There are a number of steel-workers here, all men who have been making good wages for years, and yet they have not saved a cent. It has all gone in gambling or drink. The worst of it is that they play into the hands of sharks in the towns, who are out for nothing else but to rob men coming in from the camps with money in their pockets. A fellow whom I know well told me he had a drink at a respectable hotel in Edmonton. He is not a man who drinks too much, and on this occasion he had just one glass of port. Almost immediately he fell down in a torpor, and lost consciousness. When he woke up three and a half hours later, his pockets had been turned out, but fortunately he had practically no money with him.

If this kind of thing is done once, it is done scores of times every day in the big towns. The sharks take care to drink little or nothing themselves, and too often the bartender is in league with them. I could tell you of man after man who has been "doped" and "rolled"—in other words, drugged and robbed. It is impossible to persuade the men of the folly of going into a saloon with their pockets full of money. They would run almost any risk to get a drink. They are extraordinarily happy-go-lucky. One day you may find a fellow working in some camp out West, and a few months later you may run up against him in Edmonton looking affluent and well-groomed. One year he will be working his way across the Atlantic in a cattle-boat, the next, travelling first-class. Money is easily earned and as easily spent.

Captain Bernier Readies for the Arctic, 1914

UNKNOWN

One of Canada's great, if unsung, explorers was Captain Joseph-Elzéar Bernier, who for years took government ships into the High Arctic and claimed much of the north for Canada. In 1914, acting on his own, he readied himself and his ship, Guide, *for another long voyage.*

Le capitaine Bernier, l'explorateur arctique qui a fait, dans les solitudes du nord, plusieurs croisières au compte du gouvernement canadien, est à organiser une nouvelle expédition au nord glacé, celle-ci à son compte, sur un navire qu'il a acheté lui-même, le *Guide*, qu'il dirigera dans son voyage.

C'est la seconde expédition que fera, à son propre compte, le capitaine Bernier, la première s'étant terminée, il y a plus d'un an, par son retour heureux à Québec, après une saison de chasse très fructueuse.

Pour sa prochaine expédition dans le nord, le capitaine Bernier a acheté le vapeur *Guide*, construit d'acier en 1891, par le gouvernement d'Angleterre. Il est à l'approvisionner pour une croisière d'au moins 30 mois.

Rencontré par un reporter du *Soleil*, le capitaine Bernier, qui ne semble pas s'apercevoir que les ans s'accumulent sur sa tête et qui reste toujours jeune et alerte, a parlé en termes enthousiastes de son prochain voyage dans les mers du nord.

"Je compte partir vers le mois de juillet", dit le navigateur, mais la date n'est pas encore définitivement arrêtée.

"Je n'ai pas encore terminé tous mes arrangements relativement à l'engagement de mon équipe, mais cela est un détail. J'aurai probablement avec moi, dans mon prochain voyage quelques-uns des navigateurs et officiers qui ont déjà voyagé avec moi, précédemment, mais rien n'est décidé.

"Quant à mon navire, j'en suis plus que satisfait. Il a été construit avec le plus grand soin en 1891, par le gouvernement anglais qui l'a fait travailler ferme dans bien des circonstances difficiles.

"Il est vrai que le *Guide* n'a pas été construit pour des expéditions arctiques, mais il est si fort, si solide et sûr, que je me sentirai parfaitement à l'aise à son bord.

"Il est tout construit d'acier fort et possède sept (7) compartiments étanches dans toutes ses parties, de sorte que quand bien même les glaces avarieraient quelque partie de sa coque, ses cloisons étanches lui éviteront un sort funeste.

"Le *Guide* n'est pas pourvu d'engins pour la rapidité, mais il est très fort. Il mesure 120 pieds en longueur, 23 pieds en largeur, et sa hauteur est de treize pieds. Il jauge 156 tonnes et ses engins l'ont déjà poussé à une allure de 13 noeuds à l'heure, mais il y a quelques années de cela, et jusqu'ici, ce que j'ai fait de plus vite avec lui, a été 9 noeuds à l'heure."

Le capitaine Bernier, quoiqu'il ne soit pas très avancé en âge, a déjà une histoire dans la navigation. Il a été plusieurs années dans la marine marchande, puis est entré au service du Département de la Marine Canadienne faisant pour le compte de ce département, plusieurs expéditions lointaines.

Le *Guide* est le 67ème vaisseau que commandera le capitaine Bernier et, s'il n'a pas plus d'accidents avec lui qu'il n'en a eu avec les navires précédents, on peut prédire l'heureux retour du *Guide* à Québec au petit printemps 1916.

Canadians Go to War, August 1914

ROY MACFIE

From rural Ontario, Macfie was one of the men who volunteered for the Canadian Expeditionary Force when war broke out in Europe in August. His letters from the new camp at Valcartier convey the mood of the men.

Roy to Mary
Valcartier, Quebec
Aug. 23, 1914

I suppose you will be wondering where I have gone to[.] Well I had no chance to write before[.] I couldnt get paper or anything[.] Not much of a chance yet, just sitting on the ground and men singing, yelling, working, playing all kinds of music, and making enough noise to waken the dead. This is a sight worth going across the world to see[.] There is a gang in a tent right near us singing a hymn now that would down any church Choir you ever heard, every kind of voice there is I think. . . It doesn't matter where you go they are singing and yelling everybody seems to be wild. . . The grounds are seven miles by four and covered with tents. . . surrounded by great high hills. And when you get up and look down on the tents it is the prettiest sight I ever saw. . . It is the real soldiers life, alright, the first night we were here there was fourteen men slept in each of those little round tents, it is alright now tho, just seven in ours.

There are fifteen thousand men here now. . . and hundreds of men and teams drawing loads of tents and supplies from daylight to dark. . . I guess there is about a dozen or more train loads of men arrive every day, and trains as long as ever they can draw[.] It was a great trip coming[.] I had my head out of the window all the time it was daylight, every town we passed there were crowds at the station waving flags and yelling goodbye and every farm house the women would be out waving there aprons dish cloths and anything else they could get hold of. . .

Well I am not sorry yet for coming, although I may be before I am through. But don't you worry about me for I would'nt be contented if I had stayed at home, for I would be in misery when I would hear about what they were doing here and I would want to be with them. But it is no picnic I'll tell you, we are just chased and ordered around like a lot of cattle[.]

The 23rd is 104 strong and just a Company here[.] Well how is everything at home? I had no idea that I would get away so quick when I left[.] I was sure we would be in the Sound for some time in fact I didn't expect to leave there at all. . .

Tom [Buchanan] and I have managed to stick together so far[.] Well I had to stop writing for dinner, you could hardly call it dinner either you just have to march up past the cook and get a chunk [of] bread with a little bit of butter stuck on top of it, and a bit of tough beef, and go and sit down and eat it[.]

I want the girls and all to write if possible[.] I may not be able to answer them all but write anyway and very soon too for I don't know the minute we may be moved away some place else[.]

Roy to Frank
Valcartier
undated.

I received your letter the first of the week and was surprised to hear from you so soon, I didn't think you knew where I was. . . .

This camp must be an awfull expense to the Country[ ] Just to stand on one side of the main roads for a while, you would wonder where all the stuff could be got in such a hurry, strings of waggons and Autos as far as you can see piled high with bread, and meat, uniforms boots and everything imaginable[.] We just got our new uniforms yesterday[.] . . .

It seems a very funny thing this is supposed to be a Canadain Contingent and I think that two thirds of the men that are here are Old Country men, if not more[.]

There are an awfull lot who have been through the Boer war, a lot of them have medals. There must be something nice about it when they want to try again[.]

Learning to Ride the Army Way

RAYMOND MASSEY

A son of the farm machinery dynasty, Raymond Massey joined the artillery soon after the outbreak of war. He was "taught" to ride in Kingston. After the war, he became a well-known actor.

There were about fifty of us in the third course at Tête du Pont, Kingston. About two-thirds of us were completely new to artillery. During the First World War, everything in the artillery was different from other arms, even the foot drill, and the months of training in the c.o.t.c. had gone for nothing. Some fifteen of us were taking the course as a refresher, several field officers among them. But we all got the same treatment: foot drill, stables, section gun drill, the works. We all had comfortable quarters in the officers' mess.

The course was rugged. We worked nearly twelve hours a day.

Of the junior officers, half had never ridden a horse and few had more than a little riding experience. We knew nothing of gunnery and the science of artillery. What was worse, we raw ones had no sense of soldiering. Though some of us had had some military training at school, Canada had not felt war near for a hundred years and showed it.

Eight weeks later we might not have been the best gunners in the army, or the best horsemen, or the smartest officers, but we had learned something about discipline, about the duties and responsibilities of an officer. The man who had hammered these virtues into us was Captain Thomas Duncan John Ringwood, Royal Canadian Horse Artillery, acting commandant and gunnery instructor of the Royal School of Artillery, Horse and Field.

Ringwood was a bull of a man, a fine athlete and first-rate boxer, and having "won his jacket," as a commission in the Horse Gunner was termed, he had passed out of the Royal Military College near the top of his class. He was an excellent horseman, despite his weight, with hands as gentle as a woman's. The perfect regimental officer, Ringwood's misfortune was that, in a small regular force geared to supplying instructors at just such a time as this, he should be denied service in the field. Though a good instructor, he had no empathy with his trainees. He did not conceal his burning contempt for the young, would-be officers who came to the school. Later, Ringwood would have his wish for action. He was killed commanding a 4th Division battery in France in 1918.

Ringwood's chief concern was equitation. He said to us, "An officer can be a genius in gunnery and he can lose his guns if he can't ride a horse." We had two hours every afternoon either on the road or in the riding school and Ringwood was a very fine riding master. I had ridden all my life and I was in good shape but much of the riding was "strip saddle" (stirrups crossed over the withers) or on a folded blanket and surcingle. I felt the unused muscles crying out and the fellows who had never ridden were really suffering.

On our third day two or three were a few minutes late for C.O.'s parade. Just a minute or so but there was hell to pay and we got a dressing down, innocent and guilty, then and there from Ringwood. He finished his harangue by announcing that because of this breach of discipline the whole course would go on a punishment ride that afternoon. We didn't know, we young officers, what this meant. If we had, we would have brought a second pair of breeches. We also didn't know that such a ride was inevitable, regardless of our imperfections. Every course suffered at least one.

We paraded at 2:00 p.m. and were marched to the stables and given the order, "To your horses!" I had an idea that this would be what was called a "numnah" ride or the blanket and surcingle job. A numnah pad is a thickness of felt which is placed under an officer's saddle. We would use blankets only. I spotted a comfortable looking horse and quickly moved to him.

"May I ask why you came over to this horse?" Ringwood asked.

"Sloping pasterns and low withers, sir," I answered with confidence.

"Oh, a smart ass, eh! I have just the horse for you . . . come with me." He pointed to a huge beast about seventeen hands high with cow hocks, perpendicular pasterns and withers like the Rockies. I found out later that he was used to pack the heavy reels of telephone wire.

"There," he said, "I think you will be quite happy . . . you and your goddamn pasterns!"

Jimmie Burns, who lived opposite our house in Toronto and was the son of a Methodist minister, laughed at my discomfiture. He was promptly transferred to a mount with vicious vertebral malformation.

"We aim to please," murmured Ringwood.

We filed out of the stable and lined up.

"Ride, prepare to mount. . . MOUNT!"

I never thought I'd make it all the way up but I did with a mighty effort. I was mounted on a gigantic razor-back hog!

"Half-sections right. . . walk . . . MARCH!"

It had begun.

An hour later we were near Gananoque, twelve miles from Kingston, and had turned for home. We had trotted half the time. I could feel the blood soaking my breeches and could see the blood on Jimmy Burns' behind. Try as I would, I was unable to sit back, and Ringwood's repeated exhortation, "Sit back on your asses, gentlemen!" fell on unheeding ears.

"Ride, TURROT!"

The agony of the great clodding beast jolting my bleeding backside on the row of saw-toothed vertebrae was almost more than I could bear. The trotting seemed interminable but at last came some slight solace: "Ride. . . WAALK!"

Two of the older officers had to dismount and walk in but the rest of us finished the ride. Ringwood walked us through the barrack gate, over to the stables and wheeled us into line.

"Ride, prepare to dismount. . . DISMOUNT!"

What a blessing is gravity which makes dismounting relatively easy, that is if your legs don't give way on touching the ground!

"Dismiss to stables!"

Ringwood passed along the stable with acid comments as to our abilities with brush and currycomb. He came to me and as I stood to attention he rubbed a flank of old "Hog's Back" with his white-cotton-gloved hand. I thought of Van and James in the stable at "519." Apparently he was satisfied for he asked, "How are those pasterns?" I took a chance of dire penalties and replied, "Quite solidified, sir, thank you." Ringwood smiled.

There were more numnah rides but they were not for punishment; and muscles, hardened in the riding school, made them tolerable. For the next road ride, Captain Ringwood unobtrusively motioned me over to a smart little mare stabled among the battery headquarter party horses. I put her bridle on and a standing martingale which was hanging on her post, and as I cinched up the surcingle I wondered what was in store for me. Apparently Ringwood was making a peaceful gesture, for the mare gave me a beautiful ride. I saw the need for the martingale soon enough for she was a happy little thing and tried to throw her head all over the place but she rode like thistledown. I found out afterward that she was the first trumpeter's horse and in her exuberance she had recently removed two of his front teeth as he sounded "Prepare to mount" at a parade of "C" Battery.

The eight weeks came to an end quickly. It had been a bone-crushing experience but most of us finished it fit and eager and with caudal lesions healed. Thanks to Ringwood, we had a fairly good idea of elementary gunnery knocked into us. It was the only real instruction I would have before going to France.

Ours was the third course since the war had started. Eighteen months later, Ringwood was still grinding his teeth in frustration and conducting his tenth course. I don't know how many officers of the Canadian Field Artillery he qualified but it must have amounted to over half of those who were the junior gunner officers of the Canadian Corps in France. As far as I know, not one failed to acknowledge the debt he owed to Ringwood. At long last he got to France in command of a 4th Division Battery. Most of his fellow battery commanders had been taught by him at Kingston. Major Ringwood was killed in action in 1918, about the same time as James Burns, D.S.O., and Major Vernon Powell, M.C.

The Princess Pats Fight in Polygon Wood, 1915

AGAR ADAMSON

Polygon Wood. 2nd May 1915.

My dear Mabel,

The situation is somewhat changed, but hardly for the better. Last night in our immediate right in the next Division, the Germans attacked in considerable force and shelled their whole line of trenches, as well as the wood at the back and machine guns opened from all directions. Our Artillery opened up and supports were rushed down to fill the trenches to over-flowing. We were not allowed to take any part in it, as it was feared this was an attack with the object of drawing us into it and then rushing our advance position, so we stood to Arms in slight rain all night, and the attack, after a few hours, tuckered out without results on either side.

It has now been decided that the new back line of trenches upon which so much work has been done with the object of making them a little better than ditches, has been condemned as being in the wrong place, and would be nothing but a death trap and could not be held very long against artillery fire coming as it would do, from both sides. So a line further back about two miles from here, behind a village named Westhoek was started last night and our orders are to be ready tonight to fall back and occupy them, if we get the order. This will straighten the line; but will give the Germans, in places, more than two miles of new ground and very good position. At the present moment our line twists and curves so that it takes a great many more men to man than if they were straight, but this seems also to apply to the Germans.

For the last three months the regiments at rest have been building a most magnificent back line of trenches with drains, cement, bomb-proof dugouts and everything that could be devised, including wonderful wire entanglements. This line, in this particular districts runs between Poperinghe and Vlamertinghe; the Army for months has been priding itself on this wonderful back line. They now find it is not facing the right way and instead of facing the enemy is almost at the right angle to it. It is things like this that make one very angry and wonder how we are ever going to win the war against so skilled and alert an enemy who leave nothing to chance or luck while we muddle ahead in the same old British way, losing magnificent men for the want of a little common sense or at least judgment.

We discovered that by sinking a shaft 15 to 18 feet down we came to sand, and a great quantity of the water in trenches would drain off. We told the R.E. and a Major at that. He said he would have to get authority to experiment as to the nature of the sub-soil.

This morning we were all served out with cotton wool with a piece of elastic sewn on to put over the mouth when gas is being used. Each man carries one now in his pocket. The instructions are to breath in through the mouth and out through the nose. Some people can not breath through their noses but they will have to try. I hear the effect of the gas is almost instantaneous collapse and if not fatal, puts you out of business for several weeks, affecting the lungs. Gray was hit in the head with a piece of glass from a bullet smashed periscope. The one piece of glass is still in his head. Keenan says it is better to let it come out at its own free will, rather than be taken out before the wound starts to heal. He is on duty again in his trench with a very much bound up head.

I have an idea we won't retire from here unless driven out, but as time goes on we shall see. In what does Mrs. Houston's Blue Cross work consist. Let me know if any of my friends are in the list of Canadian Casualties.

The grass is now growing so high that the Germans can but shoot from their ground level loop holes and have to make new ones in the same position as ours and we are making it uncomfortable for them while they are putting them in their parapets. Ever Thine.

Agar

Prohibition Comes to Manitoba

JAMES H. GRAY

The campaign against the liquor trade was one of the great Canadian moral struggles. Booze ruined families, and the war gave prohibitionists their chance.

My father and mother were both deeply involved in the prohibition crusade. Curiously enough, despite my father's addiction to alcohol, he supported the "banish-the-bars" crusade just as enthusiastically as did my mother. Like her, he was convinced that if the temptation were removed he would have no more trouble with demon rum. So in the election campaign in the summer of 1915 he worked actively for the Liberals, who promised to bring in prohibition, and against the Conservative administration of Sir Rodmond Roblin, which supported temperance in principle and the booze business in practice. After supper that summer I used to go with my father to a temperance rallying point in the St. Stephen's Church Hall on Portage Avenue and we would each take an armload of literature to distribute along pre-selected routes. I enjoyed this immensely and even volunteered to help with the deliveries during the day. But such was the bitterness of the feelings aroused in Winnipeg that the people in charge thought it unsafe for a nine-year-old to go out on his own. I remember being completely baffled by the decision, for it was rare indeed that any householder objected to our leaving the material. Perhaps that was an augury of the vote to come because the Liberals led by T.C. Norris went in by a landslide, aided mainly by the Legislature Building scandal which all but destroyed the Roblin regime.

Instead of enacting a prohibition law of his own, Premier Norris announced that he would re-enact the law drafted by Sir Hugh John Macdonald in 1900 but never proclaimed. First, however, there would have to be a plebiscite. That set the wets and drys off on another six-month battle during which there seemed to be some sort of public meeting every night. If the meeting was close by, my mother and father would often decide to attend and leave me to look after my younger brothers, much to my chagrin. I can remember becoming apprehensive when my father was reading the paper aloud after supper and discussing attending a meeting that was announced. I always felt completely comfortable, and safe without question, on the streets, in daylight or after dark. But I was fearful of staying home alone at night with my brothers, even in an apartment block full of people. No matter how late it got, or how tired I got, I can never remember going to sleep before their return.

Often, after my parents had come home, they would sit for an hour hashing over what they had heard. It was an age of oratory in religion, law, and politics, and every Winnipeg preacher who was at all prominent took to the sawdust trail that winter to crusade for prohibition. Such noted clergymen as the Reverend Salem Bland, the Reverend C.W. Gordon (Ralph Connor, the most famous author Winnipeg had produced), and the Reverend J.S. Woodsworth, were among the divines who were supported by social workers, business leaders, and trade unionists galore. Periodically, for special rallies, they would bring in Nellie McClung, the famous Edmonton author and temperance lecturer. The wets, of course, were equally active. They once imported Clarence Darrow, the Chicago criminal lawyer, in an effort to swing labour against the temperance cause. Darrow had recently defended Eugene Debs, the American labour leader, and the MacNamara brothers in the *Los Angeles Times* dynamiting case, and was the best-known labour lawyer on the continent. My parents never even considered going to *his* meeting.

In addition to promising the electors prohibition, the Liberal Party had also pledged itself to compulsory school attendance and to bring in woman suffrage. While the plebiscite campaign was at its height, the votes-for-women issue threatened to divide the temperance legions. People such as Nellie McClung were all for granting women the vote before the plebiscite. They reasoned that this would assure a whopping majority, even if the wets went on the ballot-stuffing blitzes they had used to defeat previous votes on the question. The Norris administration decided against granting the women the vote before the plebiscite, on the grounds that it would be impractical to put a new voters list together in time. On March 1916, the adult males of Manitoba went to the polls and voted in prohibition by a count of 50,484 to 26,502. When the liquor licences came up for renewal in May the government stopped issuing them and the prohibition era arrived in Winnipeg.

But I needed neither the temperance lecturers nor the prohibition campaign to inform me about the ramifications of the liquor problem in Winnipeg. By the time I was ten I knew more about the devastating effect of booze on family life than a beer truck filled with Nellie McClungs and Ralph Connors.

On a payday night in the winter of 1913, my father was waylaid behind a bar, beaten to a pulp, robbed of what was left of his pay and left to die in the snow. He was found some hours later and hospitalized for five weeks with pleurisy that turned into double pneumonia. Yet, curiously enough, this experience had less permanent effect on my father than it did on my mother, or on me. Once back on his feet, he was quickly able to erase the beating from his mind. When he got another job and collected another pay he resumed where he had left off the night of the attack, but with one small change. He did his drinking as far away as possible from the North Main bars. Although my father was able to forget his experience my mother never could. Thenceforth on paydays she would begin to get edgy if my father was not home when she started to make supper. By the time the meal was cooked, she was beside herself with anxiety.

"Jimmie," she'd say, after the umpteenth trip to the window, "You'd better get on your things and run down to the corner and see if you can see Daddy. He may have fallen and hurt himself."

Only she didn't mean the corner. We had been through this so often that she no longer had to spell out what had to be done. She wanted me to backtrack along my father's route home from the Clarendon Hotel opposite Eaton's to the Queen's Hotel at the corner of Notre Dame and Portage Avenue. I was about eight at this time and my mother knew that I'd walk as far as the Queen's Hotel, sneak a peek into the "longest bar in the West" and if my father was inside I'd go in and try to talk him into coming home. This was illegal, of course, since children, women, and Indians were all forbidden by law to enter bars. If the Queen's bartender spotted me he'd bang on the counter with his fist and shout at my father, "Harry get that God-damn kid the hell out of here! You want to get me fired and lose the hotel its licence?"

I have a memory of once running out the door when the bartender shouted, and sitting on a big leather-bottomed chair in the Queen's Hotel lobby until my father came out. On another occasion, I stood my ground, and my father swung his arm at me and almost fell over. Then he left and we went home, with him leaning on my shoulder for support most of the way.

The Parliament Buildings Afire, 1916

ARTHUR R. FORD

It was a dull evening, with the estimates of the Fisheries Department under consideration. Sir Douglas Hazen was leading the House. I was writing my daily report and keeping one eye on W.S. Loggie, MP for Northumberland, who was drearily discussing the question of improved transportation for fish from the Maritimes. There was barely a quorum of members, and fortunately the spectators' galleries were almost deserted. Suddenly I noticed a commotion at the main door of the chamber facing the Speaker's chair. I saw two men rush in. One was C.R. Stewart, the chief door-keeper, and the other Frank Glass, MP for East Middlesex. One of them called out, "There is a big fire in the reading room. Everybody get out quickly!"

Hon. E.N. Rhodes, who was deputy speaker, was in the chair at the time and at once, and without ceremony, adjourned the House. Everyone seemed dazed. The alarm was not taken seriously. I thought there was a fire in some part of the building, but did not imagine there was a disaster or that one was imminent. The two of us in the Gallery slowly picked up our papers, taking our time, and went down the winding stairs to the corridor. To our amazement we saw thick black smoke was pouring along the passage, although the passage south to the main lobby and the front doors was clear. I glanced into Room 16, the Conservative headquarters just back of the chamber, and saw that everyone had been warned and was gone.

By this time the black, almost oily smoke was rolling heavily. I ran to the main corridor and thence to the Press room on the west side of the building. I met Sir Robert Borden and his secretary without hats or overcoats, running towards the exit. Sir Robert shouted to me to get out. I dashed into the Press room, where only a dozen newspaper correspondents were working, and shouted "Fire!" They thought I was crazy. John MacCormac, then representing the Montreal *Gazette* and today the New York *Times* correspondent in Vienna, went to the door and as he opened it the smoke poured in. There was a mad rush. We all got out safely, although Albert Carle, the correspondent of *Le Devoir*, had to crawl on his hands and knees to escape.

One of the first men I met when I reached the lobby was the late Hon. Martin Burrell. His face was badly burned, and he was rushed to the hospital. Mr Burrell's office was off the reading room, where the fire started, and he and his secretary, William Ide, had to rush through the flames to safety. Several members of the House took their time getting out of the chamber, and when the lights suddenly went out were nearly trapped. George Elliott, MP for North Middlesex, was given credit for presence of mind in saving all those in the chamber. He called to the members to join hands and he led them to safety. There were seven lives lost in the catastrophe, including B.B. Law, member for Yarmouth, who was in his room at the time on an upper floor. . . .

The newspapermen moved down to a little office the CPR provided, and there most of us worked all night and most of the next day until the fire was under control. The government took speedy action and moved into the Victoria Museum, where there was a fair-sized auditorium which was used as a House of Commons chamber. The House met here briefly on Wednesday and Thursday and adjourned until Monday. In the four days the Public Works Department showed that they could work fast and expertly if necessary. By Monday quarters had been arranged for the Cabinet Ministers, the members, the officials, and the staff. The dinosaurs, the pictures in the National Gallery, the Indian relics and the geological specimens were packed in the basement or moved to other buildings. Here until the new building was ready for opening the House of Commons met. It was the scene of many historic debates, including the one on conscription, which led to the formation of Union Government and the debate on the nationalization of the Canadian National Railway.

Life and Death in the Trenches, 1916: I

ARCHIE MACKINNON

Belgium,
May 13, 1916

Dear Sister,

Received your letters and 3 parcels OK and certainly was pleased to receive them. I have been very busy lately and had some experience. You say I am a lot fatter in the picture. Gee you ought to see me now. You seem to think I have an awful load to carry. But that is only 3 parts of it. I certainly can stand some awful knocking around. We were in trenches for 16 days counting Reserves and Front Line and am out for 16 days rest as they call it. I think when 58 comes back, Ray will be saying "My Archie isn't there". It only takes one small bullet. It is too bad about Ray being sick. I hope he never stutters. Too bad about Mrs. McArthur. Gee there seems to be a lot of fellows enlisting. I can tell them something and I hope from the bottom of my heart Ronnie never gets here. You want to know what to send me. Well biscuits or cake—anything to eat and all kinds Keatings. This is some place for lice! Good night! I have seen Percy Veale twice and Steve Mould once. You ask me if I were scared when I first went in trenches. Well no I wasn't. I thought nobody could wish for a better place until I seen wounded fellows and fellows getting killed along side of me and have to pick up pieces and put them in a blanket for to be buried. War is no joke. I have been hit 5 times but not serious. It was shrapnel. I was hit 4 times in a battle where your girl's friend was wounded. All Canadian battalions are here together. I was buried in, too, covered clean up once and my friends dug me out. So you can imagine how I like warfare but don't think I don't get back at them. They shelled us hard for 2 hours and tried to take our trench. When they come over the parapet believe me I put bullets and bombs into them as fast as I could but they didn't get our trench. We were only 35 yards apart so you know how quick we act. Poor old Fritz dead men lay in No Mans Land all that night and next day. We only got 15 prisoners. Two were officers. I went after them and I was so excited I didn't know what to do only give it to them. So you think 58 isn't in those battles? Well I am glad to be on this side of the firing line anyway but would sooner be at [home].

Your affec. bro. Archie

PS I received 2 letters from Pa last night. I met Ron Meek (cousin). I am sending his photo to Pa.

Life and Death in the Trenches, 1916: II

GEORGE ADKINS

Dear Mother

Just a line to let you know that we are both all right for which we must thank God for we have been through a terrible ordeal. I don't know if I am allowed to say much about it but you will see by the papers what a fierce fight the Canadians have been into. How we Mart & I came through without a scratch I can not tell as we have had terrible losses. It has been simply awful I cannot describe it in words but I know there has been nothing worse in this war. We did our [?] days in all right and were bombarded pretty heavy all the time but did not suffer much. Then we came out for a rest. The next night they broke through and we had to go back. We had to make a charge in broad daylight but they were ready for us and opened up an awful fire on us we took what cover we could get in old trenches and were there all day. They opened up again two or three times in the night but we kept them back. That night we were supposed to be relieved but the relief could not get in so we had another awful 24 hrs during which they sent over the terrible high explosives & shrapnel but we held firm. Two or three times they nearly landed one in our trench. The force of the explosion threw us down and I could'nt hear nothing but ringing in my ears. I was hit on the head about four times but my steel helmet saved me. Then I had a bullet go right through a mess tin strapped on my back. I am going to keep it as a souvenir. But I wasn't very frightened although the strongest nerves could'nt stand it for long while the shells are bursting around & above. We had to stay in that trench for 8 hours without water & no food but about two dry biscuits each. It was up to our shoe tops in water and we got all stiffened & cramped up. We were thankful when the relief came at last. Of course we had some very close shaves but God must have been watching over us and it made one think about that. The wounded were very brave and bore the pain and suffering like heroes, and some had ghastly wounds. I expect to be home soon now, then I can give you a good account of it. We were so tired when we got home that we just fell down and slept for a long time. I will close now, as I am pretty shaky to-day through nervous strain & loss of sleep etc. We hav'nt seen [?] but we are trying to find them now. They suffered heavy too. I think we are out for a good rest now. Good by with love

George

Life and Death in the Air, 1916

JOHN BROPHY

John Brophy was a pilot in France with the Royal Flying Corps.

Friday, July 21st, 1916

Was blasted out of my downy bed at 5 a.m. muttering imprecations. Devoured a couple of contraband eggs, that had come out with the First Contingent, smacked lips, and seized the control handles of my old bus. Ascended into the blue vault of heaven, followed by six other *garcons* in similar busses, formed up at a given hour, fired a series of signals, and set out for Epehy station in Hunland, with the avowed intention of blowing the whole neighborhood of said station off the map of Europe.

Journeyed to Amiens, passed Albert, and crossed the French advanced lines near Peronne. The archies cut loose as soon as they sighted us, and gave me the most unpleasant few minutes I've had since I went to school. They came unpleasantly close, and some shrapnel hit under my steel seat, and I saw the bullets fly. I also saw some huns beginning to come up to us, and hoped to get bombs off before they caught us up.

I bombed the station and turned around. Immediately I heard the old pop-popping of a machine gun, and looked around to see two hun Rolands sitting above me and peppering me. I dodged about a bit, but my observer couldn't get his gun on them. They put a few holes through my bus, and hit the strut next to me, but our escorts finally got at them, and we got back across our lines. There were about a dozen huns, and they attacked all of us.

After we got back I went into Doullens until noon, then we came back to the aerodrome for lunch. At two I set out on another bomb-raid, this time to Le Transloy, where the huns have billets. We crossed the lines near Longueval, and I could see hun machines coming up to take a few rounds out of us. We got archied all the way over, and when it stopped the huns were amongst us.

Cooper was flying just ahead of me. The huns dived past us, firing as they went. Cooper turned sharply and dived under me, and went down. His machine broke to pieces at about 4,000 feet. Oliver-Jones was his observer. Our escort dived at the huns and let them have it. A hun in front of me, turned up on his nose, and went down in a dive.

I was first to reach Le Transloy, and registered two hits in the village. Going back we also got archied, but our scouts had beaten off the huns. I've been on six consecutive bomb-raids, as we are short of pilots. We went for a walk in the evening, and retired early.

Staff Officers

LIEUT.-GEN. MAURICE A. POPE

Soldiers at the front hated the red-tabbed staff officers who sent them to their deaths in fruitless attacks—or so they believed. Maurice Pope, later a senior staff officer in World War II, shared this impression in 1916.

12th September, 1916

Fair. At work on Div. H.Q. from 9.00 A.M. to 6 P.M. today.

I have had a good opportunity today to size up the Staff Officers. They are moving in tonight (IIIrd Div. staff). They have been about all day and although their Division is, I believe, to take part in a huge attack within a few days, they have been greatly worried about their own personal comforts and about nothing else. The C.R.E. had some beds and tables made for them. These came up and then the fun started. Colonels, Majors, galore, all wearing D.S.O.'s, besides being otherwise decorated like old maids at a wedding or perhaps like matadors each made a dive for a bed and wrestled it into the dugout he had appropriated for himself. I have never seen such an example of egotism and pure selfishness. I shudder to think that my life and those of my men are in the hands of these men. As the army says, they know damn all.

These chaps were no doubt the parasites of the staff, i.e., the extra men who have landed "jobs" while the real ones were probably busy elsewhere. The higher staff work, Army or G.H.Q., for the big affair on the 15th was all that could have been desired.

M.P. 25.9.16

A Pacifist Objects to Registration of Men for Conscription, 1916

J.S. WOODSWORTH

Woodsworth was a pacifist and a man of the left, neither of which were popular positions in wartime Canada. He lost his job as director of the Bureau of Social Research for the governments of the three prairie provinces after this letter's publication.

Sir:

Yesterday morning there came to me a circular letter asking my help in making the National Service registration scheme a success. As I am opposed to that scheme, it would seem my duty as a citizen to state that opposition and the grounds on which it is based. For this end I would ask the courtesy of your columns in presenting the following considerations:

(1) The citizens of Canada have been given no opportunity of expressing themselves with regard to the far-reaching principle involved in this matter.

(2) Since "life is more than meat and the body more than raiment", conscription of material possessions should in all justice precede an attempt to force men to risk their lives and the welfare of their families.

(3) It is not at all clear who is to decide whether or not a man's present work is of national importance. It is stated that the brewery workers in England are exempt. What guarantee have we that Canadian decisions will be any more sound, and who are the members of the board that decides the question of such importance to the individual?

(4) How is registration or subsequent conscription, physical or moral, to be enforced? Is intimidation to be used? Is blacklisting to be employed? What other method?

Is this measure to be equally enforced across the country? For example, in Quebec, or among the Mennonites in the West?

This registration is no mere census. It seems to look in the direction of a measure of conscription. As some of us cannot consciously engage in military service, we are bound to resist what—if the war continues—will inevitably lead to forced service.

(Signed) J.S. Woodsworth.

Scrounging at the Front

J.R. MUTCHMOR

> All soldiers "scrounge"—a polite way of saying that they steal from other units and sometimes from civilians. This account by Mutchmor, later the Moderator of the United Church, documents the practice.

On active service, particularly among the Canadians and I assume New Zealanders and Australians, a very thin line was drawn between scrounging and stealing. The *Concise Oxford Dictionary* defines to scrounge as to "appropriate things, cadge, acquire." Canadians early learned to be expert scroungers.

The general view was that all property, including such movable items as tarpaulins, rubber boots and horses, were just part of the King's stores. Often a gunner or driver's need was not met by an indent, that is a formal request to the quartermaster. It was often supplied much quicker by scrounging. Officers, as well as men, played this game, in so far as "exchanging" or even acquiring horses was concerned. Canadians enjoyed this form of appropriation best when gains were made at the expense of the English artillery. For example, the day before a battery move was to be made, even a captain or lieutenant would let it be known that a certain bay mare on a nearby Royal Artillery horse line was a desirable object. As the 43rd Battery moved off after dark, one or more of the better horses from an English line moved off too. Occasionally a spavined "crock" would be left so that there would be no statistical discrepancy.

At war's end in Canadian artillery lines in Belgium, horses disappeared, bound for meat markets. Within an hour or two, a live horse became steaks, roasts, stewing beef and soup bones. This traffic put money into the purloiners' pockets against a leave in Paris. Naturally it was opposed by the officers, who were held responsible, but some of the would-be law-enforcing post-armistice officers had been supporters of horse-scroungers during wartime.

On the whole, Canadians were far more resourceful than English or even Scottish soldiers.

Getting Wounded, January 1917

HARRY MORRIS

In Hospital,
Lewes Sussex,
April 5th, 1917.

My dear Lillian, Mother & Son:—

Having lots of time on my hands and being now completely out of danger, I thought perhaps you three, also my other loved ones, and also my good friends in Canada would be interested to hear exactly what a wounded soldier passes through from the time he is hit by a little "Made in Germany" until the time he arrives safely in "Blighty."

The word "Blighty" is used for the word England by the boys in the trenches, so I will put a title to this letter and call it "from the Front Line to Blighty—Wounded."

It is noon of the 27th January, Anderson, Maingot, Jackson, Pete and myself are taking our mid-day meal of good old "Bully" and hard tack. The weather is cold (below zero) and we are sitting round a little fire, which really provides more smoke than actual heat. Bang goes a "Fritzie" shell which shakes the roof of our dug out, making it now quite unsafe should another shell land near it. We finish our lunch and decide to make a new dug out so as we will have a place for the night. Fritz is giving us lots of work, as our gun pit, known by us as 206, has also been blown in; we certainly have some work ahead of us, but it is all in the game.

Our boys have now opened up our other seven guns, and the German line must be a pretty hot place. Fritz retaliates with heavy shells, and as we work the air around us is anything but healthy. At 1 p.m. we were having a regular scrap, the German shells making craters all around us. At 1.05 Jackson is shell shocked, and goes off for a rest; the rest of us keep plugging along, very busy dodging shells. At 1.30 I am hit with a piece of a 128 lb. Shell, which knocks me over. I try to walk but can't, and so as you may realize how fast this iron travels through the air, I may state that I heard the report of the explosion after I was hit. Shrapnel travels at a greater velocity than the sound of the explosion.

The boys dragged me into their old dug out and, with their help, I soon had a bottle of iodine into the wound, and a very tight bandage round my whole leg, no stretcher bearers being near us, I am carried by Anderson, Maingot, Pete and a sapper, who comes to my assistance. No stretcher being handy, I lay on a piece of galvanized iron, an awkward thing to carry a fellow on, and not the warmest thing in the world to lie on in zero weather. The boys have an exceedingly hard time to get me to the dressing station, but in a couple of hours I arrive there, where my leg is put into a cardboard splint. Anderson turns to the doctor and asks the question, "Is it a Blighty?" The doctor says, "Well, it is not only a Blighty, but it means Canada for this boy." I cannot explain the feeling that came over me at that moment, to realize that I was going back to my beloved country and dear ones.

I was soon on the stretcher and, after thanking the boys, and shaping a farewell to them, was placed in a dug out to wait for a field ambulance. After being in the dug out about five hours, where I thought I would any minute freeze, the ambulance arrives. I am soon placed inside, two stretcher cases only myself and a poor Lieut. who has been sniped in the head. The balance of the wounded with us were walking cases.

Before we start across the land, which is covered with shell holes, the officer commands the driver to be very careful. "Two dangerous cases inside," he shouts, "Look out for holes and drive slowly." The night is pitch dark and I don't envy the driver.

We were going on fairly well for about ten minutes when we got stuck in a large shell hole. The ambulance is now on an angle of 45 degrees and I thought we would upset any minute. Fritz is saying good-bye to me by dropping an occasional shell near the ambulance. The driver is doing his best to get us out, but it is too much for the horses. Every jerk goes through my leg like a knife, and my feelings are with the poor Lieut. beside me, but I find that he is unconscious—a blessing in this rough sea.

In a few minutes some mules, loaded with ammunition, pass us. The mules are hitched to our ambulance and we are on our way again. In an hour and a half we arrive at cross roads, where we are transferred to motor ambulances, a relief for my leg after the rough cross country trip.

A short run of 15 or 20 minutes, we arrive at dressing station, where my leg is washed. I am inoculated against lock-jaw and wooden splints put on the full length of my leg. By this time I am nearly frozen and I can tell you all truthfully that I have never been so cold in my life before.

In a very few minutes I am back in the motor ambulance. As I am being put in, I notice by aid of the stretcher bearer's lamp the following words on the outside of the ambulance: "Presented by The Children of Nova Scotia, Canada." The Lieut. is still beside me. He was terribly wounded in the head. His batman has been travelling with us all the way, looking after his comfort as well as he could.

We start again and at 12.15, a little after midnight, arrive at 23 C.C.S. I am met by the doctor, who, after looking over my papers, which are tagged on me, asks me how I would like a nice warm bed and a hot drink. By this time I am so cold that I could hardly talk, my teeth are chattering and making an awful noise. A piece of stick is placed between my teeth, my clothes are ripped off me. I am rolled up in a blanket, then hot water bottles are placed around me, lots of blankets over me, and a hot brandy makes me feel a little more comfortable.

It was three or four days afterwards before I really was warm.

Capt. McMullin, an English surgeon, told me I must be operated on first thing in the morning. My thoughts drifted back at this time to the day when I broke my arm, and Mother, who was so patient, fixing pillows around my arm. As I tried to sleep, my leg on each side was braced with sandbags against the splints, but my thoughts were with you all in Canada as I knew how worried you would all be. The night nurse took my pulse, 130, gave me something to make me sleep and I was soon in the Land of Nod.

I woke at four, had a cup of milk as I was still shivering. At 9.30 a.m. I was the first to be taken to the operating room, Nurse Hester fixing me up for the operation. I asked her if she would write a letter home and she very kindly consented to do so.

At about 11.30 the operation was over, as I found out afterwards, that is, after I wakened from ether. Capt. McMullin told me I must keep very quiet, that this operation was very successful, some bone and foreign matter being taken out of my leg.

I also had a compound fracture of femur, and my knee joint was split in two. My wound was stitched up and, to tell you the truth, I now felt fine. My leg was swollen to twice its normal size, but it did not bother me much. I had far too quick a pulse and, as I learned afterwards, my blood pressure was very bad. (The blood pressure was tested twice a day with a gauge and another instrument.)

I was not allowed to write but, when Sister Hester was off duty, managed to get a letter off to my good wife and Mother.

I made very good progress, thanks to the good care I received from Capt. McMullin and Sister Hester, although I suffered a good deal of pain in the 23 c.c.s. I shall never forget the kind manner in which I was treated by every one, from the orderlies to the Col.

On Tuesday, February 6th, the Col. came to see me, personally, and told me he had got a cable off to the Red Cross (Canadian) about my condition. The wound being in the kneecap made it very dangerous, but he was glad to see me doing so well. Getting a cable off to you relieved my mind so much.

A poor fellow died in the next bed to me this morning. He was literally riddled with bullets; he was a Canadian from Toronto. Just before he died, he asked me the question "Am I reported wounded, dead or missing?" and then he just slept away.

At a c.c.s. a patient is hardly ever kept longer than two days. My case being a dangerous one, I was kept until Friday, Feb. 9th, when I left at 9 a.m. for Boulogne. The weather was exceedingly cold. My good friend, Capt. McMullin, was at the station to fix my leg so as it would not move about. The steam pipes had burst in the train, and the temperature was below zero. We were all supplied with hot soup and cocoa at intervals to keep us warm. A boy died in our car a few moments after leaving. It was a long, trying trip and I was very glad to reach Boulogne at 11 p.m.

Crowds were round the station and a French woman gave me a cigarette, as I was carried to the ambulance. Reached Canadian General Hospital at about 11.30 p.m. Night Nurse in charge belongs to Sydney, c.b. Being tired, I was soon asleep, but not before a boy very near my bed passed away, and another report "Died of wounds" will be published in Canada. Day Nurse, a Miss Anderson, married a Doctor, who is in France with her, brother of Major Anderson, who married the little Baby Girl.

Wound dressed first thing this morning. I am at least beginning to feel warm again.

Left Boulogne at 8.30 a.m., Feb 12th, for England. About 1200 on board Red Cross ship, arrived at Dover about 3 p.m.; hustled into Red Cross Train, which was nice and warm, given a good bowl of soup, a package of tobacco, and was now enjoying my pipe. Train did not leave Dover until 7 p.m. and we arrived in Brighton at 1 o'clock in the morning, Feb. 13th. Was soon in a motor ambulance on my way to 2nd Eastern General Hospital and was glad to get to bed in a beautiful room. A photo which I have to show you will speak for itself re this room.

The night nurse met me with a smile, and right here I cannot say too much for the British women. They work long hours, nothing is a trouble for them, and work most of them without receiving a cent. Some of them work under trying circumstances. One girl who was looking after me, I was told, had just a week before been advised that the man she was to marry had been killed. Another her Father had been missing for months, and still another had a husband a prisoner of war. Still, to all appearances, they were happy, but one must guess and think otherwise. They work 12 hours a day, and smile nearly all the 12 hours. . . .

I hope that this letter will give you a little idea of a wounded soldier's trip from the trenches to England on a stretcher. . . .

The Taking of Vimy Ridge: I — Easter Monday, 1917

LIEUT. STUART KIRKLAND

Well, we know for some time before that we were going to take part in a big offensive. We had been practicing and rehearsing the details for several days, but didn't know the hour it was to start 'till the very night before. Then the officers were informed of the zero hour. (The zero hour is the hour at which the attack begins.) All watches were synchronized, that is compared and set the same, so that there could be no mistake. All the battalions taking part were to be in the front line trenches ready by the appointed hour. Well our battalion moved off from billets early on Sunday evening and marched to our part of the line where we were to go over. It was one o'clock in the morning before I had my platoon in position in the jumping off trench, and we stood there in mud to our waists all night waiting for the eventful hour. I can never describe my feelings as I stood there waiting for the moment to come. At a certain hour our artillery was to all open up on Fritz's front line and we were to jump out and advance as near as possible, ready to rush his front fine when our artillery fire raised. After fifteen minutes before the time set, I took two-water bottles or rum and gave each of the men a good swallow, for it was bitter cold standing in the mud all night. Then I stood watch in hand, waiting, waiting!

Precisely on the moment the most wonderful artillery barrage ever know in the history of the world started. Hundreds, thousands of big guns, from 18-pounders to 15-inch guns, opened at the same second. Imagine 15-inch guns firing from miles behind the line and throwing each of them about 14,000 pounds of explosives. The very earth rocked, and the noise and thunder was awful and maddening. Then I jumped over the top and called to the boys to come on. I had gone about 15 yards when I felt a stinging sensation and looking down saw a trickle of blood on my left hand. A Heinie machine gun had got me. At the same time a sergeant just to my right crumpled up in a heap, riddled with machine gun bullets. How lucky I was! I can never thank God enough for my escape. It was miraculous. How I only got one instead of a dozen I can never tell, and through my left arm of all places, when it might just as well as not have been through my head.

I dived into a shell hole and got my arm tied up a bit. A wounded man came along and I helped to bandage him up in return for him helping me to tie up my own. By that time our company was ahead of me, in to Fritz's front line and following our barrage on to the second line. Our men, you know, were going ahead on a frontage of 12 miles long. Thousands and thousands of men, imagine the scene if you can.

I got up and started ahead again, but I found my arm was going to be a bother so I turned back to go to a dressing station. By this time the German artillery was throwing everything they had at our old front line and on No Man's Land to harass our supports coming up. It took me a long while to get back the few yards to our front lines. Heinie shells were dropping all around me. I got into a mine-crater with a couple of other wounded men, but a big shell dropped on the other side and then one dropped right in the crater not far from us and we thought it time to leave those parts. We finally got into the front line but a long way from where I had gone out a while before. The first thing I saw when I got into the trench was an officer I knew lying badly wounded and his batman near him dead. Just then a Heinie came along on his way to the rear. Hundreds of prisoners went back that way without escort. Our boys, when they surrendered, gave them a kick and told them to keep moving toward our rear, when they gathered them in droves and put them in big wire enclosures. The Heinie who came along while I was examining the wounded officer happened to be a Red Cross fellow, so I got him to bandage the wounds. Then we got the officer into a deep dug-out out of harm and I continued on my way.

In one place where the trench had been blown in and it was very narrow I came on a poor fellow lying lengthwise of the trench and everyone had been tramping right over him till he was almost buried in the mud. Of course he was dead so I suppose it didn't inconvenience him any. But imagine the sensation of having to tramp on dead bodies. In another place I came on one of my own [?] company lying with both legs blown off at the knees but still alive and conscious. I stopped and talked to him for a few moments. Scenes like these are not uncommon in war.

After dodging shells for sometime and seeing more than one party of men blown to atoms I finally found a dressing-station. The doctor sent me down the line after dressing my arm, and after passing through the field ambulance and then the c.c.s. I was put on a hospital train for Boulogne, where I stayed just one night and was then packed in a hospital ship and ultimately arrived in Dover, thence by rail to Reading, and here I am.

I will tell you more of my experiences in my next letter. I may say just here that the Canadians "got there" anyway and showed they could fight as well as anyone and a little better than Heinie. We had him beat to a "farewell."

Well I must close. My arm is doing nicely and doesn't pain much. It was a lucky scratch. The bullet went through clean as a dollar making a nice clean wound.

The Taking of Vimy Ridge: II — The Casualties

CLARE GASS

April 10, 1917

This morning hundreds of Canadian wounded admitted, so tired, but the majority with only slighter wounds—

In D—we received over one hundred & fifty & had stretchers & mattresses on the floor for the lighter cases.

April 11

We received the stretcher cases from Vimy this morning—many sick men—. . .

Over 100 of yesterdays walkers went to Eng[land]—Munroe Lindsay admitted to Ward W & Ralph Proctor of the 85th to L. The 85th on the 9th at 6 p.m. went over in support to attack strong positions not captured in the first advance.

April 12

We are still very busy & the wounded are being admitted to Ward D daily—Many 85th men but most of them of D Co[mpany]. I can get no news of Blanchard though C & D Co both went over without a barrage on the evening of the 9th. Munroe said he last saw Blanchard on the eve of the 9th as they were filing down the tunnel.

April 13

I went this evening to write some letters for Ralph Proctor who is shot through the chest & spine & is in serious condition. He also asked me to send a cable to his father—

April 14

NO ENTRY

April 15 and April 16

The casualties though reported as small from last week's action have simply filled all the hospitals hereabouts to over flowing. Robert O'Callahan who is at an English hospital in Wimereux says he never saw worse wounds than those they have & some of ours are heart breaking—Gas gangrene is very prevalent & we have lost several cases. We have had no hours off for a week & have been on duty late at night & are beginning to feel the effects of the extra work.

A Québec Soldier at the Front, 1917

ARTHUR LAPOINTE

The battalion has returned to Marqueffles after sustaining heavy casualties during night duty on the front line at Lens. Now I know why we have set up so many munitions depots near German lines. We are going to attack the left flank of the city of Lens. Today we are getting ready for the assault, repeating many exercises over and over. The plain is dotted with various coloured ribbons that indicate enemy trenches. A and B companies will be part of the first wave, so I will be one of the first to reach German trenches if I am not hit in no man's land. During the rest periods between exercises I chat about the affair with veterans who have lived through tragic times; they are a little anxious, but they also show flashes of pride. They tell me that Lens is probably well defended. The enemy, which has been there since the beginning of the war, must be well entrenched. In the afternoon the men in my platoon go to the armoury to have their bayonets sharpened. Brrr . . . it gives me a chill. I have a feeling that this time it's going to be rough . . . This evening I climbed the hill lined with bushes just to be alone for a while . . . I don't have any combat experience. This is my first . . . and maybe my last . . . I know that many . . . of us will not come back. Will I be one of them? As I went down the hill . . . I thought how good it would be, when the war's over . . . to see the people I left back home.

Life and Death in the Trenches, 1917

BOB GARDNER

Private Gardner of the 21st Battalion of the Canadian Expeditionary Force sent this letter home.

Yes I was at Vimy and Hill 70. I didn't go over on the 9th of April tho. We joined the Bn. just afterwards and had to go over below the Ridge to advance the line around Fresnoy. The Lens business was the worst ever though. It is fairly well described in "Canada in Khaki" No. 2 which I am going to try and send you. Old Fritz had everything barricaded and armed. In places before we went over (the German line), our line was in cellars on one side of the street and his were on the other side. During the scrap, there were fights in cellars, dugouts, tunnels and everywhere imaginable. I can't describe anything on paper but I'll tell you all about it later on after Fritz realizes that he is beaten which might be quite a long time yet as things look now. I'll tell you something to think about on a very dark spooky night. Imagine leaving the shelter afforded by a three foot trench on a dark pitchy rainy night and creeping over No Man's Land towards Fritzie's which is only about a hundred yards away. Every time a flare goes up it is death to move so progress has to be made by lying perfectly flat in the mud and sliding along by pushing with your toes and pulling with your hands. Everything is unusually quiet. After progressing this way for about an hour which takes you probably fifty yards, you stop for a rest and then you hear a faint sound like someone's breathing and so shut the windpipe to hear better. Then a flare goes up and you are staring right into a German's face which is less than a foot away. I had this experience once and it gives me the creeps to think of it now. Of course we daren't start a scrap because we would have been "napoo" in a jiffy by the machine guns of both sides so we waited till the flare died out and then each backed away. Anyway I had found out all I was sent out to learn so I hadn't to take any chances of a mix up. There were some of our men out to get water one night and as there was a pump in No Man's Land, it was much shorter than going away back behind the support lines to Petit Vimy so they used to go up to this pump. It was in a backyard of a house in Avion? One night two of my pals were sent over and while they were there a Fritz came out of a cellar. The boys were going to capture him but he started jabbering away about something like this: "You British, me Allemand. You get water here. Me get water here. You no get water here. Go way back by Vimy. Me no get water here, me go way back. You kill me, Allemand kill you" and he pointed to the cellar. Whether or not there was anyone in there, nobody but himself knew I guess. Anyway one of the men went to the officer and he said to let him go so they did. We got our water after that about ten o'clock every night and we could hear the pump squeaking about midnight. Anyway it saved us a long tiresome walk. I can't describe these things on paper but probably you can imagine them. I was buried five times in four days at Hill 70, four of the times I got out by myself; twice I was in shell holes with chums when a five-nine buried me and both times killed my mates by concussion but I couldn't get the skin broken enough to get down to the dressing station. If we had had more men I'd have gone down with bruises etc. from being buried but there were only five men and three (Cpls?) left in our platoon so I stayed but I didn't feel like taking out any souvenirs that trip. At Passchendale when I was hit I couldn't leave the line for an hour on account of Fritz's barrage which was behind us. Then when I left, I had just gone about a hundred yards when another 5.9 (the plaguey things) lit behind me. It felt as if it lit right under me. Anyway I remember scrambling out of a shell hole a few yards away. It was the effects of this that got me to Blighty and the wounds were only an aid to it. I don't feel any ill effects now so I am expecting to get out of here soon. If you think it unwise you needn't tell Mother of this because she might be unnecessarily hurt because I haven't told the whole thing. I am fine now and feel just like giving you a big hug but I guess you'll have to hug yourself and I'll do the same.

Love Bob.

Billy Bishop's Story

MAJOR WILLIAM A. BISHOP

> *The great air ace Billy Bishop, V.C., published a wartime account of his flying experiences.*

Like nearly all other pilots who come face to face with a Hun in the air for the first time, I could hardly realise that these were real, live, hostile machines. I was fascinated by them and wanted to circle about and have a good look at them. The German Albatross machines are perfect beauties to look upon. Their swept-back planes give them more of a bird-like appearance than any other machines flying on the western front. Their splendid, graceful lines lend to them an effect of power and flying ability far beyond what they really possess. After your first few experiences with enemy machines at fairly close quarters you have very little trouble distinguishing them in the future. You learn to sense their presence, and to know their nationality long before you can make out the crosses on the planes.

Finally the three enemy machines got behind us, and we slowed down so they would overtake us all the sooner. When they had approached to about 400 yards, we opened out our engines and turned. One of the other pilots, as well as myself, had never been in a fight before, and we were naturally slower to act than the other two. My first real impression of the engagement was that one of the enemy machines dived down, then suddenly came up again and began to shoot at one of our people from the rear.

I had a quick impulse and followed it. I flew straight at the attacking machine from a position where he could not see me and opened fire. My "tracer" bullets—bullets that show a spark and a thin little trail of smoke as they speed through the air—began at once to hit the enemy machine. A moment later the Hun turned over on his back and seemed to fall out of control. This was just at the time that the Germans were doing some of their famous falling stunts. Their machines seemed to be built to stand extraordinary strains in that respect. They would go spinning down from great heights and just when you thought they were sure to crash, they would suddenly come under control, flatten out into correct flying position and streak for the rear of their lines with every ounce of horse power imprisoned in their engines.

When my man fell from his upside down position into a spinning nose dive, I dived after him. Down he went for a full thousand feet and then regained control. I had forgotten caution and everything else in my wild and overwhelming desire to destroy this thing that for the time being represented all of Germany to me. I could not have been more than forty yards behind the Hun when he flattened out and again I opened fire. It made my heart leap to see my smoking bullets biting the machine just where the closely hooded pilot was sitting. Again the Hun went into a dive and shot away from me vertically toward the earth.

Suspecting another ruse, and still unmindful of what might be happening to my companions in their set-to with the other Huns, I went into a wild dive after my particular opponent with my engine full on. With a machine capable of doing 110 to 120 miles an hour on the level, I must have attained 180 to 200 miles in that wrathful plunge. Meteor-like as was my descent, however, the Hun seemed to be falling faster still and got farther and farther away from me. When I was still about 1,500 feet up, he crashed into the ground below me. For a long time I heard pilots speaking of "crashing" enemy machines, but I never fully appreciated the full significance of "crashed" until now. There is no other word for it.

I have not to this day fully analysed my feelings in those moments of my first victory. I don't think I fully realised what it all meant.

Homefront Tragedy: The Halifax Explosion I

UNKNOWN

The war has touched Halifax. Sorrow and anguish are left in its trail. Where only a few hours ago, "the most prosperous city in Canada" stood secure in her own defences, unafraid and almost apathetic, there are now heaps of ruins. No one, even yet, can estimate more than approximately, the loss of life and property, and words fail to describe the mental anguish of those who have lost home and dear ones by one cruel stroke. The busy, thriving North End from the sugar refinery to Creighton's Corner is just a mass of broken, splintered timbers, of powdered brick and stone and human bodies crushed to pulp or charred and blackened by fire.

Five minutes before the explosion men were going about their business, women were busy in their homes and children played about the floors or went hurrying to school. Upon the harbor steamed a ship laden with munitions, and down the harbor came a ship flying the Norwegian flag. They drew nearer and in some way, the two vessels came into collision. It was twenty-five minutes after the collision before the explosion occurred. At the first shock, houses rocked, vessels broke from their moorings, bits of shell whistled through the air, buildings fell upon their occupants, shrieks and moans rose for a second above the awful din, and in all parts of the city, men, women and children ran into the streets, many of them insufficiently clad. To add to the horrors fire broke out in a hundred places at once and those who were pinned down by debris met the most horrible death.

Orders were at first given that everybody flee to the south of the city and in a short time Barrington Street resembled a road in Belgium or Serbia when the people fled before the advancing Hun. Every variety of vehicle was pressed into service for the sick and infirm. Men, women and children hurried along the pavements and blocked the street. Stores were deserted, houses forsaken, and the entrance to the Park was soon black with human beings, some massed in groups, some running anxiously back and forth like ants when their hill has been crushed. There were blanched faces and trembling hands, a few had tears pouring down their cheeks, but there was no undue excitement and no disorder. The wildest rumors were in circulation and the bearer of tidings was immediately surrounded. The stories lost nothing in the telling, until the brain reeled and the heart grew sick trying to picture the horror and desolation. When the flying automobiles brought the good word that the danger was under control, and the people might return to their homes the crowd trekked back.

Many, relieved of immediate fear for themselves, bethought them of relatives and friends in the North End, and started to walk there. Most of them returned heart-sick from the sights they saw. From North Street on the horrors and the wreckage grew. On the one side the King Edward Hotel stood a practical wreck, on the other the central portion of the Railway Station no longer existed. But the wreckage up to and including this point was as nothing to that beyond. Houses were simply indistinguishable masses where they had not been devoured by the flames that rose and fell, that roared and seethed and made the place like a smelting oven.

Most pathetic stories, so tragic that they almost benumb the sensibilities, seeped through. One possessing all the elements of horror was told by two white-faced sailors who came to ask if The Morning Chronicle could help them in their search. They were both looking for their wives and children. They had lived on Hanover Street and when they had got to what had been their homes, there was nothing but ruins, and search among the debris revealed nothing. They had then made the rounds of the hospitals with hope and fear gnawing at their hearts, but all to no avail. A list of the temporary hospitals and shelters was furnished them, but at last accounts they were still torn by hope and uncertainty. Nothing is more terrible than the suspense, and, strong men as they were, their faces showed the strain.

There were many miraculous escapes as well as appalling disasters, as is always the case at such times, but the pall that hangs over Halifax, will not be lifted in many months. Every effort was soon bent to providing succor and shelter for the injured and homeless. Every available building was turned into a shelter-house or hospital. The Academy of Music was one of the first big buildings to post the notice "Free Shelter Here." The headquarters of the Terminal Construction Company and the big sheds on their piers were soon being hastily equipped for hospital purposes. St. Mary's Young Men's Hall and a score of others were freely opened. Everywhere people whose homes were intact made room for those who had no homes, and all day long the work of removing the dead and wounded went on. Hundreds of bodies lie in temporary morgues awaiting recognition and burial. Whole families are wiped out; parents are left childless, and children have been made orphans.

All day and night the agonizing search for the missing went on. Rescuers tell harrowing tales of their experiences. Houses in most instances simply settled down, story on story, crushing everything into one awful mass. Though the inmates had been only on the street floor it was necessary to remove the wreckage layer by layer beginning at the roof and working down. One party of soldiers worked with almost superhuman strength and energy for an hour and a half to release a young girl pinned under such debris, whose moans urged them to still greater effort. Just as they lifted the last of the mass from her, her spirit fled, and it was merely a body they lifted out.

Passengers on the ferry-boat near the Dartmouth shore felt the concussion from the water even before it was felt in the air. Glass crashed in and passengers were cut and bruised. Reports say that not only were windows and doors in every part of the City shattered, but as far as Lawrencetown houses suffered severely. Dartmouth had perhaps fewer casualties than might have been expected, but there are enough to sadden the homes there.

The Learment Hotel at Truro, 62 miles away, had windows blown in by the force of the shock, while a barn at Meagher's Grant, 30 miles out of the City, was turned around and blown off its foundation, a trick as queer as some reported of cyclonic disturbances. Nearly two hundred miles away as the crow flies, at Orangedale and Sydney, the shock was distinctly felt, and a hospital ship, 60 miles out at sea, thought at first that she had struck a mine, so severely was the concussion felt. . . .

The alarm to citizens to leave their houses in case of a second explosion was given shortly after ten o'clock on Thursday morning, while those in the down town precincts of the City were warned to get back into the interior. Automobiles went all over the City with military men giving the warning with the result that in a very short time crowds of people gathered on the Citadel Hill, the Commons, in the districts around the North West Arm and Ritchie's Woods, and in the fields in the West End.

In all these places of refuge, grief and distress prevailed. Men, women and children were to be seen bleeding, bandaged and heartbroken. A large number had both friends and relatives in the North End whose fate was unknown. Wives were crying for their husbands and mothers for their children. Husbands from the North End were in despair for their children and wives, whom they had left safe and sound when they went off to work in the early morning. In addition there were those who had relations and dear friends in every part of the City, seriously ill and near to the vale of the shadow of death.

In the Western and Northwestern part of the City many poor people stood in the fields, sadly surveying the wreckage of their homes. Homes which both husband and wife had worked so hard to have for their own when old age came upon them. Practically every house had its windows shattered and the ceilings fallen through. Pianos, pictures and valuable cutlery and dishes were smashed to pieces. Family relics handed down from generation to generation, all were included in these ruined homes, which such a short time ago had been the pride of the hard-working citizen striving his utmost to secure independence.

The message came through shortly after noon that it was safe for the people to go back to their homes and immediately the unfortunate ones went back to the wreckage to fix a place to eat and sleep, for the time being. Despite their misfortunes, the hearts of all were with those who were in distress and many deeds of kindness were performed by people who were themselves in the same plight.

Although the extent of the tragedy of Thursday has been described as amazing, appalling and incalculable, an expert in explosives has made a statement that should cause Halifax, shrouded in grief as she is, to realize that she has had a miraculous escape.

The Mont Blanc carried between three thousand and four thousand tons of high explosive munitions and had the same quantity of explosives been stored on land when the explosion occurred, it would have wiped out every living thing within an area of ten square miles. Not even a cat or a rat would have been left to show that life had ever existed here. The Mont Blanc lay across the Narrows, bow on towards the Halifax shore. Small wonder that the North End of the City was wiped out in the twinkling of an eye almost. Terrible as the tragedy is it might have been a hundred fold greater and swept every vestige of human habitation on both sides of the harbor from Point Pleasant to Bedford, out of existence. There would have been none left to tell the story, for not even Louvain was so thoroughly demolished as Halifax would have been.

Homefront Tragedy: The Halifax Explosion II

LAMBERT B. GRIFFITH

> *Able Seaman Griffith of the Royal Canadian Navy Volunteer Reserve sent this letter to his wife Dorothy in Esquimalt, B.C.*

Sat Night
8 Dec 1917
HMCS *Niobe*
Halifax

My Darling;

Just a few lines to let you know that I am <u>alive</u> & have not received a single scratch. I wrote to you on Tues the last day I was ashore. This is Sat & I have only had time to get one little wash so you can imagine how I look. I am alive but do not know why. Walter was out on the Boom & escaped quite a lot. I got your telegram & just had time to rush to the ships office & get them to answer it. There is no shore leave, in fact the town is in absolute darkness & ruin. I will try & tell you something about what happened. We had just finished breakfast at 7:30 am Wed morning & were having our usual smoke before falling in for carrying on coaling ship. A Belgian relief boat had just come in also a French boat. The French boat was getting ready to dock when the Belgian boat ran in to her stern Apparently a very slight blow. Shortly after this the French boat was seen to be in flames. She put in to shore about <u>500 yards</u> from the stem of the Niobe. A lot of us boys went up on deck to see the sight. It did not look very bad. There were three pretty loud explosions & everyone just imagined that it was the oil blowing up. All at once there was a most hideous noise & I saw the whole boat vanish, a moment after I saw something coming can't describe it. I was hurled on the deck & there was an awful noise going on. I got to my feet & ran with a whole lot of fellows. My one fixed idea was to get below. We all tried to get down the one ladder without any success. I had presence of mind enough to dig my head in between all kinds of legs & c. After that I ran along the deck & heard all kinds of things falling. It was shrapnell & bits of the side of the ship. I did not know this at the time. I managed to get to the gangway unhurt & found that the ship had broken her big cables & the gangway gone. As she crashed in to the jetty I jumped off & got ashore just before she shoved the jetty over. Once safe on shore & finding I was <u>unhurt</u> I started in to assist the wounded. I helped first to take a wounded man out of the water. By this time all the houses round the dockyard were on fire. I joined a party on the run to the ammunition magazines just on shore beside the jetty where the old Nobler was tied up. We worked like slaves, pulling out cases of cordite & shells of all kinds & dumped them in the water. It was a perfect miracle they did not go off, as the 3 buildings where they were stored had been completely wrecked, but luckily had not caught fire. The ship that blew up had about 2000 ton of a more powerful explosive than nitro glycerine. The explosion was felt 10 miles away by ships. It makes it the more wonderful our escape. There is not a single pain of glass in Halifax. The yard is a complete wreck. A train coming on from Montreal was wrecked, also a street car. Our steam cutter along with her crew were lost. Several men here have lost their wives & children. Thank goodness you were not here. I have not seen a paper. I have not been thru' anything so awful in my life. We have been working so hard that I for one have not had time to realize what I have escaped. The dead are just laid out anywhere. I saw a basket on the jetty this morning & in it was a little baby, quite dead. Next to it was a stoker with his face all crushed in. I need not say any more. I have never seen death in this form before. I am sure that for ten minutes we have all been thru' worse than in the trenches. The whole town is a wreck, even the roof off the station. A German fleet could not have done so much damage. An Imperial cruiser was just on the other side of us in the stream & they have lost their Commander & about 45 men. All the wood work on board the Niobe has been shattered & water cut off. The day after the accident it blew a blizzard & made rescue more difficult but kept down the fire. Lots of ships have been sunk. The Belgian boat that caused the explosion is lying on her side on the opposite shore. The new YMCA in the yard of course is a complete wreck like everything else. I don't suppose I shall go up town till I return from the boom. Well darling, we have lots to be thankful for after all. There will be no Xmas leave now. Unless one went away there would be no way to go. Even the theatres are wrecked. Well love there are lots more details I could go on to but just as well not to.

Write soon to your lucky old Lofty. Every minute I thought I was dead. Ever your loving hubby

Bert

xxxx

We'll be working pretty near night & day for a long time yet.

Bitterness About Québec's Role in the War

JOHN W. DAFOE

Québec enlistments were low in proportion to population and, as the war's costs rose, many English Canadians became embittered. Dafoe was editor of the Manitoba Free Press.

Do you not know my dear Côté, that in Australia, 14 per cent of the whole population enlisted voluntarily? On that basis there would be in the Canadian armies today about 150,000 French Canadians in place of 15,000 or 20,000 at the outside. When you have done half as much as Australia it will be time for you to talk.

The trouble between the English and French Canadians has become acute, because French Canadians have refused to play their part in this war—being the only known race of white men to quit. They try to excuse themselves by alleging that they have domestic grievances, which should first be righted. The excuse, if true, would be contemptible. In the face of any emergency like this domestic questions have to stand.

Do not flatter yourself with the idea that the English Canadians are disturbed by your attitude of injured innocence, or your threats of reprisals. You can do precisely as you please; and we shall do whatever may be necessary. When we demonstrate, as we shall, that a solid Quebec is without power, there may be a return to reason along the banks of the St. Lawrence.

Wartime Changes in Women's Roles, 1918

NEHNUM MORR

"I understand that you have some vacancies on your line for conductors, Mr. Nickle, I wonder if I could fill the bill?" timidly questioned a female voice.

The manager of the Kingston, Portsmouth and Cataraqui Electric Railway Company swung round in his easy chair at his desk and sure enough, there was a tall, handsome young woman looking down at him appealingly. For a moment Hugh C. Nickle was taken aback at the daring request, but a twinkle soon came into his eye as his look of surprise wore off. The young lady was invited to sit down and give her qualifications for a position hitherto always held by a man.

She explained that she had seen the advertisement in the daily papers for conductors, and that she thought she was quite capable to take over the arduous duties. The exigencies of war, she remarked, were taking women into new fields of endeavour, and there was a great need for men in the ranks of the Canadian forces at the front. Women were doing all kinds of work to win the war, and she was quite willing, therefore, to act as conductor while the boys were away doing their bit. The women of England were running trams, and she considered it high time that the Canadians did the same.

The general manager was in a unique position and her argument could not go unheeded. Here was a young lady anxious to do a patriotic service in a time of need, and to release a man for the service of King and country. She was healthy and vigorous and apparently quite able to assume the new duties. Her earnestness did much to convince the perplexed Superintendent that she would "make good" and the name of Miss Maude Chart, the first conductorette in Canada, was added to the payroll of the company on October 15th, 1917.

When the girls first came on the cars, and they were somewhat of a novelty, the dear old gentlemen would put their heads together and if the man in the seat behind were to listen he might, too, become the victim of the contagious pessimism.

"You'll see that I'm right," he would hear the first old gentleman remark. "Some of those girls will break down some day when the temperature is about twenty below, and their hands are half frozen to the fare boxes."

And his friend would not be slow in adding, "You know that I think it's criminal to allow them to expose themselves to pneumonia and influenza these cold days. They'll come to an early end, poor dears."

What a dismal picture those pessimists did delight to paint! But they looked at the situation from the wrong angle and they are just now getting the right perspective. The girls did meet with discouraging difficulties, but even in the most trying days when their fingers were blue with cold, they carried on and collected the fares for ten hours at a stretch. Their unfailing politeness and courtesy at all times were commended by visitors as well as citizens, who did not fail to congratulate them on the splendid spirit of service they manifested. As the winter wore on the pessimists became disheartened at their inability to convince themselves and others that the conductorettes were bound to be failures.

A gleam of hope, however, came with the dawn of spring. Summer would soon be here, and the closed winter cars would have to be replaced by the open cars. Ha! ha! Perhaps they were not so wrong after all.

"They may be pretty fair in the winter, but what about the summer?" queried the omniscient pessimist. "They'll never be able to climb along the sides of the car to collect the fares. Mark my words. If Nickle keeps these girls in the summer, there are going to be some dead conductorettes under the sod before the snow comes round again."

And just to make it emphatic the companion in gloom remarked, "I don't see how they'll be able to walk along the sides with their skirts flying around like a couple of flags in a wind storm."

Again the pessimists were to be disappointed. During the summer months the girls have handled tremendous crowds on holidays and on other special occasions, and up to the present only one has been injured —and she was only off duty for half a day with a few bruises. Some of the "Etties" have collected as many as eleven hundred fares during one day, and registered them on an automatic recorder. It has been really wonderful to see them skip along the side steps with remarkable agility and facility. They have been especially gracious in assisting old gentlemen and ladies on and off the cars. They have easily replaced the trolleys on the wires when they slipped off. They have even turned the switches for the motormen. In a word they have performed a score of duties devolving upon them with a grace and cleverness that is exceedingly creditable and gratifying.

Clad in their natty khaki suits, they are an addition to the car service, and their courteous "Fares, please" is a delightful change from the gruff "Fares." Each girl is provided with the material for two uniforms, a peaked, brown straw cap sitting at a jaunty angle on her head under which her hair is neatly tucked, a "slicker" fisherman's hat and rubber boots for rainy days, as well as brown boots and stockings, which complete their attire on sunny days. Their suits are quite plain, consisting of a short skirt and Norfolk coat with shining brass buttons. On very warm days the girls remove their coats, and they look refreshingly cool and comfortable in pongee blouses and khaki middies. They are very business-like in appearance, and in the performance of their duties they will stand no nonsense from any of the male passengers who are of a "flirty" nature, which responds to the attractiveness of the Limestone City's conductorettes.

Their wages are also very generous and many of them make as much as eighteen and nineteen dollars a week. They are paid $2.25 for a ten hour day, and receive double pay for overtime. At the end of the summer those who have been in the service during the whole of the season are to be granted a substantial bonus by the company as a mark of appreciation for their steady work. Altogether the majority will have averaged about $18.50 a week when their bonus is given.

Some of the girls start as early as six o'clock in the morning on their trips, and Mr. Nickle stated that as a rule they were more regular than the men in arriving for the "dawning" cars. During the day they have few idle moments until the last car enters the barns shortly before eleven o'clock at night.

Mr. Nickle is very proud of them and is extremely gratified at the success they have made in the work. "They have acquitted themselves nobly," said he, "and I have absolutely no fault to find with any of them. They are punctual in arriving for work, courteous while performing their duties, and I am convinced that they have been able to collect as many fares as the men. In comparison from every standpoint they are their equal. It was a somewhat radical departure to engage them for the work but they have surpassed our most sanguine expectations and we are proud to be the one company in Canada employing conductorettes. Some of the other cities might gain by our experience in these times when labor is so scarce. The motormen show no antipathy to our employment of them and indeed are co-operating with us in splendid fashion. We are proud to have such patriotic and efficient girls in the employ of the company."

Such a testimony from one who knows should dampen the ardor of those who don't. The world never had any place for the pessimists anyway.

Heroism in the Hundred Days: I

BELLENDEN S. HUTCHESON

A Medical Officer, Capt. Hutcheson won a Military Cross and a Victoria Cross during the Hundred Days, the Canadian Corps' great battles from August 8, 1918, to the Armistice.

The bombardment lasted from 1 p.m. until 10 p.m., with a few periods of lull, and was apparently counter battery work on the part of the enemy. Our guns were not in action.

As you surmise, the gun crews had taken refuge in cellars, not anticipating a bombardment of such intensity with heavy stuff. Gas shells and high explosions were intermingled. My work consisted in dressing the wounded, checking hemorrhage, giving a hypo of morphine when necessary and seeing that the injured were evacuated to the rear. The gas used that day was the deadly sweetish smelling phosgene. It was my first experience with gas in warfare and I wore a mask part of the time and instructed the men to do so whenever there was a dangerous concentration. You ask about my own reaction. It was of course very disconcerting to endeavor to dress wounded while shells were showering debris about, and the possibility of being in the next few seconds in the same plight as the terribly wounded men I was dressing, occurred to me every now and then. The whole thing seemed rather unreal, particularly when it occurred to me, busy as I was, that the killing was being done deliberately and systematically. I felt particularly sorry for the young artillery men, (and many of them were about 19) who were being subjected to the ordeal. I remember one man who had a ghastly wound which would obviously prove fatal in a short time, pleading with me, amidst the turmoil of explosions, to shoot him. Every soldier who has seen action since knows that it requires the highest type of stamina and bravery for troops to lie in a trench and take a heavy shelling without being demoralized and panic stricken, therefore I shall always remember the orderly rescue work carried on by the officers and men of the artillery in the face of the concentrated shelling that occurred that afternoon. . . .

As we advanced we were frequently under direct observation by enemy balloons directing artillery fire. When one shell landed half a dozen others were pretty sure to land in a very short time within a radius of 50 yards or so of where the first one did, consequently when the first few caused casualties they had to be attended in a shower of debris caused by the explosion of succeeding shells.

It was necessary to pass through the streets of Le Quesnel several times during the barrage in order to find the wounded who were scattered throughout the town. I supervised their collection during lulls in the shelling in a cellar I used as a dressing station. The platoons furnished stretcher bearers. My medical section, consisting of a sergeant, corporal and two privates were with me part of the time, or were in the dressing station when I was out, or they themselves were engaged in looking for wounded.

As the 4th C.M.R. and tanks pushed through the village the shelling again became intense. The Germans were about 240 yds. outside the village. As Corporal Adnitt, and Private Marigold and myself were attending to some wounded in a d[iner]y near a street corner that was being heavily shelled, a company of the 4th C.M.R. went by. As the hind of the company reached the street corner about a hundred feet away a shell landed in their midst. About six men went down. As they were going into an attack they could not stop to take care of their wounded. Adnitt, Marigold and I ran to them. The Company Commander lay on his face with the back of his head sheared off. I recall that he had the rank and name of "Captain MacDonald" written on some of his equipment. Three other men were killed and lay beside him. The Company Sergeant Major had his leg blown off just above the knee and several men had less severe injuries. We put hurried dressings on the wounded and got them off the corner, which was a very hot spot, into shelter as quickly as possible. One of the men who had been killed was evidently carrying phosphorous smoke bombs. These set his clothing on fire. We tried to extinguish the fire, but his clothing and body seemed shot through with the phosphorous and it was impossible to put it out. The nature of his wound made it evident that he had been instantly killed and as shells were falling about at a lively rate, we left him. Later in the day when the enemy had been pushed back and things had quieted down I saw his body again. He was almost incinerated.

I dressed very few enemy wounded in Le Quesnel, as they had evidently been able to evacuate them before we took the village. A day or so later we came across a temporary tent hospital of the Germans full of wounded. These, my men and I dressed until they could be evacuated as a matter of ordinary humanity. I might add that they were very grateful. . . . The Germans did not use very much gas that day in our sector. I do not think they used the bayonet much either, though I was not in a position to know. . . .

Concerning Capt. Dunlop. . . He was first hit in the abdomen by a rifle bullet, as he led his company over the crest. He had advanced in the face of a [wither]ing fire, swinging his walking stick nonchalantly. There wasn't much chance for conversation as I dressed him but he did ask if we were having many casualties. Twenty or thirty minutes later when I was near him again he told me that he had been hit in the thigh as he lay there. We put him in a shell hole. His first wound being in the abdomen it was advisable to get him back to the C.C.S. for operation as soon as possible, so Sergeant Munnell and I stopped three or four German prisoners to press them into service as stretcher bearers. An enemy field gun about a mile away, ahead and to our right, began firing at us and the first or second shell landed among us, or so it seemed to me, I was knocked into the shell hole with one of the Germans on top of me; Munnell was knocked to the ground, a wounded man who was lying near had his ear nearly taken off and the other two Germans, wounded and shrieking, ran toward our lines. As I struggled out from under the German, he was groaning and crying, and I spoke to him sharply to get him to remove his weight from me. Dunlop said, "He's badly hit Doc. Look at his face." I looked, and the face was gray. At the same time I saw a wound in his thigh with the blood spurting from a severed femoral. As I put a tourniquet above the wound he moved a little and I saw that the whole side of chest was torn out. He expired in less than a minute. Meanwhile the field gun continued to fire at us, about every 10 or 15 seconds, I should say, landing its shells usually within 15 or 30 yards. As the four of us, Munnell, Dunlop, another wounded man and myself lay in the shell hole the din was terrific, with machine gun and rifle fire ahead, our low flying planes swooping to within 50 feet of the ground and firing at the enemy and shell explosions all about. Someone remarked that it was no place to sit and read the paper and another observed that there would be an awful mess if Fritz ever got a direct hit on our shell hole. In a short time the enemy fell back and the fire abated, and we were able to get Dunlop and the other casualties scattered along the crest, back a couple of hundred yards or so, to a trench in which we were collecting our wounded.

Heroism in the Hundred Days: II

GEORGES VANIER

Later Canada's Governor General, Vanier served with the 22nd Regiment at the front. This letter, written to his mother, describes his being seriously wounded on August 28, 1918.

On the 28th of August the battalion attacked. As Major Dubuc had been wounded the previous day (I cannot say yet exactly how seriously), I happened to be in command. Very shortly after zero hour, I was shot (machine-gun or rifle bullet) through the right side splitting a couple of ribs. The wound however was a very clean one (most bullet wounds are) and I should have been very fortunate indeed to come off with it only. But this was to be one of my bad days: as I was being dressed by the bearer a shell exploded at my side causing rather unpleasant shrapnel wounds to my right and left legs. I was evacuated in good time from the battlefield and taken to the Casualty Clearing Station at Ligny St. Flochel which I reached at about 9 p.m. and where I received every possible medical and surgical treatment. They were splendid to me.

The right knee was shattered and the Medical Officer then said even if the leg were saved I would never be able to use the knee. I asked him if he might wait until the following day for a reply. He agreed and the leg was amputated next day. A short time after my return to bed following the operation, I suffered a severe hemorrhage and was hurried back to where the operation took place. There a transfusion was done in direct contact with the donor. The immediate effect was a feeling of active physical resuscitation. I have no doubt whatever that the transfusion saved my life. When it was over, somebody suggested—perhaps I did—that a glass of port might do me good. Everybody agreed, and another voice was heard (it was the man next to me who had given blood) saying: "I'd like one too."

The End of the War

ARCHIE KEAT

France
November 11, 1918.

My Dear Mother,

Well, Dear folks here it last the great Day that we have all been waiting for so long. It has and is a great Day—

It is now about 7 P.M—and of course quite dark.

Will tell you about the place we are in, and then about the doings of the day—

We are in a Belgian town and it is just a great place. When we came here the Germans had only left it a little over a day—They left the place without even breaking a window. It is in perfect condition. They left all the civilians and of all the happy people that I have ever had the pleasure of seeing they I think are the happiest. It was Sunday and they were dressed in their best and all out in the street, cheering the Boys as they passed, with a smile and a cheery word for them all—I saw old women catch the boys by their hands and kiss them.

And the kids, the young women and even the old folks they would get around you and pull the Badges off for souvenirs, even the Buttons. They were just crazy to get them. One old woman grabbed me and before I could say a word had my Canada's off—

Had the coffee. My word! They had us drinking it every five minutes and it was good too. They all had a bag of sugar hidden away. These they produced and used with the coffee. The stores seem fairly well stocked considering.

The people welcomed the Boys and offered their houses as billets, Joe and myself met a woman coming down the street and she took us to her house. (I am writing it in one of the rooms now) and gave us the freedom of it. A dandy bed, etc. etc. She has a pretty little Girl about seven years old with lovely light hair—

The houses have electric lights so it is quite a treat.

The towns are large and quite close together. I can quite believe that this is the most densely populated country in the world. They are also perfectly clean. One can hardly realize that these places were occupied by the Huns only such a short time ago. This morning early we left this village & started to walk to the main lorry road some three kilometers away. On the way we fell in with two men on their way to work in one of the mines. They knew a short cut to this place and so we went with them. They showed us the place one of them where the Contemptibles fought. It was very interesting. They also showed us bullet marks in the steel posts that support the tramway wires. A few days ago we saw a German cemetary and it was a beautiful place, such lovely flowers, shrubs, Head stones etc. It was beautifully laid out. In one part by itself were the men of 1914, and side by side with his own dead were the dead of the British. All had the same head stones with the names, numbers rank and regiment of the ones buried there. Also the graves were covered with plants and flowers just the same as their own. One must give them credit for this act of respect—for the Brave dead.

Now, to continue with our travels of today. We walked to the main road and in due time caught a lorry going our way. Another chap climbed in too and he told us that the Armistice was to begin at 11. AM. We were a bit sceptical as to the truth of his statement. We have been of course expecting something of this sort to happen, but it seemed to good to be true. However as we went along everyone was talking about it—so we at last decided it was a Jolt. We got back this afternoon and the church bells were ringing and the streets were crowded with people old & young of all ages, sizes and descriptions. And the excitement, it was everywhere—

The Boys told me about the civilians. They dug up their old band instruments and came running up to the hall brushing off the dust as they ran—they practiced for an hour or so and then started to tour the town with a procession following them. Such a time—

Of course the Battalion Bands were out playing too—

Tonight our pipe Band as usual played after the sounding of retreat. They marched around a bit and then formed a circle. Outside this circle were the civilians. As soon as they formed the circle a Girl wearing "Sabots"—They are the wooden shoes that they wear in this country. They wear cloth slippers around the house and slip these wooden shoes on when they go out. Well, this Girl sprang into the circle and stepping out of these shoes she commenced to dance and such a dance it was. I have never seen anything so graceful or wild before. She made me think of one of Tennysons poems where a poor girl danced for one of the Kings who said, "This beggar maid shall be my Queen." There are a dozen other happenings that I will be able to tell you about later. Last night the parcel with the lovely cake, chocolate, cigars, peppermints, Note paper etc came along and was enjoyed more than I can say—

The cigars & cake were particularly good. We have the cigars to celebrate with. Alf & Rex are not back as yet. They should get back any day now. I don't suppose leave will stop yet. Won't they be excited over there and in Canada and all the other countries tonight. Such a Day.

Now I must close for tonight.

Love to All.

Archie

The Influenza Pandemic, 1918

DR. T. ROGERS

The war was scarcely over before the Spanish flu, as it was called, devastated the armies at the front and the civilians at home. A Nova Scotia doctor complained to Ottawa about the way prohibition was interfering with his ability to treat his patients.

Honored Sir:—

The people here are infested with the terrible malady called Spanish Influenza. I am medical practitioner in this small farming district. In order to save lives I cannot get or procure Scotch whisky or wine as when pneumonia sets in these intoxicants protect the patients from fatal results. The prohibition act debars any such aid. Will your Lordship please send me permission to any reliable liquor known to you in Montreal where I can get a case of wine and Scotch whisky occasionally. Also a letter of permission to be used to Rail Roads in transit.

I feel that your Lordship will acquiesce in this great favor in view of terrible fatalities from the scourge.

Prompt action will be appreciated by this community as your Lordship can realize.

With highest consideration
my Lord, I remain sincerely

T. Rogers, M.D.

The Winnipeg General Strike, 1919: I

ERNEST ROBINSON

Ernest Robinson, one of the leaders of the General Strike that paralyzed Winnipeg through May and June 1919, explained the strikers' aims.

I say that, geographically speaking, this strike will continue until it extends from Halifax to Victoria. We have received word from all intermediate points between here and the coast that Winnipeg is the leader, and that they will follow Winnipeg's example and do as we do. We have withdrawn labour from all industry, and it will stay withdrawn until the bosses realize that they cannot stand against the masses of labour. If we can control industrial production now, at this time, we can control it for all time to come, and we can control the Government of this country, too.

The Winnipeg General Strike, 1919: II

ARNOLD HEENEY

> *Later one of Canada's most distinguished public servants, Heeney was in the militia called up for service during the strike. He explained to his mother the events of the pitched battle on the streets of the city.*

The strike's over at last and it can't be long now before I 'get my ticket' (probably in less than a week). I am certainly 'fed up' with the soldier's life and with guards in particular. If the strike had gone on a few days longer I would have had two stripes. . . .

Last Saturday was quite exciting when the fight came off downtown I was detailed to a machine gun as a covering party. The gun (a Lewis) was mounted on a truck. We tore down town on orders about 3 p.m. at a fierce lick. The fighting was practically over and we didn't open up at all. The Mounties got all the fighting and several were badly battered up. I was down town on picket [i.e., patrol] until 11 p.m. in the pouring rain. Very exciting. Hundreds of troops, filling the main streets between the City Hall and the Post Office. . . Mounted Police in their wonderful scarlet Mounted Rifles, Infantry with fixed bayonets, Fort Garry Horse, Ambulances, Machine Guns and Crews, 2 armoured cars . . . and even Winnipeg's only aeroplane overhead. Very grim in appearance. This display of force has broken the opposition.

Growing Up in a Ghost Town

PIERRE BERTON

> *After the gold rush ended, Dawson remained frozen in time. Pierre Berton grew up there in the 1920s.*

It occurs to me that there are few people living today who enjoyed the kind of childhood I had. For I was raised, in the 1920s, in the most unusual ghost town in Canada. When my parents arrived back in Dawson in 1921, after the war and a brief hiatus in Whitehorse, the town was a shell. It had once enjoyed a settled population of some twenty thousand and a floating population of ten thousand more. But in my day, twelve hundred of us, and sometimes fewer, rattled around in a community of empty buildings.

Empty it certainly was, and sometimes lonely, but there was a richness of texture there not to be found in the average Canadian small town of the period. When I rode my CCM bicycle along its wooden sidewalks it was as if I was pedalling through some deserted Hollywood set. Here were streetscape after streetscape of vacant emporiums, saloons, dancehalls, theatres, brothels, hotels, and boarding houses all padlocked and boarded up. They may have been old and decaying, these two-storey frame structures—slanting every which way like drunken old men, because of the unstable permafrost—but they had *style*. For all of my childhood I was surrounded by the faded elegance of Victorian frontier architecture: false fronts, fretted porticos and pediments, elaborate bay windows and cornices, pillars and dormers and neo-classical façades, all created from dressed lumber or stamped out of metal to counterfeit the architectural glories of the European past.

And the interiors! Squinting between the boards that protected the windows, I could distinguish, in the gloom, an unholy tangle of bric-à-brac and old junk, heaped together and left to tarnish, decay, and rot because it was too expensive to take it back Outside. Here were brass spittoons, seltzer bottles, carved walking sticks, embroidered pillows, framed portraits, and glass decanters, piled up on top of Morris chairs, overstuffed sofas, gaming tables, fancy pianos and organs, all stacked against mountains of picks, shovels, gold pans, and bits of mining machinery.

I took it all for granted, of course. Wasn't every town like this? Only in later years, looking back on this great, crowded attic of a community, did I realize the uncommon nature of my background....

Dawson was a junkyard, crammed with the artifacts of history, but I didn't know that. To me most of these were gigantic toys, expressly designed for my pleasure. Behind the school were two enormous Keystone drills, discarded long ago by the mining companies, over which we boys crawled and clambered. Close by were a couple of monstrous boilers in which more than one of us could hide. I remember spending most of a summer's afternoon concealed in one of those boilers. It was my own sanctum, a magic retreat that rendered me invisible to the world....

I didn't have an electric train; I had something far better. I had only to cross the bridge across the Klondike River to come upon a real train complete with locomotive and passenger cars, sitting on its tracks in the scrub bush. The Klondike Mines Railway, which once served as a link between Dawson and the miners working on upper Bonanza Creek, had long since been abandoned. But the train was still there and so were the rails. One day when I was about nine, a group of us boys, following the old track along Bonanza, came upon a handcar in perfect working order. We couldn't believe our eyes! Here, waiting for us in the wilderness, was a marvellous device that we could actually operate. Off we clattered along the rusty right of way at a spanking pace, each fighting for his chance to pump the handles.

When we got tired of playing trainman and conductor we could always play at being steamboat men. Few of us had ever seen an actual working locomotive, but we were all familiar with the sternwheelers that plied the upper and lower river. Six of these sat abandoned in an old shipyard a few miles downstream. We'd take the ferry across the Yukon and then make our way through the woods until we saw the silhouettes of the smokestacks and the old pilothouses rising above the birches. Our excitement grew as we reached the base of the first trio of ships—the ones that were in the best condition. Off we'd go in a rush to climb aboard the *Julia B.* or the *Schwatka* or the *Lightning*, each of us racing up the stairs to try to be the first on the upper deck so he could be captain. And so we frolicked away the summer afternoons, clambering down into the engine room, pretending to be passengers and crew, taking our turn in the pilothouse working the big wheel high above the surrounding forest and shouting "Full speed ahead!" Those days are long gone. All too soon the old boats crumbled away, the sternwheels rotted, the superstructures collapsed under the weight of the winter snows until only the hulls were left, warped and splintered, soon to be hidden in a tangle of alders. No more can Dawson's children play steamboat captain or railway engineer.

As a child, I lived surrounded by decay. Every season at least one building burned down. The hockey rink, the library, the theatre all went, for these were frame buildings overheated by wood furnaces and red-hot stoves. My parents lived with a dread of fire. I could not understand why they refused to allow me to go to the movies unaccompanied. But when the movie house burned down I knew why. Nothing was safe. The Eagle Hall—my father's lodge—was consumed. To my mother's horror the only thing saved was my father's photograph; she had never liked it. Apparently herculean efforts had been made to salvage this one framed portrait, which showed my father staring blankly ahead with glazed eyes, like a stuffed eagle.

"Why in hell would they bother with that?" I remember my mother asking, using an expletive rare to her. "Wasn't there something better they could have chosen? Now I am supposed to congratulate the heroes who saved that dreadful portrait from the fate it deserved."

Travelling Abroad, 1921

JAMES MAVOR

> *Soon after World War I ended, Canadians began travelling abroad. Like Professor James Mavor of the University of Toronto, they carried their prejudices and a strong currency.*

Praha, 24 Aug. 1921.
Kemp and I expect to sail on the 15th Sept. by the Empress of France from Liverpool. He is now in Berlin, feeding the poor children and otherwise conducting himself in a Quaker-like fashion. I strongly suspect Kemp of being a Pacifist. As matter of fact, now that the war is over I am Pacifist myself, as I was before it began, and have none but the friendliest feelings towards the enemy, who have indeed for the past five weeks behaved themselves very nicely to me. I am not so sure about the perfection of our

friends the Allies—the French are extraordinarily obstinate and the people here have of course their own interests to consider. I have been waiting for a train and have written this during a solitary dinner. I shall give you my menu and my bill:

1/2 chicken (most excellently cooked) and rice
Camembert
Long bread and butter

To drink I had as aperitif:
1) a small cognac
2) 1/2 bottle Bohemian white wine
3) a small Kümmel

My total bill including tip came to 70 Korum, which at the exchange of this morning is equal to 4/6d. . . .

I shall have to post this in Vienna as I find I have now to go to my train. Yours sincerely

James Mavor

Immigration, 1920s Style

UNKNOWN

For the information of folks ashore, who have never been in the steerage of a ship, it may be well to describe the quarters of the third-class passengers.

First in importance are the bedrooms, or staterooms as they are termed aboard ship. These as a rule contain four beds, or bunks, there being two on a side. The beds are framed in iron pipe, fitted with an elastic bottom of metal strips. The bedding consists of mattress, sheets, pillow with slip, blankets and coverlet, or bed spread. Each room has electric light, linoleum floor covering, white enameled walls, mechanically controlled ventilation, and heat when needed.

Next in importance is the steerage dining room. Some ships have two. A third-class dining-room is always large—more than 300 persons can sit down at the tables at once—and it is well lighted and well ventilated. The long tables are covered with neat cloths. Individual swivel chairs permit the passengers to sit at table in comfort, and the food is served on good crockery.

As to the food itself, it is wholesome and abundant. Here are some sample bills of fare on a recent voyage of the Adriatic, when she brought 1,250 passengers in third class:

Breakfast.

Rolled Oats and Milk.
Grilled Bacon.   Fried Eggs
Tea or Coffee.   Marmalade.
Bread and Butter.
11 a.m.—Beef tea and broth as required for women and children.

Dinner.

Barley Broth.
Roast Ribs of Beef.   Brown Gravy.
Dressed Cabbage.   Boiled Potatoes.
Plum Pudding.   Sweet Sauce.
Cheese.Biscuits.

Tea

Vegetable   Stew.
Cold Meats.   Pickles.
Beetroot and Ring Onions.
Bread and Butter.   Jam.
Tea or Coffee.
Apples and Oranges.

Supper

Gruel.   Biscuits.   Cheese.   Cocoa.

The third-class passengers have their own kitchen, which is as clean as the proverbial pin. Every pot and pan is bright and every dresser well scrubbed.

On most large ships the third cabin also has its lounge, or public room, which cuts quite as great a figure in the daily lives of the people who use it as that of first or second class.

It is a large room, with neatly paneled walls, well made benches or settees with curved backs of polished wood, and many small tables at which games may be played or drinks served—for prohibition does not place its restraining hand on the immigrant until he reaches this side of the ocean and he may have his beer or wine at sea when he wants it.

The entertainment of the public room of the steerage usually is informal, and also usually is spontaneous and interesting. On most voyages the conversation is in many tongues, and seldom lags.

The steerage has a piano of its own, and players are never wanting. There is also much volunteer music on the harmonica mouth organ, accordion and other favorite instruments of the passengers. To such music it is easy to improvise jig or reel, or dance a quadrille; and many a vigorous measure is beat out upon the linoleum floor, or in fine weather the deck, by stamping young feet as the ship drives steadily along through the pathless deep.

On the Lapland a popular feature in the musical programs of the steerage in times past has been the playing of a band composed of members of the ship's fireroom force. A band concert on deck for the benefit of third-class passengers usually is accompanied by dancing. On such occasions the saloon passengers usually gather to see the sport, and a carnival spirit prevails. It would be an uphill task at such a time to convince anyone on board the ship that a steerage passage is a voyage of gloom.

Hemingway Reports on Dr. Banting

ERNEST HEMINGWAY

> *Dr. Frederick Banting, co-discoverer of insulin and Nobel Prize winner, was a hugely famous figure in 1920s Canada. Ernest Hemingway, not yet famous, was a young reporter for the* Toronto Daily Star. *The two met in 1923.*

The report that he has been working on a serum to combat pernicious anemia is absolutely unfounded, Dr. Frederick G. Banting, winner of the Nobel prize on research told the *Star* today.

"It is an absolute lie," Dr. Banting stated. "Ever since the report got around, I have been having letters, telegrams and messages of all sorts coming in on us. The greatest service people could do to us is to leave us alone to work."

Dr. Banting spoke in his usual slow, careful way.

"I feel very badly that Mr. Charles Best was not mentioned in the Nobel award. I am very anxious that it should be known that Mr. Best had an intimate part in the discovery of insulin. I am sure that Mr. Best will feel it too. I am of course going to share the award with him in every way and want everybody to know the part he played. He ought to be back here from Boston on Wednesday.

"I am more than gratified that the award should have come to Canada and to the university but I think it is very important that everyone should give the proper credit to Mr. Best."

The Political Mood of the West, 1925

JOHN W. DAFOE

> *Editor of the* Free Press, *Winnipeg's John Dafoe was a shrewd observer of the political scene.*

My idea of the political objective to be aimed at is to keep the Conservatives out for the next few years at any rate. If by any chance Mr. Meighen were to get into office with a substantial majority behind him he would probably smash this country trying to make it conform with his theories. Fortunately this is not very probable. . . .

I should think it a safe prediction that there will be fewer straight supporters of Mr. King in the next parliament from the constituencies east of the lakes. The situation in the Maritime provinces is obviously bad and will probably get worse. No gains are possible in Quebec, and there may be losses in high tariff Liberals who might go into a combination such as that suggested above; and I am very skeptical about these reports of a great increase in Liberal strength in Ontario. It seems clear to me that if the Liberal Government is to remain in power a very large measure of Western support will be necessary. I should hope that Mr. King and the party managers realize this. Are they, I wonder, coolly studying the situation, putting aside their wishes and hopes, and trying to see things as they really are? My experience of politicians is that they are peculiarly subject to pipe-dreams. . . .

One thing certain here in the West is that in very few constituencies, perhaps none, will there be a clear fight between Liberals and Conservatives. If the next election were to be a fight in the Western constituencies between King and Meighen, there would be no occasion for alarm. King would carry three-quarters of the seats; but there will be three candidates in every seat and in some four. As I see it, in the average constituency the chance of the Liberal being elected falls with every candidate who takes the field.

In every rural constituency there will be a third candidate, a Progressive or a Gingerite. The division of the Progressive movement into right and left wings is progressive and will ultimately force a split; but except where the feud goes to the length of putting two candidates into the field, the vote will come together on election day. The Progressive vote, of course, will not be so large as in 1921 when it swept everything before it. But it will be large enough to bring to naught Liberal expectations of securing a large measure of support for the Government. (I write of things as they are; conditions might change if the Progressives go wrong on the question of ocean freight rates). My judgment—and it is at least disinterested and not altogether uninformed—is that in the average rural seat, in a three-cornered fight, the chances favor the Progressive, and where this candidate cannot be elected the chances favor the Conservative. It is true that at the moment the Conservatives seem pretty dead; but there is some Conservative organization work going on in Manitoba and Saskatchewan, and if the opportunity looked good, through the development of a fierce fight between the Liberals and Progressives, they might come back pretty strong, especially in those constituencies where they used to be the dominant political force. If Meighen picks up twenty seats in the prairie provinces the whole political future of Canada might be changed. He might do this quite easily under the conditions foreshadowed; he might get half of them right here in Manitoba. . . .

The Progressive strength is certainly not going to disappear, certainly not before the next election; but there is a possibility that it can be transformed into an ally of the Liberals and ultimately into an element of the Liberal party. There is here a political problem of the first order. I don't see anybody studying it except perhaps Mr. Dunning. One factor of great potential importance is that, with considerable exceptions, the Progressives, as distinct from the Gingerites, are in reality Liberals; and if some magician could only make the necessary shift for them they would be quite content to serve as a sort of Western wing; but the stream divides them and no one is able to throw a bridge over it.

A British Official's View of Canada, 1928

GEOFFREY WHISKARD

> *Britain had worries about Canada—its policies, its loyalty to Empire, its increasing Americanization. Geoffrey Whiskard of the Dominions Office wrote this confidential memo after a visit to the Dominion early in 1928.*

First. Of all the Dominions Canada differed most from my previous conception and differed by being so much better than I had imagined. The standard of civilization is very greatly superior to that of the other Dominions. Leaving aside South Africa, where owing to the presence of a very numerous black population the conditions are very different from those in the other Dominions, the civilization of Canada is much higher than that of New Zealand and enormously higher than that of Australia. In architecture, in the sort of pictures and decorations one sees in houses and hotels, in the kind of music one sees advertised, in their idea of the way to treat a travelling visitor such as Mr. Amery, in their manners and customs and the comfort of their houses and hotels, their food,—in everything— they are comparable to, and in some respects superior to, Great Britain. Only their press is definitely worse than either the Australian or the New Zealand press.

Secondly, apart from her superiority in her general standard of civilization, Canada has a very great advantage over Australia and a substantial advantage over New Zealand in the level of ability of her public men. We were all struck with the apparent competence and force of intellect and character displayed by the Provincial Governments as compared with the ignorance and incompetence of the State Governments in Australia. One of the Provincial Premiers at least—[A.L.] Taschereau [of Quebec]

—would be an outstanding figure in almost any collection of politicians, and [E.N.] Rhodes of Nova Scotia probably comes not far behind him. Of the Federal politicians I only met Mackenzie King, [minister of railways Charles] Dunning, [immigration minister Robert] Forke, and [R.B.] Bennett, the Leader of the Opposition. Of Mackenzie King I need say nothing, except that with all his obvious defects he compared pretty favourably with any of the other Dominion Prime Ministers at the last Conference. Dunning I imagine to be a good man—I should put him above any of the Commonwealth Ministers except [Australian prime minister Stanley] Bruce himself. Forke's only prominent characteristic is his amiability. Bennett is, I imagine, considerably better than [former Conservative prime minister Arthur] Meighen, with whom I had a few words, but I should imagine that he has neither a subtle nor a penetrating mind, and he appears to be incapable of really understanding the conception of inter-Imperial relations laid down at the Conference of 1926.

Thirdly, Canada, so far as I can see, is very much less Americanized than I had anticipated. Certain unessential external features of life, such as the make-up of their press, the perfection of their plumbing arrangements, the enormous consumption of iced water, down to such comparative trifles as the adoption of college yells and Greek Letter Societies, have been lifted bodily from the States: but in fundamentals they seem to me to be farther removed from the American outlook than, for example, the Australians, and in particular to have left room in their lives for something other than the mere thirst for wealth. Such indications of public taste and of the intellectual outlook of public men as the after dinner speeches which we heard may perhaps serve to illustrate this point. The level of speaking was really high: we heard no bad speech in the whole of Canada, except one at Quebec and one at St. John. Elsewhere the speeches were sober, well-phrased, really thoughtful, with some conception of an ideal as well as a material side to politics and policy—in short very far removed from the mixture of slush and anecdote which seems to take the place of oratory in the States.

Fourthly, I had no previous idea that Quebec was quite so French as it is, and that the difference between French Canada and the rest of Canada was so marked and apparently so permanent as seems to be the case. Coghill said to me what seems to me to be very true, that Quebec is loyalist but not imperialist. Certainly, while they display in Quebec every mark of a real devotion to the person of the Crown I could perceive no understanding of the real meaning of the Crown as an institution or of the real value of their community under the Crown with the rest of the Empire. It may well be that the conception of the Empire laid down in the Report of the Conference of 1926 may tend to widen rather than to bridge the gulf between French Canada and the rest of Canada and all the other Dominions.

Mussolini's Italy, 1928

ESCOTT REID

The Fascists had a firm grip on Italy by the late 1920s, and their attitudes and ambitions were beginning to worry the world. Reid, a Canadian and a Rhodes scholar, visited Italy at the end of 1927.

Castor oil, mob law, railways running on time, suppression of the press, fewer beggars, one hundred per cent. Italianitis, noisy nationalism, a rejuvenated Italy, a menace to the Mediterranean—which of these make up the essence of fascism? Is the fascist party nothing more than the Ku Klux Klan with a black shirt instead of the white sheet, or is the black shirt rather a cloak behind which hides a capitalist feudalism? Mussolini, a theatrical ass in the lion's skin of Napoleonism, or the rightly worshipped "Il Duce Magnifico," the savior of his country? Does fascism rest upon the fervent assent of the Italian people or is it a dictatorship, abhorred by the majority?

All these questions I asked myself as I prepared to sail to Italy on an Italian steamer—and now after an Atlantic voyage and some three weeks in Italy I find I still ask myself the same questions and the answer I get is not very much more definite than before. A few incidents I experienced may throw a little light on fascism. I give them for what they are worth.

The second day at sea. I am standing on the upper deck at the stern of the boat talking to an Italian of about thirty-five. He is a Sicilian. He has lived in the United States for twenty years and he is now returning for a visit to his old home. He has been in some kind of fairly skilled labor. I mention the fascists. We are quite alone; we are standing where no one can hear us; but before he replies he looks carefully all about him. Then, "It is not wise to say anything about the fascists. In Italy everyone is supposed to be fascist."

The same day. In the dining saloon I have been sitting beside an Italian who has been living in the States for a few years. He is a man of about twenty-seven, an officer in the Italian cavalry, a graduate in law of one of the oldest Italian universities. He introduces me to an Italian liqueur after dinner—the strega. We talk of everything, war and peace, Italy and Jugo-Slavia, the necessity for birth control in Italy, socialism, bolshevism. He is a socialist, he says. What does he think of fascism? He will say nothing. "It is too dangerous."

Mustn't Joke About Fascism

The fourth day out. I meet the Italian gentleman (let us call him the Signore) strolling along the deck with an American lady who also sits at the same dining table. I raise my arm in the fascist salute. In half seriousness the Signore returns it. We smile.

"What's that? It looks like a secret society," exclaims the American.

"That's the fascist salute," I reply.

"Oh, yes," says the Signore, "I am a fascist."

"And I, I am a Balliolist," I added.

Two men, Italians, are standing by the doorway, about eight feet away. One looks very displeased. He turns and mutters something to his friend. I am worried. I break in on the others' conversation. "I don't think these men liked the way we were making fun of the fascists." The Signore looks over his shoulder at them, he seems almost nervous, at least as nervous as a man looks who tries to show no feelings.

He leans to me to give me advice. I cannot help but smile as I listen. I half know what he is going to say. It is always the same, but I never can quite believe it.

"You must remember it is not wise in Italy to make fun of the fascists. It is better to pretend to know nothing about them. Say you have not been following events. You don't know anything about fascism—never heard of it. That is what I said a few years ago, the last time I was in Italy. You may be a [non-]fascist in Italy that is, not-fascist; you cannot be anti-fascist. It was different before the fascist revolution. When the communists were in control I would frequently argue with one of their leaders. We would have a bottle of wine together in a cafe and talk for three hours or so, and I would explain why I was no longer a communist. But now, the fascist would just say, 'That's enough,' and refuse to listen. When the fascists were first in power I used to give speeches against them. I was a Mason, and the Masons were opposed to fascism. But one day some of my friends who were fascists came to see me. They said to me, 'Even though we are your friends, if we were told to beat you to death we should do so. You had better be careful.' After that I disappeared for a year. Now I don't know anything about fascism."

The next day. At lunch we notice that a member of the American Legion at the next table (he says he is to marry an Italian countess) wears the button of the fascisti. Immediately the Signore says, "Perhaps he is a spy!"

My room in a small hotel in Naples, four days after landing. The boy of the hotel is practising his French on me. He brings me his card of record as a member of the fascist militia. He shows me a ribbon with three stars, one for 1921, one for 1922, one for 1923. He has been with the fascists from the beginning. After 1923 there are no stars. "Why?" I ask. "Are you not still a fascist?" He shrugs his shoulders in reply. "Oui, mais maintenant tout le monde est fasciste." (Yes, but now everybody is fascist.)

Political Discussion Banned

The streets of Naples. Everywhere on the walls of the buildings Mussolini's face stencilled—and nothing more. In other places scrawls, "Vive Mussolini," "Vive Il Duce."

Rome. A little beer parlor on a side street near the Colosseum. On the wall a placard with these words, "It is forbidden in this place to blaspheme or to discuss politics."

Rome. The House of Deputies. The conference of which I am a member is being officially shown around the Eternal City. We are seated in the Chamber of Deputies. A government official enters and invites us all to have refreshments at the house bar. Unfortunately for me the drink I am given tastes as if the fascists had mixed the liqueurs intended for their friends with the castor oil intended for their enemies.

The "Super Cinema" in Rome. Our international conference is again the guests of the government at a showing of the widely advertised film, "Il Duce." It is a bit of fascist propaganda. First the march on Rome is shown, Mussolini everywhere, striding along at the head of his legions in Naples, on the way to Rome, at Rome, being received by the king, then at his desk as prime minister. Then the achievements of fascism—in agriculture, industry, army, navy, air force—and everywhere Mussolini, driving a plow, caressing babies, launching ships, visiting Tripoli, now dressed as a sailor, now as a soldier, now acting the part of the vote-hunting politician, now the Napoleon. And then Mussolini on his latest triumphal tour throughout Italy, Milan, Florence, Rome, everywhere giving speeches—"The Mediterranean is 'Mare Nostrum.' If need be we shall carry the march on Rome further."

The coffee room of the conference hostel in Rome. The heads of four delegations are requested to meet one of the fascists after dinner, a Scot, a South African, a Canadian, a Hollander. We sit around a little table where the young man is drinking coffee. He is a very likeable youth; he has spent several years at the Boston Institute of Technology and speaks English very well. He is plainly very nervous. He does not seem to relish his task. He speaks sadly: "This morning a picture of Mussolini was removed from one of the dormitories. It has been found in the lavatory. Someone in your dormitory must have done it. You represent the various nationalities in that room. All I can say is, if it was meant as a joke it was a very poor joke indeed, and if it was meant in any other way then it was not the courtesy due to your hosts."

We look at each other, overcome by astonishment and suppressed emotions of laughter and of sorrow. The South African is the first to speak. He speaks gently as if he is explaining something to a child. "I assure you no insult was intended. You see there are no mirrors in our room. The only way we can shave is by taking down the two framed pictures from the wall, and by placing them in a certain light use them as mirrors. But I cannot understand how the picture came to be found in the lavatory. We always used it in our room." We all express our concurrence in this explanation. We had intended no insult. A mirror of some sort was a necessity for shaving. The fascist youth appears unconvinced and still with a look of inexpressible sadness on his face, he dismisses us.

Naples, Rome, Florence, Milan, on the docks, railways, streets, stations, everywhere, armed men. Soldiers of all kinds, fascisti in their black shirts, the national army, carabinieri, other policemen, and then more black shirts, special fascist military police, everywhere in Italy, armed men. Armed for what? For display, for civil uprising, or for international war?

Vancouver's Sprinter at the Olympics, 1928

R.T. ELSON

Amsterdam, Aug. 1—A scene of riotous joy was enacted in this great stadium here today when Percy Williams, Vancouver's brilliant schoolboy flash, achieved a second glorious victory in winning the 200-metre championship, after winning the 100-metre event on Monday.

The whole Empire wildly acclaimed the young winner, who in every heat had beaten the much-vaunted American track stars.

The Canadians in the stands broke through the police barriers and draped Williams with the Union Jack. P. J. Mulqueen, Canadian Olympic president, fought his way through a force of police and kissed the Canadian victor.

Williams, as in the 100 metres, had tremendous speed left for the final dash after trailing the leaders until near the finish. The curly-haired Canadian boy was unbeatable. It was the first double sprint victory since 1912.

Williams' victory meant defeat for the United States in the first two finals of the day and again the reverses were at the hands of representatives of different sections of the British Empire, the 110-metre hurdle championship having been won by Sydney Atkinson of South Africa. In both events the U.S. held the Olympic championships and failed in their defence.

Williams came through today as no other sprinter in history, because of the fact that he fought off the greatest sprinters the world has ever seen. Most of his opponents were three or five years older and one of them was three times an Olympic champion. He remains modest in his victory.

After the race he said: "I can't say how I won. I just ran. I am glad all competition is over, and I want The Daily Province to be sure to tell Mother, Mr. Graham Bruce and the High School of Commerce." Mr. Bruce was Williams' coach at the high school.

Percy adds that when he gets home, he hopes to have some fun hunting.

It is a grand and glorious day for Canada here.

The Great Crash of 1929

UNKNOWN

Unnerving stock market declines since Thursday paled into insignificance beside the tidal wave of liquidation which flooded the Toronto and Montreal Stock Exchanges yesterday, and set prices crashing downward in the greatest collapse ever witnessed in Canada.

Hundreds of undermargined trading accounts, which successfully withstood the tremendous pressure of preceding breaks, cracked under the strain, and forced liquidation added its pressure to the overwhelming volume of selling.

Trading on both Toronto and Montreal Exchange and curb markets far exceeded all previous records. At Toronto 331,100 shares changed hands, and at Montreal 525,000 shares participated in the most drastic slump in the history of the Montreal Stock Exchange. New low prices were established in all parts of the Canadian list, and no less than 62 stocks reached new low ground for the year on the Toronto Exchange alone. Forty-five issues set "new lows" on the Standard Stock and Mining Exchange.

The immediate cause of the decline was a terrific volume of early selling on the New York Stock Exchange, and almost simultaneously the Toronto and Montreal lists began the steep descent to new low prices for the year or longer. . . .

As selling orders continued to pour into the market a condition of panic arose among the more nervous nonprofessional traders, who threw their holdings into the market with scant regard for what they believed to be their intrinsic value. . . .

Reassuring statements by bankers and other financial authorities, and reports that banking support was acting as a brake on the decline, were not without their influence, but the main purpose of the speculative element was to get out of the stock market before it became completely demoralized. The very efforts to avoid participation in a panic led to even greater confusion, and the floor of the Toronto Stock Exchange developed into a madly milling mass of men whose main purpose was to sell. Bids at prices five or more points below the market were often snapped up with eagerness. . . .

Nellie McClung Celebrates Victory in the "Persons" Case

NELLIE MCCLUNG

> *The British North America Act had confined membership in the senate to "persons"; the Canadian courts had decided women were not persons. A group of women fought this case all the way to the Empire's highest court, the Judicial Committee of the Privy Council, and won. Women could now become senators.*

Our discontents are passing. We may yet live to see the day when women will be no longer news! And it cannot come too soon. I want to be a peaceful, happy, normal human being, pursuing my unimpeded way through life, never having to stop to explain, defend, or apologize for my sex. . . I am tired of belonging to the sex that is called the Sex. And it is because the finding of the Privy Council that we are "persons," once and for all, will do so much to merge us into the human family, that we are filled with gratitude and joy. The *Winnipeg Tribune* is before me, and I have just read the interviews given by several prominent women. The lead says "indulgent laughter, mock congratulations and ironic expressions of gratitude greeted the news from London that their lordships had decided that women were legally persons within the meaning of the B.N.A. Act and were consequently entitled to sit in the Senate."

It does sound humorous. But there had to be a ruling on it. Women have been regarded as creatures of relationships rather than human beings with direct responsibilities. That is why one senator said women could not sit in the Senate, and give unbiased judgments, that is, married women, because they would naturally have to do what their husbands wished them to do. He might have gone on, and said any woman who had a male relative would owe her first allegiance to him. The world has gone on since that law prevailed, but the dear old fellow hasn't noticed. . . .

We cannot understand the mentality of the men who dare to set the boundaries of women's work. We object to barriers, just as the range horses despise fences. For this reason we protested the action of the Alberta Hotelmen's Association when they decided that women must not enter their beer parlors. Not but what we knew it was much better to be out than in, but we believe in equality.

A Communist Goes to Jail, 1931

FREDERICK GRIFFIN

> *Tim Buck was leader of the Canadian Communist Party, a small group that frightened many in Depression-era Canada. In 1931, he was sent to the Kingston Penitentiary for his actions.*

They sat in the row of seats . . . until the judge, sharply, told them to stand up. They stood in line, without plea or fear, without mockery and without rebellion. Certainly in this drama of Canadian justice these Communists did not, by word or deed, detract from its dignity.

Thus standing, they met their punishment.

For them there was no procession of clergymen, no neighbours, no comrades, no score or more of character witnesses to say that they were good citizens, churchgoers, kind fathers, philanthropists, honest men who had never taken an unearned nickel, honourable men who had never broken their word. Their character was not in question, merely their ideas and ideals. For them their single lawyer spoke but briefly. A few words, and he was done.

The judge invited them to speak. The small Tim Buck alone responded. He did not beg; he did not plead; he took a pace forward like a soldier and, looking front, said, "I accept the sentence of the court. I only hope that those who trusted me will find that I proved worthy."

Then he stepped back. . . .

The court was silent when Mr. Justice Wright pronounced sentence that sent these men to Kingston Penitentiary for terms up to five years. A full-voiced man, he spoke quietly, as if he felt that the occasion was historic, the outlawing of Communism as a philosophy and force in Canada. . . .

The condemned men stepped out smartly as a file of soldiers. Only a wave of Buck's hand, a short smile of farewell to a friend, showed that they were really men and not ideas who were going to jail.

Riding the Rods

UNKNOWN

The number of unemployed increased exponentially during the Depression years. Many men rode freight trains from one end of the country to the other looking for work.

On the Saturday night of April 15 my friend and I took the last street car out to Sutherland having previously found out that a freight train was leaving for Winnipeg during the early hours of Sunday morning. We slunk around the yards till we came upon a brakeman and asked when the freight for the East was pulling out. Before he could reply a torch light beamed in our faces and the "bull" asked "Where are you guys going?" "East"—"Winnipeg." "Well that freight won't pull out till seven to-morrow morning." We thanked the policeman for this information and retired to the shadow of a nearby Pool Elevator, lighted cigarettes and attempted to keep warm. Even I, with 2 pairs underclothing, 2 shirts, a sweater, my brown suit, overalls, overcoat, winter cap & 2 pairs sox was getting chilly.

Presently we became restless & walked out onto the tracks to espy an ancient looking empty coach with a light in it. Prowling lower we observed a notice on the side telling us it was for the use of stockmen only. A brakeman informed us that the coach was to be put on the freight to Winnipeg for the use of some stockman travelling. We entered the coach, found a fire burning in the stove, wiped the dust off the seats, spread them out bed fashion & were soon asleep. We were suddenly awakened by the guard who informed us that the train was pulling out in 5 minutes and that a "bull" was going to travel with the train. Observing the "bull" walking down the side of the train we waited till he rounded the end before ourselves, hopping out, walked after him & inspected the box cars. All but one were sealed, this "one" being half full of coal. There were already about ten other travellers sprawling in various positions amongst the coal.

The first division stop was Wynyard and here my friend turned back. He had a warm bed in Saskatoon, a mother, father and home—not work. He explained that he was a decent fellow, had never been in jail in his life &, didn't like freight riding. What would his mother say if he was arrested? Besides, supposing there was no work in Toronto what would we do? We'd be arrested, vagrants. He had never been in a big city before, our money would not last long, we might even starve to death! In other words, he'd had enough—just chicken hearted.

The sun was warm and I rode on top of a box car all day. Towards evening the train pulled in at the next division stop, Bredenbury. I was hungry & made for the town semi-satisfying my appetite in a "Chinks". Returning to the train I fell in with two of my fellow passengers of the coal car who had been "bumming" the houses. They were lads of 23 also heading for Toronto—happy but broke. Arriving at the tracks we walked boldly towards the freight & walked right into the "bull" who instantly showed his ignorance. "What the hell d'you fellows want here." We put him right as to our wants whilst he accompanied us to the entrance of the yards and the freight steamed out. He informed us that should he see us around again he would put us all in "clink". One of my new-found confederates thanked him very much and suggested that as we had lost the freight and had nowhere to sleep we should very much appreciate his hospitality. But the "bull" was not so hospitable & we slept in the C.P.R. roundhouse beside a boiler. I slept well inspite of the sudden change from feather to concrete mattress. Following morning a pail & water from the boiler brightened our appearance & we made for town agreeing that the inhabitants should pay dearly for their ignorant railway cop. Meeting the oldest resident, I think he must have been, on "Main Street" we enquired as to the whereabouts of the local "town bull", the mayor, the residences of the station agent, the railway cop and the R.C.M.P. local. With this information we commenced our labours for breakfast. Seeing a man working in a garden we wondered whether he would like our aid or company. He was not impressed by either but gave us $1 for "eats". Entering the local hotel we explained our circumstances and gorged for 25 cents per head. During the morning we lay down on some open prairie & slept till roused by a crowd of children who had come to inspect us. One yelled "Hobo, hobo we've got some candy for you", but as I got up hopefully they took to their heals and ran for town. Our stomaches informed us dinner time had arrived, one of the boys set out for the mayors house and brought back a fine "hand out" which we consumed. The other set out for another of our addresses, split some wood & received a "sit-down." Then it was my turn to go "bumming". I set out for a large house set back from the town which looked hopeful. I tapped at the door nervously and a large man poked his head cautiously out of the door letting out an equally large dog as he did so. My knees knocked and I stuttered something about work & eat. The man told me he did not feed tramps & would set his dog on me. I moved towards the dog which instantly fled with its tail between its legs and the man slammed the door. As I was walking down the path the man popped his head out of an upstairs window and threatened to inform the police if I did not "get clear" immediately.

Towards evening the Winnipeg freight pulled in and we boarded it as it pulled out of the yards. There were no "empties" but a stock coach on the back, so we sat on the steps of this. As dusk fell we stopped for water at some place & the guard sighted us. He came up & inspected us, then unlocked the coach & told us to get in there for the night, we might go to sleep on the steps & fall off. Next morning we awoke to find our freight standing in the Portage La Prairie yards. Two "bulls" walked up the train, inspected the seals, glanced at the stock coach where we had assumed an attitude of sleep once more, and walked off. We left the freight at a street crossing outside Winnipeg, yelled at a passing truck driver and were whirled into the city. The two lads I was with got a free shave at the Barber College and we learnt that the city was handing out meals to transients. After much walking and enquiring we obtained meal tickets and set out for the soup kitchens, which used to be the c.n.r. Immigration Hall where I stopped when first in Canada. The meal was awful! We walked down a counter gradually accumulating our ration which consisted of a piece of bread & square of butter, a small dish containing about a spoonful of sugar, a tin bowl containing a green fluid sometimes called soup, a tin plate on which had been dumped, dirty potatoes, two large hunks of fat, some carrots and thick gravy, and a mug contain hot water the same colour as weak tea. We sat on a bench containing males of all types, nationalities and descriptions and attempted to eat. The gentleman on my right had developed a strange habit of wiping a running nose with the back of his hand between each mouthful which did not increase the flavour of my meal. A large bowl of rice was placed on the table for desert but as I had my plate already filled with leavings I did not try any.

We left the soup kitchens and made enquiries about the times of freight trains. There was one leaving from the c.n.r. Transcona yards at around midnight for Toronto. We commenced the 9 miles walk to Transcona.

On the way we passed over a bridge on the side of which some humorist had written with chalk "I'm fed up; for further information drag the river." Over the bridge is St. Boniface where there is a large catholic church, seminary, school, nuns home etc. etc. Whilst passing the seminary and admiring its size and beauty we espied the kitchen through a basement window. Thoughts concerning the higher arts vanished from our heads, we looked at each other, looked for the nearest door, and entered, coming upon a fat cook. I moved my hand over my chest and wore my most pious expression and one of the boys addressing the cook as "brother" explained that we were extremely undernourished and should be pleased with some bread. The cook prepared some sandwiches containing cold slabs of steak and we departed praising the Lord, the cook and ourselves.

Towards late afternoon we arrived at the yards, parked ourselves on the grass outside the fencing and built a fire of old ties—and commenced a 7 hour wait. We consumed our sandwiches which were delicious— I think I'll become a priest.

Gordon Sinclair Encounters India

GORDON SINCLAIR

> Toronto Daily Star *reporter Gordon Sinclair wrote in a breezy style that made him famous. His newspaper sent him around the world, hoping that his prejudices—and eye for a good story—would appeal to its readers. They did, and when turned into books, to all Canadians.*

When I got back to my own diggings a hairy Hindu all done up like the Grand High Potentate of the Punjab was waiting on the threshold. I thought sure he had some message of might for me, but he solemnly announced that he was barber,—"To the excellent gentlemen of this hotel."

He was more erect than a pre-war Prussian guardsman. A huge bristly beard stuck out from his handsome face. He resembled Abyssinia's modest monarch who claims to be king of all the kings.

"Barber?" I asked in dismay. "Yes, sahib. I have been assigned to you. I am ready sahib." He unstrapped a brace of leather cases and took out enough instruments for a base hospital.

"Who assigned you?" "Your servant, sahib." "Well, he's all wrong Baron, I go to the barber shop."

His majesty of the shears smiled one of those smiles which say, "tut, tut, my child; Santa Claus won't come to bad little boys." Then he said; "a misunderstanding, sahib. You see there are no barber shops."

As it turned out the rajah of the razor was quite right. If you crave a head rub in this distant land you make an appointment with one of these wandering shearsmen and he comes to your room or, if you are hard up, you squat at any street corner and have the job done there and then. Bombay, Calcutta and Madras have their barber shops but in the plains there are none.

Practically every corner in the Jhandi Chow bazaar sports a curb barber, doctor, ear cleaner, and chemist. You can get a leg cut off while you wait or have a glass eye fitted in no time. I saw a man get a glass eye one day and a second one get the rotting end of a diseased finger nipped off with a pair of scissors.

An open sewer ran along the road where the anatomists were doing their stuff, and if there was one less than a billion flies to the square yard I must be first cousin to the Nyzam of Hyderabad, who is India's richest potentate.

Not only can you get yourself tatooed, shaved, trimmed, operated on, fitted with glasses, teeth, trusses or turquoise tiaras but you can get almost anything on earth made to measure while you squat among the holy heifers and the Brahminee bulls. High boots for example. Any white man going into the jungle without high boots plays hookey from a mausoleum. I had been advised to wear knee-high leather if I went to Benares and since I plan to go both there and into the Bengal tiger country, thought it worth pricing knee boots.

While in one boot shop—if you can call it "in"—a girl of twenty or so, filthy but good looking, came to buy sandals. This was a great luxury to her but she dare not, under any condition, enter the sacred presence of the shop. Oh, no. That would contaminate the place. Word of it would spread far and wide and before the merchant could open again he'd have to buy a cow and give it to the temple or kick in with many rupees.

So the girl shouted out her demands while the merchant pretended not to listen. Then he sorted out a cheap bit of junk, told the girl to lay her money on the sidewalk and tossed the sandals out. An assistant scurried out to pick up the square coins. Whether the sandals fitted or not didn't matter a hoot. The girl will probably have them stolen anyhow as she sleeps on an ant-covered slice of sidewalk.

When I barged back from the bazaars the baffled barber was still waiting, but this time he was joined by another imposing gent in silk and fur. This boy had a spiked beard and a long pigtail. Not a short pigtail like bull fighters wear but a long one so that when he dies the goddess of creation can reach down from her place in paradise and jerk this man quickly to her side.

"I have come to look over your clothes," he declared. It all looked like a gag to me and since there were newspapermen in the hotel from seventeen papers I thought they were pulling my leg.

"Well," I said, "The way things are going you'll be able to look them over any day next week in the nearest pawn shop."

"Pawn shop, sahib?" "Yes pawn shop; where men who forget to say no have to leave their clothes."

"You mean sell them, sahib?" "Call it that if you like." "Ah, so, the gods favor me. You have clothes to sell." I gave up and unloosened the only Hindustani I have learned. The last word rhymes with jell, well and Nell. It worked.

Founding the CCF

EUGENE FORSEY

Forsey was present at the creation of a democratic socialist party, the Cooperative Commonwealth Federation, in Regina in 1932.

Democratic socialism began in Canada fifty years ago this month when the provisional council of the Co-operative Commonwealth Federation adopted the Regina Manifesto and solemnly vowed to eradicate capitalism.

Fifty years ago King Gordon and I drove from Montréal to Regina via Chicago for the first annual convention of the Co-operative Commonwealth Federation, the forerunner of the New Democratic Party. Our friend Jacques Bieler was with us for a certain distance, though I forget where we dropped him off. The joke was that either Bieler or Gordon had known a girl in practically every stop along the way. I wasn't in their class at all. I was never a success with the ladies and I hadn't travelled across Canada as often as they had. Gordon and I were members of the League for Social Reconstruction, which had been founded in 1932 as "an association of men and women who are working for the establishment in Canada of a social order in which the basic principle regulating production, distribution, and service will be the common good rather than the private profit." In that same year various groups and parties had come together in Calgary to form the CCF under J.S. Woodsworth, the socialist member of parliament who was also the LSR's honorary president. He was a saintly figure. There was nothing priggish or self-righteous about him, he never made you feel that you were a lower kind of being, but you soon had the feeling that he was a higher type of being.

He was a very easy person to get along with, but occasionally he could put his foot down rather hard. People were led astray—to their subsequent discomfiture—by his mild and kindly manner. There's a story told about when he was in his final illness and on his way to the west coast. His train passed through Winnipeg and some of the faithful visited him in his Pullman.

"Winnipeg North Centre must be held," he told them.

"Oh yes, J.S.," they replied.

"And the candidate has got to be chosen absolutely democratically."

"Oh yes, of course."

Then, as they left the compartment, he called out, "And the candidate must be Stanley Knowles!"

In January, 1933, the research committee of the LSR was invited to draft a manifesto for the new party. The draft was largely the work of Frank Underhill, the University of Toronto historian who with Frank Scott, the McGill law professor and poet, had founded the League as a Canadian version of the Fabian Society. Underhill prepared the first draft at his summer home in Muskoka that June and circulated it among a group of us—notably Frank Scott and King Gordon—before sending it on to the provisional national council just before the Regina convention. I saw it and made some very minor comments, possibly suggesting that a sentence might be broken here or a comma put in there.

The convention was held in the Regina city hall between July 19 and July 21, 1933. I'm vague about how many attended, but according to Frank Scott's account that year in The Canadian Forum, there were 131 delegates from six provinces, including nine members of parliament and five members of the national executive, plus 100 or so visitors. The 4,000 word draft was read aloud and then debated. It had a rousing preamble and sections on planning, the socialization of finance, social ownership, agriculture, external trade, co-operative institutions, the labour code, socialized health services, the BNA Act, external relations, taxation and public finance, freedom, social justice, and an emergency programme to deal with the Great Depression.

The section on social justice, which then meant law with a social angle, had been put into Underhill's draft by St. George Stubbs, a district judge from Manitoba. He was a man of great ability and integrity, but very much a Stubbsian. Once, when one of his judgements was overruled by the court of appeal, he hired a hall, held a meeting, and made a speech saying what he thought of the ruling. Not surprisingly he was removed from the bench. He went on to become a CCF member in the Manitoba legislature and later sat as an independent, which is what he should have been in the first place.

There were a lot of characters representing very different interests in Regina and in the party. Bill Irvine of the United Farmers of Alberta had been touched by Social Credit and was anxious to get some Social Credit stuff in the manifesto. Ernie Winch from British Columbia wanted to get something in about nudism. The rest of us were somewhat leery. I told him to imagine the *Winnipeg Free Press* headline, "J.S. Woodsworth goes nudist."

"But I admire the human form," he said.

That was all very well, but I don't think he got much support. Winch was a dear old soul, a rip-roaring Marxist but the gentlest of men. In the B.C. legislature his great subjects were people in mental hospitals and animals in the zoo.

The discussions were lively, particularly about compensation for nationalized industries and the use of violence. The whole thing seemed on the verge of breaking up over and over again. The people from B.C. were more Marxist than Marx. They didn't think much of the Communist Party, not for the usual reasons but because it wasn't *orthodox* enough. They most admired some British party that had about a dozen members.

"There aren't very many of them, are there?" I once asked.

"No. But sound, very sound," came the reply.

At the other extreme were the United Farmers of Ontario, represented by W.C. Good and Agnes Macphail. They were terrified by all the socialist rhetoric. Good, who was as good as his name but not a very clear thinker in my judgement, confided to Frank Scott on the train to Regina his fear that the CCF would become a party! For that outfit of Progressives, "party" was a dreadful, wicked, dirty word. Their idea was to get everyone around the table in a committee and everyone would co-operate without any party feeling. In the end, I believe, Good cast the sole vote against the manifesto.

Agnes Macphail, then a member of parliament and part of the Ginger Group with Woodsworth, used to get into terrific fights with Angus MacInnis, the B.C. Marxist who had married Woodsworth's daughter Grace. Once I said something nice about him and Agnes said, "Oh, he must have some good points. I don't know why Grace would have married him if he didn't." But her real fury was reserved for the feminists.

There was a feminist warhorse named Mrs. Lucas, accompanied by her small, grey husband who was never referred to as anything but Mrs. Lucas's husband. On every conceivable and inconceivable occasion she got up and moved that "there be a woman on this committee," until John Queen, the mayor of Winnipeg, got in ahead of her and boomed, "I move that there be a man on this committee!" Agnes Macphail got fed up with this woman business and showed her displeasure when the ladies at the convention had a luncheon for her. She swept in, dressed in her opera cloak, and said, "All the time I've been in the House and I've never asked for anything on the grounds that I was a woman. If I didn't deserve something on my own merits, I didn't want it. This woman stuff makes me sick." Then she wrapped her cloak around her and shot from the room, leaving behind an infuriated mass of seething feminists.

The line between left and right became confusing at times. In Montréal Scott and Gordon and I were regarded by the respectable citizens as Stalin's right-hand men. Of course, you didn't have to be very left-wing to get into bad odour politically in Montréal. I first got into it with an article in *defence* of Arthur Meighen. I was described as a Bolshevik. Then we got to Regina. We had heard vague stories about the Saskatchewan Farmer-Labour Party's scheme for land tenure called "use tenure," so one of the first things we did was to ask George Williams to explain exactly what this meant. He was sitting in a corner and he shrank back into his armchair and roared, "No one is coming here from the East to take our socialism away from us!"

We sat bolt upright. "But Comrade Williams (or Brother Williams, or whatever we called him in those days), nothing could be further from our minds." But we never did get anything out of him. It was perfectly clear that he regarded us as the personal representatives of the Canadian Pacific Railway and the Bank of Montreal. The tables were turned completely, and we hardly knew whether we were on our heads or our heels.

Scott and Gordon played a much more prominent role than I did. I was more in the background, but I may have been more vocal than I recall. Woodsworth, Irvine, MacInnis, Macphail, Scott, Gordon, Stubbs, Good, Underhill, Winch—they were highly individualistic people. These were people who had reacted against the political culture of the day, against the injustices of the economic system, against the injustices of the law. It was a kaleidoscopic group brought together by the terrible unemployment, the terrible drought, and practically no social security.

We thought we were doing something historic and important, that the Regina Manifesto would be the beginning of something great. We were going to get labour and the farmers together to become a major force in the life of this country. It was not altogether an extravagant hope, with economic conditions as they were. And we succeeded in patching up many of the differences. We had high hopes.

R.B. Bennett and the Farmers, 1932

UNKNOWN

> Conservative R.B. Bennett won power in 1930 on the promise to blast Canada's way into the markets of the world. His way of dealing with his rural constituents and their concerns for markets did not go over well with one small-town newspaper.

Three thousand representative farmers went to Ottawa last week to lay their suggestions before Premier Bennett for guidance at the Imperial Conference. The farmers located at the Fair Grounds and sent a committee to ask the Premier to confer with them there. Mr. Bennett would not go; said he was too busy. So three thousand farmers went back home. Whose fault? It seems incredible that such a gathering, costing from $50,000 to possibly three times that amount would go from all parts of Ontario and Quebec without some definite arrangement, for an interview. Yet it seems equally incredible that with all those representatives in Ottawa the Premier would fail to keep an appointment. Anyway it must have been a great disappointment. Meantime the stage is all set for the

Conference. Whether the Farmer interests are provided for or not, we are informed the fleet of specially built Buick cars are ready; the Chateau Laurier suites are perfectly fitted and all other arrangements perfect. As usual the big guns may acknowledge Farmers as the backbone of the country and legislate to leave them skin and bone.

A Glimpse of Canada's Prime Minister, 1932

SIR A. LASCELLES

> *The British, when they stood in Bennett's way at the 1932 Imperial Conference, were roughed up, and there was some resentment in London. Sir A. Lascelles tried both to explain "R.B." and to smooth over matters in this letter sent to a senior British Cabinet minister.*

It seems probable that Mr. Bennett will shortly be going over to London for a few weeks.

The impressions he will bring back from such a visit are bound, I imagine, to have considerable effect on the future working-out of the Ottawa agreements in this country, and, as I've had many opportunities of studying R.B. at close quarters during the past 20 months, I should very much like to send you a few purely personal observations, if you won't think it impertinent of me.

It was perfectly obvious to those of us who were able to observe the day-to-day progress of the [1932 Imperial Economic] Conference from the shelter of Rideau Hall, that R.B. was behaving in a manner that must have seemed to all of you remarkable (to put it mildly). It is just because it did not seem remarkable to me, but quite natural, from my knowledge of the man, that I feel now that I might be of some small assistance if I tried to pass that knowledge on to you. For the next two years, in all probability, R.B. *is*, and will continue to be, Canada; and, the relations of Canada to U.K. being of such great importance just now, one naturally wants to make any contribution one can towards their betterment. . . .

Aggression is the only method of negotiation that he knows. Consider his background: he was never at a University, save as a day-student; at 22, he was pitchforked into the law-courts of the West, where abusing the Plaintiff's attorney, & beating the table in one's shirt-sleeves, are the recognized, & only, forensic methods; Western politics are equally crude; great wealth came to him early & unexpectedly; he has never had a wife or child to dragoon him, as only wives and children can; he has never even had a close, and candid, friend; and his only home, since he grew up, has been a series of hotels, so that he has not even had the valuable social training that a man gets from dealing with his own cook. These may seem trivial circumstances, in an estimate of a statesman; but, personally, I believe that a knowledge of such circumstances is of considerable help in attempting to understand the causes of the curious behaviour of some of our fellow-creatures! One who has known Bennett for many years is reported to have said of him, "R.B. is partially educated, but wholly uncivilised." With this somewhat primitive habit of mind go several other primitive characteristics; an almost savage sensitiveness to ridicule, small vanities, a child-like impatience of obstacles, an equally child-like appreciation of sympathy & small acts of friendliness—traits that are, perhaps, not . . . infrequently found with first-rate intellectual capacity, which he certainly has.

One such trait is a passionate devotion to England & things English; to the King, as King & as a man; to the English language (though he is an incurable splitter of infinitives!) . . . to all the things which you yourself have spoken, and written, about so infinitely better than I can express them.

And so I come to the gist of this letter: that, if R.B. comes to London and is not welcomed as a friend, it will, I believe, be a terrible shock to him, & the result might be disastrous to the relations of the two countries in the immediate future. When he discusses possible places for his much-needed holiday, he refuses to consider any except England; and if England sends him back happy, any bad vapours of the Conference that may still be hanging over Ottawa would finally be blown away.

Hitler in Power, 1933

MATTHEW HALTON

> *Journalist Matthew Halton was a close observer of the new Nazi regime in Germany. In a 1933 series of articles, notable for their clearsightedness, he laid out the practices and aims of Hitler's government.*

Vienna, Oct. 15—During the last month in Germany I have seen and studied the most fanatical, thoroughgoing and savage philosophy of war ever imposed on any nation. It is this philosophy which gives the chief and fateful significance to Germany's tragic withdrawal from the league and the disarmament conference, and the consequent destruction of fifteen years of the most difficult political reconstruction.

My overwhelming impression as set forth in the ensuing series of articles deals not with the economics of Hitlerism nor the Jewish question, but with the mental preparations of Germany for war. This is not a sensational dream, but a cold fact, and anyone who can read and hear could learn the same in 24 hours in Germany.

"War is both inevitable and necessary and therefore it is imperative. The nation's mind should be directed toward it from childhood," says the latest manual for high school teachers—a book which makes Attila seem in comparison pacifistic. "Only war can change our prevailing need and children must be prepared for war from the age of six. They must learn military tactics from the birds, hills and streams. They must learn to infect the enemies' drinking water with typhoid bacilli and to spread plague with infected rats. War is the only inexorably just test for all will and ability." That is but a sample of this ferocious primer for German children.

In a military hour on the radio, Germans are taught that all else must be subordinated to preparations for war.

God has again become a pan-German satellite. In the churches people chant "God has made me German. Germanism is a gift of God. God wishes I should fight for my Germanism."

Students at Heidelberg and everywhere else are urged and trained in the art of arms. People are inflamed by lurid posters of the Versailles treaty, crying "Death rather than slavery."

Nazis say, "No declaration of war next time." Sixteen-year-old boys bear arms and throw hand grenades at dummies.

There is a nation-wide campaign teaching that the new Germany must be built on a system of military eugenics. "German mothers must exhaust themselves bearing children for war," said Von Papen, and teachers' manuals go into more detail. Germany is literally becoming a laboratory and breeding ground for war, unless I am deaf, dumb and blind. The old myth about the German superman being destined to conquer the world is being taught and believed again. You cannot even pass one book shop without seeing it all yourself.

Hitler's radio speech on Saturday night, swearing that Germany wants peace, made a fairly good impression, but was sheer blatant mockery to anyone who has seen Germany in the last few months. Germany is being taught for war. Nazi rulers are teaching crude absurdities regarding race, war, history, women and everything, and imprisoning everyone who dares dissent . . .

Toronto the Good: I

UNKNOWN

There are interesting developments every summer in one or other of the cities of Canada on the subject of the law concerning proper wearing apparel for bathing; but Toronto has provided much the most interesting development of 1936, in the discovery that there is apparently no law against indecent exposure of the person except during the act of bathing, swimming or washing. Some thirty men were charged last week with violation of a city by-law which reads: "No person shall bathe, swim or wash the person in public water in or near the municipality of the city of Toronto without wearing a proper bathing suit to prevent indecent exposure of the person." All the cases were dismissed for the good and sufficient reason that none of the accused had swum, bathed, paddled or even washed; they were all lying on the sand sunbathing. Foiled on this crucial point, the police gave up. . . Evidently [they] considered the costume worn by these men—which consisted of trunks, with nothing above the waist—as involving indecent exposure. . . We should have expected the sartorial requirements for bathing to be less, not more, than those for occupations which are carried on in the bright and transparent air of a Toronto afternoon. Water, even public water, affords a certain measure of kindly concealment which air denies. But no; the nude manly bosom is illegal in Lake Ontario but lawful on the old Ontario strands. Public discussion of this situation has gone off at a tangent and ranges around the wholly irrelevant and non-legal question of whether the nude manly bosom is pleasing to the eye. . . . Our own opinion on this point is quite clear. Some manly bosoms are excellent, but most are terrible. But how anybody got the idea that beauty and . . . legal decency have anything to do with one another we cannot imagine. . . If we are going to start using the police to suppress ugliness, goodness only knows where we shall end.

Newfoundland Under the Commission of Government

SIR JOHN HOPE SIMPSON

> *Bankrupt, Newfoundland surrendered Dominion status in 1934 and reverted being run by London. A Commission of Government provided the executive direction. One member, Simpson, provided this comment on Newfoundland's sectarianism, public service, and economic condition in 1934.*

J.H.S. to Edgar and Eleanor, Newfoundland Hotel, 14 May 1934
. . . We have to thank you, Eleanor, for a jolly long letter, which arrived yesterday and brought us a vivid whiff of an English spring. . . You may imagine how it made us long for home, though we also have the spring. The fields are green and there are lambs everywhere and the fishermen are busy caulking and painting their boats and repairing their schooners, and the little leaves are coming out with the lilacs and the wych-elms and presently it is going to be unpleasantly hot. . . .

Here all goes well. The work is still exceedingly heavy, but I am having more efficient assistance, and shall have still more efficiency in the office when we bring in the 65-year rule and get rid of the fossil crust which is ubiquitous. That happens on 30th June. And in June, we are to hold the first public competition examination for the civil service in the history of

N.F.L. Incidentally, that is a much more important reform than appears on the surface. Hitherto, one of the criteria of appointment has been religion. If you appoint a Catholic, a similar appointment must be earmarked for a member of the Church of England and another for one of the United Church of Canada. Now we are asking for education rather than for religion in our candidates. This religious question has been one of the banes of the island. A contract given to a Methodist implied one to a Catholic and another to a C. of E., and because two Catholics running have been in charge of the General Hospital that position is now regarded as a Catholic preserve. . . .

This weekend, I am going to make a short tour down to Trepassey & then back & out to St. Mary's & back again via Whitbourne, where we are settling 10 ex-service unemployed families on the land as an experiment. They have been out there a fortnight now & have one house nearly completed and the foundations of three others laid. I trust very heartily that the experiment will succeed, as it will then be the first of 50 others of the same kind. The trouble is that once we began the experiment, there are scores of other unemployed ex-servicemen who want to do the same. . . .

The On-to-Ottawa Trekkers Meet Bennett

RONALD LIVERSEDGE

> In 1935, the Depression continuing unabated, a number of unemployed men set off from Vancouver to Ottawa to confront the government. At Regina, a committee went east to meet R.B. Bennett in a fruitless meeting. Within days, the RCMP broke up the trekkers' camp in a major police riot.

In Regina we tightened up our regulations, as we were receiving authentic news of police reinforcements arriving steadily, and being stationed around Regina. Militia being warned to be ready for call. Ominous signs. We were having routine marches around town, but one division now was always left at the Exhibition Grounds on guard. The boys played baseball and other sports. Everyone was getting more than enough to eat, as at this time our greatest diversion was "phoneying up" on the authorities who distributed the meal tickets.

Each morning the officials came out to the stadium with the meal tickets, two men to each division. The boys would file past the men, go out of one door and back in at another, to line up again at the tail end for more tickets. Tactics had to be constantly changed. The men never considered it dishonest to get as much to eat as possible, and relief authorities always tried to hold the handouts to a bare minimum.

Then came the news of our negotiations. All of Canada was agog with the news that night. Our delegation, after a night's rest in an Ottawa hotel, had been summoned to the cabinet chamber for the meeting with the Prime Minister.

There sat Bennett behind his desk, surrounded by officials and guards. There were the press, and in front of Bennett the eight representatives of the trek. The Prime Minister wasted no time, but went into his diatribe of abuse, condemnation, and threats, his face crimson with hatred.

He then singled out Slim Evans, and roared, "We know you down here, Evans! You are a criminal and a thief!" At this Slim calmly rose to his feet, and looking the Prime Minister in the eye, he said, loudly and distinctly, "And you're a liar, Bennett, and what is more, you are not fit to run a Hottentot village, let alone a great country like Canada."

The delegation was hustled out, and that was our negotiations.

Toronto the Good: II

DONALD W. BUCHANAN

In Canada, prudery has lately been allied with prejudice. By prejudice, we mean the godhead that many of our artists and most of our public, that prides itself on being modern, place in the virtues of landscape. You show your nationality and your awareness by depicting rocks and old barns. This cult of the heavy externalities of a new land, or, conversely, of what the English critic, R.H. Wilenski would call its "emotive fragments", is hailed as necessary to the birth of a Canadian culture.

If you must be a figure painter, and even the high priests of the nature dogma are willing to admit that taste and talent may incline some that way, then you had best, they advise, go paint French-Canadian farm girls standing in hay fields with the St. Lawrence as a background. But to sit in a city studio and do a Russian model, surrounded with a formal, subjective pattern of objects, is heresy. The Montreal painter, Lilias Torrence Newton, it will be remembered, committed this sin last year. The board of the Toronto Art Gallery refused to hang her painting in the show of the Canadian Group of Painters. They called the model a naked lady, not a nude, you see, for she wore green slippers. The jury had previously accepted the picture, but even some of them had their qualms. Why, they asked, had the artist dared to paint a Russian! Were not Canadians good enough! The result: the canvas reposes in the private collection of a discriminating connoisseur, the public have not and are not very likely to see it, and Mrs. Newton, not wishing aggressively, like Manet in his generation, to rush ramrods of realism down the throats of her public until they are converted, has sorrowfully put away the painting of nudes for the moment and concentrated on portraits.

Edwin Holgate is another figure painter in Montreal who has, through capable sincere work, offended the Presbyterian elders. The Art Gallery of Toronto bought one of his paintings and then, because the evil-seeking busy bodies of the town saw evil in it, the gallery meanly hid the canvas in the cellar. The effect on Mr. Holgate seems to have been, we fear, retrogressive. He continues to paint nudes but he is careful to add back-drops of forests and lakes, which soothe the prurient elders, but which unhappily at the same time, by their incongruity, destroy the harmony of his compositions.

The converse side of the medal lies in a deliberate pandering to perverted sensibilities. In 1927, several Toronto newspapers fostered an ill-conceived controversy over three paintings of nudes then being shown at the Canadian National Exhibition. With cynical glee, the press raised a stink of corruption round the canvases. Half of North America, eventually was smiling upon the evil thoughts of Toronto. Not a few of us chuckled also over the interview accorded at the time by a leading landscape painter to the *Toronto Star* in which he defended the rock and stump school against the figure painters. The headline, "Have to Substitute Pines for Models," was a gem.

The Vimy Memorial Unveiled, 1936

GREGORY CLARK

> *The site of the Canadian Corps' great victory on Easter Monday 1917 was the natural place to erect this memorial. A huge "pilgrimage" of veterans and their families gathered at Vimy in July 1936.*

It was all so beautiful it is hard to know where to begin to tell the story of the unveiling of the Vimy memorial. Spahi sabers flashing in the sunlight, as our yellow haired King set foot upon these Canadian acres so far from home, the massed splendor of 30,000 exalted people simply swept into a storm of emotion. The memorial itself like some white temple of a new and vibrant faith, the horn-like sound of 6,000 pilgrims singing "O Canada," the all-surrounding sense of something stately done worthily at last. Canada said "Rest in peace" to her 60,000 dead.

With a sincerity wholly sublime, nothing that has been or can be said about the memorial does it justice. It is painfully beautiful. It is far larger than the pictures imply. On its lonely hill, with no village or house within miles, it is sanctified by silence. It seems to rise out of the very hill itself, enchanting mystically toward it. Almost at break of day the first pilgrims began to march.

The Vimy slope has all been planted with Scottish pines, and through this forest winding paths lead out from Arras, Douaè, Lille and Armentieres. The incredible pilgrimage of Canadians and their friends began until by mid-morning the whole ridge for miles was alive with people. Hundreds of buses, borrowed from all over France, poured their throngs on to the ridge.

French infantry regiments marched in, their trumpeters flourishing their trumpets in the thrilling French way. A regiment of spahis from Morocco rode up: Arabs in white flying cloaks and scarlet uniforms, turbaned, bearded like a movie, until with a ringing command these wild warriors rose, standing in their stirrups, to swing out, as one man, their swords in salute to our King.

Strange and Lovely

Bands of Scottish pipers and of the Royal artillery, a guard of honor of British marines incomparably drilled, joined the flowing horde past our slowly-walking aged mothers and soldiers and blind men and lame men; past us, who are the elders and the grandchildren of these who are dead for that is so. The regiment marched and the buses rolled and the color parties of a 100 French veteran bodies swept until presently we began to understand that something very strange and lovely was taking form around us. . . .

It Was Colossal

I slept in a seminary and a young priest waited on us, made our beds and fed us. After some sort of a night we were roused with the lark to come in buses again swarming back to Vimy. It was like a dream to be walking over this utterly unfamiliar ridge where not even the skyline resembles the place we called home for two years, like a dream to hear behind the clatter of hoofs and a long drawn cry and see 3,000 Arabs in white and crimson take the road from us.

Hours before the ceremony began we were scattered far and wide, continuing the wholly pathetic search for familiar scenes which we had begun the day before, veterans seeking the spot from which they jumped off, husbands trying to show wives where it really happened, mothers seeking the places their boys last felt the gift of life. The French police and soldiers swarmed on the ridge and the traffic grew so dense it became difficult to move. I say 30,000 stood around the memorial at the moment of unveiling but others who count better than I say there were 100,000. It was colossal.

Find Old Crater

What all the others were doing I can best describe by telling what I did. I met Major Harry McKendrick of Toronto who was a lieutenant with me in the Vimy battle. We set out to rediscover the site of our greatest adventure. It took us hours toiling through baby Scottish pines, waist deep in French brambles and weeds, to locate a great hole in the earth that we identified as Devon crater around which our regiment attacked the enemy. So McKendrick took his side of the crater and I mine and we walked around the edge and met at the far side where the Fritzies trenches

still remain and there with a curious sense of embarrassment we shook
hands violently and dared not meet each other's eyes.

Same All Over

So it was all over the ridge, men and women, with dedication growing
momentarily in their hearts, hunting for the past where the past was mercifully hidden. Then the smoke bombs signalled, the Klaxons sang and
bugles called and we went north to the memorial. It is on what we called
the Pimple; Hill 145 which was captured by the fourth division.

Like Bach Chorales

Instead of being wholly draped, which would have been impossible, due
to its immense size, the memorial was wholly exposed all save one figure, so tremendously moving when it was revealed, which was draped with
a Union Jack. There the cleft column rose so white, so sublimely simple,
the carven figures at its base and top somehow woven into that immense
simplicity like a theme in one of Bach's chorales.

All I could think of as I stood blasted stock still before this majestic
stone was the sort of music Toscanini conducts with every instrument
storming. So felt we all. The veterans in their khaki berets assembled in the
amphitheatre, facing the monument, it looks out over Lens, the women
of the pilgrimage gathered on the sides and for acres on all hands the multitude of French guests took their places.

King Arrives

In the rear of the memorial the ceremonial guards were drawn up, for the
King and the president of the republic of France were to approach from the
back. Those spahis and the band of the first regiment of France, the British
marines and the Scottish pipers were lined here and a selected guard of
honor of about 100 veterans. Oddly enough this great park being Canadian
soil dedicated to Canada by the French, our King, who travelled here by
train came incognito but the instant he set foot on Vimy memorial park he
became His Majesty at once, a King on his own soil and it was he who welcomed the president of France, not the president who welcomed the King.

There we were waiting a little breathless with the unexpected power
of the monument. We 6,000 pilgrims, we 4,000 guests from Britain. We
unaccountable throngs from all these towns around rebuilt unrecogniz-
ably, thriving—then a chill went through us. Far back of the memorial
we heard the unmistakable hoarse crying of French trumpets sounding a
hurrying pulse-chasing flourish, a tune as old as the hills.

King Looks Young

Before we could quiet our hearts, a black car swept in the drive. Those
flaming spahis rose in their stirrups, standing above their wild-eyed Arab

mounts and into the bright afternoon air, 1,000 gleaming swords rose to full arms length above their wild heads. The guards of honor were at the present. The bugles and trumpets screamed and there thundered out old "God Save the King" and we did not know where to look.

Out of the car stepped the King slight, young with that almost indescribable yellow tousled head—bare headed he went right through the ceremony in a morning coat, not in uniform.

I said to myself, if he is in uniform it will be out of respect for these 60,000 dead of ours; if in civies, out of respect for 1,000,000 Britishers yet unborn. There he was in civies leaning slightly forward, the wind in his bright reddish yellow hair, going back to walk before these guards, these hundred chosen veterans, these spahis standing wild in their stirrups, swords on high in the attitude of striking. We massed out in front could not see but when he walked up the steps of the memorial and came into view it must have knocked his hat off if he had it on, for such a roar you never heard in war or peace as we gave Edward VIII.

Wore Military Cross

After one long proud stare at us he turned and walked straight down the front steps and into our midst hatless and wearing on his coat not any of the high and mighty decorations and honors a King has to accept, but, first and foremost, and leading all that he wore, just the military cross, the cross he got as a little lieutenant in the army with us back in the days when he envied us so our freedom to come and go, and live and die.

That was a lovely touch, that white and purple ribboned military cross to the fore. First, he walked straight to the men without legs and arms, the blind and the helpless. He was surrounded by big-wigs, Hon. Ian Mackenzie, our minister of defence, and good old General "Turkey" Ross, the leader of our pilgrimage, but Edward VIII pushed farther than they right into the midst, remembering suddenly to turn and walk past the veteran color party, to accept the salute of those bright flags, but immediately turning to push his way back into the heap, not just along the front, but into the heart of us.

It was a great thrill to men who thought they were not to see anything but a silhouette against the afternoon sun, to have had the King come smiling up under his sunburned blond eyebrows at them at less than arms' length in this curiously unplanned manoeuvre. He did many kind things without any steering.

Speaks to Mrs. Wood

Dear old Mrs. C.S. Wood of Winnipeg, the mother of whose twelve sons eleven saw France and five of them lie here forever, was greeted by the King, and their conversation was as follows:

"Madam, you had sons in the war?"

"It is a great honor, sir, to have you speak to me."

He had hold of her old hand.

"What do you think of our beautiful memorial?" he asked.

"It is lovely, but I went and saw the trenches. I did not know until now. Wasn't it dreadful our boys had to live like that?"

"Please God," said the King, "it shall never happen again."

He pressed her hand again and went over to the legless, the armless, the blind.

Parnall and Jones, two of the Toronto boys, were among those he halted with a long moment while all the bigwigs waited, hat in hand, and you in Canada waited at the radio and we in ranks craned our necks.

Dreadful to See

It was dreadful to see those blind men with an intensity, pitiful beyond all description, staring straight at the King who held their hand, wanting so to see that man with his clipped, bright word whose hand grips when it takes yours. I do not know how long it was intended he should stay down there but he stayed as long as he liked.

He turned and spoke to whoever he liked and he waved his topper to the 1,000 French veterans who stood back of us with their dipping regimental flags and then back up the great stone steps of the memorial he walked to his job.

Absolute Silence

Then the King stepped out and said: "I unveil this monument," and quite suddenly the flag on that draped figure, the one small bit of all that huge prayer in stone that we had not seen, fell away.

Storm Monument

Beauty hid this last shaking blow of beauty to the last. But after that one sharp instant of silence we let go and we cheered, and the far bugles ranged Last Post and Reveille as usual, and the Marseillaise was played, and the president of the French Republic spoke his dedication taking our lost comrades as a trust forever. And when it was over it was our King in France who escorted the president of France to his car and bowed him away, since this was Canada the King was standing on, and then he got into his own car with the golden royal standard on its fore.

Then we stormed the monument. It was dusk before the last of us went up its steps and down. Not until you are within a few feet of it do you realize that the whole immense base of marble, a giant foundation, is wholly covered front, back and sides, with names—11,000 names of Canadians whose bodies have never been found, known as it says unto God.

Calling on Haile Selassie

ROBINSON MACLEAN

Haile Selassie (or John Hoy, as his title in Amharic sounded to Western ears) was emperor of Ethiopia until he was driven into exile by Mussolini's Italy. Selassie ruled with some style in Addis Ababa, as this correspondent for the Toronto Evening Telegram *discovered.*

A grey afternoon four days after my arrival in Addis Ababa. John Hoy will see me. I dress in the palm beach black trousers that mistaken information has made me bring to what I thought was a tropical country, and borrow Barber's dinner jacket. Over it I throw a long black rain cape and take a camera with a flash bulb that I have nursed across the Red Sea. The taxi is waiting. Hailou hasn't come into the picture yet. Through the streets to the New Palace, with the customary jolting over the rain-slicked cobbles and the incessant honking to clear the path of burros, camels, and leisurely Ethiopians.

The car stops at the New Palace steps, and Beattie and myself enter. Mahmu, the driver, of undistinguished birth, can't set foot in the palace grounds. He drives away, and Lorenzo and David usher us into the anteroom. We stroll uneasily through the tall corridors. We feel the blue morocco leather of the chairs, gaze at the initialled photographs of Wilson and the Prince of Wales, and admire the two huge elephant ivories that flank the entrance to the dining-room.

Everything is sotto voce. Servants sneak a-tiptoe along the carpets, and the five of us, who are to gain an interview, fidget. My turn comes, and Lorenzo ushers me along a side hall and pushes me into a door. I have been warned that Imperial Majesty gets three bows, so, before I take my bearings, I double deeply on the doorsill, stalk half-way into the room and bow again, and in front of the big Louis Quinze desk do a third obeisance. The little brown man sticks out a tiny hand and waves me to a chair. I perch uncomfortably on its edge and wait for Majesty to speak. Nothing happens. I clear my throat. I start to say something. I think better of it. I subside. Next time the speech comes out of me in some sort of muttered gratitude to His Imperial Majesty for receiving me. David, behind me, translates, and while he speaks I try to see against the glare of the tall windows behind him what the little fellow looks like. Then he speaks, asking me how I like the country and how long it has taken me to arrive. He knows I am the first reporter direct from the American continent, and he nods in seeming satisfaction when I tell him that it can be done in twenty-one days. He asks me if I speak French. I start to explain, in French, that I don't, but it doesn't sound nearly convincing enough to make the sentence worth finishing.

It trails off into an awkward silence. I try to ask him some question with a political background, and he says that those things are matters for written questions and written answers. That seems to be that. I squirm and ask if I may take his picture. He nods assent, and David scurries out to get my camera. Probably it isn't more than three minutes, but it seems ages long. I look at Selassie. Selassie looks at me. We have no interpreter. There isn't anything we can do about it. Every twenty seconds or so I grin a feeble grin and try to see if he is grinning back. (When I knew him better I knew that he was enjoying the situation as much as I was suffering, but my camera's arrival was a welcome relief.)

My camera has a flashlight on the front that would confuse a bull elephant. Little John Hoy flinches in the glare while I focus. I shoot the bulb and start backing out. Outside the windows the rain is whispering against the glass and the fronds of the eucalyptus sway damply. I'm not thinking about that. I am only thinking about whether I'll hit the door and whether it would be against the rules to take one quick aiming sight before I smack a doorpost with my ample and unprotected posterior. I am remembering, too, how one diplomat cracked his friend's dress trousers, didn't dare turn around, and missed the door, leaving him to feel with his bare stern along the wall until he hit the exit. Except for tramping David as he makes his exit bow, my departure is unscarred by incident. I hop the taxi for the radio station to inform the world that I have spoken to Haile Selassie, and to wish that I hadn't spent most of my French lectures in drawing caricatures of the teacher.

Later I asked Hailou why the Emperor didn't speak first.

"He believes that people to whom he gives interviews have something to say or they wouldn't be there," said Hailou. Sound enough, too.

Hitler's Olympics, 1936

MATTHEW HALTON

Based in London, Halton visited Germany again to report on the 1936 Olympic Games—and on Hitler's popularity.

Berlin, Aug 10.—The Hitler parade, consisting of Hitler and his chief satellites driving in some 40 high-powered cars, moves from the centre of Berlin towards the Olympic stadium. Hitler, standing erect in the front seat beside his chauffeur, acknowledges with outstretched arm the frenzied, thunderous and unceasing heiling of the two million people who line the route, fenced in from the street by over 50,000 storm troops in brown uniforms, policemen in blue uniforms and Black Guards in black uniforms and steel helmets, and every man over six feet tall.

When the King passes in London, one policeman stands every six feet, their backs to the crowd. When Hitler passes in Berlin, the police join hands and make a cordon facing the crowd. In front of them, one man facing the crowd and the next the street, stand Brownshirts or Black-shirts. Every man is armed. And in front of these, their feet wide apart, bayonets fixed on their rifles, stand the great, black-helmeted, sinister-looking giants of the Black Guard, Hitler's personal bodyguard, his corps d'elite.

The 40 shining black cars roll by—first Hitler, then Goering, Goeb-bels, General von Blomberg, Deputy Rudolf Hess, Police President Himm-ler and other luminaries. . . When they enter their "honor seats" in the stadium, the world becomes for a few moments nothing but a sea of out-stretched arms and a crashing roar of "Heil! Heil! Heil!" and when you turn this way and that examining men's eyes you see in them something like mystic hysteria—a glazed, holy look as of men hearing voices.

This is the important event of each day's Olympics to the Germans at least, though I heard foreigners wonder whether they had come to Berlin to pay homage to Caesar or to see men running and jumping.

Caesar, dressed in his brown uniform, sits down to watch the gladia-tors. His face is whiter, but plumper, than I have seen it before. When he is not talking to someone, his eyes have an unseeing look—as of a man hearing voices, or at least thinking of something not in that stadium. His hands seem to be in his way.

Caesar's right hand man, Goering, sits near him. One glance at him and you smile. He looks so pleasant, amiable and good-natured that it is hard to believe the things you know. For once his colossal front and rear are garbed not in a resplendent uniform covered with medals, but in an ordinary gray flannel suit—yards of it. He laughs and chatters and turns this way and that, peering through huge binoculars at one thing and then another.

Caesar's left hand man, Herr Dr. Paul Josef Goebbels, sits between Goering and Caesar. He is a thin little man: Goering dwarfs him. But he has more brains than Hitler and Goering put together and then much to spare. His face is extremely intelligent, and in my opinion, even pleasant. But anti-Nazi Germans hate him far more than they hate Hitler. They call him "the Fox." He it is who has killed thought in Germany and welded most of those 65,000,000 people into one vast, sentient mass whose emotions, feelings, loves and hates he controls with diabolical skill. Every single instrument of publicity in Germany, whether it be school books or newspapers, radio or moving pictures, is part of his great pipe-organ; and that pipe-organ has one, and only one tune, played with varia-tions; the preparation of Germany for the domination of Europe.

Goering and Hitler are present every day, with other famous Nazis and visiting Italian princes. How can they afford seven full afternoons a week for watching games . . . Let us leave them there at the games and slip round behind the Olympic facade.

A pathetic, unforgettable sight meets your eyes as you leave the stadium. Outside the gates scores of thousands of people are massed, just standing there, their faces pressed to the grilles—people with a great hunger in their eyes for color and life and for ordinary sensations unconnected with politics and militarism . . . Yet how they love their militarism. There is something about a deep, heavily-massed column of marching men that arouses extraordinary emotion in the German soul. When the Bulgarian contingent to the Olympic games entered the arena goosestepping, I thought it was stupid but it seemed to drive the German crowds frantic. In London, straggling little groups gather every day to watch the changing of the guard; in Berlin, they gather on the Unter den Linden 50 deep.

Secret police and Black Guards keep close watch on Hitler's car while he sits in the stadium. Just before he leaves the stadium to enter the car, every wheel is thoroughly examined. Near his car are two or three others, with tarpaulins stretched over the machine-guns in the back seat. And wherever there were a handful of people gathered, there also were policemen and s.s. "You guard the leader well," I remarked to a policeman. "Jawohl," he replied, "he is the most precious thing we have."

Then I mentioned the dangerous word "assassination." "In my opinion," I said, "there isn't much danger of attempts being made on Hitler's life. He is so popular with most of the people." "Jawohl," said the policeman, but he said no more. Then to my surprise, an officer of the Black Guard spoke up: "And every month he becomes more popular," he said—and he said "he" almost with a capital H. "Even people who once were Socialists have seen Hitler get things for Germany which no one dreamed we would get without war, and have become enthusiastic supporters of the regime."

This is perfectly true, except for one word. I have met dozens of Germans, once radicals—that is, radical for Germany—who have seen Germany go from strength to strength in her foreign policy while the democracies, making no effort to prevent such happenings as the rape of Abyssinia and Germany's violation of one treaty after another, lose prestige almost every week. These Germans say to themselves: "Well, maybe the Nazis were right after all. They are getting what they want by force and bluff when everything else had failed." One admitted to me frankly that it wasn't much of an effort in any case for a German to go over to the cult of force and might. . . .

Perhaps I am pessimistic, but it does sometimes seem that the kind of sadistic nostalgia which has already reconquered Germany is spreading over Europe—a sort of "nostalgie de la boue," as if the fair prospect which a few years ago seemed within the grasp of humanity was too much for the smallness of us, as if there were some cancer in men making them thirsty for blood and death.

This cancer is subtly masked in a garb of belligerent nationalism called Fascism. Watch for the first signs of Fascism in your own country, and operate on them quickly, because in spite of their seductive exterior virility, they are signs of decay. They are signs that we are despairing of reason, despairing of our fine dreams, of a sane world.

John David Eaton Recalls the Depression

JOHN DAVID EATON

Thirty years later, a member of the department store family recalls the Great Depression.

. . . He can remember the Depression, a time when the company spent millions to shield its employees from the desperation of unemployment. That was a good time for John David Eaton, and he remembers it with affection. "Nobody thought about money in those days," he said, "because they never saw any. You could take your girl to a supper dance at the hotel for $10, and that included the bottle and a room for you and your friends to drink it in. I'm glad I grew up then. It was a good time for everybody. People learned what it means to work."

Boondoggling in Winnipeg

JAMES H. GRAY

While the Depression mainly affected the poor, some members of the middle classes found themselves forced to go on relief. James Gray recalls being on the dole in Winnipeg.

The closest any of us on relief ever got to socially useful labour was sawing cordwood, but we were drafted periodically for all the make-work projects, like raking leaves, picking rock, digging dandelions, and tidying up back lanes. These "boondoggles" as the Chicago *Tribune* was later to christen them, were devised to enable us to work off the assistance we received, and our services were demanded for a couple of days once a month. It was all justified on the grounds that the exercise would be good for us, that working would improve our morale, and that, by providing us with a token opportunity to work for our relief, we would be freed of the stigma of accepting charity. None of these dubious propositions had much validity. The fatuous nature of the projects the authorities invented quickly brought the entire make-work concept into disrepute.

My first boondoggle assignment came with the first issue of relief I collected. A printed work-slip instructed me to report to the Woodyard foreman to work for three afternoons. The foreman explained the system. There were 4,000 or 5,000 cords of wood in the piles, which extended clear around the yard on four sides. Strung out down the centre of the two- or three-acre courtyard were a dozen saw-horses, or "saw-bucks" as the foreman called them. Beside each saw-horse was stacked half a cord of wood in four-foot lengths. This wood was to be cut into three pieces— stove-lengths. Half the work-gang would saw and the other would load and pile. The pilers would pick up the cut wood and throw it on a heap in front of the saw-horses. One piler would serve two cutters. The rest would help load cordwood onto the horse-drawn sleighs. When the cutters finished their quota, they could go home. Everybody else would stay until 4.30 to load the trucks with cut wood, for the social welfare families, and the sleighs with cordwood, for the unemployed on relief who were supposed to saw it themselves. After my experience with a buck-saw the first afternoon, I never did. We always managed to have seventy-five cents on hand with which to hire a truck-mounted circular saw that followed the wood sleighs around the city.

When the foreman finished his instructions, my instinct was to choose the piling job. Not only had I never held a cordwood saw in my hands, I had never done any manual labour. But I became somehow caught up in the rush for the saws, and almost before I knew it I was headed for a saw-horse with a saw in my hand. This was one of the crowning blunders of my life, a fact that must have been obvious to any half-observant beholder. From any angle, I cut a ludicrous figure as I moved towards the field of combat. I was costumed in a soft felt hat, silk scarf, and form-fitting overcoat with a small velvet collar. I wore light chamois gloves, silk socks, and light oxfords. I could not even carry a buck-saw gracefully, let alone saw with it, but I located a vacant saw-horse and went to work.

How far below zero the temperature was that day, I never knew. I remember only that a cold wind was blowing and there were gusts of snow in the air. The first piece of wood fell from my log, and the second. Soon I was gasping for breath, and my arms started to ache. I tried resting, but that was no good, for the wind fanned the perspiration into ice on my hair.

It was while I was catching my breath that I saw the discarded gasoline-powered circular saws standing in the corner of the yard. Either machine could have sawed as much wood in an afternoon as our entire work-gang. The two machines, in a couple of days, could have cut all the wood the welfare families consumed in a week, perhaps in a month. But they stood idle in silent mockery of our puny efforts as the administrators of unemployment relief repudiated the machine age and set their course back through history in the general direction of the stone age.

My hands and feet were numb with cold before I discovered it was permissible to leave the saw-horses and go into the shack to get warm and have a smoke. Darkness fell, and I was not half through my pile. All the other buckers, save two, had long since finished their stint and departed. At 4:30 I was more dead than alive, and then the foreman unveiled another rule. Those who failed to finish their piles would have to come back the following morning!

"And look, you," he said, meaning me, "when you come back, put on some work clothes. Don't come around here all dressed up like a dude to buck wood!" His disgust was awesome, and I was almost too exhausted to reply.

"These", I said, "*are* my work clothes. I've been going to work all my life in clothes like these. They're the only clothes I have."

"Then for God sake get yourself some rough clothes."

I got mad.

"Look, damn it, if I had money to buy work clothes with, I wouldn't be on relief. And anyway, what clothes I wear is none of your goddam business!"

The other less printable things I said taught me my first lesson in relief deportment—never, under any circumstances, swear at a straw-boss who is ordering you around. He rode me continually the next two days. That foreman's name was the first I put down on my son-of-a-bitch list of men with whom I would some day settle some scores. The list grew and grew during the next couple of years. The day I got a job again I forgot them all.

Edward VIII and Mrs. Simpson

SIR ROBERT BORDEN

Borden, prime minister from 1911 to 1920, had an active retirement. One practice he followed was writing letters to himself commenting on public affairs. In 1936, he described the events that led to the abdication.

The nations of the British Commonwealth and its dependencies have passed through deep waters during the past two weeks; they are still passing; the end is not yet.

For more than twenty years I have known King Edward. On the occasions of his visits to Canada during my premiership I came into intimate association with him, and I conceived for him not only sincere admiration but warm affection. Now I am disillusioned, shocked, amazed; and I cannot free myself from the abhorrent thought that, early in the year, when he requested parliament to make provision for his marriage, he had in mind a woman whose husband was then living and undivorced. I hope and pray that in this I may be mistaken.

During the past month, the King's insensate folly in determining to marry a woman twice divorced created a scandal which has been exploited to the fullest extent by lewd newspapers of the baser sort in the United States; and that scandal has now developed into a constitutional crisis. Apparently, the King places before all obligation of duty, and above all concern for the welfare of the Empire his silly infatuation for this woman, and his desire to make her his queen. Endowed with two living husbands, other than the King, imagine her coronation! Would it not be appropriate that her former husbands, original and secondary, should have foremost places at the coronation?

It would be difficult to exaggerate the intense concern that disturbs our people. Last week, during a temporary indisposition which confined me to my room, I spent two sleepless nights in grieving over this deplorable incident and in endeavouring to forecast the future. For I was fully conscious that the issue of the present crisis might be so grave as eventually to disturb the Empire's unity. And all this because of the absurd infatuation of a middle-aged man for a twice-divorced woman. Physicians of this city are convinced that the King is suffering from a certain type of psychosis.

Since the growth of nationhood in the self-governing countries of the Empire, the Crown has been the perpetual symbol of the Empire's unity; and each Sovereign has been its living symbol. For the last hundred years there has been a reverence so deep and so abiding for the Crown, and indeed for each succeeding sovereign, that the unity of the Empire has withstood the severest shocks. This symbolic significance of the Crown has suffered grievously from the fantastic whim of a man who had vowed to follow in his father's footsteps. The lustre of the Crown has been tarnished; the King and the Throne discredited.

Bethune, Blood and Spain

NORMAN BETHUNE

The Spanish Civil War, which began in 1936, seemed to pit democracy against Franco's fascism. Dr. Bethune was caught up in the crusade. He created a blood transfusion unit to work with the Republican forces.

Madrid, Jan. 11, 1937

We have had a very hectic ten days as you may know and I haven't really had the time to sit down and write you a letter but as an Englishman is leaving to-day for Paris I felt I should take advantage of this and let you know the news.

Frank Pitcairn—author of "A Reporter in Spain" promised to write an article on our unit for the "Daily Worker" of London whose correspondent he is. But as he hasn't turned up to-day—he stays with us—I expect he has left for another front. Professor J.B.S. Haldane who stayed with us for two weeks, has returned to London and has promised to send "The Clarion" articles on us. I think these would be better than one I might write myself.

As you know, we have withstood the heaviest attack and the most serious effort of the Fascists to take the city since the first and second weeks of November. Their losses have been terrific—at least 5,000. Our papers say 10,000 Germans have been killed and Franco has taken the Moors away from Madrid and replaced them with fresh German troops. They thought they had a walk-over and advanced in exactly the same massed formation as they did in 1914–1915 in France. Our machine guns simply mowed them down. Our losses were one to five of theirs.

The International Brigade has suffered badly of course as they are shock troops, but large re-inforcements of French, German, English, Polish, Austrian and Italians with some Americans and Canadians, are arriving.

We have been having two and four raids a day for two weeks now and many thousands of non-combatants, women and children, have been killed. I was in the Telephone Building the other day when it was shelled. However, it is very modern and strongly built. No great damage was done—a handful of people were killed only. You simply can't get these people to take shelter during shelling and bombing!

Our night work is very eerie! We get a phone call for blood. Snatch up our packed bag, take two bottles (each 500 c.c.)—one of group IV and one of group II—out of the refrigerator and with our armed guard off we go through the absolutely pitch dark streets and the guns and machine guns and rifle shots sound as if they were in the next block, although they are really a half mile away. Without lights we drive. Stop at the hospital and with a searchlight in our hands find our way into the cellar principally. All the operating rooms in the hospitals have been moved into the basement to avoid falling shrapnel, bricks and stones coming through the operating room ceiling.

Our bag contains a completely sterilized box of instruments, towels, etc. so we can start work at once. The man is lying most frequently on a stretcher so we kneel down beside him, prick the finger and on a slide put one drop each of Serum type II and type III. If his red blood cells are agglutenated by II and not by III—he is type III. If agglutenated by III he is a II, if by both he is a type I, if neither, he is group IV. So now we know what blood he can take safely. If I, III or IV he gets our bottle of blood group IV (the universal blood). If he is a II, he gets blood group II. He could also take IV but as these "universal donors" are about only 45% of the people, we must use II's when we can.

Then the proper blood is warmed in a pan of water and we are ready to start. The man is usually as white as paper, mostly shocked, with an imperceptible pulse. He may be exsanguinated also and not so much shocked, but usually is both shocked and exsanguinated. We now inject novocaine over the vein in the bend of the elbow, cut down and find the vein and insert a small glass Cannula then run the blood in. The change in most cases is spectacular. We give him always 500 c.c. of preserved blood and sometimes more and follow it up with Saline or 5% Glucose solution. The pulse can now be felt and his pale lips have some colour.

Yesterday, we did three transfusions—this is about the average daily, besides the blood we leave at hospitals for them to use themselves. We collect 1/2 to 3/4 gallon daily, mix it with Sodium Citrate (3.8%) and keep it just above freezing in the refrigerator in sterile milk and wine bottles. This blood will keep for about a week. We are working on the use of LOCKES' SOLUTION to preserve the red blood cells longer and are making up Bayliss *Gum Solution*. (Gum Arabic in Saline.) Bayliss was (or is!) an English Physiologist who brought out this gum solution for shock during the war of 1914–18.

There is a Barcelona Unit who are putting up blood in sterile ampules. I will go there and see the method. It looks O.K.

The International Brigade Hospital needs male and female French and German speaking nurses—not English speaking at present although these may be needed later. Brain surgeons also.

Well, this is a grand country, and great people. The wounded are wonderful.

After I had given a transfusion to a French soldier who had lost his arm, he raised the other to me as I left the room in the Casualty Clearing Station, and with his raised clenched fist exclaimed "Viva la Revolution." The next boy to him was a Spaniard—a medical student shot through the liver and stomach. When I had given him a transfusion and asked him how he felt, he said "It is nothing—Nada." He recovered—so did the Frenchman. . . .

The Royal Visit, 1939

GUSTAVE LANCTOT

George VI and Queen Elizabeth visited Canada in the spring of 1939, one goal being to shore up Canadian support for the war against Hitler that loomed on the horizon.

An afternoon drive brought the King and Queen to the Battlefields Park, where more than sixty thousand persons were assembled in the grand setting of the Plains overlooking the river and the Laurentides. Soon silence prevailed, and twenty-five thousand voices of school children, fervid and youthful, sang *Dieu sauve le roi* and *O Canada*, with a stirring crescendo that made nerves and hearts tingle with emotion. It was Quebec at its best. So was it also in the evening, when at the banquet given at the Château Frontenac by Premier Duplessis and his Government, Their Majesties on leaving were greeted with a spontaneous ovation.

Next morning (May 18), the King and Queen boarded the famous silver and blue train, from now on their moving residence across Canada. From the Quebec station for miles, spectators lined the right of way and at every station groups of country people were waiting to catch a glimpse of the Royal train. At Trois-Rivières, a stop of fifteen minutes, when Their Majesties appeared on the platform, welcomed by Mayor Atchez Pitt, civic and clerical notables, there rose from the 80,000 spectators, as closely jammed as could be, wave after wave of cheering.

On the alert from Viauville to Notre-Dame de Grâces, headed by its dynamic Mayor, Camillien Houde, artistically decorated Montreal was eagerly waiting for the Royal visitors. Over a twenty-five mile route, draped in gala colours and lined with militiamen and blue-beretted veterans, one million people or so were stretched along the street curbs and crowded on stands and verandahs, on roofs and garages, cheering the Sovereigns. The feature of the day was the Stadium with 35,000 school children massed in the circular stands, one thousand of whom formed with red, white and blue dresses, a huge Union Jack, an enchanting colour scheme, while the whole multitude chanted, between two cheers: *Vive le roi, Vive la reine!* At the City Hall, a civic address with the usual bouquet was presented, while at the Chalet on Mount-Royal, after the unveiling by the King of a commemorative tablet, a delightful tea was served in a drawing-room atmosphere by a bevy of young girls in pastel dresses.

In the evening, at the Windsor Hotel, the metropolis of Canada was host to Their Majesties at a dinner attended by one thousand guests, the largest of the tour. Throwing formality aside at the King's command, Mayor Houde kept the Royal guests in continuous merriment. But the climax of the occasion was reached when Their Majesties appeared on the light-flooded balcony overlooking Dominion Square. In the midst of an ethereal white light from powerful reflectors, 100,000 people filled the large area. Suddenly the Royal couple walked into the limelight, and instantly the crowd went wild with delirious cheers. Then at the Mayor's request, silence fell and the multitude, in the still of the night and the silver light of the foliage, gathering voice and mind together sang *God Save the King* with such deep feeling and reverence that men's hearts vibrated with emotion, the King's eyes glistened with tears and the Queen's heart was overflowing.

Nazism in Montreal, 1940

LOUIS FRANCOEUR

Francoeur was the best-known Radio-Canada broadcaster. His report on Nazi sympathizers in Montreal made news.

La police est allée faire une petite excursion, ce matin, dans un établissement de la rue St-Laurent à Montréal. C'est une librairie tenue par un yougoslave naturalisé du nom de Kilbertus. Depuis assez longtemps déjà, la police recherchait la provenance d'illustrés qui circulaient parmi la nombreuse population non-canadienne-française, non-canadienne-anglaise de Montréal. Ces périodiques consacrés à l'éloge du nazisme, entretenaient chez nos coloniaux venus d'Europe centrale un sentiment dangereux. Après enquête, la police s'est rendue chez le sieur Kilbertus; elle a visité la maison de la cave au grenier, et elle y a trouvé d'abord 15,000 magazines de propagande naziste, puis une quantité difficile à déterminer de brochurettes et documents en plusieurs langues, et enfin un poste récepteur de radio d'une puissance inusitée, réglé de façon à capter exclusivement toutes les émissions allemandes.

Le plus intéressant, pour nous, Canadiens français, c'est qu'au moment où le raid s'effectuait, on distribuait dans certains quartiers de Montréal, de porte en porte, une circulaire imprimée sur carton qui disait ceci: "Ne vous enregistrez pas; résistez à la circonscription; répandez partout ce message". Et c'était signé: "Ligue québecoise contre la conscription".

L'ennemi continue donc d'être actif parmi nous. Il procède de toutes les manières: il endoctrine secrètement; il manoeuvre certains de ses affidés, qui font de la cabale dans la rue, chez le marchand de journaux, au café, au salon. Plusieurs de ceux qui se livrent à cette besogne ne se rendent pas le moindre compte qu'ils sont les agents innocents de l'ennemi. Innocents quelquefois, mais pas toujours. . . .

France et Angleterre, politiquement brouillées pour l'instant, ont tout de même autre chose dans leurs annales qu'une couple de crimes et une demi-douzaine d'erreurs. Ce sont ces deux peuples qui incarnent l'Occident, terres de paysages doux, de travail intense et d'équilibre, nations cousines, puisque l'Angleterre est une colonie normande, et que la Normandie est la première nourricière de la France. Terres si apparentées qu'on y trouve les mêmes noms, qu'il s'agisse de Colgate ou de Houlgate, du Tréport ou de Newport, de Grandville ou de Granville, du Mont St-Michel ou de St. Michael's Mount, du Finistère ou de Land's End, du Mont Ste-Catherine ou de St. Catherine's Point, des innombrables églises dédiées dans les deux pays à Notre-Dame, à saint Pierre, à saint Paul, à saint Martin.

C'est de cette double ascendance que vient notre héritage, puisque plusieurs d'entre nous ont dans leurs veines du sang anglo-saxon, et que celui qu'on appelle anglo-saxon est aux trois-quarts normand. C'est pourquoi malgré les vicissitudes et les douleurs qu'une politique, bien accessoire, somme toute, inflige aux deux grands peuples civilisés, il ne nous appartient pas, à nous qui en sommes, de juger leurs vertus et leurs vices à la petite équerre de nos rancunes de coloniaux.

Portons sur des faits précis une appréciation raisonnée . . . c'est notre droit. Personne ne peut nous l'enlever. Mais voyons dans les deux pays, à qui nous devons tout, de très grandes et de très nobles nations, sans lesquelles il n'y aurait pas d'Occident, pas d'Europe, sans lesquelles nous n'existerions point. En temps de guerre, il est des sujets que l'on s'épargne de traiter. Ceux-là qui, de façon inconsciente, ne voient que le mal, ceux-là qui ne jugent leurs parents que d'après leurs infirmités physiques, leurs accidents de digestion, ou leurs crises de mauvaise humeur, n'apportent pas, comme point de balance a leur pesée, ce sens de l'équité respectueuse et bienveillante qui incite à voir d'abord les beaux côtés, les gestes nobles, les actes valeureux.

A Defence Alliance with the U.S.

JAY PIERREPONT MOFFAT

In August 1940, with France out of the war and Britain in grave peril, Prime Minister Mackenzie King and President Franklin Roosevelt met at Ogdensburg, N.Y., to plan for the future.

August 17, 1940.

The Prime Minister and I reached Prescott about half-past six; a special ferry was awaiting to take us to Ogdensburg; there we were met by a motorcycle escort, which took us to the President's special train. He was seated in the observation room of the rear car with Colonel Stimson, Governor Lehman, and General Drum. The two latter left almost immediately.

The President had just come in from several hours inspecting troops in the field: he was tired but exhilarated. We all had long cooling drinks while he talked at random about whatever came into his head. His talk on the whole was brilliant and the charm of the man, a happy blend of Chief of State, man of the world, and host, was never more vivid. He wanted to get the text of the Willkie speech of acceptance, but the only flash that came through was that Willkie had challenged him to a series of joint debates. "If that is true," he declared with emphasis, "Willkie is lost." He chuckled at "stealing half the show" because of the fact that his visit to Ogdensburg and his conference with Mackenzie King—although this was not on purpose—happened on the very day of Willkie's speech. He said that there were times when it was wiser and more effective not to campaign and this was one of them. He talked about Canadian politics and jollied Mackenzie King about interning Mayor Houde of Montreal. He thought Grand Marian with its high cliffs and icy waters would be an ideal spot for an internment camp. . . As to the war, the news he got from England was good. The English were well satisfied with the progress with the war in the air, but their men were getting tired and they wanted more pilots. As to the possibility of selling destroyers he was momentarily expecting a message from the Attorney General as to the law governing the situation.

Sunday, August 18th.
At ten we all went to the review: the President, Mr. King, and Colonel Stimson in the first car . . . Then back to the train where the President and Mackenzie King drafted a joint handout reading as follows:

> The Prime Minister and the President have discussed the mutual problems of defense in relation to the safety of Canada and the United States.
>
> It has been agreed that a Permanent Joint Board on Defense shall be set up at once by the two countries.
>
> This Permanent Joint Board on Defense shall commence immediate studies relating to sea, land and air problems including personnel and material.
>
> It will consider in the broad sense the defense of the north half of the Western Hemisphere.
>
> The Permanent Joint Board on Defense will consist of four or five members from each country, most of them from the services. It will meet shortly. . . .

About one o'clock Mr. King left the President's car and we motored back together to Ottawa. He gave me at great length the account of his talks with the President. . . .

The essential features of the President's talks with Mr. Mackenzie King as given me by the latter were as follows:

A. The President will sell about 50 destroyers to the British. He will do this without submitting the matter to Congress. His lawyers are working on the ways and means of doing it legally. Politically, the President believes that the public will accept it, given the fact that the United States is getting the naval bases it desires. Strategically, the President believes that the Navy will now favor it, since the new naval bases are a greater asset to our defense than 50 old destroyers. Churchill had said that they would be more valuable than rubies.

B. The President will announce the sale, probably within the week. The destroyers will be sent shortly thereafter to Halifax where they will be turned over. Mr. King is telegraphing this very day to Mr. Churchill to send over crews to take them across. A skeleton crew of 75 men per ship should suffice. If more men can be spared they can learn about the ships during the crossing and save time. Canada has enough trained men to man about 5 destroyers. If, however, Canada wants these ships for convoy work, she will have to ask the British for them.

C. The President told Mr. King that Mr. Churchill had at last given a sufficient pledge that he would under no circumstances surrender the British Fleet to the Germans. Mr. King told the President that he thought Mr. Churchill, in hesitating during the month of June to give a satisfactory pledge, had been motivated by a desire to observe all the Constitutional niceties and not bind the hands of a possible successor. (Mr. King reminded me that he had cautioned Mr. Churchill not to try to use the British fleet to bargain with the United States. He had urged him to offer the United States naval bases in the Western Hemisphere. He regrets the two months lost, but now all was well.)

D. With regard to the naval bases to be leased to the United States on 99 year leases, these could be divided into three parts: the West Indian bases, which would be selected by the United States and Britain alone; the Newfoundland base, where Britain held title, but Canada had more immediate geographic and defense interests; and the Canadian base or bases, which would be selected by the United States and Canada alone.

E. The Canadian base or bases would be granted by the Government under its war powers without submission to Parliament. In effect, it would involve a limited free port where the United States could bring in its supplies and equipment, and install docks, dry-docks, repair shops, etc. To prevent its wounding Canadian susceptibilities, there would be no objection to having Canadian artillery either on, or dominating, the bases.

F. There would be set up at once a Permanent Joint Board on Defense. The first meeting would be held in Ottawa probably this coming week. Although no final selections have been made, probably Mr. Forrestal will head the American group at the first meeting, the others being the heads of the different services.

G. Among the problems to be worked out are the following: bases to select in Newfoundland and Canada; what supplies and equipment are needed; how an American army of 300,000 men could at need be sent into Nova Scotia without delay; what Canada could do in the event of a thrust toward Maine; what alterations should be made in Canadian railways, particularly with a view to strengthening bridges, enlarging tunnels, etc; what should be done about equipment, interchangeability of type, etc.

H. The President having grown eloquent about the Canadian-American frontier, was startled to have Mr. King declare that we were "creating a frontier" by our passport and visa requirements. He explained the situation at some length, and found the President knew very little about it. He said he had been told, he thought by the State Department, that Canada desired the system as it would prevent men of military age from leaving the Dominion. He promised to speak to Mr. Hull about the matter without delay and try to get the system rescinded in so far as it relates to Canada.

Taking a U-Boat, 1941

HAL LAWRENCE

The Battle of the Atlantic was critical for Britain's survival in World War II. The fledgling Royal Canadian Navy played its part fully.

My captain in *Moose Jaw* was Lieutenant Frederick Grub, RCN, the only pre-war officer on board. He regarded his officers with gloom, but also with the enthusiasm of a dedicated teacher who hoped to get his backward boys out of the primary grades.

The night before, I had had to call him because I lost contact with *Chambly*; she was guide and we were to keep station on her. I flogged around the ocean for thirty minutes before I told the Captain. That made it worse, and it was an hour before he got me back on station. The night before that, it was the opposite. I was too close, close enough to make his experienced eye stare in horror while mine was tranquil with the ignorance of one who has never heard the grinding, tearing, and shrieking of metal in the agony of collision.

The twelfth day had not yet ended. About 2130 the Captain said, "I'm going to get my head down." (He never slept; he either got his head down or put his feet up.) "Aye aye, sir," I replied.

"About one-two-oh revolutions should hold her."

"Aye aye, sir."

"You shouldn't need to alter more than five degrees to keep station."

"No, sir."

"Zigzag Eleven we're doing. You're familiar with that one?"

"Aye, sir."

"You've read my night orders?"

"Yessir."

He paused. Was there anything else? There was so much else, but my training would take years. There was nothing he could do tonight. He sighed and went below. The rigging creaked rhythmically. The bow wave hissed. All serene.

We jogged along comfortably enough for ten minutes, then the radio telephone (RT) blurted a message from *Chambly*: "Have good contact; am attacking". She veered to port. I followed. I heard a dull thud, and felt a tremor run through the ship. Two white rockets streaked up ahead.

Chambly said "Submarine". I rang "Action stations". Four more white rockets to port. Star shell blossomed ahead in a sector search. Fireworks galore! A tanker was hit: the flame mounted. *Chambly* said "Firing now", and "thuck thuck" went her depth-charge throwers. Snowflake flares were everywhere, bright as day. The RT was a babble of messages; the ocean surface boiled white and soapy. A black metal snout reared out—U-501!

Just then the Captain arrived and in a tone of honest exasperation demanded, "Lawrence, what *are* you doing?"

Water streaming from her sides, U-501 set off in the general direction of Germany. We gave chase, the Captain manoeuvring to ram. With our primitive weapons this was the surest way for a kill; a corvette in exchange for a U-boat was a bargain. A white light blinked from the U-boat bridge; could it be the night identification signal? Could she be friendly? Impossible! What was the correct identification? Where was the signalman? The Captain was altering around now. Where was the bloody signalman? He arrived with a damp and grubby bit of paper and we peered at it in a dim light. Was the submarine one of ours? No!

The Captain roared, "Stand by to ram." U-501 altered away and we were staring up her stern tubes. The Captain eased over to her quarter, but she pointed her stern at us again. We eased back. Spinney's gun made a hit just for'ard of the conning tower. The Captain edged out again to U-501's port beam. U-501 swung violently to port and suddenly she and *Moose Jaw* were side by side about thirty feet apart, on a parallel course and at the same speed. Germans were on their deck, but our guns wouldn't depress enough to fire. For a few eerie seconds we regarded each other in silence. More Germans erupted out of various hatches; a long swell lifted us within fifteen feet.

"Stand by to repel boarders," sang out the Captain.

Now, there was a thought. U-501 was bigger than us, and probably had more men. A bit theatrical on the Captain's part, though.

The navigator was at my side. "Hal, have you the key to the rifle rack?"

"No. I gave it to Spinney."

"Oh, well, Father wants . . ."

"I know what Father wants but I haven't got it."

"Oh, all right, I'll ask Spinney, but he's pretty busy; his gun's stuck, I think."

I decided to do something myself about the Germans massing on the U-boat's bridge and deck.

"Lewis gunner," I shouted, "knock those Germans off."

No Lewis gunner.

I grabbed the strip Lewis gun from its rack, smacked on an ammunition pan, rotated it anti-clockwise (as taught by CPO Bingham, bless him), cocked it, hooked my arm around a stay to steady myself against the lurching of the ship, and fired.

Click.

No tension on the spring? Recocked. Pulled the trigger.

Click.

Still no tension on the spring.

The Captain swung slowly to port to open the range. U-501's bridge was crowded with Germans. Both ships were rolling about twenty degrees in a beam sea. On opposite sides of a trough the superstructures were close now, although the hulls were thirty feet apart. One German climbed the edge of his bridge, balanced precariously for a few moments, then hurtled through the air in an astonishing standing broad-jump. He landed in the break of the fo'c's'le.

"See what he wants," said the Captain, putting on more port helm to open the range more quickly. At the break of the fo'c's'le I was met by a groggy figure struggling to his feet.

"We are not fighting. Let me speak to your captain," he said.

I led the way up the ladder, thinking half-way up that turning my back on an enemy at the height of an action was unwise. The Captain had manoeuvred into the position he sought, and was bearing in to ram. We hit, rocked over, metal screaming on metal. I arrived on the bridge with our guest.

"I am the Captain of the submarine. We surrender. Do not fire on my men, please. Do not fire any more."

There was no need. U-501's speed was reduced to about three knots, and beaten men crowded her decks. They jumped in the water and swam toward us. *Chambly* pulled up to U-501. Prentice shouted, "Stop your engines or I'll open fire."

Chambly's boarding-party pulled over in a skiff. The boarding officer, Ted Simmons, grabbed a German who was speaking English.

"Take me below," he ordered.

"No, no. It is not safe. We will sink. We have opened sea-cocks."

Thrusting him aside, Simmons grabbed two more and, jabbing their backs with his .45 and kicking their behinds, propelled them to the conning tower. On the conning tower the Germans refused to go below.

The swell was pounding the skiff badly; two seamen jumped in and lay off. A Lewis gunner covered the prisoners. U-501 was sinking by the stern; there was not much time. Simmons clambered down the hatch. If it were too late to salvage her, he might at least find code-books. The lights were out. By a dim torch he saw water gurgling up; then it flooded in with a rush. The stern sank further. Too late!

Pulling himself out, Simmons gestured the prisoners and his men over the side. Only the conning tower and the bow were awash now. With everyone off, Simmons jumped in the water. The bow reared and U-501 plunged down, sucking Simmons with her. He fought his way to the surface and struck out for the skiff. Hauling himself over the gunwale, he mustered his men. Stoker Brown was missing. Calling his name, they searched. No reply.

We in *Moose Jaw* had been circling the stopped *Chambly* and U-501. When we could we picked up prisoners. The U-boat captain, Hugo Förster, was uneasy about the lights we showed to do this. Twenty-nine Germans were plucked out of the water, frightened and exhausted. Two were dead and were dropped back in. Gunfire was continuous. And always there was the keening of the wind through the rigging and the rush of water down the scuppers.

FDR in His Prime

BRUCE HUTCHISON

> *The President of the United States for twelve years, Franklin Delano Roosevelt mixed charm and guile in equal parts, or so Hutchison told his Canadian readers.*

It is a startling experience to stand on the other side of the desk from President Roosevelt. To any man of the slightest imagination it is at once an awful experience and a joyful experience—awful because of this man's power for good or evil over all living men. Joyful because he bears his task so gaily, so strongly, so well. And any man who stands across the desk from him goes away sure that for permanent good or evil, Mr. Roosevelt's mark will remain forever on our age as long as history is written; that if he is spared his greatest work still lies ahead of him.

The president looks well. He looks much stronger, less worried, brighter than when I last saw him in the spring. The lines are not so deep below his eyes, his smile is quicker, his air more jaunty. It is an astounding fact of human chemistry, beyond the explanation of psychologists, how this man, under the weight of his responsibilities, with the whole democratic world literally leaning on him, can appear to have no troubles, no fears, no doubts.

He sits tilted back in his chair, smiling, cigarette holder tilted at a rakish angle. He wears a loosely-fitting, grey flannel suit and soft white shirt without a vest. On the arm of his coat is a black mourning band and his tie also is black in memory of a beloved mother. It is hard to realize, in the presence of obvious human power and physical health, that this man, cruelly crippled, cannot walk alone, is a prisoner in his chair. Here is the personal tragedy which he turned into personal victory, for if he had not lain ill four years, between life and death, he would never have been president; he would never have acquired the spiritual strength which has risen above the physical infirmity and equipped him for his present task.

Most Difficult Position

Today the happy-looking man on the other side of the desk is holding the most difficult position in the world. It is incomparably more difficult than the position of Hitler or Stalin because they are dictators and can do as they please. It is more difficult even than the position of Churchill, because Churchill has behind him a closely-concentrated, united nation, acting almost like a single family. Roosevelt cannot dictate like Hitler and Stalin. He does not have behind him a united and closely-knit nation. He stands in the centre of a kind of vacuum here in Washington, where gigantic social forces clash and heave in perpetual struggle. He cannot govern these forces absolutely. He can only swerve, moderate and balance them. Out of the conflict of America's economic divisions, its racial divisions, its divisions of thought, tradition, and blood, he can only strive to effect the best compromise, the safest balance, for this is democracy and Roosevelt is one of the first half dozen democrats in history. The defects of his character are the typical defects of democracy itself.

Here is Roosevelt's great task, the final test of his career. He has already succeeded in laying the groundwork of a new American society which will guarantee the poor man a square deal. Can he finish his giant's task by extending this principle throughout the world, as promised in the noble words of the Atlantic Charter? Can he persuade America to pay the price of that dream—the price, perhaps, of temporary loss, of damaged individual industries, of low tariffs, of world-wide responsibilities and power?

There dimly is the shape of the task facing this man. No other president but Wilson ever attempted it and Wilson failed. Roosevelt, who was close to Wilson in the failure, is evidently determined not to fail. On his success—his ability to marshal the basic forces of American life, to hold his people, to lead his people in the final peace settlement—will depend very largely the future of democracy everywhere. Today Roosevelt has the air of a man who looked death long in the face, has drunk life to the lees and is not afraid.

Declaring War on Japan

M.J. COLDWELL

> *The Japanese attack on Pearl Harbor brought the United States into World War II. It is little known that Canada declared war on Japan before the U.S. Coldwell was CCF leader at the time.*

When we got back, it was agreed that I would take a non-political tour, to address service clubs as well as our own people across the country. I got as far as Biggar and I was there on the night of Saturday, December 6, 1941.

The next day, we went up to the north part of the constituency, and we were there all day. When we drove back to Biggar that evening, as we came to the edge of town, there was a man standing there, in the middle of the road. He put up his hand as soon as he saw our car, and we stopped. He said, "Mr. Coldwell, will you please go to the telephone exchange at once. You are wanted urgently on the telephone."

So I went to the telephone booth and almost immediately a voice came on and said, "This is Walter Turnbull speaking from Ottawa. The Prime Minister would like a word with you."

So on came Mackenzie King.

"Well, Coldwell," he said, "Isn't this terrible news? A terrible disaster!"

"I don't understand you, Mr. King. What news and what disaster?"

"Where have you been all day?"

"I've been up in the north of my constituency."

"No telephones up there?"

"No," I said.

"No radio?"

"No."

"Well then," he said, "I must tell you that for the last five or six hours there have been broadcasts all over the radio networks telling us of the terrible disaster that happened this morning at Pearl Harbour. Virtually the whole American Pacific Fleet was wiped out by a Japanese attack this morning. The reason I am so anxious to get in touch with you is that we've had a cabinet meeting. The Americans have been very good to us all through the war. They've done everything they could, even to the extent of risking their own neutrality and you know," he said, "we'd like to be the first nation to stand beside them and declare war on Japan. In fact, we'd like to declare war before they can declare war, because they can't do that until tomorrow. Congress alone can declare war and they've got to wait for a meeting of Congress but, as far as we are concerned, if you'll agree, we can do this by Order-in-Council. We have an Order-in-Council drafted with a proclamation declaring war on Japan. I've been in touch with Mr. Manion and Mr. Blackmore. They have both agreed and all I want now is your agreement and we'll issue the proclamation."

So I said, "Well, Mr. King, you know we've been critical of the export of scrap iron and concentrate to Japan for a long time. I'm quite sure that my colleagues will not object to my saying that this proclamation should be issued and we should declare war on Japan immediately."

The proclamation was issued immediately that evening, and I have sometimes said, "And so I declared war."

Captured at Hong Kong, Christmas, 1941

WILLIAM ALLISTER

Canada dispatched two battalions of infantry to Hong Kong in the autumn of 1941. The soldiers were all either killed or captured when the Japanese attacked, and the colony surrendered on Christmas Day, 1941.

The alarms were coming in more frequently now. The city was surrounded, the water supply cut off, the population rioting. Small isolated units were being mopped up. Resistance was growing more meaningless. All that was going on now was a continuing slaughter. On Christmas Eve we lay down to sleep on the concrete floor with our Lee-Enfields clutched to our chests. This had to be the gloomiest Christmas Eve on record. There were several alarms during the night with machine-gun fire close by.

On Christmas Day there was a fresh alarm and a strange hubbub. Bodies charged to and fro—Middlesex, Punjabs, Canadians—confused cries I'd never heard before, with a new and terrifying timbre to them. What were they shouting? Were they attacking? Where? I couldn't catch it! *Something had changed!* I grabbed a Middlesex soldier dashing by. "Hey! What's up?"

"Packin' in!" he yelled in a panicky voice and rushed away.

"What's that mean?" But he was gone. I didn't know the phrase. The corridor was a bedlam of smoke and dust and incoherent shouting. My heart raced.

"Surrender!" a voice cried. "Throw away your arms!"

"What?!"

"The *end*!" someone yelled. "It's all over!"

Over? Could it be? What did it mean? I couldn't think—couldn't grasp it. The Signals gathered in a cluster, faces registering disbelief, relief, foreboding. Lay down your arms? I couldn't! It was all wrong. But the others *were actually doing it.*

"Pile them here!"

My precious Lee-Enfield? My security? My protector through all the mad chaotic events, my faithful friend, the only thing I didn't discard. Without it I was half a man, helpless. The others were laying theirs down, man after man. Slowly I followed suit, overcome by a terrible, alien sensation of nakedness, of being totally helpless, an act of ritual self-destruction. I was trying . . . grappling with the enormity of what was taking place. A faint glow flickered in the recesses of my being and expanded . . . *It's over. . .* The idea was filtering into my brain: no more terror, no dying, no fighting to the last man! It spelled "life," hope rekindled, a respite at least. I would not die today. The frightful weight was lifting and a flood of light filled me like a joyous roar: I was *alive*. To hell with tomorrow!

Tony's face was stiff with anger. "What's wrong with *you*?" I demanded. "This is great!"

"Great! It's a goddam disgrace! It's disgusting. We should have fought it out."

My irritation was mixed with admiration. "And died? No thanks. Look—we're beaten. Face it. Prolonging it just means more killing— what the hell for? What's so honorable about suicide? They did what they had to do!"

"Bullshit."

I walked away. Stupid, stupid . . . life was life and death was death, and the choice seemed simple. And here he was loading me down with guilt. Then fear took over.

There were suicides here and there by those who had no hope, no faith in the mercy of an enemy who had never taken prisoners. Would we be slaughtered? And how? It was *unconditional* surrender. We had no rights, no appeal, none of the dignity that was the essence of being human.

Fear in British Columbia, 1942

GWEN CASH

After their victories in 1941 and early 1942, the Japanese seemed to be supermen. There was great fear of an invasion in British Columbia, and fear of Japanese Canadians.

Feb. 11.—Two days after the affair at Pearl Harbor every window in Tree Tops was fitted with neat three-ply window screens inside, and the French windows to my studio with stout wooden shutters outside. Not a chink of light can be seen anywhere when a warning is sounded.

This morning before I left for the office, Bruce took me across the gully below the house to show me a bit of a fissure between what might be called, if you stretched your imagination, two small fern-fringed cliffs. Several stunted oaks grow out of the fissure, now deep in crackling leather-brown fallen leaves. Said he, "Come down here if I happen to be out on patrol and there's a raid. You should be safe from blasts though I don't know about shrapnel. Anyway, it's the best we can do. And I want to know where I can expect to find you. Don't for God's sake try to go look- ing for me. The roads will be a mess anyway."

Yes, this small fissure between two rocks is the best we can do. For right now, though the Forces may be prepared for eventualities—only we won't know that either till the time comes—civilians certainly aren't. I've seen members of the Forces with gas masks and tin helmets, and I believe the A.R.P. people have them too—there's a rumour to that effect. Civilians certainly haven't.

The island is of course filled with rumours and seething with indignation about the way the Japanese situation here is being handled.

We can't understand the Ottawa Government. With all the examples of Japanese wiliness and guile before them they simply refuse to admit any danger in the situation here. And what on earth is the good of moving just the Japs of military age east of the Mountains? It's the older Japs who would naturally be most loyal to Japan, just as it's the older English-born who are most loyal to the Mother Country. And anyway, why should any Jap feel any particular allegiance to Canada? We have never treated them as citizens. We have denied them voting rights. It's just foolishness to kid ourselves any of them like us particularly well. Disguise it as they do, I'm sure there is a smug, tittering satisfaction over our grief and horror about Singapore behind their inscrutable slant eyes. It would be queer if they didn't feel that way.

I suppose Ottawa really thinks there is no chance of a landing on this Island. How foolish! Day and night planes fly up and down the length and breadth of it, far out to sea and above its treacherously indented coast line. But I have an uneasy feeling their winged watchfulness won't prevent some sort of landing, somewhere, some time—perhaps pretty soon. And there will almost certainly be raids.

Oh well, what's the odds? Maybe it would be a good thing, if it would wake up the rest of Canada. Men, money, nothing really matters save that the spiritual meaning of democracy should go marching on down the centuries.

If Tree Tops has to go, O.K. But I bet my ghost will haunt the complacent halls of Ottawa.

Feb. 15.—Today Singapore fell. I went down into the gully to weep a little. Bruce does not like tears. Mr. Churchill's well-rounded phrases and impressive voice brought me no comfort. Singapore has fallen. It's more than a place. It's a symbol.

Afterwards I took a willow fork and tried for water among the blackberry brambles at the entrance to the gully. It twisted and leapt in my hands and gave every indication there is a good supply, but how far down I'm not a good enough diviner to hazard. And whether it would dry up in the summer it would be difficult to say. We shall have to get an expert. It would be a good thing to have a well dug.

Yesterday Sir Shenton Thomas, Singapore's Governor, said the city's water supply was very badly damaged and unlikely to last twenty-four hours. With sick and wounded, and women and children to care for, to be without water is a terrible thing.

Victoria's water supply comes from the Sooke Hills. Its storage reservoir is Sooke Lake. Concrete pipes carry it twenty-seven miles above ground to the city. There are two small catch-basins in those twenty-seven miles. A high road margins most of Sooke Lake. The pipe-line is easily accessible every bit of the way.

The City Fathers have six old men guarding the pipe-line, twenty-seven miles of it, its lake and two catch-basins. One man has a pistol. Once he fired it. They have asked for help from Military District Number Eleven. Of course the matter had to go to Ottawa. Ottawa said troops couldn't be used to guard civic property.

I ask you, did the City of Victoria declare war on Japan, or the Government of Canada? Did the Province of British Columbia declare war on Japan, or the Government of Canada? Is Vancouver Island Canada's first line of defence, or isn't it? On what was Macaulay Point Golf Links, a camp for ten thousand soldiers is being built. Dozens of soldiers stop your car and ask to see your registration papers when you drive in the direction of Sooke.

But there are no soldiers to guard the water supply of Victoria and district, on which the Army, Navy, Air Force as well as the civil population depend.

This evening I wrote to Jack that in case his father and I met some untoward end, there was a small safety deposit box in the Bank of Commerce, Government Street, and in it what war savings certificates and bonds we'd been able to buy, and my rings. I'd hate those damn Japs to stop him getting what little we have, if Tree Tops cops it.

Torpedoed at Sea

PIERRE SIMARD

Moving in convoy or on their own, merchant ships and their crews had to face Nazi U-boats and other terrible risks of the Battle of the Atlantic.

So I joined this old broken-down coal-burning ship—*SS Skotland*—in September '41, the worst ship I could have joined. I joined as a seaman to begin with and then they ran short of trimmers. You do a lot of shovelling and you have to be in good shape. I was perhaps not in good shape to begin with, but certainly was a few months later. Small, about 4,000 tons, she was built and served as a coastal vessel around the Scandinavian countries. A coastal vessel is made differently than an ocean-going vessel, but this was war and they didn't give a damn what you were, away you went. She was very old—forty-two years old—and of course in a storm great stresses are applied to the ship, so rivets popped and water came in and we used the pumps. It was very rough. You had to be young to go through that, young and stupid; the two go together.

We were carrying timber. We went to various places all around the British Isles, then we went to Philadelphia to load timber. We did a couple of those trips to the States to overseas. When we left the States one time, we were torpedoed three days out of Philadelphia. We were the first ship, I believe, to be torpedoed so close to the American coast. We were torpedoed on the seventeenth of May, I believe it was, National Norwegian Day. We were alone. The crew was only made up of twenty-five people and we were invited to the captain's cabin for a drink. We had a drink and we went back to our jobs. Somebody thought they'd seen a submarine, but this happened all the time because it could be a log, could be anything. At the time of the torpedoing we were at the gun platform at the afterdeck. It was Norwegian National Day, as I said, and we were there to celebrate. We fired two or three rounds at nothing.

The u-boat thought he could sink us with gunfire, so he pumped quite a few shells at us and into us. We had only one old American gun, I don't remember what it was, but it was breechloading. We had one Norwegian gunner, the only naval person on board. We were firing back—we had been trained more or less—and we did such a good job of coming close that he thought "The hell with this" and pumped two torpedoes into us. It was a hell of an explosion, two of them. Course we had timber on board and splinters went all over the place. I remember that I was on the gun platform and I went straight into the air. I was not hit; nothing was broken, just twisted. We lost three or four and those people just disappeared. I think two of them were in the boiler room and that is a bad place to be at any time.

It took the ship awhile to sink. We had only one lifeboat, the other one was destroyed. We had a bit of a time to lower it to the water because she was leaning fifteen to twenty degrees to starboard. We were just about to shove off when the captain's steward, a wonderful old man with one glass eye, suddenly came out saying, "Hey, wait for me!" He had a case of whiskey with him. This was lowered into the boat and he came down. He had gone into the captain's cabin and saved the photographs of the captain's family, the last that had been taken before he escaped from Norway.

We shoved off and then we had nothing to do but look after the people who were wounded. A lot of people were seriously wounded from shrapnel, large pieces of wood that exploded at the time of the torpedoing. The engineer officer was in bad shape; he had a piece of wood sticking out of his back, in his kidneys. We sawed off the piece of wood sticking out of his back and left what was in there in. Some had splinters in their faces and legs. It was very unpleasant because they were in pain and we had no morphine or anything like this. We had whiskey and we had biscuits and we just waited. My leg was the size of a telephone pole; my back was all twisted.

We were very fortunate, the sea was calm the whole time and it wasn't too cold. The next day we were spotted by an aircraft. Two days after that, a fisherman came alongside and picked us up. That was a bit of a job because by that time those who were badly wounded were in really bad shape. It took us another day and a half to get to Boston. When we got there the U.S. naval ambulances were waiting for us. We went to the USN hospital in Chelsea across the Charles River where we were extremely well treated.

The Conscription Plebiscite, 1942

W.L. MACKENZIE KING

In 1939, Prime Minister King had promised that Canada would not adopt conscription for overseas service. But the severity of the war and the growing demands for support of the British in English Canada led him to ask the people to release the government from its promises

Monday, 27 April 1942

My own guess as to the result of the plebiscite is that the affirmative vote should be about 70 percent over the Dominion as a whole. If it is that, it will be good indeed. That will mean it would run up to 80 percent and more in some of the provinces. It might be between 75 and 80 percent in all the provinces outside of Quebec. Quebec, I feel, might give 30 percent for the affirmative. It might even reach 35. That the vote will amply justify the taking of the plebiscite, in that it will make quite clear the wish of the people as a whole to have a free hand and no longer be bound by past pledges or promises in the nature of restrictions, I feel quite sure. Some of the Tories will immediately be after declaration of conscription for overseas. My belief is that we shall never have to resort to conscription for overseas. We will repeal the clause in the National Resources Mobilization Act, which limits the government's power to the confines of Canada. I will announce that we intend to extend the application of the provisions of the N.R.M.A. to cover the coasts of Canada possibly going the length of using Canadians anywhere in the northern half of this hemisphere. I doubt if we shall ever have to go beyond that, as our people will become increasingly concerned about keeping men within Canada itself. All we shall have to be sure of is reinforcements of the army at present in Britain. If there is any pressure on the part of our men to enforce conscription, just for the sake of conscription, I will fight that position to the end. Quebec and the country will see that I have kept my promise about not being a member of the government which sends men overseas under conscription. The only exception I will make in that will be that our men need additional numbers which could not be obtained voluntarily, but I do not think this will be the case. I am particularly pleased that there has been no need for conscription thus far, which could not have been applied, as we had not the power, but no need to use it if we had had the power. . . .

Around 9.30 I began to get the returns from different constituencies. I got particulars of several polls from the Maritimes, all showing an affirmative vote, First Quebec polls—three gave NO vote, and one gave YES.

By 10.30, many returns, including some from Manitoba. Returns from Quebec were quite depressing. I found it difficult to shape up anything for the press that would help to save the feelings of the Quebec people. Pickersgill was quite depressed, and I found it more than usually difficult to discover suitable words for the occasion. As it got on towards midnight, I thought once of leaving everything over until tomorrow, but concluded it would be best to make at least a tentative statement, as the B.C. returns began coming in.

By midnight, I had begun to make the different revises and shortly after got a copy to the Press Gallery of what, I thought, seemed on the whole, a pretty satisfactory statement. It made clear that the plebiscite had given the government and parliament a free hand, and that the will of the people would now prevail. I cannot say I felt any real elation over the result, though an amazingly large affirmative vote made clear the people had trust in myself and the government to see that their rights would be wholly protected. A table showing the returns by constituencies made it perfectly apparent to me that the governing factor was the racial and, possibly, race and religion combined, the French Catholic minority feeling it would be at the mercy of English Protestant majority. I felt very strongly that to keep Canada united, we would have to do all in our power from reaching the point where necessity for conscription for overseas would arise. As I looked at the returns, I thought of Durham's report on the state of Quebec when he arrived there after the rebellion 1837–38, and said he found two nations warring in the bosom of a single state. That would be the case in Canada, as applied to Canada as a whole, unless the whole question of conscription from now on is approached with the utmost care. The returns show clearly the wisdom of not attempting any conscription through coercion and in violation of pledges. Whatever is done now will be done with the will of the majority, expressed in advance, and which, if proceedings are taken in the right way, will be gradually acquiesced in by those in the minority. The returns show clearly the deplorable lack of an educational campaign in the parts of Quebec other than the Montreal district. There, the vote was surprisingly evenly balanced. . . .

Women in the Munitions Plants

OLIVE VILLENEUVE RENAUD

One of my sisters worked in the office at the Plant Bouchard. Not only was there a great deal of the stereotypical office work for females, they were also hired to work on the actual production lines. The men were then free to join up and serve their country, to defend the liberties of freedom.

By the spring of 1941 I was tired of working in private homes. A girl, named Margo Lefebvre, who lived at the home where I worked, had a job in the office at Plant Bouchard. She asked why I did not work at the Plant. I told her I had applied, but had not heard from the company yet. She said I should go back and speak to her, and she would personally handle my application.

I must tell you, my father was not very happy—he didn't even want me to ride with him and his friends to the plant the following Monday. After all, I was just a girl. But I told him it was too bad, I was going with them anyway. Then somehow the local priest, father Odias Valois, got wind of my plan to go work at the plant. He came to my parents' house and told me he had found me a job at yet another private home: a lady had given birth, and I was to go help out. I told him I wouldn't go; that was over, and I was going to work at the plant. He said I could not do that— I would be "lost" if I went to work there. He was afraid that I would learn bad things, I would become debauched and that my reputation would be ruined!

That's how things were in those days: parents were very strict, and parish priests made it their business to oversee the behaviour of their parishioners. I told him I was going. I said the same thing to my father, and I asked my mother to make me a lunch. My mother was very happy, and supported my decision. But of course, she couldn't say much, since my father was so dead set against it—and in those days, of course, the man was the head of the household. Women's opinions did not count for very much. But next day I got into the car with my father and the other men, and headed off to work at the plant.

My first paycheque was for 23 dollars and 5 cents. After a while, I was promoted to work in the service department, and my pay was raised from 23 cents an hour to 30 cents. A normal ten-hour day paid me 3 dollars— far better than the measly 5 dollars a week I had been earning as a house-keeper!

My next job at the plant was in the cordite department. The cordite was like long strings of spaghetti of different lengths. We had to wrap it around a sort of anvil, tie it with elastics and special wrapping cord, secure it with a special knot, and cut it. It was very precise work, with no room for error. The inspectors were always checking the work. I worked for two Scottish sisters named Mary and Florence Glenn. They were from Côte St. Louis, near Ste. Thérèse, and were completely bilingual. There were about forty-five workers, with some five more inspecting our work. They would check to make sure that the charges were well sewn, and that the igniter's needle did not cross over into the inner circle.

I spent three years on the cordite, and after a while I was made fore-woman, or "contre-maîtresse." I remember particularly having to con-trol the Wiser scissors we used: they were of very high quality, and the women used to steal them all the time. They all sewed, mended, quilted, knitted and crocheted, and had been extremely poor until recently—so these scissors were very attractive to them. I had to explain to the girls that it wasn't worth losing such a high-paying job just for the sake of a pair of scissors!

In 1941, two government employees came to speak to us at a lunchtime meeting. They were very uncomfortable announcing the news: from now on, we would all have something called "income tax" taken off our pay cheques. These would be provincial and federal taxes, along with a few pennies going towards a new plan called "Unemployment Insurance." Before then, whatever salary you made was yours, clear of any taxes.

They made such a big thing of this announcement, and assured us that these taxes were only temporary and would be lifted after the war. I wonder if those two gentlemen actually believed what they told us! But it was not as though we had a choice in the matter.

Women in Khaki

SUE WARD

Most clearly recalled was the one toilet for the forty of us. Not only that, it didn't function very well. In fact the whole water system was totally inadequate, and Vermilion Training Centre became known as the Pee Parade Camp. There was no way the women could be bedded for Lights Out at 10 p.m. without using the facilities. Those who had travelled with me from Vancouver felt I could do something about the matter so I, with my very inactive three stripes as a trainee, tracked down the Company Sergeant Major (CSM) who, new to her job, thought she should scare the hell out of everyone, even her own training staff.

That's the thing about the Army, you could always unload the problem to a higher rank or shift the order to a lower rank. After she conferred with her company officer, leaving the lot of us hopping around and growing more irritable, permission was granted to scurry outside and water the shrubbery. Those with greater needs were to get back into uniform and fall into ranks outside the front entrance, where they would board an army truck. Then they would be hauled to the one small Vermilion hotel in the village a mile away, there to line up the stairs in the lobby to use the upstairs washroom.

This incredible situation would happen upon arising and it was some challenge to make up the room, attend breakfast parade, and Fall In on the parade square with a full bladder. This emergency was covered by marching the whole outfit over to the few outhouses at the fair grounds, sans TP which was doled out by the NCO with a cheery "There's room for one more in this one!" As soon as new recruits arrived, each platoon officer was made responsible for taking them on a tour which included an in-depth explanation of the water workings, the septic tanks and disposal fields.

For the longest time, Vermilion, it seemed, boasted a plumber with every washroom at the camp making for screams as naked trainees, battling for the four shower stalls on our floor, met with a plumber. For sanitation purposes, the showers boasted no curtains. It was truly the survival of the fittest as the entire company of over one hundred trainees would conclude each day's program with physical education followed by supper parade. There were actually over 300 throughout the building, so the hot water would quickly disappear, encouraging further screams after the plumbers had made their smiling escapes. Some trainees found the nakedness overwhelming, never mind the presence of the plumbers. For an only daughter or a farm girl, stripping off one's clothes in front of others was intimidating and showering became a total shock to more than one's body. Some young women would avoid showering altogether so sometimes, when the roommates could stand it no longer, the screams and scramble as they dragged the girl to the shower would produce a permanent cure. It may be hard to believe in these days of TV commercials for shampoos and deodorants that cleanliness was much more difficult to come by in those shabby times. Sponge baths and weekly hairdos were the result of rationed fuel, heat, water and soaps.

Of course a facility, which was built to handle probably 150 staff and pupils, had limited laundry facilities. And the water was SO HARD, and ORANGE in colour. Most of us had no more than three pairs of panties to go with our three pair of lisle stockings. This meant there would be washings going on in the pails, found in washrooms to be used for "bathroom fatigues." Every few days some hassled CWAC would throw more than the soapy water into the toilet. The panties would get through the pipes all the way to the septic tank system to be caught by the screen, and the water would back up, up, up, to the top toilets. I've often thought the small crew of engineers, the only men on the station, deserved a special citation for keeping the flow on the go!

Dieppe

SHERWOOD LETT

Brigadier Lett commanded a brigade at Dieppe, the abortive Canadian raid on the small coastal port in France in August 1942.

We first landed at Red Beach where the Essex [Scottish] composed the first wave of the main landing force. We got one tank ashore under very heavy fire but it got bogged down in the shingle and stuck there but with all its guns blazing away at the Huns in the houses in front of us. Our Engineer party, which tried to land, was mowed down by machine-gun fire and our craft came under very heavy shell and mortar fire. So Johnny Andrews said he could not land any more tanks there and asked if we could land further west along the beach on White Beach, where we had already landed our first flight of tanks.

To this [suggestion] I agreed, so we pulled off and turned west to go into White Beach, opposite the Casino. The craft was under quite heavy fire but we were having few casualties and I was in good wireless communication with the Essex and the RHLI [Royal Hamilton Light Infantry] and the Force Command Ship, and had good control of the battle on my sector except that I had not had a word at all from the Royals [The Royal Regiment of Canada] who had landed earlier a mile or so to the east of the town on another beach.

I was, of course, very busy with the battle giving targets for the air [forces] to bomb or smoke, getting the naval fire on to a position, and passing back information to the Force Ship. Then they came and told me the craft was heading for Green Beach (the South Saskatchewan Beach) instead of White Beach. So I went up to the bridge and got that straightened out with the naval commander. We got headed in again for White Beach and ready for our second touch down. I had learned that our tanks were unable to get through the roadblocks as the roadblock demolition parties had been shot down on landing. So Col. McTavish [the senior engineer officer] had agreed to use men and explosives which he had and we would have another try at the roadblocks. As we approached White Beach, we really did come under fire of all kinds. But we kept on going on to the shore. Johnnie Andrews drove off in his command tank and just as he did so they shot away his water-proofing and he sank with only his turret showing above water. He baled out and swam to a small landing craft and was taken aboard but, in a few minutes, it was set afire and we did not see him again.

Meanwhile we were under a regular hail of fire of all kinds from in front and from the headlands on either side. They shot away the ramp in front so that we could not land any more vehicles or get ashore, they disabled the engines and finally the steering gear of our craft so we could not move in or out, and twice they shot away the aerials from my wireless set which ran up about six feet over our heads and the boys replaced them twice so that we kept touch throughout.

Then the skipper ordered "abandon ship" and we were all supposed to jump into the water and set out swimming the sixty miles back, I suppose, but the idea didn't appeal to me, particularly as I had good communication still and was able to give supporting fire to my units as they requested it and I had control of the tanks on shore through the remaining control tank which was still with me and which was in touch with the tank squadrons ashore.

It was as we lay there that we suffered our very heavy casualties. Col. McTavish was killed as was Captain Insinger, the Intelligence Officer and Murray Fairweather, my Liaison Officer, the crew of my pom-pom gun. My two signallers were wounded but carried on. I called for some-one from the Engineers to see if they could get the [ship's] engines going and they, with two naval chaps and my Staff Captain [Garneau] suc-ceeded in getting one engine going.

We got some steering gear rigged up too and after what seemed like a couple of weeks we got off shore a bit and out of the worst of the fire. The dive bombers took an odd crack at us too but our planes looked after them in short order. It was while we were lying up, trying to get our engines going, that I was hit. They put me on a stretcher near the [wire-less] set and I was still able to take an interest in the proceedings. Finally, after we had got through the order for the withdrawal to our units and to the tanks, we pulled back out to the boat pool. A naval craft came along-side and the wounded were transferred to it. Then they decided to trans-fer everyone to the naval craft as it looked as if our LCT was going to sink. They tell me now that we had thirty-seven direct hits on the craft and she looked a bit like a sieve. However, they finally took her in tow and brought her back to England.

I was wounded about nine thirty and we finally started back to Eng-land about two o'clock and arrived safely at an English port about nine thirty at night. It was a lovely, mild August afternoon and I lay on the deck on a stretcher with the odd shot of morphia and frequent tea and cigarettes . . . The Luftwaffe tried to take the odd peck at us on the way back but without much success. They finally hoisted my stretcher off onto the dock about eleven and by midnight I was rolling along in an ambulance train towards this place [No. 7 Canadian General Hospital] where we arrived at seven the following morning. My turn in the operat-ing room came that evening. . . .

Making Soldiers from Civilians

PIERRE BERTON

We shared a common hatred of church parade, which some of us man-aged to skip. It was offensive to me to be forced to take part in any reli-gious service against my will—especially as these parades had nothing to do with turning me into an efficient soldier. In this instance the chore was especially demeaning because the padre was a confirmed British Israelite. This insufferable man did his best to convince us that the lost tribes of

Israel had somehow made their way to the British Isles—a piece of fantasy no more difficult to swallow than the burning bush or the parting of the Red Sea but so patently spurious that it caused our gorges to rise, whether we had any religion or not. The hatred of church parade was one of the elements that united us, slowly transforming us from a rabble into the beginnings of a disciplined military formation.

The other element was the platoon competition in close order drill. At first nobody cared about the competition, but as the days wore on and our drill improved we began to grow a little cocky, shouting taunts at other platoons as they marched across the square. By the sixth week of training, it was clear that something was happening to us. It no longer mattered that all but three of us had no intention of shedding blood for our country. What suddenly seemed to be important was that our platoon should be proclaimed the best—that we should be presented with a plaque before the entire camp, that we should all have our photographs taken holding the trophy, with a copy to each man to send home or to cherish.

The problem was poor Codweed. It was apparent that he was holding us back. He missed training because he was forever going off on sick parade. As a result, we were denied our break periods because the instructors were always helping him catch up. We were getting weary of hearing the sergeant continually telling Codweed to keep in step.

Gradually Codweed found himself a liability. We could scarcely win the platoon competition with him limping along behind us. The little knot of sympathizers around his bunk dwindled and evaporated. Now when Codweed complained about his back he got angry looks. On parade, when he missed a step, the man behind would kick him. From martyrdom, Codweed had become a pariah.

And then, one day something remarkable happened: Codweed's back began to improve. He stopped reporting sick. He came out on parade and began to keep in step. It was, as a few of us remarked acidly, a miracle rivalling those of Lourdes.

From that point on, there was no holding us. Perfection in close order drill became an obsession. It is hard to believe, looking back on it now, that we actually gave up our precious evenings and practised at night in our own time. Of course we won the competition and were photographed with the coveted trophy on our last day together, and celebrated and swore eternal loyalty to one another—promising to write faithfully and get together for a grand reunion after the war. The following day we broke up forever—an emotional leave-taking that saw tears in the eyes of several of us. In just ten weeks the army had taken seventy-five strangers from all walks of life and turned them, for a little while at least, into the closest of comrades.

Sex in Newfoundland: A U.S. Army View

CAPT. DANIEL BERGSMA

After the "destroyers for bases" deal was made between the United States and Britain in 1941, American forces were based in Newfoundland, then a lapsed Dominion. The soldiers and Newfoundlanders interacted freely.

Sex Mores: On the basis of reports from presumably reliable persons plus personal observations, it seems quite definite that a large proportion of unmarried Newfoundland women have no effective inhibitions relative to non-marital sexual intercourse. During the evenings when the weather is favorable—and low temperature is not an adequate deterrent for many—*bargain day* crowds of women may be seen promenading along specific streets and in definite sections or areas waiting to be noticed and favored with attention. Some of these girls will take a very active part in becoming acquainted with strange males; most of the others in the parade hope too much of the evening will not be wasted before their presence is observed by a passing male. Some of these girls specifically desire that sexual intercourse be a part of the evening's entertainment while most of the other promenaders are quite easily persuaded to consent to sexual intercourse. In taverns and dance halls it is not uncommon to see girls taking the initiative in fondling, kissing, and hugging men whom they never saw before an hour or two ago. These same girls also transfer their attention from one male to another in a very nonchalant manner. Many Newfoundland girls are averse to the use of a condom by the male and will interfere in its application or will deliberately pull it off if applied. This attitude may result from a lack of knowledge about venereal disease epidemiology, a desire to capture a *wealthy* ($50 per month) American husband or more likely from religious teachings. Many Newfoundland girls reportedly will refuse consent for sexual intercourse in the normal, horizontal position but will readily consent to, and will recommend, the use of the vertical or standing position. This is presumably due to their belief that they will not become pregnant if sexual intercourse occurs while in the vertical position. Coitus may occur anywhere. The least inhibited persons copulate while lying on the grass beside the road where passers-by can see them and often within fifty or one hundred feet of another couple similarly occupied; or the girl may have insisted on the use of the standing position in which case the female will stand with her back to the side of a building or against a fence along the roadside. The writer observed the latter while passing in a car. Reportedly, more conservative individuals will wander further from the road; go behind bushes, trees or houses; into alleys between the dwellings; into a closed vestibule in their own, a friend's or a stranger's house; or inside their own or a friend's home.

Prostitution: Commercialized prostitution as known in the United States with its combined activities of pimps, bellhops, porters, taxi drivers, madams and organized groups of girls who permit sexual intercourse for a fee is essentially unknown in Newfoundland. Commercialized prostitution does exist however. Some few girls reportedly earn their entire income by fees for sexual intercourse but they operate independently. The average civilian income in Newfoundland has been very small in recent years. Accordingly, fees for prostitution are small, but prostitutes do not need to conduct a big scale organized business to maintain their standard of living. Other girls routinely *supplement* their income by prostitution but do so on a very limited scale. Many more occasionally prostitute themselves for hire to obtain the extra funds to purchase some article for which they have developed an acute desire. Reportedly, the following is not a rare situation. A girl or woman needs or desires some garment or luxury and lacks one or two dollars of the total price. Unhesitatingly, she proceeds from her home toward the store, but she solicits en route. For each coitus she consummates at the end of an alley between two buildings, in back of some structure, or in the home of some friend nearby the place where she met her customer, she obtains from 25 cents to a dollar, occasionally more. When her earnings net her the difference between cash on hand and the purchase price of the desired article, she proceeds to the store, makes her purchase and returns to her home. Reportedly, if such a woman chanced to meet some masculine friend of hers during her described trip and he requested coitus, it would be readily granted with no fee asked for or expected.

Wartime Canada: A Soviet View

IGOR GOUZENKO

> *Soviet cipher clerk Igor Gouzenko arrived in Canada in 1943, amazed at what he saw. Two years later, his defection helped start the Cold War.*

Now, as our transport plane came in for the landing and I fastened my safety belt, the houses of Edmonton, seen through a starboard window, caused little shivers of uncertainty. I had been lectured to and drilled in the procedure to follow, yet this seemed different. When the aircraft bumped slightly, then finally rolled to an easy stop by a hangar, I unbuckled my belt slowly—actually loath to leave this last contact with my familiar Russia and step onto this strange, threatening, foreign soil. Zabotin, however, showed no hesitation. He was the first out of the plane.

As I emerged into the bright sunlight a group of young men on a truck whisked over to the plane, apparently to unload baggage and mail sacks. They were in uniform, which I did not recognize at the time as that of the

Royal Canadian Air Force. I must have been staring at them because one laughed outright and yelled:

"Hiya, chum—how's Joe these days?"

I glanced uncertainly at Romanov, who shook his head almost imperceptibly. The English words were understandable but I didn't know what was meant by "Joe". Both Romanov and I would have been flabbergasted if we had realized the query referred to Joseph Stalin. As it was, we merely followed our instructions: "When in doubt simply act as if you do not understand, and keep silent."

Our ideas about Canada were soon hopelessly confused.

We had read, of course, all the official articles in encyclopedias and brochures. The small guide-book in French, translated for me by Anna, described Canada but confined itself to dry statistics or descriptions of places.

We were not prepared for the wealth of food in the Edmonton hotel where we stayed, nor the abundance of clothing, candies and luxuries of all kinds in such windows as those of the huge Hudson's Bay store on the main street. The hundreds of automobiles, carrying people who certainly didn't seem to have an official bearing, left us gaping in astonishment. We continued our journey to Ottawa aboard a Canadian National Railways' transcontinental train. The swaying fields of wheat extending endless miles from the tracks, the rich soil, the forests, the lakes, the gardens beside homes in towns and villages, reflected a prosperous and colorful country.

But the manners of the people we met on the train were most astounding of all.

The conductor came to take our tickets while we were in the dining car and, for some reason, Zabotin mentioned that we had just flown from Russia. The waiter overheard the conversation and so did some men in Canadian military uniform at the table across the aisle. Before we knew it, the whole train seemed aware of our having just landed from the Soviet Union. It was most disconcerting since we had been schooled to keep everything a secret and to lie whenever necessary to keep people from knowing our business. But as Zabotin and Romanov were in uniform, it was almost impossible to remain incognito.

The trouble was that we did not know how to meet these people, who seemed friendly and pleasant. Practically everyone who spoke to us during the three nights and two days of that train trip started off by saying:

"How are things in Russia these days?"

Naturally we were most cautious. We told of the magnificent, wonderful country we had just left, watching the effect of our words very carefully. But, to our continued bewilderment, everybody seemed to agree with us. They would nod approval and say something like:

"You fellows sure did a swell job during the war!"

Others would say: "Stalin must have a lot on the ball, yes sir!" Or: "This Communism stuff must have something in it to produce such fighters as you people!"

On the afternoon of the day after we left Edmonton, Romanov pulled me aside in the vestibule between the club car and the first sleeper. Zabotin was back in a compartment talking and drinking with some military travelers.

"I can't make these people out," said Romanov in Russian. "They all seem to be pro-Soviet. Yet they are capitalists."

The same thought had struck me also.

"Not only that," I added, "but they don't seem the least bit afraid of secret agents. Did you hear that soldier in the club car just now criticizing the government for the way it is handling the enlistment of troops?"

Romanov made a gesture of bewilderment.

"I cannot understand it. There seems to be no restraint. I took the opportunity of asking that soldier some details about recruiting and he told me things I hesitate to put into my notebook. He even disclosed that there is serious discord between the Province of Quebec and the Province of Ontario. The Prime Minister has much critical opposition and he says Communism has a damn good chance of being installed after the war if the government doesn't act smart now."

Romanov shrugged, then continued: "I was in the rear end of the club car at the time and there were four other men beside the soldier listening. Two of them laughed while the others seemed to approve of the soldier's views. One of the men who laughed asked me if we have freedom of speech in Russia?"

"What did you say?"

"I said we do."

Both of us fell silent. The clicking of the wheels below our feet beat out a curiously exhilarating rhythm. It must have been minutes later when Romanov spoke again, this time in low tones.

"Did they seem to believe everything you told them about Soviet Russia?"

"Yes," I said.

"That is an interesting indication of public opinion here," he ventured, with a note of hesitancy that puzzled me.

Even as he spoke, the thought rushed to my mind: Why should Canada turn to Communism? It appears to have infinitely more than the Soviet in every way. Romanov must have had the same thought. He peered at me sharply then looked back over a shoulder as if suspecting some NKVD agent was lurking in the vestibule reading our thoughts.

"It is time for lunch," he said abruptly. Then, as if this had prompted another thought, he asked: "Did you notice that store window with all the wrist watches in Edmonton?"

I nodded enthusiastically. "I sure did! And everybody on the train seems to be wearing a wristwatch. I wonder if we shall be able to buy one in Ottawa?"

Nazi Atrocities

GREGORY CLARK

Somewhere in Italy, Sept. 26—(Delayed)—Monsters in victory and monsters in flight, the Germans have added to the imperishable name of Lidice in Czechoslovakia the little name of Rionero in Italy, and I am one of the witnesses. In this tousled town of 10,000 inhabitants the Germans, the night before last, perpetrated one of their foul slaughters of innocent civilians. Twenty-one young men of the town of Rionero, ranging in age from 16 years and most of them in their early twenties, with the exception of a father of a family, aged 40, were lined up and shot in cold blood.

This afternoon I visited the bloodsoaked ditch in which they died and then went up to the cemetery where the pitiful bodies, clad in their rags, were laid ready for burial. Some were riddled with tommy guns, some were shot between the eyes with pistols.

Of this little random selection of townsfolk, those who fell pretending to be dead, were sought out by calm cold Germans and four Italian Fascist paratroopers aiding and abetting them, and were shot at pistol point. All but one; Stefano Di Mattia, with his townsmen's blood sluicing him, feigned death so well that he alone out of 21 escaped, with only a leg wound. Stefano it was who took me to the scene of the slaughter and then led on to the array of dead.

Here is the story to which hundreds of citizens of Rionero bear witness:

On Friday night, Sept. 24, with 8th Army patrols already on the fringe of the town, 60 Germans with a small number of Fascist paratroopers among them were preparing to withdraw north from the town. Ever since the armistice the Germans had been lawless and contemptuous of the Italians, and looted at will.

About 5 p.m. a party of half a dozen Germans, a sergeant leading, came down the main street and in front of the house of Pasquale Sibilia stopped to shoot a chicken. Little Elena, seven-year-old child of Pasquale, ran in to tell her father and Pasquale came to the door armed with a rifle and shouted to the Germans to get away. The German sergeant laughed and shot Pasquale in the leg. Pasquale fired back and hit the German in the hand.

In five minutes the town was in an uproar, and a party of 16 Germans plus four Italian Fascist paratroopers swarmed on to Pasquale's neighbors and began herding up all the men in the immediate neighborhood.

The whole affair did not take 30 minutes. With their tommy guns and pistols the Germans and Fascist Italians, whom the Italians hate almost more than the Germans, rapidly herded together all the men they could find. The youngest they got was Marco Grieco, a shy boy of 16, and the oldest was the father of the next door family, Antonio di Perro, a farm laborer working in the vineyards about Rionero.

Let Stefano Di Mattia, the only survivor of this gruesome vengeance, speak:

"I heard shots and came up the street," said Stefano, "as did many others to see what was doing. Into the crowd charged the Germans and these four lickspittle Italian Fascist gangsters, who play along with the Germans, and before I knew it a pallid-faced German had me on the end of his tommy gun, herding me up the street into a little huddle of my townsmen. For days past, ever since the armistice, we have grown used to Germans and Fascists herding us up to do dirty work for them, or mend a road or carry their stuff. None of us dreamed what was to happen.

"It was all one confused dream, all in silence, broken only by the yells of Germans and the outcries of our women, instantly stilled. We were bustled up the street to the edge of the town, about 100 yards. There in an open field we were ordered to line up. By the faces and actions of the Germans and those four Fascists we suddenly knew what was going to happen.

"In front of us with tommy guns and pistols were fourteen Germans and those four Fascists. The German sergeant gave a command. The Italian Fascists translated to us with sneers, 'Kneel! kneel!' Before we could understand, the guns opened. We were just in a huddle. I felt the sting of a bullet on my right leg and I fell. Others, I don't know who, fell or struggled over me, drenching me with their blood. I lay still as death. I heard the voices of the Germans as they waded among us shooting at pistol point those still alive. Just across the road at the corner of the village, our women folk and a crowd of townsmen and children stared in silence.

"I know," said Stefano, "that they intended to burn us right in the ditch on the roadside, for they forbade any of the townsfolk to come near us, and I lay there till dark, while a sentry guarded the pile of dead. The women and neighbors came and pleaded to have the bodies to bury, but the sentry shouted, 'Everybody back.' Then, it seems, plans were all changed when your patrols began to be reported on the fringes of the town. At midnight 60 Germans left in a great rush with lorries and armored cars and by morning all were gone."

In the second vehicle to enter Rionero, which was the jeep of a 30-year-old lieutenant-colonel, I got into Rionero as soon as the patrols reported it clear, and we went straightaway to the scene of the atrocity. From a roadside ditch, caked with dusty blood, we went to the cemetery where we saw the still open coffins of the victims, awaiting burial. The bodies had lain all night in the ditch and were therefore placed in their caskets just as found, twisted and grotesque in their poor ragged blood-stained clothes of humble workers in the fields around these poverty-stricken Italian towns. It was the most terrible sight of my life, in this quiet cypress-shaded Italian cemetery, where the Italian dead always seem to lie so much more importantly than the living. Only the men of the town were there for the funeral. The women and children were all warned away from the cemetery by the men of Rionero, who spared the memory of their town this awful chapter. But we stood and watched it, and army cameras took pictures and army movies ground out the gruesome document of Rionero.

On the notice board of the town hall, the Germans had left this written testimony to their crime:

"There have been already killed 15 men who were responsible for having fired against the Germans. This serves as a warning to all rebels of what will happen to them if any further acts against Germans are perpetrated."

It was signed by the illegible scrawl of some officer or non-com who must have already felt the hot breath of justice on his neck.

In victory they are monsters. Here their bedraggled and harried rearguard, with the Allies on their very tails, are capable of monstrous acts. Not to enemies, but to humble, poverty-stricken, backward, gentle folk, who until two weeks ago were their allies. When the time comes soon for squaring of accounts, and I am permitted to attend the peace conference, will you, reader, please clip this story of Rionero out and save it against the day I might in those golden hours to come be guilty of one forgetting word, one sparing phrase, one apology for the dirty savage who roves these mountains now?

The Royal Canadian Regiment Celebrates, Italy, 1943

STROME GALLOWAY

Canada's oldest regular force infantry regiment marked its 60th anniversary during the heavy fighting around Ortona in December 1943.

December 21 was the regimental birthday. The RCR had been formed on that day in 1883; it was our Diamond Jubilee! "Men die, wars end, but the Regiment lives on", we had always been told. So, by field telephone I invited Spry to return to the fold and "drink a Health to the Regiment." Within the hour his jeep approached. It came under shellfire and he had to crawl along a ditch to reach us. Capt. Sandy Mitchell, my battle adjutant, prepared some grog and we raised the china cups the RSM had found in an adjoining house. Dan Spry said: "Gentlemen, The Regiment!" Just then Padre Rusty Wilkes, MC, arrived with a dozen wooden crosses under his arm. He joined in the toast, before beginning his ghastly task of shoving about thirty stiffened corpses into the narrow graves the Pioneers had dug outside.

Telling the People at Home: Ortona, 1943

MATTHEW HALTON

> *The Canadian Broadcasting Corporation sent reporters into the field to broadcast to the people at home. One of the most successful broadcasters was Matthew Halton.*

With the fall of Ortona, in the early morning of December 28th, the Battle of the Moro River is over, and there is now a new name to add to the list of great British deeds of the war.

Call them out: Dunkirk; Tobruk; Alamein; the delaying action in Burma; Sidi Omar; the last stand at Sollum; the Battle of Tunis. Call them out, and then add Moro River.

Measured on the scale of the last war, the Battle of the Somme, for instance, or Passchendaele, or the enormous scale of the fighting in Russia, this was not a big battle. But it was one of the biggest ever fought by Canadians, and neither in this war nor the last, nor in any other, has there been anything more bitter and intense. The attacking Canadians beat two of the finest German divisions that ever marched, killing them, man by man, in a long-drawn-out fury of fire and death ending in the appalling week of Ortona.

The glory and the sorrow are not all Canada's because this was an Eighth Army battle. British, New Zealand and Indian troops had heavy enough fighting in the center and on the left; but the main role was assigned to Canada on the right flank, and the quality of this battle on the right had something special that our race will never forget.

During November, British and Indian troops smashed the enemy's winter lines on the Sangro River. The enemy really thought he could hold us there throughout the winter. He had dug-outs and entrenchments of a kind not seen since the last war, and the Germans might be holding there yet except for our air support. On the Moro River, because of bad weather, we had no air support on a big scale. Moreover, the quality of the enemy troops on the Sangro was not what it was here.

And now the Canadians were brought down from the central mountains around Campobasso, where they had rested for several weeks, to take the right flank of the Eighth Army in its push for Pescara and the road to Rome.

On November 30th they were moving into action near the old town of San Vito on the sea. British engineers bridged the San Vito gorge for us under fire and every time we crossed it for the next ten days we were still under fire. The Canadians manoeuvred into position along the ridge overlooking the Moro River and on the night of December 6th we made our first attempt to cross that little creek. The Germans had rushed in their famous 90th light division of Panzer Grenadiers, to replace the beaten 65th infantry division and to meet the threat on the coast. The Canadians had to fight their way across the river at night to try and clear the enemy off the bank so that the engineers could build the crossings for the tanks and other supporting arms and supplies. There are two roads across, one a few hundred yards from the sea and another a mile to the left.

On the night of the 6th, an eastern Canadian unit crossed on the coast, and western Canadians on the right, but we were thrown back. On the right they attacked again with intense artillery support. Two companies got across, but the tanks could not get over to their support and they were pulled out under murderous fire, with losses. But at last light that day, a great officer took his men over again through a curtain of fire and the next morning, gallantly supported by British tanks, they made a desperate rush and took the high ground, and we were established across the Moro River.

Two of many great episodes of the crossing. "B" Company of a western Canadian unit, alone and surrounded across the river on the left, knocked out fourteen enemy machine-gun posts, an anti-tank gun and two tanks; and a field company of Canadian engineers built a log crossing over the river under steady small-arms fire as well as shelling.

The battle now focused on the village of San Leonardo on the crest just beyond the crossing. It was at this time that we captured a German document with the order: "The line of the Moro River is to be retaken and held, no matter what the cost in lives." In an action as close and ferocious as I have ever seen, two infantry units now tried to go through our bridgehead formations to take San Leonardo and the crossroads two miles beyond on the Ortona road. Our fine troops, our excellent men, burning for victory, and full of pride in themselves, made nearly twenty furious attacks, and every time the enemy counterattacked through hundreds of his dead. The Canadians wiped the Panzer Grenadiers right out of existence, battalion after battalion of them, and then found themselves facing a still better German outfit, the 4th Parachute Division, a formation of savage, cunning young zealots as good as anything the warrior Germans ever produced.

The once-pleasant olive groves and vineyards and gardens on the slopes leading to the Ortona road became a bloody, churned up shambles. Our artillery laid down terrific concentrations of steel for nearly every attack we made and the Germans replied with the most artillery they have ever used against us, especially mortars and 88's, so that in a few days there was a shell hole wherever you stepped, and every tree was splintered, and not a leaf was left. Still the Canadians held and fought back. The Germans then were brave. The Canadians were heroic—remember they had to attack. Exhausted, lying and fighting in a quagmire of mud, with many of their comrades killed or wounded, their zest for the attack actually increased from day to day. Yard by yard, and German by German, they fought their way up to the crossroads to the hamlet of Berardi.

Now our units were mixed up at times. Combat teams of tanks and infantry were formed and still the enemy would not give in. More than once I got forward to units in action, to see German machine-guns start shooting from behind us, and keep shooting until their crews were killed.

At last an eastern Canadian unit got into position to attack Berardi on the edge of a deep gully. Forty machine-guns awaited them, and they were counter-attacked by tanks. Then a fine Canadian unit attacked and was repulsed and surrounded, but it fought its way out and got to the crossroads. Once another unit was cut off for three days and when they fought their way out they could show a German document, announcing: "One of the most famous Canadian units is surrounded, and now will be totally destroyed."

Victory would have been impossible without the Canadian tanks, who provided our mobile artillery. Time after time, they advanced against enemy tanks and anti-tank guns to make a hole for this regiment or to come to the aid of another. One day a combat team was trying to cross the Ortona road, left of the crossroads. The group of tanks, under Captain Hugh Burns of Halifax, sent back a message advising that they could attack if necessary, though it would be suicide. The order came back, "We don't expect to see you again, but do it if you can." They did it—got two anti-tank guns with two lucky shots—and were seen again. Even with the taking of the road, the Germans wouldn't give up. They stayed on everywhere fighting in little pockets, and scores of them were killed in close action. Walking over the ghastly crossroads one day, we counted nearly two hundred dead. . . .

At first light on the 28th, when I got to the command post of one unit, the colonel grinned, and said quietly, "I think it's over." A minute or two later a signaller jerked off his headphones and said, "Sir, the Jerries are gone, or else they are all dead."

Harassing Refugee Children

KARL W. BUTZER

> *Canada admitted few refugees from Hitler before and during World War II. In the wartime mood of belligerence, even refugee children could be subjected to intolerance.*

A kind of preview to our new social environment came during the one parish picnic that we attended in the spring of 1941. Father had entered a footrace and was about to win, when someone deliberately tripped him. As he fell, a lot of people broke out in cheers. It was apparent to all of us that the "rules" in Canada were different than in England. I connect this incident with my lifelong dislike for the puffed up, officious ushers I found at the Sunday masses in most old, established Catholic communities in Canada and the United States.

Outside the home, things turned nasty in the fall of 1941. I was being called names in second grade, and then a gang of more than a dozen boys jumped me on my way back from school. I wasn't really physically hurt but was humiliated and terrified. I told the principal, and he scolded them in his office the next day. When the boys filed back into class, the young teacher, Mrs. Brawley, asked if they had gotten the "strap." They replied no, and then she said, "Good. You didn't deserve it." That gave them the license to do what they wanted, and it became a year of terror. I became afraid to go out on the playground during the breaks, and after school I was stalked by a gang of boys who regularly followed me home to line up in front of the house, shouting, "Heil Hitler!" My grades plummeted, and I slipped from third in a class of twenty to second or third last: every month we shifted class seats according to rank, the best performers sitting up front. I was regularly sitting in the last row now and began to lose my sense of self-esteem. I became ashamed of my origins. . . .

In fourth grade a school inspector came into every class once a month. After rustling through some papers behind the teacher's desk, he would ask about the children's ethnicity. All the "English" children had to stand up, and so forth. Finally he would ask, "Are there any foreigners?" Now I had to stand up in the aisle. "What are you?" he would ask. "German," I had to say. Every month the same routine, with the same effect. The other children were reminded, and the hostility, bullying, and name-calling flared up again. I remember wondering, with growing anger, why he had to do this even though he already knew the facts.

There is another incident, one of only a few that I have recounted to others, that is very applicable. When a pencil or an eraser went "missing" in class, the teacher promptly came down to search through my desk and that of Paul Laberge, the only French Canadian in the class. But eventually it turned out that Charlie Benson had the item. That happened not once but several times—the teacher predictably pounced on the desks of the only two minority students, but the stolen trinket was always in Charlie's. This was a classic reflex—you're not one of us; therefore you must look dishonest and disreputable; and so you're the obvious suspect. That is probably why police selectively stop or pick up African American motorists for "suspicious behavior."

Dealing with Fear

MURRAY PEDEN

Soldiers, sailors, and airmen put themselves in harm's way, and almost all had to cope with the fear of death.

I was beginning to find that the strain of operational flying had a pronounced cumulative effect. Each time I found myself on the battle order the ordeal of waiting—an ordeal punctuated by the ritual of air test, briefing, and flying meal—seemed intensified, the muscles of the abdomen hardening until they felt like the extended ribs of a miniature umbrella. The tension would ease briefly as we finally got started and raced down the runway on takeoff, then it returned with redoubled force as we approached hostile territory, to reign supreme and worsen progressively as the trip wore on. Time moved with the glacial slowness that overtaxed nerves can occasion, making operational flying an exacting test of nerve and self control.

To a person wanting to visualize how intense the strain could become, how suppressed fear could swell and gnaw inside, I offer the following as a comparison, perhaps easier to imagine than the unfamiliar surroundings of a darkened bomber cockpit framed in faintly luminous dials.

Imagine yourself in a building of enormous size, pitch black inside. You are ordered to walk very slowly from one side to the other, then back. This walk in the dark will take you perhaps five or six hours. You know that in various nooks and crannies along your route killers armed with machine guns are lurking. They will quickly become aware that you have started your journey, and will be trying to find you the whole time you are in the course of it. There is another rather important psychological factor: the continuous roar emanating from nearby machinery. It precludes the possibility of your getting any audible warning of danger's approach. You are thus aware that if the trouble you are expecting does come, it will burst upon you with the startling surprise one can experience standing in the shower and having someone abruptly jerk open the door of the steamy cubicle and shout over the noise. If the killers stalking you on your walk should happen to detect you, they will leap at you out of the darkness firing flaming tracers from their machine guns. Compared with the armament they are carrying, you are virtually defenceless. Moreover, you must carry a pail of gasoline and a shopping bag full of dynamite in one hand. If someone rushes at you and begins firing, about all you can do is fire a small calibre pistol in his direction and try to elude him in the dark. But these killers can run twice as fast as you, and if one stalks and catches you, the odds are that he will wound and then incinerate you, or blow you into eternity. You are acutely aware of these possibilities for every second of the five or six hours you walk in the darkness, braced always, consciously or subconsciously, for a murderous burst of fire, and reminded of the stakes of the game periodically by the sight of guns flashing in the dark and great volcanic eruptions of flaming gasoline. You repeat this experience many times—if you live.

The effects of a dozen operations, or a score, were discernible from time to time in various aircrew around the station. A Canadian gunner named Mickey Claxton, who slept opposite me in "Canada House," used to have nightmares in which he dreamed he was on operations and coming under fire. He would wake up in terror, often waking the rest of us up in the process, and then try to compose himself again. So frequently did he experience these nightmares that every night, as he punched his pillow and settled himself for sleep, he would sigh jokingly to the rest of us: "Well, chocks away."

One senior pilot, a Flight Lieutenant DFC type, when his name was on the battle order, used to grow so tense as the day wore on that his responses to unexpected questions were gasped out, and there was a note approaching the hysterical in remarks solicited from him. He would, quite literally, weep in frustration at the slightest obstacle until he got airborne, then he settled down.

In most of the aircrew, of course, the outward signs were not so readily apparent, but, with few exceptions, they were there nevertheless, in one form or another.

Jake Walters, whose tour had been far from easy, was feeling the strain. He could not hold a meal on his stomach most times when he was operating. After a raid, sitting with his coffee at interrogation, he would frequently get up abruptly, leave the little ops building hurriedly, and go and throw up outside in the darkness. Gradually we all became aware of Jake's condition, and feared that it would worsen and cause him to kill himself and his crew before he was taken off operations. Jake being Jake, we knew that he would never in this world ask or suggest that he be taken off. When we finally tumbled to the fact that his nerves were getting so bad that they were turning his stomach, someone passed the word along to George Wright. George, in turn, told the Wing Commander.

On July 22nd, 1944, Jake flew with Main Force in the attack on the railway yards at Chalons sur Marne, about 90 miles east of Paris. The following afternoon he told me the sequel.

After his return, while he sat sipping his coffee and answering the questions of the Intelligence officer at interrogation, he felt the unmistakable symptoms again, and hurried outdoors. As he stood heaving, one arm bent overhead against the corner of the building, he felt someone move in behind him, and an arm slipped firmly around his waist to support him until he finished straining. Then he heard McGlinn's voice in his ear: "I think you've had enough, Jake."

Thus came the end of Jake's tour, after his twenty-fifth operation. The rest of us on the station were almost as happy as Jake and his crew to see that they had made it, and the Wingco went up another notch in my estimation.

Landing on D-Day

CHARLES MARTIN

The Allied invasion of France on June 6, 1944, was preceded by heavy bombing and shelling, but in many places the German defences were scarcely touched.

Daylight. We had never felt so alone in our lives.

There was mist and rain. Bernières-sur-Mer became visible. Fifteen hundred yards of beach stretched from the far left to the far right. Everything was dead quiet. It could have been a picture postcard of any one of a hundred tiny French beaches with a village behind—not the real thing. There wasn't much talk. Earlier we'd worried a little about the choppy, heaving seas. Now, as we came closer, it was the strange silence that gripped us. But we were all confident. There was a job to be done, each seemed to feel. Let's do it.

Ten boats stretched out over fifteen hundred yards is not really a whole lot of assault force. The boats began to look even tinier as the gaps widened, with more than the length of a football field between each. Our initial concept of a brave attack began to seem questionable, though none of us would admit it. We could see the houses and buildings of the village. In between the village and the shore were the expected embedded obstacles and barbed wire with mines attached. In the centre there was a formidable fifteen-foot wall with three large, heavy, cement pillboxes. The entire beach was open to murderous fire from machine guns positioned for a full 180-degree sweep.

Military art puts forward a different scenario. The assault boats appear to be very close together and the troops within sight and sound of one another. This is likely necessary in order to get all the action into a reasonable frame, but in the actual event it was quite a different thing.

As our assault craft continued moving forward, B Company's No. 9 and No. 10 boats headed even further to the left and Peter Rea's No. 1 boat further to the right; our own No. 2 boat headed south; both Rea's boat and ours were looking at a breakwater and some serious-looking rocks on the right. Our first experience of action under fire started with a nervous gunner in one of the pillboxes; he opened fire prematurely and a piece of metal cut Rfn. Cy Harden on the cheek. The navy chap slapped a bandage on the wound and said, "If that's the worst you get, you'll be lucky." He was lucky. Even though later that day an 88 shell landed very close to him, turning him white as a sheet, he carried on with his section and survived to handle a concession after the war at Maple Leaf Stadium. But there were no hot dogs for him this day.

The crew of two were handling the boat well; that first burst of machine-gun fire had stopped. The engine purred steadily and didn't seem to disturb the silence. We got closer. Things might have been different if we had run into heavy shore guns or enemy aircraft. The lieutenant came forward to speak to me. We could see some of our other boats seeming to drift out, not in line at all, as we got closer. What now?

"Take us in as fast as you can," I ordered. "Don't slow up, keep us going!" It was better to move directly and at high speed than to chance drifting as easy targets or broadsiding obstacles or mines. And I thought the speed would keep the bow higher and get us as close in to shore as possible. He gave a signal to the sailor in the stern—go to speed.

Everyone seemed calm and ready. The boat commander was in charge of this part. He would give our landing order. We waited for it. In just a few inches of water the prow grated onto the beach.

The order rang out: "Down ramp." The moment the ramp came down, heavy machine-gun fire broke out from somewhere back of the seawall. Mortars were dropping all over the beach. Possibly No. 1 boat on the right took more of the fire.

The men rose, starboard line turning right, port turning left. I said to Jack, across from me, and to everyone: "Move! Fast! Don't stop for anything. Go! Go! Go!" We raced down the ramp, Jack and I side by side, the men closely following. We fanned out as fast as we could, heading for that sea wall.

None of us really grasped at that point, spread across such a large beach front, just how thin on the ground we were. Each of the ten boatloads had become an independent fighting unit. None had communication with the other, although just before our touch-down we were all in sight of one another. We were on our own and in our first action. Every single one of us, from Elliot Dalton, our commanding officer, who was the leader for his boat, and the other A Company boat leaders—Jack Pond, Peter Rea and Dave Owen—to the ordinary soldier, was on the run and at top speed. We were all riflemen on the assault and there was nothing ordinary about any of us. . . .

Our boat had landed about one hundred yards from a section where sand dunes about five to six feet in height had built up in front of the wall. The enemy had been busy reinforcing the defences. As we raced across the beach, we had no time to think much. Our training did that for us. We were men who could run sixty miles with a twenty-five-pound pack, first-class marksmen, about 30 percent in the sniper class, and all of us drilled in the credo of don't stop for anything.

Our part of the beach was clear, but there were mines buried in the sand. On the dead run you just chose the path that looked best. Bert Shepherd, Bill Bettridge and I were running at top speed and firing from the hip. To our left we spotted a small gap in the wall. It looked like it had been made so that bulldozers could get through to the beach to move obstacles and that sort of thing. They had placed a belt-fed machine gun there as part of the defence and only one man was on it. He was waving

his arms furiously, as if calling for others to come up and get on the gun.
It would take two to operate it, one to feed the belt and one to do the firing. At that time of the morning they could have been shaving, having
breakfast or just generally not ready for some fast-moving assault troops.
We knew from our training that you cannot be on the move and fire
accurately at the same time. If you stop, you become the target. In any
case, Bill did stop for a split second. He took his aim and that seemed to
be the bullet that took the gunner out, although Bert and I were firing
too. We got to the wall and over it, then raced across the railway line.
The marine from our landing craft was with us. When he had tried to get
off the beach, the boat had hit a mine and sunk. So he had picked up a
rifle and joined us in the assault. Now, as we were about to move farther
ahead, he asked if we minded if he left. He felt he should follow his
orders, get on another boat and return to the mother ship for more duty.
We didn't object.

A Medical Officer on the Beach

CAPT. DARIUS ALBERT

*Medical practice in World War II was very advanced and most wounded
survived. But the sheer numbers of the casualties sometimes overwhelmed
unit medical officers.*

To me, D-Day was the frustration. The moans of the dying, drowning,
wounded men. And my helplessness. That's what I remember of D-Day.

I waded ashore along with the regiment at Bernières at low tide with
numbing cold water up to my armpits, my waterproofed black bag (medical) strapped to my back. The men immediately dug into the beach
because about 200 feet ahead of them loomed a massive stone wall, at least
12 feet high and nesting on top of the wall were seven concrete MG posts.

It was awful. I'd never seen so many wounded men. In the first two
hours, I must have attended at least 200 of them. They didn't scream or
swear or shout. They just moaned. The most pathetic cases were the
wounded lying on the shoreline. As the tide came in, they were too weak
to swim, and I couldn't help them because my Stretcher Bearers would
have been machine gunned. So we had to stand by helplessly and watch
our comrades drown in the sea, with a moan.

On July 4, while the Chauds were storming the airport at Carpiquet,
I was wounded by an enemy shell. A 2-inch chunk of shrapnel entered
my right leg and put me out of action for the rest of the war.

It hurt. I took off my high boots and applied my own field dressing to
the wound. It hurt like hell. But I didn't yell. I remembered too keenly
the silent suffering of my comrades that first day on the beach.

Fighting the Wehrmacht in Normandy

SERGEANT ALBANIE DRAPEAU

Not long after Caen fell July 9, the North Shore Regiment along with The Queen's Own Rifles and Le Régiment de La Chaudière were ordered to attack Quesnay Wood, a part of the advance on Falaise. I was assigned to assist D Company with my mortars and attended an O Group at which Major Robichaud said he didn't like the idea of going into the attack with the very little information he had been given. That made me feel the same way. But on we went, advancing under a creeping rain of explosives.

Our first task was to clear a small wood in a field before we reached the main Quesnay Wood. At first it seemed as though the position was lightly held and we got over quite a distance when suddenly the enemy opened fire with all he had.

Then five tanks loomed out of the shadows and did their best to flatten the North Shores. I was following close behind Major Robichaud and in no time my men were wounded. There was nothing to do but go on and then I lost sight of the Major as I reached a small depression nearer the Woods. There were several men of the company nearby, but they were either dead or wounded. The tank blasts ripped four vents across my tunic, but did not draw blood.

Suddenly, I could hear someone moaning on the ground to my right. There came a lull in the firing and I up and ran to the spot. A lad about 18 was lying there with an arm terribly mangled and deep cuts across his back. I used my shell dressing on his arm, lit a cigarette for him and gave him a drink of water. I hardly dared mention his back, but he said it was all right so I knew he was still numbed. I drove his rifle into the ground, bayonet first, realized not a shot had been fired at me and figured I might fool the Germans further into thinking I was an SB (Stretcher Bearer) though I was carrying a Sten gun plus a wireless set.

I started towards the woods and they let me go five steps when over came all they had and I went down among the wheat.

Then they began shooting each time I moved the grain and I had to stay quiet. Next, they threw over some smoke shells which ignited the dry grain and at once flames licked through it and I knew I would roast alive if I stayed there, or die quickly if I stood up. In all the 11 months I served in action, this was the only time my courage left me. As the glowing redness crept near, I prayed God to help me and make quick whatever was to come.

It was like an answer to a prayer when I saw the burning wheat was sending up black smoke about a man's height and it was rolling towards the woods, clinging to the ground as it went. In a second I was up and going fast. My final sprint carried me towards a thick hedge and I jumped over it to find I was face to face with 2 German soldiers whose hands were up. Behind them, their guards were Lemidas LeBlanc and Charlie Roy of our unit. They had got into the woods in their first rush, had taken the pair prisoner, and were escorting them back. Roy was wounded, a walking case, and LeBlanc was looking after him as well as his Germans.

Army Intelligence on the Home Front

MAVOR MOORE

The job of General Staff Officer III (Intelligence and Security) for Military District No. 3, HQ Kingston, Ontario, allowed me to sport a red armband and brought me face-to-face with saboteurs, spies, the Royal Canadian Mounted Police, and the governor general—all of whom proved toothless. But to get there I had to pass through basic training in Trois-Rivières, officer training in Brockville, commando training in Camp Borden, an RCMP security check, and the intelligence course at the Royal Military College in Kingston ("Strip yourself of all inhibitions and worries and be prepared to go full out mentally and physically.")

The "I" school at RMC was run by Colonel R.O. Macfarlane, a Winnipeg historian whose chaotic moustache concealed a constant smile at his charges' naivety. He had a great respect for candour and a firm grasp of its antithesis: psychological warfare. Our chief instructor was a crack I and S colonel on loan from the British who rejoiced in the Anglo-Saxon name of Cuthbert Skilbeck. In impeccable Oxonian, Skil taught us how to break locks, codes, laws, and hearts in the pursuit of information.

At his suggestion I followed my appointment as the new district security officer with a calling card: an unannounced visit to a nearby barracks, where I posed as an emissary from the chief of staff in Ottawa and made off with their personnel records and weapons inventory. It was one of my finest performances, but went unreviewed since the adjutant could hardly admit he had no idea what was in either. On the strength of this success I was allowed to visit RCMP headquarters in Ottawa to view the secret files on individuals in my district. These included some of my close friends from school and university, whose only common error seemed to be a penchant for joining causes; this explained how I had slipped through the net. The files' contents were mere filler; their power came from being secret and being there.

All of these events went to my head, and when I caught the new Ronson Flamethrower on public display at an army demonstration in Brockville, I felt it was time to let the local brass know they were under highly sophisticated surveillance. As I reminded Int. HQ, Ottawa (copy to the commanding officer, Brockville), "the marginally noted weapon is on the secret list." Unfortunately the weapon I had listed in the margin was "Ronson Lighter." A deadpan reply came from the chief (copy to the commanding officer, Brockville), commending my vigilance but pointing out that the marginally noted weapon was readily available in any cigar store.

I lectured recruits on Nazi theories of race, and defended conscientious objectors against overzealous recruiters. But my outstanding feat was the trapping of a German spy. Our platoon's sergeant and chief censor, an aristocratic Czech 20 years my senior, flagged a curious letter addressed to a private in Camp Petawawa asking for the names of other Saskatchewan boys in the unit, with reply requested to a mailbox number. The bulb went on. A whole regimental battle order, by God, could be deduced by adding up provincial numbers! A watch on the mailbox netted a corporal in the Women's Army Corps *with a German name*. I had Sergeant Woolner arrest her in my jeep, bring her into my office, and stand by to throw in German phrases to catch her off guard. The little corporal, terrified when she realized how much we knew, said she was "only doing it for the party." Scenting big game, Woolner and I hammered her in both languages (she seemed to understand neither) to tell us who her boss was. Finally she blurted out, "Tommy Douglas!" What was this? The Great Prairie socialist parliamentarian a Nazi spy? "You're in trouble," I said hard, and she started to cry. "All right, I'll tell you! I know it's illegal to politick in the army, but we gotta win the provincial election!" As I drove her home—Woolner with his arm around her in the back seat muttering "Now, now, don't cry"—I assured her no word would pass our lips about politicking if none passed hers about false arrest.

The Liberation of Paris

MATTHEW HALTON

This is Matthew Halton of the CBC speaking from Paris.

Speaking from Paris! I am telling you today about the liberation of Paris, about our entry into Paris yesterday, and I don't know how to do it.

Though there was still fighting in the streets, Paris went absolutely mad. Paris and ourselves were in a delirium of happiness yesterday, and all last night, and today.

Yesterday was the most glorious and splendid day I've ever seen.

The first French and American patrols got into the outskirts of Paris the night before last. Yesterday morning the soldiers were coming in in force. I came in with them, with French troops, into Paris.

I believe the first Canadian to enter Paris was Captain Colin MacDougall, of the Army Film and Photo Unit, and I think I was the next.

We came in from the south, along the Avenue de l'Italie. For hours we had strained our eyes for the first sight of Paris, and then suddenly there it was, the most beautiful city in the world, and the people surging into the streets in millions.

I don't know how we got along those streets. We were among the first vehicles, and the people just went mad. We drove for miles, saluting with both hands and shouting *Vive la France* till we lost our voices. Every time we stopped for a second hundreds of girls pressed round the jeep to kiss us, and to inundate us with flowers.

But as we drove along the Boulevard St. Germain toward the river and the bridges leading to the Place de la Concorde, the crowds thinned out, because there was fighting just ahead in the Chamber of Deputies. There was machinegun fire, rifle fire by German snipers, and an occasional shot from a tank.

For half an hour we watched the fighting—battle in the streets of Paris. It was indescribably dramatic—fighting, yet the people frantic with the joy of liberation. We saw Germans stop fighting and come with white flags to surrender to the French soldiers lying behind their barricades.

Then I asked a policeman how we could get around the fighting, and across the river to the Opera and the centre of the city. I asked if there was still fighting round the Opera. The gendarme at once telephoned to the Maquis. The Maquis sent two young men and a girl in a car to lead us around.

From that moment on I knew what it was to feel like a king. These three people of the Maquis came and got me—two young men and a girl, an actress, one of the loveliest women I've ever seen. They broke into tears when they saw I was Canadian and they kissed me twenty times. Then they took me in their car, and we drove through the wildly cheering crowds with our arms round each other. We crossed the river to the Île de la Cité, the cradle of Paris history—and us there hand in hand with history—and past Notre Dame, and then up the avenue of the Opera to the Scribe Hotel. Here the crowds were just beginning to come into the streets, mad with happiness, and with my friends shouting "*Il est Canadien!*"—he's a Canadian. And I knew what it was to feel like a king. We were all kings for a day.

In fact, when I asked the proprietor of the Scribe Hotel whether it would be possible to get writing paper, he said: "You can have anything in the world you wish. You are a king."

Men, women and children kissed us and thanked us for coming. Walls were knocked down to produce stores of champagne hidden from the Germans. In a few hours I made friendships that I'll treasure all my life. The only sad thing, it seemed to me, was that British and Canadian troops, who have done so much and suffered so much, were not taking part with their American and French comrades in the entry into Paris.

They should have taken part in this glory—the most glorious thing I've ever seen. For years we have dreamed of this day, and tried to imagine what it would be like; and the reality is more wonderful than I'd ever expected.

Paris is not only the most beautiful city in the world. Paris is so much more than that. Paris is a symbol. Paris is victory, freedom, democracy. In some ways Paris is all that we've fought for during these long terrible years. The fall of Paris was one of the darkest days of History. Her liberation is one of the brightest.

The last time I was in Paris was on August the twenty-fifth, 1939. On that day the world was out of control and rushing toward the abyss, and France knew already that she was doomed. Five years later to the very day I returned to Paris with the liberating army. It's a moving thing for which I have no words.

For weeks, as we strained toward Paris, there was the fear that the city might be destroyed. If the Germans held Paris as they held places like Caen, there would be nothing for it but destruction. But happily things have gone otherwise, the city of light—Paris—is not destroyed. She hardly seems to have changed. The dream has come true. You can still stand in the Tuileries gardens in front of the Louvre and look across the Place de la Concorde and up the Champs-Elysées to the Arc de Triomphe, the most splendid view in the world. Yes, and driving up the Champs-Elysées yesterday we knew what it was to be a king.

I drove up the Champs-Elysées with my friends of the Maquis. Sometimes we were all in tears. One youth with me is a descendant of Jacques Cartier. He has fought the Germans inside Paris and elsewhere for four years; his father and his brother have been killed. The young actress I spoke of has for three years been a key link in the chain by which our aviators have been hidden, protected and got out of France. I have talked all night to these people and their friends. Sometime I shall tell their story. . . .

The armistice was signed by General LeClerc and by Colonel Pol, commander of the Maquis in the Île de France. An hour later General de Gaulle was in Paris, making a triumphal tour. He went first to the Hôtel de Ville, the historic town hall of Paris, which had been seized by the Maquis four days ago. The General made a sober speech. He said: "Germany trembles, but she is not yet destroyed. Combat is still the order of the day. We must enter Germany as conquerors."

One of the most moving things I've ever seen was the entry of French troops into Paris. French troops who had continued the fight for four years, and now had come home. The reception sent thrills tingling down our spines. They were in American battledress, in American tanks and half-tracks; but the colors of France were painted on each vehicle, and each one bore the name of a French town or a French hero or a French sentiment.

Breaking the Gothic Line, 1944

FRED AND NORAH EGENER

> *One of the great victories won by Canadian troops in World War II was*
> *to break through the Nazis' Gothic Line in Italy in late August 1944.*

Sept. 19
From the Gothic Line to Rimini

Dearest Norah:

. . . This narrative will be dotted with "I's" from start to finish. That is because it is not intended to be the story of the battle nor a part of the history of a unit, but simply all that I can recall of what I personally saw and heard. . . .

The unit had begun its move up from Spoletti after an early breakfast Aug. 24 . . . This movement was a slow one, the unit moving up behind the units of another division that was pushing the fighting line back to the Foglia river and the main Gothic defences. . . .

The area was at the bottom of the steepest hill I think I've ever had the pleasure of coming down. It was not a regular road, but a track enlarged by our use and the dust lay heavily upon it. I thought several times that we would slither down the pillar of powder. . . .

Since no one knew where we were headed or what echelon we were to join, prudence led me to order the carrying of small packs and blanket. It was prudent all right, but what a bugger of a job. When we reached the end of our trail, we were exhausted and that completely. I believe I have never been so dead beat. . . .

It was here that the matter of the packs really began to tell. The road seemed intent upon going straight up to heaven, and though we quickly peered around each bend as we came to it, believing the summit must be revealed, we were not rewarded until we were nearly too tuckered to be appreciative. . . .

When we saw the position we were in on the morning of the thirtieth, we were pleased for we surrounded a sturdy farm building that was set quite picturesquely on the gentle slope of a spur that ran off onto the top of a lesser hill. . . .

Just about 10 o'clock I found everyone retired to bed. Norm Root told me Lt. Cook had had to go to hospital sick and that I was to go up to the company. I moved fast; roused Wawro, put on my essential kit and the two of us started out for the next town. . . .

When I arrived there were numerous vehicles crowded about and five or six prisoners could be made out standing under guard by the house wall. . . .

Shell fire came down . . . intermittently during the night, but it was aimed at harassing the road more than demolishing the house so that, except for the odd bit of shrapnel striking the forward part of the house, the fire did not come dangerously close to us.

Just as the darkness was beginning to thin out, the colonel decided to go forward to recce for a headquarters on the north of the river. He took Wawro and I with him . . . We set off quickly to get benefit of what darkness was left, for it was lightening rapidly and we knew we had open ground to cover that was under enemy observation. . . .

As we came along the road, the height of Montocchio lay before us on the left. It gave the enemy complete observation of the road and was within easy range. But although it was now light, no fire came at us from the feature and we reached the road junction quite easily and there used the deep ditch for cover till the company showed signs of activity.

Sgt. Reid showed me the platoon's positions and then shared his slit trench while he told me in detail what had happened the day and night before.

By now the Jerries on Montocchio had become active and were sniping particularly at the tanks . . . The snipers were accurate. I saw one tank lumber down the hill to a safer point where its crew were able to get out the tank commander, who apparently had been shot through the head while observing from his open turret.

More tank units began to move up the road . . . At the same time the Irish came up the road, cut through our position and proceeded up the slope to line the ridge. It was the right moment for Jerry, and he quickly brought down shell fire on the road junction. Baker company got its full share of this. One shell that landed right on top of company headquarters instantly killed a wireless operator, wounded CSM Sheardown and wounded another man.

Crouching in Reid's slit trench, I got the odd piece of spent shrapnel that fell into the trench, but no more. . . .

Major Snellgrove led off company H.Q. and I came next, leading 12 Platoon. We were in the tank harbour area proceeding north from the main road and commencing to climb up a shallow draw leading to the top of the ridge when shells landed right in amongst us. I had been going along trying to see some of everything that was going on, at the same time searching the ground for hollows, furrows, folds or ditches that might give some cover. . . .

I had just sighted one narrow, shallow ditch when I was in it and the shelling was on. I shall never know whether I dove into that ditch or was blown in, for I didn't consciously hear the shell that landed on top of the platoon, catching nearly eleven in a standing position, killing Cpl. Dube and wounding L/Cpl. Droshner. . . .

The effect of the morning's trials on the men was all too apparent. They were nervous, hesitant, reluctant to go on. Nothing was said, but the major paused here and the platoons moved in closer and individuals found better spots of ground.

It is amazing what can be found to get one below the ordinary ground level: the ground turf where a tank had turned in its tracks, a grass-grown furrow where once a plow had ditched the ground, the gouges spring water had taken from the land, and the innumerable folds not normally visible to the eye, besides the more obvious ditches, banks and stream bottoms, give more hiding spots than one might expect. . . .

Fifteen or twenty minutes after the shelling, we moved off up to the ridge . . . We had proceeded to a point from which we could see north and east, and there we halted . . . The men spread out on the track, which here was sunken, and removed their equipment. It was a welcome rest.

Peters pointed out a trench cutting off at right angles from the road, the entrance barred by the limb of a tree that had been drawn into it. He wanted to go into the trench but thought the limb might be booby-trapped. I got well to one side and jerked out the limb and then went on up the track on some errand or other.

When I came back, it was to be passed by platoon members proudly escorting back seven Jerry paratroopers Peters had found when he investigated the trench . . . It was just the same when we later investigated a similarly concealed trench system on the other side of the track and took out another nine paratroopers, including an officer. They were well-equipped and armed . . . If these troopers had sallied out when we were taking it easy in the road, they might well have taken the whole company for a mighty serious loss. . . .

So long-winded . . . I tired of the task of setting down the detail. Writing what I did gave me a chance to blow off some of the excitement and desire to talk of what had happened. As you see, the narrative covers to Sept. 1. . . .

The Liberation of the Netherlands

JOHN MORGAN GRAY

In the last days of the war, First Canadian Army liberated Holland's large, and starving, cities to scenes of extraordinary jubilation.

But the early part of the day was joyful, the kind of moment for which, consciously or not, we had all been waiting. My little party was carried in two jeeps and included my friend Antz, the French liaison officer, and Captain John Stonburgh, a Cambridge University graduate of distinguished Hungarian background, who had somehow landed in the Canadian Army. My driver was a small, silent Pole, Jan Mischa, who had arrived from no one knew quite where, but had been in Dachau; he spoke almost no English and only a little French but he made it clear he was enjoying this day. Someone had supplied us with bully-beef sandwiches and hunks of apple pie, and I think we had some of the Alsatian wine with which Antz had returned laden from a quick trip to Colmar after it was liberated. We were to travel the width of Holland at almost its widest point, from Hengelo to Rotterdam.

The early part of our journey was through country that had been liberated for some weeks, and then we began reaching at areas that had been fought over only a few days before. It was a brave sunny day, a day for calling out and waving flags, and there were people out to wave and sing on the edges of the villages and towns we skirted. We were travelling on the main autobahn and began overtaking long convoys of trucks filled with troops wearing the famous Red Patch of First Canadian Division. They had only just stopped fighting a few days before but they were trim and smart and looked like the first-rate soldiers they were; we were overtaking in our little scuttling jeeps some of the most famous regiments in the Canadian Army: the Royal Canadian Regiment, the Royal 22nd, the Hastings and Prince Edward, the 48th Highlanders, the Loyal Edmonton Regiment, and many more. Up ahead somewhere, in their gleaming armoured cars, rolled the Divisional Recce Regiment, the Princess Louise Dragoon Guards—a regiment I had last seen in a splendid cavalry charge across Barriefield Common outside Kingston almost twenty years before.

The war might have been all futile madness but this seemed to me a splendid moment, if only for the excitement and the joy and the tears of the people beside the road. And then, incredibly, as we passed a big house the windows and the yard outside were full of German soldiers waving and yelling excitedly, as joyously as the liberated Dutch. This we weren't quite in a mood for yet, and we hurried by with only a perfunctory acknowledgment of this forgive-and-forget gesture. It wasn't just a rough hockey game we had all been playing, and even if these men had not committed the mindless bestialities of the Nazis—of which we had still to learn the full story—they could not expect us to stop thinking them loathsome just because pieces of paper had been signed saying the shooting would stop. We could acknowledge them as brave men and superb soldiers, not as friends. . . .

Somehow with a minimum of asking we found our way to the Stadthuis—the City Hall—fronting acres of weed-covered open spaces that the German bombers had burned out in 1940; now they were filled with people. My jeep was allowed in through a great iron gate which was with difficulty closed against the crowd. John Stonburgh, left outside and fearful that he and his jeep were going to be loved to death in the surging mass, climbed cheerfully onto the bonnet to a roar of applause and led the crowd in singing—the only song he could think of: "It ain't gonna rain no more, no more". No doubt it should have been something more splendid but as a safety valve it was just right, and the Dutch people sang it as though it was for this, too, they had been waiting for five years. My business inside was soon done; there was friendly confusion but someone was able to tell me that the headquarters of the Resistance was at Heineken's Brewery and guides were not lacking. As I came out of the Stadthuis a dozen or fifteen young men were standing around my jeep, longing to do something—to sing, to shout, to shake hands. As I was about to climb in I saw the cardboard box with the remains of our lunch—sandwiches and pie. If these men were hungry—would it be resented? I asked a man who seemed to be a leader was this of any use to them? He looked into the box and stared at me incredulously—any use? He climbed onto the bonnet of the jeep and began to break the sandwiches into little bits and to give each man a small handful. They crowded forward then, reaching up so that he had to kick at them to restore some order, then went on doling out the little shares. They ate slowly, relishing every crumb, licking at their hands to get the last taste. Some got sandwich, some pie, but all had something, relishing it, smacking their lips and raising a little chorus of "dat is heerlyk", "dat is lekker"—delicious, lovely. Many soldiers had a similar experience that first day and in the days that followed; and to many Dutch people the very taste of liberty remained for a long time a mouthful of good bread or pastry such as they had almost forgotten.

The Concentration Camps

RENÉ LÉVESQUE

> *The Nazis' extermination camps were located mainly in eastern Europe, but when American troops, including U.S. Army war correspondent René Lévesque, liberated the concentration camp at Dachau, near Munich, they were horrified by what they found.*

The sin against property was nothing, absolutely nothing, compared to the hell on earth we were to get our first sight of the next day or the day after. In the outskirts, at Dachau, we knew there were mysterious places called "concentration" camps. Rumours had already reached us, first from Poland, where the Russians were telling incredible stories that we took with a grain of salt, and more recently from French units over by the Black Forest, who had also been speaking of things to make our hair stand on end. Now it was our turn to see what it was all about.

We passed neat rows of pretty little Bavarian houses each with a niche over the door with a statute or image of a patron saint in it. In their shady gardens stood pleasant-looking old people who at a sign from us would come timidly over and very politely show us the way.

"*Konzentrazions Lager? Ja, Ja*, over there. Five minutes at the most. *Danke. Bitte.*"

Our first sight of the camp was freight trains on a siding, two lines of boxcars with some cadavers hanging out the open doors, and more scattered on the embankment. A torrid sun shone down and the smell was atrocious. We quickly entered the town, for that's what it seemed to be: behind low walls interspersed with watchtowers there was some kind of industrial complex with small factory buildings and repair shops. But this first impression was dissipated at sight of the indescribable crowd that rushed toward us. Riddled with questions in a dozen languages, pulled here and there by hands of frightening thinness attached to translucent wrists, we stood there stunned, staring at these phantoms in striped pyjamas who were staggering out of the huts where they had been hiding until we had arrived on the scene with some of the members of the first health services. In fact, the last traces of the German garrison had taken to their heels less than a quarter of an hour before.

A man who was still young but who was nothing but skin and bones told me in excellent French that he had lived some time in Montreal and, like everyone else, asked for a cigarette. I felt in my pocket; the package had disappeared. I discovered that all the pockets of my jacket had fared likewise. The depths of misery and hunger sometimes bring out the hero and the saint, at least that's what they say, but more often they debase and bring out the bird of prey.

This was illustrated by the following spectacle. Holding each other by the hand as though in some kind of children's game, a group of prisoners, surrounded by others watching them avidly, came toward us. Suddenly, savage cries of joy broke out when, from the middle of the circle, a young fellow was cast forth. He had plenty of meat on him, for he was a "Kapo," one of the prison guards who hadn't been able to escape and who had been lying low waiting for the right moment. They forced him to kneel down, held his head up straight, and a big Slav with a toothless leer came up with a stick and methodically, chuckling with pleasure, smashed the lower part of his face and jaw until it was nothing but a mass of bone and bleeding flesh.

One couldn't do a thing. We wouldn't have known what to do anyway. And wouldn't have wanted to do anything when we learned it had been literally a case of an eye for an eye and a tooth for a tooth. Before putting their prisoners to work the Germans always stripped them of all their possessions, including their gold teeth. Then they worked them to death, especially the last year when rations were becoming scarce. At the end of the road they were sent to the "baths" (*Baden*), shabby-looking sheds linked to a reservoir by a couple of pipes. When the baths were full to the seams they opened the gas, and then, when the last groans had ceased, the bodies were taken to the ovens next door.

When news of this reached Quebec, and for some time after, people refused to believe. Heavy scepticism greeted such stories, which surpassed understanding. And even today, so many years later, it's sometimes worse.

People who have the gall to proclaim themselves neo-Nazis, knowing that memory is a faculty capable of forgetting, go so far as to maintain that none of this really happened.

I can assure you that it was real, all right, that the gas chamber was real in its nightmarish unreality. The loaders had gone, trying to save their skins, leaving behind their last load of corpses, naked as worms in their muddy pallor. Near me was a cameraman whom I had promised a few words of commentary; he had to come out twice before he could film his ten seconds. On seeing it, the American Brigadier who had turned up on the scene took his revolver out of its holster and strode around with haggard eyes, muttering that he had to kill some of those bastards. His men had all they could do to calm him down.

Deloused and covered from head to foot in DDT, we retraced our steps to our billet in the harmonious-sounding village of Rosenheim. On the way, passing through the quiet suburb with its kindly old people, we asked each other with our eyes, "Did they know? How could they not have? What was behind those good, old, pious-looking faces?" But what was the use questioning? We were beginning to wish we hadn't seen anything ourselves.

V-E Day at the Front

MAJOR HARRY JOLLEY

It seems strange to mention anything about VE day or kindred subjects when it all seems so dim & distant. I was really terribly disappointed—in a sense—about it all. One would imagine that that would be one day at which an old soldier would look back & recall vivid unforgettable scenes—drama, intense emotion, relief, joy, tears & laughter. It's only a little more than a week ago. I saw a few men gathered about our Signals wagon as I went over to listen. I arrived just in time to hear the announcer say "Tomorrow will be VE day." None of us shouted, threw hats in the air, nor anything of that sort. I remember I turned away and shouted to a friend "Its all over now, Jack. Tomorrow is officially VE day in Britain." He barely acknowledged having heard what I said & continued talking to the others in the group he was with. I felt—I don't know practically nothing. If anything what I felt most was surprise, maybe an impatient vexation with myself for failing to react in a manner more in keeping with the moment. I know I had rehearsed that moment often. I had decided that I probably wouldn't be able to control my emotions & break into tears & maybe murmur a prayer of thanks. Well I didn't do anything like that nor did anyone else I saw. It was amazing.

The Halifax V-E Day Riots

ANTHONY GRIFFIN

At the end of the war, servicemen and civilians in Halifax rioted drunkenly, looting and trashing stores.

That night the shameful Halifax Riot took place, during which most of the downtown section of the city was demolished. I had changed into civilian clothes and gone out to dinner with a fellow officer. When we came out on the street, the first thing we sighted was a car overturned and on fire. Then a streetcar blazing and a big crowd of naval ratings throwing large stones through a plate glass window. There was an atmosphere of total chaos.

I stopped one of them without identifying myself and asked him what possessed these men to indulge in such an orgy of destruction. He naturally assumed I was a native Haligonian and said, "We're going to repay you bastards for the way you've treated us over six years." Then came a group of three staff cars, all blowing their horns, the leading one carrying the flag of Admiral Murray, addressing the rioters through loud-hailer, telling them they should recover their senses and go back to their ships or to barracks immediately. He was totally ignored.

After a while, seeing the downtown section of the city laid waste, and having no authority or connection with the Admiral's staff, I went back to my hotel and slept fitfully, feeling quite sick. I woke early and went back to the scene. The naval personnel were hardly to be seen; but Halifax citizens were out in full force, carrying loads of loot from the shops. I asked one citizen what he thought of such behaviour and he merely shrugged and said, "Everybody's doing it."

Taking a Break at the United Nations Conference, San Francisco, 1945

CHARLES RITCHIE

The United Nations was created at a large conference in San Francisco in May and June, 1945. The large Canadian delegation played a major role, but there was still time to enjoy the delights (!) of the city and surrounding area. This excerpt is from Charles Ritchie's diary.

15 June 1945.

Last week I saw an advertisement in one of the San Francisco newspapers which described the attractions of "a historic old ranch home now transformed into a luxury hotel situated in a beautiful valley in easy reach of San

Francisco". What a delightful escape, I thought, from the pressures of the Conference! Why not spend the week-end there? I succeeded in talking my colleagues, Norman and Hume and Jean Désy, the Canadian Adviser on Latin American Affairs, into this project, and our party was joined by a friend of Jean Désy, a French Ambassador, a senior and distinguished diplomat attached to the French Delegation. Last Saturday we all set forth by car in a holiday spirit to savour the delights of old-style ranch life in California as advertised to include "gourmet meals, horseback riding and music in an exclusive atmosphere." It seemed an eminently suitable setting for this little group of overworked and fastidious *conferenciers*. As we approached in the late afternoon up the long avenue, we saw the ranch house set amidst a bower of trees, but when we debouched at the entrance instead of the subdued welcome of a luxury hotel we were brusquely but cheerily propelled by a stout and thug-like individual to-wards a swaying tollgate which opened to admit us one by one on pay-ment in advance for the period of our stay. Once in the entrance hall we found ourselves in the midst of an animated crowd, but what was unex-pected was that all the men were sailors and young sailors at that, while the women were equally young and some strikingly luscious. This throng, exchanging jokes, playful slaps on bottoms and swigs out of beer cans, filtered off from time to time in pairs to mount the noble staircase leading to the rooms above. Our diplomatic quintet stood together waiting for guidance among the jostling throng and were soon the objects of re-marks. "Who the hell are those old guys?" Finally, seeing that no one was coming to our rescue we set off up the stairs, luggage in hand to inspect our rooms. Mounting floor by floor we found all the bedrooms in a state of active and noisy occupation, until we reached the top floor where we encountered a large female of the squaw variety. As she appeared to be in charge of operations we enquired for our rooms to find that only three rooms were available for the five of us.

It was decided among us that the French Ambassador should have a room to himself, while Jean Désy and Hume shared one and Norman and I the other. In our room we found an exhausted maid slapping at some dirty-looking pillows as she replaced them in position. "This is the fifth time I have made up this bed today," she observed. "Are you two *men* sharing this room?" With a look beyond surprise she withdrew. Norman seemingly not in the least disconcerted sank with a sigh into the only available chair and addressed himself to the evening paper. The other members of our party were less philosophical. Hume and Jean appearing in the doorway rounded sharply on me. "Why had I lured them into this brothel? Was this my idea of a joke?" I suggested that we should all be better for food and drink and we descended to the dining-room, a vast, panelled interior already packed with couples dancing to a blaring radio. After a lengthy wait we were squeezed into a corner table where we were attended by a motherly-looking waitress. "Who are all these girls?" I asked her. "And why all these sailors?" "Well, I guess you might call it a kind of meeting place for the boys off the ships and the girls who work near here in an aircraft factory." Meanwhile the French Ambassador was beginning to show signs of controlled irritation as he studied the menu that had been handed to him. Adjusting his spectacles he read out, "Tomato soup, hamburger delights, cheeseburgers, Hawaiian-style ham with pineapple." "For me," he announced, "I shall have a plain omelette." At this Jean Désy, in an attempt to lighten the gloom which was settling over our little party, clapped his hands together and in an almost boisterous tone called out to the waitress, "The wine list at once—we shall have champagne." "Wine list," she said, "I do not know about any list but we have some lovely pink wine—it is sparkling, too." "Bring it," said Jean, "and lots of it." It was not bad—both sweet and tinny but it helped. For a few moments our spirits improved and we began to laugh at our predicament. Then came the omelette. The Ambassador just touched it with the prong of his fork and leaned back in his chair with an air of incredulity. "This an omelette!" He raised his shoulders with a shrug to end all shrugs.

At this Jean Désy, perhaps stimulated by the wine or pricked by embarrassment at having exposed his French colleague to such an experience, seized the plate with the omelette upon it and said, "I shall complain to the chef myself about this outrage." With this he hurled himself into the mob of dancers and made for a swinging door leading to the kitchen. Some uneasy moments passed at our table, then the swinging door swung open. Jean still holding the plate with the omelette upon it was backing away before an enormous Negro who was bellowing above the music, "Get out of my kitchen. Who the hell do you think you are? Bugger off! Bugger off! Bugger off!" Jean returned to our table. "I shall report him," he said—but it was difficult to know to whom. Soon afterwards we repaired to our rooms. As I left the dining-room I heard a girl say to her sailor companion, "Those are a bunch of old fairies sleeping together—the maid told me." The sailor spat, not actually at us, but on the floor quite audibly.

The night was an uneasy one for me. I was kept restlessly awake by the beery hoots of laughter and the moans and murmurs of passion from the next room. Norman settled into his bed and slept peaceably with his deaf ear uppermost.

When I looked out of the window in the early morning the sun was shining, and a troop of sailors and their girls mounted on miscellaneous horses were riding by towards the adjoining fields, thus proving that horseback riding was as advertised one of the facilities of the ranch. Two small figures, Jean Désy and the French Ambassador, the latter sealed into a tight-looking overcoat, were proceeding side by side down the avenue. I later learned that they were on their way to Mass at a neighbouring church.

By mutual agreement for which no words were needed our party left the ranch before luncheon and returned to San Francisco.

On the way back in the car the French Ambassador raised the possibility that one of the assiduous gossip writers of the San Francisco press might learn where we had spent the week-end and he asked what effect this would be likely to have on the prestige of our respective delegations and indeed on our own reputations. My own colleagues reassured him by saying that in the event of publicity the episode could be attributed to my misleading them owing to my innate folly and vicious proclivities. This seemed to satisfy him.

Hiroshima

W.L. MACKENZIE KING

> *With Britain and the U.S., Canada had been heavily involved in the research that led to the development of the atomic bomb. The first bomb was dropped on Hiroshima on August 6, 1945, the second a few days later on Nagasaki. The war in the Pacific ended a week later with Japan's surrender.*

Monday, 6 August 1945
Just about noon . . . I received a note . . . saying a bomb had been dropped . . . [I]t was the atom bomb in Japan . . . We now see what might have come to the British race had German scientists won the race. It is fortunate that the use of the bomb should have been upon the Japanese rather than upon the white races of Europe. I am a little concerned about how Russia may feel, not having been told anything of this invention or of what the British and the U.S. were doing in the way of exploring and perfecting the process. . . .

Liberating the Prisoners of the Japanese

COLONEL RICHARD S. MALONE

> *After Japan surrendered, one major task for the Allies was to gain control of their prisoners of war. Canadian POWs had lived in Hong Kong and Japan; all were in dreadful condition from malnutrition and forced labour.*

Some 200 Canadian prisoners of war, taken in the fall of Hong Kong to the Japanese Christmas Day, 1941, now are in Allied hands in Japan.

Today I visited the first group of liberated Canadians from Japanese prison camps and learned first-hand details of the fighting and last days of Hong Kong when the Canadian contingent of about 1,985 men from the

Winnipeg Grenadiers, the Royal Rifles of Canada and a brigade head-quarters was part of the British force that battled overwhelming odds.

Few Have Beriberi

The group interviewed today included 15 Canadian soldiers, one merchant seaman and nine French-Canadian Roman Catholic brothers. This group, the first to see Canadians from the outside, was overjoyed to see Col. L.V.M. Cosgrave, Canadian military attache at Canberra, Australia, and me.

The Canadian Franciscan and Dominican Brothers and all Canadians in Allied hands to date are in reasonable health, although a small percentage suffers touches of beriberi.

Three of the men had been hit frequently with clubs and slapped on the face. I was told of repeated cases of inhuman treatment, poor food, few Red Cross parcels arriving and little mail reaching them.

On Hospital Ships

The prisoners told of sleeping on mats on floors of filthy camps. Sanitation was beyond description in some camps and some of the men still wore the remains of clothing they had on when Hong Kong fell.

All are being screened aboard hospital ships and those needing medical care are receiving immediate treatment and excellent food from American nurses and doctors.

From first-hand reports I received Canada can be proud of the gallantry displayed by the Canadian Hong Kong Brigade and the behavior of the soldiers, particularly the officers of the Canadian regiments. The men all were loud in praise of their officers.

The exact number of Canadians liberated is impossible to determine immediately. The main effort has been to remove prisoners to places where they will receive proper care.

Prisoners are being moved by various means toward Manila, some by plane and others by ship. Men requiring medical attention are assigned to hospital ships while others are sent to Manila-bound transports.

Official Japanese records indicate some 286 Canadians are in the Tokyo area but until a central office is functioning it is impossible to get a true picture.

Repatriation

JEAN M. ELLIS

Seven thousand of us were sailing for Halifax—servicemen, servicewomen, and a few dependents. In my stateroom, built to accommodate four comfortably, 23 girls occupied double-decker bunks. In the adjoining room were 25 girls, a six weeks' old baby, and a small black spaniel smuggled aboard by a w.r.n.s. character. Between the two staterooms, and "accommodating" the 48 girls, the baby and the dog, were four biffies and four tiny washbasins. Just to make everything completely jolly, five of the girls in my dormitory were pregnant and addicted to "morning sickness." Oh, for some of that fresh air we had failed to appreciate at Southampton! Late on a chilly October night we had stood there "Easy" in formation for two hours while Movement Control officers checked and double-checked our passage. After that each girl was handed a card indicating her stateroom number and given permission to go aboard, though some unfortunates had to be turned back because their sailing orders were not on hand. We sailed at dawn to the stirring strains of "Maple Leaf Forever" and "O Canada" played by an army band.

On board life became a series of orders and directions. Day and night the public address system belched forth instructions, completely indifferent to the idea that any small interval between darkness and dawn might be considered sleeping-time. The old goat at the microphone was continually calling for someone to report to so-and-so or such-and-such. If at any time during the trip you were fortunate enough to become part of an interesting conversation, the p.a. system was bound to interrupt you by calling off a horrible list of names, the owners of which must do this and that. Of course, everybody stopped talking to listen for his or her own name. On, on it went. When the announcer ran out of names, he read off a list of lost articles which must be returned to the Orderly Room without delay. Everything, in fact, must be done without delay. Get up without delay. Wash without delay (because water was turned off between 8 a.m. and 4 p.m.). Queue for meals without delay. Queue for a seat in the Officers' Lounge without delay. Clear the decks without delay. Before long the phrase ran through everyone's mind like the rhythm of train wheels over ties—"de-da, de-da." Then there were the m.p.'s. Their word was law. You mustn't go down this corridor in THAT direction. You mustn't leave your stateroom at any time during the trip unless you lugged along that ghastly life preserver. . . .

After five days, tension increased. We were nearing Halifax . . . and after that would come home, readjustment problems, starting a new career. I didn't know what lay ahead of me; my life would have to be completely reorganized; but whatever happened, there were many precious memories to sustain me. I would never forget the first time I cut off a soldier's boots . . . nor the lad who held my hand before going into the operating room . . . the boy who had never owned hand-knitted socks until I gave him a Red Cross pair . . . the gay comrades who sang around a bonfire on V-E Day . . . it had all been very much worthwhile.

Aircraft circled over our heads, bidding us welcome. Seagulls came out to meet us. The p.a. system nearly burst its pipes belching out do's and don'ts. According to it, everyone had to appear some place without delay, and a mad scramble ensued to get it over and done with. And even when that was past, the voice continued to rasp at us. "Don't get in the lifeboats. Don't do this, don't do that . . ."

At last land was sighted, and everybody scrambled to the top of the highest point available. Cheers went up, "acquired" binoculars were passed from hand to hand, and landmarks were pointed out by the learned.

Closer and closer we sailed. Canada WAS our own, our native land . . . never had the words meant so much. Necks were craned to catch a first glimpse of Halifax. Tears flowed down many cheeks, while other faces wore a grim, set expression which defied onlookers to detect any sign of emotion. Suddenly Halifax harbour fireboats appeared, shooting off huge sprays of water as a welcome to the thousands of Canadian boys and girls who had risked their lives and futures for their country's safety. The band on the docks started up, and "O Canada" sounded sweeter than ever before. The big ship nosed into the harbour, her passengers seething with expectancy. Above the hubbub the P.A. system screamed that disembarkation would be as follows . . . Actually, a day and a half passed before all those Canadians set foot on solid ground again.

At last we came down the gangplank . . . rushed away from the dock . . . and were stopped short by a huge sign. Before our startled eyes, like a welcoming smile, was the all-too-familiar Canadian Army road sign, enlarged, its wording slightly altered. Now it read

"Maple Leaf—Home!"

Mackenzie King Visits France

CHARLES P. STACEY

> *In the summer of 1946, Mackenzie King visited France. His tour of the battlefields was organized by Colonel Stacey, the army's historian.*

Reaching Caen at lunchtime, we proceeded to the Mairie. Here there was a *vin d'honneur*, a form of entertainment with which we became only too familiar during the next two days. The maire read an eloquent address of welcome. Then King drew from his pocket a half-sheet of notepaper on which somebody had written for him three short paragraphs in French. These he read in an accent so excruciatingly bad that I suspect most of his hearers thought he was speaking English. He then finished the speech in actual English, which Georges Vanier gracefully translated. When King had finished his remarks he folded the half-sheet of notepaper and put it in his pocket. Throughout the rest of the tour he kept producing it (it got grubbier and grubbier mile by mile) and reading one of the three paragraphs to whatever audience happened to confront him at the moment. Sometimes it was the middle paragraph, sometimes it was the last one, sometimes it was the first one; the one thing you could be absolutely certain of was that it would have no relationship whatever to the business in hand. This procedure put a distinct strain on the politeness of quite a number of French mayors; their looks of astonishment were something to see. The time came when we all winced when the P.M. reached for his pocket. . . .

And let no one think that it was not moving—far more moving than the pomps of Caen. I remember more than other places Fontenay-le-Marmion, still half in ruins—the tiny hamlet below the Verrières Ridge that had been the objective of the Canadian Black Watch when they were cut to pieces in Operation "Spring." A streamer across the street said in flowers "Honneur au Canada." The mayor (I think he was the local shoemaker) came running, adjusting his sash, to read his address and give Mr. King a present. A little girl handed the Prime Minister a bouquet, and he kissed her on both cheeks. And the youngsters from the village school, eight or ten in number, sang (under their teacher's careful supervision) "O Canada," "God Save the King" (in English) and the "Marseillaise." I stood saluting in the street, very close to disgracing my uniform with tears.

A Hanging at Bordeaux Prison

GORDON LUNAN

> *Gordon Lunan, one of the Soviet spies caught as a result of cipher clerk Igor Gouzenko's defection from the USSR embassy in September 1945, was imprisoned in Bordeaux Jail in Montreal.*

Bordeaux Prison was where death penalties were carried out. Everybody was aware that Ovilda Samson was in the death cell and tension in the cell blocks mounted as the day of execution approached. Samson was an unfortunate man in his fifties who had killed two elderly women, neighbours, in what had seemed to be a pointless, motiveless crime.

On the eve of the execution my neighbour asked me if I was going to watch it.

"Watch it? How could I possibly do that?"

He produced a piece of glass which he had smoked with a candle to make a mirror. Unknown to me the gallows were less than thirty feet from our cells, occupying an iron gallery jutting out a storey above the ground in the space where two cell blocks converged at the dome. A door in the dome opened on to the gallery. The death cell was a few paces beyond the door.

My neighbour gave me a piece of the smoked glass. It gave a surprisingly good mirror image of the gallows when held through the bars at the proper angle. The rope was already in place, attached to a thick iron bar above what was only too clearly the trapdoor, the noose ready at head level and the rest of the rope looped up out of the way and tied with a string.

The string would break with the weight of the falling body. The hangman, a conscientious man, had carefully calculated the length of rope based upon the victim's weight, and had stretched the rope by making a test drop with a sand bag of equivalent weight. He was careful about this because on a previous occasion he had failed to take into account the weight which a woman had gained while in the death cell and had pulled her head off by mistake. . . .

A few minutes after midnight the gallows were flooded with light. The door to the dome opened revealing a small group, including a priest, surrounding a surprisingly serene looking Samson. Shoeless, dressed in black pants and a collarless white shirt, arms tied behind his back, he took his place on the trap as though it had all been rehearsed. The hangman knelt and quickly bound his feet. He produced a black bag from nowhere, snapped it full of air, jammed it on Samson's head, put the noose around his neck, jerked it tight with the knot at his jaw, stooped again to insert a short metal rod into a hole at his feet, straightened up and stepped on the rod. It all took no more than a few seconds. The spring-loaded trap opened with a fearsome crash. For a split second Samson seemed to stand on air before dropping through the hole to wind up with a sickening thud below. Immediately the body began to shake convulsively and jack-knifed feet first back towards the trap then swung in huge arcs from side to side. (So it's true . . . you literally swing.) The doctor who, with a couple of witnesses now appeared from a door below, fielded the body and steadied it. At intervals he applied a stethoscope to the chest, but it was not until fourteen minutes had elapsed that he could certify death.

The legal process which had started with Justice Louis Cousineau donning his three-cornered hat and black gloves as he sat high on the bench beneath the big crucifix intoning the words (in French, of course) ". . . and there be hanged by the neck until you are dead" was now complete. A hot-blooded killing had been expiated in cold blood.

"*Maudits cochons.*" A muttered curse from my neighbour.

Finding an Apartment in Paris, 1947

CHARLES RITCHIE

> *Diplomat Ritchie sent this letter from Paris to Mike Pearson, the undersecretary of state for external affairs.*

Paris, 24th February 1947

Dear Mike

It is about time that I gave you the first instalment of my Parisian adventure, which is comprised almost entirely under the heading of "Apartment Hunting". The last month has certainly been a liberal education for me. I arrived here fresh, innocent and unsullied; now you would find me aged in corruption and wise in all the stratagems required to support life in Paris. I trust that my experiences may be of benefit to other members of the service proceeding to European posts.

I started out naïvely enough with the idea that all I had to do was to find an apartment, move in, and pay the rent. That was my initial mistake. I did not realize that every business transaction in this city involves one in a labyrinth of intrigue. At first, things looked exceptionally bright for me. A French businessman I had met during the Paris Conference rang me up on arrival and asked me whether I wanted a flat or a house. He owned, he said, a house which he thought might just suit me. He would take me out to see it. On the way out in the car I was somewhat surprised by my friend's altruistic attitude. Rent, he said, was to him a matter of little or no importance. He would let me have the house free of rent, unless I found that embarrassing, in which case I could pay a nominal rent. He would, he said, like to do something for Canada, something to show his appreciation for the many kindnesses he had received in the past from Canadians. I was surprised and touched. I said that it would *not* embarrass me not to pay any rent at all.

I was still more surprised when I arrived at the house. I had thought it might have some conspicuous flaw. Instead, it was a charming small 18th Century house, directly in the Bois, surrounded by a courtyard and set in a very pretty little garden. It was only as we were crossing the courtyard to approach the house that my friend mentioned that there was one minor difficulty concerning the house, which he should perhaps bring to my attention. It had been requisitioned at the time of the Liberation by the Chinese Military Attaché. The Military Attaché was still established in the house. He was, however, away in Washington for the time being. He had not proven a good tenant. If, however, I were to put in a requisition order with the Protocol Division of the Quai d'Orsay, he was quite convinced that they would be willing to expel the Chinese Military Attaché and install me.

The truth then broke upon me that, under the present regulations, the only hope which the owner of the house had of expelling his undesirable tenant was to get another diplomat to put in a requisition. A rapid mental picture of the result of such intervention on my part rose before my eyes. Civil war between the Chinese and Canadian Embassies, and an infuriated Chinese Ambassador coming to call on General Vanier to complain of the treatment accorded to his Military Attaché and probably a distinct cooling in Sino-Canadian relations over a period of years. "No," I said to the owner of the house, "certainly not. Nothing would induce me." But, by that time, we had reached the front door, which was opened by an extremely pretty Chinese girl in a kimono.

Then ensued one of the most embarrassing five minutes in my life. The Chinese Military Attaché is a bachelor. Far from being in Washington, he was in his house in Paris, in his dressing gown having breakfast in his bedroom. His charming girl friend in the kimono had been having breakfast opposite him when we burst in upon him. I could not but feel that this was an awkward beginning to my relations with my Chinese colleague. I hastily whispered to the owner of the house not on any account to introduce me. He for his part made a rapid but ruthless tour of the house, pointing out in caustic language the various forms of damage which the Military Attaché had inflicted on his furniture and possessions. The Military Attaché and the girl friend trailed after him apologetically.

I, for my part, had decided to assume the role of business agent to the owner of the house as there had to be some excuse for my presence. I did not speak, but restricted myself to tapping the wall and furniture in a professional manner as though I were some kind of furniture appraiser hired for the occasion. At last we escaped, but not before the owner of the house had heightened the general embarrassment by observing sourly to the Military Attaché that he had not realized that he was a married man. This malicious dig appeared to be the only revenge which he could take for the destruction which had taken over a good deal of his valuable 18th Century furniture. When we got away, I politely but firmly explained the impossibility of my proceeding further in the matter of the house. The next day at the diplomatic reception at the Élysée, as luck would have it, I found myself standing directly beside the Chinese Military Attaché. He gave me a startled and open look of recognition which I met with a blank and glassy eye.

During the course of the next two weeks, a number of minor incidents took place which I have not the time to record in the detail which they deserve. Each had its own peculiar aspect. Every variety of black market operation, payment in every conceivable currency and combination of currencies, was suggested to me by various apartment owners who had seen my advertisement in the papers or who had been told that I was looking for a flat.

There was the proposal that I should pay for the flat (30,000 francs a month) in American dollars, plus the privilege of the owner using the diplomatic bag to import such goods as he might require from across the Atlantic. There was the suggestion that I should pay 40,000 francs a month for a flat with no kitchen, but that the bathroom could be converted into a kitchen in a few months if I could get the priorities and labour and materials. There were numerous invitations to pay fantastic sums for the privilege of keeping people's houses or flats heated and occupied while they had the use of one, two or three rooms in them. There were kind and pressing invitations from members of the French aristocracy, derelict baronesses and fading marquises, to make room in their *hotel particulier* at a rent which would pay the up-keep of the entire house and share the amenities of their distinguished social existence.

Then came something serious. An English spinster, long resident in Paris, telephoned to tell me that she could let me have her flat at a very remarkably reduced rate. I went to visit her. She gave me weak tea and chatted about the weather. I reflected on the wonderful power of the English character to withstand foreign influences. I might well have been taking tea with the Vicar's sister in rural England. We arranged the details regarding the flat (I was to take possession the following day). As I was leaving she dropped the remark (ominous, although I did not realize it at the time) that she had always been much interested in psychic phenomena and that if I were interested in dreams, table turning, or thought transmission, I would find an interesting collection of books on the subject in the flat.

The next day, having packed all my possessions and made my arrangements to leave my hotel, I arrived key in hand to take possession of the flat. What was my surprise and mounting irritation when the lady told me that during the preceding night she had had a particularly impressive dream in which she had been distinctly warned by a voice coming from "the other side" not on any account to leave her flat. In the circumstances, she knew that I would not wish her to go against her psychic guide. I can only bow before a Higher Force and withdraw.

Very different was my experience with an Hungarian Lady resident in the Avenue Bugeaud. I called to see her flat one morning about 11 and was greeted by an aging beauty, clad in trousers, over which she wore a long embroidered coat. She wafted me graciously into a large salon hung with portraits of herself at various stages of what appeared to have been a highly successful career. 40,000 francs per month was the sacrifice price at which she was willing to let me have her flat. This, she explained, did not include the sheets, indicating a luxurious upholstered Louis XV bed, she pointed out to me that the sheets were of black silk. On alternate weeks she employed black silk and pink silk sheets. I would understand that she could not let me have the use of either. I eagerly agreed.

A little further conversation revealed that the lady was an Hungarian. Her life, she told me, had been full of adventure but had of late become rather sad. It would be a convenience, however, if I could let her retain one room in her flat. She could then let me have the entire apartment at a much reduced rent. Moreover, if she were in the flat while I was settling in, she could help in many little ways. Perhaps I did not know, she said, that women of the higher aristocracy in Hungary were taught to cook, but such indeed was the case. She, for example, could whip up very good pastry, if she had a mind to, and she would do that for me. She could even assist me at any dinner parties which I might give.

At this point I rose poised for flight, when looking at me earnestly she said "There is one very delicate question which I think I should mention. You certainly do not intend to live here long." She took my silence for consent. "In that case" she said, "the arrangement which I am going to suggest depends on your character and I have not had time to learn what your character is. (Not surprising, as I had only been there for eight minutes).

If you have great need for matters of love, the proposal which I am about to make to you will not prove satisfactory, but if you do not require many women in your life you could always depend on me. I should always be here—'Comptez sur moi'." All this was said in a business-like manner as if the facilities which she was offering went with the pastry, as extra comforts supplied with the flat. As I was leaving, however, she imparted her final touch. "If we could come to the arrangement" she said "which I have just suggested to you there would of course be no further difficulty over the sheets—they would be available."

I know there may be scepticism about the truth of some of these experiences but I can only assure you that they are a literal record of what took place.

Well, my dear Mike, I am not living between black silk sheets and eating Hungarian pastries, nor have I involved the Canadian Government in any black market transactions. I have, however, found a flat— too expensive for me; too large for me; too cold for me; but, all the same, a very attractive flat on the left bank in the Boulevard St. Germain. But, there is a snag about that too. I only have it for three months, so that before two months are over I must begin again my endless search. You will readily appreciate that it will be at least a year before I can devote any of my time to my official duties; but I shall keep you in touch with my unofficial activities by means of further low level communications.

Yours,
Charles

Czechoslovakia Goes Behind the Iron Curtain

RONALD M. MACDONNELL

In the winter of 1948, Czech communists staged a coup with the support of the USSR. Foreign minister Jan Masaryk "fell" from a window and was killed. Diplomat R.M. Macdonnell reported to Ottawa on Masaryk's funeral.

The state funeral for the late Jan Masaryk [Foreign Minister of Czechoslovakia at his death] provided the only opportunity that the people of this unhappy country have had, or are likely to have (barring a similar tragedy involving President [Edvard] Benes), to show their real feelings about the events that have overwhelmed them. Enormous crowds turned out to pay their final tribute to the man who was the most articulate and colourful supporter in Czechoslovakia of those democratic liberties which are fast disappearing, and the display of grief was most moving.

2. March 12th: the body lay in state at the Foreign Ministry. From the early hours of dawn until late in the evening all the approaches to the building were filled for half a mile or more with long lines of people,

patiently waiting for the few moments when they could have a last glimpse of their departed friend and perhaps touch him, as many did. There must have been at least two hundred thousand representing all strata of life. Men and women, young and old, simple peasants and sophisticated urbanites, rich and poor, all moved forward slowly together in the seemingly endless procession of mourners. The sobs and tears of men and women alike showed that this was no mere perfunctory duty.

3. The next day the state funeral began at 2 p.m., and by 11 a.m. the crowds were beginning to form along the route. The opening ceremonies were held in a rather small "pantheon" in the National Museum, and were attended by the President, Members of the Government and the Assembly, Chiefs of Diplomatic Missions and service attachés, senior army officers and officials and representatives of national organisations. The President looked very ill and almost dazed. The ceremonies themselves were short and simple, consisting of vocal and instrumental music and two speeches, one by [Klement] Gottwald, the Prime Minister, and the other by an elderly legionary of the First World War. In Gottwald's speech, as in all official references to Masaryk, great stress was laid on the way in which the late Foreign Minister had identified himself with the new government because it represented the will of the people. During the two weeks between the coup d'état and his suicide, Masaryk made a number of statements, no doubt for tactical reasons, in which he eulogized the new government, and this has given the regime a wonderful body of source material from which to quote. The general line is that Masaryk was happy to be serving the people in this most democratic of governments, and was driven to suicide by the vile reproaches of those in the West whom he thought to be his friends but who revealed themselves in this crisis as imperialists, warmongers and Fascists. The Communists are doing their best to establish a legend that Masaryk was hounded to death by the West.

4. When the brief ceremonies in the National Museum were concluded, the body was mounted on a gun-carriage and the funeral procession moved off with a large military and police escort. The route led through the heart of the business and shopping district, across the Vltava and up the hill to the Ministry of Foreign Affairs, a distance of about three miles. Chiefs of Diplomatic Missions walked in the procession, and this provided an otherwise unobtainable opportunity to witness the size and emotion of the crowds. Every inch of standing room from curb to buildings along the route was occupied, and there must have been something like half a million people on hand. The sobs and tears of the previous day were repeated by men and women, young and old. One can imagine the variety of emotions that reinforced one another to produce a sense of desolation—grief for a magnetic and popular leader, pity for the mental turmoil which found in suicide the only release from an

unbearable situation, anger on the part of those who believed in murder rather than suicide, and a poignant feeling that the flag-covered casket carried with it to burial not only the body of a staunch democrat, but the liberties of the Czechoslovak people as well. The breaking of a link with the elder Masaryk must have made many people vividly aware of the contrast between today's gloomy outlook and the hopeful days of the First Republic under the President-Liberator [Tomas Masaryk].

5. At the Foreign Ministry the casket was transferred from the gun-carriage to a motor hearse and taken to the country for burial beside the elder Masaryk [in the town of Lany]. Only the family and a limited number of Ministers and officials took part in the final ceremonies, and diplomatic representatives were not invited to attend. In connection with diplomatic representation, there was one bizarre note which may be worth recording. Attendance had been strictly limited by the Foreign Ministry to Chiefs of Mission, who formed one group, and service attachés who marched in another. A notable exception to the rule was observed in the Chiefs of Mission group, where the Soviet Chargé d'Affaires was accompanied by five unknown and tough-looking individuals whose rumpled business dress made them stand out conspicuously from the morning coats and top hats of those who preceded and followed them. One can do no more than speculate on the motives which prompted the inclusion of these individuals in the procession.

6. The Legation flag was half-masted until after the funeral, and, in addition to attending the latter, I signed a condolence book in the Ministry of Foreign Affairs, paid my respects at the lying-in-state and sent a wreath on behalf of the Canadian Government.

Newfoundland Looks Towards Canada

JOSEPH R. SMALLWOOD

> *Joey Smallwood was the great proponent of Newfoundland joining Confederation, and he fought a long battle to achieve this. One of his first victories was to win election to the National Convention in 1947 to decide on the colony's future.*

I don't remember speaking for less than three hours at any such meeting, and often it went to the full four. These meetings were not only to convert the people to Confederation, but to persuade them to elect me as their representative to the forthcoming National Convention. "Don't vote for me," I pleaded at every meeting, "unless you want to be represented by a man who will fight to get Canada's terms and conditions of Confederation. Somebody else will be asking you to elect him (I would change the tense whenever that opponent appeared at the same meeting) and if he is against Confederation, I plead with you to vote for him, not for me, if you don't want to be represented by a man who'll fight to get Canada's terms of Confederation."

There was only one place in the whole of central and northern Bonavista Bay where I met with any opposition at all. This was a large place, relatively speaking, where 500 votes were cast in the election. A lady in the audience stood up and interrupted my speech with a question. I answered the question politely. After a while, she was up again, and again I answered her politely. I noticed the restiveness of the audience when she stood up a third time, and at her fourth interruption, there were shouts of impatience. I answered her rather tartly, and the whole audience applauded their approval. It turned out that the lady was not the most popular woman in the area, and the audience was itching to have me go aboard her in my replies and was impatient with my politeness. (One vote was cast against me in that place, and for weeks the people tried to figure out who it could have been. They decided in the end that it must have been a visitor who was in the settlement that day.)

The Liberals in Convention, 1948

DALTON CAMP

When Mackenzie King finally gave up power, the Liberal Party held a leadership convention to choose Louis St. Laurent as his successor. Dalton Camp, later a prominent Conservative, was a delegate.

Now, in the summer of 1948, Mackenzie King had summoned his party to choose his successor. It took getting used to, the thought of replacing King. He had been there for so long, the processes by which he would be succeeded had been almost forgotten. The New Brunswick delegation, travelling to Ottawa by sleeper and chair car, amused themselves over cards or stared at the countryside, shimmering in the white sunlight. Few of us had ever been to a national leadership convention; the last one had been in August, 1919. Leadership conventions were for Tories.

The prospect of going to the Ottawa convention was appealing, especially after the one-sided victory of John B. McNair's Liberal Party in the June general election. With the fresh prestige of a recent and complete triumph, there were rumbles about renewing in Ottawa a half-forgotten cry—Maritime rights.

New Brunswick Liberals had political muscle. Of the fifty-two seats in the provincial legislature, McNair's party held forty-seven of them; of the ten seats in the federal parliament, seven were Liberal. This, despite southern New Brunswick's acknowledged Tory inclinations, gave lustre to the reputation of the delegation from New Brunswick. Or so we thought.

Such things as electoral victories seemed to matter in Ottawa, where everyone was patronized by someone and was patronizing to someone else in turn. Ontario's delegates were the most patronized of all; they were out of power provincially and, in the federal context, their province provided the opposition with most of its seats. Ontario delegates were leaderless, poor-mouthing, and gauche. (It seemed appropriate then, just as Mackenzie King was bidding his party a last farewell and the hall was hushed in respectful silence, that the rear doors should suddenly burst open and a rabble of Ontario supporters plunge into the back of the hall, shouting slogans about drafting Paul Martin. Only Ontario Liberals could be so crudely inept, so preposterously vulgar.)

There was the usual jocular rivalry among the provincial delegations, the same restless silence when French was spoken, the same tributes to parochialism, and the usual drunken conviviality—the pawing, back-slapping, handshaking, and fond embracing which characterize political meetings in Ottawa or anywhere else.

Politics is much too serious a business to be taken seriously by too many people. Party democracy is essentially ritual, and here, as Mackenzie King stepped down, the partisans dutifully acted out their parts. Everyone—or almost everyone—knew his place and kept it.

The old patronized the young, which is their habit, and when a feeble protest was made by some of the Young Liberals, I was abruptly called out of the Resolutions Committee to the platform, one of three Young Liberals chosen by persons unknown to address the convention. We were asked—Vernon Singer, Roland Le Francois, and I—to present "the Young Liberal point of view" to a hall of chattering, distracted delegates. Although I arrived on the platform last, I was the first called upon to speak by the chairman, who signalled our presence with words I found embarrassingly gratuitous, and almost completely false:

> I do not know what they wish to talk about, but when there are three or four men who say they have something important to say to a Convention of this kind we should hear them. They have asked for only three minutes apiece. If they stick to three minutes they must be very good. We have accepted their request to speak to you for three minutes. . . .

I had the feeling of being on the end of a string looped around someone's fingers, helplessly manipulated, obliged to respond without thought or calculation to the urgencies of unknown or unseen forces. What, I asked myself, looking out over the crowd, did they want from me? Where was the revolt our presence was calculated to quell? Why was I being tokenized?

While thinking, I began talking, saying the first and most natural thing to come to mind, which proved to be an elaborate tribute to the Liberalism of John B. McNair, whose side I had just left and for whose personal circumstances I felt an overwhelming, undifferential sympathy. Such sentiments evoked applause, which sounded like the rustling of wind through treetops, but whatever I said came from a distracted mind, annoyed by the patronizing introduction, puzzled by my selection, and ignorant of any purpose. . . .

In the press the next day I read a headline saying, "Recognize Us, Or Another Party Will" and in the story below Dalton Camp was quoted as saying, "If you will not listen to the younger members of this party, then they will leave and join another party."

But at least some listened on that day. And when I sat down and Vern Singer followed me to the podium, they were still listening, because they booed something he said, which I did not hear for I had suddenly realized that Mackenzie King was sitting on the platform too, and I had said nothing in my remarks to acknowledge his presence or to pay tribute to him on this occasion of his retiring from office.

Then someone came over and tugged my sleeve and said the Prime Minister wished to speak to me. I got up and walked over to Mr. King. He shook my hand warmly and said I had made a fine speech.

Immediately I apologized for my oversight, saying that I had not seen him when I had come to the platform from outside the hall. He dismissed this, and repeated that he appreciated my speech "very much indeed."

I never saw him again. Two years later, I watched his coffin, borne on a gun carriage, pass from the Parliament Buildings, down the gentle slope of the Hill and out through the gates for the last time.

I returned to the Resolutions Committee, taking my place beside McNair, who, along with the rest of the New Brunswick members of the committee, was waiting for some pertinence to come to the proceedings. Ontario Liberals quarrelled with one another and with Quebec and western delegates. Within the Quebec group, a visible struggle was underway between Jean Lesage and Hugues Lapointe for the leadership of that delegation. Each vied with the other for prominence, position, and the floor.

McNair bore all this with inexhaustible patience. Some of us knew of his wife's illness. So there was both languor and tension among the New Brunswick delegates, but we were all good listeners.

There was a protracted discussion on the question of a Canadian flag. The Liberal Party was not without its quota of traditionalists and colonialists with strong views as to whether a new flag should have the Union Jack on it, or the Fleur de Lis, or the Coat of Arms, or something else, or nothing.

On the edge of exasperation, McNair turned to C.T. Richard, a North Shore M.P. and an Acadian: "Clovis, did you ever hear so much nonsense?"

With a huge shrug, Clovis threw up his hands. "What's wrong with the flag we got?"

Doug Anglin, an Ontario Rhodes Scholar-elect, and I were delegated to draft a resolution on the flag, which we did; the committee, its interest waning, passed it without protest. The resolution stood as Liberal policy on that matter, unchanged and unresolved, until 1964.

The Grey Cup Goes Big Time

UNKNOWN

When the Calgary Stampeders won the Grey Cup in 1948, Canadian football became important for the first time. It was less the game than the Western showmanship that captured the nation.

The boys who put the Western brand on Toronto, the boys who grabbed the Grey Cup in their first bid for national football supremacy, were welcomed home Wednesday—and with what a welcome!

Matching in size and vocal efforts the packed mobs that annually watch Calgary mid-summer Stampede parades, 30,000 Calgarians roared a "Well done, Stampeders" to Les Lear and his rollicking cowboys as they rolled back home aboard the boisterous, hilarious, never-to-be-forgotten "Victory Special."

It was a welcome that came from the heart.

Starting in Northern Ontario where small knots of people gathered to cheer the westward-driving Stampeder special train, the welcome gained impetus across the prairies, burst into a full-throated roar when Stampeders rode out of the C.P.R. station in open-topped cars and were paraded through 12 blocks of jam-packed city streets while excited Calgarians cheered them on.

With the Grey Cup riding high in a saddle-mounted jeep, flanked by cowgirls, who combined for Calgary's great football victory, the victory parade was very much a replica of the pre-game procession that won the hearts of Toronto last Saturday.

Behind the players came Harry McConachie and his mounted Westerners who thrilled Toronto with a little bit of the Calgary Stampede.

And after them came truckloads of the Calgary football fans who had followed the team east and who had ridden up Toronto's Bay Street in similar fashion, bringing staid Torontonians out of their hard shells with vigorous renditions of Western songs. . . .

Oldtimers said the reception has only been equaled by that for the King and Queen on the Royal Tour in 1939.

Right on the dot at 1 p.m. the 16-car Victory Special arrived. The King's Own Calgary Regiment band struck up "Put on Your Red and White Sweater" and the four drum majorettes went into action. The football fans poured off the train onto the station platform followed by the Stamps themselves.

A line of automobiles for the players, their wives and friends were along the station platform, waiting for their loads.

Many of the fans were overcome with the welcome even before it started, and brought out handkerchiefs for a quick dab at their eyes.

After a few handshakes and congratulations the players piled into and onto the convertibles.

Youngsters began throwing confetti over the cars, and autograph fans, who got onto the platform, despite attempts by police to keep them off, besieged the players.

There was a short wait while the horses were taken off the Special, and saddled for the parade.

Between autographs and handshakes, Chuck Anderson managed to express his feeling to The Albertan.

"This is the grandest country I ever lived in. They are really wonderful people."

Said Fritzie Hanson, "Only Calgary can do this. I love 'em everyone."

Jimmie Dobbin remarked, "It's really wonderful isn't it?"

J.P. McCaffrey, Calgary lawyer who made the trip, said, "the people in the west really went to town." He added the Ottawa supporters were wonderful sports.

At 1.20 p.m. the parade finally moved off the platform. Immediately thousands of Calgarians packed around the station let out a tremendous cheer as the goal posts, carried by 10 football fans, came into view.

Squads of motorcycle police and policemen on foot patrolled the street to keep the surging crowds back off the parade route.

As the first of the parade turned onto 9th Ave., the crowd swung into the Stampeder song, and burst into wild cheering. Confetti and paper streamers started to fly through the air. When the first car of football players rolled onto the street it was greeted with a riot of cheers, songs, yells and applause.

The crowd was so thick there was barely room for the cars to drive down the avenue. The procession moved at a snail's pace until it reached 8th Ave.

There thousands more lined the sidewalks. Fans were hanging out windows, balancing on the edge of roofs, draped over fire escapes, and standing in show windows.

It wasn't hard for the players themselves to respond to the reception given them along the street—they took it like veterans. They waved their Stetsons in the air, they stood up in the cars and called to the crowd, they autographed pieces of paper and cigarette boxes, they kissed little children all along the line. . . .

Meanwhile in front of the platform at the station, more thousands were jostling each other and trying to wiggle their way to the barriers. Hundreds failed to see any part of the parade, they were packed in so tight. Instead they kept up a steady stream of cheers and songs.

Planes from Cal-Air Ltd., and an RCAF jet-propelled aircraft zoomed over the station at low altitudes, dropping rolls of paper over the crowd. The jet screamed up almost out of sight in a "Victory Roll.". . . .

The players were driven back onto the station platform away from the crowds, and then led through the station to the stand where they were introduced individually. Each was greeted with a fanfare from the band, and ear-splitting cheers from their fans. . . .

Les Lear was surrounded by a mob of youngsters, but one young fellow got there first and wouldn't let go of his idol. He was 11-year-old Max Pronin, 1416 4a St. E. Les put his arm around the boy and the two of them pushed their way out of the crowd.

"He's my corner-lot quarter-back," Les told The Albertan.

The youngster just wouldn't let go of the team's coach.

Observing Uncle Joe

JOHN W. HOLMES

The Cold War was in its beginning stages when John Holmes went to Moscow as Chargé d'Affaires at the Canadian embassy. His observations on Josef Stalin, the Soviet dictator, were penetrating.

What about the great man? What light can I cast on Stalin? Not much, I am afraid. Not many can, I suppose. When I once did see him fairly close I recall thinking that if he was a total stranger, I would quite like the look of him—twinkling eyes and Giaconda smile in an otherwise immobile face, but freshly painted for the occasion. As I have often noticed when I confront fabulous people—Marlene Dietrich in an airport lounge, for example—they seem inordinately small. I had a good few hours to gawk unnoticed at the great man on the occasion of a celebration at the Bolshoi Theatre in February 1948 of the thirtieth anniversary of the Red Army. During the first part of the performance he sat on the platform unostentatiously in the second row behind the senior members of the Politburo—or was it ostentatiously? He was there for the endless speeches, very bellicose and very boring. For the high-spirited singing and dancing which made the speeches worth enduring, Stalin moved to a box not far from those in which the diplomatic corps were herded on elegant little chairs. The most junior of them all, the Canadian *chargé d'affaires*, was almost out in the hall but able nonetheless to see the sight.

In more ways than one it was like seeing Santa Claus. Aside from the physical resemblance was the fact that one wasn't sure whether this man was the real thing. I could have taken him for my father, and he was said to have stand-ins. He had not been present at all when the thirtieth birthday of the October Revolution had been celebrated in November, and the game of "Where's Joe" and what disease has he had preoccupied diplomats and journalists for several months. This Stalin did venture on a few impromptu words to the cheering crowd, a performance that was not usual. It was said that he spoke seldom because his speech betrayed his thick Georgian accent, but as practically everything was said about him it was wise to be sceptical of everything.

This enigma wrapped in a mystery, as Churchill once said of Russia, seemed to be pretty deliberately wrapped. I had seen him once before in a shuttered limousine with outriders racing up the Arbat from the Kremlin to wherever. Or had I? It was said that was how he went home from the office, and my car had been roughly swept off the thoroughfare by the militia. I saw him at a good hundred meters on May Day in the Red Square on the podium, impassively raising his arm from time to time as the spontaneous demonstrations, which had been marshalled since dawn in the side-streets, leaped by. It could have been a mechanical toy as he lifted his arm rather like Frankenstein. . . .

There is no doubt that the man was fascinating, and that is a quality which, as he or his impressarios would realize, is diminished by over-exposure. Maybe they kept him away from the angry populace, as some said. Those shouting "Hail Great Stalin" could be trained seals. One of the theories to explain his absence in November 1947, which I reported to Ottawa, was that he was on his way to Olympus and that as a god (or at least a crypto-god) he was manifesting himself more rarely. There was little pretence that he, like Lenin, moved among the people. In the only pictures of him fraternizing with the citizenry at that time, he was pro-tected not only by the usual group of pistol-carrying companions, but by sixteen-inch naval guns and some miles of sea as well. The portraits and busts, however, were omnipresent, and they didn't to my eye fortify the image. The tailoring, for one thing, was ungodlike—very square. I recall touring Red Square on May Day eve with Walter Cronkite, then the United Press correspondent. When we came upon one full-length icon of Joe in a stiff overcoat neatly flapping at the bottom as in an Eaton's catalogue, Walter cracked, "Step upstairs and save five dollars."

As a crypto-god, nevertheless, he seemed at that time to have a calcu-lated personal role as the great mediator. In the spring of 1948, for exam-ple, when East-West governmental relations were frigid, he intervened from on high with a letter to [former] US Vice-President Henry Wallace in what purported to be an appeal to the peace-loving masses of America and the world. When ominous pressure was being put on the Finns in April of that year, Stalin came forth with a soothing speech, and his role was glorified as benevolent friend of the small sovereignties. Some nasty diplomats were suspicious, however. It was recalled by those who had been there some years earlier that when Molotov was negotiating their independence away from the Baltic states, Stalin would happen to enter the room and say "Come now Comrade Molotov, aren't you being a little hard in insisting on quartering 300,000 troops in Estonia? Make it 150,000." From hundreds of conflicting clues one could only put together an unreal portrait—like one of those composite pictures of a rapist, or a child's depiction of a saint.

Doukhobor Days

GEORGE WOODCOCK

In 1949, writer and anarchist George Woodcock visited Hillier, B.C., the
home of a heretical Doukhobor group led by a prophet who called himself
Michael the Archangel.

We went into the kitchen. Two young women, fair and steatopygous as
Doukhobor beauties are expected to be, were preparing the evening
meal. A small girl showed us to our room and stood, avid with curiosity,
while we unpacked our rucksacks and washed our faces. Then Joe took
us around the yard, showed us the new bake house on which a hawk-
faced man like a Circassian bandit was laying bricks, and tried to entice
us into the bathhouse. I looked through the doorway and saw naked people moving like the damned in the clouds of steam that puffed up whenever a bucket of water was thrown on the hot stones. In a couple of
seconds I withdrew, gasping for breath. The bricklayer laughed. "You
never make a Doukhobor," he said. "Add ten years to your life," said Joe,
coaxingly.

When everyone stood in a circle around the great oval table for the
communal meal we began to see the kind of people the Doukhobors
were. There were twenty of them, singing in the half-Caucasian rhythm
that penetrates Doukhobor music, the women high and nasal, the men
resonant as bells. Most had Slavonic features, their breadth emphasized
among the women by the straight fringes in which their hair was cut
across the brow. But a few, like the bricklayer, were so un-Russian as
to suggest that the Doukhobors had interbred with Caucasian Moslems
during their long exile in the mountains before they came to Canada.
They sang of Siberian and Canadian prisons, of martyrs and heroes in the
faith, "Rest at last, ye eagles of courage, rest at last in the arms of God,"
they boomed and shrilled.

The singing was solemn, but afterwards the mood changed at once
and the meal went on with laughter and loud Russian talk; now and then
our neighbours would break off repentently to translate for our benefit.
The food was vegetarian, the best of its kind I have ever tasted; bowls of
purple borscht, dashed with white streaks of cream, and then casha, made
with millet and butter, and vegetables cooked in oil, and pirogi stuffed
with cheese and beans and blackberries, and eaten with great scoops of
sour cream. Slices of black bread passed around the table, cut from a massive square loaf that stood in the middle beside the salt of hospitality, and
the meal ended with huckleberries and cherries. . . .

Sunday was the climax of our visit. Our arrival had coincided with
the community's first great festival. In the afternoon the only child so
far born there was to be handed over to the care of the community as a

symbolic demonstration against conventional ideas of motherhood and the family. Since the Archangel had forbidden fornication we were rather surprised that a being whose very presence seemed to defy his will should be so honoured. From my attempts to discuss the situation I gained an impression that the Doukhobors applied a rather Dostoevskian equation—considering that, if the ban itself was sacred, so must be the sin against it. "Free men ain't bound by reason," as one young man rather unanswerably concluded a discussion on this point. . . .

We walked back to the farmhouse with a Canadian woman who had married into the Doukhobors. "You've seen what Mike wants you to see," she said bitterly. "You don't know all there is to know about that girl. Now she'll go up to stay in Mike's house. They won't let her talk to anyone, and they'll pay her out in every way they can for having a child by her own husband. Purification! That's what they talk about. I call it prison!" The mother of the Angel Gabriel was not at the evening meal, and we never saw her again. We asked Joe what had happened to her. She had gone willingly into seclusion, he answered; for her own good, of course.

The Voice of Hockey

TRENT FRAYNE

> *"Hello, Canada, and hockey fans in the United States and Newfoundland." Using those words, play-by-play commentator Foster Hewitt called fans to the game year after year.*

April 1, 1950—There aren't many sports columnists in Canada who haven't observed at one time or another that there are two hockey games in Maple Leaf Gardens in Toronto on a Saturday night: the one on the ice and the one on the air.

The observation seldom is meant as a compliment to Foster Hewitt, who is fairly generally regarded as the most entertaining play-by-play announcer of them all, but it is, nevertheless, backhanded tribute to his artistry with a microphone. Bad game or good, Hewitt's method of describing what he sees spellbinds an audience estimated by surveys conducted by his sponsor, the Imperial Oil Company, at five million people in the United States and Canada. He has been doing it since 1931 and he will be doing it during the next couple of weeks as the annual Stanley Cup playoffs unwind.

Hewitt has become the best-known hockey announcer in the world. Everything he says about a hockey game is accurate but it's what he doesn't tell that sets him apart. He has the talent of eliminating the meaningless scrambles beneath his gondola and he gives voice only to developments of consequence. Thus, while the spectator absorbs the ragged and the brilliant, the listener hears only what is pertinent and significant. If it's a dull game the spectator is bored; the listener is entertained by its highlights.

Although Hewitt has been broadcasting hockey nationally for 20 years, employing all of the game's standard clichés, ("It was a rousing first period with neither team asking quarter or giving it," "He had the goalkeeper at his mercy and made no mistake," "They came from behind in an uphill battle," etc.) the listening public, far from falling off, has increased annually, particularly in the United States which now, surveys show, has as many listeners as Canada.

Hewitt does broadcasts in which his fee is waived to charity yet his price on his services chases more prospective sponsors whimpering back to their vice-presidents' chairs than anyone else's. Conversely, he turns down lucrative assignments on other sports because he says he feels the public gets enough of Hewitt on hockey ("We don't want to saturate the air.") Hewitt, when he is talking about himself, says "we" more frequently than "I."

It is doubtful if more than a small fraction of one per cent of the five million listeners would know Hewitt if they talked to him. His flamboyant voice with the trenchant tones of an evangelist belongs to an almost embarrassingly modest, retiring and colorless paradox. Hewitt's conversational voice is not the voice Canada hears on Saturday. Inflections are similar but the volume and energy he puts into his broadcasts are missing.

"We speak from here," he explains, pointing to the base of his breastbone. "That's the only place we feel the effects of a broadcast, a dull pain here." His throat has never bothered him although there have been reports for years that he's had cancer. "There's never a trip around the country but somebody doesn't sidle up to me, peer solicitously for a moment and then softly inquire about my throat. Why, one night one of the Leaf doctors took me aside and asked me if there was anything he could do!"...

A criticism that Hewitt frequently faces is that he is partial to the Toronto Maple Leafs. It is hissed by some that his excitement in reporting a Toronto goal far surpasses that which accompanies a goal by the visiting team and critics insist that even in these latter descriptions his enthusiasm is synthetic and forced. Hewitt admits all this but denies it proves he is partial. "We let the game and the crowd carry us," he explains. "As the noise swells the voice rolls higher. If the play culminates in a goal the noise and the excitement are at such a pitch that the voice must reflect it. Since the vast majority of our games are done in Toronto it naturally follows that there is more excitement accompanying a Toronto goal. If the visiting team scores there is no such crowd reaction and in an effort to be fair and make one goal sound as exhilarating as the other the voice, of the fans, quite possibly sounds artificial at times. It's an actual fact that we do the same thing in playoff games in Boston, say, or Detroit; we reach the most natural pitch in describing goals by the Bruins or the Red Wings."

Hewitt regards himself as an official must regard himself. He admits he has favorites but, like the referees, he feels he must be impartial. If players are hurt, he says, he must be tactful—he must neither condemn the offender nor condone the offence. "I try to sell hockey," he says. "The man who sells his product, not himself, is valuable to his sponsors."

Trudeau the Communist? 1952

ROBERT A. FORD

Diplomat and poet Robert Ford served for years in Moscow. One of his early reports concerned a young Canadian visitor to the USSR.

In separate despatches in today's bag, I am writing about the results of the International Economic Conference in Moscow and the share the Canadian delegation played in it. In this despatch, I should like to talk about Mr. Pierre Trudeau, since in many ways he is the most interesting of the Canadian delegates.

2. Mr. Trudeau has been the only Canadian delegate who, apart from the initial checking in, returned to the Embassy for advice and also to inform us of what was going on. He has been fairly useful to us in giving us information about the Conference, including copies of the daily proceedings. He is, however, a puzzling character and I have been trying to estimate from my conversations with him what his real attitude to this country is.

3. Mr. Trudeau has undoubtedly been greatly impressed by the show put on for the Conference delegates by the Russians. He was prepared to believe all he had been told concerning economic conditions, prices, the supply of consumer goods, the position of labour, and even freedom of association between Russians and foreigners. He had spent an evening talking with three Russian economists from the Academy of Sciences and assumed from this that it was possible to establish contact with the Russians. I think, however, that he has been somewhat shaken by his conversations with us.

4. I understand Trudeau, sometime before coming to Russia, had been associated with a periodical called "Cité Libre" which ran an article against participation in the Korean war. He claims his position is that of a neutralist-idealist and that it is possible for men of good will to try to act as a centre group which will gradually widen and prevent the two extremes from clashing. I am willing to believe that his feelings on this subject are genuinely idealistic but I am afraid that he fails to realize that being neutral in the present struggle seems inevitably to involve leaning over backward to justify Russian actions on the one hand, and to criticize

the western position, and particularly the United States on the other. It never seems to occur to these people, incidentally, that the neutralists inevitably have to be drawn from the western ranks and that such a thing as a neutralist or idealist from the Soviet bloc is a contradiction in terms.

5. Together with this idealist strain in Trudeau, there seems to be a kind of infantile desire to shock, which may in its place not do any harm but which, when exercised here, may do a lot of damage. For example, Mr. Trudeau was taken to Easter Saturday midnight mass at the United States Embassy. He was introduced to Mrs. Cumming, the wife of the Chargé d'Affaires, and proceeded to tell her that he was a Communist, though at the same time a Catholic, after which he proceeded to heap praises on the U.S.S.R. and attack the United States.

6. I think he did this out of desire to shock. Nevertheless, the next day at luncheon Mr. Hugh S. Cumming Jr., who knew all about Trudeau's Privy Council background, said to me, "I thought you said Trudeau was not a Red?" When I said I didn't think he was, Mr. Cumming then told me what he had said to his wife. I pointed out that if Trudeau were really a Communist he would hardly be speaking like this to Mrs. Cumming. Nevertheless, I could see what was passing through Mr. Cumming's mind, and I am sure a report will go back to the State Department that a man who only six months ago was employed in a confidential job in the Privy Council is now in Moscow for the International Economic Conference and has openly stated that he is a Communist. This may have some effect on United States estimates of our security.

7. Mr. Trudeau, along with the head of the United States delegation and a number of other western delegates, has been invited by the Chinese to visit Peking. He asked for my advice on the matter and I told him that he would have to decide for himself but that for his own personal good I thought that he would be wise not to go. If he were genuinely objective, however, I suppose there might be some interest in visiting the Chinese capital. Trudeau obviously has a very strong sense of adventure and he was clearly tempted by the prospect.

8. As I mentioned in my previous despatch, Trudeau is a correspondent of *Le Devoir*, which I believe has been toying with neutralist ideas. It will be interesting to see what kind of articles he publishes in this newspaper when he returns. I should be grateful if you could let us have copies of his reports to *Le Devoir*. I think it also might be useful if someone in the Department could invite him on his return to Canada to give his impressions about the Conference and try to set him right on some of the erroneous ideas he has concerning the U.S.S.R. and international trade. It might be a little easier to talk to him after he has cooled off a little bit from his present enthusiasm.

R.A. Ford, Chargé d'Affaires, a.i.

Fighting the Chinese Communists

ROBERT S. PEACOCK

The Korean War (1950–53) saw 25,000 Canadian servicemen, mostly army and part of the UN Command, engaged in fighting the Chinese.

Our attitude to our enemy was one of curiosity rather than hatred. In fact I don't remember any expression of hatred by anyone anywhere during my tour except by Koreans. The enemy was an enigma, a shadowy thing with no personal attributes that you met only at night and then only for brief moments. There were only a few occasions which gave us the opportunity to see the human side of our enemy. During September, 1952, after a couple of weeks of heavy patrol activity, things quieted down for a short period in which there was only sporadic shelling and light activity. Every morning at the same time, 1000 hours, a few mortar bombs would come in to remind us that the war was still on. One morning our OP reported a Chinese soldier in full view on the forward slope of one of their positions, which we called "Tombstone." This was a sight to see in daylight and everyone got his binoculars to have a look at the elusive enemy. The Chinese soldier had come out of his trench, had bared his buttocks to us, and commenced his morning defecation, probably giving us the greatest insult he could think of. This was a marvelous display of spirit and panache. It gave a dimension to the enigmatic enemy to which we could relate. For the next few days we gathered after the morning mortar shoot was over to watch as the Chinese soldier repeated his action and we had a few laughs as we cheered him on. Lieutenant Colonel E.M.D. McNaughton, commanding officer of 1 RCHA, took umbrage at the ribald insult and organized a troop of four 25 pdr field guns to silently range onto the Chinaman's position and prepare to fire on order. The next morning, on schedule, the Chinese soldier came out, bared his buttocks and commenced his morning ablutions when he became the centre piece of a perfect troop target of four bursting shells. I managed to capture the incident on film for posterity. The Chinese soldier never appeared again and I think it was a loss as we had made contact with an identifiable person with a sense of humour—not a thing to be destroyed. I hope he survived as I would have liked to have met the man. I'm sure we could have had some laughs about soldiering and war.

About the same time in September, after a two week period of intense patrolling to capture a prisoner, we were surprised to hear that a Chinese soldier had crossed over no man's land and surrendered to 5 Platoon. Apparently he had appeared out of the early morning mist to give himself up to a standing patrol at one of the gaps in our barbed wire. They thought he was a Korean Service Corps soldier who was lost so they brought him into the platoon position. Lieutenant Ed Borkofsky, 5 Platoon, was told he had a visitor and found his soldiers giving the stranger a cup of coffee and some food in one of the platoon bunkers. The Chinese soldier was still fully armed and bedecked with the red stars of the Chinese Army. Needless to say, Ed was surprised by the situation. The word spread through the company and everyone wanted to have a look at what or who it was we were fighting. It turned out he was a normal soldier who became depressed and put off with his own situation and decided to quit. He was turned over to the Intelligence people from battalion HQ and we saw and heard no more of him. The black humour of the situation was not lost on us considering the battalion had done everything possible to capture a prisoner over a two week period and had had nothing to show for it but dead and wounded and a lot of battle experience, and now, when we were taking a rest, a Chinese soldier showed up and surrendered.

A Canadienne *in Japan*

JACQUELINE ROBITAILLE VAN CAMPEN

Canadian soldiers during the Korean War required the comforts of home, so the Canadian Red Cross dispatched women volunteers to Japan.

I travelled most of the way to Japan with the famous Red Cross beret under my arm as I didn't know which way it went on my head—even with the advice of my numerous uncles, aunts and cousins. I arrived in Tokyo with two other girls, another social worker from Toronto and a Red Cross worker from Montreal who spoke French. I thought that in Japan I would be given some time to learn to speak English, but it was not meant to be. As soon as I arrived, the resident French Canadian girl in Tokyo was sent away to the South of Japan and I became "it."

I'll never forget my first day at the Maple Leaf Club in Tokyo where I was to work for the next six months. I had understood that I would be doing social work for the Canadian troops in the Far East, but nothing had prepared me for the club. The Maple Leaf Club was an R & R (rest and relaxation) centre for Canadian soldiers on leave in Tokyo. It had a lounge with music, books and papers on one side and, to my horror, a beer parlour on the other side. For me, naive as I was, I couldn't believe that I was expected to go *there* and speak to the boys.

No, my job was not what I thought it would be, but I soon realized the importance of what I was doing. My role was to make the men feel more at ease by talking with them over coffee, discussing the news and helping them make the most of their R & R in Tokyo. For the French Canadians, I was someone with whom they could talk in their own language. Some of the soldiers had really heartbreaking stories. As I listened to the men, I realized that the women of the Red Cross represented home. The men talked to us as if we were their sisters. The club was a meeting place—a social club where members of the armed forces came to relax and have fun. However, they were often very homesick and some of them were struggling with drinking problems.

I also met soldiers from other parts of the world. In fact, the first men that I met were two Kiwis, a Maori and an Australian sergeant with one of the biggest mustaches I had ever seen. I wonder what we talked about? Initially I was not able to say very much in English, but I soon became bilingual. I even acquired an Australian accent. For the first few days I felt so bad about my inability to speak English that I wanted to go home. But after two weeks, I was ready for an extension of my stay.

I had been hired before the Korean war ended, but on July 27, 1953, an armistice came into effect. My social life took a marvellous turn. With the war over, the servicemen were coming to Tokyo to have a good time, and the best clubs and hotels were reserved for the United Nations troops. In my position with the Red Cross I did not have military rank, but I enjoyed all the privileges of an officer. Japan was exotic, and my life was certainly more exciting than at the Family Welfare Agency where I had worked back home. And here I felt more appreciated and useful.

I stayed in Japan . . . for fifteen months. Kure was the administrative centre of the Canadian Brigade and Kobe was an R & R centre for American troops, as well as one of their administrative centres. I was lucky enough to be re-posted often and introduced to different parts of Japan. In each of these places, my responsibilities were the same. As well as encouraging the men to talk, I wrote letters and did shopping for them. When I wasn't working, I was able to go out and learn more about the Japanese culture, which was a wonderful experience for a young woman who had never before been outside of Quebec.

After fifteen months in Japan, I was transferred to Korea near the Armistice line on the 38th parallel and the Imjin River. I was there for three months, and it was very different from my experience in Japan. Even though the war was over, there was still a strong sense of danger. At night we had to drive without lights because we were close to the military zone. I remember one time when two of us were being driven from work to where we were staying. Suddenly a soldier jumped out of the bush and demanded that the jeep stop. We were really scared, but fortunately the soldier turned out to be one of ours.

Meeting Mr. Brown

BLAIR FRASER

Igor Gouzenko, always in hiding from the KGB, led a secretive existence in Canada after he defected in 1945.

Not more than a dozen people know where Igor Gouzenko lives, or under what name, and I am not one of them. Neither are his publishers, J.M. Dent and Sons (Canada) Ltd., of Toronto. To communicate with Gouzenko they write in care of the Royal Canadian Mounted Police, Ottawa, who deliver his mail to him by courier. Ever since September, 1945, when the then-Russian cipher clerk laid before the RCMP 109 secret Soviet documents which exposed a Communist spy ring in Canada, Gouzenko has been hiding—as he will be for the rest of his life. The Soviet secret police have a long arm, and no man living has so grievously affronted them as Igor Gouzenko. . . .

Those who know they are meeting Igor Gouzenko are not, of course, told any of his new names. When they are introduced to him, as I was in Toronto a few weeks ago, they meet a Mr. Brown. Mr. Brown was waiting for us at the home of C. J. Eustace of the Dent publishing firm, but I didn't know that when I set out. My appointment was with Eustace at his Bloor Street office. Gouzenko came alone from the home of a friend with whom he was staying, and whom Eustace didn't know. None of us could have traced him once he stepped outside Eustace's door.

I shook hands with a short stocky fair-haired man who, in spite of a receding hairline, looked rather younger than his 34 years. He wore a light grey suit of ultramodern cut—wide padded shoulders, long jacket— which accentuated his short square build. Though he apparently lives a sedentary life he looks like a man in good physical shape. . . .

At this point we all went in to lunch and the conversation became general. Among other things we talked about the trial and execution of the Rosenbergs, the man and wife in the United States who had given atomic secrets to Soviet Russia. I asked Gouzenko what he thought of the case. To my surprise he was very much against the Rosenberg trial, thought it had been very badly handled. What alarmed him was not the verdict of guilty or even the sentence of death but the fact that some of the evidence was not made public. "Once you start convicting people on secret evidence where will it end? What's to stop them from shooting anybody at all and putting it down to security reasons? A democracy must not use the methods of a dictatorship, just as a dictatorship cannot use the methods of a democracy. Soviet Russia is finding that out right now in the satellite countries. They try to give a little freedom, a little relaxation of tyranny, and what happens? Riots and rebellions break out. Dictatorships cannot afford freedom.

"But democracies can't afford not to have it—all the protections of law are for everybody. When things happen like the Rosenberg trial they are too hard to explain to outsiders. For one thing the Rosenberg trial might discourage people like myself who might be willing to help you by coming over to your side. They look at things like taking evidence in secret and they naturally wonder what is the difference between a free democracy and a dictatorship."

After lunch I asked Gouzenko whether he himself still lived in fear of discovery and revenge, or whether he now felt safe. "In the beginning we were very suspicious of everything and everybody. Fear has big eyes, you know. At the very first we were afraid the Canadian government might give us back to the Russians—they didn't seem to know what to do with us. My wife was quite calm even then, though. She is a remarkable woman—she ought to have been a man. Nowadays we don't feel frightened. The best rule is always be on the alert but don't get panicky when danger threatens."

Didn't they ever get into unexpected situations? Suppose, for example, some neighbor had a guest who really came from the country Gouzenko now pretends to have come from and suppose the neighbor asked the Gouzenkos over to tea? "All I can say is, fortunately that has never happened."

But if they felt so safe now why had they moved so often? Why had they bought three different houses in six years? "No special reason. We didn't feel in any particular danger. Partly it was just to have a better house, better location. Also, on the general principle that it's better not to stay too long in one place. The real danger is always the thing you don't see. People will notice something and you won't even know it. So—we moved. If I could afford it I would move even oftener." ...

In the course of a leisurely dinner, though, we talked of many things. Canadian politics, for one. "I don't take a very active part in politics, except of course to vote," said Gouzenko, who has been a Canadian citizen since September, 1948. "I do think we should have stronger Opposition. Opposition should be strong and vigilant. I have seen the one-party system at first hand and this makes me think no party should have too big a majority. Keep government answerable for every step. Press, also, must be absolutely free and fearless. Must not be afraid to print bad things about government."

I asked what he thought of the economic system in Canada, and of course he said he liked it. Gouzenko is a free-enterprise man: "People in Russia are kept working under the most horrible conditions by the fear of punishment or exile to concentration camps. Here in Canada much better results are achieved by competition—and all this without fear or pain. Without competition there can only be concentration camps."

The Promise of Atomic Energy

I. NORMAN SMITH

The possibility that nuclear power could produce power at low cost and minor inconvenience captivated Canadians.

I'm just back from a visit to the Atomic Energy Project at Chalk River, and I know how Alice must have felt if anyone asked her when she got home what it was like in Wonderland.

She couldn't tell it all in one sentence, but just bit by bit; the way the Caterpillar smoked his hookah and how sadly the Mock Turtle sang his song.

Now at Chalk River, for example, my mouth fell ajar at how quiet it all was. I knew they weren't actually making atom bombs, but nevertheless I expected a kind of workshop to the gods of war, sparks, fire, hail, brimstone, a clangour of steel and Beethoven's Fifth Symphony at concert pitch over the p.a. system.

Instead I found a lot of serious-minded young men (average man's age in the plant is 33) slipping quietly around in white smock coats writing mathematical hieroglyphics down in books or peering into glass boxes or attentively eyeing electric needles and indicators on vast control boards. Others were poring over textbooks and still others, more power to them, were just sitting thinking.

And the things they think of! One man, having broken a lot of nature's elements asunder, tells me he can tell to look at them that the world is six billion years old. He calls the beginning of space and earth and stuff "the incident", and the ages of time to him are not in terms of apes or Greeks or Americans, but hydrogen, carbon, aluminum, uranium and all that. Another man is pondering what kind of a monster he will create if he crosses a thorium-sparked hen with a plutonium-pepped rooster. A third and gentler man was contemplating whether he would in fact bring the world to an end if he found the substance he was searching for, and bombarded it with neutrons. He wasn't going to do it that day, though, for the community drama group was going to put on "Bell, Book and Candle" next week, and he liked plays about witchcraft and wanted to see it.

Of course knocking around with scientists like that a bit you can't help getting some on you, so to speak. I know, for instance, the difference between a reactor and a pile; none. Often their jargon is doubletalk, just to confuse the Russians.

In fact I'm now so knowledgeable I can tell you the whole thing is a misnomer. It isn't atomic energy they are dealing with up at Chalk River but nuclear energy. Atomic energy is what you have when you recombine atoms, for example in the burning of coal, gas, oil, etc. That's old stuff. Nuclear energy refers to energy released by the recombination of nuclei—or the content of the atom. Clear?

It was the pile, you'll remember, that came to grief last December 12, a Friday. Call it a pile if you wish to think of it in terms of a pile of uranium rods, plus aluminum, plus helium, plus cadmium, and the whole thing cooled off with Ottawa river water and steadied down with heavy water brought clear from Trail, B.C. Call it a reactor if you wish to think of it in terms of being a great furnace 35 feet wide and 35 feet high wherein these things react to one another so that mass disappears and becomes heat and radiation.

Take an atom; break it in two. The two parts weigh less than the former whole. The difference has gone off in heat and radiation energy. That's splitting the atom and getting nuclear energy.

That business of mass disappearing shouldn't sound too mysterious. If you put a match to a log of wood mass disappears and heat or energy replace it. In Chalk River what they are doing is taking uranium instead of wood or coal, and the match they put to uranium is a bombardment of neutrons. Don't worry about where they get the neutrons or what they are—they are agitations, the chemists and physicists cook up or "release" in that furnace and that's all we need to know.

Now out of that pile or reactor or furnace, then, the white-coated men of Chalk River produce (a) great heat which they cannot harness and which goes back into the Ottawa river and (b) radiation energy which they catch in the tiniest amounts and which we use more and more in medicine, industry and research.

They'll find a way, one of these years, of catching the heat and making power out of it—and then our river and coal power will be pigmy stuff.

Burning a pound of coal supplies power to keep 100 lamps burning for 24 minutes. The fission or breaking up of a pound of uranium would power 100 lamps for a century. That's what is at the end of the road.

But in the meantime our destructive genius has found a way of using the new energy which it cannot control by the atom or hydrogen bomb. Those bombs are in effect flying or miniature piles or reactors. We send them out in an aircraft or leave them cooking in a desert and when the stew is done to a turn they go poof. Roughly, that's all there is to an atom bomb. What the scientists are now trying to do is to devise a stew or pile or reactor that won't go "poof" but will just bubble away under wraps and light our cities, power our industries, ships and trains.

Khrushchev Out-drinks Canadian Diplomats, 1955

GEORGE IGNATIEFF

In 1955, foreign minister Lester Pearson was one of the first western leaders to visit Soviet leader Nikita Khrushchev. Diplomat George Ignatieff, his family of the Russian nobility, was with the Canadian delegation.

Both Khrushchev and Bulganin were obviously aware of my Russian origin, though Khrushchev's information was not as accurate as I would have expected. He said he knew all about me, that my father had served under Kerensky in the provisional government. I told him he was mistaken, that my father had never served anyone other than the tsar. "You know, Nikita Sergeyevich," Bulganin chimed in, "he is the son of Count Paul Ignatieff, the former minister of education." From that point on Khrushchev persisted in addressing me as "Count" or "ex-Count" until I felt compelled to point out that, as a Canadian, I preferred to be called plain Mr. . . .

At about ten o'clock Khrushchev announced that it was time to eat and led the way to the banquet room, past several washrooms which he was careful to point out to us. The significance of this hospitable gesture became disconcertingly clear once we sat down to eat, and our hosts proceeded to propose a seemingly endless series of toasts. Once again I was informed that I was expected to drink like a Russian, and it didn't take me long to realize what was the objective of the exercise. "Your husband is trying to get me drunk," I said to Mrs. Khrushchev, who had joined us for dinner and was sitting beside me. She was a pleasant, mild-mannered woman, a former schoolteacher with none of her husband's bluster. "What would you like me to do about it?" she asked. "If you can't stop him," I replied, "at least get me some black bread and butter; it will act as a blotter for all that vodka." She did as I asked, but no amount of bread could soak up all that undiluted liquor. Khrushchev and Bulganin kept their eyes fixed on me as they proposed one toast after another, making sure my glass was refilled the moment I emptied it. I was munching bread furiously and I tried to spill some of the drink over my shoulder as I drained each glassful but Khrushchev immediately spotted my stratagem and announced that the Count ("or should I say ex-Count?") was trying to cheat.

I counted eighteen vodkas, fortified with red pepper, before heading for one of the washrooms Khrushchev had so thoughtfully pointed out to us earlier in the evening. . . .

Shortly after midnight I told Khrushchev and Bulganin that Pearson was suffering from a sore throat, that he had a busy day ahead of him, and that we ought to be on our way. After two more for the road we thanked our hosts and marched out of the banquet hall with our heads held high and the dubious satisfaction that we were in marginally better shape than some of the people we left behind. I barely made it back to our quarters before I was sick all over again. Years later René Lévesque, who had accompanied us to Yalta, told my wife that, the last time he saw me, I was having a wonderful time with Khrushchev while he was just an underling with steerage accommodation. When Alison asked him what made him so sure I had such a good time, he said he could tell by the number of times I flushed the john.

Glenn Gould Plays Moscow

JOHN FAST

In 1957, the great pianist Glenn Gould visited Moscow, an event the
Canadian Embassy deemed significant enough to report on to Ottawa.

Perhaps the most interesting of all recitals which Glenn Gould gave in
Moscow was his last one, the one given on Sunday morning, May 12th
for the Piano Faculty and students of the Moscow Conservatory. He was
asked several days beforehand whether he would consider playing for the
students (I understand the concert was gratis), leaving to him the choice
of programme. In my conversations with him, prior to the concert on
Friday morning, he was frankly unenthusiastic and somewhat at a loss of
what to play. He finally expressed the opinion that the [Alban] Berg
Sonata [Opus 1] and some Bach should fill the bill. The suggested time
for the concert was a little awkward. The recital was to begin at 11:00
o'clock in the morning, and at 1:00 p.m. of the same day, he was due at
the Hotel Metropole for a luncheon given in his honour by the Ministry
for Culture. . .

2. On the evening of May 10th, at a reception for Mr. Gould at the
Embassy, I met the Russian cellist Rostropovich, with whom I had quite an
interesting conversation on the sad state of Soviet symphonic orchestras,
which was particularly evident at Mr. Gould's appearance as soloist with the
Moscow State Philharmonic, in Beethoven's 4th Piano Concerto. (During
the playing of a passage in the first movement, one of the flutes came in several beats ahead of the rest and stubbornly continued playing to the bitter
end despite the pronounced scowls and gymnastics of the conductor.) In
the course of our conversation, I mentioned to Mr. Rostropovich that Mr.
Gould shall be playing for the students of the piano faculty and that he is
somewhat at a loss of what to choose for them. Rostropovich became
rather interested in the "problem" and suggested that it should be something unfamiliar. I then told him that Mr. Gould had expressed to me the
desire to present a programme which should include not only some Bach,
but a composition, or two, of near-atonal and atonal work. However, I
added, Mr. Gould was just a little apprehensive how such a programme
would be received here. Rostropovich's reaction to my remarks was quite
amazing, to say the least. It was his opinion that he could not choose better than suggested and he concluded his remarks by saying "as much as
possible of contemporary music from which they are, unfortunately, removed." I was later told by Mr. Gould that he repeated substantially the
same sentiments to him while leaving the Embassy.

3. The following Sunday, on arrival at the Conservatory, Mr. Gould
was received at the entrance of the hall by a group of enthusiastic young

students, headed by the young and very talented pianist, Lev Vlasenko. The reception which they gave him foreshadowed what was to come.

4. The recital took place at the Small Hall of the Conservatory, with a seating capacity of 400. It was jammed to the rafters, with standers taking over every available space, and overflowing into every exit and down the staircase. Youth heavily predominated.

5. Mr. Gould's recital was rather unorthodox. He prefaced it with a few remarks explaining what he intended to do. The Alban Berg Sonata was to form the focal point, however, leading to it he demonstrated with a number of short excerpts, the influence of early Arnold Schoenberg in this Sonata. The excerpts were taken from two Schoenberg song cycles: Opus 2, "Kes Knaben Wunderhorn" and Opus 3, "Verzweitflung"; still strictly diatonic and heavy with Wagnerian overtones. This was followed by Berg's Sonata, where tonal and atonal music meet, with the former perhaps dominating.

6. After the playing of the Sonata, Mr. Gould played two pieces as an illustration of musical development since Berg's Sonata: the stark and totally atonal "Three Variations" by Webern, and the 1st and 2nd movements of Krenek's Piano Sonata [No. 3]. This last work, which Mr. Gould considers as one of the more important piano compositions of our century, he played with an unbelievable verve and intensity that swept everything and everyone along. The concert concluded with several fugues from the "Art of the Fugue", several variations of the Goldberg Variations, and several movements from the E minor Partita by Bach.

7. Mr. Gould's playing was given an unbelievable reception. The Moscow habit to applaud an excellent performance with short rhythmic clapping, became a near machine-gun staccato and quite deafening in volume. I have listened to a number of performers and witnessed some truly first class performances (including Ulanova's dancing), however, Mr. Gould's reception outdid them all. Even his well-known mannerisms seem to have added, rather than detracted from his performance. His behaviour was absolutely free and easy on this day. Dressed quite informally, without tie, as the concert progressed, and he began to feel warm, Mr. Gould first removed his jacket then peeled off his sweater, dropping the clothing on the floor of the stage, finishing the concert in shirt-sleeves with part of the shirt-tail well out.

8. The getting away from the Conservatory was a veritable march of triumph. Mr. Gould's dressing room became completely jammed with people congratulating and embracing him (in the old Russian manner, and which always startled him). From his dressing room, down the lengthy staircase and to the waiting car, Glenn Gould had to walk through a solid mass of wildly cheering students. This was not a carefully arranged and "spontaneously" conducted demonstration, rather the paying of due regards to a true artist.

U.S. Red-Hunters Drive Herbert Norman to Suicide

ANONYMOUS

Canadian Ambassador Herbert Norman leaped to his death today from a Cairo building because of a charge in the U.S. Senate sub-committee he had been a Communist.

The Canadian government had angrily denied the charge. The Canadian embassy said Norman's body was found on the street below a building housing the Swedish legation here on the banks of the Nile. Egyptian police said it was suicide.

Egypt's Middle East news agency said Norman left two letters—one to his wife and one to "my friend" Carl Eng, the Swedish minister in Cairo.

"I kiss your feet and I beg you to forgive me for what I am doing" the agency quoted him as saying in the note to his wife. "I have no option" it quoted him as writing. "I must kill myself for 'Ye live without hope'."

Officials at the Canadian embassy said Norman had been depressed ever since charges made against him in the U.S. committee had been made public. Eye-witnesses said they saw Norman before he leaped "sit on a parapet and hold his head between his hands, his body apparently shaking." They said they saw him "slowly take off his glasses and his watch and lay them on the parapet." He turned his back on the crowd below and looked at the sky. "Then he started backing up," one witness said. "He took two steps backwards and with the third he was in the air."

Norman was strongly defended by the Canadian government over continuing attempts by the American sub-committee to smear him. It released testimony by a committee counsel that the FBI had given the state department information which confirmed the previous allegations—going back to 1951—that Norman was linked with the Reds. The state department following Canada's protest had asked the sub-committee not to release the testimony because "it might be damaging to our friendly relations with Canada." The Canadian protest had come after External Affairs Minister Lester Pearson defended Norman in the Commons.

Pearson referred to the sub-committee's "slanders and unsupported insinuations" against Norman, and dismissed them as old allegations which had long before been investigated and disproved. The protest, delivered orally to the state department in Washington was reported in Ottawa to be one of the strongest exchanged between the two governments in recent years. Canada's external affairs department said Norman was cleared of Communist suspicion by a double security check. Pearson said the U.S. government was told Norman was a "highly respected and trusted senior official."

Following the latest Canadian protest, the state department said allegations in the hearing transcript "do not represent opinions of the United States government." Mr. Diefenbaker suggested that the flag on Parliament Hill's peace tower be flown at half-mast. Mr. Pearson read to the House a telegram received from Norman March 19, which said: "I have been deeply moved by the generous and forthright terms of your statement in the House concerning recent allegations against me. While, on the one hand, the persistent renewal of these allegations have a vexing and discouraging effect, yet, on the other hand, the reaction to them in (Parliament) has increased, if that were possible, my pride and devotion to our institutions and our sense of fair play."

The Emergence of "The Chief"

TOM ARDIES

The footsteps of 2,000 people took the "Follow John" path Thursday afternoon in a farmer's field at Cloverdale. Those footsteps kicked up a lot of dust—and that dust hung as a warning cloud on Canada's political horizon. Its message: John Diefenbaker, the new leader of the Progressive Conservatives, is a man to be reckoned with. He is selling himself, fast, hard, and sure.

This further evidence of a sudden surge of public interest in John Diefenbaker came at a public barbecue on Ted Kuhn's big farm on Bamford Road off the old Pacific Highway. Mr. Kuhn, PC candidate in New Westminister, had 1,500 steaks on hand, and one might have thought he had sort of overstocked. Not so. Two thousand people showed up.

John Diefenbaker, who has been pulling some big surprises since he moved into British Columbia, had pulled perhaps the biggest of them all. Drawing 2,000 people to an open farm field—much of it freshly plowed—is REAL politicking.

The crowd wasn't interested in the steaks, either.

The crowd—old people, young people, all kinds of people—brought the "Follow John" slogan to life. They followed him all over that field, pulling at his sleeve, pumping his hand; praising him, thanking him, practically worshipping him. Everybody had somebody they wanted to introduce to him.

"Mr. Diefenbaker, a lady from Weyburn. . . . Mr. Diefenbaker, a man from Mossbank. . . . Mr. Diefenbaker, a lady not from Saskatchewan, but . . . please, one of the old-timers, it means so much. . . ."

It did appear to mean an awful lot, too, such as in the case of the woman who shook hands, ran back to a circle of friends and squealed, "HE shook hands with ME!" John Diefenbaker, who said he was hungry, and just had to eat some of his steak, was kept so busy he managed only a couple of nibbles on the hamburger bun.

The "Follow John" routine started as soon as he stepped down from the platform after a short speech and swept on until PC officials were almost forced to drag him away from the crowd's clutches. He had no time for conversation. Just "Hello. How are you? Very glad to meet you," over and over again. The people pushing in around him knew this, but still persisted, as if this pat, little exchange was important, extremely important.

It wasn't that John Diefenbaker cut a spell-binding figure in that field. He looked and acted tired. It often appeared that his dark sharp eyes, the most striking thing about him, were unseeing. Nor did he seem to hear anyone beyond the person clutching him at the moment. Three times a photographer asked him to remove his black homburg and pose for a picture. Three times there was no answer. Finally a public relations man lifted the hat from his head. The photographer snapped the picture. The public relations man returned the hat.

There wasn't the slightest indication that this new miracle man of politics was aware of the little by-play.

What has he got? Just how far will this go? "Thank you, thank you, thank you," John Diefenbaker called when he finally reached the car waiting to return him to Vancouver. "Goodbye, goodbye, goodbye."

Somebody called back, "Goodbye, John, the next prime minister," as the car pulled away. Perhaps—for who can say it is impossible—that is just how far this will go.

Diefenbaker en français

PIERRE SÉVIGNY

> *Pierre Sévigny was one of Diefenbaker's few Québec supporters before he won the leadership. He became a minister in the Conservative cabinet.*

John Diefenbaker told us that he understood and could read French, but that he had some difficulty with vocabulary. This was without a doubt the understatement of his long and complicated career. At his request I tried to teach him in the correct pronunciation of a few simple words. But it was hopeless, and I almost felt like telling him to forget the whole thing, or to follow Mackenzie King's example and limit his Gallic efforts to the initial words *mes chers amis* and a final *au revoir*. This would have been use-less. My candidate was determined to speak French, and nothing would convince him that he could hardly be considered a linguist. I therefore prepared the simplest of texts, which he laboriously delivered the follow-ing day. On countless occasions during the next six years, I was asked like many others to prepare his French speeches. I worked hard at this thankless function, and I must say that some progress was achieved in his dedicated desire to be bilingual. He eventually realized that he would never speak good French, and he could be quite amusing about his harmless admission. I remember his saying, after a particularly lengthy and difficult bout with the language of Victor Hugo, "In order to prove to you that I can also speak the other language of the country, I shall now address you in English." Upon his arrival in Mexico on a state visit, he was greeted by President Lopez Mateos, and John Diefenbaker answered his friendly greetings with a short speech which he delivered in Spanish as well as in English. He then asked the President if he had understood. Lopez Mateos, who spoke good English, answered that Mexicans could understand Spanish but not Portuguese.

The Springhill Mine Disaster—and Miracle

RAY TIMSON

Springhill, N.S., Nov. 3—Byron (Barney) Martin, 42, trapped for almost nine days in the devastated depths of Springhill's No. 2 Mine, spent the 200 hours alone, face-down in the dirt, trying to scratch his way out. He lay in what could be described as a shallow grave, six feet long and three feet deep, a grave that almost claimed and kept him. Throughout the entire ordeal, he had but three drinks of water. He had no food whatever. He uttered only one word the whole time.

His legs were buried under a rockfall and his stomach was propped up on other rocks beneath him. With his face to the ground, he was in a position much like kneeling, the kneeling that's done by people who pray. He knelt that way for nine nights and eight days.

When rescued Saturday at 5:45 a.m., his fingernails were worn down past his fingertips, and the flesh of the fingertips was rubbed raw from his futile efforts to claw his way to freedom. His lips were swollen like a Ubangi's. A nine-day beard was matted into his chin and cheeks. His nostrils were almost plugged with coal dust. His lungs were heavy with gas. His stomach was wracked with the pain of hunger. His legs were numb from lack of circulation. His arms ached from the constant scratching. And yet he thought he had been in the mine for just a single night.

For this is the true tragedy of Springhill. While a world cheers every word in such a dramatic rescue, more men shake their heads. What does it do to a man who survives such an ordeal? What does it do to his mind?

There are dozens of men living and working in Nova Scotia coal towns like Springhill who were once listed as "Among those rescued," but their family physicians say they have not been the same men since.

Barney Martin started his shift of 8:04 p.m. on Thursday, Oct. 23, when he and 173 other men of Springhill—average age 42—were doing regular jobs on the 3-to-11 shift in the Cumberland Coal Company's deep No. 2 mine.

At 8:05 p.m., there was a thunderous upheaval and tons of coal and rock tumbled down on miners picking away at coal seams on the long-wall faces or engaged in moving the picked coal through the various levels to the slope and thence up to the surface.

At that instant, Barney Martin was hurled eight feet down the long-wall face at the 13,000-foot level and pinned by rockfall between two stonepacks. His miner's lamp was blown off his head. As he lapsed into unconsciousness, the din of moaning, groaning and dying men grew fainter and fainter until he heard nothing at all. He lay in the shallow cavity between the packs, rock piled up at his feet and over his legs, rock piled under his waist, and rock piled high six inches from where his head rested in the dirt.

At 8:45 p.m., up at the pithead on the surface, mine manager George Calder led a party of 20 men down the 2.7-mile slope, straight down to the bottom-most 13,800-foot level which they reached at 11:30 p.m. after restoring ventilation and removing much stone and debris. There they found Jim McManaman, an overman or foreman, with 12 other men and they joined forces to work their way 150 feet up the longwall face.

A man hollered and the rescuers rushed to him. Except for about four square inches of his face, he was completely covered and there was only 18 inches between where he lay and the roof because of the floor buckling that came with the upheaval. Men shouted and strained and clawed at the rock for four hours before they freed Leon Melanson, whose leg was broken.

But up in the shallow grave on the 13,000 wall face, Barney Martin heard nothing. He had no knowledge that Calder and his men were rescuing the first of 100 miners who survived out of the total work force of 174. By 5 a.m., Friday, Oct. 24, the crowd, drawn to the pithead by the ominous "bump" that was felt in Amherst 16 miles away, had seen 81 miners come safely out, although 19 were injured.

About this time, as can best be determined, Barney Martin awoke, spat out the dirt that had been sucked into his mouth while breathing heavily during his period of unconsciousness, and looked around him. There was nothing but blackness. He tried to move his legs but the rockfall on top of them prevented him. He reached in front of him and felt more rock and started tearing at it with his hands, trying to grasp something solid with which he could cling and pull himself free. Only handfuls of dust and crumbled rock came away.

He had not eaten. His lunch pail was back on the 13,000-foot level. He reached around for his water can, hanging from a hook on his belt.

Although there was less than a tumbler full in it, a supply that a man would ration if he knew it had to last nine days, he drank generously because he had no idea how long he had been there or how long he would remain. The water stimulated him somewhat and he began clawing at the rock again, clawing, clawing, until again, he became exhausted and his face fell in the dirt. The gas made breathing difficult and he lapsed into unconsciousness again.

As Barney slept, three crews of men, led by respirator-equipped draegermen, were tunnelling their way to the 13,000-foot face. Harold Gordon, bossman of all the company's coal mines, was telling a Friday press conference that the underground destruction had been terrific, that there was no hope of any life at the 13,800 or 13,400 levels and little hope that any of the 55 miners at the 13,000 level would be found alive. Barney was in no position to deny the report.

Some 300 feet down the longwall face from where Barney Martin lay, a group of 12 men were gathered in a space too small to stand up in, or even sit upright. They were near the bottom of the wall and Caleb Rushton, a choir singer when he's not a miner, was leading them in singing hymns as they began the first of six days of praying that they'd come out of it alive.

Less than 100 feet down from Barney, another group of seven men were doing the same thing, led by Maurice Ruddick, a father of 12 children and known to the 1,000 Cumberland employees as "the singing miner." They were in an area about 50 feet long, four feet wide and three feet high.

Saturday came and 11 bodies had been brought to the surface. Sometime during the day, Barney Martin, awake again and still clawing at the rock, took his second drink. On Sunday, about the time the first two of what will total 74 funerals were being held, Barney took his last drink, emptying the can. There had been no food in his stomach since his meal Thursday before he went to work, and the water caused instant nausea. Barney's face fell in it, and he went unconscious again and the gritty coal dust and dirt began imbedding itself in the skin of his face.

Calder and his rescuers were plodding on, and, by Sunday, they had just about reached the face of the 13,000 wall. Shortly after midnight, the seven men 100 feet down from Barney divided the last of two meat-spread sandwiches and 2 1/2 quarts of water, and sang Happy Birthday to Garnet Clarke, who was 29 on Monday. One of the seven taking his share of the food was Percy Rector, whose arm was jammed among timbers and who pleaded with the other six to take the axe they had and chop it off to free him from the painful trap he had endured 3 1/2 days.

Early Monday morning, two of the seven, Garnet Clarke and Currie Smith, started up through the debris of the wall seeking an escape. They had looked in other directions on each of the previous days they had been imprisoned, but impasses blocked them each time. They came upon Barney Martin and from the bent position of his body presumed he was dead. But as they bent over him, he raised his face from the dirt and spoke the only word he was to utter the entire nine days. "Hello," Barney said, and his face fell into the dirt again.

Clarke and Smith, having no food or water to offer the man, rearranged his position, taking away jagged rocks that were digging into the man's sides. The air was cleaner near him, they noted, and he would be safer where he lay. To move him might cause injury. They returned to their small space and sang anew for their deliverance.

Monday afternoon and breakthrough: Calder and his men reached the 13,000 face but their spirit flagged considerably when the first body they found was that of Charlie Burton, who had been a hero in the 1956 fire and explosion in No. 4 mine when he found his way out after four days of entombment and led to the rescue of 88 miners. Charlie wasn't going to do it again,

On Tuesday there were six funerals and a statement that said there could be no hope for any men being found alive. At 1:45 p.m., Wednesday, Calder's men got through more debris and came across an air pipe 80 feet from the 13,000 face. There was a lot of air coming out of it and suddenly there were three tappings on it from somewhere in the face. Then a series of taps. Blair Phillips, one of the rescuers, asked if anybody was up there. Back through the pipe came Gorley Kempt's voice: "There are 12 of us. Come and get us."

Barney Martin didn't hear the joyous cries of the rescuers and the rescued. It is safe to assume he was in an advanced state of delirium by this time, and whatever strength he had mentally and physically was not being used to concentrate on hearing sounds. He was still clawing at the rock in front of him where he had now worn two pathways the width of his hands, much like those you can make by scratching at the sand on a beach. There was no fingertip bleeding. As he wore the skin thinner and thinner, the grime he was clawing at clogged into the skin.

At 3.23 a.m, Thursday, Gorley Kempt was the first of the 12 to be brought to the surface and the other 11 followed within an hour and 25 minutes. Interviewed at All Saints' Hospital, they offered next to no hope there were others still alive in the mine although one of them, Harold Brine, said at the time. "Once we thought we heard somebody up above us but we can't be sure. It sounded like somebody trying to dig out."

Barney Martin's clawing, perhaps.

On Friday, as Springhill buzzed with word that Prince Philip would be making a personal visit to the disaster town that evening, the six men 100 feet from Barney sucked on coal and ate bark stripped from timber. There were only six: Percy Rector, 55, the man who wanted his arm cut off, had died from the shock and pain of the mangled limb. The six men with him had no idea when rescue might come, and none cared to pick up the axe and do what Percy asked. The shock of such action might kill him on the spot, they figured.

At 4:45 a.m. Saturday, a few short hours after Prince Philip had come and gone, Bud Henwood, deputy overman, climbed out of the head of the tunnel the rescuers were digging to let another man take his place. Behind him were bossman Harold Gordon, and mine and union officials who were forming the bucket brigade moving back the rock and coal the men in front were clearing. In the silence of the change-over, the ears of the rescuers picked up the sound of three slow but distinct scratches. They set upon the rock like crazy men and 50 minutes and 12 feet of rock later they came upon Barney Martin. His ceaseless scratching finally had got results.

Up the open space they raced until they broke through to the other six men. One of them, Maurice Ruddick, the singing miner, hollered: "Give me a drink of water and I'll sing you a song." Quickly, the rescuers asked whether these six had heard any noises that might indicate more men were alive.

"Just some scratching," Ruddick replied. "From down that way, where Barney Martin is." Barney Martin, rendered conscious again by sips of sugary tea, muttered to a rescuer: "Thank God I'm alive." At the hospital he spoke again to miner Norman McDonald: "God must have saved that little hole for me."

Barney Martin, a miner 17 years, had put in his toughest shift.

Interviewing Mrs. Diefenbaker and Mrs. Pearson

CHRISTINA MCCALL

Encountering Mrs. Diefenbaker at 24 Sussex was like visiting a prairie parsonage presided over by a sweet-natured minister's wife who had an unexpectedly shrewd eye for the vagaries of his parishioners and the ways in which they might do him harm. After discussing with disarming frankness the details of her everyday life, she showed me the separate bedrooms where she and her husband slept; took me into the prime-ministerial kitchens and introduced me to the domestic staff; displayed for my admiration the best set of dishes used for queens and presidents, and the second-best set, used for practising politicians and assorted lesser lights; retrieved from the safe the modest jewellery that had been given to her as the Conservative leader's wife; told me confidentially— "I know you'll understand"—how hard it was for her to watch her painfully unilingual husband try to politick in Quebec despite his party's huge majority there, won in 1958 with the aid of the still-powerful Union Nationale machine of Maurice Duplessis.

"*They* are so different from *us*," she said, smiling into my apparently credulous twenty-five-year-old face. Oh God! thought I—and it wasn't the implacable Taskmaster-in-the-Sky of my Presbyterian childhood I was invoking—she thinks we're *alike*. How can I tell this nice woman I find such notions noxiously racist?—a response that was as reflective of my generation's naive one-world idealism as hers was of her generation's sectarian tribalism.

Paradoxically, interviewing Maryon Pearson was a far more difficult task, though superficially we *were* alike, at least in several of our private interests. She had a reputation as "une dame formidable," as the wife of a Quebec Liberal MP warned in advance, advising me to watch out for an ambush.

In the cold light of a November morning, Mrs. Pearson seemed less formidable than I'd feared. She was far more sophisticated in her conversation than Olive Diefenbaker and far less circumspect in bemoaning the problems of political wives, which she described with a wit she had been honing for decades and that by now had achieved a razor-sharp edge. She talked of the ennui she experienced at political events where she had to play the wife of the leader; of the pleasure she took in the work of the Canadian painters David Milne, Lawren Harris and Joe Plaskett; and of her taste in literature (the novels of Muriel Spark, the short stories of Katherine Mansfield, and the poetry of Edna St. Vincent Millay, though she disparaged Millay's verse by saying it reflected the attitudes of "sentimental girls of my generation.")

While Mrs. Diefenbaker had introduced me to her seamstress and her cook, Mrs. Pearson treated her domestic staff as though they were automatons and basked instead in the flattering attentions of the *Maclean's* photographer, a glamorous figure who drove a Jaguar, played the piano with brio, and described his experiences in publishing pictures in *Paris Match* and *Life* while clicking away like mad.

In the wake of the articles' publication, Mrs. Diefenbaker sent me a graceful note, written in a rounded hand on a flowered card. Mrs. Pearson had a secretary ring me up and then came on the line to deliver four or five sarcastic comments in rapid succession, attacking my perfidy in having repeated in print some of her milder dissatisfactions with her lot. In summing up, she said witheringly, "You're just so *young*. Only someone as *young* as you are could be so indiscreet."

Selling the Governor General's Art Collection

G. BLAIR LAING

> *Vincent Massey, governor general from 1952 to 1959, was an art collector of note. G. Blair Laing owned a Toronto gallery.*

When, in 1958, Vincent Massey, then Governor General of Canada, decided to sell his entire collection of Milne paintings, except those hanging in his own home, Batterwood, he got in touch with me. I suggested he put a price on the whole collection, and he arranged for Alan Jarvis, the great David Milne admirer and then Director of the National Gallery, to make an unofficial valuation for him.

An appointment to look at the pictures was arranged. I arrived at Rideau Hall in Ottawa, to be greeted by Massey's son Lionel, his *aide-de-camp*. (Vincent Massey himself did not appear at any time during the transaction; I expect he felt the Milne business too crass a matter for a Governor General to handle personally.) Lionel ushered me into an enormous ballroom, where spread upon the floor, unframed, and many without stretchers, were what seemed to me acres of Milnes. The paintings were from Milne's great painting years, from 1928 to 1932; several Adirondack pictures of 1928, work from Lake Timagami, Weston, and Palgrave, and also included were three lovely early Adirondack dry-brush watercolours. After looking over this unbelievable treasure trove, the major portion of Massey's original purchase from Milne in 1934, I asked Lionel what his father wanted for the collection. "Thirty-five thousand," he replied.

In the past Massey had always been a tough and canny buyer, who never hesitated to bargain and make counter offers. I decided to try his own tactics and offered thirty-two thousand. Lionel looked distressed. Then after he had gone running back to another part of the hall to consult his father, we finally settled on thirty-three. I wrote out a cheque in Lionel's name (in accordance with his father's wishes), and proceeded to carry the paintings out to the car. The whole transaction, from the time I arrived at Government House until I left, had taken no more than two hours. There were 166 pictures in the collection, and no list of them existed at the time, nor did any kind of receipt pass hands to accompany the deal. The total cost averaged out to less than $200 per picture. The truth was that Massey had become tired of his David Milne collection and wanted to get rid of it. (In 1978, one of the paintings I had bought from Vincent Massey two decades earlier came up at a public sale. The price fetched for that one work exceeded what I had paid for the entire collection.)

Québec's Place Under Duplessis

ANDRÉ LAURENDEAU

> *Journalists are the public's eyes—but not always in Québec when Maurice Duplessis was in charge, from 1936 to 1939, and from 1944 until his death in 1959.*

Last Friday, Mr. Maurice Duplessis brutally ordered one of *Le Devoir*'s reporters, Mr. Guy Lamarche, out of his office.

The reporter was attending the premier's press conference. He had not made a move, not uttered a word. He was simply there. That was enough to provoke Mr. Duplessis' wrath. "Out!" roared the premier. Our reporter, considering that he was merely exercising his normal right in a democratic country, refused. Mr. Duplessis therefore had him thrown out by a member of the provincial police.

Three groups of journalists have since protested against this action. Spontaneously, they recognized the seriousness of the matter. A reporter who has been "duly charged by his newspaper with the task of attending the premier's press conference" must be allowed to "exercise his profession freely." These are the words used in the most moderately worded of the protests.

On the other hand, the various newspapers, in their editorials, have taken the matter very philosophically indeed. With only two exceptions, they made no mention of the incident. We would not care to insult them by concluding that they are indifferent about it. They are the guardians not only of freedom of speech, but also of that right which makes it possible and protects it, namely freedom of access to sources of information. Consequently, the expulsion of a reporter from a press conference to which everyone is theoretically invited cannot but have caused them some alarm. Let us say simply that they were able to contain their indignation more easily than the reporters who protested.

If indeed it is Mr. Duplessis' whim to exclude one person, each man knows that sooner or later his own turn may come. This time the premier acted against *Le Devoir*, but what would prevent him from taking such a step against any other newspaper next time? This time it was at a press conference—next time it might be in the parliamentary debates.

And upon what principle was this action based? It was purely arbitrary. Mr. Duplessis, quite sincerely we believe, considers power as his personal property. He does with it whatever he likes. His friends obtain preferential treatment. Counties which support him receive favourable treatment. Opposition members of the provincial Legislature, however, only deserve half-rights as far as he is concerned. He treats them as though they had not been elected as honestly as those in his own majority party.

Mr. Duplessis seems to think it right and fair to starve the Opposition. In matters of jobs, roads, schools, bridges, only his favourites are served. He has just applied the same principle to the press. An opponent, to his way of thinking, has no right to hear him speak. Choosing those newspapers he considers loyal to him, he is starting to exclude all the others.

Such an arbitrary exercise of power is against democracy and the parliamentary system.

It is usually the case that English Canadians are more sensitive than we are about any encroachments upon personal freedoms. That is why Mr.

Duplessis is not popular with the press outside Quebec. The attacks against him in Ontario and Manitoba are not of course always based on this feeling; racial and linguistic prejudices are too often given free rein as well. But it would be wrong to explain them all away on the score of national prejudice. In the British tradition, people slowly and gradually conquered their political freedom; they are usually more aware of its value, therefore, and more sensitive to any threat to it.

Usually, we say. For in Quebec this tradition is strangely anemic, at least if we are to judge from what our English-language newspapers say about what happens in this province.

Whenever the Ottawa government attempts to silence people, all the newspapers raise a great hue and cry. English-language newspapers, including our Quebec ones, protest that the government is violating important parliamentary freedoms. They whip up public opinion. This contributes to the government's defeat, as in the pipeline affair.

In the Legislative Assembly in Quebec, such events happen daily, yet our English-language newspapers endure them with very little protest. Why?

Guy Lamarche's expulsion last Friday is very hard to accept. But the English-language press has remained silent about the whole affair. In the middle of an article sympathetic to the government, *The Gazette* two days ago published the mildest imaginable criticism. Yesterday *The Star* declared that what Mr. Duplessis had done was clumsy, but could not bring itself to say it was actually wrong. Why?

Quebec's English-language newspapers behave like the British in one of their African colonies.

The British possess sound political sense. Very rarely do they destroy the political institutions of countries they conquer. Instead, they control the native ruler, while allowing him a few illusions. On occasion they will let him cut off a few heads, since it is the country's custom. It would never enter their minds to expect this native monarch to conform to Britain's own high moral and political standards.

What must above all be obtained from the native ruler is his collaboration with Britain, so that her interests are protected. Once this is ensured, the petty despot no longer matters. If he should violate the rules of democracy, well, can one really expect much more from these primitive people?

I am not saying that this is what our English-speaking minority in Quebec is actually thinking. But it seems from what is happening that some of their leaders do in fact believe in applying the theory of the native ruler. Since Mr. Duplessis is merely the ruler of the Quebec natives, they absolve behaviour in him, which would never be tolerated in one of their own leaders.

This has been made very clear in the present Legislative Assembly. It was also evident in the last municipal elections. It has just been finally confirmed in the premier's office.

As a result, a blow has been struck at democracy and the parliamentary system; instead of these, we have the rule of arbitrary power, and a continuing collusion between Anglo-Quebec finance and the province's most corrupt political elements.

Shooting Down the Arrow

CLARK DAVEY

> The Avro Arrow, or CF-105, was believed to be the best fighter aircraft in existence when the Diefenbaker government scrapped it in 1959 and opted for the Bomarc surface-to-air missile.

Toronto—The age of guided missiles came to Canada like this:

Peter Galvin, $110-a-week aircraft worker, came in the front door and stopped his wife from straightening the lamp shades on the afternoon of the first day in their new house. "I've been laid off," he said. In the tiny village of Nobel, in Ontario's rocky summer resort country, 10-year-old Brian Wilson told his mother: "I won't turn on the lights any more unless I can't see, and you don't have to give me an allowance." Canada didn't need his father, a tool and die maker, to make airplanes anymore.

Reg Dean lives close by the engine plant which produced the Iroquois—the power plant for the airplane which in a few weeks would probably have been revealed as the fastest in the world. Along the Maas River in Holland during the war he was shelled by his own regiment. When he lost his job on Friday by order of his own prime minister he said he felt much the same.

The 13,800 employees of Avro Aircraft and Orenda Engines Ltd. who lost their jobs on Friday live in scattered areas within 25 miles of Toronto's Malton Airport. The aftermath of their personal disaster is rippling out from there throughout rich industrial southwestern Ontario. At Brampton, a county high school board held an emergency meeting over the weekend and decided to slow down plans for a $1,600,000 school. If Avro's skilled workers move away there'll be no need for a new school.

Many of the farm towns which boomed with red brick bungalows built by Avro's well-paid workers face cuts in their municipal spending as grueling as the belt-tightening of their taxpayers.

Mayor Walter Cook of Acton was a government inspector at Orenda Engines himself. "We'll have second thoughts about a new 10-room public school we were going to build," he said. "We've invested $250,000 in sewers and water mains in two new subdivisions on a local improvement basis. Most of the people work at Avro . . . I don't know what will happen."

A hundred miles away the ripples reached the tiny Kelcher Engineering Ltd. in Kitchener, Ont. Only 90 men were laid off there.

But throughout Canada, and mainly in industrial Ontario, there are 650 companies with sub-contracts to supply the sister firms of Avro and Orenda. They employ as many men again as the nearly 14,000 laid off by the aircraft and engine firms struck down by the end of the Arrow.

The end came by loudspeaker, fed into the aircraft bays, and into the drawing rooms where 10 years ago there emerged North America's first jet transport (similarly abandoned). It was the tense voice of company president Crawford Gordon:

"Notice of termination . . . pending a full assessment of the impact of the prime minister's statement on our aeronautical operations."

They didn't sink in at first. Then General Manager John Plant broadcast the words which may turn Georgetown, Brampton, Acton, Milton, Nobel, and Malton back to sleepy little farm towns: "There will be no work for you."

Frustration, anger and shock brought many results. Office Overload, a placement firm for part-time office help, doubled its interviewing staff of five, said laid-off Avro stenographers would be given priority when Toronto and Hamilton companies called for office employees.

There was talk of protest marches on Ottawa. But the only march was by laid-off workers back to the plant where the Unemployment Insurance Commission set up special offices on the scene, hauled out truckloads of paper forms and began registering Avro's workers for their $36 a week in benefits.

A few hundred Avro workers were back at work today—most of them called back to their secretarial and personnel jobs to handle the paper work of dismissal and to call back a lucky few who will continue to work on a U.S. flying saucer program and on an engine order for West Germany. Would the highly skilled technicians and engineers recruited by Avro and by its predecessor company since wartime days drift to the United States? Many talked that way.

A Detroit aircraft company dispatched recruiters to Toronto Monday to hire engineers. Many of Avro's workers are British, recruited by Avro itself from British aviation firms. Their fares were paid to Canada.

James Black was a draftsman at Vickers Armstrong in England. Avro paid his fare to Canada. Avro checked off his mortgage payments of $87.50 a month from his pay cheque, as it did for 1,200 employees. "We never heard of a layoff until we came to Canada," Dorothy Black said Monday. "We're going to get our visas to go to the United States."

"This Extraordinary Disquisition":
Diefenbaker Bids the U.S. Ambassador Farewell, 1962

LIVINGSTON MERCHANT

At his last meeting with Prime Minister Diefenbaker, the U.S. Ambassador received an earful of complaints.

The gist of what the Prime Minister said was this. He could only interpret the President's devoting so much time to a personal talk with Pearson, which the latter had described to the press as covering a wide range of subjects including disarmament, NATO, and the Common Market, as an intervention by the President in the Canadian election. He was satisfied that, if not Pearson himself, then his campaign lieutenants would present this to the Canadian electorate as the President turning for advice on international affairs to a single Canadian who was the Leader of the Opposition and running for Prime Minister against the present government. The Prime Minister asserted that the night before in a speech in Toronto Walter Gordon (running on the Liberal ticket and generally regarded as likely to be Minister of Finance in a Liberal Cabinet) had stated in effect that the Liberals were more competent than the Conservatives to manage Canada, because the President had turned to Mr. Pearson a few days before for advice on the international situation.

The Prime Minister said that he fully expected this line to be increasingly used throughout the country by the Liberals in their campaign. He said that during the afternoon he had had phone calls to this effect from supporters from the Maritimes to British Columbia. The Prime Minister then went on to say that Canada-United States relations would now be the dominant issue in the campaign. He said the campaigning would be more bitter than it was in 1911....

The Prime Minister then said that he had no choice except to meet head-on the expected Liberal line that Pearson was better able to manage Canadian relations with the United States. He thought he would probably be forced into this by the middle of or end of next week. He said he was opening the Conservative campaign in London, Ontario, this evening and he would not then raise this issue himself. In countering the Liberal line, he said he would publicly produce a document which he has had locked up in his private safe since a few days after the President's visit to Ottawa last May. This document he says is the original of a memorandum on White House stationery, addressed to the President from Walt Rostow and initialled by the latter, which is headed "Objectives of the President's Visit to Ottawa." The Prime Minister says that the memorandum starts:

"1. The Canadians must be pushed into join the OAS.
2. The Canadians must be pushed into something else. . .
3. The Canadians must be pushed in another direction. . ."

The Prime Minister said that the document came into his possession a few days after the President left, through External Affairs, under circumstances with which he was not familiar, but his understanding was that it had been given by someone to External Affairs. The Prime Minister said that this authoritative statement of the intention of the United States to "push" Canada would be used by him to demonstrate that he himself, was the only leader capable of preventing United States domination of Canada. . .

As you can imagine, I was not silent throughout this extraordinary disquisition. I should note that the Prime Minister was physically tired from a return early that morning from an exhausting and frustrating whistle-stop campaign in Newfoundland, and uneasy over his self-confessed inability to put together a speech for his keynote address at London tonight, which he said, must set the tone for his entire campaign. He was excited to a degree disturbing in a leader of an important country, and closer to hysteria than I have seen him, except on one other possible occasion. Nevertheless, he interjected from time to time expressions of confidence on the outcome of the election and was willing to hear me out on my interjections and my closing summation.

Diefenbaker and the People

PETER C. NEWMAN

> *After a Cabinet revolt and a defeat in the House of Commons, Prime Minister John Diefenbaker was badly wounded. His election campaign in 1963 almost brought off a miracle.*

Diefenbaker's first tour of the campaign was scheduled as a whistle-stop journey through the Prairies. His train pulled out of Ottawa's Union Station, shortly after midnight on February 28. The next morning, at his first trainboard press conference, he was asked: "Have you given any thought to appearing on television with your competitors?" Diefenbaker glared at his inquisitor, and replied: "I *have* no competitors." It was a bold beginning for a politician who only three weeks before had very nearly been overthrown by his own followers.

Between Winnipeg and Saskatoon, Diefenbaker was scheduled to leave his train only at Melville, Watrous, and Semans, where local Tory organizers were set to produce sizable advance crowds. But the timetable had to be changed when word of his tour got around, and people began spontaneously to gather on station platforms at Ituna, Nokomis, and other flag stops. The local station agents advised the campaign caravan of the crowds, asking Diefenbaker at least to wave as his train went by. Instead, the Prime Minister ordered the train to halt at every stop.

The inhabitants of the flat, sad little towns turned out by the hundreds in the March chill to pay deference to their champion. As Diefenbaker strode the station platforms, shaking hands and patting shoulders, a scramble of adoring children followed his every move.

During his six years in office, John Diefenbaker had been discredited by most of the people who could be said to belong to Canada's Establishment. But he knew no matter how the nation might pretend it had become a great trading force or an arbiter of significance in the cold war, that the real source of political power in Canada still lay close to the soil.

Let the dwellers in the sophisticated world of the cities and suburbs deride him. Now, he was coming home to the people he understood and who understood him. When he told a cluster of his supporters, as he did at Duck Lake, Saskatchewan, "They say I've made mistakes, you know. But they've been mistakes of the heart," his audience knew exactly what he meant. "I'm going across this nation," he told them, "and I'm going to look into the face of Canada, to meet the people, to carry a message of hope. . . The last time, I flew over the people. This time, I'm down on the ground with you. I'm not asking for the support of the powerful, the strong, and the mighty, but of the average Canadian, the group to which *I* belong."

The Murder of an Assassin, 1963

PETER WORTHINGTON

Dallas, Texas—Justice, Texas-style, caught up with Lee Oswald in a dimly-lit Dallas police underground garage yesterday.

I stood barely a yard away from the alleged assassin of President Kennedy, when a grief-enraged owner of a striptease joint lunged past police guards and fired a .38 caliber snub-nose revolver into his left side.

Detective Roy Lowry, standing beside me, lunged forward to grapple with the man—Jack Ruby (real name Rubenstein).

Ruby fought desperately to shoot Oswald, 24, again, but he was smothered by policemen. For a moment no one paid any attention to Oswald, who crumpled to the pavement clutching his side and shrilly sobbing "oh . . . oh . . . oh."

He died 90 minutes later in Parkland Hospital—a few feet from where President Kennedy died 48 hours earlier and about the same time of day.

Jack Ruby: the bachelor owner of a rock and roll nightclub and a striptease bar, has admitted he shot the man.

Dallas policeman P.T. Dean said Ruby told him he shot Oswald out of concern for Mrs. Kennedy. Dean said Ruby did not want Mrs. Kennedy to go through the ordeal of returning to Dallas and testifying at Oswald's trial.

Police quoted Ruby as saying: "I didn't want to be a hero—I did it for Jacqueline Kennedy."

Henry Wade, Dallas county district attorney, filed murder charges against Ruby and said he would ask for the death penalty when he presents his case to the Grand Jury.

"A second assassination doesn't help (justify) the first one," he said. "I will seek the death penalty for Ruby even if he pleads guilty because shooting a handcuffed man deserves the death penalty."

One of Ruby's four attorneys said they planned to enter a plea of temporary insanity. He was emotionally upset because he admired the President, he said.

The drama started when Oswald was to be transferred to county jail by a bank armored car that was parked at the underground garage exit.

"Here he comes," someone shouted on the other side of the driveway where TV cameras, photographers, and most newsmen and police were gathered.

Oswald, preceded by sheriffs in cowboy hats, suddenly came through the doors. He was handcuffed and had chains on his wrists. He looked into my eyes briefly but intently. He was white-faced, tight-lipped and held his head high and defiantly. I noticed a bruise on his right forehead.

There was a bustling and shoving across the driveway. No one seemed to notice a stocky man with a hat pulled low over his eyes who suddenly lunged at Oswald. Seemingly from nowhere a gun appeared in his outstretched arm.

At first I thought he was a newsman, trying to ask a question. I heard someone (Detective Bill Combest, as it turned out) yell: "Jack, you son of a bitch you . . ." and the rest was drowned in the hollow boom of a gun shot.

The next moments were like a dream. I don't think Oswald even saw his attacker. His face was contorted as he sank clutching his stomach and emitting those dreadful sobs.

I stared through a forest of police legs and could see his feet kicking feebly.

The assailant was bustled inside. Det. Lowry grabbed Oswald's shoulders, others grabbed his legs and half-dragged him and carried him back inside. Oswald was now a greenish color. His eyes were open and rolling.

There was no blood on the spot—only the fedora of the gunman lying upside down. The initials J.R. could be seen.

Nearly 100 security police began dashing frantically about afterwards. People were grabbed, white bone-handled revolvers were loosened in studded and decorated holsters, and people were indiscriminately held for questioning.

Two TV cameramen were seized, suspected of smuggling the man in. Lt. R.E. Swain took my eye-witness version of what happened, then let me go.

"We Were Afraid"

"God, we were afraid what might happen," growled Capt. O.A. Jones. He cursed with frustrated enthusiasm, and said an anonymous phone caller had tipped them off. "We don't want any policemen hurt, but we're going to get that son of a. . ." the caller said.

Hence the armored car and security precautions, however no one asked me for identification or stopped me from walking freely everywhere, prior to the shooting. . .

An ambulance screamed into the garage. Seconds later Oswald appeared for the second time that morning. This time his face was the grey color of cement; his dark sweater was tugged back, exposing his torso.

I saw the bullet hole—neat, bloodless and ringed with black powder burn. It was in his ribs directly below his heart.

His hand dragged along the ground from his stretcher, and his head lolled sideways. He looked dead, yet there were wheezing noises coming from him.

"We asked him if he had anything he wanted to say—but he just shook his head," said Det. B.H. Combest. No deathbed confession from Oswald.

Policemen began to yell frantically because the armored car was still on the ramp, blocking the ambulance.

"Let's do something right men . . . move that damn thing," shouted an officer in a tan stetson.

The ambulance tires shrieked, sirens howled and Oswald was gone.

Soon Dead

I looked at my watch. It was 11:25 a.m. Barely five minutes had passed since Oswald had first appeared. By 1:07 p.m. Oswald would be dead, his vital organs smashed and scrambled by the point-blank blast. . . .

Vengeance strikes swiftly and deadly in Texas.

Mr. Chrétien Comes to Ottawa

JEAN CHRÉTIEN

In April 1963, at the age of twenty-nine, I was elected to the House of Commons as part of a minority Liberal government under Lester "Mike" Pearson. Members of Parliament may have lost prestige in recent times, but for them and their families getting elected is always a very emotional moment. Despite the cruelties of political life, we all take some joy and pride in that moment. I had been to Ottawa a couple of times before, once for the Liberal convention at which Lester Pearson was elected leader, but I remember first walking under the Peace Tower as an MP. I was moved, thinking of my mother, who had died when I was twenty; but I was pleased that my father's dream of having a politician in the family had come true at last.

Ottawa was a very English town in 1963. Very little French was spoken, except by security guards, waitresses, and maintenance men. French Canadians felt strange there, as if it wasn't our national capital at all. Slowly we began to change that. The arrival of a number of very rural, unilingual Créditistes made a difference. Though rather uneducated, they were quite articulate and not shy in complaining about the lack of French services. Liberals and even some Tories made similar noises, and Pearson was sympathetic. Once he said to me, "The biggest mistake we ever made in Canada was when Queen Victoria chose Ottawa over Montreal as the capital. It was a bad move because it made the capital an English city." He was determined to correct that mistake, and we made gradual progress. All sorts of services became available in both languages, and more people insisted on speaking French at work and around town. The city's character has changed completely now.

When I arrived I hardly spoke any English. I could read it a bit but communicating and understanding were very difficult. I was determined to learn, however. Since there were no language teachers on Parliament Hill, I had to develop by myself. One way was to read *Time* and *Newsweek* thoroughly every week, which also helped me learn about American issues. I kept a dictionary at hand and I got assistance on pronunciation from my wife, who was bilingual. I often joke that I resolved to learn English so that I wouldn't feel inferior to Aline, but as soon as I became functionally bilingual she learned Spanish. She has a great facility for languages, she speaks four now, and she found me a poor student.

The more practical and enjoyable way was to become friends with many of the anglophone parliamentarians, guys such as Rick Cashin from Newfoundland, Ron Basford from British Columbia, and Donald Macdonald and "Mo" Moreau from Toronto. They all went on to highly successful careers: Cashin as head of the fishermen's union in New-foundland, Basford as Minister of Justice, Macdonald as Minister of Finance, and Moreau as president of a mining company. Moreau was particularly helpful. He had been French-speaking in his youth but had become anglicized later on, so I helped him learn back his French and he helped me with my English. We were part of a group of ambitious young mavericks who used to meet regularly, usually in Rick Cashin's office. Cashin was a lively Newfoundlander whom we called "Prime Minister" because he supplied the booze. I didn't drink—that was one of the promises I had made to my wife when I went into politics—but I spent hours listening to the talk in order to improve my English. For a long while I never knew whether they were laughing at me when they were making jokes, but I picked up new words and I was never shy about try-ing out my English. That led to many funny incidents.

Once there was a big argument between Cashin and Gerry Regan, a Liberal MP from Halifax who became Premier of Nova Scotia and later a Trudeau cabinet minister, about whether Newfoundland or Nova Scotia produced the best lobsters. So I was called upon to be a judge at a party at the Cashins'. There was a lot of white wine that night so nobody cared about who won. The talk was all about politics, and since most of the guests were from the Maritimes, the talk was all in English. Someone asked me how I had won my riding in spite of the huge Créditiste majority of the previous election. I answered falteringly.

"Work hard, vary hard," I said. "I went to all the fact-or-ies and I shaked hands with every-body. Sometimes when the work was finish at five o'clock, the man and the woman were passing by so fast that I did not have the time to shake their hand, so I just touched them on the *bras.*" Of course I meant "arms." Everyone roared with laughter. "So that's how you won your election, you damn Frenchman!" they said.

Another time I was asked about Claude Ryan, then the editor of *Le Devoir*. "Vary important," I said. "Every politician read him. He love to be consulted and he give good advice. But he can be a little bit pompous. When you are in the presence of Mr. Ryan, you feel you are in front of a bishop. You almost have to put your knee on the floor and kiss his *bague.*" The word "bague" had come into my head instead of "ring." People were laughing so hard that I couldn't continue speaking, but I didn't know what I had said that was so funny.

I still have problems in English. There are mistakes that I made at the beginning and I haven't been able to shake them. But many Canadians are very sympathetic. They have followed my progress on television and in speeches over the years and that has given them a rapport with me. "You were pretty bad last year, but you're getting better," they used to say to me on the street and in airports, or "I understood everything you said tonight."

I went to a language teacher for a while. She corrected me on my grammar and my pronunciation mostly. "You should learn to say 'Japan' and not 'Chapan'" and so on. One day I asked her to help me with my accent, but she refused. "Never," she said. "When I turn on the radio and you're speaking, I know it's you and the rest of Canada knows it's you. You have to keep it." That's often led me to say that Maurice Chevalier and I had to practise to keep our French accent in English. It has become a kind of trademark.

Welcoming the Queen to Québec City

BLAIR FRASER

The Queen arrived next morning. Instead of going in to watch her inspect the guard of honor (a ritual which took place inside the big freight and Customs shed, thus screened from public view), I stood outside by the steel fence behind which about four hundred people had gathered to greet her. They raised a rather squeaky cheer as she came down the gangplank—not very loud, but almost as loud as the one at the same spot in Charlottetown four days before.

While the arrival ceremonies went on, I talked to the Mountie on duty at the gate. He told me about the security precautions. All the *real* security measures, the steps to protect the Queen from actual harm, were the work of the R.C.M.P. They had searched, with dogs, the wooded bank along the Queen's route to make sure that no Lee Oswald was hiding there with a rifle. They had checked every window that looked out on the route, and stationed men in many of them. They had binoculars trained on the crowd for every instant of the Queen's procession. All these things were done so unobtrusively that the R.C.M.P. was by far the least noticeable force on duty. The R.C.M.P.'s instructions were to pay no attention to placard-carriers or demonstrators so long as they were orderly, to use force only to make arrests or in self-defence, and in no circumstances to inflict injury on anyone. Unfortunately the Quebec City police seem to have had different instructions.

There were four major encounters between the city police and the crowd during the day, and every one took place in the absence of the Queen. Her personal security was not involved in any of them. All that she saw or heard, if anything, was a crowd chanting slogans such as "Québec aux québécois" and, on two or three brief occasions, shouting "boo" and "Elisabeth chez vous". A few young men turned their backs as the Queen's car went by. They were certainly very rude, and their parents must have felt ashamed of them, but they never offered or even threatened any violence.

It was after the Queen had passed (or, in one instance, at a place she never went near) that the Quebec City police charged into the crowd with clubs swinging. This was the only violence of the day. Nobody attacked the police and few even tried to defend themselves—mostly they ran, or tried to run, with the police beating them from behind.

I watched one incident from beginning to end, from a distance never greater than ten yards. A constable set upon a tall young man, about six foot five and wearing a Berber wool hat, who had been rather conspicuous among the chanting crowd, though he hadn't actually done anything. The constable hit him from behind, then half-prodded, half-hustled him down a side street. Two other constables joined the first. Together, they pushed the young man against a garage door and all three beat him with their clubs. The young man had a notebook in his hand. I heard him cry out, "I'm an American—I have my passport." The three constables paid no heed, but continued beating him. Finally two more constables came up; the five pushed the young man into a police car with a few farewell thumps, and he was taken away.

Other reporters saw, and in several cases photographed, dozens of similar assaults. Some were hit themselves, and painfully though not seriously hurt. The effect was one that we'd have thought impossible a few hours before—sympathy for the young demonstrators who, rude and ill-behaved though they were, had certainly not provoked this sort of treatment. There were enough policemen on duty to have arrested the entire crowd, one by one, without striking a blow, but the police didn't seem much interested in making arrests. Their object was to hit people, and they achieved it.

Another object which they didn't intend, but which they also achieved, was to create a scapegoat for Quebec's shame and embarrassment over the whole affair.

Nobody could possibly have felt proud of the boorish young separatists. Even those who agreed with their politics could only have deplored their manners to a royal guest whom the elected premier of Quebec had cordially invited. It's a commonplace to say that although the separatists are still a minority they include the leaders of French Canada's youth; if so, they certainly don't look it. It is hard to imagine any people following these singularly unattractive young men.

But however preposterous they may look as leaders, they did look pathetic as victims of police brutality. To watch two or three men armed with heavy clubs, all engaged in beating one smaller who is not armed, is a very ugly sight. So now it is the police who are denounced and whose behavior is investigated while the separatists emerge, by inference at least, as martyrs in the eyes of their own people. Quebeckers may not realize how little this sentiment is shared by the hundreds of observers from outside, who saw what actually went on.

The harsh truth is that on that dreary Saturday, every aspect of Quebec looked bad. The separatists looked like bad little boys. The police looked like brutes. The authorities, seemingly unable to control either the one or the other, looked weak and irresolute. Even the people, who were said to be "afraid" to put out flags or turn out in large numbers to welcome the Queen, looked something less than brave. Were they really intimidated by this unimposing handful of weedy, straggly-bearded youths? Or did they really share the sentiments and condone the behavior of the ill-mannered juveniles?

Leaving Montreal

DAVID BERCUSON

> *The Quiet Revolution in Québec saw French Canadians come to the fore in the province, some with bombs. The Front de Libération pour la Québec, which began bombings in the early 1960s and in 1964 killed its first victim, had a pronounced impact on Anglophone opinion.*

It changed not so much with the rise of separatism, but with the FLQ. I remember being in the Stanley tavern the night that Wilfrid O'Neill was killed at the Armoury, and somebody came running in saying that a bomb had just gone off about two blocks away. We all ran over and we got there before the police and fire department arrived, and it was all quite eerie.

I remember going home that night, saying I would probably not be in Quebec as an adult, that something would happen that would push me out, or that I would leave; and that would be the case with most of my friends. I remember this as distinctly as I have any recollection of my life, driving home that night and having this conversation with a friend, who also subsequently left Quebec. We did not equate what the FLQ was doing with the majority of the population, but we said to ourselves that here was a group of people who clearly believed that we must be disenfranchised, that we had no rights here. The nationalism of that movement was an ethnocentric nationalism. The rest of the country thinks it has created a post-nationalist nation or a pre-nationalist nation, but the FLQ was interested in creating a nationalist nation based on a certain ethnic identity. Even if I learned to be as fluently French as the premier of Quebec, I'd still be a Montreal Jew and I'd never be accepted as one of them. That was what the big change was.

Sex Scandal in Ottawa

ROBERT REGULY

*In 1966, stories of spies and sex in Ottawa absorbed Canadians. The key
to the story seemed to be one Gerda Munsinger who had had a relationship (or two) with cabinet ministers in the Diefenbaker government.
Munsinger was thought to be dead, but a reporter found her—and the
fat was in the fire.*

Munich—The girl Canada calls Olga Munsinger is alive and well.

Her real name is Gerda Munsinger. She is tall, blonde and shapely.

I found her in a chintzy flat in an affluent district of Munich, wearing
a gold September birthstone ring that was the gift of a former Canadian
cabinet minister.

I had a fifteen minute chat with her last evening and have just
returned from a longer discussion over lunch today.

I did not tell her of Justice Minister Lucien Cardin's statement yesterday that the girl at the centre of the 1961 sex-and-security case alleged
to involve Conservative cabinet ministers died of leukemia four years ago.

But I did say that her name had been mentioned in the House of Commons.

Immediately, she said: "Perhaps it's about Sevigny?"

Pierre Sevigny was Associate Minister of National Defence in the
Diefenbaker government.

Gerda said she had been his frequent companion in the years 1958,
1959 and 1960. That birthstone ring was a keepsake he bought for her in
Mexico.

She'd travelled in a twin-engine government plane with him to
Boston "for the races."

She'd visited his Beacon Arms Hotel suite in Ottawa. He'd visited her
apartment in Montreal.

Once "I attended an election banquet at the Windsor Hotel in Montreal. Diefenbaker was there and so were most of the cabinet."

Gerda said she also knew a second Conservative cabinet minister—
"very well."

One of her minister friends was once called in by "somebody in
Ottawa" for a warning to "go easy" on their relationship in public "because
an election was coming on."

I told Mrs. Munsinger, now a coffee shop manageress, that her name
was at the centre of Canada's biggest political storm in years as a result of
Cardin's statements.

She took the news calmly and said: "If the justice minister wants any
information, why doesn't he call me?

"You know where I live. If you can find me, surely he could."

She volunteered to come back to Canada to tell all she knew "if they keep pushing my name around in Canada."

Then, she seemed to have second thoughts.

She said she wanted physical protection if she returned to Canada to testify at any inquiry, expressing fears for her life from a Montreal businessman-racketeer.

At today's lunch, she apologized for having been slightly reticent at our first brief meeting last night.

She had been afraid, she said, that I might be an emissary from the racketeer in Montreal who she said "had good reason to keep me quiet."

Later, I asked her what she had to say about the charge that she had been a Communist spy. Without batting her long eyelashes, she answered: "If I were a spy, would I be working for a living?"

Then she turned to what she obviously found a more pleasant topic. She walked across the comfortable living room and came back—with a copy of the Social Register of Canada.

"I know and I can call many people in here. I tried to phone Sevigny last night in Montreal but he wasn't home."

She said she was once known as "Ricky" as well as Gerda by her Montreal friends.

She categorically denied that she had left Canada under pressure.

"No Mounties visited me before I left. I had been homesick for years for Munich and after I came back, intending a visit, I decided to stay."

She recalled her marriage to Mike Munsinger, an American GI who took his discharge in Germany. They were divorced in the 1950s.

Gerda remembered the date of her arrival in Canada as August 7, 1955.

She came aboard the Arosa Star, a ship which later became famous as the Yarmouth Castle when it burned in the Bahamas last August with heavy loss of life.

In Montreal she said she worked as a waitress and as a secretary.

Before returning to Germany she made a brief trip to Cali, Colombia in 1960. She intended to marry a newspaper heir but thought better of it and returned to Montreal.

She was born Gerda Hessler of Koensigburg, East Prussia, where her mother still lives. Gerda fled East Germany "as a refugee" in 1948—at the age of 19.

One year she was elected Miss Garmisch-Partenkirchen in a beauty queen contest in the Bavarian ski-resort town.

Friendly and uninhibited as she was in our first talk, Gerda Munsinger was waiting for her wealthy businessman boy friend, "Mr. Wagner."

Her still shapely figure dressed smartly in black dotted gray wool, her centre-parted hair curling long at the sides, she sat and eyed the clock; an attractive woman, though past the first bloom.

The Avenue Road-style one-bedroom apartment would cost around $175 a month in Toronto.

The furniture is attractive but rather heavy with fringe drapings.

A few months ago she was working as a waitress at a popular restaurant.

It was through the restaurant that I found her. And Gerda, storm centre that she is, was remarkably easy to find.

I was at the door of her apartment within three hours of my landing at Munich Airport.

I went straight to the coffee bar where, I had learned, she had been a waitress in mid-1965. The proprietor scratched his head. Yes, he remembered the street, but the number . . . no, he couldn't be sure.

He gave me the two numbers he thought most likely. At the first I tried, a smart, four-storey apartment building, it was there on the wall of the foyer—G. MUNSINGER, in capital letters on a neat nameplate. But no one answered the buzzer.

I stood on the sidewalk, watching the blondes go in. One . . . two . . . three . . . any one of them could have been the mystery girl.

At 6:45 (12:45 Toronto time) I pressed the buzzer again. A girl's voice called "herein, bitte."

I went on up, saw her in her doorway and said "Gerda Munsinger?" She said "yes." I identified myself and asked if I could talk to her.

She agreed—but even then she was apologizing for having so little time.

She answered the questions she wanted to answer and left me to guess the rest.

And the rest was plenty.

The Trudeau Phenomenon, 1968

RON HAGGART AND VAL SEARS

> *Pierre Trudeau, first elected to parliament in 1965, won a Liberal Party leadership convention in April 1968 and became prime minister. How did this relative unknown capture the country and the party?*

Ottawa—In his secluded house near the embassies of Rockcliffe Park, the prime minister-designate of Canada asked for a steak, cooked rare to his order, sipped a glass of wine and savored the last few moments of the delights of being a private man.

Three miles away in downtown Ottawa, the crowds filled two ballrooms of the Skyline hotel. They broke in through a fire exit and marched up the back stairs, they filled the lobby save for a narrow corridor across the gold broadloom, they spilled out through the glass doors to the driveway under the porte-cochere. Even a line of punching policemen had trouble getting through.

Only half-an-hour before, Pierre Elliott Trudeau had said: "There will be some action at the Skyline tonight, and I'll be there." In the new age of expectation Trudeau had created, that was enough to bring out the crowds.

At the house in Rockcliffe which Trudeau had borrowed from a friend, it was quiet enough to hear the pop of the champagne cork when those who had been with him from the start drank him a toast.

The start had been such a recent thing that some in the house could count their friendship by the weeks. They had in the space of four months turned a pleasant and impossible idea into a prime minister of Canada.

First Question

One tiny seed had been planted in November when most of the provincial premiers of Canada met in what was to become the Safari room bar of the Toronto Dominion centre. From Ottawa, Marc Lalonde came to Toronto to watch the premiers at work; a onetime professor of constitutional law and then a government policy adviser, he was one of only two men with an appointment to see the prime minister every day.

Lalonde said to Ramsay Cook, a Toronto history professor and writer on French-Canada: "What would you think of Trudeau as prime minister?"

"I couldn't think of anything better," Cook replied. A few weeks later, Cook mailed back his membership card in the New Democratic Party and joined in what appeared sometimes to be a hopeless Children's Crusade to convince a man few had ever heard of to run for a job he said he didn't want.

In Montreal, Jean Pierre Goyer, a 35-year-old MP who had made a name for himself as a student fighter of Duplessis, said to Trudeau one day that he should run for the Liberal leadership.

"Jamais," Trudeau replied.

But Goyer told him: "En politique, on ne dit jamais jamais."

The man who said "never" was being discussed quietly as a future prime minister in the summer of last year; he was being urged as a serious candidate in November and December; it was not until mid-January that Trudeau himself took it seriously; it was mid-February when he announced his intention, and seven weeks later he was prime minister-designate of Canada.

The fire had many spontaneous origins in many parts of the country. Many people high and low found themselves coming to the same conclusion at the same time, but reserving their judgments, reluctant to expose their naivete with such an absurd but beautiful idea.

In the late summer of last year, 30-year-old Gordon Gibson, one of the Ottawa corps of bright ministerial assistants, came to the conclusion that Pierre Trudeau was not the curious fellow he'd first imagined after seeing his picture in Weekend magazine wearing a yellow turtleneck sweater and red polkadot scarf.

Criminal Code

He had a beer with Marc Lalonde in the Jasper lounge of the Chateau Laurier and the two men agreed that Trudeau would make a great prime minister.

Trudeau had been minister of justice only since April, but he had been given a surprising amount of responsibility: He had introduced the divorce reform bill and the wholesale rewriting of the Criminal Code. He had therefore come quickly to public attention and had appeared on such television shows as the Public Eye, Twenty Million Questions and Newsmagazine.

Decisions to the order in which legislation shall be introduced are made by the Prime Minister himself with the help of policy advisers such as Lalonde; the minister of justice achieved in a few months a fame which his predecessors achieved only through scandal.

When the House of Commons adjourned for the 1967 Christmas recess, Gordon Gibson let it be known he wanted to meet Trudeau. He came away from his meeting not entirely discouraged, but believing that Trudeau wasn't interested in becoming prime minister.

In Montreal, in the last months of 1967, a group of young Liberals, including Goyer, Claude Frenette, Harold (Sunny) Gordon and others had been discussing the need to reorganize the stagnant federal wing of the Liberal party in Quebec. They believed that a legacy of oldtime politics left behind by Lionel Chevrier and Guy Favreau meant sure disaster in the next federal election.

Petition Plan

They were not formed originally to campaign for Pierre Trudeau, but when Lester Pearson announced his retirement on Dec. 14, the group was already in existence, a natural amalgamation of young Turks looking for a Quebec candidate of stature.

In Toronto, Ramsay Cook phoned his friend William Kilbourn, an author, also a professor, and academic workhorse of the Liberal party, in Rosedale. Almost 20 years before, when Kilbourn was on a footloose European jaunt, he had encountered Pierre Trudeau in Belgrade, Yugoslavia. Kilbourn wrote in his diary that he had talked for hours with the most fascinating Canadian he'd ever met.

Cook proposed that they send a petition to universities across Canada, to academic people who would recognize Trudeau's name, urging him to run for the Liberal leadership. They decided to launch the petition at the annual pre-Christmas cocktail party given by Macmillan, the book publishers. Many well-known writers would be there.

A message came to Cook from Pierre Trudeau that he would prefer them not to do it. He didn't want to see his friends sticking their necks out.

Then Marc Lalonde encouraged Cook to carry on despite what Trudeau himself had to say about it. The first signature on Kilbourn's copy of the petition was Pierre Berton. Eventually, about 400 from the English community and 200 from the French community signed copies of the petition and sent them to Trudeau.

Gordon Gibson went to Montreal to meet the group which had begun as young Turks trying to capture the Quebec wing of the federal-party and who were, by early in the year, a campaign nucleus for Trudeau. Gibson discussed with them the idea of opening a Trudeau campaign office in Ottawa.

Gloomy First Days

Trudeau himself was frantically busy at this time and to see him, Gibson had to fly to Toronto, where Trudeau was visiting Premier Robarts. Trudeau asked him not to open an office in Ottawa, using the same phrase that he didn't think his friends should stick their necks out.

"But what if we want to open it anyway," Gibson persisted.

"I don't think you should do it, but if you do, don't tell me about it," Trudeau told him.

In January, an office was quietly opened in an unprepossessing building on O'Connor St. in Ottawa. Into it moved Gordon Gibson, Jim Davey, a 37-year-old Montreal businessman, and Pierre Levaseur, secretary of the federal party in Quebec.

The first days were gloomy: They couldn't afford a cleaning service and cigarette butts littered the floor. They had no typists, the men answered the phones themselves. When they did hire a girl to answer the phone, she said discreetly "237-6460." The man for whom they were organizing was not yet a candidate.

The petition organized by Cook, Kilbourn and others in Toronto had gone well but Cook had deliberately tried to keep news of it away from the press. He wanted it to be a sincere and private expression of support from scholars Trudeau would respect.

But the petition was soon reported in the columns of Peter Newman of The Toronto Star and George Bain of the Globe and Mail. "This turned out to be the most important impact of the petition," Cook recalls.

A series of important and well-publicized conferences then came along in rapid succession. At the end of January, the Quebec wing of the federal party met in Montreal. It was a personal triumph for Trudeau and for the group who had organized the new wave a few months before.

The man who had been for 16 years the party's full-time secretary in Quebec lost his job. Trudeau's enemies were defeated in the elections for party positions.

The federal leadership candidates were prohibited from addressing the convention, they had to haunt the lobby and hospitality rooms of the Hotel Bonaventure to find hands to shake.

Poke at de Gaulle

But Trudeau was invited to join a panel discussion. His friends built an illuminated screen which sat on the stage beside him; down one side of the screen were listed all the options for Quebec, from separatism to absolute monarchy, and across the top were subjects such as economics and independence. The chart, and Trudeau's speech, proved that federalism was best for Quebec.

Trudeau took a poke at Charles de Gaulle for trying to give Canada a new constitution; the advice came, Trudeau said, from a country that had run through 17 constitutions in 180 years. They cheered, and one terrible doubt was removed: Pierre Trudeau could win support from Liberals in Quebec.

The Montreal meeting was the turning point. Before that convention, Gibson recalled, "it was still fun, it was still just an exercise. Then it took on a serious context."

Trudeau came to the Ontario Liberal Convention in February and was mobbed. He was carried on the shoulders of delegates at the Royal York Hotel and one woman cried "we need you, Pierre."

With less emotion but equal conviction, three men told Trudeau the same thing in his hotel room, Alderman Charles Caccia, Tim Reid, MPP, and Robert Stanbury, the MP for York-Scarborough.

At about the same time, the "Ontario-for-Trudeau committee" was organized by a number of MPs and some of them began to fly to the Maritimes and to the West, sounding out influential Liberals on the subject of Trudeau.

The dominion-provincial conference on constitutional problems followed quickly in mid-February. This was the point in time for which his Montreal friends had been waiting; he had to negotiate with the premiers as the minister of justice, not as a potential prime minister and rival.

On thousands of TV screens, Trudeau appeared at the Prime Minister's right hand.

Two Questions

He had shown his flexibility on Quebec problems in Montreal, now he penetrated into living-rooms across the country with clarity previously unknown in this tangled arena—he told them the premier of Quebec was not the only spokesman for French Canadians; the Prime Minister of Canada spoke for all Canadians, English or French.

Those who deserved special consideration were French-Canadian people, not French-Canadian politicians.

When Trudeau met from time to time with those who were now campaigning openly for him, he asked two questions: Am I a big enough man for the job? If I did enter the race, would it be a good thing for Quebec and for the country?

With the constitutional conference over, Trudeau met at the Chateau Laurier with those who had started it all. They assured Trudeau that he was not a "regional" candidate; the Montreal meeting plus the trips of MPs Russell Honey and Donald MacDonald showed that there were Trudeau fans across the country.

Trudeau went for a long walk by himself that night and the next day made his announcement. The phone girl at 124 O'Connor St. began for the first time to answer the phone, "Pierre Elliott Trudeau."

Jim Davey, the Montreal businessman, wrote a memo outlining the campaign tactics which would be followed faithfully to the last crucial minute on April 6. Their campaign would be run without attacking other candidates or inflicting wounds; they would avoid the gimmickry of politics and show their man to as many people as they could.

Thus, on the Friday night of the convention, no hired band paraded through the auditorium, as for Hellyer and Martin, no tricks were attempted (as with the snowballs which were tossed to the audience as Robert Winters ended his speech). With only a line of pretty hostesses before and after, he walked from his box to the speakers' rostrum.

92 Votes

Two days before, he had returned to Ottawa in a private parlor car from Montreal. He sat at a table in the car called Joie de Vivre and Tim Porteous helped him meld two versions of his speech into one.

As they rolled into Ottawa Union Station, they were all in a lighthearted mood. "We thought we had 800 votes on the first ballot," said one of those in the car, "but we had butterflies all the same." (It was to be 752 on the first ballot.)

Then, on the fourth ballot it was 1203, just 92 votes more than his opponents. The new Prime Minister went to his borrowed home in Rockcliffe, took a shower, had his steak and wine, and avoided the crowds at the Skyline Hotel when his car was driven into the underground garage.

In the International ballroom of the hotel he stood before the throng and cried: "We have a big party here tonight, but we have a bigger party, the Liberal party. On Monday morning we have to go back to school, back to Parliament and back to work."

Upstairs in the vice-regal suite, a diverse group of guests awaited him; they included Senator Maurice Lamontagne and David DePoe, the Yorkville hippie. Canada, in some four months, had produced a new Prime Minister and a new kind of Prime Minister.

October 1970: The Murder of Pierre Laporte

CLAUDE RYAN

In October 1970, the Front de la libération de Québec kidnapped James Cross, the British trade commissioner in Montreal, and Québec labour minister Pierre Laporte. The federal government put the War Measures Act into force and troops onto the streets.

Two weeks after the act that opened the Cross-Laporte drama, the confusion that has surrounded this tragic story, far from being dissipated, has only grown more profound. The kidnappings had at first seemed like an unusual drama that we persisted in believing would end well. Since the terrible nights of Saturday and Sunday, there can be no doubt about the seriousness of these events. The first acts of the drama assailed us as never before. All of that was nothing. The cruel assassination of Pierre Laporte has struck us like a blade, cutting without pity into what we hold most sacred, with a cold-bloodedness that arouses revulsion and horror.

The most serious aspect of the assassination of Pierre Laporte is not that he fell beneath the blows of his aggressors. In the United States, for example, more than one public figure has fallen to aggressors. But whereas the assassination of Mr. Kennedy was based, from all appearances, on obscure personal motives, that of Mr. Laporte was political. Its authors give it not only an ethical justification, but they threaten to repeat it. And it seems they can rely, towards this end, on a greater support, be it partial or indistinct, than we would have suspected.

The exclusive recourse to protective measures and manhunts will settle nothing in the long run. For every citizen we may find guilty of a crime, we risk creating, if discretionary powers are badly used, two, three, five citizens irritated by having had their rights denied. This could, if we are not careful, increase a certain climate of desperation which is not unusual in the emergence of a phenomenon such as the FLQ. The grave times through which Québec is living bring into question whether we wish it or not, the political system and the socio-economic structural order which we have lived in the past decade. Problems this serious (and this widespread) do not spring up spontaneously. They grow in appropriate soil. It is more important than ever during this crisis that citizens give full support to the reasonable decisions of their legitimate political leaders and that they even accord the benefit of the doubt in instances when complete explorations cannot be immediately provided. But it is equally important that political leaders become humbly aware of the fragility of their leadership and act without delay to consolidate their leadership by associating with it those, from various milieux, whose social influence and moral authority are of another form, not less vital but often disdained by political powers, of democratic leadership. At this moment, it is not the prestige or authority of any individual but democracy in Québec that must be safeguarded. That is the goal to which we must hold through the difficulties of this unprecedented night of darkness through which Québec is living.

Canada vs. the USSR: Hockey War

JACK LUDWIG

In 1972, Canada's best played against the Soviet Union in a contest that Canadians expected to be a walkover. Instead, the struggle was excruciatingly close. The Canadians won the series in the last seconds of the final game.

So, finally, it was here. We filed into the Forum like small kids anxious to get first crack at Santa Claus. Team Canada came out on the ice in their dazzling bright red uniforms with a huge white sunburst maple leaf disappearing down their fronts. The fans cheered loudest for the Montreal Canadiens on the team—building up to "high" for Yvan Cournoyer, a little restrained for Pete Mahovlich and Guy Lapointe, then "higher" for Frank Mahovlich, and deafeningly "highest" for Ken Dryden. Everyone was in a good mood. Even Prime Minister Trudeau, walking the red carpet to where the ceremonial puck was to be dropped, got a hand.

Almost as soon as Mr. Trudeau got back to his seat, after the national anthem was sung, silently in French, and falteringly in English, Team Canada did exactly what we all expected. Gary Bergman got the puck to Frank Mahovlich who passed it onto Phil Esposito's stick and poof— Canada was leading, 1–0, and only 30 seconds had passed. At that rate of scoring Canada would win 120–0.

But when at 1:03 Paul Henderson was called for tripping, the USSR team began to look *formidable*. Twice they got off shots that Dryden had to be good on. They didn't score, but something was quite evident. In races for the puck, they won. When a Team Canada player and a USSR player banged together the Soviet guy barely budged and the Team Canada man frequently bounced back. Ron Ellis went charging into a Soviet player whose head was seemingly down, hit what felt like a concrete pillar, and himself went down. At 6:32, however, Henderson caught USSR goaler Vladislav Tretiak nodding, and banged home a pass from Bobby Clarke. This made it 2–0. At that rate, Team Canada could only win by 10–0, a sudden drastic drop. Five minutes later, the USSR did the impossible—they put a puck past Ken Dryden.

At 11:40, a big stoop-shouldered hard-skating left winger, Aleksandr Yakushev, took a pass from Vladimir Shadrin and set up Evgeni Zimin: Dryden was *beaten*. His defence was nowhere. His forwards were being outskated, outhustled and outgunned.

A pall settled over the Forum. Team Canada so obviously lacked spark. Even explosive Yvan Cournoyer looked slow. At 17:19 Aleksandr Ragulin tripped Brad Park. Team Canada coach Harry Sinden sent out Park, Seiling and the highest-scoring line in NHL history, Ratelle, Hadfield, Gilbert. Gilbert clumsily fanned on the puck, Boris Mikhailov shot into the clear, passed to Vladimir Petrov and, unbelievably, the score was *tied*.

We could not believe what we were seeing. The USSR had more cool, better puck control, better recovery. Their goalie, when tested, showed incredible skill and command. *Tretiak*. The man, we realized, was young enough to be playing in *junior* hockey in Canada.

The crowd sat in silence: when the organist tried to get the usual NHL response to a fight, or go Canada go, the cheers were chokingly unenthusiastic. Almost no sound and even less fury. In front of TV sets fans watched in horror. Not only Canadians but Americans who believed, with us, that Team Canada was the greatest because the NHL was the greatest: hadn't Gerry Eskenazi, hockey reporter for the astute *New York Times*, said, "The NHL will slaughter them in eight straight"?

With less than three minutes to go in the second period the predicted "slaughter" began, but the victim was Team Canada: number 17, someone called Valeriy Kharlamov, stickhandled his way around the all-star defence as if he were playing against peewees, scored, and the USSR *was in the lead*! All of Team Canada looked terrible. Errant passes went skimming over the ice. Suddenly, "big leaguers" who couldn't catch up with a USSR guy tried, instead, to trip him or hack at him. Chippy bush play— from NHLers!

At 9:46 of the second period the Montreal crowd actually booed Team Canada—for icing the puck. By 10:18, when the USSR went ahead 4-2 on an incredibly fast wrist-shot release by that same Kharlamov, he was the man Montreal applauded. Kharlamov, and goalie Tretiak. At 17:50 of this same period Montreal's organist played "I'm Dreaming Of A White Christmas." A guy near the press box said, "Man, this makes the Stanley Cup pure sh——."

What was evident, by then, was not only the USSR's superb physical condition but its equally superb preparation: Bobrov and Kulagin said they had looked at films of 1971 and 1972 Stanley Cup play. They had obviously seen a lot. They came in on Dryden believing he could be *stickhandled around*, made to drop to the ice. A man his height—six feet four— had to have trouble handling low off the ice shots on his glove side.

The Montreal crowd came to life only once in the dreaded third period: when Bobby Clarke, assisted by Ron Ellis and Paul Henderson, scored. Team Canada looked alive and almost well. But at 13:32, Boris Mikhailov broke in on Dryden, drew him to one side, and lifted a backhand past him. It all looked so easy. Less than a minute later Evgeni Zimin took advantage of a Brad Park goof to make the score 6-3. With five minutes left the same people who had been dying to get into the Forum couldn't wait to get out. They were spared, as Dryden wasn't, Yakushev's backhand score and the mock cheers for Dryden that followed. They didn't hear the boos another Canadien, Guy Lapointe, got for what the crowd thought was a cheap shot at a Soviet player. Phil Esposito was booed for the same kind of chintzy play. At the buzzer Team Canada, led by Esposito, charged off the ice. Only three men—Ken Dryden, who had given up *seven* goals, Red Berenson, and Peter Mahovlich stayed around to congratulate the winners. Team Canada had not been told to line up to shake hands, Harry Sinden told me. Doug Fisher of Hockey Canada said it certainly had: the Montreal crowd took the omission to be willful. Its heroes had let the country down people said, even in deportment.

Canadian Pro-Americanism

GORDON SINCLAIR

In 1973, anti-Americanism in Canada was near its peak, thanks in large part to the Vietnam War. Not everyone shared this view of our neighbours.

This Canadian thinks it is time to speak up for the Americans as the most generous and possibly the least appreciated people on all the earth.

Germany, Japan and, to a lesser extent, Britain and Italy were lifted out of the debris of war by the Americans who poured in billions of dollars and forgave other billions in debts. None of these countries is today paying even the interest on its remaining debts to the United States.

When the franc was in danger of collapsing in 1956, it was the Americans who propped it up, and their reward was to be insulted and swindled on the streets of Paris. I was there. I saw it. When distant cities are hit by earthquakes, it is the United States that hurries in to help. This spring, 59 American communities were flattened by tornadoes. Nobody helped.

The Marshall Plan and the Truman Policy pumped billions of dollars into discouraged countries. Now newspapers in those countries are writing about the decadent, warmongering Americans. I'd like to see just one of those countries that is gloating over the erosion of the United States Dollar build its own airplane. Does any other country in the world have a plane to equal the Boeing Jumbo Jet, the Lockheed Tristar, or the Douglas 10? If so, why don't they fly them? Why do all the International lines except Russia fly American planes?

Why does no other land on earth even consider putting a man or woman on the moon? You talk about Japanese technocracy, and you get radios. You talk about German technocracy, and you get automobiles. You talk about American technocracy, and you find men on the moon—not once, but several times—and safely home again.

You talk about scandals, and the Americans put theirs right in the store window for everybody to look at. Even their draft-dodgers are not pursued and hounded. They are here on our streets, and most of them, unless they are breaking Canadian laws, are getting American dollars from ma and pa at home to spend here.

When the railways of France, Germany and India were breaking down through age, it was the Americans who rebuilt them. When the Pennsylvania Railroad and the New York Central went broke, nobody loaned them an old caboose. Both are still broke.

I can name you 5,000 times when the Americans raced to the help of other people in trouble. Can you name me even one time when someone else raced to the Americans in trouble? I don't think there was outside help even during the San Francisco earthquake.

Our neighbors have faced it alone, and I'm one Canadian who is damned tired of hearing them get kicked around. They will come out of this thing with their flag high. And when they do, they are entitled to thumb their nose at the lands that are gloating over their present troubles. I hope Canada is not one of those.

The Sinking of the Edmund Fitzgerald

DERIK HODGSON

Sault Ste. Marie, Mich.—The ore freighter Edmund Fitzgerald has sunk with all 29 hands believed lost. The U.S. coast guard offers little hope that anyone survived.

Freighters, Coast Guard cutters and aircraft that criss-crossed the eastern end of Lake Superior since late Monday found only an oil slick, shattered lifeboats, rubber rafts and broken flotation rings.

Capt. Charles Millradt of the U.S. Coast Guard said the water temperature was about 50 degrees Fahrenheit, and said the human body could not withstand that for long.

"Any hope we had is very dim now."

The ore carrier suddenly vanished from sight and radar at about 7 p.m. Monday as 75-mile-an-hour winds whipped up 25-foot waves on the lake.

Although much debris has been found, the searchers failed to find any bodies or parts of the ship. They said most of the debris was material that could have washed off the vessel.

A brief hope flared yesterday afternoon when the Coast Guard received reports that a man or body had been seen clinging to a log off the Canadian shore. This proved false.

Capt. Millradt, co-ordinating the search, said he believed the ship broached to, allowing the waves to strike it broadside, and it sank in 300 feet of water about 50 miles north-west of here.

The vessel fell victim to what fresh-water mariners here call the curse of the 11th month.

The gales of November can pile up mountainous waves, and it was 62 years ago almost to the day when a November storm shattered 71 ships on the Great Lakes, killing 248 men.

Monday night's storm was described by some local observers as the worst in 35 years.

The last sighting of the missing carrier occurred at 7:10 p.m. when the crew of the Arthur Anderson saw it ahead in the waves and on radar Then it vanished.

Shortly before the ship disappeared, the captain of the Fitzgerald asked the Anderson to shadow his ship because it was taking water and had lost several hold covers.

There was no other message, and no distress call was received.

The Anderson moored here late yesterday, and the shaken captain refused to talk to reporters.

Later, a tiny tug brought wreckage to the Coast Guard wharf and guardsmen hauled out the remains of life rings and a rubber dinghy with a cover. The dinghy was empty but the knives in the survival pouches were missing.

Freighters heading down the lakes yesterday stopped to take part in the search, and at one time there were eight lakers in line looking for signs of the Edmund Fitzgerald.

On the Canadian side, nine provincial policemen patrolled the rocky Superior coastline, picking up debris and searching for bodies. They found life-jackets and other objects from ships, but a police spokesman said there was nothing to link the debris to the missing freighter.

The ship apparently sank in U.S. waters, and the U.S. Coast Guard was the co-ordinating organization for the search.

The owners of the Fitzgerald identified its captain as E.R. McSorley, 62, Ontario-born but now of Toledo, and the chief engineer as George Holl of Cabot, Pa. The other 27 crew members, including a cadet sailor, will be identified after their families are notified.

The 729-foot freighter, which sailed out of Cleveland, was down-bound from Superior, Wis., to Detroit with 26,126 tons of taconite pellets.

It was owned by Northwestern Mutual Life Insurance Co. of Milwaukee and had been chartered by Oglebay Norton Co. of Cleveland.

The sinking was the first major Great Lakes shipping disaster in nine years. On Nov. 29, 1966, the lives of 28 men were lost when the freighter Daniel J. Morrell sank in a Lake Huron storm.

Olympic Architecture, Montreal, 1976

NICK AUF DER MAUR

*Montreal hosted the 1976 Summer Olympics in a series of architec-
turally stunning—but hugely costly—venues.*

In parliamentary committees, in public appearances and in private conversations, the Mayor consistently argued that the entire complex had to
be viewed as a whole. Nothing could be changed without altering the entire complex. Every line, every abutment, every minute detail—all were
part of an "artistic whole."

"Taillibert," the Mayor proclaimed, "is the kind of architect who
built the cathedrals of ancient times." (He failed to add that a remarkable
feature common to many of the great medieval French cathedrals is that
their towers were never completed.)

The architect designed a viaduct to allow athletes to cross over
Sherbrooke Street on their way from the Village to the Stadium. As with
everything else, he came up with an enormously complicated design.

It was an intricate 600-foot viaduct, supported by an inverted
triangular pillar system. It was originally costed at less than $5 million.
But because of structural design changes, an engineering firm later
reported to the Mayor that it would cost close to $9 million, an absurd
cost for a viaduct when one considers that some railroad level crossings
in Montreal have yet to be eliminated because at $2 million it is consid-
ered too expensive. Replacing the triangular supports on the Olympic
viaduct with straightforward pillars would in itself have saved $2 million.

When the engineers arrived at the new cost, they presented the
estimate to Mayor Drapeau at City Hall, expecting that he would order
changes and reductions. But the Mayor was annoyed at any such suggestions, saying, "I don't want a railway bridge." There was to be no economy,
and Atlas Construction was awarded the contract at cost plus a $500,000
fee.

The builders couldn't find any scaffolding in the city, because so much
of the area's materials, equipment and supplies were tied up in the Olympic
project, so they had to buy new scaffolding elsewhere for $1.5 million.

The intricacy of Taillibert's designs extended even to the cement
benches to be installed on the Sherbrooke Street viaduct. The plans were
so complicated that it took the carpenters a full night to unravel the mys-
teries of the geometry. The completed wood forms for the benches ended
up costing $400 a square yard, as compared with $30 or $40 on normal
construction jobs.

The final cost of the viaduct would be $14 million, well over twice
the amount Montreal spends on roads in the entire city each year.

Joe Who?

SANDRA GWYN

In 1976, the Progressive Conservative Party chose dark horse candidate Joe Clark from High River, Alberta, as leader.

Joe Clark and I are talking, over Air Canada ginger ale and butter tarts, on the way back to Ottawa from St. John's. He, for the past forty hours, has been hopping round the Avalon Peninsula, showing the flag for John Crosbie in the St. John's West by-election. I've been tagging after him with a notebook. For this precious, pre-arranged interview, I have in my lap a list of questions of the How-Exactly-Will-You-Save-The-Country? variety. I am not, however, looking at these questions. Instead, the interview has turned into an easy, old-shoe conversation, the kind that comes naturally to a couple of more-or-less contemporaries who discover they've quite a bit in common. The Leader and I are talking, for instance, about having grown up shy, bookish, with vague literary aspirations, and a total lack of eye-hand co-ordination in the era of sock hops, cheerleaders, and Big Men on Campus. About having been brought up Catholic, not being really serious about it anymore, but still liking to go to Mass for, as Clark puts it, "the sense of continuity." About liking Joni Mitchell, Wallace Stegner, and the one-liners in Tom Stoppard's plays, but not being able to get onto the same wavelength as rock music, Mel Brooks, or William Faulkner. About magazine writers—"If I weren't a politician," says Clark, "I think I could be a reasonably good one"—and about how our mutual idol in this regard is Joan Didion, that master of resonant, solemnly elegant prose. We talk about the sense of place in Didion's writing, her marvellous ability to evoke the spirit of California, and Clark is telling me about his own sense of place, about the foothills of Alberta which I have never seen; how once, driving back from Calgary to High River late at night when the chinook was blowing, he stopped the car and stood a long moment by the side of the road. "A moment," I suggest, "of pure happiness." "A moment," he corrects me, "of pure awe."

In the big hall next to the church in Witless Bay, just south of St. John's, Powers and O'Keefes and Keatings and Kavanaghs are getting up from hard, wooden chairs after listening to Clark's major speech of the trip. The provincial party official next to me is shaking his head. "I can't figure it out," he is saying. "Why didn't Joe tell them about meeting the Holy Father?"

At Witless Bay, as at Ferryland and St. Bride's and Trepassey, it's the ability to make the right connections that Clark is missing. Witless Bay is the southern shore, the heartland of Newfoundland Catholicism—hard ground, even in the era of ecumenicalism, for a Protestant candidate like

Crosbie. (They will tell you, down the shore, about the provincial candidate with a Scottish name and thereby, even though Catholic, suspect, who made his allegiance known by inserting an ad in the parish weekly: "Lost. Rosary Beads. Will finder please return to candidate, at Liberal headquarters.")

The Witless Bay rally is a challenge for Clark. This is also the heartland of Newfoundland oratory. James McGrath, MP for St. John's East, comes on in the manner of a Redemptorist priest giving a Holy Week retreat. "How many more fishermen must die needlessly," he bellows, pauses for effect, then shovels on the irony, with a sneer. "Before it dawns on Otto Lang and his bureaucrats that to put an efficient search-and-rescue operation in Newfoundland will indeed be 'cost-effective.'" Crosbie, jacket off, bright blue shirt damp, bawls off one-liners. "What will we send Pierre Trudeau on his fifty-seventh birthday? I know what we'll send him. Two-hundred-and-twenty pounds of John Carnell Crosbie wrapped up in blue ribbon and tissue paper. As for Otto the Buscatcher, as for Romeo LeBlanc and Juliet Jamieson, also known as Quiet Flows the Don,"— Crosbie is working the crowd like a yo-yo—"they scare me not a whit."

Clark does his leaden best. "Regional disparity is a national problem. Concern for regional problems must permeate national policy." Only once does he reach inside himself and out to the crowd. "The fire and brimstone of Jim McGrath and John Crosbie," he tells the audience, "are not lurking in my soul."

The style is the man himself, as Trudeau, once upon a time, liked to say. Clark's style is to have no style. "There isn't very much that excites me," he said earlier this year. "There are no social causes that move me to the point that I can't cope with them." Yet this is also the man who voted against capital punishment, against the spoken will of his constituents and who in a province where drunken Indian jokes are as common as Newfie jokes on Quebec radio, accords native people the same respect he accords women.

"What I owe my constituents," he explains, "is my own judgement." Talking to Clark, you're struck by his candour, his grave natural courtesy, and—something I've never remarked before in a politician—his almost total lack of ego. There are moments when he seems younger than he really is, when you get the impression of someone caught up in what the U.S. journalist Elizabeth Drew calls "the magnification process" and not quite able to cope with it. Yet the substance is there; it just hasn't had time to mature.

As the seat belt sign goes on, I finally get around to asking Clark the question that journalists always ask aspiring leaders: "What drives you?" Maybe Clark's been waiting for it. At any rate, the answer is crisp. "What drives me," he says, "is that this is the most interesting thing I could possibly think of doing. There's no sense of destiny about it. I distrust words like 'vision,' and 'grand design.' I expect to do no more than move the country forward on some priorities. Priorities that, as leader, it's entirely my responsibility to choose. I won't be able to eliminate the bitterness that's in the country. I won't be able to stop it. I believe, though, that I can help to heal it, by using my own consensual talents and by the accident of where I happen to come from."

The Gretzky Phenomenon

PETER GZOWSKI

Perhaps the greatest hockey player ever, Wayne Gretzky had some physiological advantages.

There is an unhurried grace to everything Gretzky does on the ice. Winding up for a slapshot, he will stop for an almost imperceptible moment at the top of his arc, like a golfer with a rhythmic swing. Often the difference between what Wayne does with the puck and what a less accomplished player would have done with it is simply a *pause*, as if, as time freezes, he is enjoying an extra handful of milliseconds. Time seems to slow down for him, and indeed, it may actually do so. Dr. Adrian R.M. Upton, the head neurologist at McMaster University in Hamilton, Ontario, has done some fascinating experiments with elite sprinters that suggest (the reservations about the work are that it is very hard to get a sufficiently large sample to test) that their motor neurons fire faster than those of mere mortals; the quicker their reaction times were to even simple tap tests, the faster they were liable to run. If this is true, it may account for much of what we see among the champions of a lot of sports. When Bjorn Borg, playing tennis as fast as any human can play it, appears to have the same control the rest of us would have in a casual Sunday morning knockup, it may well be that for him the pace *is* slower. His neurological motor is running with such efficiency that his response to his opponent's actions is as deliberate as ours would be at a more turgid pace. Dr. Upton, who has published several technical papers about his work with athletes, compares the difference between the neurological systems of the superstars and those of the rest of us to the difference between a highly tuned sports car and the family sedan. The sports car is simply capable of firing faster. When George Brett claims that he can see the stitches on a baseball spinning toward his hitting zone, he may be telling us something about his motorneurological capacity. Wayne, too, if Dr. Upton's suppositions are correct (and from neurological evidence alone he was able to predict the 1976 Olympic sprint victory of Hasely Crawford of Trinidad), is reacting to the situations of the games he plays as if it were being played for him in slow-motion film.

In the fall of 1980, John Jerome, a former editor of *Skiing* magazine, brought out a book called *The Sweet Spot in Time* in which he examined much of the most recent exploration of athletic anatomy. His title was an echo of one of his central observations, that just as there is a physical "sweet spot" on a tennis racquet or a baseball bat, so is there, for the exceptional athlete, an almost immeasurably brief moment in time that is precisely right for performing his action. In explaining this thesis, Jerome cited a musical analogy. He wrote:

> I happened to hear violinist Isaac Stern discuss his art one night, and a jazz musician (whose name escapes me) the next. Both of these immensely talented individuals would sing wordless snatches— "dum dum ti dum," and so on—to illustrate points about their very different forms of music. I am not a musician, and could barely catch the significant differences they were demonstrating so effortlessly. I could discern, but I'm sure I did not fully compre- hend, these differences—in emphasis and tone, but mostly just in timing. Each man would illustrate one way to play a phrase, then an alternate, varying the timing of the notes subtly without violat- ing the form, changing in major ways the emotional content of the music without changing a note. I suddenly realized that for musi- cians—and for athletes—there must be a great deal more *room*, in effect, in the flow of time than there is for the rest of us.

Gretzky uses this room to insert an extra beat into his actions. In front of the net, eyeball to eyeball with the goaltender, he will . . . hold the puck one . . . extra instant, upsetting the anticipated rhythm of the game, extending his moment . . . the way a ballet dancer extends the time of his leap. He distorts time, and not always by slowing it down. Some- times he will release the puck before be appears to be ready, threading a pass through a maze of players precisely to the blade of a teammate's stick or finding a chink in a goaltender's armour and slipping the puck into it before the goaltender is ready to react. Because of hockey's speed, the differences between his actions and those of anyone else are invisible from the stands (as they often are, for that matter, from a position next to him on the ice). If he did not repeat their results so many times it would be possible to dismiss many of them as luck. If there is such a thing as sleight of body, he performs it.

On top of his neurological advantages, Gretzky seems to bring cer- tain special qualities of metabolism to the game. With Gordie Howe, he shares an exceptional capacity to renew his energy resources quickly. Even when Howe had been out on the ice longer than any of his team- mates he would be the first man on the bench to lift his head. Similarly with Gretzky, who often, as against St. Louis, or in the turnaround of the game in Toronto in November, has his best moments in the third period. When Dave Smith, a University of Alberta exercise physiologist who tested all the Oilers in the spring of 1980, first saw the results of Gretzky's test of recuperative abilities, he thought the machine had broken.

In the simplest terms, Gretzky is an exceptional pure athlete. Bearing out Dr. Upton's suppositions, he is a runner fast enough to compete at respectable levels. (His sister, Kim, was a provincial champion.) In baseball, he batted .492 for the Brantford CKCP Braves in the summer of 1980, and he was offered—seriously—a contract by the Toronto Blue Jays. But he is hardly a superman. Smith's tests also showed him to be the weakest of the Oilers. ("Am I stronger than my Mom?" he asked when he saw the results.)

Separatism's Leader at Work

GRAHAM FRASER

Devoted to achieving the independence of Québec, Premier René Lévesque was also charismatic and sometimes forgetful.

Quebec—It is nine o'clock in the morning. Thursday, Nov. 6, 1980.

A 1978 Buick Electra limousine pulls up in front of 91 Rue d'Auteuil, a narrow street just inside the walls of Old Quebec. It waits, with engine running.

In the front seat are two tall men. Gilles Lévesque and Marcel Drouin, veterans in the provincial police and now in the eight-man security detail in the premier's office. They are waiting for the premier of Quebec.

Minutes later, René Lévesque comes downstairs and gets in. The car heads up the Grande Allée toward the National Assembly. Then it turns left, pulling in beside the austere modern fortress with the slit windows. "Administrative building J" in the language of the government bureaucracy, but known to everyone as simply "the bunker."

The day begins. A day in the life of the premier.

It is by no means a typical day—there is a cabinet shuffle, a luncheon speech, and a totally unexpected bit of confusion in the National Assembly which postpones the swearing-in of the new speaker.

But there are no typical days for René Lévesque, and this one was chosen arbitrarily 10 days earlier.

9:06 a.m.

Lévesque walks through the glass doors into the lobby, arriving at the same time as his chief of staff, Jean-Roch Boivin.

Boivin, tall, silver-haired, shaggy, has been a close friend of Lévesque's since before they left the Liberal party in 1967 to form the Mouvement Souverainte-Association.

A lawyer, son of a dairy farmer, one of a family of 12, he has never lost his earthy, rough-hewn style. He became Lévesque's chief of staff in 1977, but retained his trouble-shooter style, leaving much of the day-to-day administration of the premier's office to his assistant.

It is a decentralized office. Boivin and Lévesque touch base briefly and irregularly through the day, rather than functioning with scheduled meetings.

Lévesque nods a good morning to Daniele Tremblay, the receptionist who checks people as they come in and walks to the elevator.

"We Don't Talk"

The premier looks tired. He grimaces self-mockingly at how crummy he feels in the morning, and mutters "Ooooh, I'm beat."

Glancing at the reporter in the elevator, he growls: "There is one basic thing: We don't talk to one another."

It is an unspoken rule among those who work with Lévesque that in the morning he has little patience for long conversations. Until he has settled into the day, had his cup of coffee and a cigarette and read the papers, the exchanges are terse.

The night before, he put the last touches to the cabinet shuffle; a fairly wide-ranging re-jigging of cabinet, involving two new members and changes for 10 current members.

For 42 backbenchers, it was the last chance to be named to the cabinet of the Lévesque regime.

The premier had gone home about 9 the night before for supper with his wife, Corinne.

Then it had been a housewarming drink with Industry and Commerce Minister Yves Duhaime and his wife Lise, who recently moved in nearby. It had turned out to be a longer evening than planned.

Coming into his office, Lévesque hangs up his coat.

The office is a corner suite, where Lévesque makes his calls, studies and signs documents and reads his newspapers. There is an adjoining salon with a long table, couches, chairs and a fold-out bar.

Large Cup of Coffee

Every piece of desk space is piled high with papers and books. Lévesque gestures at the mess with a shrug. "Once a month we try, but Christ . . ."

Lighting a cigarette, he moves to the office couch. The morning papers are laid out on the coffee table: the *Journal de Quebec*, *Le Devoir*, *Le Monde*, *La Presse*, *The Gazette* and the *Globe and Mail*.

A minute or so later, his secretary, Mariette Saindon, brings in a large cup of black coffee.

This is one of the few constant elements in Lévesque's days. Each begins with time to read the papers. If he is disturbed, it is only briefly.

9:35 a.m.

This morning, the time for reading the papers is to be cut short. There was to be a swearing in of the new cabinet at 10:10 a.m., followed by a press conference, a speech at the Chambre de Commerce at noon, and the first regular sitting of the National Assembly in the new session.

Lévesque skims the papers, looking at Normand Girard's column in the *Journal de Quebec*, then turns to the editorial page of *Le Devoir*.

He then gets up from the couch, heads into the adjoining salon and begins making notes for his speech.

9:45 a.m.

Lévesque's press secretary, Gratia O'Leary, hands him the list of titles and the new cabinet. She says it's been verified by Louis Bernard (secretary-general of the executive council and cabinet clerk). "The titles are correct."

In fact, there has been an error in one draft, the alphabetical order of the ministries is wrong, and in retyping the list, a secretary typed in Denis Vaugeois as minister of communications, instead of Clement Richard, the former speaker. It was a minor slip, but it was to contribute to the confusion of the afternoon.

10:00 a.m.

Bernard arrives to accompany Lévesque to the swearing-in at the Lieutenant-Governor's suite.

Bernard, 43, is Quebec's senior civil servant. He was assistant deputy-minister of federal-provincial relations under Claude Morin when he stunned the civil service in August, 1970, by resigning to go to work for the PQ parliamentary caucus.

After the election, he became Lévesque's chief of staff, before taking over as secretary-general to the executive council and cabinet clerk in April, 1978.

Accompanied by O'Leary and Drouin, they head for the elevator. Lévesque sees Michel Carpentier in the hall.

"Salut," he says.

In denims, with long black hair and open-necked shirt, Carpentier looks like a glimpse of storefront politics in the air-conditioned world of the bunker. But it is an illusion.

At 35, Carpentier is as discreet as Bernard, and a more seasoned veteran with the Parti Quebecois.

From 1974–76, he was Lévesque's executive assistant, was director of the 1976 election campaign and the referendum campaign, and since 1976 has been deputy chief of staff and the man in charge of Lévesque's relations with the party.

The three men, Bernard, Boivin and Carpentier, are the three key senior advisers; no others have such easy access and influence.

A second rung of influence in the premier's office consists of O'Leary and advisers Marine Tremblay and Claude Malette.

Carpentier smiles laconically.

"Another one," he says, referring to the cabinet shuffle.

Lévesque shrugs slightly. "It will make a round of musical chairs."

10:06 a.m.

The route by tunnel to the Lieutenant-Governor's is complicated across the Grande Allée to the Assembly, then several twists and turns to the building directly behind. Lévesque gets a bit twitchy on the fourth turn, and mutters: "On the way back, we're going outside."

10:25 a.m.

The brief ceremony of swearing in the new ministers is over quickly. Lévesque heads out and walks to the door of the National Assembly library, where one floor above, there is a formal press conference.

He notes there is a kind of team spirit in a cabinet and tells reporters.

"So, when the moment comes when you tell yourself it has to be modified or shuffled, there is always a hesitation, and it kind of tears you apart, I can tell you."

As he speaks, Gratia O'Leary hands out the new cabinet list, complete with biographies.

Ryan Gets Wrong Copy

Some uncorrected copies are sent out—one of which is delivered to Claude Ryan, who later says that until 2:30 he thought Clement Richard was to remain speaker.

When Lévesque finishes his summary, there are questions: first in French, and then in English.

They focus on the future role of the ministers of state, three of whom have been transferred.

Lévesque replies easily, saying he felt it was time for some ministers of state to move to the firing line.

10:50 a.m.

Bernard Chabot, a TVA television reporter presiding at the press conference, says the period for questions in French is over, it's time for questions in English.

It is mainly for English-language radio and TV, since newspaper reporters generally ask questions in French. Most questions are repeated, but no one leaves: Lévesque often says things more bluntly, concisely or colorfully in English than he did earlier in French. And if someone pops an unexpected question, he will almost always answer it—often producing an unexpected story.

10:59 a.m.

The questions over, Lévesque walks to his office—outside.

11:03 a.m.

Back in the office, he asks Saindon to hold all calls. He hasn't finished working on his speech.

He walks into the salon and sitting at the end of the table, with a foolscap pad and a black felt pen, he writes longhand notes.

He writes with his pen held between the first and second fingers of this right hand, rather than resting in the joint between thumb and forefinger. It's a habit he acquired as a small boy, imitating his father.

Lévesque is one of the few politicians who writes his own speeches. Occasionally, he will use a speech prepared by his staff, but even then, he will rework it carefully. The one great exception was the notorious speech to the Economic Club in New York in February, 1977: a failure.

11:56 a.m.

His notes completed, Lévesque leaves the office and walks quickly to the elevator and the waiting limousine with Gratia O'Leary. Usually, Mariette Saindon makes a bowl of soup in the kitchenette nearby, which he drinks in the salon as he goes through documents, but today he makes one of his infrequent luncheon speeches in Quebec.

Two weeks before, Pierre Trudeau addressed the Chambre de Commerce, launching his constitutional campaign. Now it's Lévesque's turn.

1:30 p.m.

After a fulsome introduction, the premier rises, teases Quebec Mayor Jean Pelletier with a joke, and launches into his constitutional views.

It is a smaller and younger crowd than Trudeau spoke to.

Lévesque speaks for 45 minutes, going over much ground he has worked before in speeches attacking federal plans to amend and patriate the constitution.

But there are a few new wrinkles. Lévesque accuses Trudeau specifically of lying, referring to the draft proposal presented to the provinces on July 8 that imposes bilingualism on Ontario and New Brunswick, and quoting Trudeau as denying this.

2:20 p.m.

Lévesque concludes: "There is only one slogan possible. It is that it must not go through, and it will not go through. I thank you very much."

Then, as briskly as he can, he moves through the crowd and out. . . .

2:43 p.m.

Deputies, aides and wives chat in the lounge. Corinne Lévesque, striking in white blouse and black velvet slacks, has come to watch the session on TV in the lounge.

Claude Charron strides into the room: the mace is being carried into the Assembly, and the show is about to begin.

But Lévesque has not emerged from his private office.

"Quickly, quickly," implores Charron, beckoning furiously. "The secretary-general has gone in!" Gratia O'Leary shrugs. "He's in the bathroom."

2:44 p.m.

Lévesque emerges, and he and Charron walk quickly into the Assembly chamber. In the absence of the speaker, who has not yet been named, Rene Blondin, secretary-general of the National Assembly, presides. After calling for order and a moment's silence, Blondin reads Richard's resignation and calls on the premier.

But Lévesque gets only one word out when Gérard-D. Lévesque, the Liberals' house leader, rises to complain that the opposition leaders were not consulted, and that this represents an abuse of procedure.

The Assembly is plunged into three quarters of an hour of partisan procedural debate. Lévesque is caught; he has simply forgotten, and no one reminded him.

Gerard-D. Lévesque gives a vintage performance: he has caught the government out clearly, and rags Lévesque with wit and skill. A member of the Assembly since 1956, Liberal house leader for a decade, in government and in opposition, he is a superb parliamentarian.

Cherish a Good Play

In the government lounge, the aides watch: amused, exasperated, impressed. Like hockey fans at the Forum, despite their partisan fervor they are connoisseurs, and cherish a good play from either side.

Gerard-D. calls the speaker's nomination a "unilateral gesture" by the premier—a point that wins him laughter and applause from the opposition and sheepish grins from the government. He then suggests adjournment until Tuesday.

René Lévesque apologizes, saying that the decision had been taken late the night before.

"And I should tell you—it's an explanation, it's not an excuse—that I have had to endure this morning an infernal pace which took that from my mind. It's as stupid as that."

But as the needling goes on, the irritation rises in his voice.

The session suspends for a few minutes, then adjourns.

Lévesque quickly consults Charron and Bernard, and sets about reorganizing the rest of the afternoon.

He had planned to spend it listening to Ryan's reply to the throne speech, but the afternoon has suddenly opened up.

4:10 p.m.

Lévesque walks through the empty Assembly chamber to the small room known as "the hot room"—once an office for reporters, now for impromptu press conferences.

He reiterates for reporters what he said at lunch, and repeats that he just plain forgot to consult Ryan.

"That's what happens when you plan too many things for one day."

He walks back through the Assembly chamber. By his office, there is a private elevator which takes him down to the executive tunnel which leads directly to the bunker, and he begins to speculate on what the Liberals are up to.

"Maybe the delay is all for the best," he says.

4:50 p.m.

Back on the third floor, he sticks his head into Boivin's office, and says what he is thinking; perhaps a contributing factor in the Liberal determination to postpone the debate until next week was to stall for time and get some consensus on the question in the caucus.

Then he walks into his office, reaches for the phone and calls Louis Bernard on the floor below.

"How could you let that happen to me?" he blusters. But he's laughing and can't even feign annoyance.

"Look," he continues seriously, "I've just spoken to Jean-Roch about this. It may be just as well.

"I get the sense that part of the reason for this was that they want to use the time, and get some more agreement."

5 p.m.

Lévesque walks into the secretary's office and asks Esther Turgeon to put through calls to Angus Maclean, premier of Prince Edward Island, and Gerald Godin, the new immigration minister.

They Keep Copies

As the calls are being placed, Lévesque goes back to the "red book": the red leather folder in which Boivin and his staff have placed key documents they feel Lévesque should see: letters, memos, drafts of legislation.

The staff has learned over the years to keep a copy of everything they give Lévesque—partly because he may lose it, leave it in the other office or in the car, and partly because the reflex action after having absorbed a document is to tear it and dump it in the wastebasket.

The next two hours are punctuated by a series of ripping sounds.

5:20 p.m.

Angus Maclean is on the line.

Lévesque was calling to bring him up to date on the state of a request Maclean had made about the possibility of Hydro-Quebec selling power to P.E.I. They chat briefly, and agree to be in touch again the following week.

5:35 p.m.

Corinne Lévesque arrives.

"Salut. I won't be too much longer," Lévesque says, and she picks up a few magazines and walks into the salon.

A few minutes later, she is joined by Gratia O'Leary, and Corinne gets a gin and tonic for Lévesque, O'Leary and herself.

Lévesque has said they will leave for Montreal at 5:45, but there are still some odds and ends to do, and the time stretches on. . . .

6:55 p.m.

Lévesque does the last bit of paper-tearing, finding a few scraps of paper with scribbles of early versions of the cabinet shuffle.

Finally the last piece of work.

"Okay, done," he says, shoving some documents into a folder for the evening's work.

Corinne notes with a wry smile that they are not doing too badly, leaving only an hour and a quarter later than planned. They head for the elevators, and down to the waiting limousines: one for the Lévesques, while O'Leary gets into the car behind—an insurance car for all long trips, in case one breaks down.

The day is over.

The cars pull onto the Grande Allée and head for Montréal, where Lévesque will spend a quiet evening at his Pine Ave. apartment with Corinne and a full file of government papers.

The Persistent Amateurism in the Canadian Soul

BHARATI MUKHERJEE

Multiculturalism is part of the Canadian fabric in theory. In practice?

It is now the summer of 1966, and the three of us cross at Windsor in a battered vw van. Our admission goes smoothly, for I have a lecturer's position at McGill. I say "smoothly," but I realize now there was one curious, even comic event that foreshadowed the difficulties faced by Indians in Canada. A middle-aged immigration officer, in filling out my application, asked me the year of my birth. I told him, in that private-school accent of which I was once so proud. Mishearing, he wrote down "1914" and remarked, "Ah, we're the same age." He happened to be exactly twice my age. He corrected his error without a fuss. Ten minutes inside Canada, and I was already invisible.

The oldest paradox of prejudice is that it renders its victims simultaneously invisible and over-exposed. I have not met an Indian in Canada who has not suffered the humiliations of being overlooked (in jobs, in queues, in deserved recognition) and from being singled out (in hotels, department stores, on the streets, and at customs). It happened to me so regularly in Canada that I now feel relief, just entering Macy's in Albany, New York, knowing that I won't be followed out by a security guard. In America, I can stay in hotels and not be hauled out of elevators or stopped as I enter my room. It's perhaps a small privilege in the life of a North American housewife—not to be taken automatically for a shoplifter or a whore—but it's one that my years in Canada, and especially my two years in Toronto, have made me grateful for. I know objections will be raised; I know Canadians all too well. Which of us has *not* been harassed at customs? On a summer's night, which of us *can* walk down Yonge Street without carloads of stoned youths shouting out insults? We have all stood patiently in bakery lines, had people step in front of us, we've all waved our plastic numbers and wailed, "But I was next—"

If we are interested in drawing minute distinctions, we can disregard or explain away nearly anything. ("Where did it happen? Oh, *Rosedale*. Well, no *wonder* ..." Or, "Were you wearing a sari? No? Well, no wonder ..." Or, "Oh, *we* wouldn't do such a thing. He must have been French or something ...") And I know the pious denials of hotel clerks. In a Toronto hotel I was harassed by two house detectives who demanded to see my room key before allowing me to go upstairs to join my family—harassed me in front of an elevator-load of leering, elbow-nudging women. When I complained, I extracted only a "Some of my best friends are Pakis" from the night manager, as he fervently denied that what I had just experienced was in fact a racial incident.

And I know the sanctimonious denials of customs officers, even as they delight in making people like me dance on the head of a bureaucratic pin. On a return from New York to Toronto I was told, after being forced to declare a $1 valuation on a promotional leaflet handed out by a bookstore, that even a book of matches had to be declared. ("I didn't ask if you *bought* anything. Did you hear me ask about purchases? Did you? I'll ask you again in very clear English. *Are you bringing anything into the country?*")

Do not think that I enjoy writing this of Canada. I remain a Canadian citizen. This is the testament of a woman who came, like most immigrants, confident of her ability to do good work, in answer to a stated need. After the unsophisticated, beer-swilling rednecks of Iowa, British-commonwealth Canada, and Montréal in particular, promised a kind of haven. At the road-stops in Iowa and Illinois, when I entered in a sari, silverware would drop, conversations cease; it was not the kind of attention

I craved. It was never a hostile reaction (it might have been, in the Deep South, but I avoided that region). It was innocent, dumbfounded stupefaction, and I thought I would be happy enough to leave it behind. As we drove past Toronto on the 401, we picked up the strains of sitar music on the radio; Montréal had spice shops and was soon to have Indian restaurants. It should have been a decent country, and we should have been happy in it. . . .

A spectre is haunting Canada: the perfidious "new" (meaning "dark" and thus, self-fulfillingly, "non-assimilatable") immigrant, coming to snatch up jobs, welfare cheques, subway space, cheap apartments, and blue-eyed women.

The Green Paper in 1975—which seemed an admirable exercise in demographic planning, an open invitation to join in a "debate"—was really a premeditated move on the part of government to throw some bones (some immigrants) to the howling wolves. The "we" of that open question was understood to mean the Anglo-Saxon or Québec-French "founding races"; it opened up the sewers of resentment that polite, British-style forbearance had kept a lid on. My kind of Canadian was assumed, once again, not to exist, not to have a legitimate opinion to offer. ("Well, you could have made an official deposition through the proper multicultural channel whenever hearings were held in your community . . .")

Most Indians would date the new up-front violence, the physical assaults, the spitting, the name-calling, the bricks through the windows, the pushing and shoving on the subways—it would be, by this time, a very isolated Indian who has not experienced one or more of those reactions—from the implied consent given to racism by that infamous document. I cannot describe the agony and the betrayal one feels, hearing oneself spoken of by one's own country as being somehow exotic to its nature—a burden, a cause for serious concern. It may have been rhetorically softened, it may have been academic in tone, but in feeling it was Nuremberg, and it unleashed its own mild but continuing *Kristallnacht*. In that ill-tempered debate, the government itself appropriated the language, the reasoning, the motivation that had belonged—until then—to disreputable fringe groups. Suddenly it was all right, even patriotic, to blame these non-assimilatable Asian hordes for urban crowding, unemployment, and welfare burdens. And the uneducated, unemployed, welfare-dependent, native-born *lumpen* teenagers leaped at the bait.

It is not pleasant to realize your own government has betrayed you so coldly.

What about the "absorptive capacity" of the ambitious immigrant to take in all these new, startling descriptions of himself? It creates double-vision when self-perception is so utterly at odds with social standing. We are split from our most confident self-assumptions. We must be blind, stupid, or egomaniacal to maintain self-respect or dignity when society consistently undervalues our contribution. In Montréal, I was, simultaneously, a full professor at McGill, an author, a confident lecturer, and (I like to think) a charming and competent hostess and guest—*and* a housebound, fearful, aggrieved, obsessive, and unforgiving queen of bitterness. Whenever I read articles about men going berserk, or women committing suicide, and read the neighbours' dazed pronouncements ("But he was always so friendly, so outgoing, never a problem in the world . . ."), I knew I was looking into a mirror. Knowing that the culture condescended toward me, I needed ways of bolstering my self-respect—but those ways, at least to politely raised, tightly disciplined women of my age and origin, can only be achieved in society, in the recognition of our contributions.

And there, of course, I am up against another Canadian dilemma. I have always been struck by an oddity, call it a gap, in the cultural consciousness of the Canadian literary establishment. For fifteen years I was a professor of English and of creative writing at McGill. I published novels, stories, essays, reviews. In a land that fills its airports with itinerant poets and story-tellers, I was invited only once to give a reading by myself (after *Days and Nights in Calcutta* appeared, Clark and I, who had written it together, were frequently invited together). On that one occasion, I learned, after arriving in a mining town at three in the morning, that I'd been invited from the jacket photo and was expected to "come across." ("The others did.") No provisions had been made for my stay, except in my host's bachelor house. ("Oh, you let him meet you at the airport at three a.m.? And you went back to his house thinking there was a wife?") Friends explained to me that really, since nothing happened (except a few shoves and pushes), I shouldn't mention it again. Until now, I haven't.

Of course, it is possible to interpret everything in a different light. While no one likes to be pawed, isn't it nice to be acknowledged, even this way? (Don't laugh, it was suggested.) My point is simply this: an Indian slips out of invisibility in this culture at considerable peril to body and soul. I've alluded briefly (in *Days and Nights*) to the fact that I was not invited to join the Writers' Union of Canada, back at its founding, even though at that particular moment I was a Canadian and Clark was not (my Indian citizenship conferred special dispensations that his American one did not). The first explanation for the oversight was that the invitation extended to Clark was "assumed" to include me. While even a low-grade feminist might react uncomfortably to such a concoction, another, and I think truthful, explanation was offered. "We didn't know how to spell your name, and we were afraid of insulting you," a well-known writer later wrote me. She's right; I would have been insulted (just as I'm mildly insulted by Canada Council letters to "Mr. Bharati Blaise"). And then, with a tinge of self-justification, she continued: "Your book was published by an American publisher and we couldn't get hold of it, so . . ."

Well, it's an apology and an explanation and it's easy to forgive as an instance of the persistent amateurism in the Canadian soul. But if you scrutinize just a little harder, and if you've dipped into the well of forgiveness far too often, you see a very different interpretation. *If you don't have a family compact name, forget about joining us.* If you don't have Canadian content, forget about publishing here. "The only Canadian thing about the novel is that it was written by a woman who now lives in Montréal," said a reviewer of my second novel, *Wife*, in *Books in Canada* (she was herself a feminist and emerging ethnicist), not even recognizing a book aimed right at her. "How can you call yourself a Canadian writer if you didn't play in snow as a child?" asked a CBC television interviewer. And more severely: "How do you justify taking grants and then not writing about Canada?"

The answer to all that is that I do write about Canada, perhaps not as directly as I am writing now, but that I refuse to capitulate to the rawness of Canadian literature—and, more to the point, I refuse to set my work in Canada because to do so would be to reduce its content to the very subject of this essay: politics and paranoia and bitter disappointment. The condition of the Indian in Canada is a sociological and political subject. We've not yet achieved the ease that would permit us to write of the self and of the expanding consciousness. To set my work in Canada is necessarily to adopt an urgent and strident tone; I would find irony an ill-considered option in any such situation. I advocate, instead, fighting back.

In case anyone finds a copy of *Wife*, it should be read in the following way: the nominal setting is Calcutta and New York City. But in the mind of the heroine, it is always Toronto.

The Banks and Canadian Nationalism

MEL HURTIG

> *The bankers' instinct to foreclose persisted long after the Great Depression, as Mel Hurtig, the nationalist publisher, discovered.*

Late in the afternoon of Friday, May 13, 1983, I sat at my desk working on production budgets for Hurtig Publishers' fall list. My secretary came in with a registered letter from the CIBC. With much curiosity, I opened the envelope. Inside was a letter calling my entire $700,000 bank loan and giving me two weeks to pay up.

I was incredulous, flattened. With no warning, the bank was quite prepared to wipe us out—not only Hurtig Publishers but *The Canadian Encyclopedia* with it. I phoned the bank, but the manager was gone for the day. I felt a pain in my stomach. I was paralysed with despair. It was the blackest day of my life. Everything I had been working for over the space of twenty-seven years would be lost. We would be unable to pay our bills, we would default on our author and printer contracts; our home and everything else I owned were signed over to the bank on my loan guarantee. We would lose *everything*. The rotten bastards!

I left the office and went home, but said nothing to anyone. Kay made dinner but I hardly ate. We went for a walk and then went to bed early; I didn't sleep for a minute. Saturday I went to the office and sat there all day trying to figure out what I could do. There was no bloody way in the world I was going to sell the entire encyclopedia to Britannica, but even if I did, it wouldn't solve my problems. How was I going to tell my staff? My authors whose royalty cheques wouldn't arrive? My wife and family?

Saturday night I lay in bed tossing and turning. There was no answer, we were going under. Suddenly, at around three in the morning, I sat bolt upright in bed. By God! I jumped out of bed, quickly dressed, and rushed down to the office. Around six in the morning, I found what I was looking for—an early-April Zena Cherry column from the *Globe*. I read it and reread it. My, my.

Sunday night at seven o'clock I slipped into the bedroom at home, closed the door, and called Gordon Lewis, vice president and general manager of the CIBC. Here is how the brief conversation went:

"Mr. Lewis, this is Mel Hurtig from Hurtig Publishers. I apologize for disturbing you at home during the supper hour, but I have something important to discuss with you."

"Can't it wait until tomorrow morning?"

"No, sir, it cannot."

"Okay. What can I do for you?"

"Mr. Lewis, I have here in my hand a clipping about a big luncheon in Toronto, hosted by Russell Edward Harrison, chairman of the Canadian Imperial Bank of Commerce, to kick off the fundraising campaign for the new John Robarts chair of Canadian Studies at York University."

"And?"

"Mr. Lewis, what do you think the reaction will be in Toronto, in Edmonton, and elsewhere across Canada when I announce that the CIBC has just pulled the plug on the largest-ever project in the history of Canadian studies?"

There was a long silence.

"What exactly do you want, Mr. Hurtig?"

"Mr. Lewis, all I want is the time to make new arrangements and to get the hell out of your bloody bank."

There was another even longer silence.

"I will call you at your office tomorrow, Mr. Hurtig."

I slammed down the phone.

Early next morning Lewis called; we could take as long as we wanted to make new arrangements. The bank would withdraw its loan-call immediately.

It took another seven months and many new flowcharts and business plans before the Bank of Montreal's financing offer arrived. We had expected it on August 1, but it finally arrived in December after two long years of negotiations. The terms, conditions, and bank fees were onerous.

I joked afterwards that "if one of our staff had to go to the bathroom once too often, the bank would own the encyclopedia," but it wasn't too far off the mark. If we fell behind schedule, or suffered any number of other woes, the bank would be entitled to cut off further funding.

It was to me to be an absurd situation. Every day across the country more and more people were talking about the encyclopedia and sending in orders, yet still the bank made stringent demands. The bottom line was that unless we could generate a much larger number of sales in advance of having to go to press, the money we needed wouldn't be available. We could still end up with a superb encyclopedia, the product of years of work and the best minds, writers, and artists in the country, but we might not be able to publish it. And, oh yes, we'd have to close our publishing house and declare bankruptcy, and Kay and I would have to move out of our house and lose everything we owned.

But I had no choice, or so it seemed. The documents for me to sign arrived on my desk; they were several inches thick. I sent a set to my lawyer's office for him to review. He would get back to me by the end of the week.

The very next morning, totally out of the blue, I received a phone call from Gerry McLaughlan, president and CEO of the Canadian Commercial Bank. "Mr. Hurtig," he said, "I would like to introduce myself. We're a new bank. I hear you're looking for some money. Can I come over for a talk?"

Within six days the CCB had a contract on my desk. In every respect, it was more attractive and more reasonable than the Bank of Montreal offer: interest rates, life-insurance requirements for my senior staff and me, Hurtig Publishers' operating line of credit, collateral demands, production schedules. It didn't take me long to sit down with my lawyer and accountant. We quickly accepted the CCB's offer.

When I called the Bank of Montreal to inform them that I had received a much better all-around offer, they asked me not to make an immediate decision—to wait at least through the weekend. On Monday morning the Bank of Montreal called me; they were willing to match the CCB's terms, item for item. No way, I thought. I owed the CCB a huge debt of gratitude. Very politely I told this to the Bank of Montreal.

In December the CCB paid the CIBC the $607,000 we still owed them. We bought a million dollars' worth of life insurance for me and three-quarters of a million each for Frank McGuire and Jim Marsh. According to William French, writing in the *Globe and Mail*, "Surely this must be the highest value ever put on the life of a Canadian publisher."

Dic Doyle, then the editor of the *Globe*, said I had obviously made a serious mistake in my attempts to raise funds from Canadian banks. If I had called it *The Mexican Encyclopedia*, I wouldn't have had any problems.

The Personality of Brian Mulroney

MICHEL GRATTON

> *When journalist Michel Gratton worked for Prime Minister Brian Mulroney, his main job was to keep the "boss" informed on what the "boys" were saying.*

On trips outside Ottawa, he and Mila would get out and mingle with ordinary Canadians, and inevitably a crowd would gather around them, perhaps to exchange a few words, or maybe touch one of them as they passed along, much as they would mob a rock star who strayed into town. The Boss loved these scenes; they were like a drug for him, and would lift his spirits for days. Inevitably, afterwards, he would ask me what the Boys were saying. I'd have to tell him that he'd performed well, but that the Boys wouldn't give him much credit for it this time, either. He'd shake his head.

"If it was Trudeau," he'd say, "they'd be talking about Trudeaumania."

He did have something of a point. It bothered Mila, too. One day, when we were flying back to Ottawa on the Challenger, she told him, "Why don't you stop talking about that? You know it's never going to change."

As he'd often do when reproached by his wife, Mulroney smiled softly at her and reached out to take her hand. They were still intensely in love. I've rarely seen two people who were so frankly smitten with each other. It struck me from the very start of the election campaign, but it was even more evident during some of the dark days to come.

He showed the same warmth to his children. I never heard him raise his voice to any of the four youngsters, who often came with us on trips. Mila sometimes bridled at this.

"'Hello, nice baby. Hello, nice baby.' That's all you can say," she complained when he refused to take a tougher line with their youngest son, Nicolas. The Boss would talk to me about my own three daughters, and ask how they were doing. Whenever I said I was going to visit them, he'd say, "Ah, that's fun, that." Mulroney, with one daughter and three boys, said, "You're lucky, Michel; girls are a lot of fun."

I was always happy to see the kids along; it always put the Boss in a better mood. There were practical considerations, too. A picture of Nicolas or Mark had a far better chance of getting on the front pages than a hundred shots of Brian and Mila alone. Canadians, being vastly less cynical than reporters, were delighted to see the Mulroney family together, so it was heartening to hear The Boss chirrup to Nicolas, "Get ready, baby, we're going out on campaign!"

Although I never heard the Prime Minister shout at his children, I can't say the same thing for adults.

There has been much talk about Mulroney's towering rages, and I've been witness to a few. One came early in the new administration, when Finance Minister Michael Wilson, during an interview with Canadian Press, cast doubts on the continuation of universal social programs. Perhaps they should be provided free only to some Canadians, he suggested, although, during the election, Mulroney had spoken of universality as "a sacred trust." This plunged the government, and the Prime Minister in particular, into an embarrassing imbroglio of backtracking and explaining. When I first showed Mulroney the CP wire story, he went white as a sheet, then started shouting that it was "terrible," and "outrageous," along with some phrases that would make a stevedore blush. Turning to me, he said, "I want you to pick up the phone, talk to Wilson or his chief of staff, and tell them. . ."

Then, seeing my helpless expression—I was going to bawl out Wilson?—he stopped in mid-sentence, and decided to make the call himself. On the phone, he did no shouting, for one of the curious things about his rages was that he would rarely explode in front of the person he was angry with. Someone else would get it, by deflection. So, whenever he started screaming in my presence, I knew that I was safe, at least for the time being. On the other hand, I'd start worrying when he'd fold his hands on his desk, look at me over the tops of his glasses, and talk in his deepest tone. It would always start with, "You know, Michel . . ."

I knew then I was in for a sermon.

While Mulroney had an explosive temper, his humour and his desire to make people laugh were far more important to his makeup. On a trip to Zimbabwe, where the President—a strictly honorary title—rejoiced in the name, Banana, (actually, the Rev. Canaan Banana) we had a hard time restraining ourselves from making cracks, lest we wind up in somebody's column saying something that would breach protocol. The reporters, of course, were not so constrained. The Prime Minister finally had his meeting with President Banana, and, in the staff briefing that followed, dwelt primarily on the far more important meeting he had had with Prime Minister Mugabe. When I was able to slip in a question, I asked, "And how was your meeting with President Banana?"

"Very fruitful," he replied.

Ben Johnson, Drugs and Sport, 1988

JAMES CHRISTIE

For Canadians, the 1988 Olympics brought amazing joy and dashed pride in just a few hours.

It has started. The cruel, snide, persecuting snickers about Ben Johnson are in the breeze all around the Olympic city.

Across from Canadian media headquarters, hung high between a U.S. flag and the logo of the Seoul Olympics, was a handpainted banner that reads: "Just say no, Ben."

And, like the banner, Ben Johnson, who still holds a world record of 9.83 for the 100 metres, has been hung out to twist in the breeze. Canada's gold-medal pride and joy became, overnight, a universal bad example.

Forget the thrill of watching him fly down the track. Sport Canada won't touch him anymore.

This morning, the man who received a Commonwealth Games medal from the Queen, the Order of Canada from Governor General Jeanne Sauvé and, a few nights ago, the heart of an enthralled nation, is just an unemployed ex-athlete.

Johnson's agent, Larry Heidebrecht, says neither he, nor coach Charlie Francis, nor Jamie Astaphan, Johnson's physician, could explain how the drug Stanozolol came to be found in Johnson's urine specimen.

At the news conference to announce Johnson's expulsion from the Games for the use of anabolic steroids, a team of uneasy Canadian sport bureaucrats sat and carefully deflected questions to colleagues.

It was as bewildering to onlookers as the passing of political bucks from federal to provincial jurisdictions—and just as unsatisfying. They all share the guilt, but they all keep their jobs.

Now a politician says there will be more money from the Ministry of Fitness and Amateur Sport for drug tests.

Now the Canadian Track and Field Association says it can go ahead with random, monthly testing.

Now the Canadian Olympic Association is making apologies to Seoul organizers for causing embarrassment.

Where was all this righteousness a month ago when the team was being pulled together? Did we need "a disaster" as it was termed by Prince Alexandre de Merode, head of the medical commission of the International Olympic Committee? It ought to have been discovered and punished at home instead of before a world-wide television audience.

Johnson is being painted as singular villain in this. But how could the members of an entourage, such as Johnson had, have failed to notice that their leader was ingesting large quantities of a substance sport-medicine doctors consider carcinogenic and dangerous?

The Blue Jays Go for the Pennant— and Free Trade

RICK SALUTIN

> Neither baseball fans nor anti–free traders are necessarily cerebral. But fans and anti–free traders, an unlikely pairing, can be.

That awful weekend at the start of October, when the free trade deal was made, was a watershed for me culturally. Not just politically, nationally, emotionally and cosmically. A cultural watershed. Because of the Blue Jays. The watershed for me lay not in the fact that they lost their drive for the pennant; nor was it that, because of the deal, I didn't *care* that they lost. It's that I was *glad* they lost.

On Friday, Reisman had returned to Washington, the deal that seemed scuttled was clearly back on. I was sunk in depression but had to attend a meeting with a varied group about a project involving film, broadcasting, books—the whole grisly concoction. In late came the president of the Canadian branch of a large multinational publishing house. He sat down across the room, sighed with a great weight and said, "We'll know in three days." I felt a surge of sympathy and surprise. "I didn't know he was worried about free trade," I thought, "he's the head of a multinational, I didn't think a deal would be troubling him." It wasn't. He meant the Blue Jays and their final weekend series against Detroit.

So, as that weekend unfolded, as Reisman, Carney and Wilson played out the tragic farce of their deal with the Americans, I paid some sideways attention while the Jays lost their fifth, sixth and seventh in a row to conclude the season disastrously and deprive themselves of victory. And with each defeat, I quietly exulted.

Let me put this in context. I was at the very first Blue Jays game ever during a blizzard in April 1977: you couldn't see the ball for its whiteness. I suffered through the lean years, and then the rise of the fine, fast, smart and mostly non-white young team we now have. I have followed game after game, not just live and on radio or TV, but even scrambled over the pay sports channel: there is nothing like devoting hours of an evening which ends with a sudden loss in extra innings; you feel, as John Saul says, like you have lost an irreplaceable period of your life to no end, and learned something about your capacity for misery you'd rather not know. This past summer a Mozambican friend was visiting while the Blue Jays went through their worst patch prior to that final week. I told her I tried to put the Jays' difficulties in perspective by thinking of famine and massacre in southern Africa. "Doesn't help a bit, does it?" she said. I even think of the Blue Jays as a basically Canadian team—though none are Canadian and many come from the Dominican Republic—because of their quiet competence, lack of flamboyance, absence of superstars and so forth.

But think what would have happened had they won on that free trade weekend. The catastrophe of the deal would have been alloyed with baseball triumphalism. The two would have vied on the front pages and, at least in central Canada, baseball would have been on top. Then, through the American League playoffs, attention would have divided between the details of the agreement pro and con, and the most recent news about starting pitchers. Had the Jays won and gone to the World Series, we'd have seen a veritable orgy of joy over the fact "we" were in the *World* Series. There'd have been jocular idiocy and rivalry between politicians on both sides of the border, terrible jokes and camaraderie, the nauseating sight of Mulroney in glory at the games . . . The terrible humiliation over the deal would have been, at best, diffused—and I'm talking about the reaction among many of the die-hard *nationalists* I know, never mind people who aren't certain how they feel about free trade. Worst of all, had the Blue Jays won the Series, we'd have been subjected to endless comment about how we can play the Americans' own game and beat them, we needn't fear to compete in the *American* league, it's proof Canadians are ready to move out into the world—fill it in yourself. I was in New York in 1969 when the miracle Mets won their first World Series and a deeply unpopular John Lindsay was re-elected mayor in the citywide afterglow. The only possible good effect of a Blue Jay success might have been a backlash in the US, with demands for rejection of the deal because that so-called Canadian team had the bad grace to win our championship—a sort of sports protectionism spilling over.

Instead, it seems to me, the odious if vague specifics of the deal got the attention they deserved, and the debate got off to a properly rowdy start. Rather than drowning national sorrow in baseball glory, those prone to the affliction had an almost immediate way of forgetting the definitive loss on the diamond, by turning to a defeat which was still not sealed; and rising to fight on. In place of a honeymoon on the issue, which the government surely anticipated as just reward for its last-minute histrionics, within hours huge holes and unfulfilled promises were showing in the deal; by noon, Monday, the political and popular opposition were marshalling arguments. "It ain't over till it's over," as Yogi Berra said, anticipating the free trade debate. I don't mean to suggest we've won, or even that we are likely to win, but there is a fight on, and it wasn't delayed or diluted by the diversions of baseball.

I think this is a good omen and bespeaks the differences that still remain between our society and the United States. In Canada, it appears there is still room for politics and public debate. Those areas remain distinguishable from matters like culture, entertainment and sports. There is no politics in American public life today: there is gossip, titillation and entertainment. Culture. Comparatively, we're doing well. Free trade here is an actual issue; people and parties take sides; discussion of the issue proceeds, more or less, in relation to real interests and effects. Public life has not been replaced by the meagerest elements of pop culture.

It seems to me that much of the role played in social life by culture today used to be played by religion. Marx commented in his time that religion was the opium of the people; it would not be farfetched to say the Blue Jays occupy a similar function today, especially if you think of what would have happened had they won instead of lost on free trade weekend. I say this in spite of what seem to me many positive, even politically positive, aspects of professional sports in our society. Those elements include: a presentation of the elegant, aesthetic, truly beautiful possibilities of human beings; and the maintenance of a realm, in the midst of this grimy society, in which success depends more or less on merit rather than on birth, wealth or influence; a protected little moral universe, you might say.

The Blue Jays have therefore a dual potential: for good or for ill. This is not much different from what Marx said about religion. It's true he called it the opium of the people; but he also said, in the very same passage, that it—religion—is "a sigh from the oppressed, the soul of a heartless world, the spirit of a spiritless situation." One might well describe the place of the Blue Jays in the hearts of their fans in the same manner.

Still, I've made a (perhaps temporary) retreat from the ballpark; but in honesty I've felt my legs taking me in another direction: back toward the hockey rink. For I felt no ambivalence at all watching the Canada Cup this past summer, especially the wondrous final three games between Canada and the USSR. Hockey is so clearly our game; it contains far less potential for perversion in the current political context. This feels to me like a sensible solution. The need for culture will not melt from our lives just because it is capable of playing a devious and dangerous role—nor on the current evidence will religion either—but for those of us who find in sports a part of what we mean by culture, at least for a season or so, we may find firmer ground on ice.

The Friday which began the hideous weekend, I'd agreed to go on a local radio program to discuss the merits of the "new" *Star Trek*, which aired on TV the night before. I went with a heavy heart, lightened only by the pleasant presence on the show of the Toronto vice-president of the Star Trek Fan Club—no callow media critic but a knowledgeable and impassioned *aficionado*. Next day John Saul called again. "I've spent the last twenty-four hours bathed in shame on account of you," he bellowed, "because you pointed out I was worrying over the Blue Jays while our country was being dealt away. And then someone comes along and tells me you were on the fucking radio yesterday afternoon right after we argued and you were talking about fucking *Star Trek*!"

Detroit Comes to the North

MARK STAROWICZ

Television's powerful influence—and its sometimes distorting lens—can create incongruity.

At approximately 68 degrees north latitude, where the Mackenzie River empties into the Beaufort Sea, the town of Inuvik embodies the Canadian Arctic. Three thousand Inuit, Whites, Metis and Indians co-exist in relative tranquility in this stark and treeless landscape. Inuvik resembles a frontier movie set—false-front stores, rugged architecture—and in the place of horses and buckboards hitched at the post, empty snowmobiles and four-wheel-drive trucks idle waiting for their owners in front of stores and bars, filling the air with a constant growling rumble.

One of the first observable effects of the New Age came when a few of the Inuit teenage boys started wearing narrow-brimmed fedoras, dark sports jackets and sunglasses while they generally hung around on the main street. The reason for this mildly incongruous addition to the main street soon became apparent to all: Channel 2, Detroit, 8,000 kilometres away was broadcasting *Kojak*. The Satellite Age had arrived.

Since these odd beginnings, the satellite has flooded the North with *Miami Vice* and rock videos, so that on the streets of the Territorial capital of Yellowknife, native Indian teenagers will stroll with open-collared parkas sporting gold medallions at 35 degrees below zero, and in the neighbouring Yukon Territory, the most popular program is *Dynasty*.

Throughout the high Arctic, and in hundreds of remote communities in the north, it is now common to tune into Detroit's Channel 2 each night to have the *Eyewitness News* Team unfold the list of mayhem, arson and drug violence that comprises television news in one of America's most-violent cities. Some 1,000 remote Canadian communities, one million viewers are served by a Canadian company which distributes a package of Canadian and American stations by satellite to local cable operations. In this way, northern residents can watch any of four Detroit stations and catch a feature explaining how to sterilize a needle to avoid AIDS, and how to get on the waiting list for a Crack clinic; after a Budweiser commercial, the rush-hour traffic report paints a picture of choked freeways, and Accu-weather warns that an inch of snow is expected to create even more chaos. In this way, an evening of TV viewing in the North begins without anyone finding the matter incongruous anymore.

"It is a curious and little known fact of Canadian life," observes the Southam News Service, "that four powerful Detroit television stations are among the ties that bind this country together. The magic of satellite transmission and cable television has turned Detroit into a cultural beacon, an unlikely Canadian role model with almost as much reach as Toronto, Montreal or Vancouver."

This special satellite service to Canadian remote communities is relevant for more than its incongruity. It is unsettlingly close to being a metaphor for all of Canadian broadcasting today, and perhaps, a precursor of what some national cultures might expect in the current worldwide trend towards deregulation and privatization in television systems.

Misogyny and Death in Montreal in 1989

BARRY CAME

At first, they viewed it as a prank, some kind of collegiate farce in keeping with the festive spirit that marked the second-last day of classes at the University of Montreal's Ecole polytechnique. The man was young, about the same age as most of the roughly 60 engineering students gathered in Room 303 on the second floor of the yellow-brick building sprawled across the north slope of the mountain in the heart of the city. He entered the classroom slowly, a few minutes past five on a bitterly cold afternoon. There was a shy smile on his face as he interrupted a dissertation on the mechanics of heat transfer. In clear, unaccented French, he asked the women to move to one side of the room and ordered the men to leave. The request was greeted with titters of laughter. "Nobody moved," recalled Prof. Yvan Bouchard. "We thought it was a joke." An instant later, Bouchard and his students discovered that what they were confronting was no joke.

The young man, who would later be identified as a 25-year-old semirecluse named Marc Lépine, lifted a light, semiautomatic rifle and fired two quick shots into the ceiling. "You're all a bunch of feminists, and I hate feminists," Lépine shouted at the suddenly terrified occupants of Room 303. He told the men to leave—they did so without protest—and, as one of the young women attempted to reason with him, the gun-toting man opened fire in earnest. Six of the women were shot dead. Over the course of the next 20 minutes, the young man methodically stalked the cafeteria, the classrooms and the corridors of the school, leaving a trail of death and injury in his wake. In four separate locations scattered around three floors of the six-storey structure, he gunned down a total of 27 people, leaving 14 of them dead. Finally, he turned his weapon against himself, blowing off the top of his skull. Most of the injured and all of the dead—except for the gunman himself—were women. This week, the city and the nation will mourn again for the victims as a funeral service was held for 11 of the victims at Montreal's Notre Dame Roman Catholic church.

It was the worst single-day massacre in Canadian history. And the very senselessness of the act prompted an outpouring of grief, indignation and outright rage. The City of Montreal and the Province of Quebec declared three days of mourning. Vigils were mounted in cities and towns from coast to coast. Churches held memorial services. Prime Minister Brian Mulroney and his wife, Mila, traveled to the school to offer their condolences on behalf of the rest of Canada. "It is indeed a national tragedy," he said. Earlier, with the flag atop Parliament fluttering at half-staff, the Prime Minister had asked a hushed House of Commons: "Why such violence in a society that considers itself civilized and compassionate?"

Rolling the Dice at Meech Lake

SUSAN DELACOURT AND GRAHAM FRASER

> *The Meech Lake constitutional accord was difficult to negotiate and hotly debated. Prime Minister Brian Mulroney's strategy was unveiled in this interview, a newspaper story that played a major role in building up opposition to the deal.*

Ottawa—Prime Minister Brian Mulroney says last week's first ministers meeting was deliberately timed to bring the Meech Lake constitutional impasse down to 11th-hour negotiations.

In an interview with The Globe and Mail yesterday, Mr. Mulroney recalled how he and his advisers had gathered at 24 Sussex Dr. about a month ago to map the federal strategy to deal with the Meech Lake crisis.

"Right here, I told them when it would be," Mr. Mulroney said. "I told them a month ago when we were going to (meet.) It's like an election campaign; you count backward. (I said), 'That's the day we're going to roll the dice.'"

Although he announced later yesterday that the House of Commons would be moving soon to require public hearings on constitutional amendments, Mr. Mulroney made it clear in the interview that he would not have done anything differently last week, when the public was denied any glimpse of the seven-day discussions among the first ministers.

The Prime Minister's revelation about the set date for a first ministers meeting could come as a surprise to some of the provincial players in the Meech Lake deadlock, who believed that Ottawa's delay in calling the first ministers conference came as a result of the difficult search for "common ground" among the opponents to the accord.

Since about May 17, when a special Commons committee issued its report on the Meech Lake impasse, premiers and opposition leaders were agitating for a first ministers conference, but Mr. Mulroney insisted that the time was not yet right.

He said in the interview that he had always known that the conference would be held in the first week of June.

Liberal Opposition Leader Herbert Gray criticized Mr. Mulroney
for delaying the call so long. "We believe the Prime Minister's delay led
to the crisis atmosphere," Mr. Gray said, noting that this atmosphere left
little time for a proper solution to the impasse.

New Democratic Party Leader Audrey McLaughlin also levelled
criticism at Mr. Mulroney for letting the talks carry on in crisis-style
secrecy for so long last week.

The federal plan figured that the three holdout provinces would be
brought on side one by one, with New Brunswick first, Manitoba second
and Newfoundland last, Mr. Mulroney said in the interview.

This is exactly what has happened, with New Brunswick Premier
Frank McKenna saying midway through last week's talks that he was
ready to ratify the accord, Manitoba Premier Gary Filmon signing on by
Saturday, and Newfoundland Premier Clyde Wells awaiting a vote from
his Legislature during the next two weeks before deciding whether to
put his province's support behind the Meech Lake deal.

Mr. Mulroney said the plan was not aimed at isolating any one province. "Given certain realities, this was the order we felt it would happen."

He said he has no apologies to make for the marathon seven-day session he held to obtain the first ministers deal on Saturday night, and no
regrets about the lack of public debate on the constitutional negotiations.

"That's the way it had to be done. You're asking me if I have any
regrets? None whatsoever."

The Prime Minister said the private talks among the 11 men merely
followed a tradition established by Canada's founding fathers. Citing the
first talks held to achieve Confederation in 1867, Mr. Mulroney noted
that Canada's constitutional architects, even the first prime minister, Sir
John A. Macdonald, always conducted their most important debates in
private, with plenty of liquor and unpublished remarks.

"In Charlottetown, the boys arrived in a ship—and spent a long time
in places other than the library," Mr. Mulroney said, going on to cite other
examples of hard-drinking, rough-talking sessions of constitution-building.

"This is the way it was done. This is the way Confederation came
about. There was no public debate; there was no great public hearings. It
became a kind of tradition."

Much of last week was taken up with building the "human dynamic"
among the three men who had not been at Meech Lake, Que., for the
1987 agreement, he said, acknowledging that it probably would have been
a different deal if Mr. Wells, Mr. Filmon or Mr. McKenna were there.

Again, this is why the privacy of the talks was so important, he said.
"The last thing we needed was to go into the conference centre and say,
'Look, we've come together to try to get a constitutional deal.' It's based

on an agreement whose important human dynamic is unknown to three of the participants because they weren't there when it was done."

Posing the question rhetorically to the three holdouts, he said: "How can we explain to you why certain things were done when you weren't there? And perhaps had you been there, we'd have done things differently. But you weren't there, you weren't elected, so you didn't have the right to be there. We did it, we took the responsibility."

Nor does it bother Mr. Mulroney that the news of his deal and his negotiations came through leaks to the media and that it was a CBC announcer, not the first ministers, who gave Canadians most of their information about the constitutional session and agreement.

"Not in the slightest. It doesn't bother me at all. I find out everything about what's going on from the television, everything. Why the hell should it be different for this?"

But Mr. Mulroney also vowed that the tradition of secrecy would soon be coming to a close because of the lessons he has learned from Quebec's exclusion from the negotiating table in 1982 and all the hostility that has built up over Meech Lake in the past few years.

Mr. Mulroney also announced yesterday in the Commons that Canada should move immediately to shorten the length of time between the agreement on a constitutional amendment and the actual proclamation. At present, it can take as long as three years.

Meeting Parizeau

DIANE FRANCIS

PQ leader Jacques Parizeau was a formidable intellect and zealot.

It was late, around 5:30 p.m., and Parizeau looked tired. He had just lost his wife of many years to a lengthy and lingering battle against cancer. When Alice was mentioned, tears welled up in his eyes.

He was as candid as usual but cockier than he had been before. The mood in Quebec was ugly, and a referendum on separation would have handily won, according to polls. This reversal had taken place because negative feelings towards the rest of Canada had been astutely whipped up by Parizeau and Quebec's separatist press. They billed the death of Meech Lake as English Canada's rejection of French language and culture. From my perspective, that was bunk. English Canada had signed on and only two provincial premiers, Gary Filmon of Manitoba and Clyde Wells of Newfoundland, caused its demise.

Parizeau out of power was charming, but as leader of the opposition Parti Québécois, which was enjoying unprecedented popular support, he was frightening. He stated for the first time that a separate Quebec would agree to assume only 17 percent of the federal debt, even though it represented 24 percent of the population. He said that, like it or not, Quebec would use Canadian currency and demand seats on the Bank of Canada's board of governors. He threatened that if Canada did not like those terms and others, Quebec might simply disrupt traffic on the St. Lawrence Seaway. He said that Quebec would demand to be a third-party signatory of every treaty or free trade agreement that Canada had signed. Or else. This was important, because Canada had negotiated a veto over new entrants to its U.S. or Mexico free trade agreements, providing Ottawa with a major bargaining chip if Quebec separatists ever obtained a mandate from voters to leave.

"What we want is everything to have a third, Quebec signature. What if the Americans don't want a third signature and push Quebec out of the Free Trade Agreement? Then Quebec must have the right to look at each treaty signed in our name. NORAD, the St. Lawrence Seaway, and dozens more. Either Quebec countersigns all these treaties in one afternoon, or we renegotiate them one by one. It'll be one incredible mess."

Besides such threats, he said Quebec had to leave because of egregious past events, not merely because it was a "pain in the neck" as he had said previously. He told me, for example, that francophone geologists were unable to find jobs in Canada until the 1970s. He agreed that wasn't the case any longer. He also agreed that any ambitious Quebecer should, like himself, speak English. "Yes," he said, surprisingly, and on the record, "and I'd like them to speak a third language, too."

In his mind, another justification for leaving was that Quebecers could only trust their own provincial government in Quebec City. "No one says that what was done at the federal civil service [in terms of bilingualism] was puny or ridiculous. But more often than not, when our own [Quebec] government opened the doors, intense conflict resulted on the so-called language front [with English-Canadians]. Language rights would not have been given to us. Doors were opened only by the Quebec government. Federal bilingualism came too late. We're not mad, and we understand full well you don't operate in international markets without English."

The interview was interesting as always; but he was different this time, threatening and talking about reneging on obligations such as debts. He also openly admitted the hypocrisy of imposing French-only policies on francophones in Quebec while at the same time agreeing that a knowledge of the English language was imperative in the new economic reality.

Chaos in Haiti, 1992

FRANCINE PELLETIER

Port-Au-Prince, Haiti

«Arrêtez!» Le ton du petit caporal assis à l'entrée du poste de garde du palais présidentiel se veut autoritaire. Sa mine renfrognée aussi. Quiconque a le culot de se présenter au palais national n'a qu'à bien se tenir, semble-t-il dire. Et surtout, attendre. Une vingtaine de personnes sagement alignées sur des bancs d'église, affichant cet air mi-ennuyé mi-fatigué qu'on remarque souvent chez les Haïtiens, laissent croire que l'attente sera longue.

Heureusement, on est mardi. Le jour où—c'est écrit en petites lettres pâles au-dessus de la tête du caporal—«le premier ministre reçoit.» Au-dessus de la tête du soldat, six ou sept mitraillettes bien astiquées pendent au mur. Inévitablement, des images du dernier coup d'État, le 30 septembre 1991, le quatrième en six ans, s'imposent. La prise du palais par l'armée, la tuerie dans les rues, la fuite du prêtre-président, Jean-Bertrand Aristide . . . Ces mitraillettes ont-elles servi depuis? On se le demande.

Enfin, un soldat, un autre, un peu serré dans son uniforme kaki recyclé de l'armée américaine, me conduit, solennellement, jusqu'à l'entrée du palais national. L'énorme bâtiment blanc trône comme un gros gâteau de noces à l'extrémité ouest de la place des Héros de l'Indépendance—plus familièrement appelée place des Zéros. A l'intérieur de ce monument à la vacuité et à la prétention, les taches de sang séchées sur le tapis du grand escalier surprennent un peu. Tant de grands airs mériteraient plus d'attention aux détails.

«M. le premier ministre n'est pas encore arrivé, me dira sa secrétaire. Patientez.»

Bienvenue en Haïti. Pays de l'intimidation et de la grandiloquence. De l'ambition démesurée et du n'importe quoi. Plus que toute autre chose, plus que la misère, le vaudou et les bains de sangs. Haïti, c'est ça: un pays qui fait semblant. («Demain appartient à Haïti» annonce, absurdement optimiste, une affiche à l'aéroport de Port-au-Prince.) Un pays qui s'est doté au cours de ses 192 ans d'existence de 25 constitutions—un record, après la Bolivie, dans l'histoire des peuples—et qui n'en a respecté aucune. Un pays où les dirigeants font semblant de gouverner et les gens, semblant de ne rien voir.

Comme le vieux Thompson, par exemple, ombre permanente du jadis chic, aujourd'hui décrépi, hôtel Oloffson à Port-au-Prince. «Connaisseur d'art haïtien», Thompson, qui fait aussi une prodigieuse consommation de rhum, évite généralement de parler politique. La politique fait fuir les touristes, il ne le sait que trop. Déjà, l'Oloffson doit offrir des soirées vaudou, le vendredi, pour attirer la clientèle. Ah! ils sont loin les jours où Graham Greene, Irving Stone et autres grands écrivains venaient trouver l'inspiration sous les éventails et les hauts plafonds de cette ancienne résidence présidentielle. Même les journalistes fuient l'Oloffson depuis que l'électricité fait quotidiennement défaut, à cause de l'embargo.

«Haïti a aucune chance de réaliser rien avec ce gouvernement», dit enfin le vieil homme, frêle comme un cure-dent. Comme la plupart des Haïtiens, Thompson a fini par admettre son écoeurement. Le pays a beau avoir la couenne dure, et l'habitude des coups d'État, celui du 30 septembre 1991 s'est avéré une catastrophe sans pareille pour la majorité des Haïtiens. «Arracher un morceau de pain des mains, alors qu'on y goûte pour la première fois, explique l'ancien directeur de Radio-Soleil, Hugo Trieste, est un plus grand crime que de retenir ce morceau de pain.»

C'est un recul de taille, donc, que connaît actuellement le pays. Haïti *faire back*, comme on dit en créole. Huit mois après un coup d'État qui a tué, estime-t-on, 3 000 personnes et en a fait s'exiler 35 000 autres, une chose est sûre: la vieille classe politique, imbue d'elle-même et assoiffée de pouvoir, est en selle à nouveau. Mais avec un brin de sophistication, cette fois, un je-ne-sais-quoi de retenue dans l'air, un désir de plaire—ou d'en imposer—au monde extérieur.

Les rituels vaudouisants de Papa Doc Duvalier et les fastes cérémonies de son fils Jean-Claude ont cédé le pas à un parlementarisme douteux certes, mais présent. Et les «présidents à vie» ont fait place à des dirigeants plus distingués, certainement plus intellectuels. Comme Raoul Cédras, par exemple, commandant en chef de l'armée, «un pion des États-Unis depuis longtemps», dit Edwidge Balutansky, correspondante de l'agence Reuter, «mais qui n'est pas la pire crapule.» Ou encore, comme Marc Bazin, nouveau premier ministre du gouvernement «de consensus et de salut public», lui-même étroitement lié aux États-Unis et surnommé «M. Net» par la presse américaine, du temps qu'il était ministre des Finances de Jean-Claude Duvalier.

Nouveaux hommes forts d'Haïti, ces deux personnages redonnent un certain vernis à la «perle des Antilles.» Ils croient, en fait, explique Mme Balutansky, elle-même haïtienne, qu'ils ont «un devoir à faire, un ordre à maintenir.» Si la violence en principe leur répugne—ni l'un ni l'autre n'y ont été directement associés avant le coup d'État—ils sont prêts à l'utiliser, ou à fermer les yeux, au besoin. Comme dit le ministre de l'information, Gérard Bissainthe, «des gentils, vous savez, n'ont qu'un oeil.»

La dictature est donc de retour en Haïti, mais à double visage. Au sommet de la pyramide, on retrouve les «comme il faut», Cédras, Bazin, Bissainthe et cie qui font belle figure et savent se tenir. Ce sont les Dr

Jekyll du régime actuel. Derrière eux, oeuvrant désormais dans l'ombre et le mystère, on retrouve les «crapules», les M. Hyde du régime. Le redoutable chef de la police de Port-au-Prince, Michel François, par exemple, que tout le monde soupçonne d'avoir mené le coup d'État. Du moins, de s'être acquitté de la sale besogne. Il aurait été l'exécutant du coup et Cédras, le maître-d'oeuvre.

Une façon de faire que le leader du Mouvement pour l'instauration de la démocratie en Haïti (MIDH), Marc Bazin, connaît bien lui aussi. Un reporter de Radio-Antilles, Pierre-André Pacquiot, raconte comment, quelques semaines avant les élections de décembre 1990, deux autres journalistes et lui ont été interceptés par les gardes du corps de Bazin, accompagnés de militaires. «Ils ne nous ont pas posé de questions, dit-il. Ils nous ont frappés, puis ont cassé la voiture. Ils nous ont accusés ensuite de les avoir dépassés.»

La vraie raison de cette bastonnade tenait au fait que le candidat du MIDH ne prisait guère la mauvaise presse dont il était victime depuis le début de la campagne. Récoltant à peine 13% de la faveur populaire (selon un sondage de Radio-Métropole en avril, Bazin fait toujours piètre figure), il tenait les médias, de toute évidence, responsables.

Si la dictature pure et dure semble chose du passé, il n'y a pas de rupture avec le pouvoir des tontons macoutes (les fiers-à-bras de Duvalier) comme tel. Marc Bazin a d'ailleurs toujours dit qu'il fallait «s'appuyer sur les structures traditionnelles du pays», c'est-à-dire inclure les macoutes dans le processus politique.

Par contre, on remarque un net relâchement de la discipline dans les rangs de l'armée. «Les soldats sont plus arrogants, ils ne se laissent pas diriger par la hiérarchie militaire», explique le père Trieste. Ce qui fait qu'aujourd'hui «même les militaires ont peur des militaires.»

Quiconque a vu les images télévisées du départ précipité des membres de l'Organisation des États américains, en octobre 1991, en sait quelque chose. Mitraillettes en main, les soldats, qui devaient protéger le départ des visiteurs, se sont mis tout à coup à bousculer, à pointer leurs armes et à proférer des menaces. Excès de mauvaise humeur? Montée de fièvre nationaliste? Ou directives venues d'en haut? Impossible à dire. C'est d'ailleurs ce qu'il y a de plus terrifiant en Haïti: de ne jamais savoir exactement à qui on a affaire et ce que ces individus—armés, toujours—pourraient avoir en tête.

«Sous Duvalier, dit le directeur de l'agence France-Presse, Dominique Levanti, on ne pouvait pas tirer une balle sans être immédiatement interpellé. Aujourd'hui c'est une pétarade après l'autre!»

Sous les Duvalier, tout était rigidement contrôlé. D'un côté, les militaires, de l'autre, les tristement célèbres Volontaires de la sécurité nationale (tontons macoutes), créés pour équilibrer les forces armées. Le tout minutieusement supervisé par un chef absolu. Aujourd'hui, il n'y a plus de contrôles aussi stricts. Le ministre de l'Information, Gérard Bissainthe, l'admet volontiers, d'ailleurs. «L'armée intervient malheureusement avant que nous puissions faire fonctionner l'appareil judiciaire», dit-il pour expliquer les exactions, arrestations, menaces de toutes sortes qui pullulent. Et il ajoute, débonnaire: «Comme disait le général de Gaulle, le pouvoir, c'est l'impuissance.»

Bref, si le climat actuel paraît plus calme, plus «civilisé», il est aussi plus imprévisible et plus dangereux. «Avant, on pouvait nous arrêter, nous battre, dit le journaliste Sylvain Chanel. Aujourd'hui, on pourrait nous éliminer.»

Duvalier est mort, vive le duvaliérisme. La situation en Haïti se résume à ça, en fait. Et aussi, à une polarisation accrue entre la classe dirigeante—ceux «qui ont un ego gros comme le palais national», dit le ministre de la Planification sous Aristide Renaud Bernardin—et ceux qui ont moins que rien, la majorité de la population. Ceux qui ont en horreur Jean Bertrand Aristide, et qui n'hésiteraient pas à l'éliminer advenant son retour, et ceux qui ont vu en «Titid» un miracle, et n'hésiteraient pas à le défendre. Haïti court-elle donc vers la guerre civile?

Au contraire, dit l'ex-premier ministre, Jean-Jacques Honorat, qui occupait encore le palais national au moment de ma visite. «C'est nous qui avons sauvé le pays de la guerre civile.» Suivent une longue diatribe contre la «catastrophe appelée Aristide» et un rappel du «devoir» qu'a tout pays de se protéger de l'ignominie. À écouter cet ex-défenseur des droits et libertés, on jurerait que la violence, c'est avant le coup d'État qu'elle s'est produite, pas après. «Les parlementaires ont été battus . . . tout le monde avait peur de se retrouver un pneu autour du cou», poursuit-il, passionné, n'hésitant pas à qualifier le seul président haïtien démocratiquement élu d'«Hitler» et d'«ayatollah.»

Maître démagogue, Jean-Jacques Honorat exagère bien sûr. En ce qui concerne les violations de la personne, il n'y a pas de comparaison entre le gouvernement Aristide et le régime autoproclamé actuel. Tous les organismes de défense des droits humains, d'Amnistie Internationale au Lawyers' Committee to Protect Human Rights à New York, sont formels là-dessus. Néanmoins, Honorat soulève un point important: l'intolérance qu'on retrouve partout en Haïti. «C'est le fléau numéro un du pays», déplore le doyen de la presse étrangère, Dominique Levanti.

C'est d'ailleurs le seul point sur lequel tout le monde s'entend là-bas: la difficulté d'accepter un point de vue adverse. Et, le cas échéant, l'envie de battre, la rage qui s'empare des gens. Si vous avez le malheur de renverser quelqu'un sur la route, par exemple, il ne faut surtout pas vous arrêter: vous risqueriez de vous faire empoigner et battre par la foule. «Ce ne sont pas les macoutes qu'il faut combattre, ajoute Levanti, c'est l'esprit du macoutisme en permanence!»

Tout se passe, en fait, comme si la vengeance populaire, celle des petits soldats ou celle d'une foule en délire, était la seule issue, la seule possibilité d'expression pour une population trop longtemps brimée et méprisée. Tout se passe comme si Haïti n'avait toujours pas fini de payer une indépendance trop précoce, faite avant tout le monde, mais sans autre modèle en tête que celui du maître tortionnaire.

«Les traumatismes coloniaux, vous ne pouvez pas comprendre, mais ça marque pendant des centaines d'années, poursuit l'ex-premier ministre. Surtout l'esclavage. Nous étions sous la férule du colon armé d'un fouet. Celui qui a le droit d'exercer la coercition. Et qui frappe. N'importe qui. C'est un modèle et nous l'avons reproduit. C'est malheureux à dire mais Haïti est une société foncièrement intolérante.»

À l'Oloffson, les quelques clients de l'hôtel pataugent dans le noir, silencieux tout à coup. Interruption de courant. L'heure des ténèbres a sonné. «Au moins si c'était tous les jours à la même heure», dit Thompson en haussant les épaules.

Bientôt, les chiens se mettront à aboyer. Comme toutes les nuits, dans un concert de lamentations inimaginables, couvrant les coups de feu qui retentissent dans le noir. Toutes les nuits de Port-au-Prince sont comme ça. Au petit matin, quand les chiens auront fini d'aboyer, on trouvera un ou deux cadavres dans les rues, qu'on fera semblant de ne pas voir.

On peut tout faire avec une baïonnette, dit-on, sauf s'asseoir dessus. Mais en ce pays incroyable qu'est Haïti, on y arrive. On arrive même à sourire et à se parer de grands airs pour mieux dissimuler le coup. Mais pour combien de temps encore?

Voilà la question.

Teaching and Learning History

KEN DRYDEN

Hockey great Ken Dryden turned himself into a fine reporter, as this account of what went on in a high school in 1994 demonstrates.

Wednesday, May 11, 11:22 a.m.

No Willy, no Chad, no Pat, no Marv, no Calvin. History class begins. Rick Ray writes on the board: "The Countdown to War: June 28, 1914 to August 4, 1914." Calvin arrives, then Marv, then Pat, then twenty minutes into the class, Willy. Rick stops.

"Sit down, William, and get this down."

"Sir, I don't have my books. Chad has them and I don't think he's here today." Sandee hands him a sheet of paper and a pen; he begins writing. Less than a minute later, he stops, less than a minute after that, he starts again.

Rodney looks lost. He had been doing so well; something has happened to him this week. He had started the semester cautiously, waiting to see which way the class would go for him. Not too loud or too late or too absent, not a troublemaker or a troubleseeker, he'd always back off the fooling around just before Rick's limit was reached. Then gradually he seemed to get interested in the course itself.

Rodney likes the games, choosing teams, feeling himself on one side against another, strutting right answers, a little "two thumbs up," a little "in your face," depending on how the mood strikes. Needling Calvin, flirting with Monika, he is a lively, harmless presence in the class. But today, Rodney wants nothing to do with anybody. He sits slumped in his seat, his binder open, his eyes closed. "What's wrong?" Rick asks finally. "I'm sick, sir," he says with conviction. After he is certain Rodney is not too sick, Rick lets him be.

But Calvin doesn't. Every few seconds, he yammers a burst of words at Rodney who, without opening his eyes, as if swishing away a bothersome pest, twists his head, contorts his face, and yammers back some words of his own. This distracts Ahmed, who sits in front of Rodney, across from Calvin. Ahmed is a good student who has had a disappointing semester. At the beginning, Rick thought he would be one of his strong students, a rival to Fahad, but Ahmed has other priorities. He does adequately, but he has come to enjoy the social life of the class more than the work. He starts out today facing ahead in his seat, interested, intending to be involved, but slowly his head turns. He finds Rodney and Calvin irresistible. Marv sits in front of Calvin and would ordinarily join whatever fray was available, but today he seems so out of it that nothing gets his attention. Not so Monika, who sits in front of Ahmed. Every so often, Calvin says something to Rodney just loud enough for Monika to hear, and she swirls around flashing an exasperated, affectionate smile towards him. But Monika is strong enough to decide for herself which way the pull of the room will take her, and she faces the front most of the time attending to the business of the class.

Rick can see what's going on, of course. He offers a few quiet, stern words at first, then lets things go as he gets absorbed in his own lesson. He holds either side of his lectern, his head tilted forward, his face and voice hitting the highs and lows of his message. He acts out the build-up to World War I, playing to one side of the room, then the other. He talks, writes on the board, then searches for answers among the students. He ignores Fahad's hand as often as he can, saving the harder questions for him, saving for him those moments when the class bogs down. When the kids are trying to puzzle through to an answer and can afford some temporary misdirection, he calls on Jamie. He asks Calvin, to give him something to do, Monika and Charlene because, capable but quiet, they need to be pushed. He asks Sandee and Karen, who never offer an answer on their own, because he will forget they are here if he doesn't.

He drops the class into Austria-Hungary, into Serbia, into Germany and Russia. He describes each nation's state of mind, the nature of European geopolitics at the time. He describes the escalating arms race. Germany has built up its navy; what does England do? Archduke Franz Ferdinand is assassinated, the Austro-Hungarians march into Serbia, Russia mobilizes; what about Germany? What about England and France? He talks of the psychology of war: "'If you fail to prepare'" he thunders, as if both houses of parliament were before him, "'you are preparing to fail.'" He stops himself and changes character. "Some of you might want to keep that in mind with exams coming up," he smiles. The change comes too fast for Willy. "What was that, sir?" he asks. Rick repeats himself. Willy flops back into his chair, "Ah, that's beautiful, man." He remains back in his chair a few moments longer, then raises his hand.

"Yes, William, you have a question?"

"Can I be excused, sir?"

It is twelve noon. Each day Willy is here, he asks the same question at the same time. Sometimes Rick lets him go, sometimes not. He knows Willy can't give more than forty or fifty good minutes a class; ask him for more and he would probably get less. Today, Rick says yes. Ten minutes later, Willy returns. Though Rick doesn't know it for sure, he could guess: Willy was in the Caf, earphones in his ears, Walkman turned up, a small tub of French fries in his hands, dancing up and down the aisles, greeting his buddies. He returns as Rick finds himself tuning in more to Rodney, Calvin, and Ahmed than to what he is saying himself.

"Calvin! Ahmed!" Rick explodes, "I've had enough with you two. Face the front!"

The room goes quiet, Rodney goes back to sleep, Calvin and Ahmed turn their bodies more or less to face the front.

At the end of class, Rick tells Calvin that tomorrow he's going to move him closer to the front, away from Rodney.

"I won't be here tomorrow, sir," he says.

"You won't be here? Where will you be?"

"I don't know, sir."

"What do you mean, you don't know?"

"I won't be here."

"You won't be here, but you don't know why?"

"It's my birthday."

The Hell of Rwanda

UNKNOWN

A Canadian Navy officer, attached to the UN mission to Rwanda, reports on genocide.

Kibeho, Rwanda
April 22, 1995

I arrived at approximately 0745 at Kibeho Camp by UN helicopter with journalists from *Reuters, Magnum* and *Die Deit.*

The RPA [Rwandan Patriotic Army] at the first roadblock, located between the helipad and the ZAMBATT [Zambian Battalion] Company HQ, denied the journalists access to not just the camp, but also to the ZAMBATT Company HQ.

As I was in uniform, we agreed that I would go into the camp and find out what was going on and return and brief the journalists later that morning.

At this time, across the hill, we saw a man being chased by two armed RPA down the hill—he was shot at a few times, but not hit and a few minutes later, apprehended.

Throughout the rest of the morning, there were sporadic bursts of gunfire either into or above the crowd, or at specific persons trying to run through the cordon

On entering the camp. I first made my way to Medécins Sans Frontieres [Doctors Without Borders or MSF in French] building, located next to the ZAMBATT Company HQ. On entering the compound, I faced approximately 50 persons with severe, fresh machete wounds to the head, face, neck, back, arms and legs. There appeared to be only two local MSF staff on hand, with no medical supplies and there was not much they could do.

I then passed by the back of the ZAMBATT Company HQ where the Zambians showed me an IDP who had tried to hide in one of their pit latrines and was buried up to the head in excrement and was either dead or unconscious.

By 0825, I had made my way along the road towards the ZAMBATT Company HQ location, found in the centre of the camp. The crowd was very tense—likely from being packed together as they were, but also from four days of little sleep, food and water, horrendous sanitary conditions, night machete attacks and fear of their future, but specifically, I would say, as a result of the sporadic gunfire that was occurring.

At 0830, I witnessed a man trying to run through the cordon past the RPA. He was shot in the back at very close range by an RPA soldier chasing him. I tried, along with two Zambian soldiers, to get over to see if he had survived, but we were prevented from doing so by the RPA.

For the next hour-and-a-quarter, I made my way to the back of the ZAMBATT Company HQ location, but due to the crowds, was unable to gain access to the compound. The crowds were crushing up to the compound and there was a general tenseness and misery about the situation amongst the IDPs.

At some point, I saw another man being shot by the RPA as he tried to run down a hill. Again, we were denied access to his body, but within 15 minutes, he had been buried on the spot by the RPA.

During this time, ZAMBATT soldiers began to move the very frightened crowd back from the ZAMBATT company location. This was a slow, but steady process. People were generally confused, fatigued and despondent. As they passed by us, some would indicate that if they left their throats would be cut, others made halfhearted attempts to walk towards the RPA who pushed them back into the crowd and others were dehydrated enough to drink muddy water from plastic sheets strewn about the ground. Many children had lost their parents and were wandering around aimlessly.

A UN truck had been overtaken by the crowd and men could be seen atop the cab and others trying to get in. It had to stop as it made its way towards the compound due to the density of the crowd.

After assisting in directing people back, I made my way through the crowd to the ZAMBATT compound. I had been in Kibeho on Wednesday and Thursday that week, but never had the crowd been packed together so tightly. It was essentially a question of forcing our way through the crowd and for the first time in my many visits to Kibeho over that past week and over the past three months, I distinctly felt that there was an air of danger, fear and tension among the IDPs.

As we pushed our way through the crowd towards the entrance of the compound, the crowd cleared, but only because the road was covered in bodies of dead, dying or injured people—to the point where it was impossible not to pass by without at some point stepping on someone. I would estimate that there were about 20 people: men, women and children, laying in front of the compound. However, these were injured not by bullet wounds, but rather machete wounds or having been crushed, suffocated or dehydrated.

I finally gained access to the ZAMBATT compound and over the next two and one quarter hours, we assisted with bringing in injured people—some with machete wounds to the face, having babies/children, both alive and dead, passed to us from the crowd and giving what water we had to the sick and dying. Some of the ZAMBATT soldiers would go out into the crowd and help bring in bodies or injured people. They also were able to clear the pile of bodies at the front entrance, by bringing them into the compound. They also provided a sense of stability to an impossible situation and kept the crowd as calm and organized as they could. However, with the sporadic firing taking place at all points of the camp, as the morning went on, the situation appeared more and more grim. Some healthy men fought their way into the compound, but were apprehended by ZAMBATT and pushed outside the barbed wire perimeter.

At approximately 1035, the ZAMBATT compound received fire to the degree that we all immediately dove behind sandbags for a few minutes. It is impossible to say whether the fire was directed at us, but is certain that it passed all around us—no one was injured in the compound, but could have been in the crowd.

At 1045, I confirmed with an UNREO [United Nations Rwanda Emergency Office] representative who had made his way illegally past the cordon and into the compound, the MSF, UNICEF [United Nations Children's Fund], Save The Children, etc. [aid workers] were all being blocked by the RPA cordon and no medical assistance was getting in.

By this time, there were over 125 people inside the compound to whom we were providing safety, security and sanctuary as well as humanitarian and medical assistance as best we could. I counted 35 dead babies/children that were lined up in the compound. Of the other victims, I would say that the majority were still alive, however, about 15 adults and youths were dead from trampling, suffocation, dehydration, etc. There were also about 75 children sitting in the compound. Throughout, the ZAMBATT troops were providing water to them and those in the crowd and generally maintaining some semblance of control around the compound, in fact, doing a magnificent job given the conditions.

At approximately 1100, the prefect of Gikongoro [Province located in Southeast Rwanda] drove through the crowd and through the compound, accompanied by [the] RPA. He continued on towards the transportation/screening point at the opposite end of the camp.

Shortly thereafter, I watched another man shot who had been walking past the compound down the hill at the back of the ZAMBATT location. Again, we were denied access to his body and he was buried by [the] RPA within five to ten minutes on the hillside in a shallow grave.

Throughout this time, there was sporadic gunfire throughout the camp. Also, I could see that people walking through the screening point towards the transportation points—as they were, they were being beaten severely by [the] RPA with long, heavy sticks and rifle butts.

In the opposite direction, in a clearing on the hill, a woman was beaten to the ground by three RPA [soldiers] with sticks, then chased and beaten back up into the crowd. If you are wondering why we couldn't do anything, these occurrences were taking place hundreds of yards and tens of thousands of people away, and our hands were full taking care of the sick and dying around the compound and also providing security to the compound. At the same time, ZAMBATT soldiers would venture into the crowd to assist those that they could.

More people with machete wounds stumbled into the compound area and we had them sit in the shade of some UN vehicles in the area.

By this time, the women and children were hiding under the vehicles inside the compound.

At 1150, more shots were heard around the camp, this time a more serious and intense volley—the crowd was bordering on panic.

At 1155, a severe rainstorm approached the camp and by 1200, the rain started coming down hard on the crowd. The ZAMBATT soldiers held their positions at the barbed wire perimeter of the compound shouting to the crowd to stay where they were and calm down—others helped move the 35 to 40 dead babies/children into the building for dignity from the rain.

As the rain beat down and the crowd shifted for shelter, heavy gunfire erupted from all over the camp. Within one minute, despite the best efforts of ZAMBATT soldiers to prevent it, the crowd poured over the barbed wire and overran the outside part of the compound, which included the jeep I was in. They did not make it into the walled part of the compound.

Our vehicle instantly disappeared under the crowd. We couldn't see outside the windows or the windshield due to the people crushed against the car, on the hood, on the windshield, on the roof and under the vehicle. For the next one-and-a half hours, we remained in the vehicle, not only physically unable to open a door for the crush of people, but when I started to roll down my window for air, people tried to force their way inside.

The firing continued from 1200 to about 1250, relatively continuously, then died down to sporadic fire. The people on the roof had broken our antennae so we could not send messages out about our situation, but as we were about 20 yards from a UN truck that had three ZAMBATT soldiers on the cab keeping people from overtaking it, we remained inside the vehicle rather than risking the impossible of forcing our way out of the vehicle and through the crowd.

At about 1300, someone told us through the window that people were being macheted in the crowd behind the vehicle—one minute later, a man's face appeared in one of the windows, split in half with a machete.

Throughout, people were passing babies and children above their heads towards the ZAMBATT compound, which may explain the 250 abandoned children found there later.

At about 1330, the crowd was still crushed together, but two ZAMBATT soldiers forced their way to the vehicle and using sticks, were able to clear a path for us towards the end of the camp. As they did so, they had to pick up and remove bodies from before us, and as we passed, the crowd swallowed up any space that had been provided.

By 1345, we were at the transportation point outside the perimeter of the camp. Sporadic firing could still be heard. After waiting for instructions for about [an] hour, then we were told to go to Butare [the district capital of the province of Butare located in Southeast Rwanda].

On the road to Butare, we measured a 13-kilometre steady stream of IDPs making their way along the road. They were being beaten by the RPA with sticks, were being stopped and having what little possessions they

had with them taken, and were being forced to run down the road by the
RPA chasing them. On more than one occasion I witnessed local civilians
along the sides of the road beating the IDPs [Internally Displaced Persons]
as they passed by.

At this point, I stopped being a witness to the events, but am told that
at approximately 1730, heavy firing into the crowd took place for an
extended period, including machine gun firing, grenades and, I am told,
mortar rounds.

Quebec's 1995 Referendum

EDISON STEWART

Montreal—Lucien Bouchard no sooner told separatists to accept last
night's defeat than he promised a new vote could be held soon.

"The idea (of independence) is alive in too many Quebecers to extinguish it now," the Bloc Québécois leader declared.

"On the contrary, it is more alive than ever.

"The Yes has never been as numerous as tonight," he said to cheers
from a crowd of a few thousand who had hoped to see the birth of a new
country.

"It Hurts"

"Let's keep hope, because the next time will be the one.

"And that next time could come more rapidly than we think!" he
vowed to a roar from the crowd.

Bouchard spoke for only seven minutes and appeared grim despite the
fighting stance. His wife, Audrey Best, appeared on the verge of tears.

"I am, like you all, disappointed by tonight's verdict," began Bouchard,
who plans to face a victorious Prime Minister Jean Chrétien in the House
of Commons today.

"Never has the victory of the Yes appeared so close than these last
days.

"To see it escape at the very moment we thought it was within our
grasp, it hurts.

"But, dear friends, let us recognize that democracy has spoken.

"And democracy, we have to remember tonight, is the foundation of
everything."

Bouchard drew boos when he said the separatist government must
now bow to the will of the majority, as slim as it is.

"Yes, I tell you, whatever our sadness, our first duty is to behave as
democrats and accept, with calm and dignity, the decision of Quebecers,"
he said.

"Let us be proud of the democratic exercise that is ending.

"The referendum debate has demonstrated discipline, political maturity, the profound attachment of Quebecers to democratic values."

But then he shifted gears and began speaking about a future referendum, saying campaign workers had "planted deep, for the future, the roots of hope."

The federalists have won but Canada's unity problem is worse than ever, he declared.

"If the federalists in Ottawa do not realize that the Canadian federal regime has never been so fragile as it is tonight, they will have understood nothing from what has just happened.

"More than ever, we must put reconciliation at the centre of our concerns.

"But more than ever also, we must be vigilant given the results of tonight. Solidarity is more necessary than ever.

"There are people in Ottawa tonight who may think they now have a free hand (to do what they want with Quebec).

"They must know that they're wrong!" he declared to more cheers.

Bouchard gave no indication what will now happen to the 53-member Bloc in Parliament.

In the past he has variously hinted he might quit if the referendum was lost; at other times he has left open the possibility the Bloc would stay in the House to defend Quebec's interests.

The latter now seems more likely, at least in the short term, given the closeness of last night's result.

Bouchard ended the campaign with a warning that this could be Quebec's last chance to be an independent country.

"Seize it and vote yes . . . say Yes to ourselves. Say Yes to the people of Quebec," he declared at a rally Sunday.

"We don't have the right to let this chance pass us by. God knows when there will be another chance."

The last-minute warning was in stark contrast to his declaration at the outset of the campaign that separatists would never give up until Quebec is out of Canada.

Bouchard, the most popular politician in Quebec by far, was absolutely critical to the separatist campaign.

Even before Premier Jacques Parizeau appointed him *de facto* leader Oct. 7, Bouchard weighed in heavily both on the timing of the referendum and the wording of the question.

In last year's Quebec election, Parizeau had promised the question would be short and clear, something like: "Do you want Quebec to become a sovereign country, as of (date)?"

But when Parizeau barely won the election, Bouchard publicly warned Parizeau conditions weren't right for a quick referendum.

"There is no way sovereignists will engage in a losing referendum," he declared last September.

Bouchard intervened again this spring to demand that the separatist campaign place much greater emphasis on plans for a post-independence partnership—"equal to equal"—with what would be left of Canada.

Selling "Partnership"

Parizeau ultimately agreed and the two brought in the leader of a tiny third party, Mario Dumont of the Action democratique, to sign a deal June 12 setting out the terms of the proposed partnership.

The referendum question made no mention of Quebec becoming a "country." Instead, it read:

"Do you agree that Quebec should become sovereign, after having made a formal offer to Canada for a new economic and political partnership, within the scope of the bill respecting the future of Quebec and of the agreement signed on June 12, 1995?"

Bouchard's self-acknowledged role was not to sell sovereignty as much as it was to sell the proposed "partnership."

All the polls showed that, with a guarantee of an economic and political association with what would be left of Canada, a majority of people said they would vote Yes.

But without such guarantee, they said they would vote No, and polls early in the campaign found separatist support suffering as a result.

"I think perhaps we waited too long before speaking about the partnership," Bouchard explained to one interviewer after he took over in mid-October.

"We've talked a fairly long time about sovereignty; I decided to focus my message on the partnership," he told La Presse a few days later.

Bouchard quickly whipped up separatist passions, tapping feelings of pride, fear, and vengeance.

The latter came with repeated references to the 1982 changes to the Constitution by Ottawa and the other nine provinces which slightly reduced Quebec's power over language issues over its strenuous objections.

And mention of the defeat of the Meech Lake constitutional accord, and its proposed recognition of Quebec as a distinct society, was never far behind.

Bouchard used fear by speaking in apocalyptic terms about the consequences of a No vote, saying Quebecers would be left defenceless against the actions of a sinister federal government.

Thirty Years of Bilingualism

MURRAY CAMPBELL

Did the Official Languages Act change Canada and Canadians? A generation after the Act's passage, a report card on successes and failures.

Thirty years after official bilingualism became a fact of Canadian life it is perhaps time to issue a report card on just how it is doing. What has been the point of the language laws, the bilingual signs, the school programs, even the bilingual corn flakes packages?

If we grade it on the basis of whether a once cranky English Canada has learned to speak French, it qualifies as a success beyond most expectations: About 4.4 million people—more than 16 per cent of the population—can speak both English and French. The delivery of federal services from coast to coast in two languages is a reality. Hundreds of thousands of students have learned French in immersion programs. In Ottawa, the men and women who were in on the ground floor of official bilingualism wear Order of Canada buttons and pronounce themselves well pleased with their effort.

"It is, in my view, one of the most extraordinarily successful social revolutions ever brought about peacefully in a democratic country anywhere," says Max Yalden, a Torontonian who learned French as an adult and served for five years as the Official Languages Commissioner.

But if, as many anglos believe, the 1969 official Languages Act was freighted with a higher design—the use of language to bind together two nations into one country—the marks on the report card get much lower, particularly in the West. "Canadian politics has been dominated by a language policy that provides no more than a chimera of the justice it promised nor of the unity it was supposed to guarantee," says Scott Reid, the bilingual author of a 1993 study, *Lament for a Notion*, that is highly critical of bilingualism.

Neither the supporters or opponents of Canada's language policies are likely to prevail anytime soon, but thanks to piles of government data and exhaustive academic analysis, the major linguistic trends in Canada can be identified. John Richards, a bilingual Simon Fraser University professor and former NDP politician, summarized them in a recent paper for the C.D. Howe Institute:

- French-English bilingualism has increased in both Quebec and the other nine provinces, from 13 per cent nationally in 1971 to 16 per cent in 1991. In Quebec, the rate rose to 35 per cent from 28 and in the rest of Canada to 10 per cent from 7.

- Outside Quebec, French is in decline with the exception of regions adjacent to Quebec, such as eastern Ontario and northern New Brunswick. Expressed in terms of mother tongue, francophones represented 4.8 per cent of the population of the nine English-speaking provinces in the last census, compared with 6 per cent in 1971. If home language is used, francophones are just 3.2 per cent of the population now and the vast majority are concentrated in New Brunswick and Ontario.
- The proportion of those who learn French as infants and still use it at home as adults is nearly 100 per cent in Quebec and 90 per cent in New Brunswick. But in the rest of Canada the retention rate is just 65 per cent, compared with 70 per cent two decades ago. Take away New Brunswick and Ontario and the rate falls to 40 per cent, compared with 51 per cent 20 years ago.
- Within Quebec, French has retained its status as the overwhelmingly dominant language. The proportion of anglophones has declined since 1971 after remaining stable for the previous 20 years, mostly in reaction to laws guaranteeing the primacy of French within the province.

The scope of the Official Languages Act was modest. It dealt with the public service and the provision of services in two languages. It said nothing about obliging Canadians to become bilingual or about securing Quebec's place in Confederation.

But there's no doubt the spirit of the times transformed Ottawa's initiative into something bolder, and for many people, particularly anglophones, the quest for linguistic equity was framed by the question of national unity.

But there's no doubt that it has transformed Canada in the past 30 years—a fact viewed with considerable satisfaction in Ottawa, no doubt because it has been most affected by the zeal of the B&B era.

Today, more than 63,000 public-service positions—about 31 per cent of the work force—are designated bilingual and meetings conducted in two languages are commonplace. Francophones now make up about 28 per cent of the public service.

This remarkable achievement reflects the toil of thousands of people over a great deal of time (it takes about 1,000 hours—at a current budgeted rate of $27 an hour—to make someone bilingual).

Many came grumpily and many left with atrocious accents in their adopted language, but the inarguable fact is that about 100,000 public employees have taken up a second language and that a public service that was once unrelentingly English-speaking is now irreversibly bilingual. "I believe that on the scale we've done it, Canada is unique in the world," says Judith Moses, executive director of the Public Service Commission's training programs branch. "I'm told by world experts that this is an unparallelled experiment."

This education of the public service is mirrored by the phenomenal growth of French immersion school programs in English Canada. In 1976, there were fewer than 18,000 students in French immersion; today there are more than 310,000—about 7 per cent of the English-speaking school system. Quebec does not offer an English-immersion program but English as a second language is compulsory from Grade 4 to the end of high school.

The experience of how much French these immersion children retain as they become adults is so far not encouraging. Birgit Harley of OISE concluded, after reviewing all the research, that the pattern of French use is generally rather limited for most immersion graduates and that, consequently, skills decline although perhaps not irretrievably.

So how much has it all cost? Can we do a cost-benefit study of bilingualism? Despite its successes, the larger criticism that current Official Languages Commissioner Victor Goldbloom has to deal with is whether the whole enormous bilingualism machinery is worth the cost.

He estimates the overall cost to the government last year—including two-language service delivery and federal transfers to the provinces for education—at $549-million (out of federal program expenditures of about $109-billion). The spending is about $105-million less than it was in 1992 because of cuts to in transfer payments and reductions in support for minority-language activities.

Critics, noting the interwoven costs of everything from public-service language training to the labelling requirement on packaged goods, say the cost is much, much more.

Scott Reid's "preliminary stab" in 1993 was an annual cost to the Canadian economy of $5-billion—of which $2.7-billion represented direct federal expenditures, $300-million was provincial spending resulting from federal initiatives and $2-billion arising from private sector compliance with federal language regulations. He suggests that more than $50-billion has been added to the federal debt in the past two decades because of "the official-languages monster."

Dr. Goldbloom, relying on Treasury Board figures, dismisses Mr. Reid's figures. A recent report he commissioned, for example, found the average cost of compliance with bilingual laws and regulations was about $100-million a year—not the $2-billion that Mr. Reid suggested.

Whatever the price tag, bilingualism's defenders, as often as not, will shrug and say this is the cost of being a country. The real issue, they say, is what would be the cost of *not* having some sort of language regimen. "I think the language thing has always been fundamental to this country," says Mr. Yalden, who was language commissioner from 1977 to 1984. "You either come to terms with that or it tears the country apart."

Supporters of the federal official-languages policy believe it has been key in keeping Quebec in Confederation. Trouble is, it might also be contributing to Quebec's uneasiness.

Somehow, Canada has ended up with a system that also allows Quebec to operate under a more protectionist philosophy. While anglophones, for the most part, feel enriched by a culture in which two languages flourish, Quebec is suspicious of the federal power over language matters that makes this possible.

Québécois accept both languages—their 35-per-cent rate of bilingualism is the highest in the country—but they resist the idea of official bilingualism inside the province for fear that French would be swamped.

Thus, the federal government and Quebec remain devoted to different language-policy visions. Ottawa pursues the notion of equality of French and English across Canada but tolerates the French-only unilingualism in Quebec.

Quebec's language charter, passed in 1978, declares French to be the province's official language and is antithetical to the linguistic duality of the Official Languages Act. Polls show it is very popular among Québécois.

Dr. Goldbloom says Quebec's sense of collective destiny continues to clash with the rest of Canada's strong attachment to individual freedoms: "So unfortunately, even if we're bilingual and can communicate with one another we're . . . not speaking the same language when we talk about individual and collective interests."

The result is that while anglophones in the rest of Canada accept official bilingualism, they detect a whiff of hypocrisy in Quebec's stance—manifest in its restrictive sign legislation—and increasingly endorse the so-called "tough-love" approach to constitutional negotiation. If this approach fails and Quebec does leave Confederation, the prospects would not be good that the elaborate official-languages structure would remain in the nine anglophone provinces.

Can anything be done? Does anything need to be done?

The Reform Party argues that the Official Languages Act should be scrapped and bilingual services continue only in areas with high concentrations of minority-language speakers.

Prof. Richards at Simon Fraser University argues that Quebec ought to be given explicit jurisdiction over language (subject to the maintenance of bilingualism within federal institutions) to calm the "perfectly reasonable" fears of Québécois about the survival of the French language.

Dr. Goldbloom makes the case for staying the course. He admits English Canada's good will has been tested in recent years by the discourse over Quebec. He argues that political leaders worry about these matters much more than the average person but accepts, nonetheless, that there is continuing tension about language matters all across Canada and pressure for radical changes.

"I think that we are doing reasonably well—not well enough, but reasonably well in responding to the historic existence of two languages in this country," he says.

The Great Ice Storm of 1998

LYSIANE GAGNON

Ice Storm, The Sequel: Freezing rains, high winds, fallen trees, dangling wires, broken bones, dead computers . . . a timeless natural disaster with a postmodern twist, as Quebeckers realize once again that they cannot live without electricity.

On Day One, it was kind of fun. "We moved all the mattresses around the fire place," recalls my friend Catherine. "We lit candles, ate take-out Chinese, played Scrabble and went to bed giggling, dressed in our warmest clothes. The kids were elated: Schools were closed; it was Christmas holidays all over again."

On Day Two, the cold settled in—deep into their bones. They moved in with Catherine's brother.

By Day Three, it was pure hell: Her brother's electricity went out too, and an enlarged family of nine was now frantically calling hotels in and around Montreal. "Sorry, we're full," was the reply everywhere. They finally found shelter with a family friend who is lucky enough to live in a new housing development that has underground hydro lines.

Other friends of mine, a colleague and his wife settled in a motel for the night. They awoke at 4 a.m. with frozen feet—the power was off at the motel too.

Our own apartment has been turned into a camping site; two of our friends just moved in with luggage, portable computer, boxes of perishable food and exams to grade.

As I write this, more than 16,000 trees are severely damaged in Montreal alone, and throughout the province, more than one million households (1,025,000, buildings according to the latest Hydro-Québec account) are without electricity. Since the number includes apartment buildings, it could mean that more than one-third of the Quebec population is temporarily homeless. The best-known homeless person is Premier Lucien Bouchard, whose Outremont house is without power; so is the house of Hydro-Québec's president André Caillé.

Nature is sometimes a great equalizer. One striking aspect of this natural disaster is that the victims live on the rich side of the tracks. Usually it's the other side that suffers. Floods and hurricanes hit the poor first because they settle on cheaper land, often on exposed river banks; earthquakes hit the poor first because their houses are not as solidly built. This ice storm is the poor man's revenge.

People living on tree-lined streets, near parks, are the most severely affected. In Montreal, the worst damage has occurred in the tony district of Notre-Dame-de-Grâce; the most affluent suburbs—Outremont, Town of Mount-Royal, Saint-Lambert—are the most devastated areas. The more modest districts, where people sweat in the summer heat and vainly look for shade, where the only lush gardens and green parks one can see are on calendar pictures, have escaped the worst effects of the storm.

As for downtown Montreal, where I live, life goes on pretty much as usual, because there are practically no trees around.

One must admit, Montreal is at its most beautiful when it is like this, encased in bright, gleaming ice. Under grey skies, it is a silver city. If the sun shone, it would turn to pure gold. Fallen branches covered in ice look like stunning sculptures lying on the streets.

There is magic in this strange, still scene. There is also a bit of magic in the air, as friends and family excitedly exchange news on the telephone or huddle together in makeshift accommodations.

All natural disasters bring their share of excitement, especially when there is no widespread risk of death. (But this is the worst time ever to be sick: Hospitals, already hit by drastic budget cuts, are crowded with patients seeking treatment for broken bones and respiratory diseases.)

Mercifully, public shelters are opening everywhere. Relief crews, including the Canadian Armed Forces, are at work day and night. The city's sidewalks are slippery and dangerous, but the roads are safer than ever since most people won't drive unless they really have to.

There is a solidarity that can be felt everywhere, as neighbours who never exchange smiles benevolently help each other.

But when the ice melts and the magic subsides, what will be left is stark devastation. All these fallen trees already are an awfully painful sight. By and large, Montreal is not a green city. Trees were savagely cut during the construction boom of the 1960s. Since then, Montrealers have cherished the relatively few century-old trees that were left. Now the city has lost at least one tenth of its trees, especially the largest and oldest ones. Many things in life can be replaced, but how do you replace a very old tree?

And of course, the other costs—the damage to property and to the overall economy—will be astronomical. But, right now, people are too busy looking for a warm place or welcoming unexpected guests to begin the depressing task of computing their losses.

My Jack

ANDREW COHEN

Reflective and informed, Canadian journalists ventured far afield in their reportage. This article on Seymour Hersh's interpretation of John F. Kennedy's Camelot tells us as much about reporter Andrew Cohen as it does about either Hersh or Kennedy.

Seymour Hersh leaps from his chair. He skitters across the room like a waterbug, digging into the files, producing a shower of letters, photocopies, faxes and newspaper clippings. "There, read that!" he says, pulling out another declassified document. "That's my boy! That's my Jack!"

There is, about him, a sense of the maniacal. The eyes glare, the hands flail, the body coils. Conversation comes in a torrent, without pause or punctuation. "Outrageous!" he shouts, pointing at the latest example of lie, falsehood or half-truth.

The facsimile machine peeps. More lousy reviews? The voice mail blinks. More leads? The mailman knocks. More brown envelopes? The telephone rings, incessantly. Yes, we have a German sale. No, he won't go on television to discuss the death of Michael Kennedy. Yes, the book is in its fourth printing.

"I am not only a historian now," says Mr. Hersh, "I am a merchandiser, I am a pimp."

It's all about Jack. "My Jack," as he calls John Fitzgerald Kennedy, the 35th president of the United States. This is not a term of endearment but an allusion to Mr. Kennedy's immorality. He has spent five years linking private and public recklessness. *The Dark Side of Camelot*, his much-maligned bestselling book, is the most withering portrait of Mr. Kennedy from a writer of stature in this country.

Since last autumn, when the book was published, it has been open season on Seymour Hersh. The book has been savaged by critics and denounced by the Kennedys, an auto-da-fé that still consumes him three months later. It has dealt a blow to the reputation of Mr. Hersh—perhaps the foremost investigative journalist of his time—from which he may not recover. The chorus of criticism has been unrelenting....

The book has no sense of balance, the allegations are old, the sources are suspect, the evidence is hearsay, rumour or innuendo. Sy fi.

But that is only part of it. The story behind the story is more than about Mr. Hersh's reputation and the negative reception of his book. The attacks have been too personal, the denials too practiced, the vengeance too gleeful.

No, there is something else at work here. The river of recrimination in which Seymour Hersh swims flows only in part from the incendiary allegations of his book. The other source of its poisoned waters are the lowlands of the national psyche. *The Dark Side of Camelot* desecrates an icon, as it seeks to replace an old truth with a new one. In doing so, it threatens the mythology of a generation. "There is still a literary and historical class protecting the flame of Kennedy," says Nigel Hamilton, the British historian who fled the U.S. after he was pilloried for his revisionist biography of the young JFK in 1992. "They will pounce on anyone making criticism of the great liberal god. To question it is *lèse majesté*."

In questioning the god, there emerges another dark side in which everyone has something at stake. Seymour Hersh has his reputation. The Kennedys have their honour. The acolytes have their careers. The historians have their history. The idealists have their idealism. It is a struggle among memories, in which all the principals have their interests. Truth be told, I have mine too.

From the time he flunked out of law school and entered journalism as a police reporter in Chicago in 1959, Seymour Myron Hersh has looked for trouble. He broke the story of the My Lai massacre, exposed the excesses of the CIA, unveiled the machinations of Henry Kissinger. First in newspapers and then in half a dozen books, he unveiled skulduggery at home and abroad. He has won the Pulitzer Prize, the National Book Critics Circle Award and the George Polk Memorial Award (four times).

I knew about his formidable reputation when I heard that Mr. Hersh had turned his steady gaze on Camelot. It was said he had explosive revelations that would be "the death rattle of the Kennedys." Seymour Hersh, it seemed, had the power to debunk much of what I believed about John Kennedy and his brothers, Robert and Edward. That unsettled me. I had read and written about the Kennedys, visited their shrines, followed their careers, sought out their chroniclers and contemporaries. When one of JFK's old friends once told me, "you know, Jack would have liked you," I was strangely touched.

I was too young to cry over Jack's death and too old not to over Bobby's. My attachment deepened when I went to Choate, the same boarding school in Connecticut as had JFK, worked in George McGovern's presidential campaign in 1972 (convinced he was carrying the torch) and attended quadrennial conventions of the Democratic Party. . . .

I could put the things of childhood away, but I never put away the Kennedys. I still listen to recordings of their speeches, absorbing the rhythms of JFK's Inaugural Address or the anguish of RFK's elegy to his brother (from Shakespeare: "When he shall die, take him and cut him out in little stars and he will make the face of heaven so fine that all the world will be in love with night, and pay no worship to the garish sun"). I still make visits to their graves at Arlington National Cemetery, after hours, when the sun slants in the sky and the imperial city glows.

But then, last November, along come hitman Hersh. He says it ain't so. Jack Kennedy was a bigamist. A cad. An invalid. An addict. A cheat.

He stole the election of 1960, he collaborated with the Mafia, he tried to kill Fidel Castro, he provoked the Cuban missile crisis, he prolonged Vietnam, he had been married before his marriage to Jackie. He was blackmailed by Lyndon Johnson, J. Edgar Hoover and General Dynamics Corp. His legacy isn't courage, grace and idealism, but corruption, nuclear gamesmanship, assassination and assignation.

Oh, of course, we've heard this before. But never in this detail, with this authority. Camelot was a junk bond. The emperor has no clothes, largely because he couldn't keep them on. It was a lie. Burn the books. Erase the speeches. Banish the memory. If you're looking for heroes, try Mother Teresa. . . .

By the time I met Seymour Hersh, he had weathered a siege worse than Stalingrad. The bombardment had begun before publication of the book with unflattering magazine profiles condemning him for using forged documents alleging a contract between Mr. Kennedy and Marilyn Monroe to buy her silence over their alleged affair. Mr. Hersh never published the information in the documents but they offered his critics a chance to denounce him before the book was published. Vanity Fair, in particular, portrayed him as arrogant, venal and intimidating, the kind of guy who throws typewriters from windows and screams at people . . .

The repudiation of *The Dark Side of Camelot* was total; the problem wasn't Camelot, but Mr. Hersh. He had aimed low and missed. Wasn't it safe to believe again?

Talk to Seymour Hersh, hear his side, and the story becomes "complicated," to use one of his favourite words. Like the fabled 50 million Frenchmen, all those reviewers cannot be wrong. But the news is that Seymour Hersh may be more right then we know, particularly in suggesting that there is more to the criticism than his credibility.

"I understood, I really, truly understood what I was doing when I wrote the book," he says in his cluttered downtown office in Washington, where he lives with his psychiatrist-wife and their three children. "I understood I was taking a cut at something big. This wasn't like taking down Henry Kissinger, who was controversial anyway, or even mass murder by American boys in Vietnam. This was going to be real war."

War. The image is invoked often in the course of several conversations. "I'm in a public war. I won't back off," he vows. Mr. Hersh believes he is taking on "the cult of Kennedy."

Contrary to his hooves-and-horn reputation, Mr. Hersh, 60, is open, attentive and frank, artlessly if crudely frank. After listening to him, the thought occurs: Has the messenger become the victim? What is going on here?

According to Mr. Hersh, plenty. There wasn't an organized conspiracy to suppress his work, though he had reason to wonder when he received a letter from Jack Miller, a lawyer for the Kennedys, warning him to stop harassing a widow of a former government employee for her husband's papers. ("I won't go away," Mr. Hersh replied.) He also couldn't understand how, on his promotion tour, a list of tough questions had been faxed, anonymously, to interviewers.

Some of the criticism was motivated by jealousy, and by anger that he was getting rich on the Kennedys. But Mr. Hersh maintains that his advance of $1.2 million was paid over five years, he had $130,000 a year in expenses and he had to borrow money to finish the book. When Robert Sam Anson, himself an investigative journalist, attacked him in Vanity Fair, says Mr. Hersh, it was largely a case of professional rivalry. Mr. Hersh had refused to leak the contents of the book. Mr. Anson, claims Mr. Hersh, repeated material from off-the-record interviews Mr. Anson had obtained surreptitiously. Then he acted as his own fact-checker. "Outrageous," Mr. Hersh sniffs.

The historians? Mr. Hersh, unrepentant, says they are either wrong or self-interested. Garry Wills, for example, dismisses an interpretation of the Cuban missile crisis close to the one he suggested in his book, *The Kennedy Imprisonment*, in 1981. Could it be that he only wanted to sustain his version of the truth? Could it be the same for Kennedy biographer Herbert Parmet, who mistakenly awards Mr. Hersh *two* Pulitzers and seems to consider him unworthy of both?

"Well, of course," says Mr. Hersh. "They have their biases. If I'm right, their version of history is wrong." . . .

To Mr. Hersh, there is a double standard. The Washington Post could publish a false story and return a Pulitzer Prize, but attacks him for the Monroe papers he didn't use. Sometimes it's more subtle. He cites a footnote in historian Michael Beschloss's much praised account, *The Crisis Years*. Mr. Beschloss suggests there that Mr. Johnson may have blackmailed Mr. Kennedy into making him his running mate in 1960. Mr. Hersh has been discredited for the allegation, which he takes further. No one criticized Mr. Beschloss.

Some suggest that Mr. Hersh, a self-described liberal democrat, is being punished for turning on his own. He does argue that many Kennedy contemporaries—from historian William Manchester to journalist Benjamin Bradlee—know what he learned. If that's true, the great question about John Kennedy is no longer how he died, which has so preoccupied assassination scenarists, but how he lived. It is the conspiracy of silence.

And what about the loyalists? Mr. Hersh believes that Arthur Schlesinger, Theodore Sorensen and Dave Powers, all advisers or assistants who deified Mr. Kennedy in their best-selling memoirs, cannot confront the demons of their past. Mr. Hamilton calls it a form of "pyschological corruption."

After all, they made him a saint, and we believed it. Here was how Mr. Powers described the nightly ritual when Jack was in the White House, alone. "Dave would watch him kneel beside the bed and say his prayers.

Then he would get into bed and say to Dave. 'Goodnight, pal, would you please put out the light?"

Before prayers, there would be prostitutes, whom Mr. Powers arranged and shared. It suggests a less wholesome image of the president than the one drawn from the pages of Boy's Life. For his part, the 80-year old Mr. Schlesinger wrote of *A Thousand Days* of glory and light. Today, Mr. Schlesinger is saying he cannot recognize any room in Mr. Hersh's White House.

This is the Mr. Schlesinger, who, in a memo obtained by Mr. Hersh dated five days before the aborted invasion of the Bay of Pigs in Cuba, introduced the notion of "plausible deniability": "When lies must be told, they should be told by subordinate officials. At no point should the president be allowed to lend himself to the cover operation . . . Someone other than the president [should] make the final decision and do so in his absence, someone whose head can later be placed on the block if things go terribly wrong."

When Mr. Hersh showed me that, I winced. I have always admired Arthur Schlesinger. But it is reasonable to ask what he knew, about Cuba, Castro and the mob, the compromises of conscience he made to be a jester in the Court of Camelot.

If Mr. Hersh needs moral support, he will find it in Nigel Hamilton and others. "Now is the time to rejoice that someone in America had the gumption to do it," he says of Mr. Hersh. "Historians owe him a great debt."

A.J. Langguth, a professor of journalism at the University of Southern California, says "Seymour Hersh is one of the great reporters in America. The degree that the Kennedy cult has tried to paper over legitimate problems with his person and presidency is striking. Some people have a glow and nothing can tarnish it."

But let it be said: If the others in this story have their dark side, so does Seymour Hersh. His logic is often unpersuasive, his allegations unfounded. He lacks a biographer's patience, sympathy, subtlety or care. Feverish, impulsive and erratic, he can say something one day and deny it the next. How to explain his maze of contradiction and admission? "I am amazed at myself," he says. "I yap so much."

Over the course of several weeks, we talk, many times, and sometimes I wonder who is writing about whom. He leaves hilarious messages on my answering machine ("The Canadians are all over me on this story! Help."). He lowers his voice, suggesting Camelot was worse, far worse, than he writes.

He lets slip what he did not use, letters to Jack from Mary Meyer, a lover mysteriously murdered in 1964; allegations of an affair between Jacqueline and Bobby Kennedy, the magnitude of the president's sexual adventures; friends and associates on the take in the White House.

Mr. Hersh lives by his own code of conduct. He refused to allow the television networks to broadcast a tape recording of Caroline talking to her father because he thought it would be too unsettling for her. Similarly, he declined to use a classified oral history of Arthur Schlesinger's wife because it was "private." He honours anonymity, and says he uses only on-the-record sources.

Amid the storm, Mr. Hersh remains serene. The book is selling well—425,000 in print—but that may not be enough. "The hurt is that they didn't do for me what I did for others," he says meaning that having unearthed all this material, he hoped others would verify it. The sex, he allows, was a sideshow to the main attraction, which was Vietnam, the Cuban missile crisis, the plot to kill Castro. "It's a different business today," he sighs.

In the end, it is both cloudy and clear. The romantic in me says that Mr. Hersh is largely wrong, that his story doesn't entirely hang together, the picture is incomplete. He has his Jack, and I have mine. Mine is a good but not a great president, who inspired a generation, who showed restraint in Cuba and Berlin, who supported civil rights and established the Peace Corps and the space program.

But the journalist in me says the evidence of Kennedy's personal recklessness is beyond question. An honest observer has reason to wonder. There is too much here to be ignored. Mr. Hersh has found not the Truth, as he implies, but he found a truth, which is undeniable and arresting. As journalist David M. Shribman argued in The Wall Street Journal, "the presence of facts does not mean that the truth is present. The truth is a more complicated thing than mere facts alone."

I never discussed "my Jack" with Mr. Hersh and he never asked. Nor did I raise truth or context or perspective with him, and I think if I had, he would have shrugged. But when I opened my copy of *The Dark Side of Camelot* the other day, I found this inscription:

"To Andrew: There may not be truth, but there will always be history. May we learn. . . . Seymour Hersh."

The Multi-Hued Metropolis

ELAINE CAREY

> *As Canada's greatest magnet for immigrants, Toronto by the end of the 20th century was a far cry from the very British city a hundred years before.*

In less than 18 months, the majority of people in the new city of Toronto will be non-white, according to a new report.

And if steps aren't taken to address the "huge inequalities" faced by many visible minority groups in employment, education, income and housing, the disparities and frustrations will get worse, warns the report on diversity in Toronto to be presented to city councillors tomorrow.

A newly established task force on access and diversity will announce Tuesday a series of public meetings to be held this month and next to try to find solutions to those problems.

Toronto is the most ethnically diverse city in the world, the report says, and does far more than any other to help that mix cope.

"We do not simply recognize and tolerate this diversity, but respect, value and nurture it as an exciting and integral part of our collective experience and identity."

But while immigrants are the "economic engine" driving the new global economy, not everyone is benefitting, says the report by Tim Rees, co-ordinator of Toronto's Access and Equity Centre.

The most disadvantaged groups are First Nations people, Africans, Jamaicans, Tamils, Sri Lankans, Pakistanis, Bangladeshis, Vietnamese, Iranians, Latin Americans and Hispanics.

Toronto's immigrant communities make up 48 per cent of the population, but they continue to be underrepresented in important positions of influence and on issues and policies that have an impact on their lives, the report says.

"If this situation is not addressed, as well as the incidents of hate activity and discriminatory practices and prejudicial attitudes that unfortunately continue to plague our city," it warns, "it can only lead to a growing sense of frustration."

The centre analyzed data from the 1996 census, separating Toronto from the 905 area, and found:

- By the year 2000, visible minorities will make up 54 per cent of the population of Toronto, up from 30 per cent in 1991 and only 3 per cent in 1961.
- Toronto is home to 42 per cent of the total non-white population in Canada, including almost half the South Asian and black population, as well as two-fifths of the Chinese, Korean and Filipino.
- Over 70,000 immigrants come to Toronto every year. Immigrants have come from 169 countries, speaking 100 different languages and 42 per cent speak neither English nor French when they arrive.
- One in five Toronto residents arrived in Canada after 1981 and one in 10 came after 1991. The population of immigrants grew at four times the rate of the non-immigrant between 1991 and 1996.
- The largest concentration of immigrants is found in the North York, Scarborough and Toronto community council areas, accounting for three-quarters of the total.
- About one-third of Toronto's residents speak neither English nor French at home and the top three languages are Chinese in many dialects, Italian and Portuguese.

Despite the problems, "there is nowhere in the world where diversity works as well as it does here," Mayor Mel Lastman said in an interview, "The more we talk about it, the better it will be for everyone."

Lastman said he was "shocked" when he first saw the figure that 48 per cent of Toronto's population is foreign-born, "but it's working out better and faster here than anywhere else in the world."

The report says Toronto has a higher proportion of its population who are foreign-born than any other city.

While New York, with the Statue of Liberty, is the city most symbolic and celebrated as an immigrant destination, only 28 per cent of its population was foreign-born, compared to Toronto's 48 per cent. In fact, the Greater Toronto Area has 11 municipalities with more than 28 per cent immigrants—surpassing New York's numbers.

Contrary to popular myth, immigrants are not a drain on the system but contribute more to the economy than they receive, the report says.

One study found that all post-1951 immigrants have in fact "subsidized the Canadian-born population," and they have done better economically than their Canadian-born counterparts, "not by taking away jobs but through their own initiative."

But while Toronto celebrates its diversity—the key to competing successfully in the new global marketplace—prejudice persists, it says.

In order to encourage potential investment, attract high-skilled immigrants and win the bid for the 2008 Summer Olympic Games, it calls for:

- A new and comprehensive framework for recognizing that diversity affects every area of public policy and public service.
- Removal of all the barriers to ensuring "the full and equal access and participation of all residents, regardless of their origin or background."
- Including the entire community—not just minority groups—in the diversity debate "to minimize animosities or competition based on perceptions of difference."

"If we're going to really address some of the problems and inequalities, we're only going to do it by drawing on everyone—not just the minority groups talking to each other," Rees said in an interview.

Other institutions and groups would like to be involved in some way in the discussion "but it's somewhat difficult," he said.

"We've sort of isolated ourselves over the years into separate silos."

The new access and equality task force, chaired by Councillor Joe Mihevc (York-Eglinton), will hold a series of public meetings.

These will be aimed at getting the public's input on race, gender, disability, aboriginal and gay and lesbian issues.

The task force has to find a way of putting together the "hodge podge" of programs that existed in the cities that now make up the new Toronto, Mihevc said in an interview.

The 1996 census was the very first time Statistics Canada asked Canadians about their race.

Ethnic Cleansing in Kosovo

MICHAEL IGNATIEFF

Historian Ignatieff, here a thoughtful commentator, witnessed the killing in Kosovo in 1999.

Celine is a small village on the road between Prizren and Djakovica in western Kosovo. It is a hot July morning and about a hundred villagers are waiting for a helicopter to land in the meadow beside what remains of the local school. It has been torched: the roof timbers are lying among charred children's desks. The red and black Kosovo flag flies over the ruins.

A clutch of brown-faced schoolchildren are standing against a rope line, holding bunches of wilting flowers picked from their family's gardens. They have been told that an important woman is coming to see them. They do not know who she is, but they like the idea that she is coming in a helicopter and so they peer up into the sky and cock their ears for the sound of rotor blades.

The older men of the village sit on the meadow grass in a circle, smoking, running their fingers through their mustaches and staring at the mountains across the valley. They are wearing the *kelesche*, the conical cap of Albanian country people. The women, in their best white embroidered dresses and kerchiefs, sit in a separate circle, talking among themselves. One of them wipes away tears with the back of her hand.

As the sun rises in the sky, camera crews begin to arrive: young people in wraparound sunglasses, shorts, T-shirts and Caterpillar boots. They are from CNN, Reuters, Sky and Channel Four Television from London, plus the *Washington Post*, National Public Radio, and Deutsche Welle.

About forty yards from the cameras and reporters, on the other side of the rope line, there is a Dutch armored personnel carrier with signalers inside talking on the radio phone. Next to the APC are a couple of military tents with camouflage nets spread between them. Inside one of the tents, a heavy-set man in white shirt and chinos is poring over a map. He looks glumly at the gathering of the TV crews, lights a cigarette and comes out to talk to them. His name is Bill Gent and he is a senior officer with London's Metropolitan Police. He is in charge of the forensic team—pathologists, archeologists, anthropologists, ballistics specialists—who are digging in the ravine behind Celine.

After a long wait, a Huey with German markings comes up over the hill behind the village, circles twice and settles down gently beside the school, while Dutch soldiers positioned on the perimeter duck and shield their faces from the rotor blast. A short female figure wearing black glasses, her shoulders hunched and head bowed, steps down from the helicopter and, with a small entourage following behind, approaches the villagers, gathering against the rope line.

Louise Arbour doesn't like scenes like this: she is a criminal prosecutor, not a celebrity, yet she plunges into what the scene requires, taking the bouquets held out by the children, stroking their cheeks, clasping some of the hands held out to her and saying over and over: "Thank you, thank you."

Kosovo has been in NATO's hands for a month. Since then, the troops, together with Arbour's investigators from the International Tribunal at the Hague have been finding "sites" everywhere. The whole of Kosovo, she has been quoted as saying, was "one vast crime scene." She had been up in the French sector that morning at Mitrovica and next she will be visiting a site near Gnilane where the Canadian RCMP is digging; now she wants to see what her team has found at Celine. She gets into Bill Gent's Land Rover and they drive down the hill, followed by the reporters' jeeps. The villagers stay where they are: they know what there is to see. But the crews don't: they push and shove each other to get a shot of Louise Arbour looking down into the pit and slowly shaking her head.

I do not go down in the ravine—I know what is there. So I wait for her to return. When she comes back up to the forensic team's tent, she does not look shocked or dismayed, just tired. The crowd is about fifty yards away, watching her every move. While she has not said she will bring them truth and justice, that is what they expect. I ask her whether there isn't something cruel about these expectations. How likely is it that she or anyone else will find the men who killed the villagers of Celine—twenty-one of them—for no other reason than that they were Kosovar Albanians? She thinks about this, hands on hips, head down and then says fiercely: "We have no choice. We owe it to these people. If there are expectations, we just have to meet them."

They are calling her over to the rope line, and she duly goes and shakes hands, and bows her head in thanks, and then her staff turns her towards the helicopter—rotors now whirring up the dust—and she climbs aboard, and is suddenly airborne, whirling overhead. A tiny hand is just visible waving down at us and then the chopper wheels around and vanishes behind the next hill.

Hi-Tech Hijinks

CHARLOTTE GRAY

As Mac Brown pads through his 12,000-square-foot mansion in Manotick, an expensive dormitory village outside Ottawa, his eyes linger on the life-size bronze leopard on the kitchen counter, the weight machines in the exercise room, the blue-tiled swimming pool. Mac is a short, balding guy, a forty-one-year-old engineer with well-toned muscles. He shows off his toys with barely suppressed glee. There's the home theatre with its black lambskin couch, real theatre seats, and a videodisc of the Eagles in concert playing on the ten-foot screen. Upstairs, there's the vast master bedroom, with its king-size bed, faux tiger-skin throw, life-size stuffed toy leopard, and a pulsating remote-controlled sound system. Through a glass door to the left I can see a heart-shaped Jacuzzi set in an echoing marble-tiled bathroom. Mac (he's Mac to everybody, never Mr. Brown) flexes his shoulders under his blue silk shirt as he remarks: "You'll like the bathroom. Most women do."

Mac is CEO of Rebel.com, one of Canada's fastest-growing companies. It's a small enterprise with only 140 employees, but in the past ten years its revenue from sales of customized computer systems for large and small businesses have jumped 1,789 percent, to $45 million a year. The company has the backing of Michael Cowpland, the controversial chairman of Corel Corporation and a founding father of the high-tech boom in the national capital. Mac and Ottawa native Mike Mansfield, president of Rebel.com, plan to take the company public this year. The Rebel.com Web site and promotional materials feature an image of the all-time rebel hero James Dean and the tag line "Technology with Attitude."

Mac Brown embodies technology with attitude. Part of this attitude involves an appetite for conspicuous consumption that is *de rigueur* among the Californian cyber-rich of Portola Valley or Los Altos Hills, but unfamiliar—until recently, anyway—in Ottawa. As he shows me around Horizon Point, which is what he calls his high-tech megalo-mansion, I feel as though I'm in a millionaire teenager's dream rec room. It is stuffed with hockey memorabilia (the Ottawa Senators are prominently featured), model cars, Mac's collection of fifty baseball hats, a pool table, and stacks of reggae CDs. Mike Mansfield, who has joined the tour and wears a leather jacket with the Rebel.com logo emblazoned on the back, points out to me the Boston Steinway baby grand, which is also a CD player-piano. I cannot see a book anywhere, but, through the enormous picture windows, I can see examples of Mac's eclectic taste in sculpture on the grassy slope between the house and the Rideau River: a woolly mammoth, a prowling lion, and an Art Nouveau-style maiden. In the six-car garage, Mac proudly shows me his $86,000 black Lexus LX470, with "RBEL1" on its plate, and his little summer runaround, a snarling scarlet $90,000 Plymouth Prowler. "I bet there are only twenty-five of those in Canada," Mac brags.

Mac and his house typify the testosterone-charged high-tech vigour that is transforming Ottawa. He is just the latest basement-to-big-time story in Silicon Valley North.

The Death of Pierre Trudeau

JOHN GRAY AND TU THANH HA

Under clear blue skies and brilliant October sunshine, Pierre Trudeau returned from Ottawa yesterday to be buried today in Montreal, the city he always called home.

Thousands of mourners were expected in the narrow streets of Old Montreal this morning for the 90-minute state funeral in the monumental grey stone Notre Dame Basilica that has long been the spiritual focus of Quebec.

The funeral will be the final stage in the extravagant outpouring of emotion that began with the announcement on Thursday that the 80-year-old former prime minister had died as a result of complications from Parkinson's disease and cancer.

Governor-General Adrienne Clarkson, Prime Minister Jean Chrétien and most of the leading political figures in the land will be in the basilica for the televised funeral service.

But Mr. Trudeau's sons Justin and Sacha have asked that the burial be away from the public eye, to be attended by only family and close friends of the man who was prime minister for almost 16 years.

After a weekend in which tens of thousands waited for hours in Ottawa in the hot sunshine or in the cool of the night to pay their respects, the crowds appeared again on Parliament Hill to say goodbye yesterday morning.

As it had been throughout the weekend, it was a humble crowd— windbreakers, T-shirts, jeans and baseball caps, in contrast to the black suits of the official mourners.

Again it was a time for weeping as the crowd silently watched tears pour down the tortured face of Justin Trudeau while RCMP pallbearers carried the coffin to the hearse.

A military band played *Auld Lang Syne* and the crowd of thousands broke into applause as the limousines pulled away from the Peace Tower and headed for the Ottawa train station.

The train ride was a majestic procession through the lush Eastern Ontario countryside, the fields still green from the summer's heavy rains but the leaves on the trees warning that winter is not far off.

At the request of Mr. Trudeau's two sons, the train slowed to a crawl through towns along the route as townspeople, especially children who had been liberated from their classrooms, gathered along the tracks to wave farewell.

Some mourners stopped their cars and waved to the train from the road. Occasionally, lonely figures in the fields stopped work to wave, hats over their hearts.

Everywhere were the red roses that were the trademark of Mr. Trudeau in life and have become his symbol in death.

In one village, someone threw a red rose that was caught by Sacha as he leaned out the window to wave gently to the crowd.

There were more roses when the hearse carried Mr. Trudeau's flag-draped coffin to the Montreal City Hall to lie in state.

There were significantly fewer spectators than in Ottawa, either because it was a working day or because Montreal has always had a more complex relationship with the former prime minister.

One of the little ironies of history and politics is that the coffin was carried into city hall just under the balcony from which French President Charles de Gaulle had delivered his famous cry of *Vive le Québec Libre*.

Mr. Trudeau, then justice minister in Lester Pearson's cabinet, had counselled a hard Canadian response to that kind of meddling.

Politics made its own intrusion in Montreal yesterday as Heritage Canada distributed small Canadian flags to mourners at city hall.

The most eager of the flag-wavers led a number of people in singing *O Canada* as the coffin was carried up the steps and into city hall, although much of the anthem was drowned out by a helicopter.

But apparently spontaneous applause swept through the crowd when Justin and Sacha emerged from the lead mourners' car.

Noticeably absent from the official ceremonies yesterday was Margaret Trudeau, who stayed on Parliament Hill and talked to spectators gathered around the pile of roses, letters and other mementos left at the Eternal Flame in front of the Peace Tower.

She broke down in tears when a television reporter reminded her that yesterday was the birthday of the third Trudeau son, Michel, who died two years ago.

In Montreal, as eight RCMP officers, sporting black armbands on their red serge uniforms, removed the coffin from the hearse, the crowd applauded.

Inside the foyer of city hall, the first minutes were kept private for Justin and Sacha Trudeau and friends of their father.

Among those accompanying the two young men were former federal minister Marc Lalonde, Senator Jacques Hébert, former Quebec lieutenant-governor Jean-Louis Roux, former governor-general Roméo Leblanc and his son Dominic, and Roy Heenan, senior partner of Mr. Trudeau's law firm, Heenan Blaikie.

Sacha had a sad, benign smile as he touched his father's casket. Justin, his teary face showing more emotion, bent down and kissed the coffin before following his younger brother out of the building.

The two sons were still young when Mr. Trudeau was in office and have led a private life, Dominic Leblanc said later. "They're not used to this kind of public ceremony."

Several dignitaries, such as current and former federal ministers Lucie Pépin, Denis Coderre, Francis Fox, Warren Allmand, Céline Hervieux-Payette, then paid tribute, along with members of Heenan Blaikie, including former Parti Québécois premier Pierre-Marc Johnson.

One Heenan Blaikie lawyer, Bruce McNiven, had his young children, 4-year-old Yan Maurice and 2-year-old Céleste, deposit roses at the foot of the casket, the first of what would become a knee-high mound of flowers.

As the general public came in, some dabbed tears from their eyes. Many made acts of religious devotions, expressed in their respective faiths.

Christians made the sign of the cross. One man knelt down and cupped his hands to heaven in a Muslim prayer. Another man, when he arrived before the casket, put on his head a *kipah*, the Jewish skullcap.

One woman, a small Canadian flag tucked into her hair, snapped a picture of the coffin with a disposable camera.

Marcelle Lapierre, 80, came with her friend, 79-year-old Françoise Blackburn, who clutched a cane and a framed black-and-white photo of Mr. Trudeau, autographed, "to Françoise with my best memories."

As she stood before the casket, Mrs. Blackburn presented the photo, then slowly walked away, tucking the portrait back into a plastic bag.

Downstairs from the main foyer, she joined others who put their thoughts in condolence books. "To my handsome Pierre, in memory," she wrote.

Mrs. Blackburn and Ms. Lapierre said they grew up as neighbours of Mr. Trudeau. "I remember going to the ball with him. I was 20 and he was 22. He was so nice," Mrs. Blackburn said.

"I wonder if there'll be as many people here as there were in Ottawa," Ms. Lapierre said. "There's a lot of Péquistes here in Montreal."

The sun hadn't risen yet and it was still chilly when the first well-wishers showed up outside the steps of Montreal's city hall.

Around 6:10 a.m., nearly an hour before sunrise and five hours before the bronze doors of the city hall would open to the public, Yvonne

Orneau, a 49-year-old hairdressing instructor, became the first person to arrive at the scene. Shortly after, she was joined by Jeannette Gaboton, 55, a health-sector clerk.

Ms. Orneau was an immigrant from Martinique, Ms. Gaboton from Haiti.

"He was someone who was close to immigrants, who made us feel at home here," Ms. Orneau said.

"It's important to be here today to salute him. He gave me the opportunity to be here. Immigrants are the heirs of Mr. Trudeau," Ms. Gaboton said.

Those who came were a reflection of Mr. Trudeau's Canada: immigrants who started a new life here, older members of the Quebec bourgeoisie who still consider themselves French Canadian rather than Québécois, those who had travelled the country in the military, the young people intrigued by the Camelot-like magic of a past age.

"I'm in awe of him. I can only imagine what Trudeaumania was like in his days," said 22-year-old Matthew Glick, a Concordia University communications student who was six when Mr. Trudeau retired.

Despite having had only three hours of sleep, he was among those who arrived early, "so I won't miss too many classes."

By mid-afternoon, about 1,200 people were passing through each hour and the average wait was an hour. The line-up was smaller than in Ottawa—where the wait could be up to four hours.

Teachers, Students and Sex

CHRISTIE BLATCHFORD

On the telephone, the young mother dropped her voice to a whisper.

"He's here," she said of her five-year-old son, Christopher, who was underfoot. "How do I tell him there's a B-A-D teacher?"

In this brief, sad exchange yesterday with Leslie Horn, is told the astonishing story of the crisis, at Holly Meadows Elementary School in Barrie, where the parents of 750 students are still struggling to come to grips with the unbelievable: One of the teachers at their brand-new school is listed on the provincial child-abuse registry because of her sexually charged relationship with one—and there are hints of perhaps even two—of the boys in a previous class.

"How?" Mrs. Horn asked wearily, can you teach your child to go to teachers for help, when the teacher is the one who needs help?"

The 30-year-old woman named Laura Glen Sclater who is at the centre of this storm doesn't actually teach Christopher Horn, who is in kindergarten; Mrs. Sclater now teaches a class of Grade 3 students.

But her troubled past and the secrecy surrounding her reinstatement last summer after a lengthy suspension has affected the entire school, which just opened last month, and at least two parents whose children were in Mrs. Sclater's room this fall have pulled their youngsters out of Holly Meadows and enrolled them elsewhere.

Brad and Susan Lumbers have found a new school for their eight-year-old, Laura, who learned about Mrs. Sclater from a local TV newscast and tentatively asked her mother, "It's not good news, is it?" Her mom replied gently, "Well no, honey, it's not." As she told the *National Post* yesterday, "This [Ms. Sclater] is the kind of person you warn your child about."

And Christine Campbell's seven-year-old son, Jordan, also started at his new school yesterday, about three weeks after he approached his mother and said, "Mom, that's my teacher on the news," and in the next breath asked, "What are sex letters?" The Campbells fought unsuccessfully to have Jordan transferred to another Grade 3 class at Holly Meadows, but the school and the Simcoe County Board of Education flatly refused.

"I just didn't feel comfortable with her," Mrs. Campbell said yesterday. "She shouldn't be teaching. I don't need my children to be taught by a woman who herself needs a babysitter."

Indeed, that's pretty much true—under a series of conditions set out by the governing Ontario College of Teachers, Mrs. Sclater must report every two weeks to a so-called mentor appointed by the college to counsel her.

And notwithstanding the board's assertions that things are pretty much back to normal at the school, furious parents in the new subdivision where Holly Meadows is located have banded together, formed a group (called the Simcoe County Association for Responsible Education, or SCARE), demanded a hearing at the board's regular meeting later this month, and are now in the midst of producing a petition and posters seeking more support.

The parents are stunned that after the tumultuous last month, Mrs. Sclater's own acknowledged wrongdoing, and the massive publicity the entire case has generated, she is still indisputably there, in the school that many of them, and their children, excitedly watched rise from the ground.

As Mrs. Horn said yesterday, "What we really can't believe is just how powerless we are."

How it came to this—that families came to be in essence street-proofing their young children *against* a person in a position of trust; that youngsters should be preoccupied with vigilance instead of "trading Pokémon cards," as protest organizer Laura Armitage put it yesterday—began in February of 1998.

Mrs. Sclater, a York University graduate, was then teaching a combined class of Grade 7s and Grade 8s at another Simcoe County school, Goodfellow Public School—her fifth year there.

According to documents filed with the Ontario divisional court, in February of that year, she began writing notes—64 of them in total, generally described by two experts as having "both romantic and sexual innuendo"—to a 13-year-old boy identified only as "R," and the two developed a relationship outside the classroom.

In one excerpt that became part of the public record in court, Mrs. Sclater wrote, "There can *never* be another honey for me. 'J' last year and you this year? It doesn't get any better." It is this reference to the boy J, and another in which she wrote, "I miss J, but I miss you more," which suggest that her relationship with R may not have been her first improper one.

Other excerpts show her signing off with, "Love, your woman," calling R "a big stud" and "Big sweety" and herself his "hottie," and are replete with giddy talk of an upcoming field trip to Ottawa, where, she said, "I trust you to keep your hands where they belong" and joked that if she fell asleep on the bus, "The Ottawa police might have to dust me for prints!!! . . . If I go swimming," she teased, "I have decided to wear an undershirt over my bathing suit, so relax, please!!!"

The letters were discovered by the boy's mother in April of 1998. She promptly called the Simcoe County Children's Aid Society, which investigated and produced a damning report recommending, among other things, that Mrs. Sclater "not be allowed direct duties that involve children" and seek a psychiatric assessment "of her maturation and emotional state." It is also this agency that reported Mrs. Sclater to the provincial child-abuse register.

As a result of this report, Mrs. Sclater was suspended without pay by the board on Sept. 1, 1998.

At first, the board insisted she adhere to the Children's Aid Society recommendation, but later changed its position—by this stage, Mrs. Sclater was being ably represented by a lawyer appointed and paid for by her union, the now-defunct Federation of Women Teachers Association of Ontario—and referred the case not to a discipline committee, but rather to a fitness-to-practise committee.

In September of last year, over three days of meetings, the three member, all-female committee accepted an "agreed statement of facts" approved by lawyers for both parties, Mrs. Sclater and the Simcoe board—this, essentially, meant a plea bargain was reached going into the hearing.

Among the agreed-upon evidence accepted as fact were reports from Dr. Peter Collins, a forensic psychiatrist with the Ontario Provincial Police, who pronounced Mrs. Sclater's behaviour with the boy "a serious boundary violation" and another that said "teachers who breach such boundaries either tend to have psychological problems or emotional needs and are likely to repeat the behaviour" and concluded that "students are potentially at risk should she continue in a teaching role."

But, in accepting the plea arrangement, the committee agreed that Mrs. Sclater was "incapacitated" and was suffering from "a mental condition"—defined by psychiatrist Dr. Hy Bloom as one "born of naïveté, some measure of psychological and emotional immaturity and poor judgment."

In other words, though Mrs. Sclater was found to have behaved, at best, with gross immaturity and with carelessness about the impact on the boy R., that immaturity and attitude were, remarkably, also somehow deemed to be the mental condition that rendered her incapacitated.

On Oct. 20 last year, the committee ordered her suspended until she had completed at least 20 sessions with an approved therapist—more than the number of sessions the lawyers recommended—and was reassessed by Dr. Bloom.

Arguing the additional sessions were unfair, Mrs. Sclater and her lawyer, David Matheson, appealed this decision to the divisional court, where, in February of this year, a three-member panel upheld the original committee recommendation.

It is because of this court hearing that any of the documents and notes became public.

But in July of this year, Mrs. Sclater was back before the same fitness committee, and on July 14, was duly reinstated.

And all that is publicly available about this proceeding are the conditions the committee imposed upon her reinstatement—that she be restricted to teaching younger children, apparently on the grounds they will be less likely to pique her improper interest; that she can't even supervise the older students at Holly Meadow unless another adult is present; that she regularly consult the mentor; that she not communicate to any students by e-mail or write any notes not directly related to a student's work, and that her supervising principal report on her three times during the school year to the board.

As Mrs. Armitage said, because she's on the abuse register, Mrs. Sclater likely wouldn't be an acceptable Block Parent or daycare provider and she can't supervise Mrs. Armitage's five-year-old at lunch or in the playground at recess, but she's allowed to teach.

"How can they say she's been rehabilitated? If she's fine back in the classroom, then why not remove the restrictions on her and let her go back to Grade 8s? She doesn't teach my son, but he's in the classroom right next door, and I can't tell him to go to her if he needs help. And I resent the fact that I had to tell him *anything*, that I have had to put this in his mind. He should never have to look at a teacher like this."

The rationale for Mrs. Sclater's reinstatement—the psychiatric reassessment and reports from the therapist she saw—are considered confidential, Denys Giguere, spokesman for the College of Teachers, confirmed yesterday.

Mr. Matheson, Mrs. Sclater's lawyer, wouldn't make any comment yesterday, and though he promised to pass on a message to his client, he said she had declined such media requests before, and indeed, Mrs. Sclater couldn't be reached.

And even when she was ostensibly available, at an emergency meeting called last month to settle down the parents of children in her class, Mrs. Sclater was accompanied by Mr. Matheson. She made only a brief statement, and deferred to him on more pointed questions.

As Mrs. Horn noted, the current edition of the school bulletin, the *Holly Meadows Herald*, proudly trumpets on its front page the importance of communication. "Communication! Communication!" the headline blares.

How good is that, Mrs. Horn wondered aloud, "when the teacher isn't allowed to talk unless her lawyer is there?"

9/11 and Canadian Anti-Americanism

MARGARET WENTE

"The Americans are reaping the fruits of their crimes against humanity."

That's Saddam Hussein speaking. But you don't have to go to Baghdad to hear such views. Just hang around any college campus. Or chat with your well-heeled neighbours in downtown Toronto. Anti-American sentiment is nearly as popular among Canadians—especially well-heeled ones—as Starbucks lattes.

You'd think anti-Americanism would have gone discreetly underground this week. Not so. My inbox is crammed with e-mail such as the following: "The values that I venerate as a Canadian are not the same as those values venerated by Americans. Where is your indignation when NATO bombs Iraq or when the CIA perpetrates deathly intrigues worldwide every day?"

The anti-Americans, of course, don't believe that the thousands of innocent people who were blown to smithereens deserved to die. They're as horrified as anyone at the carnage. But they also believe the United States was asking for it.

One first-year student at a leading university described her political science class this week. "Everyone was saying it's a terrible thing, but America brought it on itself because it's against the other countries," she said. "The whole attitude was: America sucks." There was no other point of view expressed. The professor didn't bother to suggest there might be one.

At first, I thought these rants against America were confined to the usual anti-globalization crowd. But here's a sampling of opinion culled from lawyers, managers, teachers and various other people in Toronto:

"Isn't this really a symbol for people's discontent all over the world?"

"Well, what do they expect? They've been messing about in everyone's business. The only thing that's shocking is that it took so long."

"What goes around comes around. It's hubris."

I don't think these views represent the majority of Canadians. Certainly, the cafeteria lady, the liquor-store clerk and the guy who fixes my plumbing don't blame the victim. They're outraged. Their attitude is: "Terrorism must be stopped, so that this never happens again." They think that the United States must strike back and that Canada ought to help them.

But what do they know? Among the more sophisticated set, people say, "They should have known this was coming," and "Retaliation will make it worse." I heard well-meaning people phone in to CBC talk shows to ask just what it was America did, anyway, because they weren't exactly sure. I heard other well-meaning people describe the attack as an act of "misdirected anger," as if the suicide hijackers had been badly informed, and if only someone had sat down and explained things properly to them, they would have changed their minds.

It hadn't occurred to them that there are some people in the world who hate us and want us dead because they believe Western civilization is profoundly corrupt.

The bill of indictment against the United States is both very vague and very specific. Some people blame the gap between rich and poor, which the U.S. is either inadvertently or advertently responsible for creating. The feeling is that the poor are so desperate, so hopeless and so oppressed that it's not surprising they would lash out like this.

Other people blame the long record of alleged U.S. atrocities abroad, including its efforts to overthrow Fidel Castro, the war in Vietnam, the secret war in Cambodia, its support for various strongmen and dictators, the Persian Gulf war, the oppression of Palestinians, the deliberate starvation of Iraqi children etc. etc. They also like to argue that the CIA trained and backed Osama bin Laden in the first place, so it serves them right. (History professor John Kirton, at the University of Toronto, says the links weren't close, but a popular theory circulating on the Internet says the CIA really did it.)

Most kids have not mastered the bill of indictment in very much detail. Nonetheless, they know for a fact that America sucks, and that George W. Bush really sucks. "The kids in my school won't stop talking about how they hate the U.S.," says a young woman I know. Her Grade 12 classmates are multicultural children of the intelligentsia. "They think it's intellectually sophisticated. It means, 'I'm cynical, I'm hard.'"

Her generation has embraced anti-racism and multiculturalism. They believe in tolerance and respect for difference. But they have not been taught to believe that some values are better than others. "Sometimes, I'd like to ask them what would happen if a country like Afghanistan had the power the U.S. has," she says. "But you can't bring that up because it's perceived as racist."

Among these kids, reflexive anti-Americanism is as much a fashion statement as the jeans they wear. Their teachers haven't challenged their beliefs. Their parents haven't, either. Chances are their teachers and their parents think George Bush sucks, too. They've all been raised in a country where recreational bitching at the United States is just as much fun as going to Disney World. And they've never learned how much their lives depend on the liberal democratic values our nations share.

It's not just Muslims who are afraid of being stigmatized by mindless prejudice. So is any kid who's not entirely sure that George Bush sucks. "My American friend who's a student here has been crying all week long," says the first-year student at the first-rate university. "That's all she's heard."

It probably wouldn't do any good for these girls to remind their friends that Saddam Hussein is a warmonger who attacked four countries before the Americans moved against him or that he's a mass murderer who did not hesitate to gas his own women and children, or that he was a hair away from being able to make a nuclear bomb and chemical weapons, which he would have been most happy to use on all the rest of us. It wouldn't help them to point out that the United States imposed a virtuous peace after the Second World War, and converted Germany and Japan into robust democracies. Or that Canada is full of countless Afghans and Pakistanis and Muslims from many nations who are here because they want what we have, not what they had in the lands they left behind.

It probably wouldn't do any good for them to remind their friends that the people who perished in the World Trade Center and the Pentagon were doing work that makes it possible to go shopping at the Gap whenever we want, with money in our pockets and without fear for our personal safety. Work that makes it possible to express any political belief you want and not get locked up.

They're just kids, of course, so I guess you can forgive them for their ignorant prejudice against America. But the grownups—the many, many grownups—should know better.

Fighting Terrorism, 2001

MIRO CERNETIG

The impact of the al-Qaeda attack on the World Trade Center in New York was both political and personal.

Sept 16.
Islamabad, Pakistan
It's midnight in Islamabad, CNN's new arena of good versus evil, and hundreds of foreign correspondents are streaming into the capital, declaring

that this will be the biggest thing since the war in the Persian Gulf, maybe even bigger than the Second World War.

An Aussie, dressed in a war jacket and slinging two laptops over his shoulder, puts the sentiment best: "Mate, when your grandkids ask where granddaddy was in September, 2001, you're not going to want to answer anything but Islamabad."

Certainly, our jet is touching down on risky territory. It is still not clear what way 140 million Pakistanis were going to go: Will the country explode in riots of Islamic fundamentalists, made all the more dangerous given that their military wields nuclear bombs? Or will cooler heads, and the military regime, prevail?

The ride in the taxicab doesn't comfort me any.

As we move through the dimly lit streets, there are men with AK-47s everywhere. Some are army soldiers, holding submachine guns and wearing bulletproof vests. Others are the private security guards of Pakistan's rich, an unpredictable private army standing in front of guesthouses and hotels, mansions and banks, usually under 40-watt bulbs that lend them film-noir shadows. The taxi hits a pothole and something rolls out from under the seat and bounces around my shoes. It is a grenade, with a patina of rust.

"What's that for?" I ask the driver, who calls himself Mohammad.

He looks down, spots the object in question and deftly uses his hand to shove it back under the seat. "You've been to Pakistan before, sir?" he enquires.

"No," I answer.

"Always good to have such things."

A week ago, I was a world away from the weirdness of the war, on one of those spectacular Manhattan mornings when all that marred a peerless blue sky was the contrails of jets passing overhead. The Globe and Mail was moving me from my Beijing post to New York, and my wife, Beatrice, and I had just signed a lease on our first New York apartment, in Battery Park—the neighbourhood that in 48 hours would come to be known as ground zero.

We didn't know that then, of course, and just felt relief at finally finding a place. To celebrate, we decided that we would get up early and take our first real walk through what everyone told us was the most vibrant, egotistical and unpredictable city you could ever find.

Leaving the Gramercy Park Hotel at 7:30 a.m., we were reflecting on almost four years of living in China, during which we mostly trotted through Third World police states, where guns and possible chaos were staples of life. It was exotic and often fun, but it was also a life that sometimes got you caught in the middle of a curfew, when the soldiers were loading their weapons and you were running down strange streets, looking for your hotel.

As we walked through Manhattan, we laughed easily at the doyens of Gramercy Park, who walked in Gucci spikes, noses held high as their pedigreed poodles tinkled on the sidewalks. We marvelled at the $7 (U.S.) lattes in Soho and wondered if I might be getting a raise. And we passed Little Italy and were soon transported back to Beijing: Everyone was haggling in Mandarin and its various dialects. We wouldn't be that far from China after all.

Of course, we quickly got lost, as most new New Yorkers do. But like all the denizens of pre-Sept. 11 Manhattan, we just had to gaze upward to find a beacon to orient us: the twin towers of the World Trade Center, the sliver monoliths that rose on Manhattan Island's southern tip, just around the corner from our new pad on the Hudson River.

Before we knew it, we were standing directly under the towers, touching their smooth, carefully milled steel. It being a Sunday, there was nobody around. But we did notice a circular object at one end of the plaza, the memorial to the dead and wounded from the 1993 truck bomb that was the first terrorist attack meant to bring down America.

In a moment I still wonder about, I turned to my wife: "You know, they're so beautiful, such a target, I can't believe someone hasn't tried to bomb them again."

She looked at me and shrugged it off. We crossed the West Street Highway, walked past the tower where The Globe's office once was, and headed to our new apartment. We passed the neighbourhood movie theatre, watched the waiters getting tables ready at Lili's Noodle Shop and then sat at the man-made pond by the Hudson, drinking in the skyline. We didn't dream that we'd never be able to do that again.

Sept. 11, Beijing

"Wake up, wake up!"

It is my wife, telling me she has just heard from a friend that a plane has just hit the World Trade Center.

"Don't worry," I say. "It'll be okay."

My head is fuzzy with jet lag from our return to China, and I think that one of the small Cessnas I'd seen buzzing over lower Manhattan like mosquitoes had hit the towers by accident. I roll over and go back to sleep.

"They're gone, Miro. They're gone." It is my wife again, her face white with shock.

"What's gone?" I ask.

"The World Trade Center, it's gone," she answers as we rushed into the other room and flick on CNN to see the slow-motion image of the towers collapsing and the first, and never repeated, video clips of men cascading from the towers, fluttering through as the sky they fell.

I call a friend who lives at ground zero, who had been instrumental in telling me to live in Battery Park. Somehow I get through on the first try. He is on the 42nd floor, with a full view of the trade centre. "I saw them come down," he says. "I could see the people jumping out. It's all still burning."

As for our new apartment, "it's still there," he advises. But the building was enveloped in the great cloud of dust and smoke, and has been evacuated. The Globe's office, across the street from the twin towers, is in ruins. Windows have been shattered and the threat of asbestos is everywhere.

I hang up and find my passport, making sure it has pages for extra visas. As any foreign correspondent knows, it is time to pack a suitcase and charge up the laptop and be ready to fly.

But it won't be to New York, not yet. . . .

Dec. 12, New York

At JFK airport, upon our arrival at midnight, there's a new sight: Soldiers in battle fatigues, with both hands on their M-16s, stare at the passengers as they enter the arrival lounge. We find our bags and head into Manhattan.

Still jet-lagged, we can't sleep. So we head toward our apartment. Ground zero is lit up by massive klieg lights, and the ruins of Building 5 are still standing.

In the dimly lit streets nearby, a few late-night figures stand at memorials, some praying, quietly praying. The soldiers and police are everywhere, making America seem eerily like Beijing.

In the days to come, we find that Manhattan is not the model of First World efficiency we thought it was. People's mail is being opened at the border, just like back in China, and some moving men tell me that it may take longer than usual to get our furniture. Everything is being checked.

In the days ahead, we're overwhelmed by the bureaucracy of America, which is saying a lot when you're used to the nightmare of Communist China. To get a cellphone, AT & T wants a $1,600 deposit, something the Chinese never demanded. It takes 25 phone calls and two weeks to get the long-distance lines set up, an unthinkable delay in Beijing or Shanghai.

Waiters are also a shock: In Beijing, they stand at your table, instantly filling a teacup after every sip. In New York, most don't pay you any attention until they figure out if you've left at least a 15-per-cent tip.

But mostly it's the sense of unease that now pervades New York, at least near ground zero. Many of the apartments around us are vacant, their occupants having either fled or never made it home on Sept. 11. The threat of getting cancer from asbestos has left the movie theatre closed. Lili's Noodle Shop stands empty, its tables still set as they were for lunch on Sept. 11.

At New York dinner parties, people now discuss whether it's okay to open mail. Others say New York is safe, because the police and army are patrolling with Geiger counters to sniff out nuclear bombs. Outside our apartment, a man comes around every day to test the air, for asbestos.

It doesn't seem a bad idea to have all that Cipro in the medicine cabinet.

Games at the Olympics, 2002

CHRISTIE BLATCHFORD

Hockey aside, what galvanized Canadians most at the 2002 Winter Olympics was the judging scandal in pairs figure skating.

Even in the pretty muck of the figure skating world, where almost no one speaks bluntly for fear of retribution against their athletes or themselves, the consensus is plain: Jamie Salé and David Pelletier got screwed.

The young Canadians who two nights ago skated a flawless free skate but saw the gold medal awarded instead to a struggling Russian pair appear to have been either crucified upon the sport's traditional cross—political vote-trading in internecine back-rooms—or sacrificed upon the altar of an unnamed judge's ambition, or both.

"It certainly wasn't the skating," Frank Carroll, a veteran American coach in the self-described twilight of his 40-year-long career, said flatly yesterday.

Mr. Carroll wasn't alone in his view, only uniquely outspoken.

So outrageous were Monday's results that Mr. Carroll wondered aloud if it isn't time for the International Olympic Committee to give skating the boot from the Olympic Games until the International Skating Union, which controls the judges, cleans up its act, and Sally Rehorick, a veteran skating judge who has worked both Olympics and world championships and who is in Salt Lake as the chef de mission of the Canadian team, felt so sick as the scores were posted that "I didn't want to judge again.

"I was horrified. As a judge, you want things to be fair. . . . I was hoping for a clear-cut result, and when Jamie and David finished skating, I thought, 'Oh, this is easy.'"

At a press conference yesterday, Ms. Rehorick went through the Russians' and Canadians' program almost step for step, pointing out places where Elena Berezhnaya and Anton Sikharulidze were shaky or actually stumbled, and was unequivocal in her conclusion that "This is not the right decision."

She also put to rest the notion that perhaps European judges, particularly those from the former Soviet Union—the five who placed the Russians ahead of Ms. Salé and Mr. Pelletier are from France, Poland, Russia, China and Ukraine—bring a different artistic sensibility to their work and may have genuinely preferred the more classical program skated by Ms. Berezhnaya and Mr. Sikharulidze.

"I don't see it as an issue of esthetic preference," she said curtly, adding that judges are supposed to award the best marks to the best skaters on that night.

She said the Canadian Olympic Association was asking the ISU to conduct an investigation.

But the ISU announcement later yesterday that it will hold an internal review was met with almost universally low, even bemused, expectations—there isn't a soul in skating who holds out a prayer that Monday's marks will be reversed, and few who harbour any hope for longer-term changes.

Mr. Carroll, who is here coaching U.S. singles' competitor Timothy Goebel, said Ms. Salé and Mr. Pelletier were so clearly superior to Ms. Berezhnaya and Mr. Sikharulidze that there is simply no benign explanation for the Canadian couple's second-place finish.

The answer, he said bluntly, lies with the panel of nine judges.

He suggested that some of them voted for the Russians in order to secure votes for their skaters in either ice dancing or the men's singles, or that one of them, whom he wouldn't identify, was seeking a place on the ISU's powerful technical committee and was in need of votes from other nations.

"You look at the panel [on Monday].

"All kinds of things go through your mind, like why, why, why? Why could they do this?

"Now, you've got a French judge [Marie Reine Le Gougne] on the panel. The French dance team [of Marina Anissina and Gwendal Peizerat] just lost to the Canadians [Shae-Lynn Bourne and Victor Kraatz, at the recent Grand Prix].

"Does that mean now the Russian [judge] possibly is going to give the French dance team first [as payback for Ms. Le Gougne voting for Berezhnaya and Sikharulidze]? Does it mean now it's locked in, that the French will get first from the Russian judge?

"These are the things that go through people's minds.

"It may not be true, but I'm just saying these are things.

"Now, you have the Chinese boys, they're very, very good skaters, they do quadruple jumps beautifully, they're very strong.

"Does this mean now that the Chinese have made sure [with Chinese judge Jiasheng Yang voting for Berezhnaya and Sikharulidze] that the Russian [judge in men's singles] is going to put one of the Chinese boys third? That's the thing that goes through my mind because I have a boy [in the singles, Goebel].

"Or is there someone on this panel looking to be on the ISU technical committee? Are they trying to get the votes of the Soviet bloc?"

Whatever else, Mr. Carroll said, what happened to Ms. Salé and Mr. Pelletier has its roots in "ambitions and motives," and is "the worst thing that has happened in a long time in figure skating."

These sentiments were heard everywhere skaters gathered yesterday, particularly at the ice centre, scene of Ms. Salé and Mr. Pelletier's short-lived triumph on Monday, when Mr. Pelletier fell to his knees and kissed the ice after they finished skating, only to sit in the waiting area known as the "kiss 'n' cry" to receive their shocking marks, the lowest they have

ever received for that particular program, skated to the theme from the
1970 movie *Love Story*.

Canada's Elvis Stojko, who was competing in the men's short program
last night, said that in his opinion, Ms. Salé and Mr. Pelletier "skated
pretty much perfectly" and outperformed the Russians. "But in my position [with his own competition looming], I'm not going to comment any
more. . . . It's a very touchy situation."

Former Olympic gold medallist American Scott Hamilton, who is now
a television commentator, concurred with Mr. Carroll that the Russian
pair, whom he said he likes and admires, struggled, while Ms. Salé and
Mr. Pelletier had a "perfectly skated program."

Mr. Hamilton also joined a chorus of voices yesterday in praise of the
graceful manner in which the Canadians have accepted their fate. "They're
better as people than the sport is [as a sport]," he said. "You rise above
it, and they have. Jamie Salé and Dave Pelletier are straight-up, quality
people."

Indeed, this was one key note of the theme most often sounded yesterday: Judging controversies are hardly new to skating; athletes know
this going in; there's nothing one can do and nothing will change, so the
best course is to suck up the unfairness and the blow with grit.

Ms. Salé and Mr. Pelletier themselves, who head off to the world
championships in Nagano next month, were still wearing this brave face
yesterday, albeit wearily.

"Sometimes," the 27-year-old Mr. Pelletier said, "a silver medal is
won by a gold-medal performance and that's what we did. . . . We have
no comments on the judging. We do our job; we're just figure skaters."

Only Mr. Carroll, who has been punished before for his outspoken-
ness and who is now at the close of his honourable career and has little
left to lose, saw it differently. He said Ms. Salé and Mr. Pelletier "were
screwed," that the skating game is rife with abuse and open to corruption, "too easily manoeuvred and manipulated," a rich sport peopled
with impoverished judges and hungry athletes.

"And if we keep our mouths shut," Mr. Carroll concluded sadly, "they
really win."

Olympic Hockey Gold

ROY MACGREGOR

*The Salt Lake City Olympics ended on a high note for Canadians when
our hockey team defeated the United States in the gold medal game.*

Four minutes left in the biggest hockey game in the 30 years of his life—
biggest in the last 50 years of Canada's—and Owen Nolan suddenly
bolted from the bench to the dressing room.

Nothing to do with injury, but an equipment problem.

He wanted his camera. Sixty seconds to go in the final match at the 2002 Winter Games and Nolan, like his teammates, was on his feet at the Team Canada bench.

The big Canadian forward, however, was the only one not holding his stick. Gloves off and stick down, he was recording the final seconds so he would never forget.

As if he will ever be allowed.

All around him, the crowd was singing *O Canada;* behind him, coach Pat Quinn was dealing with the first of many tears, so perhaps he didn't notice. Nor would it have mattered if Quinn had and tapped the player to take the next shift.

"I wasn't going on!" a smiling Nolan said when it was all over. "I was too busy."

His camera lens had captured what all Canada had been dreaming about for four long, torturous, soul-searching and at times panicking years: the first Olympic gold medal in hockey in 50 years, to the very day. Canada's Perfect Golden Anniversary.

"Words can't describe what was going on," said Nolan.

They can try: The horn went and the scoreboard said Canada 5, U.S.A. 2. Sticks and gloves and helmets were in the air. Goaltender Martin Brodeur—he of the endless doubts—was being mobbed by those who now believed they had believed in him forever. Quinn used the back of his sleeve to wipe away a tear.

They rushed Brodeur and someone tossed a Canadian flag to Team Canada captain Mario Lemieux and he thought about wearing it and then thought it would be too much and carried it to the bench. Paul Kariya blew kisses up to his mother and girlfriend in the stands. Lemieux then led his team in a hand shake with the Americans that ended, charmingly, with Brodeur hugging American goaltender Mike Richter.

Such a modest, gracious, classy celebration—the moment the horn blew the Canadians ceased to be fierce, driven hockey players and suddenly turned back into the shy and humble men who have taken their lead from the likes of Gordie Howe and Bobbie Orr and, yes, the one who put this team together: Wayne Gretzky.

They shook hands and the American team saluted the crowd that cheered for them all over again, and they gave out the medals—the classless Russians not even bothering to show up for their bronze—and the Canadian flag rose highest in the E-Center for the second time this week. And Quinn wiped away a tear, just as he had when the Canadian women took the gold medal Thursday night.

"A big monkey is lifted off Canada's back," said U.S. forward Jeremy Roenick, who played his junior hockey in Hull, Que., and knows what this day meant to Canada.

"Today was their day."

"This," said Quinn, "is a legacy for Canadian hockey we want to pass on."

"Fifty years ago today," mused Canadian defenceman Al MacInnis. "Maybe some things are meant to be."

Asked what he thought the reaction might be back home, MacInnis smiled and suggested, "They're having a cold one on us—and well deserved."

The Canadian team, assembled over this past year by Gretzky and his Team Canada brain trust, was widely held to be the greatest hockey team ever iced by the country that invented the sport—and yet it had been plagued by questions. Patrick Roy, the best goaltender, had elected not to play. Other key players—Lemieux, Nolan, Steve Yzerman—were injured coming in. The team collapsed against Sweden, struggled against Germany, but seemed to find itself against the Czech Republic. They then beat Finland and Belarus to reach the final, which they won in convincing fashion.

"There's no question there was a great deal of pressure on us," said a relieved Gretzky. "There was pressure on all the teams, but ours seemed to be a little bit greater, maybe because we hadn't won in 50 years."

Gretzky himself conceded he "probably" handled the pressure better as a player, and claimed his emotional outburst last week had been deliberate, in order to "get all the focus off those guys and turn the focus in a different direction."

Whatever, the players still felt the pressure, intensely. Paul Kariya said he was so "numb" he found it difficult to play the third period.

"It was like I got shot by a shotgun," defenceman Adam Foote said when it was over, "and all the air was seeping out, all the pressure."

The pressure going into this match was extraordinary. No Canadian team had won since the Edmonton Mercurys in the 1952 Oslo Games. Canada had twice reached silver in the 1990s and fallen in a shootout four years ago in Nagano. The Americans were enjoying their best Winter Games ever, and were talking up their own anniversary: 22 years since the "Miracle on Ice" at Lake Placid that had given the U.S. its last gold medal in hockey. The Americans had not lost an Olympic hockey game on home ice since 1932—a 70-year anniversary to lord over Canada's 50-year benchmark.

It was not quite the game expected. The Americans had dominated throughout the tournament but could not use their speed against the pounding Canadian defence. Nor could the Americans get the Canadians to play their European hybrid puck-control game. The Canadians simply played NHL hockey on a big ice surface, up and down, dump and chase, pound and jam—and it worked wonderfully.

Herb Brooks, the American coach in both 1980 and today, sounded the only sour note, claiming that the Canadians had been given an easier route to the final and Team U.S.A.'s tougher matches had meant the Canadians had "better legs" when it counted.

It had been anticipated that Canadian nerves and American patriotism would fire up Team U.S.A. right off the mark, and the U.S.A. did score first when Tony Amonte came in on a two-on-one and fired a hard, low shot through Brodeur's pads. It was Brodeur's only bad moment of the day.

Canada tied the game on a gorgeous cross-ice pass from Chris Pronger to Kariya, moving fast up the left side, and Kariya had the open side to put the puck in behind Richter.

The Canadians went ahead on a second lovely pass, this time from Sakic to Jarome Iginla, the NHL scoring leader, and Iginla jammed the puck in along the post.

Canada should have run away with the match in the second but for an extraordinary number of missed opportunities. Theoren Fleury flubbed a chance, Scott Niedermayer failed to slip a puck into the open net and—in the shocker of the day—Lemieux missed a wide-open net, hitting the goalpost as Canada enjoyed a two-man advantage and Richter was so far out of the play that Lemieux could have shoved it in with his nose had he so chosen.

In a brief but ominous turn, the Americans then immediately tied the game 2–2 when a power-play pass from defenceman Brian Rafalski was tipped by Pronger into his own net.

Canada took the lead again, however, when Sakic fired a floater from the top of the left circle that seemed to deflect off American defenceman Brian Leetch, for there seemed no other explanation for Richter missing so easy a shot.

Richter, incidentally, was named all-star goaltender for the tournament, in a media vote that must have been counted in Florida. He was joined by American defencemen Chris Chelios and Leetch, U.S. forward John LeClair, Swedish forward Mats Sundin and, mercifully, Canada's Sakic.

The best forward in the tournament, however, may well have been Canada's Steve Yzerman.

The Canadians put it away in the third period when Iginla one-timed a nice pass from Yzerman and the puck simply trickled on in after an initial stop by Richter.

It was 16:01, and Nolan was already hurrying down the hallway in his skates, racing for his video camera. Gretzky, high in the stands, was also on his feet, pumping his fist in the air and shouting something we will presume was "Hip, Hip, Hurrah."

Then, with only 1:20 left in the game, Sakic broke up the right side, drove to the net and slipped a quick low shot into the far side.

The crowd was already singing *O Canada*. Nolan had it on film, just in case anyone ever doubted that Canada did not win the gold medal at the 2002 Winter Games.

And Pat Quinn was wondering if anyone was noticing that he was crying.

Copyright Acknowledgments

Louis Fornel, from *Documents of the Enquiry into the Labrador Boundary by the British Privy Council* (London: William Clowes and Sons, 1929); "The Expulsion of the Acadians, 1755," Lieut.-Col. John Winslow, from *Report of the Public Archives of Canada, 1905* (Ottawa: Public Archives, 1906); "Governor General Vaudreuil Reacts to Montcalm's Defeat, 1759," Marquis de Vaudreuil, from Abbé H.R. Casgrain, ed., *Collection de Manuscrits du Maréchal de Lévis*, vol. VIII (Quebec: L.J. Demers, 1889–95); "Wolfe's Men Gain the Heights at Québec," unknown, from National Archives of Canada, Dobbs Collection, Microfilm A652; "The Death of Wolfe, 1759," Captain John Knox, from A.G. Doughty, ed., *Historical Journal of the Campaigns in North America 1757–1760 by Captain John Knox* (Toronto: The Champlain Society, 1906); "The Governor Reports on the Isle of St. John, 1770," Walter Patterson, from *Report of the Public Archives of Canada, 1939* (Ottawa: Public Archives, 1940); "Captain Cook's Crew Enjoys Nootka Sound, 1778," David Samwell, from J.C. Beaglehole, ed., *The Journals of Captain James Cook on His Voyages of Discovery: The Voyage of the* Resolution *and* Discovery, *1776–1780, Part Two* (Cambridge, England: Cambridge University Press, 1967); "The Fur Trade, 1784," Benjamin and Joseph Frobisher, from W.S. Wallace, ed., *Documents Relating to the North West Company* (Toronto: The Champlain Society, 1934); "Saint John— 'The Most Magnificent and Romantic Scene,'" Edward Winslow, from W.O. Raymond, ed., *The Winslow Papers* (Saint John, NB, 1901); "The Well-off Loyalist Comes to Québec," William Smith, from L.F.S. Upton, ed., *The Diary and Selected Papers of Chief Justice William Smith, 1784–1793* vol. II (Toronto: The Champlain Society, 1965); "Love and Marriage in Upper Canada, 1800," Amelia Harris, from J.J. Talman, ed., *Loyalist Narratives from Upper Canada* (Toronto: The Champlain Society, 1946); "French–English Tensions in Lower Canada, 1804," Lord Selkirk, from P.C.T. White, ed., *Lord Selkirk's Diary, 1803–1804* (Toronto: The Champlain Society, 1958); "Lac la Biche," Gabriel Franchère, from W. Kaye Lamb, ed., *Journal of a Voyage on the North West Coast of North America During the Years 1811, 1812, 1813, 1814 by Gabriel Franchère* (Toronto: The Champlain Society, 1969); "The Americans Take York, 1813," Dr. William Beaumont, from Jesse S. Myer, *Life and Letters of Dr. William Beaumont* (St. Louis: C.V. Mosby, 1912); "Laura Secord's Heroism," James FitzGibbon, from Mary Agnes Fitzgibbon, *A Veteran of 1812: The Life of James FitzGibbon* (Toronto: William Briggs, 1899); "The Indians in the War of 1812," Lieut. John Le Couteur, from Donald E. Graves, ed., *Merry Hearts Make Light Days: The War of 1812 Journal of Lieutenant John Le Couteur, 104th Foot* (Ottawa: Carleton University Press, 1994); "Seven Weeks at Sea to Québec," James Wilson, *Narrative of a Voyage from Dublin to Quebec, in North America* (Dublin: T. Courtney, 1822); "Sir John Franklin Explores the Arctic Lands, 1820," Sir John Franklin, from Richard C. Davis, ed., *Sir John Franklin's Journals and Correspondence: The First Arctic Land Expedition, 1819–1822* (Toronto: The Champlain Society, 1995); "Alcohol and the Indians," George Simpson, from National Archives of Canada, Lord Selkirk Papers, Simpson to

(January 28, 1870); "The Riel Rebellion, 1870 II: Executing Thomas Scott," Alexander Begg, from W.L. Morton, ed., *Alexander Begg's Red River Journal, 1869–1870* (Toronto: Champlain Society, 1956); "Marking the International Boundary," Samuel Anderson, from C. Ian Jackson, *Letters from the 49th Parallel, 1857–1873: Selected Correspondence of Joseph Harris and Samuel Anderson* (Toronto: Champlain Society, 2000); "Bread and Beans in a Lumber Camp, 1883," Joshua Fraser, *Shanty, Forest and River Life in the Backwoods of Canada* (Montreal: Lovell, 1883); "Sandford Fleming Breakfasts on a Lake Steamer, 1884," Sandford Fleming, *England and Canada: A Summer Tour Between Westminster and New Westminster* (London, England: n.p., 1884); "Opium Smoking in British Columbia, 1884," Emily Wharton, from House of Commons Sessional Papers, 1885, No. 54A, testimony of Emily Wharton, August 9, 1884; "Anti-Chinese Sentiment in British Columbia, 1884," R.F. John, from House of Commons Sessional Papers, 1885, No. 54A, Letter R.F. John, MPP, to the Secretary, Chinese Commission, August 30, 1884; "Canada's National Game: Lacrosse," the Marquis of Lorne, *Canadian Pictures Drawn with Pen and Pencil* (London, England: The Religious Tract Society, 1884); "A Diary of the 1885 Northwest Rebellion," Walter F. Stewart, from Walter F. Stewart Collection, Diary, at www.mala.bc.ca/davies/letters .images; "Victory over Riel, 1885," Major-General Frederick Middleton, from Desmond Morton and R.H. Roy, eds., *Telegrams of the North-West Campaign, 1885* (Toronto: The Champlain Society, 1972); "Riel's Last Interview," Nicholas Flood Davin, from "Interview with Riel," *Regina Leader* (November 16, 1885); "Exploring for the Beothuck, 1886," James P. Howley, from W.J. Kirwin et al., eds., *Reminiscences of James P. Howley: Selected Years* (Toronto: The Champlain Society, 1997); "The Great Hull Fire of 1886," anonymous, from "Hull Ablaze," *Ottawa Evening Citizen* (May 10, 1886); "Women's Advice to Prairie Settlers, 1886," Mrs. J. Alexander et al., from n.a., *What Women Say of the Canadian North West* (n.p., 1886); "A Frenchman on Québec, 1891," Paul Blouet, *A Frenchman in America: The Anglo-Saxon Race Revisited* (Bristol: Arrowsmith, 1891); "The Bounty of the Okanagan, 1892," Charles Mair, from National Archives of Canada, George T. Denison Papers, Mair to Denison, October 6, 1892; "On the Klondike Trail, 1898," W.H.T. Olive, from *The Right Way On: Adventures in the Klondyke of 1898. Memoirs of W.H.T. Olive* (Langley, B.C.: Timberholme Books, 1999); "The Dangers of Americanization," Ishbel, Lady Aberdeen, from National Archives of Canada, Aberdeen Papers, Lady Aberdeen Journal; "The 1896 Election: Sir Charles Tupper Leaves Office Grudgingly," Ishbel, Lady Aberdeen, from National Archives of Canada, Aberdeen Papers, Lady Aberdeen Journal, July 4, 1896; "Ukrainian Immigrants Come to Canada, 1897," Dmytro Romanchych, from V.J. Kaye, *Early Ukrainian Settlements in Canada, 1895–1900* (Toronto: University of Toronto Press, 1964); "Canada Goes to War, South Africa, 1899," Lord Minto, from P. Stevens and John Saywell, eds. *Lord Minto's Canadian Papers, 1898–1904* (Toronto: The Champlain Society, 1981); "Getting the Royal Canadian Regiment to South

Africa," C.F. Hamilton, from National Archives of Canada, J.S. Willison Papers, Hamilton to Willison, November 11, 1899; "The Victory of Paardeberg," Albert Perkins, from National Archives of Canada, Albert Perkins Papers, "One of Our Boy's Diary," Fredericton *Daily Gleaner*, n.d. [March–April 1900]; "The Brutal Sameness of Prairie Towns, 1902," Bernard McEvoy, *From the Great Lakes to the Wide West* (Toronto: William Briggs, 1902); "The Red Light District in Dawson," Laura Berton, *I Married the Klondike* (Toronto: McClelland & Stewart, 1954); "Signor Marconi and Wireless Telegraphy," unknown, from *The Evening Telegram* (St. John's) (December 16, 1901); "Pauline Johnson on the Blackfoots, 1902," Pauline Johnson, "Among the Blackfoots," *The Globe* (August 2, 1902); "The Crack Shot of the Empire," unknown, from "The Empire's Best Shot Welcomed to His Home," *The Globe* (August 10, 1904); "Making a Life on the Prairies, 1903," C. Schack, from C. Schack to W. Toole, October 27, 1903, in Canadian Pacific Railway, *Western Canada, How to Reach It, How to Obtain Lands, How to Make a Home* (1904); "Sir Wilfrid Laurier on the United States," Sir Wilfrid Laurier, from House of Commons, *Debates*, February 21, 1905; "Dining in the West," Howard A. Kennedy, *New Canada and the New Canadians* (London: H. Marshall, 1907); "The Railway Comes to Lloydminster," Mrs. W. Rendall, from Letter, November 1905, quoted in E.H. Oliver, "The Settlement of Saskatchewan to 1914," *Transactions of the Royal Society of Canada*, Third Series, vol. XX; "The Salvation Army Takes Over Joe Beef's Saloon, Montreal," W.H. Davies, *The Autobiography of a Super-tramp* (London: A.C. Fifeld, 1908); "The Collapse of the Québec Bridge, 1907," anonymous, from "End of Quebec's New Bridge Collapsed; Over Eighty Workmen Met Terrible Fate," *The Globe* (August 30, 1907); "Election Campaigning in Newfoundland, 1909," Major Peter Cashin, *My Life and Times, 1890–1919* (St. John's: Breakwater Books, 1976); "A Home Helper on an Alberta Ranch, 1911," anonymous, from "Canadian Life: Canada for Home Helps," *The Imperial Colonist* (August, 1911); "Nellie McClung on Discrimination Against Women," Nellie McClung, *The Stream Runs Fast: My Own Story* (Toronto: Thomas Allen, 1945); "The Sinking of the *Titanic*," M. Grattan O'Leary, from "*Titanic's* Officers Shot Cowards," *Ottawa Journal* (April 19, 1912); "Reaching a Prairie Homestead," James M. Minifie, *Homesteader: A Prairie Boyhood Recalled* (Toronto: Macmillan, 1972); "Bunkhouse Men and Booze," J. Burgon Bickersteth, *The Land of Open Doors: Being Letters from Western Canada* (London, England: Wells Gardner, Darton, 1914); "Captain Bernier Readies for the Arctic, 1914," unknown, from "Le Capitaine Bernier Prépare une Expédition," *Le Soleil* (May 29, 1914); "Canadians Go to War, August 1914," Roy Macfie from John Mafie, *Letters Home* (Meaford, ON: n.p., 1990); "Learning to Ride the Army Way," Raymond Massey, *When I Was Young* (Toronto: McClelland and Stewart, 1976); "The Princess Pats Fight in Polygon Wood, 1915," Agar Adamson, from National Archives of Canada, Agar Adamson Papers; "Prohibition Comes to Manitoba," James H. Gray, *The Boy from Winnipeg* (Toronto: Macmillan, 1970); "The Parliament Buildings Afire,

1916," Arthur R. Ford, *As the World Wags On* (Toronto: Ryerson, 1950); "Life and Death in the Trenches, 1916 I," Archie MacKinnon, from Archie MacKinnon Papers, Private Collection (Toronto); "Life and Death in the Trenches, 1916 II," George Adkins, from George Adkins Collection, Adkins to His Mother, June 5, 1916, at www.mala. bc.ca/davies/letters.images; "Life and Death in the Air, 1916," John Brophy, from B. Greenhous, ed., *A Rattle of Pebbles: The First World War Diaries of Two Canadian Airmen* (Ottawa: Department of National Defence, 1987); "Staff Officers," Lieut.-Gen. Maurice A. Pope, *Letters from the Front 1914–1919*, edited by Joseph Pope (Toronto: Pope & Co., 1993); "A Pacifist Objects to Registration of Men for Conscription, 1916," J.S. Woodsworth, from Letter, *Manitoba Free Press* (December 28, 1916); "Scrounging at the Front," J.R. Mutchmor, *Mutchmor: The Memoirs of James Ralph Mutchmor* (Toronto: Ryerson, 1965); "Getting Wounded, January 1917," Harry Morris, from Harry Morris Collection, Morris to Lillian, Mother and Son, April 5, 1917, at www.mala.bc.ca/davies/letters.images; "The Taking of Vimy Ridge I: Easter Monday, 1917," Lieut. Stuart Kirkland, from The Dutton Advance Collection, Lieut. Stuart Kirkland letter published May 10, 1917, at www.mala.bc.ca/davies/letters.images; "The Taking of Vimy Ridge II: The Casualties," Clare Gass, from Susan Mann, ed., *The War Diary of Clare Gass, 1915–1918* (Montreal: McGill-Queen's University Press, 2000); "A Québec Soldier at the Front, 1917," Arthur Lapointe, from A.S. Lapointe, *Souvenirs d'un soldat du Québec* (Drummondville, PQ: Editions du Castor, 1944), translated in S. Bernier, *The Royal 22e Régiment, 1914–1999* (Montreal: Art Global, 2000); "Life and Death in the Trenches, 1917," Bob Gardner, from M.G. Millman, ed., *Letters Home, 1915–18* (unpub. ms.); "Billy Bishop's Story," Major William A. Bishop, *Winged Warfare* (Toronto: McClelland, Goodchild & Stewart, 1918); "Homefront Tragedy: The Halifax Explosion I," unknown, from "Death Roll Grows," *Halifax Morning Chronicle* (December 8, 1917); "Homefront Tragedy: The Halifax Explosion II," Lambert B. Griffith, from Griffith Papers, L.B. Griffith to his wife, December 8, 1917, [In possession of Major John G. Armstrong, Ottawa]; "Bitterness About Québec's Role in the War," John W. Dafoe, from National Archives of Canada, J.W. Dafoe Papers, Dafoe to Thomas Côté, January 1, 1918; "Wartime Changes in Women's Roles, 1918," Nehnum Morr, "Street Railway Conductorettes," *Daily British Whig* (Kingston, ON: August 24, 1918); "Heroism in the Hundred Days I," Bellenden S. Hutcheson, from Hutcheson to Captain Gunyon, n.d., on the Veterans Affairs Canada web site; "Heroism in the Hundred Days II," Georges Vanier, from Deborah Cowley, ed., *Georges Vanier: Soldier. The Wartime Letters and Diaries, 1915–1919* (Toronto: Dundurn Press, 2000); "The End of the War," Archie Keat, from Keat to His Mother, November 11, 1918, in the North Shore Archives Collection on www.mala.bc.ca/davies/letters.images; "The Influenza Pandemic, 1918," Dr. T. Rogers, from Dr. T. Rogers, Rosedale, NS, to Hon. Mr. Doherty, Chief Justice [sic], November 30, 1918, on National Archives of Canada web site;

"The Winnipeg General Strike, 1919 I," Ernest Robinson, from *Manitoba Free Press* fly-sheet (strike edition), May 20, 1919; "The Winnipeg General Strike, 1919 II," Arnold Heeney, from Arnold Heeney to his Mother, June 27, 1919, in Brian Heeney Papers (Peterborough, ON); "Growing Up in a Ghost Town," Pierre Berton, *Starting Out, 1920–1947* (Toronto: McClelland & Stewart, 1987); "Travelling Abroad, 1921," James Mavor, quoted in Vincent Bladen, *Bladen on Bladen: Memoirs of a Political Economist* (Toronto: Scarborough College, 1978); "Immigration, 1920s Style," unknown, from "Immigrants Travel in State," *Saturday Night* (June 18, 1921); "Hemingway Reports on Dr. Banting," Ernest Hemingway, from "An Absolute Lie, Says Dr. Banting, of Serum Report," *Toronto Daily Star* (October 11, 1923); "The Political Mood of the West, 1925," John W. Dafoe, from National Archives of Canada, Clifford Sifton Papers; "A British Official's View of Canada, 1928," Geoffrey Whiskard, from Public Record Office, Kew, England, Dominions Office Records; "Mussolini's Italy, 1928," Escott Reid, "Where Mussolini Rules," *Toronto Star Weekly* (January 21, 1928); "Vancouver's Sprinter at the Olympics, 1928," R.T. Elson, "Percy Williams Captures Second World Title," *Vancouver Province* (August 1, 1928); "The Great Crash of 1929," unknown, from "Utter Collapse in Stock Market Narrowly Averted," *The Globe* (October 30, 1929); "Nellie McClung Celebrates Victory in the 'Persons' Case," Nellie McClung, "A Retrospect," *The Country Guide* (December 1929); "A Communist Goes to Jail, 1931," Frederick Griffin, *Variety Show: Twenty Years of Watching the News Parade* (Toronto, 1936); "Riding the Rods," unknown, from "Experiences of a Depression Hobo," *Saskatchewan History* (Spring 1969); "Gordon Sinclair Encounters India," Gordon Sinclair, *Foot-Loose in India* (Toronto: Gundy, 1932); "Founding the CCF," Eugene Forsey, "Remembering Regina," *Saturday Night* (July 1983); "R.B. Bennett and the Farmers, 1932," unknown, from *The Bracebridge Gazette* (July 21, 1932); "A Glimpse of Canada's Prime Minister, 1932," Sir A. Lascelles, from Sir A. Lascelles to S. Baldwin, November 22, 1932, Cambridge University Library, Cambridge, England, Baldwin Papers, vol. 98; "Hitler in Power, 1933," M.H. Halton, "As Child Reaches Six Prepare Him for War Hitler Tells Germany," *Toronto Daily Star* (October 16, 1933), reprinted with permission of the Toronto Star Syndicate; "Toronto the Good I," unknown, from "The Manly Bosom," *Saturday Night* (April 1933); "Newfoundland Under the Commission of Government," Sir John Hope Simpson, from Peter Neary, ed., *White Tie and Decorations: Sir John Hope and Lady Simpson in Newfoundland, 1934–1936* (Toronto: University of Toronto Press, 1996); "The On-to-Ottawa Trekkers Meet Bennett," Ronald Liversedge, *Recollections of the On-to-Ottawa Trek, 1935*, ed. Victor Hoar (Toronto: McClelland & Stewart, 1973); "Toronto the Good II," Donald W. Buchanan, "Naked Ladies," *Canadian Forum* (April 1935); "The Vimy Memorial Unveiled, 1936," Gregory Clark, "In Storm of Emotion Temple of New Faith is Unveiled at Vimy," *Toronto Daily Star* (July 27, 1936); "Calling on Haile Selassie," Robinson MacLean, *John Hoy of Ethiopia* (Toronto: S.B. Gundy, 1936); "Hitler's

Strome Galloway, *Bravely into Battle: The Autobiography of a Canadian Soldier in World War II* (Toronto: Stoddart, 1981); "Telling the People at Home: Ortona, 1943," Matthew Halton, from A.E. Powley, *Broadcast from the Front: Canadian Radio Overseas in the Second World War* (Toronto: Hakkert, 1975); "Harassing Refugee Children," Karl W. Butzer, "Coming Full Circle: Learning from the Experience of Emigration and Ethnic Prejudice," in Peter Suedfeld, ed., *Light from the Ashes: Social Science Careers of Young Holocaust Refugees and Survivors* (Ann Arbor: University of Michigan Press, 2001); "Dealing with Fear," Murray Peden, *A Thousand Shall Fall* (Stittsville, ON: Canada's Wings, 1979); "Landing on D-Day," Charles Martin, *Battle Diary: From D-Day and Normandy to the Zuider Zee and VE* (Toronto: Dundurn Press, 1994); "A Medical Officer on the Beach," Capt. Darius Albert, in Jean E. Portugal, *We Were There: The Army: A Record for Canada*, vol. V (Toronto: Royal Canadian Military Institute Heritage Society, 1998); "Fighting the Wehrmacht in Normandy," Sergeant Albanie Drapeau, in Jean E. Portugal, in *We Were There: The Army: A Record for Canada*, vol. V (Toronto: Royal Canadian Military Institute Heritage Society, 1998); "Army Intelligence on the Home Front," Mavor Moore, *Reinventing Myself: Memoirs* (Toronto: Stoddart, 1994), copyright © 1994 by Mavor Moore, reprinted by permission of Stoddart Publishing; "The Liberation of Paris," Matthew Halton, "Speaking from Paris," CBC (August 26, 1944); "Breaking the Gothic Line, 1944," Fred and Norah Egener, from Fred and Norah Egener, in Joan Barfoot, ed., *A Time Apart: Letters of Love and War* (Owen Sound, ON: Ginger Press, 1995); "The Liberation of the Netherlands," John Morgan Gray, *Fun Tomorrow: Learning to Be a Publisher and Much Else* (Toronto: Macmillan, 1978); "The Concentration Camps," René Lévesque, *Memoirs* (Montreal: Amerique, 1986); "V-E Day at the Front," Major Harry Jolley, from Major Harry Jolley Papers, in possession of Carol Sures, Annapolis, Maryland; "The Halifax V-E Day Riots," Anthony Griffin, *Footfalls in Memory* (Toronto: privately published, 1998); "Taking a Break at the United Nations Conference, San Francisco, 1945," Charles Ritchie, *The Siren Years: A Canadian Diplomat Abroad, 1937–1945* (Toronto: Macmillan, 1974); "Hiroshima," W.L. Mackenzie King, from National Archives of Canada, W.L.M. King Papers, Diary; "Liberating the Prisoners of the Japanese," Colonel Richard S. Malone, "Canadians at Kowloon, Hong Kong Liberated," *Globe and Mail* (September 4, 1945); "Repatriation," Jean M. Ellis, from Jean M. Ellis with Isabel Dingman, *Face Powder and Gunpowder* (Toronto: S.J. Reginald Saunders & Co., 1947); "Mackenzie King Visits France," Charles P. Stacey, *A Date with History: Memoirs of a Canadian Historian* (Toronto: Deneau, 1983); "A Hanging at Bordeaux Prison," Gordon Lunan, *The Making of a Spy* (Montreal: Robert Davies Publishing, 1995); "Finding an Apartment in Paris, 1947," Charles Ritchie, from *Bout de Papier* (winter 1992); "Czechoslovakia Goes Behind the Iron Curtain," Ronald M. Macdonnell, from National Archives of Canada, Department of External Affairs Records; "Newfoundland Looks Towards Canada," Joseph R. Smallwood, *I Chose Canada: The Memoirs of the Honourable*

Joseph R. "Joey" Smallwood (Toronto: Macmillan, 1973); "The Liberals in Convention, 1948," Dalton Camp, *Gentlemen, Players and Politicians* (Toronto: McClelland & Stewart, 1970), copyright © 1970 by Dalton Camp, reprinted with the permission of the estate of Dalton Camp; "The Grey Cup Goes Big Time," unknown, from "30,000 Welcome Grid Champs," *The Albertan* (December 2, 1948); "Observing Uncle Joe," John W. Holmes, "Moscow, 1947–1948: Reflections on the Origins of My Cold War," in J.L. Black and Norman Hillmer, eds., *Nearly Neighbours: Canada and the Soviet Union from Cold War to Détente and Beyond* (Kingston: Ronald P. Frye & Co., 1989); "Doukhobor Days," George Woodcock, *The Rejection of Politics and Other Essays* (Toronto: New Press, 1972); "The Voice of Hockey," Trent Frayne, "Foster Hewitt: Play-by-Playboy," *Maclean's* (April 1, 1950); "Trudeau the Communist? 1952," Robert A. Ford, from National Archives of Canada, Department of External Affairs Records; "Fighting the Chinese Communists," Robert S. Peacock, *Kim-chi, Asahi and Rum: A Platoon Commander Remembers Korea, 1952–1953* (Lugus, 1994); "A *Canadienne* in Japan," Jacqueline Robitaille Van Campen, "It Changed My life Forever," in F. Day et al., eds., *Women Overseas: Memoirs of the Canadian Red Cross Corps* (Vancouver: Ronsdale Press, 1998), reprinted with the permission of Ronsdale Press; "Meeting Mr. Brown," Blair Fraser, "A Secret Rendezvous with Igor Gouzenko," *Maclean's* (September 1, 1953); "The Promise of Atomic Energy," I. Norman Smith, *A Reporter Reports* (Toronto: Ryerson, 1954); "Khrushchev Out-drinks Canadian Diplomats, 1955," George Ignatieff, *The Making of a Peacemonger: The Memoirs of George Ignatieff* (Toronto: University of Toronto Press, 1985); "Glenn Gould Plays Moscow," John Fast, from National Archives of Canada, Department of External Affairs Records; "U.S. Red-Hunters Drive Herbert Norman to Suicide," anonymous, from "Canada Envoy to Cairo Dies in Suicide Leap," *Globe and Mail* (April 4, 1957); "The Emergence of 'The Chief,'" Tom Ardies, "2000 Persons 'Follow John' into Plowed Field," *Vancouver Sun* (May 24, 1957); "Diefenbaker *en français*," Pierre Sévigny, *This Game of Politics* (Toronto: McClelland & Stewart, 1965); "The Springhill Mine Disaster—and Miracle," Ray Timson, "Star Reporter Recreates Miner's Face-down Eternity," *Toronto Daily Star* (November 3, 1958), reprinted with permission of the Toronto Star Syndicate; "Interviewing Mrs. Diefenbaker and Mrs. Pearson," Christina McCall, "The Unlikely Gladiators: Pearson and Diefenbaker Remembered," in Norman Hillmer, ed., *Pearson: The Unlikely Gladiator* (Montreal: McGill-Queen's University Press, 1999); "Selling the Governor General's Art Collection," G. Blair Laing, *Memoirs of an Art Dealer* (Toronto: McClelland & Stewart, 1979); "Québec's Place Under Duplessis," André Laurendeau, "Is Quebec Led by a 'Negro King'?" *Le Devoir* (July 4, 1958), translated in R. Cook and M. Behiels, eds., *The Essential Laurendeau* (Toronto: Copp Clark, 1976); "Shooting Down the Arrow," Clark Davey, from Ron Haggart, "A Close-up View: They Marked the Arrow's Fall," *Vancouver Sun* (February 24, 1959); "This Extraordinary Disquisition": Diefenbaker Bids the U.S. Ambassador

and National Culture," Quebec City, April 1989; "Misogyny and Death in Montreal in 1989," Barry Came, "Montreal Massacre," *Maclean's* (December 18, 1989); "Rolling the Dice at Meech Lake," Susan Delacourt and Graham Fraser, "Marathon Talks Were All Part of Plan, PM Says," *Globe and Mail* (June 12, 1990), reprinted with permission of the *Globe and Mail*; "Meeting Parizeau," Diane Francis, *Fighting for Canada* (Toronto: Key Porter Books, 1996); "Chaos in Haiti, 1992," Francine Pelletier,"Au pays de l'intimidation," *L'actualité* (November 15, 1992); "Teaching and Learning History," Ken Dryden, *In School: Our Kids, Our Teachers, Our Classrooms* (Toronto: McClelland & Stewart, 1995); "The Hell of Rwanda," unknown, from Jane Snailham, *Eyewitnesses to Peace: Letters from Canadian Peacekeepers* (Clementsport, NS: The Canadian Peacekeeping Press, 1998); "Quebec's 1995 Referendum," Edison Stewart, "Quebec Gone in 'Next' Vote—Bouchard," *Toronto Star* (October 31, 1995), reprinted with permission of the Toronto Star Syndicate; "Thirty Years of Bilingualism," Murray Campbell, "Canada Talks the Talk," *Globe and Mail* (February 22, 1997), reprinted with permission of the *Globe and Mail*; "The Great Ice Storm of 1998," Lysiane Gagnon, "Trees Paying Heavy Price for Ice Storm," *Globe and Mail* (January 10, 1998), reprinted with permission of the *Globe and Mail*; "My Jack," Andrew Cohen, "The Savaging of Seymour," *Globe and Mail* (January 10, 1998), reprinted with permission of the *Globe and Mail*; "The Multi-Hued Metropolis," Elaine Carey, "Minorities Set to Be Majority," *Toronto Star* (June 7, 1998), reprinted with permission of the Toronto Star Syndicate; "Ethnic Cleansing in Kosovo," Michael Ignatieff, from Michael Ignatieff, *Virtual War: Kosovo and Beyond* (Toronto: Viking, 2000); "Hi-Tech Hijinks," Charlotte Gray, "Ottawa dot com," *Saturday Night* (March 2000); "The Death of Pierre Trudeau," John Gray and Tu Thanh Ha, "Trudeau Goes Home," *Globe and Mail* (October 3, 2000), reprinted with permission of the *Globe and Mail*; "Teachers, Students and Sex," Christie Blatchford, "Teacher on Abuse Registry Still in Class," *National Post* (October 13, 2000); "9/11 and Canadian Anti-Americanism," Margaret Wente, "They Had It Coming?" *Globe and Mail* (September 15, 2001), reprinted with permission of the *Globe and Mail*; "Fighting Terrorism, 2001," Miro Cernetig, "'China Knows How to Fight Terrorism," *Globe and Mail* (January 5, 2002), reprinted with permission of the *Globe and Mail*; "Games at the Olympics, 2002," Christie Blatchford, "If We Keep Our Mouths Shut, They Really Win," *National Post* (February 13, 2002); "Olympic Hockey Gold," Roy MacGregor, "Canada's Moment of Truth," *National Post* (February 25, 2002).

Index